Mike Holt's Illustrated Guide to

ELECTRICAL EXAM PREPARATION

Theory • Code • Calculations

D1712388

Mike Holt Enterprises
MikeHolt.com • 888.632.2633

BASED ON THE
2023 NEC®

NOTICE TO THE READER

Mike Holt's Illustrated Guide to Electrical Exam Preparation, based on the 2023 NEC®

Second Printing: March 2024
Author: Mike Holt
Technical Illustrator: Mike Culbreath
Cover Design: Bryan Burch
Layout Design and Typesetting: Cathleen Kwas
COPYRIGHT © 2023 Charles Michael Holt
ISBN 978-1-950431-71-7

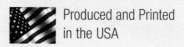
Produced and Printed in the USA

This logo is a registered trademark of Mike Holt Enterprises, Inc.

NEC®, NFPA 70®, NFPA 70E® and *National Electrical Code®* are registered trademarks of the National Fire Protection Association.

Are you an Instructor?

You can request a review copy of this or other Mike Holt Publications:

888.632.2633 • Training@MikeHolt.com

Download a sample PDF of all our publications by visiting MikeHolt.com/Instructors

I dedicate this book to the
Lord Jesus Christ, *my mentor and teacher.*
Proverbs 16:3

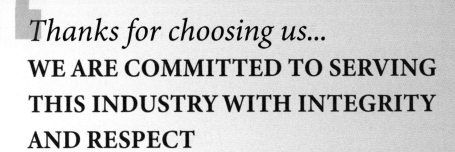

"*Thanks for choosing us...* WE ARE COMMITTED TO SERVING THIS INDUSTRY WITH INTEGRITY AND RESPECT

Since 1975, we have worked hard to develop products that get results, and to help individuals in their pursuit of success in this exciting industry.

From the very beginning we have been committed to the idea that customers come first. Everyone on my team will do everything they possibly can to help you succeed. I want you to know that we value you and are honored that you have chosen us to be your partner in training.

You are the future of this industry and we know that it is you who will make the difference in the years to come. My goal is to share with you everything that I know and to encourage you to pursue your education on a continuous basis. I hope that not only will you learn theory, *Code*, calculations, or how to pass an exam, but that in the process, you will become the expert in the field and the person others know to trust.

To put it simply, we genuinely care about your success and will do everything that we can to help you take your skills to the next level!

We are happy to partner with you on your educational journey.

God bless and much success,

TABLE OF CONTENTS

THEORY

Table of Contents

CODE

CALCULATIONS

ABOUT THIS TEXTBOOK

Mike Holt's Illustrated Guide to Electrical Exam Preparation, based on the 2023 *NEC*

Mike Holt's Illustrated Guide to Electrical Exam Preparation, based on the 2023 NEC® provides a review of electrical fundamentals, questions on the *National Electrical Code®*, and in-depth instruction on calculations. It all starts with an overview of basic math functions and electrical theory. The second module provides extensive *NEC* practice in answering questions on the *National Electrical Code* in sequential order. The final modules give step-by-step instruction on calculations. They give you the background you need to learn to solve the types of electrical calculations you will see on your exam. This textbook can be used alone or as part of one of our Exam Preparation study programs that include videos and additional instruction on theory and the *NEC*.

Electrical exams contain questions on electrical theory, the *Code*, and a variety of *NEC* calculations. The illustrations, examples and practice questions in this book hit all three of these points. To complete the work in this textbook, you will need a calculator, the 2023 *National Electrical Code,* and a notepad or paper to work through the calculations.

Passing your electrical exam is an important step in your career and it can be life changing. Many electricians are unsuccessful in passing their exams because they haven't properly prepared for the technical section, or they simply don't know how to take an exam. This textbook, along with our other exam preparation products can address these concerns and give you confidence!

The questions in this material are similar to the ones you'll see on Journeyman, Master, Contractor, or Inspector exams and written in a clear easy-to-understand way that will allow you to build skills with the least amount of confusion.

Although you may experience a few "aha" moments while reviewing this material, you won't find any "gotcha" type questions to discourage you. The goal of this material is to let you review things that are familiar, learn to answer calculations questions, and (most importantly) elevate your test-taking confidence before you sit for your exam.

Mike's writing style is informative, practical and applicable for today's electrical professional. As with all of Mike's textbooks, this one contains hundreds of detailed illustrations and step-by-step examples to help you visualize what's being explained, making it easier to understand challenging technical topics.

The learning material is presented in four modules:

Module I—Electrical Fundamentals. This module focuses on simple math equations and electrical theory. There's a summary of the theory principles, and simple math equations with graphics that will help you refresh your basic electrical fundamental knowledge and prepare you for the types of theory questions you might find on your exam.

Module II—*NEC* Practice Questions. Each set of review questions is ordered incrementally through the *NEC*. For example, the first set of review questions covers Article 90 in *NEC* order, the next covers Chapter 1 in *NEC* order, and so on. By completing each set of review questions, you'll be working your way through the *NEC* until you're able to answer questions from Article 90 all the way through to Article 830. The final *NEC* exam consists of 100 questions in random order.

Module III—*NEC* Calculations. In this module you will cover the fundamental topics and calculations typically included in journeyman exams. You'll work through each of these topics, step-by-step, one example, and one calculation at a time. You'll learn to consider the conditions necessary for the types of questions you will be required to answer on most electrical exams.

Module IV—Advanced *NEC* Calculations. The calculations in this section are the ones most likely found on Master exams, and not typically found on Journeyman exams. The advanced calculations covered in Module IV are the most time-consuming questions you will encounter in an exam, so it's important to become proficient at completing these correctly.

Taking an electrical exam? Here are the modules you should study:

Journeyman Exam. Focus your studies on Modules I–III. Go through the Review Questions and Practice Questions in those sections. If you don't score an 85% or better on those questions, review that section of the textbook before moving to the next.

Master/Contractor Exam. In addition to Modules I–III, you'll also need to complete Units 7 and 8 found in Module IV. Go through the Review Questions and Practice Questions in all units. If you don't score an 85% or better on the unit questions, review the content in the textbook and/or videos before moving to the next segment.

For additional help in preparing for an exam, we recommend you supplement your study program with the videos that accompany this textbook, and with additional in-depth instruction on electrical theory and *Code* topics. To order these videos at a discounted price or to get additional instruction on *Code* and theory, call 888.632.2633.

Important Note: The first step in preparing for your exam is to have a copy of the 2023 *NEC* to be used along with this textbook. When answering the *NEC* and calculations questions in this textbook, you'll need to reference your *Code* book.

 Make sure to watch our video on how to prepare for your exam. Scan the QR code or visit MikeHolt.com/Studytips.

Now you are ready to get started. Find a quiet space and designate a routine study time in your busy schedule. Relax and remember that you are NOT testing! You're practicing, learning, and building confidence to pass your exam!

The Scope of This Textbook

This textbook covers those installation requirements that we consider to be important and is based on the following conditions:

1. Power Systems and Voltage. All power-supply systems are assumed to be one of the following nominal voltages or "voltage class," unless identified otherwise:

- ▸ 2-wire, single-phase, 120V
- ▸ 3-wire, single-phase, 120/240V
- ▸ 4-wire, three-phase, 120/240V Delta High-Leg
- ▸ 4-wire, three-phase, 208Y/120V or 480Y/277V Wye

2. Electrical Calculations. Unless the question or example specifies three-phase, they're based on a single-phase power supply. In addition, all amperage calculations are rounded to the nearest whole number in accordance with Section 220.5(B).

3. Conductor Material/Insulation. The conductor material and insulation are copper THWN-2, unless otherwise indicated.

4. Conductor Sizing.

Circuits Rated 100A or Less. Conductors are sized to the 60°C column of Table 310.16 [110.14(C)(1)(a)(2)]. Where equipment is listed and identified for use with conductors having at least a 75°C temperature rating, the conductors can be sized to the 75°C column of Table 310.16 [110.14(C)(1)(a)(3)].

Circuits Rated Over 100A. Conductors are sized to the 75°C column of Table 310.16 [110.14(C)(1)(b)(2)].

5. Overcurrent Protective Device. The term "overcurrent protective device" refers to a molded-case circuit breaker, unless specified otherwise. Where a fuse is specified, it's a single-element type fuse, also known as a "onetime fuse," unless the text specifies otherwise.

6. Raceways. All raceways are metal unless otherwise noted. All PVC raceways are Schedule 40 unless otherwise noted.

7. Continuous Loads. All loads are considered noncontinuous unless specified otherwise.

How to Use This Textbook

This textbook can't be used without the *NEC*—be sure to have a copy of the 2023 *National Electrical Code* book in hand when working through the material. You'll need to reference it to answer the *NEC* and calculations questions. You'll notice that we simplify much of the *NEC* language, so some of the article and section titles appear different here than in the actual *Code* book. We believe doing so makes it easier to understand the content of the rule, so keep this in mind when comparing this textbook to the *NEC*.

Always compare what's being explained in this material to the *Code* book to become familiar with what it actually says. Get with others who are knowledgeable about the *NEC* to discuss any topics you find difficult to understand or join our free *Code* Forum at www.MikeHolt.com/Forum to post your question.

This textbook doesn't cover every rule in the *NEC*. The focus is specifically for exam preparation. For example, it doesn't include every article, section, subsection, exception, or Informational Note. So, don't be concerned if you see that the textbook contains Exception 1 and Exception 3, but not Exception 2.

Cross-References. This textbook might contain *NEC* cross-references to other related *Code* requirements. We've done this to help you develop a better understanding of how one *NEC* rule relates to another. These cross-references are indicated by *Code* section numbers in brackets, an example of which is "[90.4]."

Informational Notes. Informational Notes contained in the *NEC* will be identified in this textbook as "Note."

Exceptions. Exceptions contained in the *Code* book will be identified in this material as "Ex" and not spelled out.

As you read through this textbook, allow yourself enough time to review the text along with the detailed graphics and examples to give yourself the opportunity for a deeper understanding of the *NEC*.

Answer Keys

Digital answer keys are provided for all your purchases of Mike Holt textbooks, and can be found in your online account at Mike Holt Enterprises. Go to MikeHolt.com/MyAccount and log in to your account, or create one if you haven't already.

 If you are not currently a Mike Holt customer, you can access your answer key at MikeHolt.com/MyAK23EP.

Watch the Videos That Accompany This Textbook

Mike, along with an expert panel, recorded videos to accompany this textbook. Watching these videos will complete your learning experience. The videos contain explanations and additional commentary that expand on the topics covered in the text. Mike and the panel discuss the nuances behind the rules, and cover their practical application in the field, in a way that is different from what can be conveyed in written format.

 To watch a sample video clip, scan this QR code with a smartphone app or visit MikeHolt.com/23EPvideos. To get the complete video library that accompanies this book, call 888.632.2633 to find out how to upgrade your program, or visit MikeHolt.com/Upgrade23EXB.

Technical Questions

As you progress through this textbook, you might find that you don't understand every explanation, example, calculation, or comment. If you find some topics difficult to understand, they are discussed in detail in the videos that correlate to this book. You may also find it helpful to discuss your questions with instructors, co-workers, other students, or your supervisor—they might have a perspective that will help you understand more clearly. Don't become frustrated, and don't get down on yourself.

 If you have additional questions that aren't covered in this material, visit MikeHolt.com/Forum, and post your question on the Code Forum for help.

Textbook Errors and Corrections

We're committed to providing you the finest product with the fewest errors and take great care to ensure our textbooks are correct. But we're realistic and know that errors might be found after printing. If you believe that there's an error of any kind (typographical, grammatical, technical, etc.) in this textbook or in the Answer Key, please visit MikeHolt.com/Corrections and complete the online Textbook Correction Form.

Textbook Format

The layout and design of this textbook incorporate special features and symbols designed to help you navigate easily through the material, and to enhance your understanding.

Formulas

$$P = I \times E$$

Formulas are easily identifiable in green text on a gray bar.

Modular Color-Coded Page Layout

Modules are color-coded to make it easy to navigate through each different part of the textbook.

According to Article 100

Throughout the textbook, Mike references definitions that are easily identified by colored text "**According to Article 100**," at the start of the paragraph.

Indexes

At the end of a module there will be an index of the topics covered in that module, with a reference to the related content for that topic. This will make it easier to go back to a module to review specific topics, or to reference the *Code* rule or section in one of our other supporting books, like *Understanding Electrical Theory*.

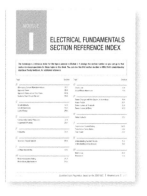

Caution, Danger, and Warning Icons

These icons, when they appear in the textbook, highlight areas of concern.

Danger

DANGER: An explanation of possible severe injury or death.

Caution

CAUTION: An explanation of possible damage to property or equipment.

Warning

WARNING: An explanation of possible severe property damage or personal injury.

Key Features

Examples and practical application questions and answers are contained in yellow boxes.

Detailed full-color educational graphics illustrate the rule in a real-world application.

Author's Comments provide additional information to help you understand the context.

Each first level subsection is highlighted in yellow to help you navigate through the text.

If you see an ellipsis (● ● ●) at the bottom right corner of a page or example box, it is continued on the following page.

6.16 | Dwelling Unit Calculations

Cooking Equipment Neutral Load [220.61(B)(1)]

The neutral load for household cooking appliances, such as electric ranges, wall-mounted ovens, or counter-mounted cooking units, is calculated at 70 percent of the demand load as determined by 220.55.

▶ **Neutral Load—Cooking Equipment, Example**

Question: What is the neutral load for one 14 kW range? ▶Figure 6–31

(a) 3,510W   (b) 4,910W   (c) 5,710W   (d) 6,160W

Dwelling Unit Standard Calculation
Range Neutral Demand Load
220.61(B)(1) Example

14 kW,
120/240V range.

Range Demand Load = 8 kW x 110% = 8.8 kW
Neutral Demand Load = 8.8 kW x 70%
Neutral Demand Load = 6.16 kW

▶Figure 6–31

Solution:

Step 1: Since the range exceeds 12 kW, we must comply with Note 1 of Table 220.55. The first step is to determine the demand load as listed in Column C of Table 220.55 for one unit which is 8 kW.

Step 2: The Column C value (8 kW) must be increased by 5 percent for each kVA that the range exceeds 12 kW [Table 220.55, Note 1]: 14 kW – 12 kW = 2 kW.

2 × 5% = 10 percent increase of the Column C value resulting in 110 percent

Cooking Equipment Demand Load = 8 kW × 110%
Cooking Equipment Demand Load = 8.8 kW

Neutral Demand Load = 8,800 VA × 70% [220.61(B)(1)]
Neutral Demand Load = 6,160W

Answer: *(d) 6,160W*

6.16 Service Neutral Calculation [220.61]

(A) Neutral Calculated Load. The neutral calculated load for feeders or services is the maximum calculated load between the neutral conductor and any one phase conductor.

Author's Comment:

▶ Line-to-line loads do not place any load on the neutral conductor, therefore line-to-line loads are not considered in the neutral calculation.

(B) Neutral Calculated Load Reductions

(1) Electric Ranges, Ovens, Cooking Units. The neutral load for household electric ranges, wall-mounted ovens, or counter-mounted cooking units can be calculated at 70 percent of the cooking equipment demand load as determined in accordance with Table 220.55.

(1) Dryer Load. The neutral load for household electric dryers can be calculated at 70 percent of the dryer calculated load as determined in accordance with Table 220.54.

▶ **Example**

Question: What is the service neutral load for 6,000 sq ft. dwelling unit containing the following loads?

• *Dishwasher, 12A at 120V*
• *Disposal (Waste), 10A at 120V*
• *Microwave, 16A at 120V*
• *Water Heater (Tankless), 40A at 240V*
• *Dryer, 4,000W at 120/240V*
• *Cooking, Range, 14,000W at 120/240V*
• *Trash Compactor, 8A at 120V*
• *A/C Condenser, 30A at 240V*
• *Electric Heating, 9.6 kW*

(a) 58A   (b) 68A   (c) 78A   (d) 88A

Solution:

Step 1: Determine the general lighting and general-use receptacles, and the laundry circuit demand load [Table 220.45].

General Lighting and Receptacles		
Load [220.41]	6,000 sq ft × 3 VA	18,000 VA
Small-Appliance Circuits [210.52(B)]	1,500 VA × 2	3,000 VA
Laundry Circuit [210.52(F)]	1,500 VA × 1	+1,500 VA
Total Connected Load		22,500 VA

PASSING YOUR EXAM

Electrical Exam Study Tips

Preparing for your exam means more than just knowing electrical fundamentals, *Code*, and calculations; it also means being prepared for the anxiety and stress of studying and test-taking. Many good and knowledgeable electricians have not passed their exams because they did not know the proper way to get ready for an exam, or how to take a test. Preparing for your exam is a process, and the following suggestions are designed to help you pass your exam with confidence.

Mentally Prepare Yourself and Your Family

Identify your goals. One of the ways to keep yourself motivated is to figure out why you are taking the exam. When you keep your goals in mind, it makes it easier to stay disciplined when studying for your exam.

Stay positive. The way you talk to yourself has a huge influence on how you approach studying. If you stay positive and view the process as a good one, it makes it much easier to stay on task. Say positive affirmations like: "I've got this," "I can do this," and "It will all make sense in the end."

Visualize success. Imagine how passing your exam will feel, and how it will change your life. See yourself passing and holding the passing grade in your hand. This is how professional athletes prepare for competition, and studying for an exam is very similar.

Focus on your successes. Focus on how much you have already accomplished and not on your fears or worries about the outcome.

Manage the stress of studying for an exam. Some ideas to de-stress include a walk with family or a pet, listening to music, exercising, spending time with family, praying, meditating, or sitting down with a favorite book during a break.

Communicate with your family. Studying is hard work, and it will take you time, and will impact your entire family. Communicate to them how passing this exam can change all of your lives. Explain to them the specifics of why you need to study and when you need to study. If you do a good job of including them in the process it will be easier for them to understand the changes that will affect the family dynamics. Remind them that this is a short-term commitment that will have life-time benefits.

Take Care of Your Health and Increase Your Energy Level

Eyes. Visit the eye doctor to make sure that your eyes are healthy and confirm that you don't need glasses. You will be doing a lot of reading and you don't want to strain your eyes by not having the proper glasses, if needed.

Sleep. Make sure you get plenty of rest at night—this gives your body (and mind) time to recharge. Most adults need 7–9 hours a night to be well rested. This may not be possible but great sleep habits will be important to help you retain the information you have learned.

Exercise. Try to add physical activity every day to feel more energized. Stretch if you start to feel yourself tense up while studying.

Eat well. Fuel your body with a diet low in fats, sugars, and salt. Avoid excessive red meats, which can make you feel drained and run-down. Instead, try foods that provide a slow, steady release of energy, like fish, blueberries, nuts, yogurt, and seeds.

▸ Time yourself while taking the exam so you can get practice answering questions in a timed format.

Research the Exam Details and Select the Right Study Material

Review state requirements and identify what you will be tested on.

▸ Check with your Local or State Examining Board to get as much information as possible, as each exam is different. To find out the requirements for your state visit www.MikeHolt.com/Statelicense.

▸ Review the Candidate Booklet.

▸ Which Edition of the *NEC* is the exam based on?

▸ Is the exam open-book?

　▸ If yes—can you use your own copy? What kind of markings can you use? What kind of notes or highlighting, if any, are you allowed to take in the exam room?

▸ What items can you have while taking the exam? This includes both professional items, like reference books, extra tools such as calculators and pencils, and personal items, like a watch, bottle of water, or jacket.

▸ What reference books will be used on the exam?

▸ What types of questions will you be asked, and how many of each type?

Identify your strengths and weaknesses. What works for someone else may not be as effective for you!

▸ Every person has a different work and educational background. Your study program should be based on what you already know and your experience with taking exams. Some questions you should ask yourself:

　▸ How strong am I in *Code*, Electrical Calculations, Fundamentals?

　▸ Am I a visual learner or can I learn well directly from a book? Or, am I an auditory learner, or tactile learner?

　▸ Am I a good test-taker?

▸ Take a practice exam so you can test your skills and understanding of Theory, *Code* and Calculations, and are comfortable with the time constraints.

Make a Plan

Schedule study time and other commitments.

▸ Know the date of your exam, and work backwards to create a study schedule that fits your needs. Give yourself enough time to study! One of the biggest reasons people fail their exams is that they simply didn't give themselves enough structured study time.

▸ Put your study times into your calendar and try to plan it for the same time each and every week.

▸ Study at the times where you can be the most productive, whether that is in the morning when you first start the day, or at night, when the stresses of the day are behind you and handled. You know when you are most able to absorb new material and should plan your study schedule accordingly.

▸ If you feel yourself drifting while studying, then give yourself a 5- or 10-minute break to rest, and start again. This will help you keep your study time productive.

▸ Make sure you also schedule time for more than just studying. Factor in time around your work and study for rest, meals, and time with friends and family. By setting aside time to spend with your family it will be easier for them to support you if they know what to expect.

▸ Sticking to a routine each week and pacing yourself will help avoid cramming at the last minute.

Organize your study area.

▸ Set up a private study location that is quiet with good lighting. If it's not quiet enough, invest in good quality noise-cancelling headphones.

▸ All your work material should be in one place, so you don't waste time setting up each time you sit down to study. Find space in your home to keep your reference books, mobile devices, supplies and study materials.

▸ Keep organized folders for notes and miscellaneous items—if you are allowed to use resources during your exam, it will be quick and easy for you to find what you need.

▸ Keep organized folders for notes, exams and answer keys, and miscellaneous items—if you are allowed to use resources during your exam, it will be quick and easy for you to find what you need.

▸ If possible, always have an extra copy of your book(s) with you, so you can study anytime, anywhere! A digital version of this textbook is a great way to study on the go. Be creative!

Successful Study Tips

Really get to know your *Code* book and other reference books.

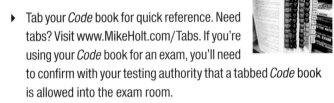

▸ Tab your *Code* book for quick reference. Need tabs? Visit www.MikeHolt.com/Tabs. If you're using your *Code* book for an exam, you'll need to confirm with your testing authority that a tabbed *Code* book is allowed into the exam room.

  ▸ The quicker you can find information during a timed exam, the easier the exam will be. One of the best ways to pass your exam is to be completely confident with your *NEC* book, and this only happens with practice.

▸ If your State Board allows it, highlight important details in your *Code* book. Remember to confirm this with the board.

Stay hydrated and satisfied. Drink water and have a light snack if you haven't recently eaten.

Eliminate distractions. Turn off your phone and let your family know that you are in "official study mode."

When using your textbook focus on the following:

▸ Review the headings before reading, so that your brain knows ahead of time what material you are mastering.

▸ Continually ask yourself questions while reading through the content. This helps you stay focused, retain more information, and learn where specific topics are in your materials.

▸ Pay attention to the graphics; they support the learning, and in many cases will explain the specific topic you are learning.

▸ Work through the practice questions. Research tells us that testing improves learning and the ability for your brain to retrieve the information later. So those questions not only help you determine if you have mastered a concept, but they also help you learn it.

Making marks in books. Remember that any marks you make in your books should be in accordance with the rules of your Exam Board.

Take a break. Every person is different, but plan to take a 5- to 10-minute break every 30–50 minutes so you can stay focused and productive during your study time. Try moving around during your break, or just get up and stretch instead of checking your phone or messages.

Use music. If listening to music helps you study, make sure it is low and instrumental.

Rest your eyes. Be sure to look up occasionally while studying. Our eyes are designed for survival, and the combination of small text with close-up continuous reading puts a large amount of strain on our eyes.

Study with others. You are more likely to study if you have a friend to be your "accountability partner."

▸ Students who study together perform above average because they try different approaches and discuss ideas and solutions. So, if possible, set up an occasional study session with others preparing for their exam.

Take advantage of your natural learning style. Everyone learns differently, and you can improve your retention by recognizing the method that best suits you. There are different schools of thought about how people learn, but one of the most popular breaks down learning into three styles:

▸ **Auditory.** If you are an auditory learner it is important for you to hear the material. Watch videos, read sections from your textbook out loud if they're difficult for you to understand, study with someone else so you can discuss the material. Remember to work in a quiet area so that noise is not distracting to you.

▸ **Visual.** Since you learn better seeing pictures and visual stimuli, really study the graphics in this textbook. Here are additional ways to utilize your learning style. If you aren't taking a class, watch a video so you can see the instructor interact with the images and content. Create your own pictures to work through difficult concepts, color-code your notes, work with flash cards, and take notes or create outlines to memorize the material.

▸ **Tactile.** A tactile learner is a "hands-on" person who prefers to touch, build, or physically interact with what they are learning, taking them apart and putting them back together. As a tactile learner, hands-on activities like physically highlighting your textbook, or finding ways to create a physical connection with the content will be the best way for you to learn.

Don't get overwhelmed. Often students make studying harder because they get intimidated by the work ahead. Take it step by step and understand that with time and practice the material will start to make sense. Break up your studying into manageable sections. This way you can conquer the content section by section.

If you are in a class, speak up! There are valuable ideas to be shared in the classroom setting, and there is nothing wrong with asking for clarification or more explanation. Others may have the same questions that you do!

Time yourself while taking tests. Ultimately, timing is an element of your exam, so the more you can practice, the faster you will work through your questions on exam day, and the less stressful the timing element will be for you mentally.

Tips for Passing Your Exam

You've done the preparation: read books and materials, watched videos, studied, and hopefully even did a practice exam or two. Now comes the second part: taking and passing your official exam. Here are some helpful tips to ace your exam:

The Week Before the Exam

Checklist. Create a checklist of everything you need to do before the exam and bring to the exam.

Back-up. Make sure you have a back-up calculator, batteries, and any other supplies so that you are prepared. If you use glasses to read, bring an extra pair of these as well. If you are taking a paper exam, have 6 sharpened #2 pencils with erasers.

The Night Before the Exam

Pack. Make sure everything is ready and packed the night before. Go through your supplies list one more time and have your clothes already selected and laid out.

Confidence. You have already done your work, so while there is nothing wrong with a quick refresher, don't try to cram the night before. Feel confident and calm. Create some positive affirmations, such as "I am prepared for this test, and I will do well!"

Directions. Review directions to the testing facility. Know where the exam is going to take place and how long it will take to get there. The last thing you need is to get lost on your way to the testing facility. NOTE: If the facility is more than an hour away from your home you may want to consider getting a hotel near the testing facility.

Sleep. You have done what you can, and now is the time to get a good night's rest. Get to sleep early so you can get to the exam well-rested.

The Day of the Exam

Healthy Breakfast. Have a healthy, high-protein breakfast like eggs, yogurt, whole grain cereal with milk, or oatmeal with milk.

Drinks and Snacks. Get a water bottle, insulated mug, and energy snacks ready if you are permitted to bring them into the exam.

Reference Books. Take all your reference books with you. If you are unsure if you are permitted to use a particular book in the exam, bring it and let the proctors tell you what you can and can't use.

Get there early. Know where the exam will be held and leave early so you can arrive early.

▸ This gives you time to find a comfortable seat, organize your test taking materials, review your *NEC* book, and use the restroom (for privacy and accuracy, some testing centers do not allow restroom breaks during the examination).

I.D. and Supplies. Bring your identification, confirmation papers from the licensing board, and any additional information and supplies you may need to be successful.

Take a quick walk to get centered. If time permits, one of the best ways to harness your energy is to take a quick walk to reduce the over-flow of nerves. If you don't have time for a walk, try a few stretches before you head out the door.

Music. Listen to music that relaxes you while you are driving to your exam.

Be positive. Don't engage in negative talk with others beforehand (for example, "I'm so nervous—I don't know if I studied enough," or "You seem so much more prepared than me, I'm not ready!"). Instead, focus on your positive affirmations.

FIVE Success Strategies for Your Exam

1. Get centered

It is normal to be a little bit nervous as you sit for the exam. The key is to control that energy, so it can help you with your exam. Here are a few techniques:

▸ **Breathing technique.** Breathe in slowly for a count of 4 seconds, then breathe out slowly for a count of four. Repeat. Imagine that there is a balloon in your stomach and you are trying to fill it. As you breathe in, watch your stomach rise and as you breathe out, watch it deflate. This will help reduce any last-minute stress as you sit for your exam.

▸ **Single-Muscle Relaxation.** If you find that you carry your tension in your muscles (clenching your jaw, tensing your shoulders), purposefully tense and then relax that group. Repeat every few minutes, and the rest of your muscles will automatically relax, too.

▸ **Prayer.** For many people, prayer is exactly what is needed to mentally prepare for the stress of an upcoming exam. They find that prayer provides comfort when it is needed the most, and some studies have shown a correlation between prayer and stress relief.

2. Understand the question

Read. Make sure you fully and carefully read and understand each word of the question. What are they really looking for in the question?

Review Answers. Read all the answers before selecting the first one that looks correct.

Circle important words. Remember that one word can change the entire meaning, so underline or circle any key words that stand out.

Move on if confused. If you find that a question is difficult, skip it and come back to it later if this is possible in your test format.

▸ If you are stuck on a question, you will likely spend more time dwelling on it, and then worry about completing on time, setting off a chain reaction.

▸ Make sure you mark the questions you are coming back to, so you don't miss them.

Guessing. When you don't know the answer, rule out those answers that are completely wrong through the process of elimination. Never leave a question unanswered—not answering a question is guaranteed to be wrong, but your best guess could be correct.

3. Check your work

Review. Before completing your exam go through all questions to make sure that you have understood and answered correctly and filled in all blanks.

Bubble sheets. In written exams, make sure if using a bubble sheet that you fully and completely fill in the circle for your answer.

Second guessing. Be careful when changing answers. Your first answer is best in most cases, and if you aren't certain, stick with that choice. On written exams, be sure to completely erase to change your answers if necessary and erase any stray pencil marks from the answer sheet.

4. A good strategy to take your exam is by "passing" over it several times

Pass 1. Answer the questions that you know and can answer within 30 seconds, with or without your reference book. If it takes longer than 30 seconds, go on to the next. Chances are, you'll come across the answer while finding another one.

Pass 2. Go back to the beginning of the exam, and do the same as before, but allow more time for each question. A good timeframe is double the amount of the first pass, so allow 60 seconds this time through.

Pass 3. Spend your remaining time on each question equally. If you still haven't answered, make an educated guess, you don't want to leave questions unanswered on your exam, by eliminating several options you increase your chance of getting it right even if you don't know the exact answer.

Pass 4. Use the last 30 minutes of the exam for review. Reread each question and ensure that they are answered correctly (or with your educated guess). Make sure your answers were transferred correctly for paper exams, and make sure all answers are saved (if applicable) for computer exams. With any remaining time, see if you can find an answer for those that you guessed on. Remember though that your first answer is usually the correct one.

5. A note about rounding answers

You should always round your answers to the same number of places as the exam's answers.

Example. If an exam has multiple choice options of: (a) 2.1, (b) 2.2, (c) 2.3, or (d) none of these, and your calculation comes out to 2.16; don't choose the answer (d) none of these. The correct answer is (b) 2.2, because the answer choices in this case are rounded off to the nearest tenth.

Example. It can be rounded to tens, such as: (a) 50, (b) 60, (c) 70, or (d) none of these. For this group, an answer such as 67 will be (c) 70, while an answer of 63 will be (b) 60. The general rule is to check the question's choice of answers and then round off your answer to match it.

Final Thoughts on Taking a Test

Walk in with confidence, knowing that you have done your best to get ready for this exam. If you pass the first time, GREAT! If you don't pass this time, ask if you can review your exam so that you can see what you need to work on, and come into the exam confident for the next time.

Good luck and God Bless. Please let us know when you pass! We love to hear good news stories, email us at Info@MikeHolt.com.

We are here to help you in every way that we can. If you need anything, please call us at 888.632.2633.

ADDITIONAL PRODUCTS TO HELP YOU LEARN

Upgrade Your Textbook with the 2023 *Electrical Exam Preparation* Videos

One of the best ways to get the most out of this textbook is to use it in conjunction with the corresponding videos. These videos showcase dynamic discussions as Mike and the video team of industry experts deep-dive into the topics in this book. They analyze each rule, its purpose, and its application in the field.

Whether you're a visual or an auditory learner, watching the videos as you work through the textbook will enhance your knowledge and provide additional in-depth insight into each topic. Upgrade your program today, and you will broaden your understanding of the rules and their impact on your work. All upgrade purchases include the corresponding videos plus a digital copy of the textbook.

UPGRADE PACKAGE INCLUDES:

▸ *2023 Electrical Exam Preparation videos*

Plus! A digital version of the book

 Ready to get started? To add the videos that accompany this textbook, scan the QR code or call our office at 888.632.2633 to upgrade your product.

Have questions? You can e-mail Info@MikeHolt.com.

Product Code: [23EXBUPGRADEVI]

Understanding the *NEC* Complete Video Library

Do you want a comprehensive understanding of the *Code*? Then you need Mike's best-selling Understanding the *NEC* Complete Video Library. This program has helped thousands of electricians learn the *Code* because of its clear explanations, and easy-to-use format. Mike guides students through the most utilized rules and takes you step-by-step through the *NEC*, in *Code* order, with detailed illustrations, great practice questions, and in-depth video analysis. The full-color instructional graphics in the textbooks help students visualize and understand the concepts being taught; the videos provide additional reinforcement with Mike and the panel discussing each article, its meaning and its application in the real world. When you need to know the *Code*, this program is the best tool you can use to start building your knowledge—there's no other product quite like it.

PROGRAM INCLUDES:

Understanding the *National Electrical Code*—Volume 1 Textbook
▸ *Understanding the NEC Volume 1 videos*

Understanding the *National Electrical Code*—Volume 2 Textbook
▸ *Understanding the NEC Volume 2 videos*

Bonding and Grounding Textbook
▸ *Bonding and Grounding videos*

Fundamental *NEC* Calculations Textbook
▸ *Fundamental NEC Calculations videos*

Understanding the *National Electrical Code* Workbook (Articles 90-480)
Digital answer keys
Plus! A digital version of each book

Product Code: [23UNDLIBMM]

To order, call 888.632.2633 or visit MikeHolt.com/Code.

Mike Holt's Journeyman and Master Intermediate Library

When you know *Code* and Theory, but need additional instruction on Electrical Calculations, the Intermediate Library is your perfect study program. This library includes the calculations videos that accompany this book to provide more instruction. Mike's *2023 Changes to the NEC* textbook and videos are a great companion to help you review and refresh your *Code* skills. The Simulated Exams give you the opportunity to apply the knowledge you have learned.

The Master Intermediate Library includes everything in the Journeyman Library, plus advanced calculations videos.

PROGRAM INCLUDES:

Changes to the *NEC* Textbook
▸ *Changes to the NEC videos*

Electrical Exam Preparation Textbook
▸ *Electrical Exam Preparation videos*

Journeyman or Master Electrician Simulated Exams

Digital answer keys

Plus! A digital version of each book

Product Code: [23MAINMM] or [23JRINMM]

For information about adding the videos and additional textbooks, call us at 888.632.2633.

Mike Holt's Journeyman and Master Comprehensive Library

This is our best-selling exam preparation library and has helped thousands of electricians across the country pass their state and county exams. The Comprehensive Program will help you master essential concepts with in-depth training on *Code*, Calculations and Electrical Fundamentals. Completing this program will give you confidence on your exam, as well as in the field.

PROGRAM INCLUDES:

Understanding Electrical Theory Textbook
▸ *Electrical Theory videos*

Understanding the *National Electrical Code*—Volume 1 Textbook
▸ *Understanding the NEC Volume 1 videos*

Understanding the *National Electrical Code*—Volume 2 Textbook
▸ *Understanding the NEC Volume 2 videos*

Bonding and Grounding Textbook
▸ *Bonding and Grounding videos*

Fundamental *NEC* Calculations Textbook
▸ *Fundamental NEC Calculations videos*

Electrical Exam Preparation Textbook
▸ *Electrical Exam Preparation videos*

Journeyman or Master Electrician Simulated Exams

Digital answer keys

Plus! A digital version of each book

Product Code: [23MACOMM] or [23JRCOMM]

Ready to upgrade? Contact our office to get the additional components, 888.632.2633.

Very happy about how well this is put together and easy to understand. Excellent products—definitely recommend this to anyone in the electrical trade who wants to improve their knowledge. —Jose J.

HOW TO USE THE *NATIONAL ELECTRICAL CODE*

The original *NEC* document was developed in 1897 as a result of the united efforts of various insurance, electrical, architectural, and other cooperative interests. The National Fire Protection Association (NFPA) has sponsored the *National Electrical Code* since 1911.

The purpose of the *Code* is the practical safeguarding of persons and property from hazards arising from the use of electricity. It isn't intended as a design specification or an instruction manual for untrained persons. It is, in fact, a standard that contains the minimum requirements for an electrical installation that's essentially free from hazard. Learning to understand and use the *Code* is critical to you working safely; whether you're training to become an electrician, or are already an electrician, electrical contractor, inspector, engineer, designer, or instructor.

The *NEC* was written for qualified persons; those who understand electrical terms, theory, safety procedures, and electrical trade practices. Learning to use the *Code* is a lengthy process and can be frustrating if you don't approach it the right way. First, you'll need to understand electrical theory and if you don't have theory as a background when you get into the *NEC*, you're going to struggle. Take one step back if necessary and learn electrical theory. You must also understand the concepts and terms in the *Code* and know grammar and punctuation in order to understand the complex structure of the rules and their intended purpose(s). The *NEC* is written in a formal outline which many of us haven't seen or used since high school or college so it's important for you to pay particular attention to this format. Our goal for the next few pages is to give you some guidelines and suggestions on using your *Code* book to help you understand that standard, and assist you in what you're trying to accomplish and, ultimately, your personal success as an electrical professional!

Language Considerations for the *NEC*

Terms and Concepts

The *NEC* contains many technical terms, and it's crucial for *Code* users to understand their meanings and applications. If you don't understand a term used in a rule, it will be impossible to properly apply the *NEC* requirement. Article 100 defines those that are used generally in two or more articles throughout the *Code*; for example, the term "Dwelling Unit" is found in many articles. If you don't know the *NEC* definition for a "dwelling unit" you can't properly identify its *Code* requirements. Another example worth mentioning is the term "Outlet." For many people it has always meant a receptacle—not so in the *NEC*!

Article 100 contains the definitions of terms used throughout the *Code*. Where a definition is unique to a specific article, the article number is indicated at the end of the definition in parenthesis (xxx). For example, the definition of "Pool" is specific to Article 680 and ends with (680) because it applies ONLY to that article. Definitions of standard terms, such as volt, voltage drop, ampere, impedance, and resistance are not contained in Article 100. If the *NEC* does not define a term, then a dictionary or building code acceptable to the authority having jurisdiction should be consulted.

Small Words, Grammar, and Punctuation

Technical words aren't the only ones that require close attention. Even simple words can make a big difference to the application of a rule. Is there a comma? Does it use "or," "and," "other than," "greater than," or "smaller than"? The word "or" can imply alternate choices for wiring methods. A word like "or" gives us choices while the word "and" can mean an additional requirement must be met.

An example of the important role small words play in the *NEC* is found in 110.26(C)(2), where it says equipment containing overcurrent, switching, "or" control devices that are 1,200A or more "and" over 6 ft wide require a means of egress at each end of the working space. In this section, the word "or" clarifies that equipment containing any of the three types of devices listed must follow this rule. The word "and" clarifies that 110.26(C)(2) only applies if the equipment is both 1,200A or more and over 6 ft wide.

Grammar and punctuation play an important role in establishing the meaning of a rule. The location of a comma can dramatically change the requirement of a rule such as in 250.28(A), where it says a main bonding jumper shall be a wire, bus, screw, or similar suitable conductor. If the comma between "bus" and "screw" was removed, only a "bus screw" could be used. That comma makes a big change in the requirements of the rule.

Slang Terms or Technical Jargon

Trade-related professionals in different areas of the country often use local "slang" terms that aren't shared by all. This can make it difficult to communicate if it isn't clear what the meaning of those slang terms are. Use the proper terms by finding out what their definitions and applications are before you use them. For example, the term "pigtail" is often used to describe the short piece of conductor used to connect a device to a splice, but a "pigtail" is also used for a rubberized light socket with pre-terminated conductors. Although the term is the same, the meaning is very different and could cause confusion. The words "splice" and "tap" are examples of terms often interchanged in the field but are two entirely different things! The uniformity and consistency of the terminology used in the *Code*, makes it so everyone says and means the same thing regardless of geographical location.

NEC Style and Layout

It's important to understand the structure and writing style of the *Code* if you want to use it effectively. The *National Electrical Code* is organized using twelve major components.

1. Table of Contents
2. Chapters—Chapters 1 through 9 (major categories)
3. Articles—Chapter subdivisions that cover specific subjects
4. Parts—Divisions used to organize article subject matter
5. Sections—Divisions used to further organize article subject matter
6. Tables and Figures—Represent the mandatory requirements of a rule
7. Exceptions—Alternatives to the main *Code* rule
8. Informational Notes—Explanatory material for a specific rule (not a requirement)
9. Tables—Applicable as referenced in the *NEC*
10. Annexes—Additional explanatory information such as tables and references (not a requirement)
11. Index
12. Changes to the *Code* from the previous edition

1. Table of Contents. The Table of Contents displays the layout of the chapters, articles, and parts as well as the page numbers. It's an excellent resource and should be referred to periodically to observe the interrelationship of the various *NEC* components. When attempting to locate the rules for a specific situation, knowledgeable *Code* users often go first to the Table of Contents to quickly find the specific *NEC* rule that applies.

2. Chapters. There are nine chapters, each of which is divided into articles. The articles fall into one of four groupings: General Requirements (Chapters 1 through 4), Specific Requirements (Chapters 5 through 7), Communications Systems (Chapter 8), and Tables (Chapter 9).

Chapter 1—General
Chapter 2—Wiring and Protection
Chapter 3—Wiring Methods and Materials
Chapter 4—Equipment for General Use
Chapter 5—Special Occupancies
Chapter 6—Special Equipment
Chapter 7—Special Conditions
Chapter 8—Communications Systems (Telephone, Data, Satellite, Cable TV, and Broadband)
Chapter 9—Tables–Conductor and Raceway Specifications

3. Articles. The *NEC* contains approximately 160 articles, each of which covers a specific subject. It begins with Article 90, the introduction to the *Code* which contains the purpose of the *NEC*, what is covered and isn't covered, along with how the *Code* is arranged. It also gives information on enforcement, how mandatory and permissive rules are written, and how explanatory material is included. Article 90 also includes information on formal interpretations, examination of equipment for safety, wiring planning, and information about formatting units of measurement. Here are some other examples of articles you'll find in the *NEC*:

Article 110—General Requirements for Electrical Installations
Article 250—Grounding and Bonding
Article 300—General Requirements for Wiring Methods and Materials
Article 430—Motors, Motor Circuits, and Motor Controllers
Article 500—Hazardous (Classified) Locations
Article 680—Swimming Pools, Fountains, and Similar Installations
Article 725—Class 2 and Class 3 Power-Limited Circuits
Article 800—General Requirements for Communications Systems

4. Parts. Larger articles are subdivided into parts. Because the parts of a *Code* article aren't included in the section numbers, we tend to forget to what "part" an *NEC* rule is relating. For example, Table 110.34(A) contains working space clearances for electrical equipment. If we aren't careful, we might think this table applies to all electrical installations, but Table 110.34(A) is in Part III, which only contains requirements for "Over 1,000 Volts, Nominal" installations. The rules for working clearances for electrical equipment for systems 1,000V, nominal, or less are contained in Table 110.26(A)(1), which is in Part II—1,000 Volts, Nominal, or Less.

5. Sections. Each *NEC* rule is called a "*Code* Section." A *Code* section may be broken down into subdivisions; first level subdivision will be in parentheses like (A), (B),..., the next will be second level subdivisions in parentheses like (1), (2),..., and third level subdivisions in lowercase letters such as (a), (b), and so on.

For example, the rule requiring all receptacles in a dwelling unit bathroom to be GFCI protected is contained in Section 210.8(A)(1) which is in Chapter 2, Article 210, Section 8, first level subdivision (A), and second level subdivision (1).

Note: According to the *NEC Style Manual*, first and second level subdivisions are required to have titles. A title for a third level subdivision is permitted but not required.

Many in the industry incorrectly use the term "Article" when referring to a *Code* section. For example, they say "Article 210.8," when they should say "Section 210.8." Section numbers in this textbook are shown without the word "Section," unless they're at the beginning of a sentence. For example, Section 210.8(A) is shown as simply 210.8(A).

6. Tables and Figures. Many *NEC* requirements are contained within tables, which are lists of *Code* rules placed in a systematic arrangement. The titles of the tables are extremely important; you must read them carefully in order to understand the contents, applications, and limitations of each one. Notes are often provided in or below a table; be sure to read them as well since they're also part of the requirement. For example, Note 1 for Table 300.5(A) explains how to measure the cover when burying cables and raceways and Note 5 explains what to do if solid rock is encountered.

7. Exceptions. Exceptions are *NEC* requirements or permissions that provide an alternative method to a specific rule. There are two types of exceptions—mandatory and permissive. When a rule has several exceptions, those exceptions with mandatory requirements are listed before the permissive exceptions.

Mandatory Exceptions. A mandatory exception uses the words "shall" or "shall not." The word "shall" in an exception means that if you're using the exception, you're required to do it in a specific way. The phrase "shall not" means it isn't permitted.

Permissive Exceptions. A permissive exception uses words such as "shall be permitted," which means it's acceptable (but not mandatory) to do it in this way.

8. Informational Notes. An Informational Note contains explanatory material intended to clarify a rule or give assistance, but it isn't a *Code* requirement.

9. Tables. Chapter 9 consists of tables applicable as referenced in the *NEC*. They're used to calculate raceway sizing, conductor fill, the radius of raceway bends, and conductor voltage drop.

10. Informative Annexes. Annexes aren't a part of the *Code* requirements and are included for informational purposes only.

Annex A. Product Safety Standards
Annex B. Application Information for Ampacity Calculation
Annex C. Conduit, Tubing, and Cable Tray Fill Tables for Conductors and Fixture Wires of the Same Size
Annex D. Examples
Annex E. Types of Construction
Annex F. Availability and Reliability for Critical Operations Power Systems (COPS), and Development and Implementation of Functional Performance Tests (FPTs) for Critical Operations Power Systems
Annex G. Supervisory Control and Data Acquisition (SCADA)
Annex H. Administration and Enforcement
Annex I. Recommended Tightening Torque Tables from UL Standard 486A-486B
Annex J. ADA Standards for Accessible Design
Annex K. Use of Medical Electrical Equipment in Dwellings and Residential Board-and-Care Occupancies

11. Index. The Index at the back of the *NEC* is helpful in locating a specific rule using pertinent keywords to assist in your search.

12. Changes to the *Code*. Changes in the *NEC* are indicated as follows:

▸ Rules that were changed since the previous edition are identified by shading the revised text.

▸ New rules aren't shaded like a change, instead they have a shaded "N" in the margin to the left of the section number.

▸ Relocated rules are treated like new rules with a shaded "N" in the left margin by the section number.

▸ Deleted rules are indicated by a bullet symbol " • " located in the left margin where the rule was in the previous edition. Unlike older editions the bullet symbol is only used where one or more complete paragraphs have been deleted.

▸ A "Δ" represents partial text deletions and or figure/table revisions somewhere in the text. There's no specific indication of which word, group of words, or a sentence was deleted.

How to Locate a Specific Requirement

How to go about finding what you're looking for in the *Code* book depends, to some degree, on your experience with the *NEC*. Experts typically know the requirements so well that they just go to the correct rule. Very experienced people might only need the Table of Contents to locate the requirement for which they're looking. On the other hand, average users should use all the tools at their disposal, including the Table of Contents, the Index, and the search feature on electronic versions of the *Code* book.

Let's work through a simple example: What *NEC* rule specifies the maximum number of disconnects permitted for a service?

Using the Table of Contents. If you're an experienced *Code* user, you might use the Table of Contents. You'll know Article 230 applies to "Services," and because this article is so large, it's divided up into multiple parts (eight parts to be exact). With this knowledge, you can quickly go to the Table of Contents and see it lists the Service Equipment Disconnecting Means requirements in Part VI.

Author's Comment:

▸ The number "70" precedes all page numbers in this standard because the *NEC* is NFPA Standard Number 70.

Using the Index. If you use the Index (which lists subjects in alphabetical order) to look up the term "service disconnect," you'll see there's no listing. If you try "disconnecting means," then "services," you'll find that the Index indicates the rule is in Article 230, Part VI. Because the *NEC* doesn't give a page number in the Index, you'll need to use the Table of Contents to find it, or flip through the *Code* book to Article 230, then continue to flip through pages until you find Part VI.

Many people complain that the *NEC* only confuses them by taking them in circles. Once you gain experience in using the *Code* and deepen your understanding of words, terms, principles, and practices, you'll find it much easier to understand and use than you originally thought.

With enough exposure in the use of the *NEC*, you'll discover that some words and terms are often specific to certain articles. The word "solar" for example will immediately send experienced *Code* book users to Article 690–Solar Photovoltaic (PV) Systems. The word "marina" suggests what you seek might be in Article 555. There are times when a main article will send you to a specific requirement in another one in which compliance is required in which case it will say (for example), "in accordance with 230.xx." Don't think of these situations as a "circle," but rather a map directing you to exactly where you need to be.

Customizing Your *Code* Book

One way to increase your comfort level with your *Code* book is to customize it to meet your needs. You can do this by highlighting and underlining important *NEC* requirements. Preprinted adhesive tabs are also an excellent aid to quickly find important articles and sections that are regularly referenced. However, understand that if you're using your *Code* book to prepare to take an exam, some exam centers don't allow markings of any type. For more information about tabs for your *Code* book, visit MikeHolt.com/Tabs.

Highlighting. As you read through or find answers to your questions, be sure you highlight those requirements in the *NEC* that are the most important or relevant to you. Use one color, like yellow, for general interest and a different one for important requirements you want to find quickly. Be sure to highlight terms in the Index and the Table of Contents as you use them.

Underlining. Underline or circle key words and phrases in the *Code* with a red or blue pen (not a lead pencil) using a short ruler or other straightedge to keep lines straight and neat. This is a very handy way to make important requirements stand out. A short ruler or other straightedge also comes in handy for locating the correct information in a table.

Interpretations

Industry professionals often enjoy the challenge of discussing, and at times debating, the *Code* requirements. These types of discussions are important to the process of better understanding the *NEC* requirements and applications. However, if you decide you're going to participate in one of these discussions, don't spout out what you think without having the actual *Code* book in your hand. The professional way of discussing a requirement is by referring to a specific section rather than talking in vague generalities. This will help everyone involved clearly understand the point and become better educated. In fact, you may become so well educated about the *NEC* that you might even decide to participate in the change process and help to make it even better!

Become Involved in the *NEC* Process

The actual process of changing the *Code* takes about two years and involves hundreds of individuals trying to make the *NEC* as current and accurate as possible. As you advance in your studies and understanding of the *Code*, you might begin to find it very interesting, enjoy it more, and realize that you can also be a part of the process. Rather than sitting back and allowing others to take the lead, you can participate by making proposals and being a part of its development. For the 2023 cycle, there were over 4,000 Public Inputs and 1,956 Public Comments. This resulted in several new articles and a wide array of revised rules to keep the *NEC* up to date with new technologies and pave the way to a safer and more efficient electrical future.

Here's how the process works:

STEP 1—Public Input Stage

Public Input. The revision cycle begins with the acceptance of Public Input (PI) which is the public notice asking for anyone interested to submit input on an existing standard or a committee-approved new draft standard. Following the closing date, the committee conducts a First Draft Meeting to respond to all Public Inputs.

First Draft Meeting. At the First Draft (FD) Meeting, the Technical Committee considers and provides a response to all Public Input. The Technical Committee may use the input to develop First Revisions to the standard. The First Draft documents consist of the initial meeting consensus of the committee by simple majority. However, the final position of the Technical Committee must be established by a ballot which follows.

Committee Ballot on First Draft. The First Draft developed at the First Draft Meeting is balloted. In order to appear in the First Draft, a revision must be approved by at least two-thirds of the Technical Committee.

First Draft Report Posted. First revisions which pass ballot are ultimately compiled and published as the First Draft Report on the document's NFPA web page. This report serves as documentation for the Input Stage and is published for review and comment. The public may review the First Draft Report to determine whether to submit Public Comments on the First Draft.

STEP 2—Public Comment Stage

Public Comment. Once the First Draft Report becomes available, there's a Public Comment period during which anyone can submit a Public Comment on the First Draft. After the Public Comment closing date, the Technical Committee conducts/holds their Second Draft Meeting.

Second Draft Meeting. After the Public Comment closing date, if Public Comments are received or the committee has additional proposed revisions, a Second Draft Meeting is held. At the Second Draft Meeting, the Technical Committee reviews the First Draft and may make additional revisions to the draft Standard. All Public Comments are considered, and the Technical Committee provides an action and response to each Public Comment. These actions result in the Second Draft.

Committee Ballot on Second Draft. The Second Revisions developed at the Second Draft Meeting are balloted. To appear in the Second Draft, a revision must be approved by at least two-thirds of the Technical Committee.

Second Draft Report Posted. Second Revisions which pass ballot are ultimately compiled and published as the Second Draft Report on the document's NFPA website. This report serves as documentation of the Comment Stage and is published for public review.

Once published, the public can review the Second Draft Report to decide whether to submit a Notice of Intent to Make a Motion (NITMAM) for further consideration.

STEP 3—NFPA Technical Meeting (Tech Session)

Following completion of the Public Input and Public Comment stages, there's further opportunity for debate and discussion of issues through the NFPA Technical Meeting that takes place at the NFPA Conference & Expo®. These motions are attempts to change the resulting final Standard from the committee's recommendations published as the Second Draft.

STEP 4—Council Appeals and Issuance of Standard

Issuance of Standards. When the Standards Council convenes to issue an NFPA standard, it also hears any related appeals. Appeals are an important part of assuring that all NFPA rules have been followed and that due process and fairness have continued throughout the standards development process. The Standards Council considers appeals based on the written record and by conducting live hearings during which all interested parties can participate. Appeals are decided on the entire record of the process, as well as all submissions and statements presented.

After deciding all appeals related to a standard, the Standards Council, if appropriate, proceeds to issue the Standard as an official NFPA Standard. The decision of the Standards Council is final subject only to limited review by the NFPA Board of Directors. The new NFPA standard becomes effective twenty days following the Standards Council's action of issuance.

Temporary Interim Amendment—(TIA)

Sometimes, a change to the *NEC* is of an emergency nature. Perhaps an editing mistake was made that can affect an electrical installation to the extent it may create a hazard. Maybe an occurrence in the field created a condition that needs to be addressed immediately and can't wait for the normal *Code* cycle and next edition of the standard. When these circumstances warrant it, a TIA or "Temporary Interim Amendment" can be submitted for consideration.

The NFPA defines a TIA as, "tentative because it has not been processed through the entire standards-making procedures. It is interim because it is effective only between editions of the standard. A TIA automatically becomes a Public Input of the proponent for the next edition of the standard; as such, it then is subject to all of the procedures of the standards-making process."

Author's Comment:

▸ Proposals, comments, and TIAs can be submitted for consideration online at the NFPA website, www.nfpa.org. From the homepage, look for "Codes & Standards," then find "Standards Development," and click on "How the Process Works." If you'd like to see something changed in the *Code*, you're encouraged to participate in the process.

MODULE

I

ELECTRICAL FUNDAMENTALS

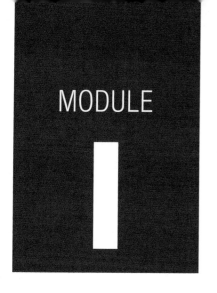

Introduction to Module I—Electrical Fundamentals

The units in this module review electrical fundamentals that relate to math, electrical circuits, and formulas and constitute a short review of the core principles of electricity. Some of the concepts might seem very basic, but rest assured, they're important. Establishing a good foundation of knowledge as you prepare to take your exam will include reviewing simple math, equations used for basic electrical calculations, refreshing your basic electrical theory knowledge, and putting it all together so you can use it to answer questions on the exam. Most electrical exams contain questions on electrical theory, so it should be considered a vital component of your studies.

The material covered in this module is extracted from *Mike Holt's Understanding Electrical Theory for NEC Applications* textbook and includes only certain portions from that book. It does not include Units 1-9; it starts with Unit 10, and does not contain many of the units between 10 and 29. It does, however, use the unit numbers and the style of the original textbook. In addition, the figure numbers and references correspond to the *Understanding Electrical Theory* textbook. All of this will make it easier for you to cross-reference that original textbook. The units covered here are:

▶ **Unit 10–Basic Math**
▶ **Unit 12–Ohm's Law**
▶ **Unit 13–Watt's Law**
▶ **Unit 14–Series Circuits**
▶ **Unit 15–Parallel Circuits**
▶ **Unit 16–Series-Parallel Circuits**
▶ **Unit 17–Alternating Current Fundamentals**
▶ **Unit 20–True Power, Power Factor, and Apparent Power**
▶ **Unit 21–Motors**
▶ **Unit 22–Generators**
▶ **Unit 23–Relays**
▶ **Unit 24–Transformers**
▶ **Unit 25–Overcurrent Protection**
▶ **Unit 29–The Formula Wheel**

We recommend that you invest in your own understanding of electrical fundamentals by reviewing the book and videos in the Theory Library. For more information about those products, visit MikeHolt.com/Theory.

UNIT
10

BASIC MATH

10.1 Introduction

Understanding math is the foundation to becoming a successful electrician. Many people have, unfortunately, been taught to fear math, but as you work through this material you will see that math enables you to do things faster and easier than you otherwise could have. In fact, you will begin to see math as a convenient short cut. In this unit you will learn:

▶ The difference between whole numbers and fractional numbers

▶ How to convert a percentage into a decimal to use as a multiplier

▶ The differences between a reciprocal, a square root, and squaring a number

---

10.2 Whole Numbers

Whole numbers are exactly what the term implies; these numbers do not contain any fractions, decimals, or percentages.

10.3 Fractional Numbers

Parts of a whole number are called "fractions" from the Latin word "fractus," meaning broken into parts. ▶Figure 10–1

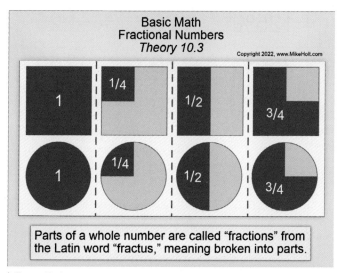

Parts of a whole number are called "fractions" from the Latin word "fractus," meaning broken into parts.

▶Figure 10–1

10.4 Decimal Numbers

(A) General. A decimal number is a number that is a fractional part of a number separated by a decimal point.

(B) Fractions Converted to Decimal Numbers. A fraction represents part of a whole number. If you use a calculator for adding, dividing, subtracting, or multiplying fractions, you need to convert the fraction to a decimal or whole number. To change a fraction to a decimal or whole number, divide the top number of the fraction by its bottom number. ▶Figure 10–2

(C) Number of Decimal Places. The decimal system places numbers to the right of a decimal point to indicate values that are a fraction of "one." For example, the first digit on the right of the decimal is one-tenth of a whole number, the second is one-hundredth of a whole number, and the third digit is one-thousandth of a whole number. ▶Figure 10–3

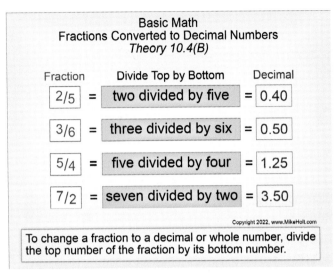

Basic Math
Fractions Converted to Decimal Numbers
Theory 10.4(B)

Fraction	Divide Top by Bottom	Decimal
2/5 =	two divided by five	= 0.40
3/6 =	three divided by six	= 0.50
5/4 =	five divided by four	= 1.25
7/2 =	seven divided by two	= 3.50

Copyright 2022, www.MikeHolt.com

To change a fraction to a decimal or whole number, divide the top number of the fraction by its bottom number.

▶Figure 10–2

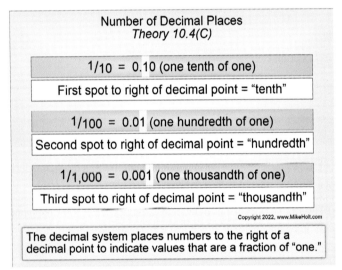

Number of Decimal Places
Theory 10.4(C)

1/10 = 0.10 (one tenth of one)

First spot to right of decimal point = "tenth"

1/100 = 0.01 (one hundredth of one)

Second spot to right of decimal point = "hundredth"

1/1,000 = 0.001 (one thousandth of one)

Third spot to right of decimal point = "thousandth"

Copyright 2022, www.MikeHolt.com

The decimal system places numbers to the right of a decimal point to indicate values that are a fraction of "one."

▶Figure 10–3

If the decimal number is greater than "one," the whole number will be to the left of the decimal point such as 1.25, 1.732, and 2.50.

10.5 Percentages

(A) General. A percentage is another method used to display the value of a number. One hundred percent means the entire value; 50 percent means one-half of a value, and 25 percent means one-fourth of a value. ▶Figure 10–4

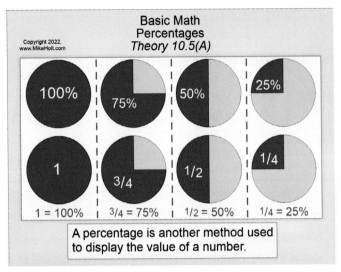

Basic Math
Percentages
Theory 10.5(A)

Copyright 2022. www.MikeHolt.com

100%   75%   50%   25%

1   3/4   1/2   1/4

1 = 100%   3/4 = 75%   1/2 = 50%   1/4 = 25%

A percentage is another method used to display the value of a number.

▶Figure 10–4

(B) Convert a Percentage to a Decimal. For convenience in multiplying or dividing by a percentage, convert the percentage value to a whole number or whole number with a decimal, and then use that value for the calculation.

When changing a percent value to a decimal or whole number with a decimal, drop the percentage symbol and move the decimal point two places to the left. ▶Figure 10–5

Convert a Percentage to a Decimal
Theory 10.5(B)

Copyright 2022, www.MikeHolt.com

Percentage	Drop "%"	Decimal
32.50%	0.325 X	0.325
80%	0.80 X	0.80
125%	1.25 X	1.25
250%	2.50 X	2.50

Move the decimal point two places to the left.

▶Figure 10–5

10.6 Parentheses

In a math problem, parentheses are used to group steps of mathematical functions together. Whenever numbers are in parentheses, complete the mathematical function within the parentheses before proceeding with the remaining math functions.

▶ Parentheses Example

Question: What is the sum of 3 and 15 added to the product of 4 and 2?

Note: A "sum" is the result of adding numbers, and a "product" is the result of multiplying numbers.

(a) 6   (b) 12   (c) 16   (d) 26

Solution:

$(3 + 15) + (4 \times 2)$
$18 + 8 = 26$

Answer: (d) 26

10.7 Squaring a Number

Squaring (^{2}) a number is the process of multiplying a number by itself.

▶ Squaring a Number Example 1

$8^2 = 8 \times 8$
$8^2 = 64$

▶ Squaring a Number Example 2

$12^2 = 12 \times 12$
$12^2 = 144$

10.8 Square Root

The square root ($\sqrt{\ }$) of a number is the number that, if squared (multiplied by itself), would equal the original number. You must use the square root key ($\sqrt{\ }$) on your calculator to perform this function.

▶ Square Root Example 1

Question: What is the square root of 100? ▶Figure 10–6

(a) 1   (b) 10   (c) 21.52   (d) 31.62

Answer: (b) 10

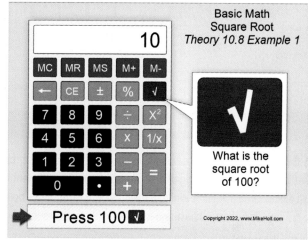

▶Figure 10–6

▶ Square Root Example 2

Question: What is the square root of 3?

(a) 1.255   (b) 1.55   (c) 1.732   (d) 1.935

Answer: (c) 1.732

10.9 Kilo

The letter "k" is the abbreviation for "kilo" which means "1,000." To convert a number that includes the "k," multiply the number by 1,000. To convert a number to a "k" value, divide the number by 1,000 and add "k" after the number.

▶ Kilo Conversion Example 1

Question: What is the value of 8k?

(a) 8   (b) 800   (c) 4,000   (d) 8,000

Solution:

$8 \times 1,000 = 8,000$

Answer: (d) 8,000

▶ **Kilo Conversion Example 2**

Question: *What is the "k" value of 3,000?*

(a) 0.30k   (b) 3k   (c) 30k   (d) 300k

Solution:

k = 3,000/1,000
k = 3k

Answer: *(b) 3k*

10.10 Rounding

(A) General. There is no specific rule for rounding numbers, but; rounding to two or three "significant digits" should be sufficient for most electrical calculations. When rounding is desired, numbers below five are rounded down, while numbers five and above are rounded up. ▶Figure 10–7

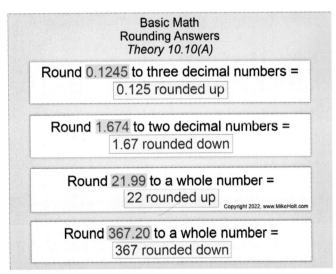

**Basic Math
Rounding Answers
Theory 10.10(A)**

Round 0.1245 to three decimal numbers =
0.125 rounded up

Round 1.674 to two decimal numbers =
1.67 rounded down

Round 21.99 to a whole number =
22 rounded up

Copyright 2022, www.MikeHolt.com

Round 367.20 to a whole number =
367 rounded down

▶Figure 10–7

(B) Rounding Answers for Multiple-Choice Questions. When selecting an answer for a multiple-choice question, you need to round your answers in the same manner as the multiple-choice selections are given.

▶ **Rounding Answers for Multiple-Choice Questions Example**

Question: *The sum of 12, 17, 28, and 40 is approximately equal to _____.*

(a) 70   (b) 80   (c) 90   (d) 100

Solution:

12 + 17 + 28 + 40 = 97

The multiple-choice selections in this case are rounded off to the nearest "tens," so the answer is 100.

Answer: *(d) 100*

10.11 Surface Area of a Rectangle or Square

The surface area for a rectangle or square is calculated using the formula: **Area = Length (L) × Width (W)**

▶ **Surface Area—Rectangle or Square Example 1**

Question: *What is the surface area of a bedroom that is 10 ft wide and 12 ft long?* ▶Figure 10–8

(a) 10 sq ft   (b) 50 sq ft   (c) 80 sq ft   (d) 120 sq ft

**Surface Area of a Rectangle or Square
Theory 10.11 Example 1**

Area = Length (L) x Width (W)
Area = 10 ft x 12 ft
Area = 120 sq ft

Copyright 2022, www.MikeHolt.com

▶Figure 10–8

Solution:

Area = L × W
Area = 12 ft × 10 ft
Area = 120 sq ft

Answer: *(d) 120 sq ft*

▶ **Surface Area—Rectangle or Square Example 2**

Question: What is the surface area of a house that is 30 ft wide and 40 ft long? ▶Figure 10–9

(a) 1,000 sq ft   (b) 1,200 sq ft   (c) 1,800 sq ft   (d) 2,000 sq ft

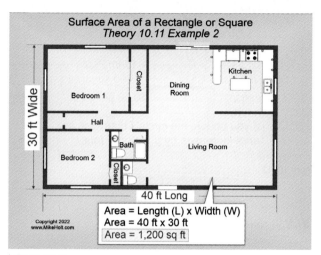

▶Figure 10–9

Solution:

Area = L × W

Area = 40 ft × 30 ft

Area = 1,200 sq ft

Answer: (b) 1,200 sq ft

10.12 Surface Area of a Circle

The surface area of a circle is calculated using the formula: **Area of a Circle = π × r²**

Use 3.14 for **π** (pi).

The radius (r^2) is equal to one half the diameter of the circle.

▶ **Surface Area—Circle Example 1**

Question: What is the surface area of an 8-in. pizza? ▶Figure 10–10

(a) 25 sq in.   (b) 50 sq in.   (c) 64 sq in.   (d) 75 sq in.

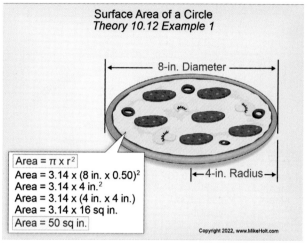

▶Figure 10–10

Solution:

Area of a Circle = π × r²

π = 3.14

Radius = ½ the diameter

Area = 3.14 × (8 in. × 0.50)²

Area = 3.14 × 4 in.²

Area = 3.14 × (4 in. × 4 in.)

Area = 3.14 × 16 sq in.

Area = 50 sq in.

Answer: (b) 50 sq in.

Note: If you prefer to use a calculator, then follow these steps:

Step 1: Find the radius (½ the diameter) of the circle by multiplying 8 in. by 0.50:

8 in. × 0.50 = 4 in.

Step 2: Press the square "x²" key = 16 sq in.

Step 3: Multiply 16 sq in. (Step 2) by 3.14.

16 sq in. × 3.14 = 50.26 sq in.

Step 4: Round to match the answer options: 50 sq in.

Answer: (b) 50 sq in.

▶ Surface Area—Circle Example 2

Question: *What is the surface area of a 16-in. pizza?* ▶**Figure 10–11**

(a) 100 sq in.   *(b) 150 sq in.*   *(c) 200 sq in.*   *(d) 256 sq in.*

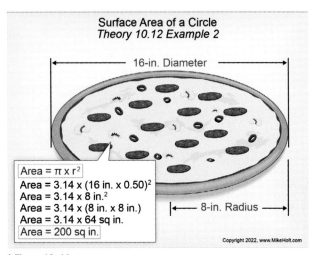

▶Figure 10–11

Solution:

Area of a Circle = π × r²

π = 3.14

Radius = ½ the diameter

Area = 3.14 × (16 in. × 0.50)²

Area = 3.14 × 8 in.²

Area = 3.14 × (8 in. × 8 in.)

Area = 3.14 × 64 sq in.

Area = 200 sq in.

Answer: *(c) 200 sq in.*

Author's Comment:

▸ As you can see, if you double the circle's diameter (an 8-in. pizza versus a 16-in. pizza), its area is increased by a factor of four. By the way, a large (or extra-large) pizza is always cheaper per square inch than a small one! ▶Figure 10–12

10.13 Volume

The volume of an enclosure is expressed in cubic inches (cu in. or in³), and is determined by multiplying the enclosure's length, width, and depth together: **Volume = Length (L) × Width (W) × Depth (D)**.

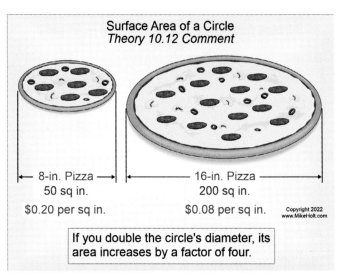

▶Figure 10–12

▶ Volume Example

Question: *What is the volume of a 6 in. × 6 in. × 4 in. box?* ▶**Figure 10–13**

(a) 134 cu in.   *(b) 144 cu in.*   *(c) 154 cu in.*   *(d) 164 cu in.*

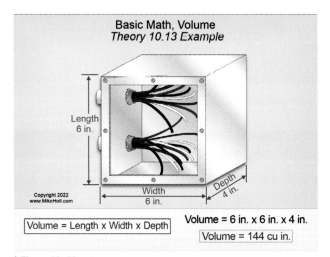

▶Figure 10–13

Solution:

Volume = Length (L) × Width (W) × Depth (D)

Volume = 6 in. × 6 in. × 4 in.

Volume = 144 cu in.

Answer: *(b) 144 cu in.*

10.14 Reciprocal

A reciprocal is the value of 1 divided by the number. All whole numbers shown as a fraction are over 1, a reciprocal flips the top number and puts it on the bottom for the mathematical function.

▶ **Reciprocal Example**

Question: What is the reciprocal of 0.80?

(a) 0.80   (b) 1.10   (c) 1.25   (d) 1.50

Solution:

1/0.80 = 1.25

Answer: (c) 1.25

10.15 Testing Your Answer

Never assume a mathematical calculation you have done is correct. Always do a "reality check" to be sure your answer makes sense. Even the best of us makes mistakes. You may have part of the problem jotted down incorrectly, or perhaps you pressed the wrong key on the calculator. Always examine your answer to see if it makes sense.

UNIT
10

REVIEW QUESTIONS

The following questions are based on the material you just reviewed. If you struggle with any of the answers, go back and review that unit again, or refer to Mike Holt's Understanding Electrical Theory Video Library.

10.2 Whole Numbers

1. _____ numbers do not contain any fractions, decimals, or percentages.
   - (a) Decimal
   - (b) Fractional
   - (c) Real
   - (d) Whole

10.3 Fractional Numbers

2. Parts of a whole number are called "_____" from the Latin word "fractus," meaning broken into parts.
   - (a) decimals
   - (b) fractions
   - (c) percentages
   - (d) integers

10.4 Decimal Numbers

3. A(An) _____ number is a number that is a fractional part of a number separated by a decimal point.
   - (a) decimal
   - (b) fractional
   - (c) percentage
   - (d) integer

4. To change a fraction to a decimal or whole number, _____ the top number of the fraction by its bottom number.
   - (a) divide
   - (b) multiply
   - (c) add
   - (d) subtract

5. The decimal equivalent for the fraction "½" is _____.
   - (a) 0.20
   - (b) 0.50
   - (c) 2
   - (d) 5

6. The approximate decimal equivalent for the fraction "$4/18$" is _____.
   - (a) 0.22
   - (b) 2.52
   - (c) 3.52
   - (d) 4.52

7. The decimal system places numbers to the _____ of a decimal point to indicate values that are a fraction of "one."
   - (a) left
   - (b) right
   - (c) left or right
   - (d) none of these

10.5 Percentages

8. To change a percent value to a decimal or whole number, drop the percentage sign and move the decimal point two places to the _____.

    (a) right
    (b) left
    (c) right or left
    (d) none of these

9. The decimal equivalent for "75 percent" is _____.

    (a) 0.075
    (b) 0.75
    (c) 7.50
    (d) 75

10. The decimal equivalent for "225 percent" is _____.

    (a) 0.225
    (b) 2.25
    (c) 22.50
    (d) 225

11. The decimal equivalent for "300 percent" is _____.

    (a) 0.03
    (b) 0.30
    (c) 3
    (d) 30.00

10.6 Parentheses

12. Whenever numbers are _____, complete the mathematical function within the parentheses before proceeding with the remaining math functions.

    (a) in brackets
    (b) in parentheses
    (c) underlined
    (d) none of these

13. What is the sum of 5 and 10 added to the product of 5 and 10?

    (a) 26
    (b) 32
    (c) 46
    (d) 65

10.7 Squaring a Number

14. Squaring a number means multiplying the number by _____.

    (a) itself
    (b) two
    (c) four
    (d) none of these

15. The numeric equivalent of 4^2 is _____.

    (a) 2
    (b) 8
    (c) 16
    (d) 32

16. The numeric equivalent of 12^2 is _____.

    (a) 3.46
    (b) 24
    (c) 144
    (d) 1,728

10.8 Square Root

17. What is the approximate square root ($\sqrt{\ }$) of 25?

    (a) 5
    (b) 6
    (c) 7
    (d) 8

18. What is the approximate square root ($\sqrt{\ }$) of 1,000?

    (a) 3
    (b) 32
    (c) 100
    (d) 500

10.9 Kilo

19. What is the "k" value of 75,000?

    (a) 0.07k
    (b) 0.75k
    (c) 7.50k
    (d) 75k

10.10 Rounding

20. The sum of 2, 7, 8, and 9 is approximately _____.

    (a) 15
    (b) 20
    (c) 25
    (d) 30

10.11 Surface Area of a Rectangle or Square

21. What is the surface area of a bedroom that is 10 ft by 20 ft?

    (a) 100 sq ft
    (b) 150 sq ft
    (c) 200 sq ft
    (d) 250 sq ft

10.12 Surface Area of a Circle

22. What is the surface area of a 10-in. pizza?

    (a) 25.50 sq in.
    (b) 55.50 sq in.
    (c) 64.50 sq in.
    (d) 78.50 sq in.

23. What is the surface area of a 20-in. pizza?

    (a) 255 sq in.
    (b) 275 sq in.
    (c) 299 sq in.
    (d) 314 sq in.

10.13 Volume

24. The volume of an enclosure is expressed in _____, and it is calculated by multiplying the length, by the width, by the depth of the enclosure.

    (a) cubic inches
    (b) weight
    (c) inch-pounds
    (d) none of these

25. What is the volume (in cubic inches) of a 4 in. × 4 in. × 1.50 in. box?

    (a) 20 cu in.
    (b) 24 cu in.
    (c) 30 cu in.
    (d) 33 cu in.

10.14 Reciprocal

26. What is the reciprocal of 1.25?

    (a) 0.80
    (b) 1.10
    (c) 1.25
    (d) 1.50

10.15 Testing Your Answer

27. Never assume a mathematical calculation you have done is correct. Always do a "_____" to be sure your answer makes sense.

    (a) reality check
    (b) quick scan
    (c) fast review
    (d) none of these

UNIT
12

OHM'S LAW

12.1 Introduction

To understand electrical circuits, you must understand electrical terminology. In this unit you will learn:

▸ What electromotive force, intensity, and resistance are

▸ What voltmeters, ammeters, and ohmmeters are

▸ How to use the Ohm's Law formula

12.2 The Electrical Circuit

All electrical circuits contain a power source necessary to produce the pressure to move electrons through the circuit wires to supply the load. ▸Figure 12–1

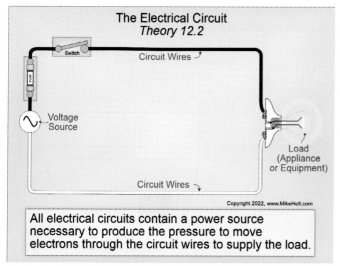

The Electrical Circuit
Theory 12.2

All electrical circuits contain a power source necessary to produce the pressure to move electrons through the circuit wires to supply the load.

▸Figure 12–1

12.3 Electromotive Force (Pressure)

(A) General. In a circuit, the electrical pressure necessary for current flow is called "electromotive force" and is measured in the unit called a "volt" (V). Electromotive force is abbreviated as "EMF." It is also simply referred to as "Voltage."

(1) Residential Voltage. In the United States, circuits for residential lights and receptacles operate at 120V, while large demanding loads like ranges, dryers, and air-conditioning equipment operate at 120/240V or 240V. ▸Figure 12–2

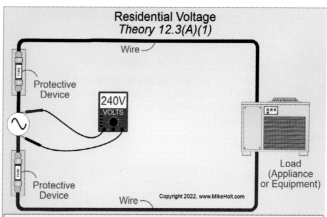

Residential Voltage
Theory 12.3(A)(1)

In the United States, circuits for residential lights and receptacles operate at 120V, while large demanding loads like ranges, dryers, and air-conditioning equipment operate at 120/240V or 240V.

▸Figure 12–2

---

(2) Commercial Voltage. In commercial and industrial occupancies, the voltage is often 277V for lighting and 480V for commercial loads like motors, air-conditioning units, and other equipment. ▶Figure 12–3

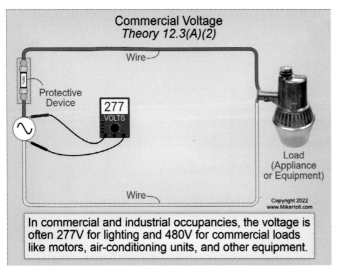

Commercial Voltage
Theory 12.3(A)(2)

In commercial and industrial occupancies, the voltage is often 277V for lighting and 480V for commercial loads like motors, air-conditioning units, and other equipment.

▶Figure 12–3

(B) Voltmeter. Voltmeters are connected in parallel with the load and are used to measure the difference of potential between the two test leads. ▶Figure 12–4

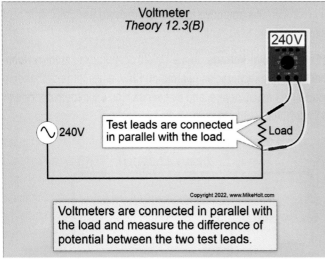

Voltmeter
Theory 12.3(B)

Test leads are connected in parallel with the load.

Voltmeters are connected in parallel with the load and measure the difference of potential between the two test leads.

▶Figure 12–4

12.4 Circuit Resistance

(A) General. In a circuit, resistance is the opposition to current flow. Every component of an electrical circuit contains resistance, which includes the power source, the circuit wiring, and the load. Resistance is represented by the letter "R" or "Ω," which is the ancient Greek letter Omega capitalized as "O," in honor of Georg Simon Ohm (1787–1854). ▶Figure 12–5

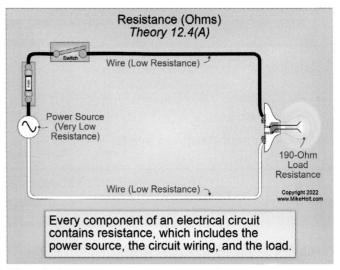

Resistance (Ohms)
Theory 12.4(A)

Switch
Wire (Low Resistance)
Power Source (Very Low Resistance)
190-Ohm Load Resistance
Wire (Low Resistance)

Every component of an electrical circuit contains resistance, which includes the power source, the circuit wiring, and the load.

▶Figure 12–5

(B) Ohmmeters. Ohmmeters are used to measure resistance in the unit called an "ohm" (Ω). ▶Figure 12–6

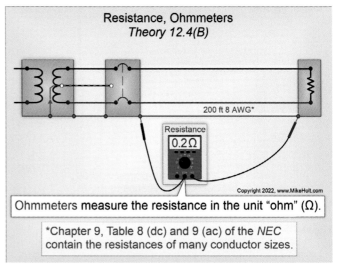

Resistance, Ohmmeters
Theory 12.4(B)

200 ft 8 AWG*
Resistance
0.2Ω

Ohmmeters **measure the resistance in the unit "ohm" (Ω).**

*Chapter 9, Table 8 (dc) and 9 (ac) of the *NEC* contain the resistances of many conductor sizes.

▶Figure 12–6

12.5 Circuit Intensity

(A) General. In an electrical circuit, the intensity of the current flow is measured in the unit called an "ampere," which is represented by the letter "I" for intensity. ▶Figure 12–7

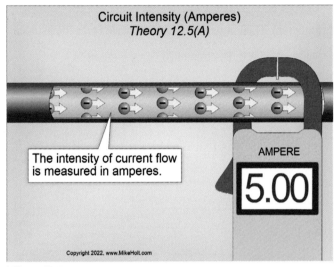

▶Figure 12–7

(B) Current Measurement. Ammeters are used to measure current flow in the unit called amperes.

(1) Series-Connected Ammeters. Series-connected ammeters measure current in amperes and are connected in series with the circuit. Handheld series-connected ammeters are typically limited to a maximum current of 10 amperes. ▶Figure 12–8

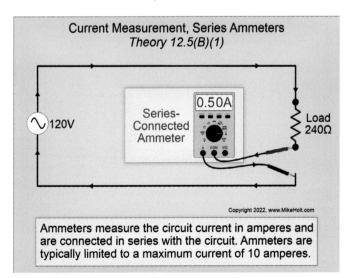

▶Figure 12–8

(2) Clamp-On Ammeter. Clamp-on ammeters measure the circuit current without opening the circuit wires as is required for a series-connected ammeter. In addition, these meters can measure current in the thousands of amperes.

A clamp-on ammeter has a sensor that is clamped around the wire and detects the rising and falling electromagnetic field being produced due to the ac flow through the wire. ▶Figure 12–9

▶Figure 12–9

12.6 Ohm's Law

(A) General. The German physicist Georg Simon Ohm (1787–1854) discovered that current is directly proportional to voltage and inversely proportional to resistance.

(1) Directly Proportional. Ohm's Law states that current is directly proportional to voltage. This means that current will increase in direct proportion to the voltage increase if the resistance of the circuit remains the same. If the voltage decreases and the circuit resistance remains the same, the circuit amperes will decrease in direct proportion to the voltage change. ▶Figure 12–10

(2) Inversely Proportional. Ohm's Law also states that current is inversely proportional to resistance. This means that current will decrease in direct proportion to the increase in resistance if the voltage remains the same. If the resistance decreases and the voltage remains the same, then the circuit amperes will increase in proportion to the change in resistance. ▶Figure 12–11

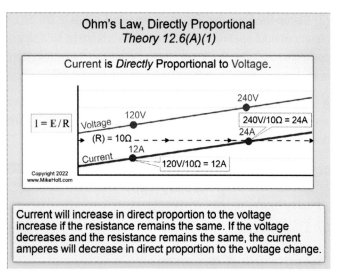

Ohm's Law, Directly Proportional
Theory 12.6(A)(1)

Current is *Directly* Proportional to Voltage.

$I = E/R$

240V
120V
240V/10Ω = 24A
24A
Voltage
(R) = 10Ω
12A
Current
120V/10Ω = 12A

Copyright 2022
www.MikeHolt.com

Current will increase in direct proportion to the voltage increase if the resistance remains the same. If the voltage decreases and the resistance remains the same, the current amperes will decrease in direct proportion to the voltage change.

▶Figure 12–10

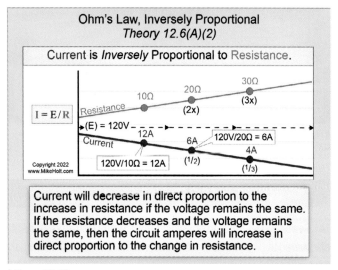

Ohm's Law, Inversely Proportional
Theory 12.6(A)(2)

Current is *Inversely* Proportional to Resistance.

$I = E/R$

30Ω
20Ω
10Ω
(3x)
Resistance
(2x)
(E) = 120V
12A
6A
120V/20Ω = 6A
Current
4A
120V/10Ω = 12A
(1/2)
(1/3)

Copyright 2022
www.MikeHolt.com

Current will decrease in direct proportion to the increase in resistance if the voltage remains the same. If the resistance decreases and the voltage remains the same, then the circuit amperes will increase in direct proportion to the change in resistance.

▶Figure 12–11

(B) Ohm's Law Formula. The Ohm's Law formula demonstrates the relationship between the circuit intensity (I) or current measured in amperes, the electromotive force (E) or pressure measured in volts, and the resistance (R) measured in ohms as expressed in the formula: $I = E/R$.

The Ohm's Law formula can be transposed as follows:

I (Amperes) = E/R, Intensity = Electromotive Force/Resistance

E (Voltage) = I × R, Electromotive Force = Intensity × Resistance

R (Ohms) = E/I, Resistance = Electromotive Force/Intensity

UNIT 12

REVIEW QUESTIONS

The following questions are based on the material you just reviewed. If you struggle with any of the answers, go back and review that unit again, or refer to Mike Holt's Understanding Electrical Theory Video Library.

12.3 Electromotive Force (Pressure)

1. Electrical pressure is called "_____," and it is measured in volts.

    (a) EMF
    (b) potential
    (c) EMF or potential
    (d) none of these

2. Voltmeters are connected in _____ with the circuit and measure the difference of potential between the two test leads.

    (a) series
    (b) parallel
    (c) series-parallel
    (d) none of these

12.4 Circuit Resistance

3. Every component of an electrical circuit contains _____, which includes the power source, the circuit wiring, and the load.

    (a) resistance
    (b) voltage
    (c) current
    (d) power

4. The circuit resistance includes the resistance of the _____.

    (a) power source
    (b) circuit wring
    (c) load
    (d) all of these

5. Ohmmeters measure the _____ of the circuit in the unit "ohm."

    (a) voltage
    (b) current
    (c) power
    (d) resistance

12.5 Circuit Intensity

6. In an electrical circuit, the volume of the current flow is measured in the unit "amperes" which is represented by the letter "I" for _____.

    (a) resistance
    (b) power
    (c) pressure
    (d) intensity

7. The intensity of the circuit is measured in _____.

    (a) voltage
    (b) ohms
    (c) watts
    (d) amperes

12.6 Ohm's Law

8. Ohm's Law states that current is _____ proportional to the voltage, this means that current will increase in direct proportion to the voltage increase if the resistance of the circuit remains the same.

   (a) indirectly
   (b) inversely
   (c) aversely
   (d) directly

9. Ohm's Law states that current is _____ proportional to the resistance, this means that current will decrease in direct proportion to the increase in resistance if the voltage remains the same.

   (a) indirectly
   (b) inversely
   (c) aversely
   (d) directly

10. The Ohm's Law formula demonstrates the relationship between circuit _____.

    (a) intensity
    (b) EMF
    (c) resistance
    (d) all of these

11. The symbol "I" in Ohm's Law represents the circuit _____.

    (a) coulomb
    (b) in-rush
    (c) intensity
    (d) impedance

UNIT

13

WATT'S LAW

13.1 Introduction

Wattage is a measure of the amount of power that is being used in a circuit. In this unit you will learn:

▶ What Watt's Law is

▶ How to use Watt's Law

▶ What a wattmeter is

13.2 Watt's Law

Power is defined as the rate of work measured by the unit called the "watt."

(A) Watt's Law Formula. Watt's Law states that power (P) in watts is equal to intensity (I) in amperes, times the electromotive force (E) in volts. ▶Figure 13–1

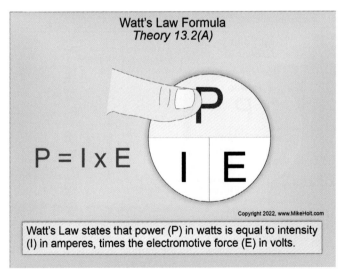

Watt's Law Formula
Theory 13.2(A)

$P = I \times E$

Watt's Law states that power (P) in watts is equal to intensity (I) in amperes, times the electromotive force (E) in volts.

Copyright 2022, www.MikeHolt.com

▶Figure 13–1

The formula for Watt's Law can be transposed as follows:

P (Watts) = I × E, Power = Intensity × Electromotive Force

I (Amperes) = P/E, Intensity = Power/Electromotive Force

E (Volts) = P/I, Electromotive Force = Power/Intensity

(B) Wattmeter. A wattmeter measures power by connecting it in parallel with the circuit to measure voltage, and in series with the circuit to measure amperes to calculate watts. ▶Figure 13–2

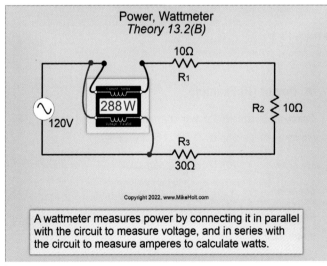

Power, Wattmeter
Theory 13.2(B)

288 W

120V

R1 10Ω

R2 10Ω

R3 30Ω

A wattmeter measures power by connecting it in parallel with the circuit to measure voltage, and in series with the circuit to measure amperes to calculate watts.

Copyright 2022, www.MikeHolt.com

▶Figure 13–2

▶ **Example**

Question: A(An) _____ is used to measure power.

(a) wattmeter   *(b) voltmeter*   *(c) ohmmeter*   *(d) megger*

Answer: (a) wattmeter

13.3 Power Formula Circle

The Power Formula Circle demonstrates the relationship between power, current, and voltage. To apply Watt's Law using the Power Formula Circle, place your finger on the unknown value for which you are looking and the two remaining variables "show" you the formula to be used. ▶Figure 13–3

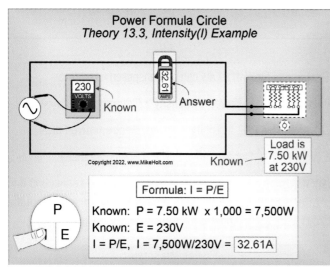

▶Figure 13–3

▶ **Power (P) Example**

Question: What is the power consumed by a circuit carrying 24A having a voltage drop of 7.20V? ▶Figure 13–4

(a) 125W   *(b) 175W*   *(c) 235W*   *(d) 350W*

Solution:

Step 1: What is the question asking you to find? What is the wire power loss? "P."

Step 2: What do you know about the wires?

  I = 24A

  E = 7.20 VD

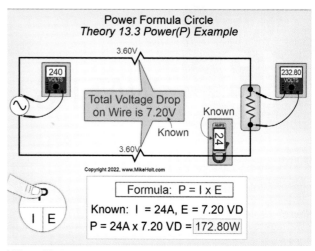

▶Figure 13–4

Step 3: The formula is $P = I \times E$.

Step 4: Calculate the answer.

  P = 24A × 7.20 VD

  P = 172.80W, round to 175W to match answer options ``

Answer: (b) 175W

▶ **Intensity (I) Example**

Question: What is the current through a 7.50 kW heat strip rated 230V? ▶Figure 13–5

(a) 25A   *(b) 33A*   *(c) 39A*   *(d) 230A*

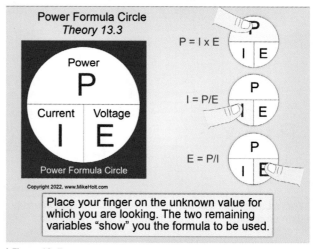

▶Figure 13–5

Solution:

Step 1: *What is the question? What is "I"?*

Step 2: *What do you know?*

Heat Strip Power Rating, P = 7.50 kW × 1,000

Heat Strip Power Rating, P = 7,500W

Heat Strip Voltage Rating, E = 230V

Step 3: *The formula is **I = P/E**.*

Step 4: *The answer is I = 7,500W/230V.*

Step 5: *The answer is 32.61A, round to 33A to match answer options*

Answer: (b) 33A

13.4 Power Changes with the Square of the Voltage

The voltage applied to a load affects the power consumed by that load. The voltage can dramatically affect the power consumed by a load because power is a function of the square of the voltage. This means that if the voltage is doubled, the power will be four times the original value. If the voltage is decreased to 50 percent, the power will be 25 percent of its original value. ▶Figure 13–6

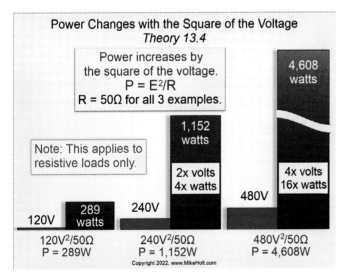

▶Figure 13–6

▶ **Power Equals the Square (^{2}) of the Voltage Example 1**

Question: What is the power consumed by a 10Ω load operating at 120V?

(a) 1,040W   (b) 1,400W   (c) 1,440W   (d) 1,444W

Solution:

$P = E^2/R$

E = 120V (given)
R = 10Ω (given)

P = (120V × 120V)/10Ω
P = 14,400/10Ω
P = 1,440W

Answer: (c) 1,440W

▶ **Power Equals the Square (^{2}) of the Voltage Example 2**

Question: What is the power consumed by a 10Ω load operating at 240V?

(a) 5,600W   (b) 5,660W   (c) 5,700W   (d) 5,760W

Solution:

$P = E^2/R$

E = 240V (given)
R = 10Ω (given)

P = (240V × 240V)/10Ω
P = 57,600/10Ω
P = 5,760W

Answer: (d) 5,760W

Note: At 240V, the 10Ω resistor consumes four times the power as compared to the 120V circuit power.

The following questions are based on the material you just reviewed. If you struggle with any of the answers, go back and review that unit again, or refer to Mike Holt's Understanding Electrical Theory Video Library.

13.2 Watt's Law

1. _____ is defined as the rate of work measured by the unit called the "watt."

   (a) Resistance
   (b) Power
   (c) Pressure
   (d) Intensity

2. _____ Law states that power (P) in watts is equal to intensity (I) in amperes, times the electromotive force (E) in volts.

   (a) Ohm's
   (b) Watt's
   (c) Kirchhoff's
   (d) Circle

3. A(An) _____ measures power by connecting it in parallel with the circuit to measure the voltage, and in series with the circuit to measure the amperes to calculate watts.

   (a) ammeter
   (b) ohmmeter
   (c) voltmeter
   (d) wattmeter

13.3 Power Formula Circle

4. The _____ Formula Circle demonstrates the relationship between power, current, and voltage.

   (a) Amp
   (b) Ohm
   (c) Voltage
   (d) Power

5. What is the power loss for a circuit carrying 20A having a voltage drop of 10.20V?

   (a) 122W
   (b) 174W
   (c) 204W
   (d) 354W

6. What is the current through a 9.50 kW heat strip rated 240V?

   (a) 25.40A
   (b) 33.50A
   (c) 39.60A
   (d) 42.70A

13.4 Power Changes with the Square of the Voltage

7. The voltage can dramatically affect the power consumed by a load because power is a function of the _____ of the voltage.

   (a) square
   (b) mean
   (c) volume
   (d) multiplier

8. What is the approximate power consumed by a 5Ω heat strip rated 240V?

   (a) 10.1 kW
   (b) 10.5 kW
   (c) 10.7 kW
   (d) 11.5 kW

9. What is the approximate power consumed by a 11.5 kW heat strip rated 240V, connected to 240V?

    (a) 10.1 kW
    (b) 10.5 kW
    (c) 10.7 kW
    (d) 11.5 kW

10. What is the approximate power consumed by a 11.5 kW heat strip rated 240V, connected to 230V?

    (a) 10.1 kW
    (b) 10.4 kW
    (c) 10.6 kW
    (d) 10.9 kW

11. What is the approximate power consumed by a 11.5 kW heat strip rated 240V, connected to 208V?

    (a) 8.7 kW
    (b) 9.1 kW
    (c) 9.5 kW
    (d) 9.9 kW

UNIT
14

SERIES CIRCUITS

14.1 Introduction

A series circuit is a circuit in which a current leaves the power source and flows through every electrical device in a single path before it returns to the power source. In this unit you will learn:

- ▸ The relationship between resistance, current, and voltage in series circuits
- ▸ About the voltage and current of series-connected power supplies
- ▸ About common applications of series circuits
- ▸ That the current is identical in each component

14.2 Series Circuits

(A) General. A series circuit can be envisioned as a circle where current leaves the power source, flows through every load in a single path, and then returns to the power source. ▸Figure 14–1

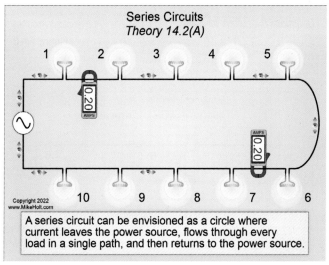

A series circuit can be envisioned as a circle where current leaves the power source, flows through every load in a single path, and then returns to the power source.

▸Figure 14–1

(B) Open Circuit. If there is a break in a series circuit, the current in the circuit will stop flowing. ▸Figure 14–2

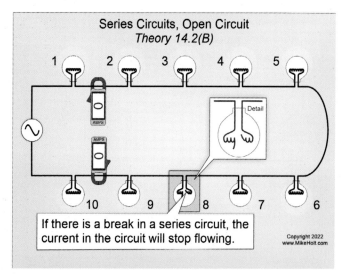

If there is a break in a series circuit, the current in the circuit will stop flowing.

▸Figure 14–2

14.3 Understanding Series Circuits

It is important to understand the relationship between resistance, current, and voltage in a series circuit.

(A) Resistance. In a series circuit, the total circuit resistance is equal to the sum of the resistance of all the resistors. It is calculated according to the total resistance formula: $R_T = R_1 + R_2 + R_3...$ ▸Figure 14–3

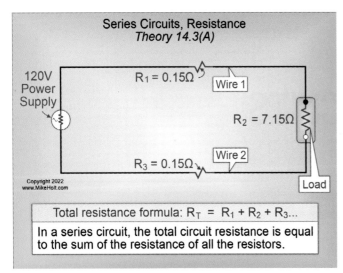

▶Figure 14-3

▶ Series Circuit Resistance Example

Question: *What is the total resistance of three resistors where R_1 is 16Ω, R_2 is 13Ω, and R_3 is 36Ω?* ▶**Figure 14-4**

(a) 50Ω　　*(b) 65Ω*　　*(c) 100Ω*　　*(d) 150Ω*

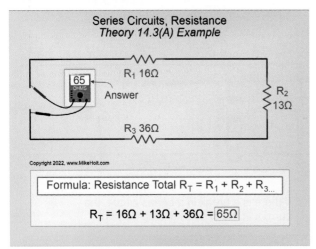

▶Figure 14-4

Solution:

$R_T = R_1 + R_2 + R_3$
$R_T = 16Ω + 13Ω + 36Ω$
$R_T = 65Ω$

Answer: *(b) 65Ω*

(B) Current.

(1) Current Remains the Same. Kirchhoff's Current Law states that the current flowing through each resistor of a series circuit will be the same value as the current leaving and returning to the power source. ▶Figure 14-5

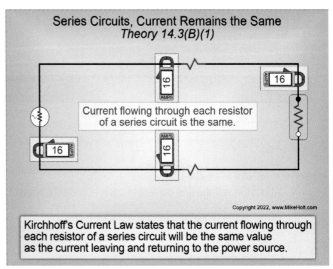

▶Figure 14-5

(2) Current Formula. To calculate the current in a series circuit, you need to know the circuit voltage and the circuit's total resistance as expressed by the formula: $I = E/R$.

▶ Circuit Current Formula Example

Question: *The current for a 240V circuit that has three resistors in series where R_1 is 5Ω, R_2 is 10Ω, and R_3 is 5Ω is _____.* ▶**Figure 14-6**

(a) 5A　　*(b) 7A*　　*(c) 9A*　　*(d) 12A*

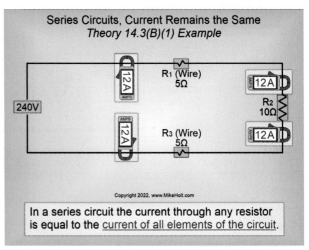

▶Figure 14-6

Solution:

$I = E/R$

$E = 240V$, voltage source

$R_T = R_1 + R_2 + R_3$
$R_T = 5\Omega + 10\Omega + 5\Omega$
$R_T = 20\Omega$

$I = 240V/20\Omega$
$I = 12A$, current of the circuit

Answer: *(d) 12A*

(C) Voltage.

(1) Voltage across Each Resistor. The voltage across each resistor is determined using the formula: $E = I \times R$.

▶ **Voltage of Each Resistor Example 1**

Question: *A 120V circuit has three resistors in series where R_1 is 10Ω, R_2 is 5Ω, and R_3 is 5Ω. The voltage across R_1 is _____.*
▶Figure 14–7

(a) 30V   (b) 60V   (c) 90V   (d) 120V

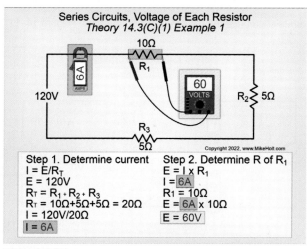

Series Circuits, Voltage of Each Resistor
Theory 14.3(C)(1) Example 1

Step 1. Determine current
I = E/R_T
E = 120V
R_T = R_1 + R_2 + R_3
R_T = 10Ω + 5Ω + 5Ω = 20Ω
I = 120V/20Ω
I = 6A

Step 2. Determine R of R_1
E = I x R_1
I = 6A
R_1 = 10Ω
E = 6A x 10Ω
E = 60V

▶Figure 14–7

Solution:

Step 1: Determine the current of the series circuit:

$I = E/R$

$E = 120V$, voltage source

$R_T = R_1 + R_2 + R_3$
$R_T = 10\Omega + 5\Omega + 5\Omega$

$R_T = 20\Omega$, resistance total

$I = 120V/20\Omega$

$I = 6A$, current of the circuit

Step 2: Determine the voltage across R_1:

$E = I \times R_1$

$I = 6A$, current of the circuit

$R_1 = 10\Omega$

$E = 6A \times 10\Omega$

Answer: *(b) 60V*

▶ **Voltage of Each Resistor Example 2**

Question: *A 120V circuit has three resistors in series where R_1 is 10Ω, R_2 is 5Ω, and R_3 is 5Ω. The voltage across R_2 or R_3 is _____.* ▶Figure 14–8

(a) 30V   (b) 60V   (c) 90V   (d) 120V

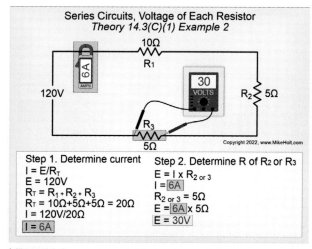

Series Circuits, Voltage of Each Resistor
Theory 14.3(C)(1) Example 2

Step 1. Determine current
I = E/R_T
E = 120V
R_T = R_1 + R_2 + R_3
R_T = 10Ω+5Ω+5Ω = 20Ω
I = 120V/20Ω
I = 6A

Step 2. Determine R of R_2 or R_3
E = I x R_2 or 3
I = 6A
R_2 or 3 = 5Ω
E = 6A x 5Ω
E = 30V

▶Figure 14–8

Solution:

Step 1: Determine the current of the series circuit:

$I = E/R_T$

$E = 120V$, voltage source

$R_T = R_1 + R_2 + R_3$
$R_T = 10\Omega + 5\Omega + 5\Omega$

$R_T = 20\Omega$, resistance total

$I = 120V/20\Omega$

$I = 6A$, current of the circuit

• • •

Step 2: *Determine the voltage across R_2 or R_3:*

$E = I \times R_1$

I = 6A, current of the circuit

R_2 *or* $R_3 = 5\Omega$

$E = 6A \times 5\Omega$

Answer: *(a) 30V*

(2) Voltage Source. Kirchhoff's Voltage Law states that the source voltage of a series circuit is equal to the sum of the voltages across all circuit resistors as expressed by the formula: $E_s = E_1 + E_2 + E_3...$

▶ **Voltage Source Example**

Question: *A 20Ω circuit has three resistors in series where R_1 is 60V, R_2 is 30V, and R_3 is 30V. The voltage source is equal to _____.* ▶Figure 14-9

(a) 30V   (b) 60V   (c) 90V   (d) 120V

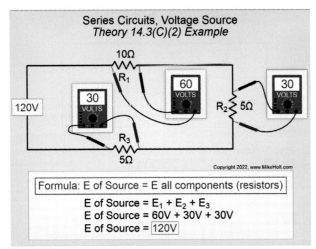

Series Circuits, Voltage Source
Theory 14.3(C)(2) Example

Formula: E of Source = E all components (resistors)

E of Source = $E_1 + E_2 + E_3$
E of Source = 60V + 30V + 30V
E of Source = 120V

▶Figure 14-9

Solution:

Determine the voltage source of the series circuit:

$E_S = E_1 + E_2 + E_3$
$E_S = 60V + 30V + 30V$
$E_S = 120V$

Answer: *(d) 120V*

(3) Voltage Law of Proportion. The voltage of a power source is distributed among all the resistors in a series circuit according to the Voltage Law of Proportion. The Voltage Law of Proportion states that the voltage across each resistor is relative to the resistance of that resistor as compared to the total circuit resistance. ▶Figure 14-10

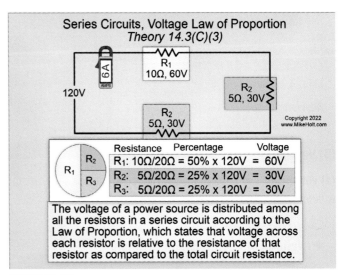

Series Circuits, Voltage Law of Proportion
Theory 14.3(C)(3)

Resistance	Percentage		Voltage
R_1: 10Ω/20Ω =	50% x 120V	=	60V
R_2: 5Ω/20Ω =	25% x 120V	=	30V
R_3: 5Ω/20Ω =	25% x 120V	=	30V

The voltage of a power source is distributed among all the resistors in a series circuit according to the Law of Proportion, which states that voltage across each resistor is relative to the resistance of that resistor as compared to the total circuit resistance.

▶Figure 14-10

14.4 Series Circuit Summary

A series circuit has the following characteristics: ▶Figure 14-11

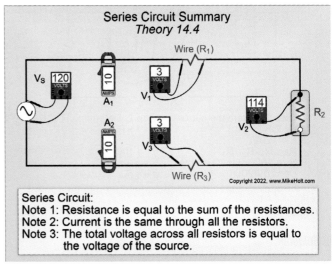

Series Circuit Summary
Theory 14.4

Series Circuit:
Note 1: Resistance is equal to the sum of the resistances.
Note 2: Current is the same through all the resistors.
Note 3: The total voltage across all resistors is equal to the voltage of the source.

▶Figure 14-11

Note 1: Circuit resistance is equal to the sum of the resistances.

Note 2: Current is the same through all the resistors.

Note 3: Total voltage across all resistors is equal to the voltage of the source.

14.5 Series-Connected Power Supplies

(A) Additive Voltage. When power supplies are connected in series, the voltage of the series-connected power supplies is equal to the sum of the power supply voltages as expressed by the formula: $E_s = E_1 + E_2 + E_3...$ ▶Figure 14–12

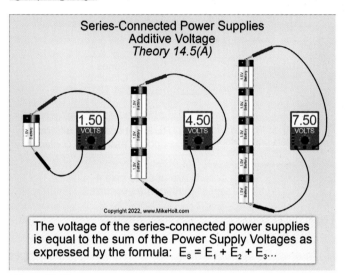

▶Figure 14–12

(B) Subtractive Voltage. If series-connected power supplies are not arranged positive (+) to negative (-), the circuit voltage will not be equal to the sum of the power supply voltages. ▶Figure 14–13

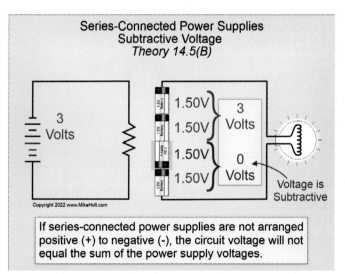

▶Figure 14–13

▶ Series-Connected Power Supplies Example 1

Question: The voltage across two 12V batteries connected in series is _____. ▶Figure 14–14

(a) 12V   (b) 24V   (c) 120V   (d) 240V

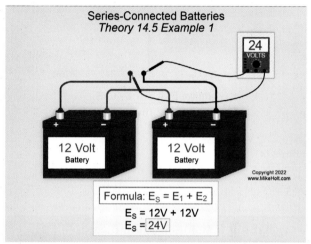

▶Figure 14–14

Solution:

$E_S = E_1 + E_2$
$E_S = 12V + 12V$
$E_S = 24V$, two series-connected power sources

Answer: (b) 24V

▶ Series-Connected Power Supplies Example 2

Question: The voltage of ten 42.70V solar panels in series is _____. ▶Figure 14–15

(a) 120V   (b) 240V   (c) 427V   (d) 480V

Solution:

$E_S = E_1 + E_2 + E_3... E_{10}$
$E_S = 42.70V \times 10$ solar panels
$E_S = 427V$, ten series-connected power sources

Answer: (c) 427V

• • •

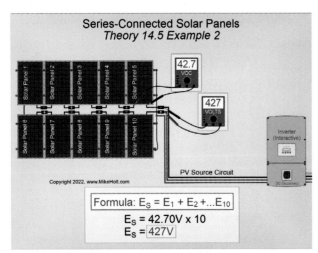

▶Figure 14–15

14.6 Applications of Series Circuits

Series circuits are used for equipment control, signaling, and (at times) the internal wiring of equipment.

(A) Control Circuits. Series circuits are often used for control applications (starting and stopping) for electrical equipment. ▶Figure 14–16

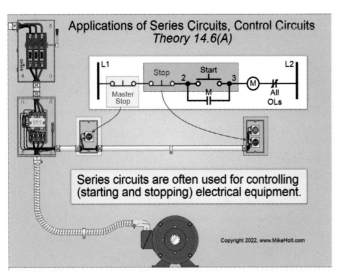

▶Figure 14–16

(B) Signaling Circuits. Series circuits are used to give a signal that something has occurred. They can indicate that a door is open, a process is operating, or there is fire or smoke. ▶Figure 14–17

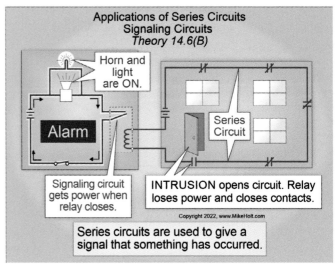

▶Figure 14–17

(C) Internal Equipment Wiring. The internal wiring of many types of equipment, such as motor windings, are connected in series for higher voltage application. ▶Figure 14–18

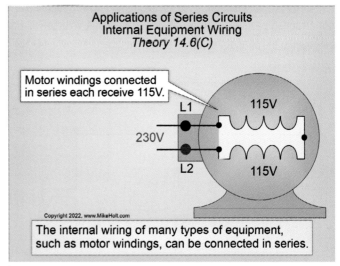

▶Figure 14–18

UNIT
14

REVIEW QUESTIONS

The following questions are based on the material you just reviewed. If you struggle with any of the answers, go back and review that unit again, or refer to Mike Holt's Understanding Electrical Theory Video Library.

14.2 Series Circuits

1. A series circuit can be envisioned as a circle where current leaves the power source and flows through every load in a _____ path before it returns to the power source.
   (a) single
   (b) parallel
   (c) multiple
   (d) various

2. If there is a break in a _____ circuit, the current in the circuit will stop flowing and none of the loads in the circuit will receive voltage.
   (a) series
   (b) parallel
   (c) multiwire
   (d) any of these

14.3 Understanding Series Circuits

3. In a series circuit, the total circuit resistance is equal to the _____ of all the resistances of all the resistors.
   (a) sum
   (b) product
   (c) square
   (d) square root

4. What is the total resistance of three resistors in series where R_1 is 15Ω, R_2 is 20Ω, and R_3 is 35Ω?
   (a) 50Ω
   (b) 70Ω
   (c) 100Ω
   (d) 150Ω

5. What is the total resistance of three resistors in series where R_1 is 35Ω, R_2 is 40Ω, and R_3 is 55Ω?
   (a) 50Ω
   (b) 70Ω
   (c) 130Ω
   (d) 150Ω

6. Kirchhoff's Current Law states that the current flowing through each resistor of a series circuit will be _____ the current leaving and returning to the power source.
   (a) directly proportional to
   (b) inversely proportional to
   (c) added to
   (d) the same value as

7. The current for a 240V circuit that has three resistors in series where R_1 is 15Ω, R_2 is 20Ω, and R_3 is 25Ω is _____.
   (a) 4A
   (b) 7A
   (c) 9A
   (d) 12A

8. The current for a 120V circuit that has three resistors in series where R_1 is 8Ω, R_2 is 12Ω, and R_3 is 30Ω is _____.
   - (a) 2.40A
   - (b) 3.70A
   - (c) 4.90A
   - (d) 5.20A

9. The current for a 208V circuit that has three resistors in series where R_1 is 1Ω, R_2 is 5Ω, and R_3 is 14Ω is _____.
   - (a) 10.40A
   - (b) 12.70A
   - (c) 12.90A
   - (d) 15.20A

10. The current for a 277V circuit that has three resistors in series where R_1 is 10Ω, R_2 is 10Ω, and R_3 is 10Ω is _____.
    - (a) 4A
    - (b) 7A
    - (c) 9A
    - (d) 12A

11. A 120V circuit has three resistors in series where R_1 is 10Ω, R_2 is 15Ω, and R_3 is 25Ω. The voltage across R_1 is _____.
    - (a) 24V
    - (b) 30V
    - (c) 104V
    - (d) 110V

12. A 120V circuit has three resistors in series where R_1 is 10Ω, R_2 is 15Ω, and R_3 is 15Ω. The voltage across R_2 or R_3 is _____.
    - (a) 30V
    - (b) 45V
    - (c) 60V
    - (d) 95V

13. A 240V circuit has three resistors in series where R_1 is 15Ω, R_2 is 15Ω, and R_3 is 15Ω. The voltage across R_2 or R_3 is _____.
    - (a) 50V
    - (b) 65V
    - (c) 80V
    - (d) 95V

14. A 240V circuit has three resistors in series where R_1 is 25Ω, R_2 is 25Ω, and R_3 is 30Ω. The voltage across R_1 is _____.
    - (a) 45V
    - (b) 55V
    - (c) 65V
    - (d) 75V

15. Kirchhoff's Voltage Law states that the source voltage of a series circuit is equal to the _____ of the voltages across all circuit resistors.
    - (a) sum
    - (b) product
    - (c) square
    - (d) square root

16. A 40Ω circuit has three resistors in series where R_1 is 60V, R_2 is 60V, and R_3 is 120V. The voltage source is equal to _____.
    - (a) 60V
    - (b) 90V
    - (c) 120V
    - (d) 240V

17. A 50Ω circuit has three resistors in series where R_1 is 60V, R_2 is 60V, and R_3 is 88V. The voltage source is equal to _____.
    - (a) 60V
    - (b) 90V
    - (c) 120V
    - (d) 208V

18. A 10A circuit has three resistors in series where R_1 is 4Ω, R_2 is 4Ω, and R_3 is 4Ω. The voltage source is equal to _____.
    - (a) 120V
    - (b) 130V
    - (c) 140V
    - (d) 200V

19. A 20A circuit has three resistors in series where R_1 is 4Ω, R_2 is 4Ω, and R_3 is 4Ω. The voltage source is equal to _____.
    - (a) 230V
    - (b) 240V
    - (c) 277V
    - (d) 480V

20. No matter how many resistances there are in a series circuit, the sum of the voltages across all of the resistances equals the voltage of the source according to the _____ Law of Proportion.
    - (a) Voltage
    - (b) Current
    - (c) Resistance
    - (d) Power

UNIT
15

PARALLEL CIRCUITS

15.1 Introduction

"Parallel" is a term used to describe a method of connecting an electrical circuit so there are two or more paths through which current can flow simultaneously. A parallel circuit has different characteristics and calculations than a series circuit. In this unit you will learn: ▶Figure 15–1

▶ The relationship between resistance, current, and voltage in parallel circuits

▶ About the voltage and current of parallel-connected power supplies

▶ About common applications of parallel circuits

▶ That the voltage is equal in all branches of the circuit

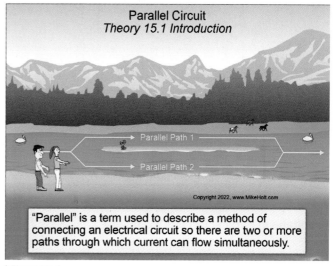

Parallel Circuit
Theory 15.1 Introduction

"Parallel" is a term used to describe a method of connecting an electrical circuit so there are two or more paths through which current can flow simultaneously.

▶Figure 15–1

15.2 Understanding Parallel Circuits

(A) Voltage. In a parallel circuit, the voltage across each component of the circuit is equal to the voltage source. ▶Figure 15–2

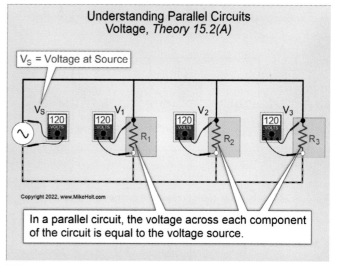

Understanding Parallel Circuits
Voltage, Theory 15.2(A)

V_S = Voltage at Source

In a parallel circuit, the voltage across each component of the circuit is equal to the voltage source.

▶Figure 15–2

▶ Voltage in Parallel Circuits Example 1

Question: A 240V circuit has three 15Ω resistors connected in parallel. The voltage across any one of these resistors is _____. ▶Figure 15–3

(a) 60V   *(b) 90V*   *(c) 120V*   *(d) 240V*

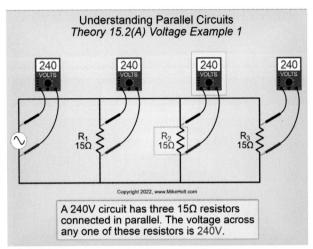

▶Figure 15–3

Answer: (d) 240V

▶ Voltage in Parallel Circuits Example 2

Question: A 24V circuit has two 5Ω resistors connected in parallel. The voltage across any one of these resistors is _____. ▶Figure 15–4

(a) 12V   *(b) 24V*   *(c) 48V*   *(d) 120V*

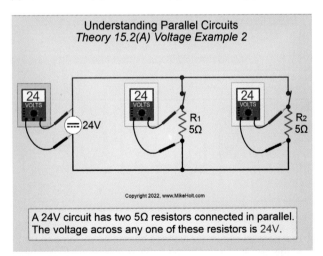

▶Figure 15–4

Answer: (b) 24V

(B) Circuit Current.

A parallel circuit has two or more paths through which current can flow simultaneously. Kirchhoff's Current Law states that the total current of a parallel circuit is equal to the sum of the currents of all the parallel branches. In other words, current in a parallel circuit is additive as expressed by the formula:

$I_T = I_1 + I_2 + I_3...$ ▶Figure 15–5

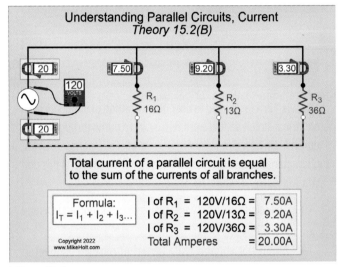

▶Figure 15–5

▶ Current in Parallel Circuits Example

Question: A circuit has three 15A resistors connected in parallel. The current of this circuit is _____. ▶Figure 15–6

(a) 15A   *(b) 25A*   *(c) 35A*   *(d) 45A*

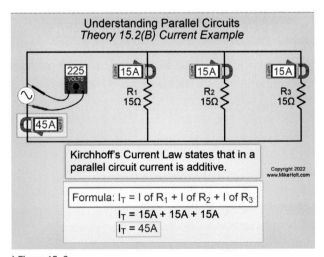

▶Figure 15–6

Solution:

$I_T = I$ *of* $R_1 + I$ *of* $R_2 + I$ *of* R_3
$I_T = 15A + 15A + 15A$
$I_T = 45A$, *circuit current*

Answer: (d) 45A

15.3 Parallel Circuit Resistance Calculations

There are three methods for calculating the total resistance of a parallel circuit:

▸ Equal Resistance method

▸ Product-Over-Sum method

▸ Reciprocal method

Author's Comment:

▸ The total resistance of a parallel circuit is always less than the smallest individual branch's resistance. ▸Figure 15–7

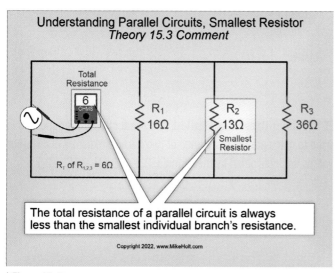

▸Figure 15–7

(A) Equal Resistance Method. When all components of a parallel circuit have the same value, the resistance can be determined by the formula: R_T = **Resistance of One Resistor/Number of Resistors**.

▸ Equal Resistance Method Example 1

Question: The total resistance of three 10Ω resistors connected in parallel is _____. ▸Figure 15–8

(a) 3.33Ω   *(b) 10Ω*   *(c) 20Ω*   *(d) 30Ω*

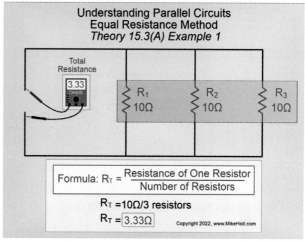

▸Figure 15–8

Solution:

R_T = *Resistance of One Resistor/Number of Resistors*
$R_T = 10Ω/3$ *resistors*
$R_T = 3.33Ω$

Answer: (a) 3.33Ω

Note: The total resistance is always smaller than the smallest resistor.

▸ Equal Resistance Method Example 2

Question: The total resistance of ten 10Ω resistors connected in parallel is _____. ▸Figure 15–9

(a) 1Ω   *(b) 10Ω*   *(c) 50Ω*   *(d) 100Ω*

Solution:

R_T = *Resistance of One Resistor/Number of Resistors*
$R_T = 10Ω/10$ *resistors*
$R_T = 1$ *ohm*

Answer: (a) 1Ω

Note: The total resistance is always smaller than the smallest resistor.

• • •

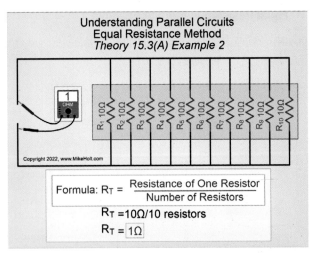

▶Figure 15–9

▶ Equal Resistance Method Example 3

Question: *A 240V circuit has three resistors in parallel where R_1 is 15Ω, R_2 is 15Ω, and R_3 is 15Ω. The resistance of this parallel circuit is _____.* ▶Figure 15–10

(a) 5Ω   (b) 15Ω   (c) 30Ω   (d) 45Ω

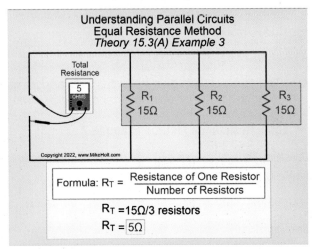

▶Figure 15–10

Solution:

R_T = Resistance of One Resistor/Number of Resistors
R_T = 15Ω/3 resistors
R_T = 5Ω

Answer: *(a) 5Ω*

Note: *The total resistance is always smaller than the smallest resistor.*

▶ Equal Resistance Method Example 4

Question: *A circuit has three 20Ω resistors connected in parallel. The resistance of this circuit is _____.* ▶Figure 15–11

(a) 3.20Ω   (b) 4.20Ω   (c) 5.70Ω   (d) 6.70Ω

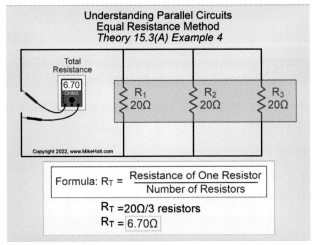

▶Figure 15–11

Solution:

R_T = Resistance of One Resistor/Number of Resistors
R_T = 20Ω/3 resistors
R_T = 6.70Ω

Answer: *(d) 6.70Ω*

Note: *The total resistance is always smaller than the smallest resistor.*

(B) Product-Over-Sum Method. The Product-Over-Sum method is used to calculate the resistance of two parallel resistors of different values as determined by the formula: $R_T = (R_1 \times R_2)/(R_1 + R_2)$

▶ Product-Over-Sum Method—Two Resistors Example

Question: The resistance of a coffee pot is 16Ω (R_1), and the resistance of a skillet is approximately 13Ω (R_2). What is the total resistance of the two appliances if they are connected in parallel? ▶Figure 15–12

(a) 7.20Ω   (b) 13Ω   (c) 16Ω   (d) 29Ω

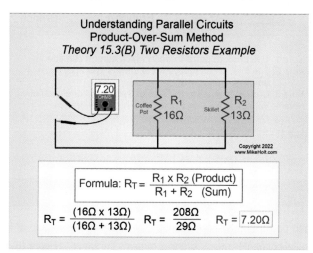

▶Figure 15–12

Solution:

$R_T = (R_1 \times R_2)/(R_1 + R_2)$
$R_T = (16Ω \times 13Ω)/(16Ω + 13Ω)$
$R_T = 208Ω/29Ω$
$R_T = 7.20Ω$

Answer: (a) 7.20Ω

Note: The total resistance is always smaller than the smallest resistor.

(C) Reciprocal Method. The Reciprocal Method for determining the total resistance of a parallel circuit is used when there are more than two resistors of different values. Use the formula:

$R_T = 1/(1/R_1 + 1/R_2 + 1/R_3...$

▶ Reciprocal Method Example 1

Question: What is the resistance total of a 16Ω, 13Ω, and 36Ω resistor connected in parallel? ▶Figure 15–13

(a) 6Ω   (b) 13Ω   (c) 16Ω   (d) 36Ω

Solution:

$R_T = 1/(1/R_1 + 1/R_2 + 1/R_3)$
$R_T = 1/(1/16 + 1/13 + 1/36)$
$R_T = 1/(0.0625Ω + 0.0769Ω + 0.0278Ω)$
$R_T = 1/0.1672Ω$
$R_T = 6Ω$

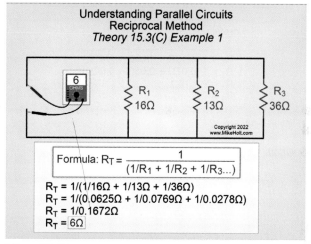

▶Figure 15–13

Note: If you use your calculator, add the reciprocals of all the resistors together.

$R_T = 1/(1/R_1 + 1/R_2 + 1/R_3)$
$R_T = 1/(1/16 + 1/13 + 1/36)$
$R_T = 1/(16 [press "1/✕"] + 13 [press "1/✕"] + 36 [press "1/✕"])$
$R_T = (0.1672Ω) [press "1/✕"]$
$R_T = 5.98Ω$; round up to 6Ω

Answer: (a) 6Ω

Note: The total resistance is always smaller than the smallest resistor.

▶ Reciprocal Method Example 2

Question: *A circuit has three resistors in parallel: 15Ω, 30Ω, and 45Ω. The circuit resistance is _____.* ▶Figure 15–14

(a) 8.33Ω (b) 9.10Ω (c) 10.99Ω (d) 12.22Ω

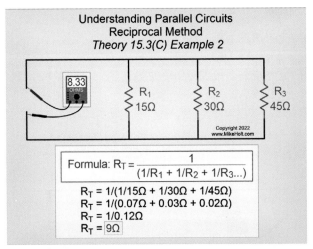

Understanding Parallel Circuits
Reciprocal Method
Theory 15.3(C) Example 2

Formula: $R_T = \dfrac{1}{(1/R_1 + 1/R_2 + 1/R_3...)}$

$R_T = 1/(1/15Ω + 1/30Ω + 1/45Ω)$
$R_T = 1/(0.07Ω + 0.03Ω + 0.02Ω)$
$R_T = 1/0.12Ω$
$R_T = \boxed{9Ω}$

▶Figure 15–14

Solution:

$R_T = 1/(1/R_1 + 1/R_2 + 1/R_3)$
$R_T = 1/(1/15Ω + 1/30Ω + 1/45Ω)$
$R_T = 1/(0.07Ω + 0.03Ω + 0.02Ω)$
$R_T = 1/0.12Ω$
$R_T = 8.33Ω$

Answer: *(a) 8.33Ω*

Note: The answer will always be less than the smallest resistor.

15.4 Parallel Circuit Summary

A parallel circuit has the following characteristics: ▶Figure 15–15

Note 1: Two or more paths through which current can flow.

Note 2: The total circuit resistance is always less than the smallest component.

Note 3: Current is equal to the sum of the current of all branches.

Note 4: Voltage is the same across each parallel branch.

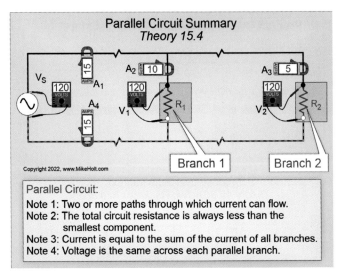

Parallel Circuit Summary
Theory 15.4

Copyright 2022, www.MikeHolt.com

Branch 1   Branch 2

Parallel Circuit:
Note 1: Two or more paths through which current can flow.
Note 2: The total circuit resistance is always less than the smallest component.
Note 3: Current is equal to the sum of the current of all branches.
Note 4: Voltage is the same across each parallel branch.

▶Figure 15–15

15.5 Parallel-Connected Power Supplies

When power supplies are connected in parallel, the voltage of the parallel-connected power supplies remains the same. ▶Figure 15–16

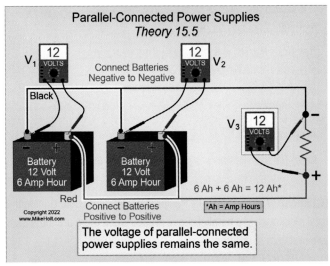

Parallel-Connected Power Supplies
Theory 15.5

Connect Batteries
Negative to Negative

Black

Battery
12 Volt
6 Amp Hour

Battery
12 Volt
6 Amp Hour

Red

Connect Batteries
Positive to Positive

6 Ah + 6 Ah = 12 Ah*

*Ah = Amp Hours

Copyright 2022
www.MikeHolt.com

The voltage of parallel-connected power supplies remains the same.

▶Figure 15–16

Caution

⚠ **CAUTION:** When jumping a battery in parallel, place the red cable clamps on the battery's positive (+) terminal and the black cable clamps on its negative (–) terminal. Pay close attention when terminating the cables on batteries to avoid causing a short circuit (+) to (-) connection which could lead to an explosion. ▶Figure 15–17

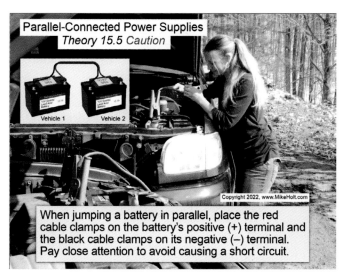

When jumping a battery in parallel, place the red cable clamps on the battery's positive (+) terminal and the black cable clamps on its negative (−) terminal. Pay close attention to avoid causing a short circuit.

▶Figure 15–17

15.6 Practical Uses of Parallel Circuits

(A) General. Parallel circuits are commonly used for wiring receptacles, lighting, appliances, and equipment.

(1) Receptacles. Receptacles on a circuit are connected in parallel. This results in each receptacle having the same operating voltage. ▶Figure 15–18

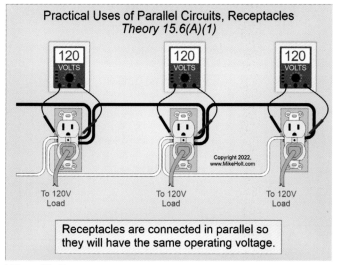

Receptacles are connected in parallel so they will have the same operating voltage.

▶Figure 15–18

▶ **Receptacles Example**

Question: Receptacles are connected in parallel so they will have the same operating _____.

(a) power   (b) power factor   (c) voltage   (d) current

Answer: (c) voltage

(2) Lighting. Lighting is connected in parallel, and each light will have the same operating voltage. ▶Figure 15–19

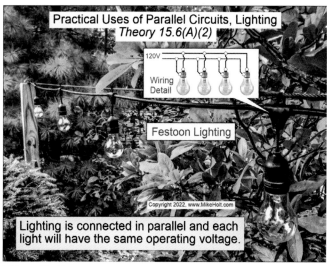

Lighting is connected in parallel and each light will have the same operating voltage.

▶Figure 15–19

(3) Appliances and Electrical Equipment. Appliances such as heat strips, water heaters, and some types of motors have their internal electrical components connected in parallel. ▶Figure 15–20

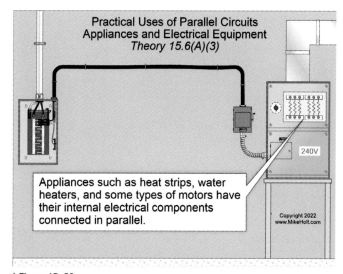

Appliances such as heat strips, water heaters, and some types of motors have their internal electrical components connected in parallel.

▶Figure 15–20

(B) Advantage of Parallel Circuits. One advantage of parallel circuits is that if one branch of a parallel circuit is opened, voltage is still provided to the other parallel branches. ▶Figure 15–21

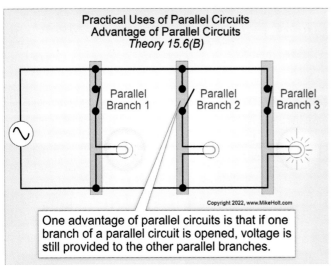

Practical Uses of Parallel Circuits
Advantage of Parallel Circuits
Theory 15.6(B)

Parallel Branch 1
Parallel Branch 2
Parallel Branch 3

Copyright 2022, www.MikeHolt.com

One advantage of parallel circuits is that if one branch of a parallel circuit is opened, voltage is still provided to the other parallel branches.

▶Figure 15–21

UNIT 15

REVIEW QUESTIONS

The following questions are based on the material you just reviewed. If you struggle with any of the answers, go back and review that unit again, or refer to Mike Holt's Understanding Electrical Theory Video Library.

15.2 Understanding Parallel Circuits

1. In a parallel circuit, the voltage across each resistance of the circuit is _____ the voltage source.
   (a) less than
   (b) equal to
   (c) greater than
   (d) less than or greater than

2. A 12V circuit has two 5Ω resistors connected in parallel. The voltage across any one of these resistors is _____.
   (a) 12V
   (b) 24V
   (c) 48V
   (d) 120V

3. A 120V circuit has two 20Ω resistors connected in parallel. The voltage across any one of these resistors is _____.
   (a) 12V
   (b) 24V
   (c) 48V
   (d) 120V

4. According to Kirchhoff's _____ Law, the total current of a parallel circuit equals the sum of the currents of all the branches.
   (a) Current
   (b) Voltage
   (c) Resistance
   (d) Power

5. A circuit has three 25A resistors connected in parallel. The current of this parallel circuit is _____.
   (a) 35A
   (b) 45A
   (c) 65A
   (d) 75A

6. A circuit has three 15A resistors connected in parallel. The current of this parallel circuit is _____.
   (a) 35A
   (b) 45A
   (c) 65A
   (d) 75A

7. A circuit has three 10A resistors connected in parallel. The current of this parallel circuit is _____.
   (a) 30A
   (b) 40A
   (c) 60A
   (d) 70A

15.3 Parallel Circuit Resistance Calculations

8. The total resistance of a parallel circuit can be calculated by the _____ method.
   (a) Equal Resistance
   (b) Product-Over-Sum
   (c) Reciprocal
   (d) any of these

9. In a parallel circuit, the total circuit resistance is always _____ the smallest resistance.

    (a) greater than
    (b) less than
    (c) equal to
    (d) the square of

10. According to the _____ method, when all the resistances of the parallel circuit have the same resistance, divide the resistance of one resistance by the number of resistors in parallel.

    (a) Equal Resistance
    (b) Product-Over-Sum
    (c) Reciprocal
    (d) none of these

11. The total resistance of three 15Ω resistors connected in parallel is _____.

    (a) 5Ω
    (b) 10Ω
    (c) 20Ω
    (d) 30Ω

12. The total resistance of ten 50Ω resistors connected in parallel is _____.

    (a) 5Ω
    (b) 10Ω
    (c) 50Ω
    (d) 100Ω

13. A 240V circuit has three resistors in parallel where R_1 is 25Ω, R_2 is 25Ω, and R_3 is 25Ω. The resistance of this parallel circuit is _____.

    (a) 5.30Ω
    (b) 8.33Ω
    (c) 13.30Ω
    (d) 15.33Ω

14. A circuit has three 5Ω resistors connected in parallel. The resistance of this parallel circuit is _____.

    (a) 1.66Ω
    (b) 2.26Ω
    (c) 4.76Ω
    (d) 5.66Ω

15. The Product-Over-Sum method is used to calculate the resistance of _____ parallel resistances of different values.

    (a) two
    (b) three
    (c) four
    (d) five

16. The resistance of a coffee pot is 16Ω (R_1), and the resistance of a skillet is approximately 13Ω (R_2). What is the total resistance of the two appliances if they are connected in parallel?

    (a) 7.20Ω
    (b) 13Ω
    (c) 16Ω
    (d) 29Ω

17. The resistance of a microwave is 15Ω (R_1), and the resistance of an oven is approximately 30Ω (R_2). What is the total resistance of the two appliances if they are connected in parallel?

    (a) 7.20Ω
    (b) 10Ω
    (c) 16Ω
    (d) 25Ω

18. The resistance of a toaster is 6Ω (R_1), and the resistance of a warming drawer is approximately 12Ω (R_2). What is the total resistance of the two appliances if they are connected in parallel?

    (a) 4Ω
    (b) 8Ω
    (c) 16Ω
    (d) 20Ω

19. The resistance of a rice cooker is 5Ω (R_1), and the resistance of an air fryer is approximately 10Ω (R_2). What is the total resistance of the two appliances if they are connected in parallel?

    (a) 3.33Ω
    (b) 5.20Ω
    (c) 7.16Ω
    (d) 8.29Ω

20. The _____ method for determining the total resistance of a parallel circuit is used when there are more than two resistors of different values.

    (a) Equal Resistance
    (b) Product-Over-Sum
    (c) Reciprocal
    (d) none of these

21. What is the resistance total of a 16Ω, a 13Ω, and a 36Ω resistor connected in parallel?

    (a) 6Ω
    (b) 13Ω
    (c) 16Ω
    (d) 36Ω

22. A circuit has three resistors in parallel: 15Ω, 30Ω, and 45Ω. The parallel circuit resistance is _____.

    (a) 8.2Ω
    (b) 8.6Ω
    (c) 9.2Ω
    (d) 9.9Ω

UNIT
16

SERIES-PARALLEL CIRCUITS

16.1 Introduction

In this unit you will learn how to calculate total circuit resistance for series-parallel circuits.

16.2 Understanding Series-Parallel Circuits

A series-parallel circuit is one that contains some resistors in series and some in parallel with each other. That portion of the circuit that includes resistors in series must comply with the rules for series circuits. That portion of the circuit that contains resistors in parallel must comply with the rules for parallel circuits. ▶Figure 16–1

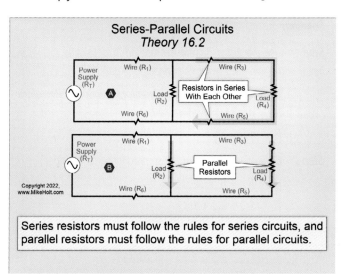

Series-Parallel Circuits
Theory 16.2

Series resistors must follow the rules for series circuits, and parallel resistors must follow the rules for parallel circuits.

▶Figure 16–1

To understand series-parallel circuits, we must review the rules for determining resistance for series and parallel circuits.

(A) Series Circuit Resistance. The total resistance of a series circuit is equal to the sum of the resistances. ▶Figure 16–2

(B) Parallel Circuit Resistance. The total resistance of a parallel circuit must be calculated with one of the three methods covered in the previous unit. ▶Figure 16–3

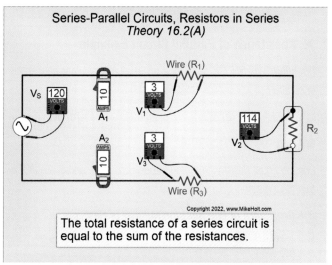

Series-Parallel Circuits, Resistors in Series
Theory 16.2(A)

The total resistance of a series circuit is equal to the sum of the resistances.

▶Figure 16–2

▶ Method 1. Equal Resistance

▶ Method 2. Product-Over-Sum

▶ Method 3. Reciprocal

16.3 Calculating Resistance in Series-Parallel Circuits

When determining the resistance for a series-parallel circuit, you need to keep breaking the circuit down to the part(s) of the circuit that is series and the part(s) that is parallel until you have only one resistance. Draw the circuit so you can see the series components and the parallel branches. Determine the series resistance and the parallel resistance, then redraw the circuit again.

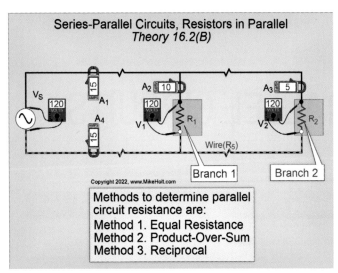

▶Figure 16–3

▶ Resistance of Parallel Circuit Example

Question: *What is the resistance of two 12Ω resistors connected in parallel?*

(a) 2Ω   (b) 4Ω   (c) 6Ω   (d) 8Ω

Solution:

Use the Equal Resistance method to determine the resistance of the two 12Ω resistors connected in parallel.

R = Resistance of One Resistor/Number of Resistors

$R = 12Ω/2$ *resistors*

$R = 6Ω$

Answer: *(c) 6Ω*

▶ Resistance of Series Circuit Example

Question: *What is the resistance of two 15Ω resistors connected in series?*

(a) 24Ω   (b) 30Ω   (c) 36Ω   (d) 54Ω

Solution:

Determine the sum of the series-connected resistors:

$(R + R_1 + R_2)$

$R = 15Ω + 15Ω$

$R = 30Ω$

Answer: *(b) 30Ω*

▶ Resistance of Series-Parallel Circuits Example

Question: *What is the total resistance of a series-parallel circuit: Resistors 1 and 4 are rated 15Ω each and resistors 2 and 3 are rated 12Ω each. Resistor 1 is in series with the parallel resistors 2 and 3, and resistor 4 is in series with parallel resistors 2 and 3.*
▶Figure 16–4

(a) 24Ω   (b) 30Ω   (c) 36Ω   (d) 54Ω

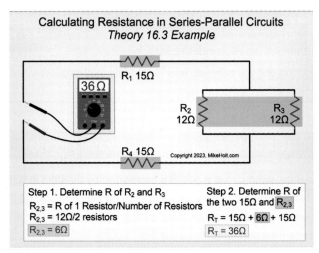

▶Figure 16–4

Solution:

Step 1: *Use the Equal Resistance method to determine the resistance of the two 12Ω resistors connected in parallel.*

$R_{2,3}$ **= Resistance of One Resistor/Number of Resistors**

$R_{2,3} = 12Ω/2$ *resistors*

$R_{2,3} = 6Ω$

Step 2: *Determine the sum of the series-connected resistors:*

$(R_1 + R_{2,3} + R_4)$

$R = 15Ω + 6Ω + 15Ω$

$R = 36Ω$

Answer: *(c) 36Ω*

UNIT
16

REVIEW QUESTIONS

The following questions are based on the material you just reviewed. If you struggle with any of the answers, go back and review that unit again, or refer to Mike Holt's Understanding Electrical Theory Video Library.

16.2 Understanding Series-Parallel Circuits

1. A _____ circuit is one that contains some resistances in series and some resistances in parallel with each other.
   (a) parallel
   (b) series
   (c) series-parallel
   (d) none of these

2. That portion of the series-parallel circuit that contains resistances in _____ must comply with the rules for series circuits.
   (a) series
   (b) parallel
   (c) series-parallel
   (d) parallel-series

3. That portion of the series-parallel circuit that contains resistances in _____ must comply with the rules for parallel circuits.
   (a) series
   (b) parallel
   (c) series-parallel
   (d) parallel-series

4. The total resistance of a _____ circuit is equal to the sum of the resistances.
   (a) series
   (b) parallel
   (c) series-parallel
   (d) parallel-series

5. The total resistance of a parallel circuit can be calculated by using the _____.
   (a) Equal Resistance method
   (b) Product-Over-Sum method
   (c) Reciprocal method
   (d) any of these

ALTERNATING CURRENT FUNDAMENTALS

17.1 Introduction

The major advantage of alternating current is that it can be transformed into different voltages to transmit power long distances. In this unit you will learn:

▸ How alternating current is produced

▸ The relationship of voltage and current waveforms

17.2 How Alternating Current is Produced

(A) Magnetism. In 1831, Michael Faraday discovered that electricity could be produced from a source other than a battery. He knew that electricity could be used to produce an electromagnet and wondered if a magnet could be used to generate electricity. Faraday discovered that when he moved a magnet inside a coil of wire, he was able to measure a pulse of electric current with a measuring instrument called a "galvanometer." When he pulled the magnet out of the coil of wire, he measured another electrical pulse of current.

(B) Current Direction. Faraday discovered that a magnet that pushes into or pulls out of a coil of wire causes the current in the wire to move in a specific direction relative to the movement of the magnetic field of the magnet. When a magnetic field moves through a coil of wire, the lines of force of the magnetic field cause the electrons in the wire to flow in a specific direction and when the magnetic field moves in the opposite direction, electrons in the wire flow in the opposite direction. ▸Figure 17–1

(C) Alternating-Current Generator. Generators can be used to produce alternating-current flow. To do so, a magnetic field must have motion relative to a coil of wire. A simple ac generator can be constructed with loops of wire rotating within the magnetic field between opposite poles of a stationary magnet. ▸Figure 17–2

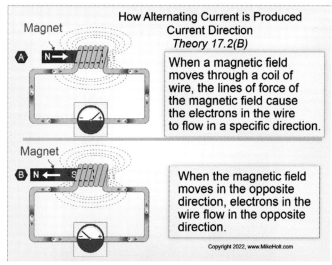

▸Figure 17–1

Author's Comment:

▸ According to the Drift Theory, electrons wiggle back and forth no more than $1/10^{th}$ an inch per ½ cycle in 60 Hz alternating-current circuits.

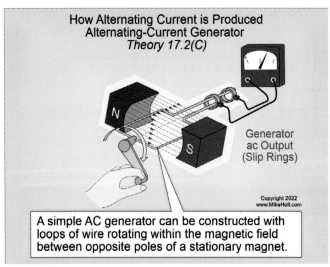

A simple AC generator can be constructed with loops of wire rotating within the magnetic field between opposite poles of a stationary magnet.

▶Figure 17–2

17.3 Waveforms

A waveform is a mathematical representation (a graph) used to visualize the level and direction of current and voltage in a circuit. One way to see the different characteristics of waveforms is by using an oscilloscope. ▶Figure 17–3

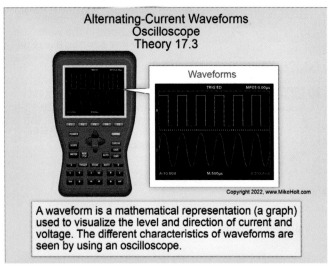

A waveform is a mathematical representation (a graph) used to visualize the level and direction of current and voltage. The different characteristics of waveforms are seen by using an oscilloscope.

▶Figure 17–3

(A) Direct-Current Waveforms. Direct-current (dc) power sources push and pull electrons in the circuit in one direction and the polarity of the voltage waveform is positive because the electrons flow from the negative to positive terminals of the power source.

(1) Battery. Direct-current voltage produced by a battery has a constant magnitude and the polarity is always the same. When dc voltage from a battery is plotted on a graph, it looks like a flat line. ▶Figure 17–4

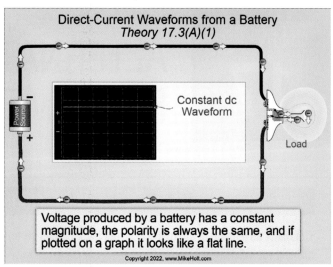

Voltage produced by a battery has a constant magnitude, the polarity is always the same, and if plotted on a graph it looks like a flat line.

▶Figure 17–4

(2) Solar PV. Direct-current voltage produced by a solar cell is a function of the irradiation of the sun's rays. At night the voltage will be almost zero, and as the sun rises, the voltage will increase to peak voltage. As the sun sets, the voltage decreases again to nearly zero. When dc voltage from a solar cell for a 24-hour period is plotted on a graph, it looks like an arc with a fairly flat top. ▶Figure 17–5

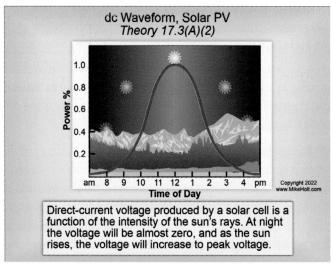

Direct-current voltage produced by a solar cell is a function of the intensity of the sun's rays. At night the voltage will be almost zero, and as the sun rises, the voltage will increase to peak voltage.

▶Figure 17–5

(3) Full-Wave Rectifier Diode. A rectifier is a device that converts alternating current to direct current. Direct current from a full-wave rectifier supplied by ac power has a varying magnitude because the polarity is always the same, so the waveform appears as a ripple with positive polarity. The combination of alternating-current and direct-current waveforms result in a pulsating waveform. ▶Figure 17–6

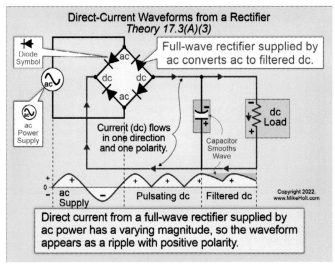

▶Figure 17–6

(B) Alternating-Current Waveforms. Most commercial alternating-current power is produced by some type of generator using wind, steam, or water. An alternating-current waveform represents the level and direction of the voltage for every instant of time during one full revolution of the generator's rotor. Alternating current can also come from electronic devices called inverters.

(1) Polarity. The voltage and current waveforms for alternating-current generators begin with a positive polarity for the first 180° and then change to a negative polarity.

(2) Sinusoidal Waveform. The waveform for an alternating-current generator is symmetrical, with positive values above and negative values below the zero-reference line on the graph. This waveform is called a "sine wave" or a "sinusoidal waveform." ▶Figure 17–7

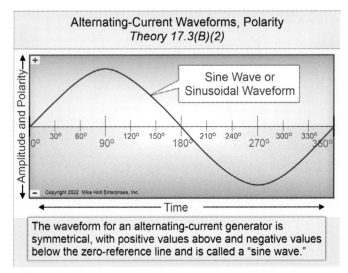

▶Figure 17–7

(a) Degrees. The relationship of the voltage and current waveforms to the generator's rotor position is from 0° to 360° as follows: ▶Figure 17–8

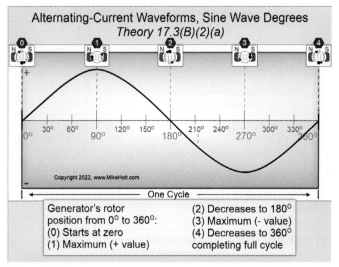

▶Figure 17–8

Point (0). The voltage/current waveform starts at the zero value when the generator's rotor is not turning.

Point (1). As the generator rotor turns through the electromagnetic field, the voltage/current increases from zero to a maximum value at 90° of the 360° in a positive polarity.

Point (2). As the generator rotor continues to turn through the electromagnetic field, the positive polarity voltage/current decreases from the maximum value at 90° to 180°.

Point (3). As the generator rotor continues to turn through the electromagnetic field, the voltage/current increases from zero to a maximum value at 270° of the 360° in the negative polarity.

Point (4). As the generator rotor continues to turn through the electromagnetic field, the negative polarity voltage/current decreases from the maximum value at 270° to 360°.

(3) Nonsinusoidal Current Waveform. A nonsinusoidal current waveform is produced when nonlinear loads distort the fundamental current sine waves. ▶Figure 17–9

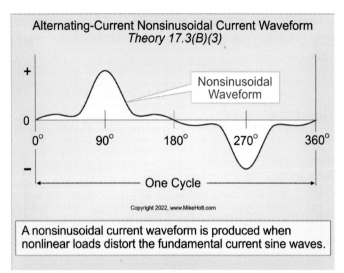

Figure 17-9

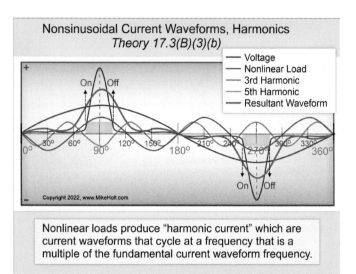

Figure 17-11

(a) Nonlinear Loads. A nonlinear load is a load where the shape of the current waveform does not follow the shape of the applied sinusoidal voltage waveform. Examples of nonlinear loads that contribute to nonsinusoidal waveforms include computer power supplies, electronic ballasts for fluorescent lighting fixtures, LED drivers, and adjustable-speed drives for motors. A nonsymmetrical current waveform is more common than a symmetrical sine wave in today's world of electronics. ▶Figure 17-10

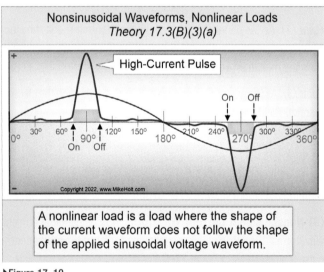

Figure 17-10

(b) Harmonics Currents. Nonlinear loads produce "harmonic current" which are current waveforms that cycle at a frequency that is a multiple of the fundamental current waveform frequency. If an electronic load has an abrupt change in impedance (such as a sudden change from high to low), it causes current pulses that reflect back into the power distribution system. ▶Figure 17-11

17.4 Frequency

The full rotation of an alternating-current generator is equal to 360° and its frequency output is expressed as "cycles per second" measured in "Hertz" (Hz) in honor of Heinrich Hertz. Electrical power generated in the United States and Canada have their generators rotate at speeds that are a multiple of 60 rotations per second; therefore, the frequency is 60 Hz. Some other parts of the world have their generators rotate at multiples of 50 rotations per second, or 50 Hz. ▶Figure 17-12

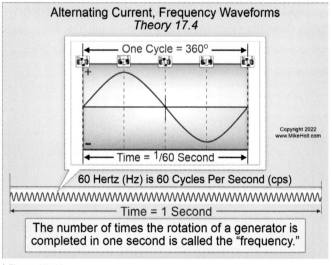

Figure 17-12

17.5 In-Phase Waveforms

If the voltage and current waveforms begin and end simultaneously, then the two waveforms are "in-phase" with each other. This means that, at every instant, the current is exactly in step with the voltage, so the current and voltage waveforms will reach their zero and peak values at the same time. ▶Figure 17–13

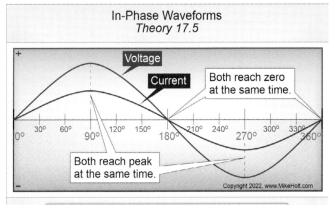

In-Phase Waveforms
Theory 17.5

Voltage

Current

Both reach zero at the same time.

Both reach peak at the same time.

Copyright 2022, www.MikeHolt.com

If the voltage and current waveforms begin and end simultaneously, then the two waveforms are in "in-phase" with each other.

▶Figure 17–13

17.6 Out-of-Phase Waveforms

When the voltage and current waveforms reach their zero and peak values at different times, the waveforms are said to be "out-of-phase" with each other. When describing the relationship between voltage and current, the reference waveform is always voltage. ▶Figure 17–14

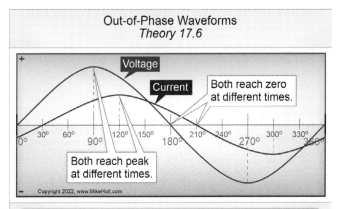

Out-of-Phase Waveforms
Theory 17.6

Voltage

Current

Both reach zero at different times.

Both reach peak at different times.

Copyright 2022, www.MikeHolt.com

When the voltage and current waveforms reach their zero and peak values at different times, the waveforms are said to be "out-of-phase" with each other.

▶Figure 17–14

(A) Capacitive Circuit. In a purely capacitive circuit, the current waveform leads the voltage waveform by as much as 90°. ▶Figure 17–15

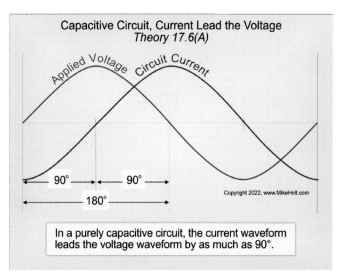

Capacitive Circuit, Current Lead the Voltage
Theory 17.6(A)

Applied Voltage   Circuit Current

90°   90°

180°

Copyright 2022, www.MikeHolt.com

In a purely capacitive circuit, the current waveform leads the voltage waveform by as much as 90°.

▶Figure 17–15

(B) Inductive Circuit. In a purely inductive circuit, the current waveform lags the voltage waveform by as much as 90°. ▶Figure 17–16

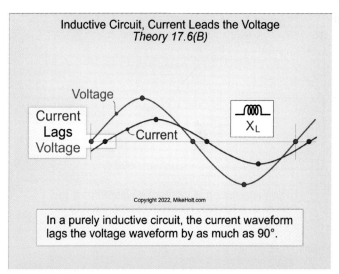

Inductive Circuit, Current Leads the Voltage
Theory 17.6(B)

Voltage

Current
Lags
Voltage

Current

X_L

Copyright 2022, MikeHolt.com

In a purely inductive circuit, the current waveform lags the voltage waveform by as much as 90°.

▶Figure 17–16

17.7 Alternating-Current Waveform Values

Alternating current waveform values include "instantaneous," "peak," and "effective root-mean-square" (RMS). ▶Figure 17–17

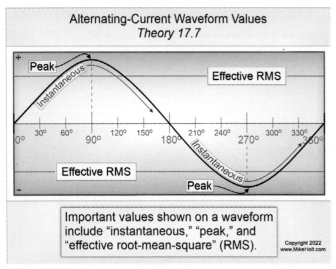

▶Figure 17–17

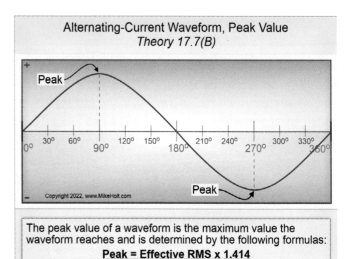

▶Figure 17–19

(A) Instantaneous Waveform Value. The instantaneous value of a voltage or current waveform is the value at a specific moment in time starting at zero, having a peak value, and ending at zero. ▶Figure 17–18

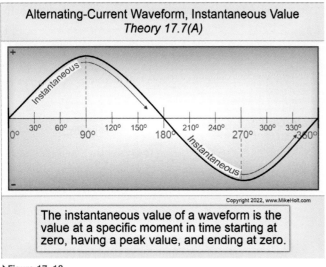

▶Figure 17–18

(B) Peak Waveform Value. The peak value of a voltage or current waveform is the maximum value the waveform reaches, for both positive and negative polarities. The peak value is determined by the following formula: ▶Figure 17–19

Peak = Effective (RMS) × 1.414

▶ **Peak Value Example 1**

Question: *The peak current, in amperes, of a circuit with a load having an effective (RMS) current of 10A is _____.* ▶Figure 17–20

(a) 14A　　　*(b) 15A*　　　*(c) 16A*　　　*(d) 17A*

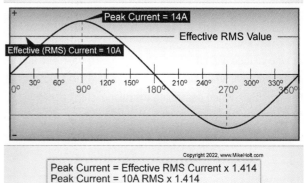

▶Figure 17–20

Solution:

Peak Current = Effective (RMS) Current × 1.414
Peak Current = 10A RMS × 1.414
Peak Current = 14.14A

Answer: *(a) 14A*

▶ Peak Value Example 2

Question: *The peak voltage of a circuit having an effective (RMS) voltage of 277V is _____.* ▶Figure 17–21

(a) 170V   (b) 277V   (c) 300V   (d) 392V

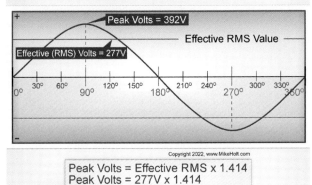

Alternating-Current Waveform, Peak Volts
Theory 17.7(B) Example 2

Peak Volts = Effective RMS x 1.414
Peak Volts = 277V x 1.414
Peak Volts = 392V

▶Figure 17–21

Solution:

Peak Voltage = Effective Voltage × 1.414

Peak Voltage = 277V RMS × 1.414

Peak Voltage = 391.68V, rounded to 392V to match answer options

Answer: *(d) 392V*

(C) Effective (RMS) Waveform Value. The effective ac voltage is equal to the dc voltage that would provide the same heat generation if applied to a resistor. The effective RMS value of a waveform is determined by the following formula: ▶Figure 17–22

Effective (RMS) = Peak × 0.707

Author's Comment:

▶ Root-Mean-Square (RMS) voltage describes the calculation steps (in reverse) necessary to determine the effective ac voltage. ▶Figure 17–23

Step 1: *Square.* Square the instantaneous ac voltage values.

Step 2: *Mean.* Determine the mean (average) of the instantaneous ac voltages from Step 1.

Step 3: *Root.* Calculate the square root value of the mean (average) from Step 2.

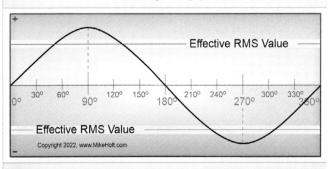

Alternating-Current Waveform, Effective RMS Value
Theory 17.7(C)

The effective ac voltage is equal to the dc voltage that generates the same heat if applied to a resistor, determined by formulas:
Effective RMS = Peak x 0.707

▶Figure 17–22

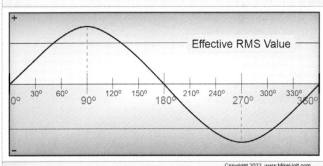

Alternating-Current Waveform, Effective RMS Value
Theory 17.7(C) Comment

Root-Mean-Square (RMS) voltage describes the calculation steps (in reverse) necessary to determine the effective ac voltage.

▶Figure 17–23

▶ Effective (RMS) Value Example

Question: What is the effective (RMS) voltage of a circuit with a peak value of 170V? ▶Figure 17–24

(a) 100V   *(b) 110V*   *(c) 115V*   *(d) 120V*

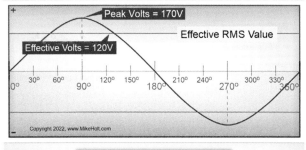

▶Figure 17–24

Solution:

Effective (RMS) = Peak × 0.707

Effective (RMS) = 170V × 0.707

Effective (RMS) = 120.18V, round to 120 to match answer options

Answer: (d) 120V

The following questions are based on the material you just reviewed. If you struggle with any of the answers, go back and review that unit again, or refer to Mike Holt's Understanding Electrical Theory Video Library.

17.3 Waveforms

1. A nonsinusoidal waveform is produced when _____ loads distort the voltage and current sinusoidal waveform.
   - (a) linear
   - (b) resistive
   - (c) inductive
   - (d) nonlinear

2. A nonlinear load is a load where the shape of the current waveform does not follow the _____ of the applied sinusoidal voltage waveform.
   - (a) shape
   - (b) color
   - (c) direction
   - (d) orientation

3. Nonlinear loads produce "_____" which are waveforms that cycle at a frequency that is a multiple of the fundamental frequency.
   - (a) capacitors
   - (b) resistors
   - (c) inductors
   - (d) harmonics

17.4 Frequency

4. The full rotation of an alternating-current generator is equal to 360° and its frequency output is expressed as "cycles per second" measured in "_____."
   - (a) degrees
   - (b) sine waves
   - (c) phases
   - (d) Hertz

17.5 In-Phase Waveforms

5. If the voltage and current waveforms begin and end simultaneously, then the two waveforms are "_____" with each other.
   - (a) in-phase
   - (b) out-of-phase
   - (c) coupled
   - (d) any of these

17.6 Out-of-Phase Waveforms

6. When the voltage and current waveforms reach their zero and peak values at different times, the waveforms are said to be "_____" with each other.
   - (a) in-phase
   - (b) out-of-phase
   - (c) in-phase or out-of-phase
   - (d) none of these

7. When describing the relationship between voltage and current, the reference waveform is always _____.
   - (a) current
   - (b) resistance
   - (c) voltage
   - (d) none of these

8. In a purely capacitive circuit, the current waveform _____ the voltage waveform by as much as 90°.
   - (a) leads
   - (b) lags
   - (c) is in-phase with
   - (d) none of these

9. In a purely inductive circuit, the current waveform _____ the voltage waveform by as much as 90°.

   (a) leads
   (b) lags
   (c) is in-phase with
   (d) none of these

17.7 Alternating-Current Waveform Values

10. The important value(s) shown on an ac waveform is(are) "_____."

    (a) instantaneous
    (b) peak
    (c) effective RMS
    (d) all of these

11. "_____" is the value of the voltage or current waveform at a specific moment in time.

    (a) Peak
    (b) Root-mean-square
    (c) Effective
    (d) Instantaneous

12. "_____" is the maximum value that ac current or voltage reaches, for both positive and negative polarities.

    (a) Peak
    (b) Root-mean-square
    (c) Instantaneous
    (d) none of these

13. The peak value is equal to the effective value _____.

    (a) times 0.707
    (b) times 1.414
    (c) divided by 2
    (d) times 0.58

14. What is the peak current of a circuit with a 12A effective RMS load?

    (a) 15A
    (b) 17A
    (c) 19A
    (d) 20A

15. What is the peak current of a circuit with a 20A effective RMS load?

    (a) 25.70A
    (b) 28.28A
    (c) 29.10A
    (d) 30.80A

16. The peak voltage of an alternating-current circuit having an effective RMS voltage of 240V is _____.

    (a) 170V
    (b) 339V
    (c) 392V
    (d) 480V

17. The peak voltage of an alternating-current circuit having an effective RMS voltage of 480V is _____.

    (a) 570.18V
    (b) 639.85V
    (c) 678.72V
    (d) 780.92V

18. _____ ac voltage or ac current is the equivalent value of dc voltage or dc current that would produce the same amount of heat in a resistor.

    (a) Peak
    (b) Effective
    (c) Instantaneous
    (d) none of these

19. The effective value of 120V is equal to the peak value of 170V _____.

    (a) times 0.314
    (b) times 0.707
    (c) divided by 0.707
    (d) divided by 0.314

20. What is the effective RMS voltage of a circuit with a peak value of 392V?

    (a) 120V
    (b) 208V
    (c) 277V
    (d) 300V

21. What is the effective RMS voltage of a circuit with a peak value of 340V?

    (a) 120V
    (b) 208V
    (c) 240V
    (d) 300V

22. What is the effective RMS voltage of a circuit with a peak value of 294V?

    (a) 120V
    (b) 208V
    (c) 277V
    (d) 300V

23. What is the effective RMS current of a circuit with a peak value of 15A?

    (a) 10.60A
    (b) 20.80A
    (c) 27.70A
    (d) 30.20A

24. "_____" describes the steps necessary to determine the effective voltage or current value.

    (a) Peak
    (b) Root-Mean-Square
    (c) Instantaneous
    (d) none of these

UNIT 20

TRUE POWER, POWER FACTOR, AND APPARENT POWER

20.1 Introduction

True power can only be produced when both the current and voltage are in-phase with each other. If the current and voltage are out-of-phase, the alternating-current circuit will have power factor. Apparent power is the power delivered to alternating-current circuits with power factor. In this unit you will learn:

▸ What true power and apparent power are

▸ The relationship between true power and apparent power

20.2 True Power

True power is the electrical energy consumed in a circuit supplying resistive loads such as incandescent lighting and resistive heating. True power, for resistive loads, is measured in watts as expressed by the formula: $P = E \times I$.

▸ **True Power Example**

Question: *What is the approximate power consumed for a 32.60A resistive heater rated 230V?* ▸**Figure 20–1**

(a) 2,353W   (b) 3,541W   (c) 5,136W   (d) 7,498W

Solution:

$P = E \times I$

E = 230V, voltage given

I = 32.60A, amperes given

P = 230V × 32.60A

P = 7,498W

Answer: (d) 7,498W

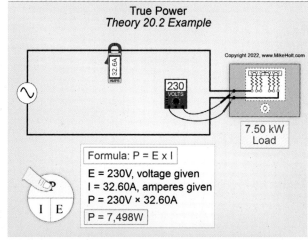

True Power
Theory 20.2 Example

Copyright 2022, www.MikeHolt.com

7.50 kW Load

Formula: P = E x I
E = 230V, voltage given
I = 32.60A, amperes given
P = 230V × 32.60A
P = 7,498W

▸Figure 20–1

20.3 Power Losses of Wires

Power in a circuit can be either useful or wasted; the wasted work is still energy used and is called "power loss." The heating of wires, transformer windings, motor windings, and many other loads result in power loss of the wires. Power loss in a wire is directly proportional to the length of the wire and the square of the current. If the current is doubled, the power loss will be increased by 400 percent. Wire power loss in watts is determined by the formula: $P = I^2 \times R$.

▶ Power Losses of Wires Example

Question: *What is the approximate power loss of a circuit carrying 16A having a total wire resistance of 0.30Ω?* ▶Figure 20–2

(a) 22.40W   *(b) 76.80W*   *(c) 154.20W*   *(d) 310.20W*

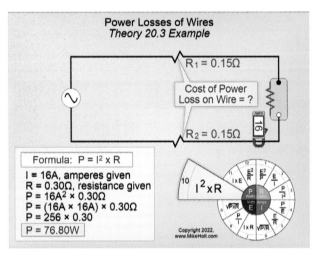

▶Figure 20–2

Solution:

$$P = I^2 \times R$$

I = 16A, amperes given

R = 0.30Ω, resistance given

P = 16A² × 0.30Ω

P = (16A × 16A) × 0.30Ω

P = 256A × 0.30Ω

P = 76.80W

Answer: *(b) 76.80W*

20.4 Power Losses at Terminals

Loose wire connections at terminals result in a high resistive contact point which can cause the terminals to overheat. Terminals for wires must be tightened to manufacturer's torque specifications to prevent fires caused by excessive heating at the terminals. The power loss in watts at a terminal can be determined by the formula: **P = I² × R**.

▶ Power Losses at Terminal Example 1

Question: *The power loss of a terminal carrying 50A with a contact resistance of 0.40Ω is _____.* ▶Figure 20–3

(a) 1,000W   *(b) 1,200W*   *(c) 1,400W*   *(d) 1,500W*

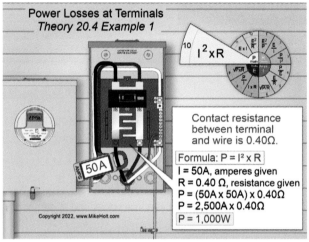

▶Figure 20–3

Solution:

$$P = I^2 \times R$$

I = 50A, amperes given

R = 0.40 Ω, resistance given

P = (50A × 50A) × 0.40Ω

P = 2,500A × 0.40Ω

P = 1,000W

Answer: *(a) 1,000W*

▶ Power Losses at Terminal Example 2

Question: *The power loss of a terminal carrying 25A with a contact resistance of 0.20Ω is _____.* ▶Figure 20–4

(a) 125W   *(b) 131W*   *(c) 141W*   *(d) 151W*

Solution:

$$P = I^2 \times R$$

I = 25A, amperes given

R = 0.20Ω, resistance given

P = (25A × 25A) × 0.20Ω

P = 625A × 0.20Ω

P = 125W

Answer: *(a) 125W*

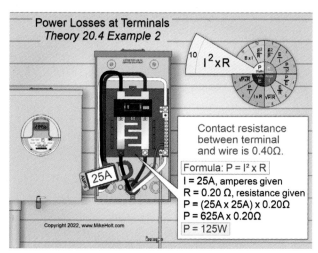

▶Figure 20–4

20.5 Equipment Efficiency

Efficiency describes how much input energy is used for the intended purpose. Efficiency is expressed as a ratio of output watts to input watts using the formula: **Efficiency = Output Watts/Input Watts**. ▶Figure 20–5

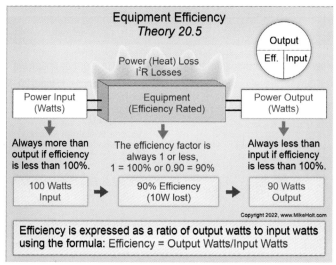

▶Figure 20–5

▶ **Calculating Efficiency Example**

Question: *The power supply output is rated 6.20A at 19.50V, and the input is rated 1.40A at 100V. What is the approximate efficiency of the power supply?*

(a) 75 percent   (b) 86 percent   (c) 90 percent   (d) 95 percent

Solution:

Efficiency = Output Watts/Input Watts

Output Watts = E × I
Output Watts = 19.50V × 6.20A
Output Watts = 121W

Input Watts = E × I
Input Watts = 100V × 1.40A
Input Watts = 140W

Efficiency = Output Watts/Input Watts
Efficiency = 121W/140W
Efficiency = 0.86 or 86 percent

Answer: *(b) 86 percent*

20.6 Cost of Power

Your electric bill is based on the energy consumed during a month, multiplied by the cost of the energy in "kilowatt hours" (kWh). ▶Figure 20–6

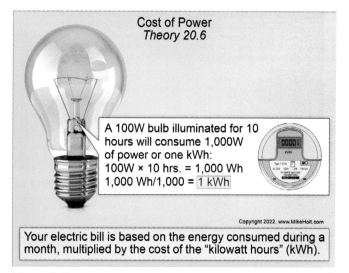

▶Figure 20–6

▶ **Cost of Power, Loss for Light Bulbs Example**

Question: *The cost of electricity is 13 cents per kWh. What does it cost to supply one 100W loads ten hours a day for 30 days?*

(a) $2.30   (b) $3.90   (c) $4.10   (d) $5.60

Solution:

Step 1: *Determine the power consumed for the month:*

> **Power for the Month = 100W × 10 Hours a Day × 30 days**
>
> Power for the Month = 30,000 Wh

Step 2: *Convert the answer in Step 1 to kWh:*

> P = 30,000 Wh/1,000
>
> P = 30 kWh

Step 3: *Determine the cost for the month:*

> Cost for the Month = 13 cents per kWh × 30 kWh
>
> Cost for the Month = $3.90

Answer: *(b) $3.90*

▶ **Cost of Power, Loss for Wire Example**

Question: *The cost of electricity is 13 cents per kWh. What does it cost for the year to heat up two 10 AWG wires having a total resistance of 0.24Ω supplying a 24A load that operates for 20 hours each day?* ▶Figure 20–7

(a) $131   (b) $141   (c) $151   (d) $161

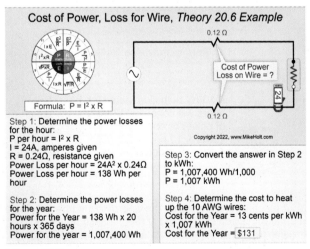

Cost of Power, Loss for Wire, *Theory 20.6 Example*

▶Figure 20–7

Solution:

Step 1: *Determine the power losses for the hour:*

> **P per Hour = I^2 × R**
>
> I = 24A, amperes given
>
> R = 0.24Ω, resistance given
>
> Power Loss Per Hour = 24A^2 × 0.24Ω
>
> Power Loss Per Hour = 138 Wh per hour

Step 2: *Determine the power losses for the year:*

> Power for the Year = 138 Wh × 20 hours × 365 days
>
> Power for the year = 1,007,400 Wh

Step 3: *Convert the answer in Step 2 to kWh:*

> P = 1,007,400 Wh/1,000
>
> P = 1,007 kWh

Step 4: *Determine the cost to heat up the 10 AWG wires:*

> Cost for the Year = 13 cents per kWh × 1,007 kWh
>
> Cost for the Year = $130.91, round to $131 to match answer options

Answer: *(a) $131*

20.7 Power Factor

Power factor occurs when the voltage waveform is out-of-phase with the current waveform due to inductance or capacitance. ▶Figure 20–8

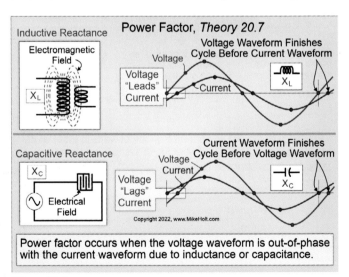

Power Factor, *Theory 20.7*

Power factor occurs when the voltage waveform is out-of-phase with the current waveform due to inductance or capacitance.

▶Figure 20–8

"Power factor percentage" is the relationship between true power and apparent power as determined by the formula:

Power Factor % = True Power (Watts)/Apparent Power (VA)

▶ Power Factor (PF) Example 1

Question: What is the power factor percentage for a 120V ballast rated 0.75A supplying two lamps, each rated 42W? ▶Figure 20–9

(a) 75 percent   (b) 89 percent   (c) 93 percent   (d) 95 percent

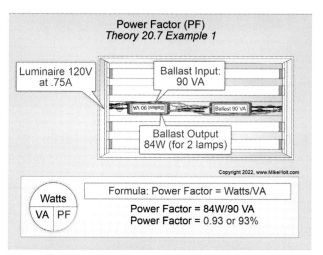

▶Figure 20–9

Solution:

Step 1: Determine the formula and knowns:

PF = Watts/VA

Watts = 42W × 2 bulbs, watts given

Watts = 84W

VA = Ballast Volts × Amperes (VA)

Volts = 120V, volts given

Amperes = 0.75A, amperes given

VA = 120V × 0.75A

VA = 90 VA

Step 2: Determine the power factor percentage:

PF = Watts/VA

Watts = 84W

VA = 90 VA

PF = 84W/90 VA

PF = 0.93 or 93 percent

Answer: (c) 93 percent

▶ Power Factor (PF) Example 2

Question: The power factor rating for a 250W high-bay light at 277V rated 1.20A is _____. ▶Figure 20–10

(a) 75 percent   (b) 80 percent   (c) 90 percent   (d) 100 percent

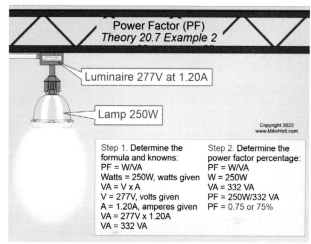

▶Figure 20–10

Solution:

Step 1: Determine the formula and knowns:

PF = W/VA

Watts = 250W, watts given

VA = V × A

V = 277V, volts given

A = 1.20A, amperes given

VA = 277V × 1.20A

VA = 332 VA

Step 2: Determine the power factor percentage:

PF = W/VA

W = 250W

VA = 332 VA

PF = 250W/332 VA

PF = 0.75 or 75 percent

Answer: (a) 75 percent

(A) Unity Power Factor. When an ac circuit supplies power to a purely resistive load, such as incandescent lighting or resistive heating elements, the voltage and current waveforms will be in-phase with each other. This condition is called "unity power factor." ▶Figure 20–11

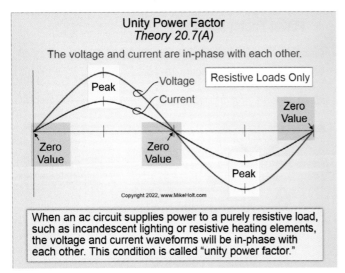

▶Figure 20–11

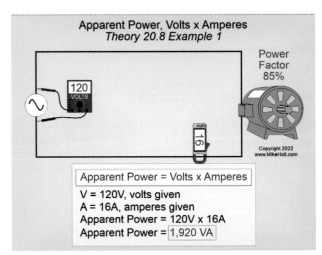

▶Figure 20–12

20.8 Apparent Power

In an inductive load such as a motor, the voltage and current waveforms do not reach their zero and peak values at the same time. Apparent power is a measurement of the amount of electrical energy supplied to a load, *not* the energy used by the load. Apparent power is determined by the formulas:

Apparent Power = Volts × Amperes

Apparent Power = True Power/Power Factor Percentage

▶ Apparent Power—Volts × Amperes Example

Question: What is the apparent power of a 120V motor rated 16A? ▶Figure 20–12

(a) 1,632 VA   (b) 1,800 VA   (c) 1,920 VA   (d) 2,400 VA
Solution:

Apparent Power = Volts × Amperes

V = 120V, volts given

A = 16A, amperes given

Apparent Power = 120V × 16A
Apparent Power = 1,920 VA

Answer: (c) 1,920 VA

▶ Apparent Power—True Power/Power Factor Percentage Example

Question: What is the apparent power of an 80W load having a power factor of 90 percent? ▶Figure 20–13

(a) 80.89 VA   (b) 80.98 VA   (c) 88.90 VA   (d) 89.98 VA

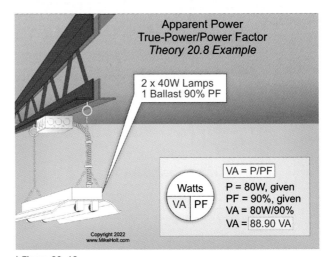

▶Figure 20–13

Solution:

Apparent Power = True Power/Power Factor Percentage

True Power = 80W, given

Power Factor Percentage = 90 percent, given

Apparent Power = 80W/90 percent
Apparent Power = 88.90 VA

Answer: (c) 88.90 VA

20.9 Apparent Power versus True Power

True power is expressed in watts and apparent power is expressed in VA. True power is equal to or less than apparent power, and apparent power is equal to or greater than true power. The formula for true power, when power factor applies, is:

True Power = Apparent Power × Power Factor Percentage

▶ Apparent Power versus True Power Example

Question: What is the true power of a 16A load rated 120V with a power factor of 85 percent? ▶Figure 20–14

(a) 1,632W   (b) 1,800W   (c) 1,920W   (d) 2,400W

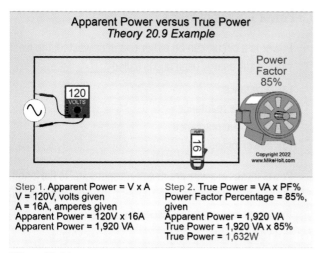

Apparent Power versus True Power
Theory 20.9 Example

Step 1. **Apparent Power = V x A**
V = 120V, volts given
A = 16A, amperes given
Apparent Power = 120V x 16A
Apparent Power = 1,920 VA

Step 2. **True Power = VA x PF%**
Power Factor Percentage = 85%, given
Apparent Power = 1,920 VA
True Power = 1,920 VA x 85%
True Power = 1,632W

▶Figure 20–14

Solution:

Step 1: *Determine the apparent power:*

Apparent Power = V × A

V = 120V, volts given

A = 16A, amperes given

Apparent Power = 120V × 16A

Apparent Power = 1,920 VA

Step 2: *Determine the true power:*

True Power = Apparent Power × Power Factor Percentage

Power Factor Percentage = 85 percent, given

Apparent Power = 1,920 VA

True Power = 1,920 VA × 85 percent

True Power = 1,632W

Answer: *(a) 1,632W*

REVIEW QUESTIONS

The following questions are based on the material you just reviewed. If you struggle with any of the answers, go back and review that unit again, or refer to Mike Holt's Understanding Electrical Theory Video Library.

20.2 True Power

1. To determine the true power for _____ loads, use the formula $P = E \times I$.
   - (a) resistive
   - (b) inductive
   - (c) capacitive
   - (d) all of these

2. What is the approximate power consumed by a 30A resistive heater rated 240V?
   - (a) 2,350W
   - (b) 3,500W
   - (c) 5,000W
   - (d) 7,200W

3. What is the approximate power consumed by a 15A incandescent light bulb rated 115V?
   - (a) 1,725W
   - (b) 2,570W
   - (c) 3,505W
   - (d) 5,200W

4. What is the approximate power consumed by a 20A water heater rated 208V?
   - (a) 2,350W
   - (b) 3,500W
   - (c) 4,160W
   - (d) 4,200W

20.3 Power Losses of Wires

5. Power in a circuit can be either useful or wasted, the wasted work is still energy used and is called "_____."
   - (a) resistance
   - (b) inductive reactance
   - (c) capacitive reactance
   - (d) power losses

6. Power losses in a wire are directly proportional to the length of the wire and the square of the current. If the current is doubled, the power loss will be increased by _____.
   - (a) 100 percent
   - (b) 200 percent
   - (c) 300 percent
   - (d) 400 percent

7. What is the approximate power loss of a circuit carrying 6A having a total wire resistance of 0.60Ω?
   - (a) 22W
   - (b) 75W
   - (c) 150W
   - (d) 320W

20.4 Power Losses at Terminals

8. The power loss in watts at a terminal can be determined by the formula _____.
   - (a) $P = I^2 \times R$
   - (b) $R = E^2/P$
   - (c) $E = I \times R$
   - (d) $I = E/R$

9. The power loss of a terminal carrying 25A with a contact resistance of 0.20Ω is _____.

   (a) 100W
   (b) 125W
   (c) 140W
   (d) 150W

10. The power loss of a terminal carrying 50A with a contact resistance of 0.40Ω is _____.

    (a) 400W
    (b) 600W
    (c) 800W
    (d) 1,000W

20.5 Equipment Efficiency

11. Efficiency is expressed as a ratio of _____ watts to input watts.

    (a) output
    (b) input
    (c) kilo
    (d) none of these

12. Efficiency describes how much _____ energy is used for its intended purpose.

    (a) output
    (b) input
    (c) kilo
    (d) none of these

13. If the output power is 1,320W and the input power is 1,800W, what is the efficiency of the equipment?

    (a) 62 percent
    (b) 73 percent
    (c) 80 percent
    (d) 100 percent

14. If the input power of a 1 hp dc motor is 1,128W and the output power is 746W, what is the efficiency of the motor?

    (a) 66 percent
    (b) 74 percent
    (c) 87 percent
    (d) 100 percent

15. If the output power is 1,600W and the equipment is 88 percent efficient, what are the input amperes at 120V?

    (a) 10A
    (b) 15A
    (c) 20A
    (d) 25A

16. If a transformer is 97 percent efficient, for every 1 kW input, there will be _____ output.

    (a) 970W
    (b) 1,000W
    (c) 1,030W
    (d) 1,200W

20.6 Cost of Power

17. The cost of electricity is 13 cents per kWh. What does it cost to supply ten 100W light ten hours a day for thirty days?

    (a) $37.00
    (b) $39.00
    (c) $41.00
    (d) $44.00

18. The cost of electricity is 13 cents per kWh. What does it cost for the year to heat up two 10 AWG wires having a total resistance of 0.24Ω supplying a 24A load that operates for 20 hours each day?

    (a) $131
    (b) $141
    (c) $151
    (d) $161

19. What does it cost per year (at 9 cents per kWh) for ten 150W recessed luminaires to operate if they are turned on for six hours a day?

    (a) $150
    (b) $300
    (c) $500
    (d) $800

20. What does it cost per year (at 8 cents per kWh) for the power loss of a 12 AWG wire (100 ft long) that has a total resistance of 0.40Ω and a current flow of 16A that operates 10 hours each day?

    (a) $30
    (b) $50
    (c) $70
    (d) $80

20.7 Power Factor

21. Alternating-current inductive or capacitive reactive loads cause the voltage and current waveforms to be _____ with each other.

    (a) in-phase
    (b) out-of-phase
    (c) in sync
    (d) none of these

22. _____ is the relationship between true power and apparent power.

    (a) Alternating-current power
    (b) Power factor percentage
    (c) Direct-current power
    (d) Reactive power

23. The formula for determining power factor percentage is Power Factor % = _____.

    (a) True Power/Apparent Power
    (b) Apparent Power/True Power
    (c) Watts/Impedance
    (d) Capacitance/Inductance

24. What is the power factor for a ballast at 120V rated 0.85A supplying two bulbs, each rated 40W?

    (a) 78 percent
    (b) 89 percent
    (c) 93 percent
    (d) 95 percent

25. The power factor rating for a 300W high-bay light at 277V rated 1.20A is _____.

    (a) 75 percent
    (b) 80 percent
    (c) 90 percent
    (d) 100 percent

26. The power factor of a 10A, 120V circuit supplying a 1,000W load is _____.

    (a) 80 percent
    (b) 83 percent
    (c) 87 percent
    (d) 82 percent

20.8 Apparent Power

27. What is the apparent power of an 84W load having a power factor of 90 percent?

    (a) 80.33 VA
    (b) 80.98 VA
    (c) 89.90 VA
    (d) 93.33 VA

20.9 Apparent Power versus True Power

28. What is the true power of a 120V load rated 18A with a power factor of 95 percent?

    (a) 1,632W
    (b) 1,800W
    (c) 2,052W
    (d) 2,400W

29. What is the true power of a 240V load rated 28A with a power factor of 90 percent?

    (a) 4,632W
    (b) 5,880W
    (c) 6,048W
    (d) 7,405W

30. The true power for a 20 kVA load having a power factor of 70 percent is _____

    (a) 13,000W
    (b) 14,000W
    (c) 15,000W
    (d) 16,000W

31. What is the power output of a power supply rated 10A at 120V with unity power factor?

    (a) 1,200W
    (b) 1,800W
    (c) 2,400W
    (d) 3,000W

32. What is the power output of a power supply rated 20A at 120V with a power factor of 90 percent?

    (a) 1,660W
    (b) 1,860W
    (c) 2,160W
    (d) 2,460W

UNIT
21

MOTORS

21.1 Introduction

Electric motors are among the most common loads connected to an electrical system. A motor is a rotating machine that converts electrical energy into mechanical energy. In this unit you will learn:

▸ Motor calculations involving horsepower and nameplate ratings

▸ About dual-voltage motors and reversing the rotation of alternating-current motors

---

21.3 Motor Horsepower Rating

The mechanical output of a motor is rated in horsepower (hp), and one horsepower of mechanical work is equal to 746 mechanical watts. The formulas to determine the horsepower size or output watts of a motor are: ▸Figure 21–4

Output Watts = Horsepower × 746W

Horsepower = Output Watts/746W

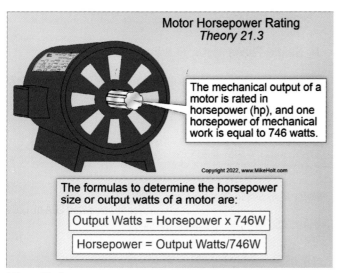

▸Figure 21–4

▸ Output Watts Example

Question: *What are the output watts of a 10 hp single-phase motor?* ▸Figure 21–5

(a) 5.46 kW   (b) 6.64 kW   (c) 7.46 kW   (d) 8.64 kW

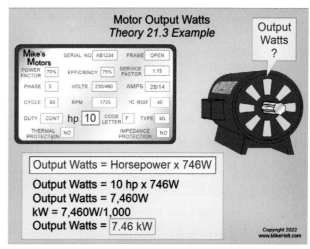

▸Figure 21–5

• • •

Solution:

Output Watts = Horsepower × 746W

Output Watts = 10 hp × 746W

Output Watts = 7,460W

Output Watts = 7,460W/1,000

Output Watts = 7.46 kW

Answer: (c) 7.46 kW

▶ Horsepower Size Example

Question: What size motor will produce 15 kW of output mechanical work? ▶Figure 21–6

(a) 5 hp   (b) 10 hp   (c) 20 hp   (d) 30 hp

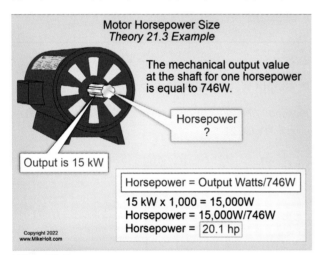

▶Figure 21–6

Solution:

Horsepower = Output Watts/746W

Output Watts = 15 kW × 1,000

Output Watts = 15,000W

Horsepower = 15,000W/746W

Horsepower = 20 hp

Answer: (c) 20 hp

21.5 Motor Nameplate Amperes

(A) Nameplate Amperes. The motor nameplate amperes indicate the current the motor is expected to draw at its rated horsepower, rated voltage, efficiency, and power factor. The motor nameplate amperes rating is commonly referred to as the motor "full-load amperes" (FLA). ▶Figure 21–12

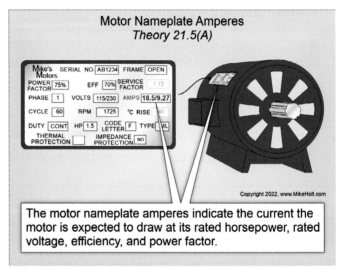

▶Figure 21–12

(B) Calculating Motor Nameplate Amperes. The motor nameplate amperes (FLA) can be determined using the following formulas:

Single-Phase FLA = (hp × 746W)/(E × Eff × PF)

Three-Phase FLA = (hp × 746W)/(E × 1.732 × Eff × PF)

▶ Single-Phase Motor FLA Example 1

Question: The motor nameplate amperes for a 7.50 hp, 230V, single-phase motor with an efficiency rating of 65 percent and a power factor of 60 percent is _____. ▶Figure 21–13

(a) 32A   (b) 42A   (c) 52A   (d) 62A

Solution:

Motor FLA, Single-Phase = (hp × 746W)/(E × Eff × PF)

FLA = (7.50 hp × 746W)/(230V × 65% Eff × 60% PF)

FLA = 5,595W/89.7

FLA = 62A

Answer: (d) 62A

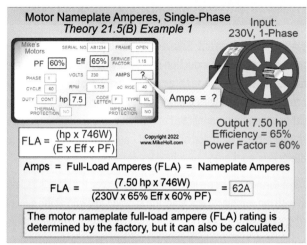

▶Figure 21-13

▶ Single-Phase Motor FLA Example 2

Question: The nameplate full-load ampere rating for a 1 hp, 115V single-phase motor will be _____ if the motor operates at an efficiency rating of 70 percent with a power factor of 70 percent. ▶**Figure 21-14**

(a) 13.20A   (b) 14.20A   (c) 15.20A   (d) 16.20A

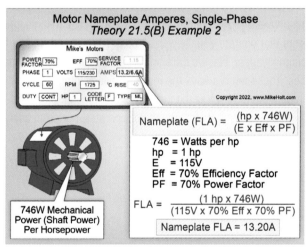

▶Figure 21-14

Solution:

Motor FLA, Single-Phase = (hp × 746W)/(E × Eff × PF)

Motor FLA = (1 hp × 746W)/(115V × 70% Eff × 70% PF)
Motor FLA = 746W/56.35
Motor FLA = 13.20A

***Answer:** (a) 13.20A*

▶ Three-Phase Motor FLA Example

Question: The motor nameplate amperes for a 10 hp, 208V, three-phase motor with an efficiency rating of 95 percent and a power factor of 90 percent is _____. ▶**Figure 21-15**

(a) 13A   (b) 19A   (c) 24A   (d) 33A

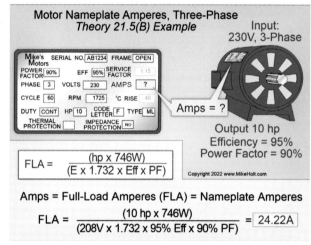

▶Figure 21-15

Solution:

Motor FLA, Three-Phase = (hp × 746W)/(E × 1.732 × Eff × PF)

Motor FLA = (10 hp × 746W)/(208V ×1.732 × 95% Eff × 90% PF)
Motor FLA = 7,460W/308
Motor FLA = 24.22A

***Answer:** (c) 24A*

21.7 Reversing the Rotation of Alternating-Current Motors

(A) Single-Phase. Some ac single-phase motors are constructed so their direction of rotation can be reversed. To reverse a single-phase ac induction motor, it is necessary to change the relative polarity of the start winding in relation to the run winding. The motor nameplate will contain the information for forward and reverse operation.

(B) Three-Phase. A three-phase motor can be reversed by swapping any two of the three-phase wires at any point in the circuit to the motor. The industry practice is to reverse the Phase A and Phase C wires. ▶Figure 21-19

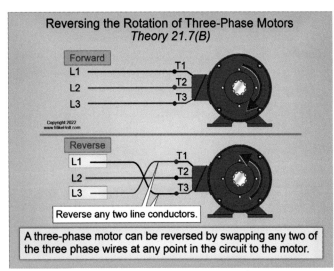

Reversing the Rotation of Three-Phase Motors
Theory 21.7(B)

Forward
L1 — T1
L2 — T2
L3 — T3

Copyright 2022
www.MikeHolt.com

Reverse
L1 — T1
L2 — T2
L3 — T3

Reverse any two line conductors.

A three-phase motor can be reversed by swapping any two of the three phase wires at any point in the circuit to the motor.

▶Figure 21–19

Caution

⚡ **CAUTION:** If a three-phase motor loses a phase while it is operating, the rotor will continue to turn but at a reduced speed and torque. Eventually, the reduced torque will cause the current flow on the other two phases to increase and will most likely damage the stator winding if the motor does not have overload protection.

21.8 Alternating-Current Motor Types

(A) Alternating-Current Squirrel-Cage Induction Motor. Three-phase ac squirrel-cage induction motors are used in almost all major industrial applications. They are called squirrel-cage motors because the rotor consists of bars that are either parallel to the shaft or at a slight angle and are connected at the ends by shorting rings. These bars resemble a hamster or squirrel cage if you remove the core material around them.

(B) Synchronous Motor. In a synchronous motor, the rotor is locked in step with the rotating stator field and is dragged along at the synchronous speed of the rotating electromagnetic field. Synchronous motors maintain their speed with a high degree of accuracy. Small synchronous motors are used for clock motors. Large synchronous motors are often found in large industrial facilities driving loads such as compressors, crushers, and large pumps.

(C) Wound-Rotor Induction Motor. Wound-rotor induction motors are used only in special applications because of their complexity. Wound-rotor induction motors only operate on three-phase ac power. They are also like induction motors; however, the rotor windings are connected in a wye configuration and the points of the wye are brought out through slip rings to an external controller.

(D) Universal Motor. Universal motors are fractional horsepower motors that operate equally well on ac and dc. They are used for vacuum cleaners, electric drills, mixers, and light household appliances. These motors have the inherent disadvantage associated with dc motors, which is the need for commutation. The problem with commutators is that as the motor operates, parts rub against each other and wear out.

The following questions are based on the material you just reviewed. If you struggle with any of the answers, go back and review that unit again, or refer to Mike Holt's Understanding Electrical Theory Video Library.

21.3 Motor Horsepower Rating

1. Motors are used to convert electrical energy into mechanical work and the output mechanical work of a motor is rated in horsepower, where 1 hp = _____.

   (a) 476W
   (b) 674W
   (c) 746W
   (d) 840W

2. What size motor in horsepower is required to produce approximately 30 kW of output watts?

   (a) 20 hp
   (b) 30 hp
   (c) 40 hp
   (d) 50 hp

3. What size motor in horsepower is required to produce approximately 60 kW of output watts?

   (a) 50 hp
   (b) 60 hp
   (c) 70 hp
   (d) 80 hp

4. What size motor in horsepower is required to produce approximately 110 kW of output watts?

   (a) 75 hp
   (b) 100 hp
   (c) 125 hp
   (d) 150 hp

5. What is the approximate output in watts of a 15 hp motor?

   (a) 11 kW
   (b) 15 kW
   (c) 22 kW
   (d) 31 kW

6. What is the approximate output watts of a 5 hp motor, 208V, three-phase motor?

   (a) 3.75 kW
   (b) 4.75 kW
   (c) 6.75 kW
   (d) 7.75 kW

7. What is the approximate output in watts of a 25 hp, 480V, three-phase motor?

   (a) 18.65 kW
   (b) 19.50 kW
   (c) 22.75 kW
   (d) 31.45 kW

21.5 Motor Nameplate Amperes

8. The nameplate full load ampere rating for a 1 hp, 115V motor is _____ if the motor operates at 70 percent efficiency and 70 percent power factor.

   (a) 11.24A
   (b) 13.24A
   (c) 15.24A
   (d) 19.24A

9. What is the nameplate current rating of a 1.5 hp, 120V motor at 90 percent efficiency at 85 percent power factor?

    (a) 9A
    (b) 10A
    (c) 11A
    (d) 12A

10. What is the nameplate FLA for a 5 hp, 230V, single-phase motor with 93 percent power factor and 87 percent efficiency?

    (a) 10A
    (b) 20A
    (c) 28A
    (d) 35A

11. What is the nameplate FLA for a 20 hp, 208V, three-phase motor with 90 percent power factor and 80 percent efficiency?

    (a) 51A
    (b) 58A
    (c) 65A
    (d) 80A

21.7 Reversing the Rotation of Alternating-Current Motors

12. Swapping _____ of the line wires can reverse a three-phase ac motor's rotation.

    (a) one
    (b) two
    (c) three
    (d) four

UNIT
22

GENERATORS

22.1 Introduction

A generator is a device that converts mechanical energy into electrical energy. Generators produce most of the electric power in the world and are used in residential, commercial, and industrial facilities for primary, backup, and temporary power. In this unit you will learn:

▸ The differences between single- and three-phase generators

▸ How to calculate generator output volt-amperes and amperes

22.4 Generator Output Current

The output current of a generator is determined by the following formulas:

Single-Phase: I = VA/E

Three-Phase: I = VA/(E × 1.732)

▸ Generator Output Current—Single-Phase Example

Question: *The output current for a single-phase, 24 kVA, 240V generator is _____.* ▸Figure 22–4

(a) 50A   (b) 70A   (c) 90A   (d) 100A

Solution:

I = VA/E
VA = 24,000 VA
E = 240V

I = 24,000 VA/240V
I = 100A

Answer: *(d) 100A*

Generator Output Current, Single-Phase
Theory 22.4 Example

I = VA/E
VA = 24,000 VA
E = 240V
I = 24,000 VA/240V
I = 100A

Copyright 2022, www.MikeHolt.com   Bob Cramer

▸Figure 22–4

▶ **Generator Output Current—Three-Phase Example**

Question: The current for a three-phase, 36 kVA, 120/208V generator is _____. ▶Figure 22–5

(a) 100A   (b) 110A   (c) 125A   (d) 150A

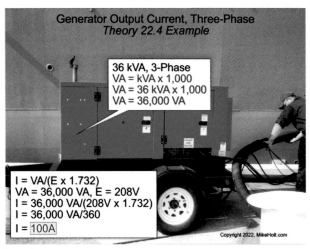

▶Figure 22–5

Solution:

$I = VA/(E × 1.732)$

VA = 36,000 VA

E = 208V

I = 36,000 VA/(208V × 1.732)

I = 36,000 VA/360

I = 100A

Answer: (a) 100A

22.5 Single-Phase and Three-Phase Generator Voltages

(A) Single-Phase Generator Voltages. Single-phase voltage can originate from a single-phase generator. ▶Figure 22–6

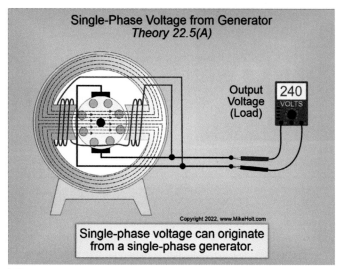

▶Figure 22–6

(B) Three-Phase Generator Voltages. Voltages in a three-phase circuit originate from a generator where there are three windings, one for each phase, that are out-of-phase with each other by 120°. ▶Figure 22–7

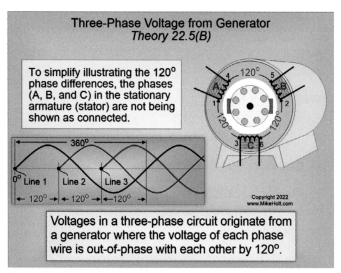

▶Figure 22–7

UNIT
22

REVIEW QUESTIONS

The following questions are based on the material you just reviewed. If you struggle with any of the answers, go back and review that unit again, or refer to Mike Holt's Understanding Electrical Theory Video Library.

22.4 Generator Output Current

1. The approximate output current for a single-phase, 22 kVA, 120/240V generator is _____.
   - (a) 72A
   - (b) 82A
   - (c) 92A
   - (d) 99A

2. The approximate output current for a 24 kVA, 120/240V generator is _____.
   - (a) 100A
   - (b) 110A
   - (c) 125A
   - (d) 130A

3. The approximate output current for a three-phase, 48 kVA, 120/208V generator is _____.
   - (a) 119A
   - (b) 121A
   - (c) 127A
   - (d) 133A

4. The approximate output current for a three-phase, 50 kVA, 120/208V generator is _____.
   - (a) 100A
   - (b) 120A
   - (c) 140A
   - (d) 160A

5. The approximate output current for a three-phase, 75 kVA, 120/208V generator is _____.
   - (a) 179A
   - (b) 180A
   - (c) 191A
   - (d) 208A

22.5 Single-Phase and Three-Phase Generator Voltages

6. Voltages in a three-phase circuit originating from a generator is out-of-phase with each other by _____.
   - (a) 0°
   - (b) 120°
   - (c) 240°
   - (d) 360°

RELAYS

23.1 Introduction

A relay is a switch that uses an electromagnetic coil to operate one or more sets of contacts. In this unit you will learn: ▶Figure 23–1

- ▶ How relays operate
- ▶ About normally open and normally closed relay contacts

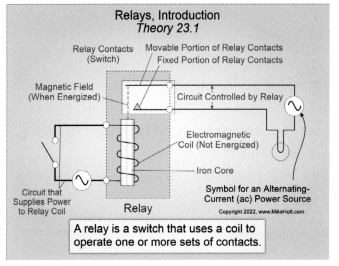

▶Figure 23–1

23.2 How Relays Operate

(A) Electromagnetic Relay. An electromagnetic relay uses an electromagnetic field to open or close a contact. One part of the relay contact is fixed, and the other part of the relay contact moves to open or close the relay contact by an electromagnetic field. ▶Figure 23–2

(B) Relay Sequence of Operation. The sequence of operation for a relay, where the contact(s) is open and when the relay is not energized is as follows: ▶Figure 23–3

Step 1: Closing the switch provides electrical energy to energize the relay.

Step 2: The coil of the relay becomes energized once the switch is closed.

Step 3: The coil creates an electromagnetic field once it is energized.

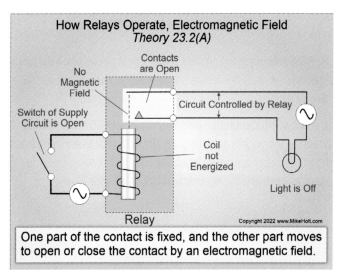

▶Figure 23–2

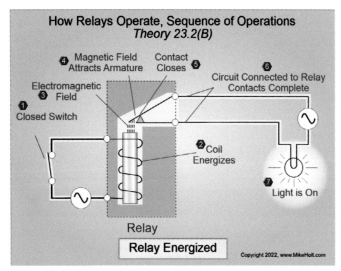

How Relays Operate, Sequence of Operations
Theory 23.2(B)

Figure 23–3

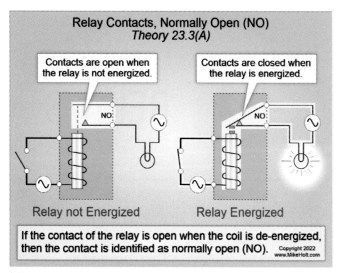

Relay Contacts, Normally Open (NO)
Theory 23.3(A)

If the contact of the relay is open when the coil is de-energized, then the contact is identified as normally open (NO).

Figure 23–4

Step 4: The electromagnetic field attracts the armature (to close the contact).

Step 5: The electromagnetic field from the coil closes the normally open (NO) contact.

Step 6: The circuit connected to the relay contacts is completed.

Step 7: The light is on.

23.3 Relay Contacts

Relays can contain contacts that are normally open, normally closed, or both normally open and normally closed.

(A) NO Contacts. If the contact of the relay is open when the coil is de-energized, then the contact is identified as normally open (NO). ▶Figure 23–4

(B) NC Contacts. If the contact of the relay is closed when the coil is de-energized, then the contact is identified as normally closed (NC). ▶Figure 23–5

(C) NO and NC Contacts. Some relays have both NO and NC contacts. When the relay coil is not energized, the NC contacts are closed, and the NO contacts are open. When the relay coil is energized, the NC contacts open and the NO contacts close. ▶Figure 23–6

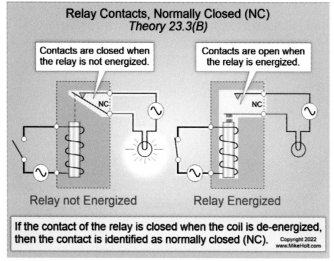

Relay Contacts, Normally Closed (NC)
Theory 23.3(B)

If the contact of the relay is closed when the coil is de-energized, then the contact is identified as normally closed (NC).

Figure 23–5

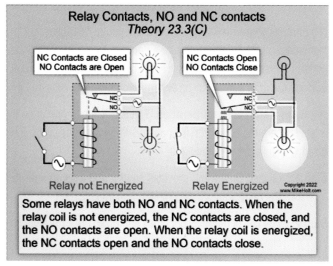

Relay Contacts, NO and NC contacts
Theory 23.3(C)

Some relays have both NO and NC contacts. When the relay coil is not energized, the NC contacts are closed, and the NO contacts are open. When the relay coil is energized, the NC contacts open and the NO contacts close.

Figure 23–6

UNIT 23

REVIEW QUESTIONS

The following questions are based on the material you just reviewed. If you struggle with any of the answers, go back and review that unit again, or refer to Mike Holt's Understanding Electrical Theory Video Library.

23.3 Relay Contacts

1. "Normally _____" means that the contacts are open when the coil is de-energized.

   (a) open
   (b) closed
   (c) powered
   (d) none of these

2. "Normally _____" means the contacts are closed when the coil is energized.

   (a) open
   (b) closed
   (c) powered
   (d) none of these

3. When the relay coil is energized, the NC contacts _____ and the NO contacts _____.

   (a) open, close
   (b) close, open
   (c) open, open
   (d) close, close

UNIT
24

TRANSFORMERS

24.1 Introduction

A transformer uses electromagnetism to convert input voltage into a different output voltage. In this unit you will learn:

▸ How to calculate the transformer winding and voltage ratios

▸ How to calculate primary and secondary current

24.6 Transformer Turns Ratios

(A) Winding Turns Ratio. The relationship between the number of primary winding turns compared to the number of secondary winding turns is called the transformer "winding turns ratio" and the formula for calculations is: ▸Figure 24–5

Winding Turns Ratio = Primary Turns:Secondary Turns

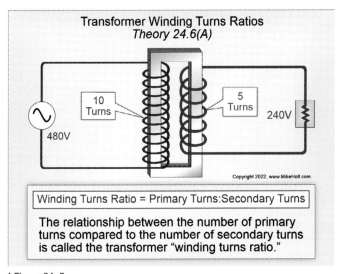

▸Figure 24–5

▸ Winding Turns Ratio Example

Question: *A transformer has a primary winding of ten turns and a secondary winding of two turns. The winding turns ratio of this transformer is _____.* ▸Figure 24–6

(a) 3:1   *(b) 4:1*   *(c) 5:1*   *(d) 10:1*

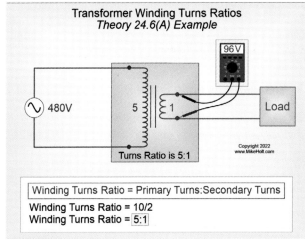

▸Figure 24–6

• • •

Solution:

Winding Turns Ratio = Primary Turns:Secondary Turns

Winding Turns Ratio = 10/2

Winding Turns Ratio = 5:1

Answer: *(c) 5:1*

(B) Voltage Turns Ratio. The relationship between the primary voltage and secondary voltage is called the transformer "voltage turns ratio" and the formula for calculations is: ▶Figure 24–7

Voltage Turns Ratio = Primary Volts:Secondary Volts

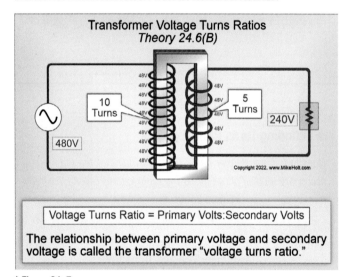

▶Figure 24–7

▶ **Voltage Turns Ratio Example**

Question: *If the primary voltage of a transformer is 480V and the secondary is 120V, the voltage turns ratio will be _____.* ▶Figure 24–8

(a) 1:4   (b) 2:4   (c) 4:1   (d) 4:20

Solution:

Voltage Turns Ratio = Primary Volts:Secondary Volts

Primary Volts = 480V

Secondary Volts = 120V

Voltage Turns Ratio = 480V:120V

Voltage Turns Ratio = 4:1

Answer: *(c) 4:1*

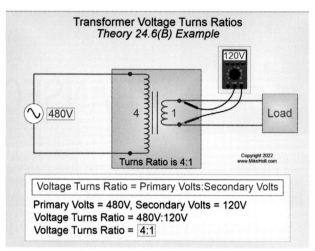

▶Figure 24–8

(C) Secondary Voltage. The secondary voltage of a transformer is determined by the following formula:

Secondary Voltage = Primary Volts/Voltage Turns Ratio

▶ **Secondary Volts Example 1**

Question: *The secondary voltage of a 5:1 transformer is _____ if the primary is 120V.* ▶Figure 24–9

(a) 3V   (b) 6V   (c) 12V   (d) 24V

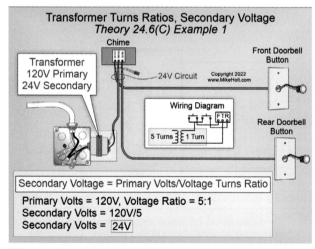

▶Figure 24–9

Solution:

Secondary Voltage = Primary Volts/Turns Ratio

Primary Volts = 120V

Voltage Turns Ratio = 5:1

Secondary Volts = 120V/5
Secondary Volts = 24V

Answer: (d) 24V

▶ **Secondary Volts Example 2**

Question: The secondary voltage of a 4:1 turns ratio transformer is _____ if the primary is 480V. ▶Figure 24–10

(a) 120V   (b) 208V   (c) 277V   (d) 480V

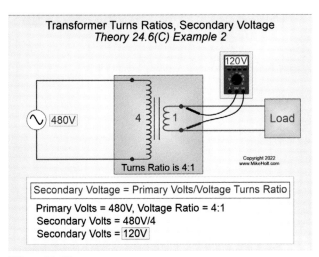

▶Figure 24–10

Solution:

Secondary Voltage = Primary Volts/Turn Ratio

Primary Volts = 480V

Voltage Turns Ratio = 4:1

Secondary Volts = 480V/4
Secondary Volts = 120V

Answer: (a) 120V

24.8 Autotransformers

Autotransformers use a single winding for both the primary and secondary and are often referred to as "buck-boost transformers."
▶Figure 24–12

The disadvantage of an autotransformer is the lack of electrical isolation between the primary and secondary windings. A short circuit between the primary and secondary wires can lead to the primary voltage being directly applied to the connected equipment.

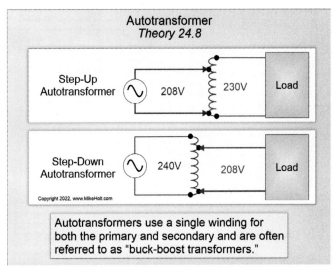

▶Figure 24–12

24.11 Transformer Current Rating

(A) Secondary Current. The secondary current of a transformer is determined by one of the following formulas:

Single-Phase Secondary Current = Transformer VA/Volts

Three-Phase Secondary Current = Transformer VA/(Volts × 1.732)

▶ **Single-Phase Secondary Line Current Example 1**

Question: What is the secondary current for a fully loaded single-phase, 25 kVA, 480V to 240V transformer? ▶Figure 24–15

(a) 52A   (b) 104A   (c) 208A   (d) 250A

Solution:

$I_{SEC} = VA/E$
VA = 25,000
E = 240V

$I_{SEC} = 25,000 \ VA/240V$
$I_{SEC} = 104A$

Answer: (b) 104A

• • •

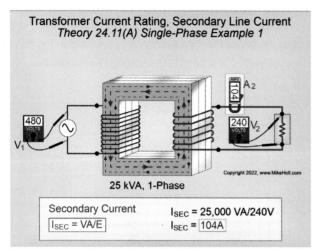

▶Figure 24–15

▶ Single-Phase Secondary Line Current Example 2

Question: The secondary current for a fully loaded single-phase, 37.50 kVA, 480V to 240V transformer is _____. ▶Figure 24–16

(a) 108A   (b) 130A   (c) 140A   (d) 156A

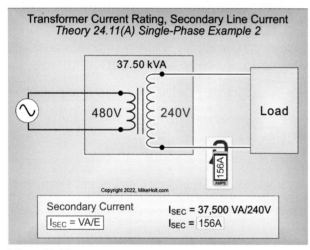

▶Figure 24–16

Solution:

$I_{SEC} = VA/E$

VA = 37,500

E = 240V

I_{SEC} = 37,500 VA/240V

I_{SEC} = 156.25A, round to 156A to match answer options

Answer: (d) 156A

▶ Three-Phase Secondary Line Current Example

Question: What is the secondary current for a fully loaded three-phase, 75 kVA, 480V to 208Y/120V transformer? ▶Figure 24–17

(a) 104A   (b) 140A   (c) 208A   (d) 500A

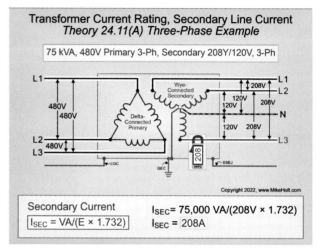

▶Figure 24–17

Solution:

$I_{SEC} = VA/(E × 1.732)$

VA = 75,000

E = 208V

I_{SEC} = 75,000 VA/(208V × 1.732)

I_{SEC} = 75,000 VA/360.26V

I_{SEC} = 208A

Answer: (c) 208A

(B) Primary Current. The primary current of a transformer is determined by one of the following formulas:

Single-Phase Primary Current = Transformer VA/Volts

Three-Phase Primary Current = Transformer VA/(Volts × 1.732)

▶ **Single-Phase Primary Line Current Example**

Question: *What is the primary current for a fully loaded single-phase, 25 kVA, 480V to240V transformer?* ▶Figure 24–18

(a) 52A   *(b) 72A*   *(c) 82A*   *(d) 614A*

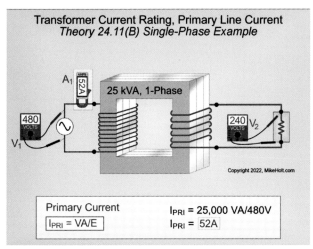

▶Figure 24–18

Solution:

$I_{PRI} = VA/E$

VA = 25,000

E = 480V

I_{PRI} = 25,000 VA/480V

I_{PRI} = 52A

Answer: (a) 52A

▶ **Three-Phase Primary Line Current Example 1**

Question: *What is the primary current for a fully loaded three-phase, 75 kVA, 480 to 208Y/120V transformer?* ▶Figure 24–19

(a) 10A   *(b) 70A*   *(c) 80A*   *(d) 90A*

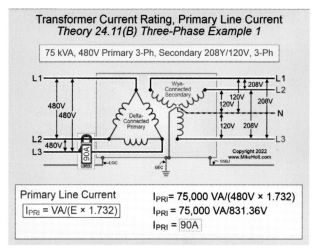

▶Figure 24–19

Solution:

$I_{PRI} = VA/(E × 1.732)$

VA = 75,000

E = 480V

I_{PRI} = 75,000 VA/(480V × 1.732)

I_{PRI} = 75,000 VA/831.36V

I_{PRI} = 90A

Answer: (d) 90A

▶ Three-Phase Primary Line Current Example 2

Question: *The primary current for a fully loaded three-phase, 37.50 kVA, 480V to 208Y/120V transformer is _____.* ▶Figure 24–20

(a) 45A   (b) 55A   (c) 65A   (d) 75A

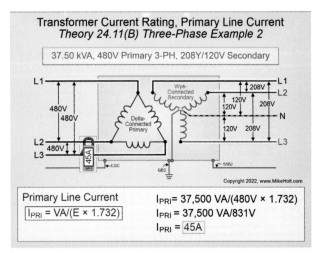

▶Figure 24–20

Solution:

$I_{PRI} = VA/(E \times 1.732)$

VA = 37,500

E = 480V

I_{PRI} = 37,500 VA/(480V × 1.732)
I_{PRI} = 37,500 VA/831V
I_{PRI} = 45A

Answer: *(a) 45A*

UNIT
24

REVIEW QUESTIONS

The following questions are based on the material you just reviewed. If you struggle with any of the answers, go back and review that unit again, or refer to Mike Holt's Understanding Electrical Theory Video Library.

24.6 Transformer Turns Ratios

1. The relationship of the number of turns of wire on the _____ as compared to the number of turns on the _____ is called the transformer "winding turns ratio."

   (a) primary, secondary
   (b) secondary, primary
   (c) primary, primary
   (d) secondary, secondary

2. A transformer has a primary winding of twenty turns and a secondary of ten turns. The winding turns ratio of this transformer is _____.

   (a) 2:1
   (b) 4:1
   (c) 5:1
   (d) 10:1

3. The relationship between primary voltage and secondary voltage is called the transformer "_____ turns ratio."

   (a) resistance
   (b) voltage
   (c) power
   (d) current

4. If the primary phase voltage is 480V and the secondary phase voltage is 240V, the voltage turns ratio is _____.

   (a) 1:2
   (b) 1:4
   (c) 2:1
   (d) 4:1

5. A single-phase transformer has a primary voltage of 480V and a secondary voltage of 96V. The voltage turns ratio of this transformer is _____.

   (a) 3:1
   (b) 4:1
   (c) 5:1
   (d) 10:1

6. The secondary voltage of a 5:1 transformer is _____ if the primary is 240V.

   (a) 6V
   (b) 12V
   (c) 24V
   (d) 48V

7. The secondary voltage of a 4:1 transformer is _____ if the primary is 240V.

   (a) 60V
   (b) 210V
   (c) 208V
   (d) 277V

8. The secondary voltage of a 4:1 transformer is _____ if the primary is 480V.

   (a) 120V
   (b) 208V
   (c) 277V
   (d) 480V

9. The secondary voltage of a 2:1 transformer is _____ if the primary is 480V.

    (a) 52A
    (b) 104A
    (c) 208A
    (d) 240A

24.11 Transformer Current Rating

Secondary Current

10. What is the secondary current for a fully loaded single-phase, 25 kVA, 480V to 240V transformer?

    (a) 52A
    (b) 104A
    (c) 208A
    (d) 250A

11. What is the secondary current for a fully loaded three-phase, 75 kVA, 480V to 208Y/120V transformer?

    (a) 104A
    (b) 140A
    (c) 208A
    (d) 500A

12. The secondary current for a fully loaded single-phase, 37.50 kVA, 480V to 240V transformer is _____.

    (a) 148A
    (b) 156A
    (c) 168A
    (d) 178A

13. The secondary current for a fully loaded 20 kVA, 480V to 208Y/120V three-phase transformer is _____ per phase.

    (a) 49A
    (b) 51A
    (c) 53A
    (d) 56A

14. The secondary current for a fully loaded 30 kVA, 480V to 208Y/120V three-phase transformer is _____ per phase.

    (a) 83A
    (b) 91A
    (c) 97A
    (d) 99A

15. The secondary current for a fully loaded 15 kVA, 480V to 240V three-phase delta-delta transformer is _____ per phase.

    (a) 24A
    (b) 36A
    (c) 41A
    (d) 46A

16. The secondary current for a fully loaded 36 kVA, 480V to 240V three-phase delta-delta transformer is _____ per phase.

    (a) 82A
    (b) 87A
    (c) 95A
    (d) 99A

Primary Current

17. What is the primary current for a fully loaded single-phase, 25 kVA, 480V to 240V transformer?

    (a) 52A
    (b) 72A
    (c) 82A
    (d) 614A

18. The primary current for a fully loaded three-phase, 37.50 kVA, 480V to 208Y/120V transformer is _____.

    (a) 45A
    (b) 55A
    (c) 65A
    (d) 75A

19. What is the primary current for a fully loaded three-phase, 75 kVA, 480V to 208Y/120V transformer?

    (a) 10A
    (b) 70A
    (c) 80A
    (d) 90A

20. What is the primary current for a fully loaded three-phase, 112.5 kVA, 480V to 208Y/120V transformer?

    (a) 135A
    (b) 271A
    (c) 406A
    (d) 469A

21. What is the primary current for a fully loaded three-phase, 300 kVA, 480V to 208Y/120V transformer?

    (a) 131A
    (b) 271A
    (c) 360A
    (d) 461A

UNIT
25

OVERCURRENT PROTECTION

25.1 Introduction

Overcurrent protection is a complex subject because different types of overcurrent protective devices serve different purposes. In this unit you will learn:

▸ How to calculate the available short-circuit current in different points of the electrical system

▸ Overcurrent device interrupting ratings ▸Figure 25–1

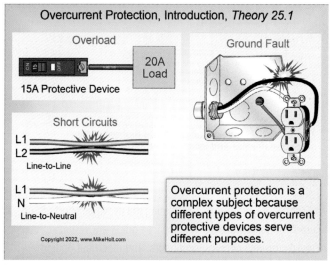

Overcurrent Protection, Introduction, *Theory 25.1*

Overload

15A Protective Device

20A Load

Short Circuits

L1
L2
Line-to-Line

L1
N
Line-to-Neutral

Ground Fault

Overcurrent protection is a complex subject because different types of overcurrent protective devices serve different purposes.

Copyright 2022, www.MikeHolt.com

▸Figure 25–1

25.6 Available Short-Circuit Current

The available short-circuit current is the largest short-circuit current capable of being delivered at a given point on the electrical system. The available short-circuit current is calculated at the line terminals of the service disconnect, panelboards, and equipment disconnects. ▸Figure 25–23

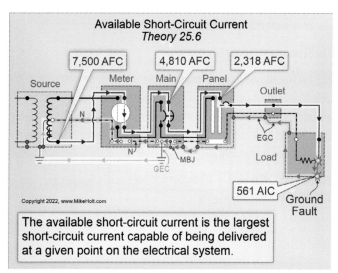

Available Short-Circuit Current
Theory 25.6

7,500 AFC   4,810 AFC   2,318 AFC

Source   Meter   Main   Panel   Outlet

N   EGC   Load

N'   MBJ
GEC

561 AIC   Ground Fault

Copyright 2022, www.MikeHolt.com

The available short-circuit current is the largest short-circuit current capable of being delivered at a given point on the electrical system.

▸Figure 25–23

(A) At Utility Transformer. The available short-circuit current is first determined at the secondary terminals of the utility transformer and is provided by the electric utility—no calculation is required. The available short-circuit current is highest at the utility transformer and lowest at the furthest branch-circuit load because of circuit wire impedance. ▶Figure 25–24

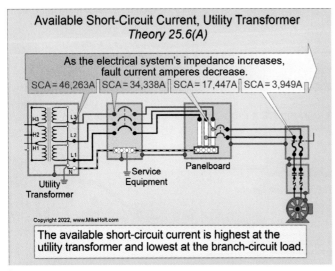

Available Short-Circuit Current, Utility Transformer Theory 25.6(A)

As the electrical system's impedance increases, fault current amperes decrease.

SCA = 46,263A | SCA = 34,338A | SCA = 17,447A | SCA = 3,949A

Utility Transformer
Service Equipment
Panelboard

Copyright 2022, www.MikeHolt.com

The available short-circuit current is highest at the utility transformer and lowest at the branch-circuit load.

▶Figure 25–24

(B) At Electrical Equipment. Calculating the available short-circuit fault current at the terminals of the service equipment, branch-circuit panelboards, branch-circuit disconnects, and electrical equipment considers the following factors:

(1) Transformer kVA, secondary system voltage, and transformer impedance.

(2) Wire material and circuit length.

(3) Steel or PVC raceway.

(C) Load-Side of Transformer. Factors that determine the available short-circuit current at the secondary terminals of a transformer include the kVA rating, impedance, and system voltage. The available short-circuit fault current at the secondary terminals of a transformer is calculated by the formula:

Short-Circuit Current = Transformer Secondary Amperes/ Transformer Impedance %

▶ **Short-Circuit Current—Single-Phase Example**

Question: What is the approximate available short-circuit current on the secondary of a single-phase, 50 kVA, 480V to 240V transformer having an impedance rating of 1.50 percent?

(a) 11,000A   *(b) 12,000A*   *(c) 13,000A*   *(d) 14,000A*

Solution:

There are two steps required to solve this problem.

Step 1: *Determine the transformer secondary amperes:*

Transformer Secondary Amperes = VA/Volts

Transformer Secondary Amperes = 50,000 VA/240V

Transformer Secondary Amperes = 208A

Step 2: *Determine the available short-circuit fault current at the transformer secondary terminals:*

Short-Circuit Current = Transformer Secondary Amperes/Transformer Impedance %

Transformer Impedance = 1.50%

Short-Circuit Current = 208A/1.50%

Short-Circuit Current = 13,866A, round to 14,000A to match answer options

Answer: *(d) 14,000A*

▶ **Short-Circuit Current—Three-Phase Example**

Question: What is the approximate available short-circuit current on the secondary of a three-phase, 112.50 kVA, 480V to 208Y/120V transformer having an impedance rating of three percent?

(a) 10,500A   *(b) 11,500A*   *(c) 12,500A*   *(d) 13,500A*

Solution:

There are two steps required to solve this problem.

Step 1: *Determine the transformer secondary amperes:*

Transformer Secondary Amperes = VA/(Volts × 1.732)

Transformer Secondary Amperes = 112,500 VA/(208V × 1.732)

Transformer Secondary Amperes = 112,500 VA/360

Transformer Secondary Amperes = 313A

Step 2: *Determine the available short-circuit fault current at the transformer secondary terminals:*

> **Short-Circuit Current = Transformer Secondary**
> **Amperes/Transformer Impedance %**

Transformer Impedance = 3%

Short-Circuit Current = 313A/3%

Short-Circuit Current = 10,433A, round to 10,500A to
*   match answer options*

Answer: *(a) 10,500A*

25.7 Overcurrent Protective Devices, Interrupting Rating

(A) General. Overcurrent protective devices are intended to interrupt a circuit during an overload, short circuit, and/or ground fault. The interrupting rating marked on circuit breakers and fuses such as 10K, 22K, and 65K, must be sufficient for the available short-circuit current at the line terminals of the overcurrent protective device. ▶Figure 25–25

(B) Hazard. Extremely high values of fault currents caused by short circuits or ground faults produce tremendously destructive thermal and magnetic forces. If an overcurrent protective device is not rated to interrupt the available fault current at the equipment, it can explode and vaporize metal components which can cause serious injury or death, as well as property damage and electrical system down time. ▶Figure 25–26

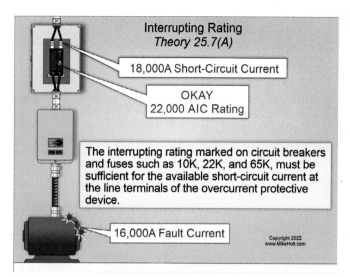

Interrupting Rating
Theory 25.7(A)

18,000A Short-Circuit Current

OKAY
22,000 AIC Rating

The interrupting rating marked on circuit breakers and fuses such as 10K, 22K, and 65K, must be sufficient for the available short-circuit current at the line terminals of the overcurrent protective device.

16,000A Fault Current

Copyright 2022
www.MikeHolt.com

▶Figure 25–25

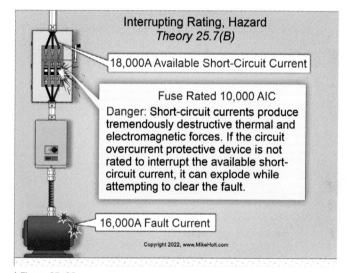

Interrupting Rating, Hazard
Theory 25.7(B)

18,000A Available Short-Circuit Current

Fuse Rated 10,000 AIC
Danger: Short-circuit currents produce tremendously destructive thermal and electromagnetic forces. If the circuit overcurrent protective device is not rated to interrupt the available short-circuit current, it can explode while attempting to clear the fault.

16,000A Fault Current

Copyright 2022, www.MikeHolt.com

▶Figure 25–26

The following questions are based on the material you just reviewed. If you struggle with any of the answers, go back and review that unit again, or refer to Mike Holt's Understanding Electrical Theory Video Library.

25.6 Available Short-Circuit Current

1. Available short-circuit current is the _____ current in amperes that is available at a given point in the electrical system.

   (a) phase
   (b) line
   (c) largest
   (d) smallest

2. The available short-circuit current is highest at the utility transformer and lowest at the _____ load because of the impedance of the circuit.

   (a) branch-circuit
   (b) feeder
   (c) service
   (d) utility transformer

3. The factor(s) that impact the available short-circuit current on the load side of a transformer is(are) _____.

   (a) system voltage
   (b) kVA rating
   (c) impedance
   (d) all of these

4. What is the approximate available short-circuit current on the secondary of a 50 kVA, 480V to 240V transformer having an impedance rating of 1.20 percent?

   (a) 10,000A
   (b) 12,000A
   (c) 14,000A
   (d) 17,000A

5. What is the approximate available short-circuit current on the secondary of a three-phase, 112.50 kVA, 480V to 208Y/120V transformer having an impedance rating of 2.40 percent?

   (a) 10,500A
   (b) 11,000A
   (c) 12,500A
   (d) 13,000A

6. The secondary available short-circuit current for a three-phase 300 kVA, 480Y – 208Y/120V transformer with an impedance of 1.5 percent is _____.

   (a) 53,533A
   (b) 55,533A
   (c) 57,533A
   (d) 59,533A

UNIT
29
THE FORMULA WHEEL

29.1 Introduction

The formula wheel combines the Ohm's Law Formula Circle and Power Formula Circle (Watt's Law). In this unit you will learn how to perform calculations using the formula wheel. ▶Figure 29–1

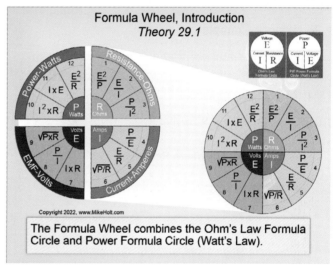

Formula Wheel, Introduction
Theory 29.1

The Formula Wheel combines the Ohm's Law Formula Circle and Power Formula Circle (Watt's Law).

▶Figure 29–1

29.2 Formula Wheel Quadrants

The formula wheel is divided into four sections with three formulas in each section. The sections include: ▶Figure 29–2

- ▶ "P" for power measured in watts
- ▶ "R" for resistance measured in ohms
- ▶ "I" for intensity or current measured in amperes
- ▶ "E" for electromotive force, or voltage measured in volts

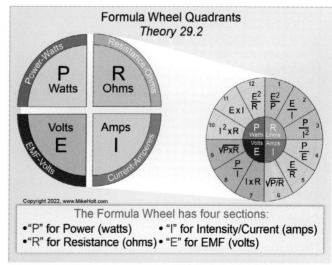

Formula Wheel Quadrants
Theory 29.2

The Formula Wheel has four sections:
• "P" for Power (watts) • "I" for Intensity/Current (amps)
• "R" for Resistance (ohms) • "E" for EMF (volts)

▶Figure 29–2

29.3 Using the Formula Wheel

When working with the formula wheel, the key to finding the correct answer is to follow these steps:

Step 1: What is the question? Amperes, voltage, resistance, or power?

Step 2: What do you know? Amperes, voltage, resistance, or power?

Step 3: Select the formula from the wheel.

Step 4: Work out the formula calculation.

▶ Resistance Example

Question: What is the resistance of two wires where each wire has a voltage drop of 1.50V and the current flowing in the circuit is 100A?
▶Figure 29–3

(a) 0.03Ω   (b) 2Ω   (c) 30Ω   (d) 300Ω

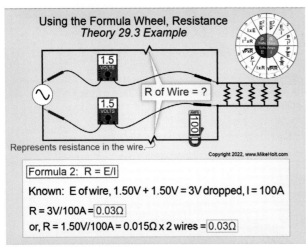

▶Figure 29–3

Solution:

Step 1: What is the question? What is "R"?

Step 2: What do you know?
   Voltage Drop = 3V
   Circuit Current = 100A

Step 3: The formula to use is **R = E/I**.

Step 4: Calculate the answer:
   R = 3V/100A
   R = 0.03Ω

Answer: (a) 0.03Ω

▶ Current Example

Question: What is the current flow in amperes through a 7.50 kW heat strip rated 230V when connected to a 230V power source?
▶Figure 29–4

(a) 25A   (b) 33A   (c) 39A   (d) 230A

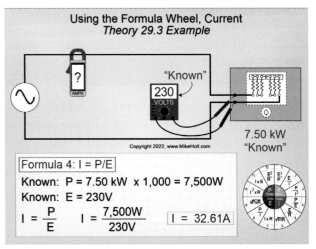

▶Figure 29–4

Solution:

Step 1: What is the question? What is "I"?

Step 2: What do you know?
   Heat Strip Power Rating, P = 7.50 kW × 1,000
   Heat Strip Power Rating, P = 7,500W
   Heat Strip Voltage Rating, E = 230V

Step 3: The formula to use is **I = P/E**.

Step 4: Calculate the answer:
   I = 7,500W/230V
   I = 32.61A, round to 33A to match answer options

Answer: (b) 33A

▶ Voltage Example

Question: *What is the voltage of a circuit carrying 1.20A supplying a 100Ω resistor?* ▶**Figure 29–5**

(a) 110V   *(b) 120V*   *(c) 160V*   *(d) 320V*

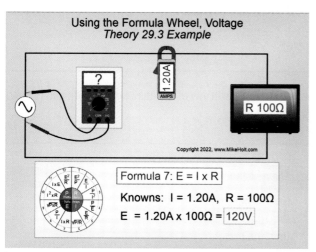

▶Figure 29–5

Solution:

Step 1: *What is the question? What is "E"?*

Step 2: *What do you know?*

    Current (I) = 1.20A

    Resistance (R) = 100Ω

Step 3: *The formula to use is $E = I \times R$.*

Step 4: *Calculate the answer:*

    E = 1.20A × 100Ω

    E = 120V

Answer: *(b) 120V*

▶ Power Example

Question: *What is the power loss of a 2-wire circuit carrying 16A having a length of 75 ft with two 12 AWG wires each having a resistance of 0.15Ω?* ▶**Figure 29–6**

(a) 67.20W   *(b) 76.80W*   *(c) 83.50W*   *(d) 96.30W*

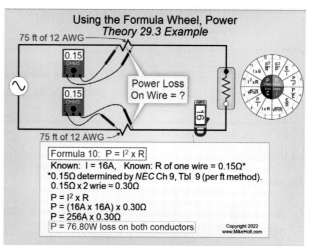

▶Figure 29–6

Solution:

Step 1: *What is the question? What is the power loss of the wires in watts ("P")?*

Step 2: *What do you know about the circuit?*

    I = 16A

    R = 0.15Ω per wire × 2 wires

    R = 0.30Ω

Step 3: *What is the formula? $P = I^2 \times R$.*

Step 4: *Calculate the answer:*

    P = 16A² × 0.30Ω

    P = (16A × 16A) × 0.30Ω

    P = 256A × 0.30Ω

    P = 76.80W

Answer: *(b) 76.80W*

REVIEW QUESTIONS

The following questions are based on the material you just reviewed. If you struggle with any of the answers, go back and review that unit again, or refer to Mike Holt's Understanding Electrical Theory Video Library.

29.3 Using the Formula Wheel

Resistance (R)

1. What is the resistance of the circuit wires when the wire voltage drop is 7.20V and the current flow is 20A?

   (a) 0.24Ω
   (b) 0.36Ω
   (c) 0.41Ω
   (d) 0.55Ω

2. What is the resistance of the circuit wires when the wire voltage drop is 3.60V and the current flow is 30A?

   (a) 0.12Ω
   (b) 0.14Ω
   (c) 0.17Ω
   (d) 0.19Ω

3. What is the resistance of the circuit wires when the wire voltage drop is 6.24V and the current flow is 40A?

   (a) 0.145Ω
   (b) 0.156Ω
   (c) 0.176Ω
   (d) 0.181Ω

4. What is the resistance of the circuit wires when the wire voltage drop is 14.40V and the current flow is 50A?

   (a) 0.29Ω
   (b) 0.34Ω
   (c) 0.36Ω
   (d) 0.39Ω

5. The resistance of a light bulb 120V drawing 1A is _____.

   (a) 120Ω
   (b) 145Ω
   (c) 160Ω
   (d) 180Ω

6. The resistance of a 240V circuit drawing 30A is _____.

   (a) 4Ω
   (b) 7Ω
   (c) 8Ω
   (d) 9Ω

7. What is the resistance of a circuit that has voltage drop of 6V and it consumes 50W of power?

   (a) 0.72Ω
   (b) 0.81Ω
   (c) 0.89Ω
   (d) 0.94Ω

Current (I)

8. What is the circuit current for ten 200 VA 277V lights?

   (a) 6.33A
   (b) 6.36A
   (c) 6.89A
   (d) 7.22A

9. The circuit current for ten 500W, 240V lights is _____.

   (a) 8.33A
   (b) 10.03A
   (c) 20.83A
   (d) 33.80A

10. If a 120V source supplies a 12Ω resistor, the current flow in the circuit will be _____.

    (a) 5A
    (b) 10A
    (c) 11A
    (d) 12A

11. What is the current of a 50 kVA three-phase load operating at 480V?

    (a) 51A
    (b) 60A
    (c) 104A
    (d) 120A

12. What is the current flow in amperes through a 10 kW heat strip rated 230V when connected to a 230V power source?

    (a) 25A
    (b) 39A
    (c) 43A
    (d) 50A

Voltage (E)

13. What is the voltage of a circuit carrying 4.80A supplying a 100Ω resistor?

    (a) 110V
    (b) 220V
    (c) 360V
    (d) 480V

14. What is the voltage of a circuit carrying 20.80A supplying a 10Ω resistor?

    (a) 110V
    (b) 208V
    (c) 460V
    (d) 500V

15. What is the voltage of a circuit carrying 7.50A supplying a 37Ω resistor?

    (a) 120V
    (b) 277V
    (c) 360V
    (d) 520V

16. What is the voltage of a circuit carrying 4.60A supplying a 52Ω resistor?

    (a) 110V
    (b) 120V
    (c) 230V
    (d) 240V

17. What is the voltage applied to a 100Ω resistor if the circuit current is 1.2A?

    (a) 100V
    (b) 110V
    (c) 120V
    (d) 125V

18. What is the voltage of a 20Ω resistor having a current of 50 mA?

    (a) 0.10V
    (b) 1V
    (c) 1.60V
    (d) 3V

19. What is the voltage of a 4.8A circuit supplying a 100Ω resistor?

    (a) 120V
    (b) 240V
    (c) 360V
    (d) 480V

Power (P)

20. What is the power loss at a terminal having a resistance of 0.20Ω when carrying 40A?

    (a) 100W
    (b) 210W
    (c) 320W
    (d) 430W

21. What is the power loss at a terminal having a resistance of 0.40Ω when carrying 20A?

    (a) 100W
    (b) 160W
    (c) 250W
    (d) 300W

22. What is the power loss at a terminal having a resistance of 0.50Ω when carrying 15A?

    (a) 112.50W
    (b) 200.40W
    (c) 230.20W
    (d) 340.30W

23. What is the power loss at a terminal having a resistance of 0.70Ω when carrying 10A?

    (a) 10W
    (b) 40W
    (c) 70W
    (d) 100W

24. The power of a 40Ω load operating at 120V is _____.

    (a) 36W
    (b) 360W
    (c) 603W
    (d) 630W

25. What is the approximate power consumed by a 5Ω heat strip at 240V?

    (a) 8.5 kW
    (b) 9.5 kW
    (c) 10.5 kW
    (d) 11.5 kW

26. What is the approximate power consumed for a 50A resistive heater at 240V?

    (a) 10,300W
    (b) 11,200W
    (c) 11,500W
    (d) 12,000W

27. What is the power of a 40Ω load operating at 240V?

    (a) 620W
    (b) 920W
    (c) 1,440W
    (d) 1,922W

28. The power consumed for a 120V circuit having a 10Ω, 20Ω, and 30Ω resistor in series is _____.

    (a) 120W
    (b) 240W
    (c) 360W
    (d) 480W

29. What is the power consumption of a 50Ω resistor at 120V?

    (a) 120W
    (b) 288W
    (c) 480W
    (d) 720W

30. The power consumed for a 2A circuit having a 10Ω, 20Ω, and 30Ω resistor in series is _____.

    (a) 120W
    (b) 240W
    (c) 360W
    (d) 480W

31. The power consumed for a 3A circuit having a 30Ω and 50Ω in series is _____.

    (a) 520W
    (b) 620W
    (c) 720W
    (d) 920W

32. The power consumed for a 3Ω load carrying 40A is _____.

    (a) 3,800W
    (b) 4,800W
    (c) 5,800W
    (d) 6,800W

33. The power consumed for a 1,000W, 240V heater connected to a 120V circuit is _____.

    (a) 250W
    (b) 500W
    (c) 750W
    (d) 1,000W

ELECTRICAL FUNDAMENTALS—
PRACTICE EXAM

The following 50-question random order Practice Exam will test your knowledge of Module I—Electrical Fundamentals. The questions are based on the material you just reviewed. If you struggle with any of the answers, go back and review that unit again, or refer to Mike Holt's Understanding Electrical Theory Video Library.

 Want to practice online? Scan the QR code to access these questions online to get familiar with the online environment in which you'll most likely be taking your exam.

1. A circuit has three 5Ω resistors connected in parallel. The resistance of this circuit is _____.

   (a) 1.66Ω
   (b) 2.26Ω
   (c) 4.76Ω
   (d) 5.66Ω

2. What is the current through a 9.50 kW heat strip rated 240V?

   (a) 25.40A
   (b) 33.50A
   (c) 39.60A
   (d) 42.70A

3. What is the approximate power consumed by a 11.5 kW heat strip rated 240V, connected to 208V?

   (a) 8.7 kW
   (b) 9.1 kW
   (c) 9.5 kW
   (d) 9.9 kW

4. What is the nameplate current rating of a 1.5 hp, 120V motor at 90 percent efficiency at 85 percent power factor?

   (a) 9A
   (b) 10A
   (c) 11A
   (d) 12A

5. The approximate output current for a three-phase, 48 kVA, 120/208V generator is _____.

   (a) 119A
   (b) 121A
   (c) 127A
   (d) 133A

6. What is the total resistance of three resistors is series where R1 is 15Ω, R2 is 20Ω, and R3 is 35Ω?

   (a) 50Ω
   (b) 70Ω
   (c) 100Ω
   (d) 150Ω

7. The total resistance of a parallel circuit can be calculated by the _____ method.

   (a) Equal Resistance
   (b) Product-Over-Sum
   (c) Reciprocal
   (d) any of these

8. The symbol "I" in Ohm's Law represents the circuit _____.

   (a) coulomb
   (b) in-rush
   (c) intensity
   (d) impedance

9. The power of a 40Ω load operating at 120V is _____.

   (a) 36W
   (b) 360W
   (c) 603W
   (d) 630W

10. The approximate output current for a single-phase, 22 kVA, 240V generator is _____.

    (a) 72A
    (b) 82A
    (c) 92A
    (d) 99A

11. The secondary voltage of a 4:1 transformer is _____ if the primary is 480V.

    (a) 120V
    (b) 208V
    (c) 277V
    (d) 480V

12. "_____" is the maximum value that ac current or voltage reaches, for both positive and negative polarities.

    (a) Peak
    (b) Root-mean-square
    (c) Instantaneous
    (d) none of these

13. A(An) _____ number is a number that is a fractional part of a number separated by a decimal point.

    (a) decimal
    (b) fractional
    (c) percentage
    (d) integer

14. The relationship of the number of turns of wire on the _____ as compared to the number of turns on the _____ is called the transformer "winding turns ratio."

    (a) primary, secondary
    (b) secondary, primary
    (c) primary, primary
    (d) secondary, secondary

15. Deriving the _____ of a number is the number that, if squared, would equal the number requested to be square rooted.

    (a) square root
    (b) square
    (c) multiplier
    (d) area

16. A nonlinear load is a load where the shape of the current waveform does not follow the _____ of the applied sinusoidal voltage waveform.

    (a) shape
    (b) color
    (c) direction
    (d) orientation

17. What is the primary current for a fully loaded three-phase, 112.5 kVA, 480V to 208Y/120V transformer?

    (a) 135A
    (b) 271A
    (c) 406A
    (d) 469A

18. What is the power loss at a terminal having a resistance of 0.20Ω when carrying 40A?

    (a) 100W
    (b) 210W
    (c) 320W
    (d) 430W

19. In a series circuit, the total circuit resistance is equal to the _____ of all the resistances of all the resistors.

    (a) sum
    (b) product
    (c) square
    (d) square root

20. What is the volume (in cubic inches) of a 4 in. × 4 in. × 1.50 in. box?

    (a) 20 cu in.
    (b) 24 cu in.
    (c) 30 cu in.
    (d) 33 cu in.

21. Ohm's Law states that current is _____ proportional to the resistance, this means that current will decrease in direct proportion to the increase in resistance if the voltage remains the same.

    (a) indirectly
    (b) inversely
    (c) aversely
    (d) directly

22. What is the effective RMS voltage of a circuit with a peak value of 340V?
    (a) 120V
    (b) 208V
    (c) 240V
    (d) 300V

23. What is the apparent power of an 84W load having a power factor of 90 percent?
    (a) 80.33 VA
    (b) 80.98 VA
    (c) 89.90 VA
    (d) 93.33 VA

24. A circuit has three resistors in parallel: 15Ω, 30Ω, and 45Ω. The circuit resistance is _____.
    (a) 8.2Ω
    (b) 8.6Ω
    (c) 9.2Ω
    (d) 9.9Ω

25. Ohmmeters measure the _____ of the circuit in the unit "ohm."
    (a) voltage
    (b) current
    (c) power
    (d) resistance

26. The numeric equivalent of 4^2 is _____.
    (a) 2
    (b) 8
    (c) 16
    (d) 32

27. What is the voltage of a circuit carrying 4.60A supplying a 52Ω resistor?
    (a) 110V
    (b) 120V
    (c) 230V
    (d) 240V

28. What is the peak current of a circuit with a 20A effective RMS load?
    (a) 25.70A
    (b) 28.28A
    (c) 29.10A
    (d) 30.80A

29. If a 120V source supplies a 12Ω resistor, the current flow in the circuit will be _____.
    (a) 5A
    (b) 10A
    (c) 11A
    (d) 12A

30. The power loss of a terminal carrying 25A with a contact resistance of 0.20Ω is _____.
    (a) 100W
    (b) 125W
    (c) 140W
    (d) 150W

31. A 240V circuit has three resistors in series where R_1 is 15Ω, R_2 is 15Ω, and R_3 is 15Ω. The voltage across R_2 or R_3 is _____.
    (a) 50V
    (b) 65V
    (c) 80V
    (d) 95V

32. A 20A circuit has three resistors in series where R_1 is 4Ω, R_2 is 4Ω, and R_3 is 4Ω. The voltage source is equal to _____.
    (a) 230V
    (b) 240V
    (c) 277V
    (d) 480V

33. The power consumed for a 2A circuit having a 10Ω, 20Ω, and 30Ω resistor in series is _____.
    (a) 120W
    (b) 240W
    (c) 360W
    (d) 480W

34. When describing the relationship between voltage and current, the reference waveform is always _____.
    (a) current
    (b) resistance
    (c) voltage
    (d) none of these

35. A nonsinusoidal waveform is produced when _____ loads distort the voltage and current sinusoidal waveform.
    (a) linear
    (b) resistive
    (c) inductive
    (d) nonlinear

36. The power factor rating for a 300W high-bay light at 277V rated 1.20A is _____.

    (a) 75 percent
    (b) 80 percent
    (c) 90 percent
    (d) 100 percent

37. The power consumed for a 3A circuit having a 30Ω and 50Ω in series is _____.

    (a) 520W
    (b) 620W
    (c) 720W
    (d) 920W

38. Power losses in a wire are directly proportional to the length of the wire and the square of the current. If the current is doubled, the power loss will be increased by _____.

    (a) 100 percent
    (b) 200 percent
    (c) 300 percent
    (d) 400 percent

39. A transformer has a primary winding of twenty turns and a secondary of ten turns. The winding turns ratio of this transformer is _____.

    (a) 2:1
    (b) 4:1
    (c) 5:1
    (d) 10:1

40. The resistance of a 240V circuit drawing 30A is _____.

    (a) 4Ω
    (b) 7Ω
    (c) 8Ω
    (d) 9Ω

41. Every component of an electrical circuit contains _____, which includes the power source, the circuit wiring, and the load.

    (a) resistance
    (b) voltage
    (c) current
    (d) power

42. What is the power output of a power supply rated 10A at 120V with unity power factor?

    (a) 1,200W
    (b) 1,800W
    (c) 2,400W
    (d) 3,000W

43. _____ ac voltage or ac current is the equivalent value of dc voltage or dc current that would produce the same amount of heat in a resistor.

    (a) Peak
    (b) Effective
    (c) Instantaneous
    (d) none of these

44. The secondary current for a fully loaded 36 kVA, 480V to 240V three-phase delta-delta transformer is _____ per phase.

    (a) 82A
    (b) 87A
    (c) 95A
    (d) 99A

45. To change a percent value to a decimal or whole number, drop the percentage sign and move the decimal point two places to the _____.

    (a) right
    (b) left
    (c) right or left
    (d) none of these

46. What is the circuit current for ten 200 VA 277V lights?

    (a) 6.33A
    (b) 6.36A
    (c) 6.89A
    (d) 7.22A

47. What is the current flow in amperes through a 10 kW heat strip rated 230V when connected to a 230V power source?

    (a) 25A
    (b) 39A
    (c) 41A
    (d) 230A

48. If the voltage and current waveforms begin and end simultaneously, then the two waveforms are "_____" with each other.

    (a) in-phase
    (b) out-of-phase
    (c) coupled
    (d) any of these

49. What is the approximate power consumed for a 50A resistive heater at 240V?

    (a) 10,300W
    (b) 11,200W
    (c) 11,500W
    (d) 12,000W

50. Nonlinear loads produce "_____" which are waveforms that cycle at a frequency that is a multiple of the fundamental frequency.

    (a) capacitors
    (b) resistors
    (c) inductors
    (d) harmonics

MODULE

I

ELECTRICAL FUNDAMENTALS SECTION REFERENCE INDEX

The following is a reference index for the topics covered in Module I. It displays the section number so you can go to that section to review questions for those topics in this book. You can also find that section number in *Mike Holt's Understanding Electrical Theory* textbook, which has additional topics.

NEC REVIEW QUESTIONS

Introduction to Module II—*NEC* Review Questions

The secret to navigating the *NEC* and passing your exam isn't your ability to memorize answers, but knowing where to look in the *Code* book for a requirement when you need it. You will find the common articles, sections, and tables as you answer each question. Once you learn to recognize the keywords, navigating to the correct section to find the answer will become second nature.

Let's face it, taking a test on the *Code* can be intimidating, but with practice, you will become confident, proficient, and successful. This module contains multiple review questions in sequential order by *Code* article. Each set of questions is designed to be completed as a whole. Review the answers to each question as you go along so you can learn from your mistakes and reinforce the correct answers.

If your state allows it in exams, highlight these rules and sections in your *Code* book. If not, check if they will provide a *Code* book for you, or if you'll need to purchase or borrow an unmarked copy.

 For more information on how to use your *Code* book effectively, make sure to watch this video.

To learn more about the *Code* and how it's organized, review our full line of *NEC* products at MikeHolt.com/Code, or scan this QR code.

ARTICLE 90

REVIEW QUESTIONS

Please use the 2023 *Code* book to answer the following questions.

ARTICLE 90—INTRODUCTION TO THE *NATIONAL ELECTRICAL CODE*

1. Article _____ covers use and application, arrangement, and enforcement of the *National Electrical Code*.
   (a) 90
   (b) 110
   (c) 200
   (d) 300

2. The purpose of the *NEC* is for _____.
   (a) it to be used as a design manual
   (b) use as an instruction guide for untrained persons
   (c) the practical safeguarding of persons and property
   (d) interacting with inspectors

3. Compliance with the *Code* and proper maintenance result in an installation that is _____.
   (a) essentially free from hazard
   (b) not necessarily efficient or convenient
   (c) not necessarily adequate for good service or future expansion
   (d) all of these

4. Electrical hazards often occur because the initial _____ did not provide for increases in the use of electricity.
   (a) inspection
   (b) owner
   (c) wiring
   (d) builder

5. The *NEC* covers the installation and removal of _____.
   (a) electrical conductors, equipment, and raceways
   (b) signaling and communications conductors, equipment, and raceways
   (c) optical fiber cables
   (d) all of these

6. The *NEC* does not cover installations in _____.
   (a) ships and watercraft
   (b) mobile homes
   (c) recreational vehicles
   (d) any of these

7. Chapters 1, 2, 3, and 4 of the *NEC* apply _____.
   (a) generally to all electrical installations
   (b) only to special occupancies and conditions
   (c) only to special equipment and material
   (d) all of these

8. The enforcement of the *NEC* is the responsibility of the authority having jurisdiction, who is responsible for _____.
   (a) making interpretations of rules
   (b) approval of equipment and materials
   (c) granting special permission
   (d) all of these

9. By special permission, the authority having jurisdiction may waive *NEC* requirements or approve alternative methods where equivalent _____ can be achieved and maintained.
   (a) safety
   (b) workmanship
   (c) installations
   (d) job progress

10. In the *NEC*, the word(s) ____ indicate a mandatory requirement.

    (a) shall

    (b) shall not

    (c) shall be permitted

    (d) shall or shall not

11. When the *Code* uses ____, it indicates the actions are allowed but not required.

    (a) shall or shall not

    (b) shall not be permitted

    (c) shall be permitted

    (d) none of these

12. Nonmandatory information relative to the use of the *NEC* is provided in informative annexes and are ____.

    (a) included for information purposes only

    (b) not enforceable requirements of the *Code*

    (c) enforceable as a requirement of the *Code*

    (d) included for information purposes only and are not enforceable requirements of the *Code*

13. Except to detect alterations or damage, qualified electrical testing laboratory listed factory-installed ____ wiring of equipment does not need to be inspected for *NEC* compliance at the time of installation.

    (a) external

    (b) associated

    (c) internal

    (d) all of these

CHAPTER 1

REVIEW QUESTIONS

Please use the 2023 *Code* book to answer the following questions.

CHAPTER 1—GENERAL RULES

Article 100—Definitions

1. Capable of being reached quickly for operation, renewal, or inspections without climbing over or under obstructions, removing obstacles, resorting to portable ladders, or the use of tools (other than keys) is known as ____.
   - (a) accessible (as applied to equipment)
   - (b) accessible (as applied to wiring methods)
   - (c) accessible, readily (readily accessible)
   - (d) all of these

2. The maximum current, in amperes, that a conductor can carry continuously under the conditions of use without exceeding its temperature rating is known as its ____.
   - (a) short-circuit rating
   - (b) ground-fault rating
   - (c) ampacity
   - (d) all of these

3. ____ means acceptable to the authority having jurisdiction.
   - (a) Identified
   - (b) Listed
   - (c) Approved
   - (d) Labeled

4. Bonded is defined as ____ to establish electrical continuity and conductivity.
   - (a) isolated
   - (b) guarded
   - (c) connected
   - (d) separated

5. The connection between the grounded circuit conductor and the equipment grounding conductor, or the supply-side bonding jumper, or both, at the service is the ____ bonding jumper.
   - (a) main
   - (b) system
   - (c) equipment
   - (d) circuit

6. A cable tray system is a unit or assembly of units or sections and associated fittings forming a ____ system used to securely fasten or support cables and raceways.
   - (a) structural
   - (b) flexible
   - (c) movable
   - (d) secure

7. A circuit breaker is a device designed to open and close a circuit by nonautomatic means and to ____ the circuit automatically on a predetermined overcurrent without damage to itself when properly applied within its rating.
   - (a) energize
   - (b) reset
   - (c) connect
   - (d) open

8. A continuous load is a load where the maximum current is expected to continue for ____ or more.
   - (a) ½ hour
   - (b) 1 hour
   - (c) 2 hour
   - (d) 3 hour

9. The circuit of a control apparatus or system that carries the electric signals directing the performance of the controller but does not carry the main power current defines a ____.

   (a) control circuit
   (b) low-voltage circuit
   (c) function circuit
   (d) performance circuit

10. A ____ is a device or group of devices that govern, in some predetermined manner, the electric power delivered to the apparatus to which it is connected.

    (a) relay
    (b) breaker
    (c) transformer
    (d) controller

11. A dc-to-dc converter is a device that can provide an output ____ voltage and current at a higher or lower value than the input ____ voltage and current.

    (a) ac, dc
    (b) ac, ac
    (c) dc, dc
    (d) dc, ac

12. The *NEC* defines a ____ as all circuit conductors between the service equipment, the source of a separately derived system, or other power supply source, and the final branch-circuit over-current device.

    (a) service
    (b) feeder
    (c) branch circuit
    (d) all of these

13. A fountain is defined as an ornamental structure or recreational water feature from which one or more jets or streams of water are discharged into the air, including splash pads, and ____ pools.

    (a) ornamental
    (b) wading
    (c) seasonal
    (d) permanently installed

14. Connected (connecting) to ground or to a conductive body that extends the ground connection is called ____.

    (a) equipment grounding
    (b) bonded
    (c) grounded
    (d) all of these

15. A system or circuit conductor that is intentionally grounded is called a(an) ____.

    (a) grounding conductor
    (b) unidentified conductor
    (c) grounded conductor
    (d) grounding electrode conductor

16. A(An) ____ is a device intended for the protection of personnel that functions to de-energize a circuit or portion thereof within an established period of time when a ground-fault current exceeds the values established for a Class A device.

    (a) dual-element fuse
    (b) inverse time breaker
    (c) ground-fault circuit interrupter
    (d) safety switch

17. A Class A GFCI trips when the ground-fault current is ____ or higher.

    (a) 4 mA
    (b) 5 mA
    (c) 6 mA
    (d) 7 mA

18. An effective ground-fault current path is an intentionally constructed, low-impedance electrically conductive path designed and intended to carry current during a ground-fault event from the point of a ground fault on a wiring system to ____.

    (a) ground
    (b) earth
    (c) the electrical supply source
    (d) the grounding electrode

19. In sight from or within sight from is defined as equipment that is visible and not more than ____ distant from other equipment is in sight from that other equipment.

    (a) 10 ft
    (b) 20 ft
    (c) 25 ft
    (d) 50 ft

20. A(An) ____ is equipment that changes dc to ac.

    (a) diode
    (b) rectifier
    (c) transistor
    (d) inverter

21. A location protected from weather and not subject to saturation with water or other liquids, but subject to moderate degrees of moisture defines a ____ location.

    (a) dry
    (b) damp
    (c) wet
    (d) moist

22. A location not normally subject to dampness or wetness but may be temporarily subject to dampness and wetness as in the case of a building under construction defines a ____ location.

    (a) dry
    (b) damp
    (c) moist
    (d) wet

23. A location unprotected and exposed to weather, subject to saturation, underground, or in concrete slabs in direct contact with the earth defines a ____ location.

    (a) dry
    (b) damp
    (c) wet
    (d) moist

24. A manufactured wiring system is a system containing component parts that are assembled in the process of manufacture and cannot be inspected at the building site without ____.

    (a) a permit
    (b) a manufacturer's representative present
    (c) damage or destruction to the assembly
    (d) an engineer's supervision

25. An ac module is a complete, environmentally protected unit consisting of ____, designed to produce ac power.

    (a) solar cells
    (b) inverters
    (c) other components
    (d) all of these

26. A(An) ____ is a point on the wiring system at which current is taken to supply utilization equipment.

    (a) box
    (b) receptacle
    (c) outlet
    (d) device

27. A ____ is an enclosed assembly that can include receptacles, circuit breakers, fused switches, fuses, watt-hour meter(s), panelboards and monitoring means identified for marina use.

    (a) marina power receptacle
    (b) marina outlet
    (c) marina power outlet
    (d) any of these

28. Electrical generating equipment supplied by any source other than a utility service, up to the source system disconnecting means defines ____.

    (a) a service drop
    (b) power production equipment
    (c) the service point
    (d) utilization equipment

29. A power supply cord is an assembly consisting of an attachment plug and a length of ____ cord connected to utilization equipment.

    (a) heavy duty
    (b) hard usage
    (c) flexible
    (d) light duty

30. A contact device installed at an outlet for the connection of an attachment plug is known as a(an) ____.

    (a) attachment point
    (b) tap
    (c) receptacle
    (d) wall plug

31. A ____ system is an electrical power supply output, other than a service, having no direct connection(s) to circuit conductors of any other electrical source other than those established by grounding and bonding connections.

    (a) separately derived
    (b) classified
    (c) direct
    (d) emergency

32. A service drop is defined as the overhead conductors between the serving utility and the ____.

    (a) service equipment
    (b) service point
    (c) grounding electrode conductor
    (d) equipment grounding conductor

33. ____ is a pliable corrugated raceway of circular cross section, with integral or associated couplings, connectors, and fittings that are listed for the installation of electrical conductors.

    (a) PVC
    (b) ENT
    (c) RMC
    (d) IMC

34. ____ is, for grounded circuits, the voltage between the given conductor and that point or conductor of the circuit that is grounded; for ungrounded circuits, the greatest voltage between the given conductor and any other conductor of the circuit.

    (a) Line-to-line voltage
    (b) voltage to ground
    (c) Phase-to-phase voltage
    (d) Neutral to ground voltage

35. A(An) ____ enclosure is constructed or protected so that exposure to the weather will not interfere with successful operation.

    (a) weatherproof
    (b) weathertight
    (c) weather-resistant
    (d) all weather

Article 110—General Requirements for Electrical Installations

1. General requirements for the examination and approval, installation and use, access to and spaces about electrical conductors and equipment, enclosures intended for personnel entry, and tunnel installations are within the scope of ____.

    (a) Article 800
    (b) Article 300
    (c) Article 110
    (d) Annex J

2. The conductors and equipment required or permitted by this *Code* shall be acceptable only if ____.

    (a) labeled
    (b) listed
    (c) approved
    (d) identified

3. Equipment that is ____ or identified for a use shall be installed and used in accordance with any instructions included in the listing, labeling, or identification.

    (a) listed, labeled, or both
    (b) listed
    (c) marked
    (d) suitable

4. Equipment intended to interrupt current at ____ levels shall have an interrupting rating at nominal circuit voltage at least equal to the available fault current at the line terminals of the equipment.

    (a) fault
    (b) overcurrent
    (c) overload
    (d) incident energy

5. Electrical equipment shall be installed ____.

    (a) in a professional and skillful manner
    (b) under the supervision of a licensed person
    (c) completely before being inspected
    (d) all of these

6. Unused openings, other than those intended for the operation of equipment, those intended for mounting purposes, or permitted as part of the design for listed equipment shall be ____.

    (a) filled with cable clamps or connectors only
    (b) taped over with electrical tape
    (c) repaired only by welding or brazing in a metal slug
    (d) closed to afford protection substantially equivalent to the wall of the equipment

7. Internal parts of electrical equipment, including busbars, wiring terminals, insulators, and other surfaces, shall not be damaged or contaminated by foreign materials such as _____, or corrosive residues.

(a) paint, plaster
(b) cleaners
(c) abrasives
(d) any of these

8. Pressure terminal or pressure splicing connectors and soldering lugs shall be _____ for the material of the conductor and shall be properly installed and used.

(a) listed
(b) approved
(c) identified
(d) all of these

9. Connectors and terminals for conductors more finely stranded than Class B and Class C, as shown in Chapter 9, Table 10, shall be _____ for the specific conductor class or classes.

(a) listed
(b) approved
(c) identified
(d) all of these

10. Conductors of dissimilar metals shall not be intermixed in a terminal or splicing connector where physical contact occurs between dissimilar conductors unless the device is _____ for the purpose and conditions of use.

(a) identified
(b) listed
(c) approved
(d) designed

11. Connection of conductors to terminal parts shall ensure a mechanically secure electrical connection without damaging the conductors and shall be made by means of _____.

(a) solder lugs
(b) pressure connectors
(c) splices to flexible leads
(d) any of these

12. All _____ shall be covered with an insulation equivalent to that of the conductors or with an identified insulating device.

(a) splices
(b) joints
(c) free ends of conductors
(d) all of these

13. On a 4-wire, delta-connected system where the midpoint of one phase winding is grounded, only the conductor or busbar having the higher phase voltage-to-ground shall be durably and permanently marked by an outer finish that is _____ in color.

(a) black
(b) red
(c) blue
(d) orange

14. Electrical equipment such as switchboards, switchgear, enclosed panelboards, industrial control panels, meter socket enclosures, and motor control centers, which are in other than dwelling units, and are likely to require _____ while energized, shall be field or factory marked to warn qualified persons of potential electric arc-flash hazards.

(a) examination
(b) adjustment
(c) servicing or maintenance
(d) any of these

15. In other than dwelling units, a permanent arc-flash label shall be field or factory applied to service equipment and feeder supplied equipment rated _____ or more.

(a) 600A
(b) 1,000A
(c) 1,200A
(d) 1,600A

16. When modifications to the electrical installation occur that affect the available fault current at the service, the available fault current shall be verified or _____ as necessary to ensure the service equipment ratings are sufficient for the available fault current at the line terminals of the equipment.

(a) recalculated
(b) increased
(c) decreased
(d) adjusted

17. If a disconnecting means is required to be lockable open else-where in the *NEC*, it shall be capable of being locked in the open position. The provisions for locking shall remain in place with or without ____.

    (a) the power off
    (b) the lock installed
    (c) supervision
    (d) a lock-out tag

18. ____ and access to and egress from working space, shall be provided and maintained about all electrical equipment to permit ready and safe operation and maintenance of such equipment.

    (a) Ventilation
    (b) Unrestricted movement
    (c) Circulation
    (d) Working space

19. Access to or egress from the required working space about electrical equipment is considered impeded if one or more simultaneously opened equipment doors restrict working space access to be less than ____ wide and 6½ ft high.

    (a) 24 in.
    (b) 28 in.
    (c) 30 in.
    (d) 36 in.

20. Working space is required for equipment operating at 1,000V, nominal, or less to ground and likely to require ____ while energized.

    (a) examination
    (b) adjustment
    (c) servicing or maintenance
    (d) all of these

21. Working space distances for enclosed live parts shall be measured from the ____ of equipment if the live parts are enclosed.

    (a) enclosure or opening
    (b) front or back
    (c) mounting pad
    (d) footprint

22. Working space is not required at the back or sides of equipment where all ____ and all renewable, adjustable, or serviceable parts are accessible from the front.

    (a) screws
    (b) connections
    (c) bolts
    (d) doors

23. The minimum working space on a circuit for equipment oper-ating at 120V to ground, with exposed live parts on one side and no live or grounded parts on the other side of the working space is ____.

    (a) 1 ft
    (b) 3 ft
    (c) 4 ft
    (d) 6 ft

24. The required working space for access to live parts of equip-ment operating at 300V to ground, where there are exposed live parts on one side and grounded parts on the other side, is ____.

    (a) 3 ft
    (b) 3½ ft
    (c) 4 ft
    (d) 4½ ft

25. The required working space for access to live parts of equip-ment operating at 300V to ground, where there are exposed live parts on both sides of the workspace is ____.

    (a) 3 ft
    (b) 3½ ft
    (c) 4 ft
    (d) 4½ ft

26. The width of the working space shall not be less than ____ wide, or the width of the equipment, whichever is greater.

    (a) 15 in.
    (b) 30 in.
    (c) 40 in.
    (d) 60 in.

27. The minimum height of working spaces shall be clear and extend from the grade, floor, or platform to a height of ____ or the height of the equipment, whichever is greater.

    (a) 3 ft
    (b) 6 ft
    (c) 6½ ft
    (d) 7 ft

28. The grade, floor, or platform in the required working space about electrical equipment shall be as level and flat as ____ for the entire required depth and width of the working space.

    (a) practical
    (b) possible
    (c) required
    (d) none of these

29. All service equipment, switchboards, panelboards, and motor control centers shall be ____.

    (a) located in dedicated spaces
    (b) protected from damage
    (c) in weatherproof enclosures
    (d) located in dedicated spaces and protected from damage

30. The minimum height of dedicated equipment space for motor control centers installed indoors is ____ above the enclosure, or to the structural ceiling, whichever is lower.

    (a) 3 ft
    (b) 5 ft
    (c) 6 ft
    (d) 6½ ft

31. A dropped, suspended, or similar ceiling that does not add strength to the building structure shall not be considered a ____ ceiling.

    (a) structural
    (b) permanent
    (c) real
    (d) drop

32. All switchboards, switchgear, panelboards, and motor control centers located outdoors shall be ____.

    (a) installed in identified enclosures
    (b) protected from accidental contact by unauthorized personnel or by vehicular traffic
    (c) protected from accidental spillage or leakage from piping systems
    (d) all of these

33. A NEMA Type 1 enclosure is approved for the environmental condition where ____ might be present.

    (a) falling dirt
    (b) falling liquids
    (c) circulating dust
    (d) settling airborne dust

34. Enclosures of switchboards, switchgear, or panelboards that may become ice covered where exposed to sleet may be installed in a ____ enclosure.

    (a) Type 3 or 3R
    (b) Type 3X or RX
    (c) Type 3S or SX
    (d) Type 4 or 4X

35. Enclosure Type 3X for switchboards, switchgear, or panelboards located outdoors are suitable in locations subject to ____.

    (a) rain
    (b) windblown dust
    (c) corrosive agents
    (d) any of these

36. A Type 4X enclosure for switchboards, switchgear, or panelboards located indoors is suitable in locations subject to the environmental condition of ____.

    (a) falling dirt
    (b) falling liquid
    (c) corrosive agents
    (d) any of these

37. The term rainproof is typically used in conjunction with enclosure type(s) ____.

    (a) NEMA 3
    (b) NEMA 3R and 3RX
    (c) NEMA 4
    (d) NEMA 4R and 4RX

CHAPTER 2

REVIEW QUESTIONS

Please use the 2023 *Code* book to answer the following questions.

CHAPTER 2—WIRING AND PROTECTION

Article 200—Use and Identification of Grounded Conductors

1. The continuity of a grounded conductor shall not depend on a connection to ____.
   (a) a metal enclosure
   (b) a raceway
   (c) cable armor
   (d) any of these

2. Where more than one neutral conductor is associated with different circuits in an enclosure, they shall be ____.
   (a) color coded
   (b) identified or grouped to correspond to the ungrounded circuit conductor(s)
   (c) tagged individually with individual stripes
   (d) together in one bundle

3. An insulated grounded conductor ____ or smaller shall be identified by a continuous white or gray outer finish, or by three continuous white or gray stripes along its entire length on other than green insulation.
   (a) 8 AWG
   (b) 6 AWG
   (c) 4 AWG
   (d) 3 AWG

4. At the time of installation, grounded conductors ____ or larger can be identified by a distinctive white or gray marking at their terminations.
   (a) 10 AWG
   (b) 8 AWG
   (c) 6 AWG
   (d) 4 AWG

5. Where grounded conductors of different nominal voltage systems are installed in the same raceway, cable, or enclosure, each grounded conductor shall be identified to distinguish the systems by ____.
   (a) a continuous white or gray outer finish
   (b) a grounded conductor with an outer covering of white or gray with a distinguishable colored stripe other than green
   (c) other identification allowed by 200.6(A) or (B) that distinguishes each nominal voltage system grounded conductor
   (d) any of these

6. A ____ shall be used only for the grounded circuit conductor, unless otherwise permitted in 200.7(B) and (C).
   (a) conductor with continuous white or gray covering
   (b) conductor with three continuous white or gray stripes on other than green insulation
   (c) marking of white or gray color at the termination
   (d) any of these

7. Receptacles shall have the terminal intended for connection to the grounded conductor identified by a metal or metal coating that is white or silver in color or by the word, ____.

    (a) green
    (b) white
    (c) silver
    (d) neutral

8. For devices with screw shells, the terminal for the ____ shall be the one connected to the screw shell.

    (a) grounded conductor
    (b) ungrounded conductor
    (c) equipment grounding conductor
    (d) forming shell terminal

Article 210—Branch Circuits

1. Each multiwire branch circuit shall be provided with a means that will simultaneously disconnect all ____ conductors at the point where the branch circuit originates.

    (a) circuit
    (b) grounded
    (c) grounding
    (d) ungrounded

2. Where the premises wiring system has branch circuits supplied from more than one nominal voltage system, each ____ conductor of a branch circuit shall be identified by phase or line and by nominal voltage system at all termination, connection, and splice points.

    (a) neutral
    (b) ungrounded
    (c) grounding
    (d) all of these

3. Where a different nominal voltage system is added to a(an) ____ installation, branch-circuit identification is only required for the new one.

    (a) new
    (b) existing
    (c) remodeled
    (d) repaired

4. In dwelling units and guest rooms or guest suites, voltage shall not exceed 120V for cord and plug equipment connected to loads rated ____.

    (a) 1,440 VA
    (b) 1,500 VA
    (c) 1,800 VA
    (d) 2,400 VA

5. A listed Class A GFCI shall provide protection in accordance with 210.8(A) through (F). The GFCI protective device shall be installed in a(an) ____ location.

    (a) circuit breaker type only
    (b) accessible
    (c) readily accessible
    (d) concealed

6. All 125V through 250V receptacles installed in dwelling unit ____ and supplied by branch circuits rated 150V or less to ground shall have ground-fault circuit-interrupter protection for personnel.

    (a) hallways
    (b) bedrooms
    (c) closets
    (d) bathrooms

7. GFCI protection shall be provided for all 125V through 250V ____ in dwelling unit basements.

    (a) receptacles
    (b) switches
    (c) outlets
    (d) disconnects

8. In dwelling units, GFCI protection shall be provided for 125V through 250V receptacles installed in areas with sinks and permanent provisions for ____.

    (a) food preparation
    (b) beverage preparation
    (c) cooking
    (d) any of these

9. In other than dwelling units, GFCI protection shall be provided for receptacles and cord-and-plug connected appliances installed within ____ from the top inside edge of the bowl of a sink.

    (a) 3 ft
    (b) 4 ft
    (c) 5 ft
    (d) 6 ft

10. Two or more ____ small-appliance branch circuits shall be provided for all receptacle outlets specified by 210.52(B).

    (a) 15A
    (b) 20A
    (c) auxiliary
    (d) supplemental

11. There shall be a minimum of one additional ____ branch circuit for dwelling unit laundry receptacle outlet(s).

    (a) 15A
    (b) 20A
    (c) auxiliary
    (d) supplemental

12. At least ____ or more 120V, 20A branch circuit(s) shall be provided to supply dwelling unit bathroom(s) receptacle outlet(s).

    (a) one
    (b) two
    (c) three
    (d) four

13. At least one 120V, 20A branch circuit shall be installed to supply receptacle outlets, including those required by 210.52(G)(1) for ____ and in ____ with electric power.

    (a) attached decks, detached gazebos
    (b) attached garages, detached sheds
    (c) attached garages, unfinished accessory buildings
    (d) attached garages, detached garages

14. All 120V, single-phase, 10A, 15A, and 20A branch circuits supplying outlets or devices installed in dwelling unit ____ shall be AFCI protected.

    (a) kitchens
    (b) garages
    (c) bathrooms
    (d) outdoor areas

15. All 120V, single-phase, 10A, 15A, and 20A branch circuits supplying outlets or devices installed in dwelling unit ____ shall be AFCI protected by any of the means described in 210.12(A)(1) through (6).

    (a) kitchens
    (b) family rooms
    (c) dining rooms
    (d) all of these

16. All 120V, single-phase, 10A, 15A, or 20A branch circuits supplying outlets or devices installed in the ____ of dormitory units shall be AFCI protected.

    (a) bedrooms
    (b) living rooms
    (c) closets
    (d) all of these

17. Guest rooms and guest suites in ____ that are provided with permanent provisions for cooking shall have branch circuits installed to meet the rules for dwelling units.

    (a) hotels
    (b) motels
    (c) assisted living facilities
    (d) all of these

18. Conductors for branch circuits [Article 210] are sized to prevent a voltage drop exceeding ____ at the farthest outlet of power, heating, and lighting loads, or combinations of such loads.

    (a) 2 percent
    (b) 3 percent
    (c) 4 percent
    (d) 6 percent

19. Where a branch circuit supplies continuous loads and/or noncontinuous loads, the rating of the overcurrent device shall not be less than the noncontinuous load plus ____ of the continuous load.

    (a) 80 percent
    (b) 115 percent
    (c) 120 percent
    (d) 125 percent

20. A single receptacle installed on an individual branch circuit shall have an ampere rating not less than the rating of the ____.

    (a) branch circuit
    (b) device listing
    (c) manufacturer's instructions
    (d) equipment current rating

21. The rating of any one cord-and plug-connected utilization equipment on a 15A, 120V branch circuit shall not exceed ____.

    (a) 12A
    (b) 15A
    (c) 16A
    (d) 20A

22. If a 20A branch circuit supplies multiple receptacles, the receptacles shall have an ampere rating of no less than ____.

    (a) 10A
    (b) 15A
    (c) 20A
    (d) 30A

23. A 15A or 20A branch circuit shall be permitted to supply lighting outlets, lighting units, or other utilization equipment, or any combination of them, if the rating of any one cord-and-plug-connected utilization equipment not fastened in place does not exceed ____ of the branch-circuit ampere rating.

    (a) 25 percent
    (b) 50 percent
    (c) 80 percent
    (d) 100 percent

24. The total rating of utilization equipment fastened in place shall not exceed ____ of the rating of a 20A multiple outlet branch circuit.

    (a) 25 percent
    (b) 50 percent
    (c) 80 percent
    (d) 100 percent

25. An appliance receptacle outlet installed for a specific appliance shall be installed within ____ of the intended location of the appliance.

    (a) sight
    (b) 3 ft
    (c) 6 ft
    (d) the length of the cord

26. The dwelling unit 15- and 20A receptacle outlets required by the *Code* are in addition to any receptacles that are ____.

    (a) part of a luminaire or appliance
    (b) located within cabinets or cupboards
    (c) located more than 5½ ft above the floor
    (d) any of these

27. A receptacle outlet shall be installed so no point along the floor line of any wall is more than ____, measured horizontally along the floor line, from a receptacle outlet.

    (a) 6 ft
    (b) 8 ft
    (c) 10 ft
    (d) 12 ft

28. In a dwelling unit, any wall space including space measured around corners and unbroken along the floor line by doorways, fireplaces, fixed cabinets, and similar openings shall be considered wall space when the wall space is at least ____ wide.

    (a) 2 ft
    (b) 3 ft
    (c) 4 ft
    (d) 6 ft

29. In dwelling units, when determining the spacing of receptacle outlets, ____ on exterior walls shall not be considered wall space.

    (a) fixed panels
    (b) fixed glass
    (c) sliding panels
    (d) all of these

30. Floor receptacle outlets shall not be counted as part of the required number of receptacle outlets for dwelling unit wall spaces, unless they are located within ____ of the wall.

    (a) 6 in.
    (b) 12 in.
    (c) 18 in.
    (d) 24 in.

31. Receptacles installed for ____ and similar work surfaces as specified in 210.52(C) shall not be considered as the receptacle outlets required by 210.52(A).

    (a) countertops
    (b) tables
    (c) peninsulas
    (d) none of these

32. The two or more small-appliance branch circuits specified in 210.52(B)(1) shall have ____.

    (a) no more than one outlet
    (b) no other outlets
    (c) unlimited outlets
    (d) supply only one appliance

33. Receptacles installed in a dwelling unit kitchen to serve countertop surfaces shall be supplied by not fewer than ____ small-appliance branch circuit(s).

    (a) one
    (b) two
    (c) three
    (d) four

34. Receptacle outlets are required for kitchen countertops and work surfaces that are ____ and wider.

    (a) 12 in.
    (b) 15 in.
    (c) 18 in.
    (d) 24 in.

35. Kitchen wall countertop and work surface space receptacle outlets shall be installed so that no point along the wall line is more than ____ measured horizontally from a receptacle outlet in that space.

    (a) 10 in.
    (b) 12 in.
    (c) 16 in.
    (d) 24 in.

36. If a receptacle outlet is not provided to serve an island or peninsular countertop or work surface, provisions shall be provided at the island or peninsula for the ____ addition of a receptacle outlet to serve the island or peninsular countertop or work surface.

    (a) future
    (b) permanent
    (c) possible
    (d) none of these

37. Kitchen and dining room countertop receptacle outlets in dwelling units shall be installed on or above the countertop or work surface, but not more than ____ above the countertop or work surface.

    (a) 12 in.
    (b) 18 in.
    (c) 20 in.
    (d) 24 in.

38. In dwelling units, the required bathroom receptacle outlet can be installed on the side or face of the sink cabinet if not more than ____ below the top of the sink or sink countertop.

    (a) 12 in.
    (b) 18 in.
    (c) 20 in.
    (d) 24 in.

39. In dwelling unit bathrooms, not less than one 15A or 20A, 125V receptacle outlet shall be installed within ____ of the outside edge of each bathroom basin.

    (a) 2 ft
    (b) 3 ft
    (c) 4 ft
    (d) 5 ft

40. For one- and two-family dwellings, at least one receptacle outlet shall be installed in each ____.

    (a) separate unfinished portion of a basement
    (b) attached or detached garage with electric power
    (c) accessory building with electric power
    (d) all of these

41. For one- and two-family dwellings, and multifamily dwellings, at least one receptacle outlet shall be installed in each separate ____ of a basement.

    (a) unfinished portion
    (b) hallway
    (c) stairway
    (d) all of these

42. Hallways in dwelling units that are ____ or longer require a receptacle outlet.

    (a) 6 ft
    (b) 8 ft
    (c) 10 ft
    (d) 12 ft

43. At least one 125-volt, single-phase, 15A- or 20A-rated receptacle outlet shall be installed within 18 in. of the top of each show window. No point along the top of the window shall be farther than ____ from a receptacle outlet.

    (a) 3 ft
    (b) 4 ft
    (c) 6 ft
    (d) 8 ft

44. A 125V, single-phase, 15A- or 20A-rated receptacle outlet shall be installed at an accessible location within ____ of equipment requiring servicing.

    (a) 8 ft
    (b) 10 ft
    (c) 25 ft
    (d) 50 ft

45. The required heating, air-conditioning, and refrigeration equipment receptacle outlet shall not be connected to the _____ side of the equipment disconnecting means.

    (a) line
    (b) load
    (c) high
    (d) low

46. The required heating, air-conditioning, and refrigeration equipment receptacle outlet can be connected to the ____ side of the equipment disconnecting means.

    (a) line
    (b) load
    (c) high
    (d) low

47. At least one lighting outlet controlled by a listed ____ shall be installed in every habitable room, kitchen, laundry area, and bathroom of a dwelling unit.

    (a) wall-mounted control device
    (b) switch
    (c) occupancy sensor
    (d) motion detector

48. At least one lighting outlet controlled by a listed wall-mounted control device shall be installed in dwelling unit hallways, stairways, and ____.

    (a) attached garages
    (b) detached garages with electric power
    (c) accessory buildings with electric power
    (d) all of these

49. For dwelling units, attached garages, detached garages with electric power, and accessory buildings with electric power, at least ____ exterior lighting outlet(s) controlled by a listed wall-mounted control device shall be installed to provide illumination on the exterior side of outdoor entrances or exits with grade-level access.

    (a) one
    (b) two
    (c) three
    (d) one or two

50. Where lighting outlets are installed for an interior stairway with ____ risers between floor levels, there shall be a listed wall-mounted control device at each floor level and at each landing level that includes a stairway entry to control the lighting outlets.

    (a) three or more
    (b) four or more
    (c) six or more
    (d) any number of

51. At least one lighting outlet ____ shall be located at the point of entry to the attic, underfloor space, utility room, or basement where these spaces are used for storage or contain equipment requiring servicing.

    (a) that is unswitched
    (b) containing or controlled by a switch or listed wall-mounted control device
    (c) that is GFCI protected
    (d) that is shielded from damage

Article 215—Feeders

1. Where a feeder supplies continuous loads or any combination of continuous and noncontinuous loads, the conductor ampacity shall be no less than the noncontinuous load plus ____ of the continuous load.

    (a) 80 percent
    (b) 100 percent
    (c) 125 percent
    (d) 150 percent

2. Feeder grounded conductors not connected to an overcurrent device can be sized at ____ of the continuous and noncontinuous load.

    (a) 80 percent
    (b) 100 percent
    (c) 125 percent
    (d) 150 percent

Article 220—Branch-Circuit, Feeder, and Service Load Calculations

1. Unless otherwise specified, for purposes of calculating branch-circuit and feeder loads, ____ system voltages of 120V, 120/240V, 208Y/120V, 240V, 347V, 480Y/277V, 480V, 600Y/347V, and 600V shall be used.

    (a) nominal
    (b) separately derived
    (c) utility
    (d) secondary

2. Outlets supplying luminaires shall be calculated based on the maximum ____ rating of the equipment.

    (a) power
    (b) true power
    (c) voltage
    (d) volt-ampere

3. Sign and outline lighting outlets are to be calculated at a minimum of ____ for each required branch circuit specified in 600.5(A).

    (a) 1,000 VA
    (b) 1,200 VA
    (c) 1,500 VA
    (d) 2,000 VA

4. Show window loads shall be calculated at ____ per linear ft of show window.

    (a) 90 VA
    (b) 120 VA
    (c) 200 VA
    (d) 240 VA

5. Nondwelling unit motors rated less than ____ and connected to a lighting circuit shall be considered general lighting load.

    (a) 1/16 hp
    (b) 1/8 hp
    (c) 1/4 hp
    (d) 1/3 hp

6. The lighting load unit values of Table 220.42(A) are based on minimum load conditions and ____ power factor and might not provide sufficient capacity for the installation contemplated.

    (a) 80 percent
    (b) 85 percent
    (c) 90 percent
    (d) 92 percent

7. The 125 percent multiplier for a continuous load as specified in 210.20(A) ____ included when using the unit loads in table 220.12 for calculating the minimum lighting load for a specified occupancy.

    (a) is
    (b) is not
    (c) is permitted to be
    (d) shall not be

8. The general lighting load for a school is ____.

    (a) 1.50 VA
    (b) 2.50 VA
    (c) 3 VA
    (d) 3.50 VA

9. Where the building is designed to comply with an energy code, the lighting load shall be calculated using the unit values specified in the ____.

    (a) *NEC*
    (b) building code
    (c) energy code
    (d) any of these

10. For other than dwelling units or guest rooms of hotels or motels, the feeder and service calculation for track lighting shall be calculated at 150 VA for every ____ of lighting track or fraction thereof.

    (a) 1 ft
    (b) 2 ft
    (c) 3 ft
    (d) 4 ft

11. Feeder and service loads for fixed electric space-heating loads shall be calculated at ____ of the total connected load.

    (a) 80 percent
    (b) 100 percent
    (c) 125 percent
    (d) 200 percent

12. For dwelling unit load calculations in accordance Article 220, a load of not less than ____ for each 2-wire small-appliance branch circuit shall be applied.

    (a) 1,000 VA
    (b) 1,200 VA
    (c) 1,500 VA
    (d) 2,000 VA

13. For dwelling unit load calculations in accordance Article 220, a load of not less than _____ for the laundry branch circuit shall be applied.
    (a) 1,000 VA
    (b) 1,200 VA
    (c) 1,500 VA
    (d) 2,000 VA

14. When sizing a service or feeder for fixed appliances in dwelling units, a demand factor of 75 percent of the total nameplate ratings can be applied if there are _____ or more appliances fastened in place.
    (a) two
    (b) three
    (c) four
    (d) five

15. Applying a demand factor of 75 percent to the nameplate rating load of four or more appliances rated ¼ hp or greater, or 500 watts or greater, that are fastened in place, and that are served by the same feeder or service in a one-family, two-family, or multifamily dwelling shall be permitted. This demand factor shall not apply to _____.
    (a) electric vehicle supply equipment
    (b) dishwashers
    (c) waste disposals
    (d) microwave/hoods

16. The load for electric clothes dryers in a dwelling unit shall be _____ or the nameplate rating, whichever is larger, for each dryer served.
    (a) 1,500W
    (b) 4,500W
    (c) 5,000W
    (d) 8,000W

17. For dwelling unit load calculations in accordance Article 220, the branch-circuit load for one 10 kW range is _____.
    (a) 8 kW
    (b) 10 kW
    (c) 12 kW
    (d) 14 kW

18. For dwelling unit load calculations in accordance Article 220, the branch-circuit load for one wall-mounted oven and one counter-mounted cooking unit shall be the _____ rating of the appliance.
    (a) nameplate
    (b) ampere
    (c) wattage
    (d) voltage

19. Using the standard load calculation method, the feeder demand factor for a duplex containing two 12 kW ranges is _____.
    (a) 11 kW
    (b) 14 kW
    (c) 16 kW
    (d) 24 kW

20. Table 220.56 may be applied to determine the load for thermostatically controlled or intermittently used _____ and other kitchen equipment in a commercial kitchen.
    (a) commercial electric cooking equipment
    (b) dishwasher booster heaters
    (c) water heaters
    (d) all of these

21. The demand factors in Table 220.56 shall apply to _____ equipment.
    (a) space-heating
    (b) ventilating
    (c) air-conditioning
    (d) none of these

22. When applying the demand factors of Table 220.56, the feeder or service demand load shall not be less than the sum of the _____.
    (a) total number of receptacles at 180 VA per receptacle outlet
    (b) VA ratings of all of the small-appliance branch circuits combined
    (c) largest two kitchen equipment loads
    (d) kitchen heating and air-conditioning loads

23. The electrical vehicle supply equipment (EVSE) load shall be calculated at the larger of _____ or the nameplate rating of the equipment.
    (a) 5,000W
    (b) 7,200W
    (c) 10,000W
    (d) 12,500W

24. If a motor or air-conditioning load is part of the noncoincident load and is not the largest of the noncoincident loads, 125 percent of either the motor load or air-conditioning load, whichever is ____, shall be used in the calculation.

    (a) less
    (b) smaller
    (c) larger
    (d) less or smaller

25. There shall be no reduction in the size of the neutral or grounded conductor on ____ loads supplied from a 4-wire, wye-connected, three-phase system.

    (a) dwelling unit
    (b) hospital
    (c) nonlinear
    (d) motel

26. If an energy management system (EMS) is used to limit the current to a feeder or service, the set point value of the EMS shall be considered ____.

    (a) at 80 percent
    (b) at 90 percent
    (c) at 100 percent
    (d) a continuous load

27. Under the optional method for calculating a single-family dwelling unit service, general loads beyond the initial 10 kVA are assessed at a ____ demand factor.

    (a) 40 percent
    (b) 50 percent
    (c) 60 percent
    (d) 75 percent

28. A demand factor of ____ applies to a multifamily dwelling with ten units if the optional calculation method is used.

    (a) 43 percent
    (b) 50 percent
    (c) 60 percent
    (d) 75 percent

29. Where two dwelling units are supplied by a single feeder or service and the calculated load under Part III of this article exceeds that for ____ identical units calculated under 220.84, the lesser of the two loads is permitted to be used.

    (a) two
    (b) three
    (c) four
    (d) five

30. When calculating a feeder or service load for existing installations, if the maximum demand data for a 1-year period is not available, the calculated load shall be permitted to be based on the maximum demand (the ____ kilowatts) reached and maintained for a 15-minute interval continuously recorded over a minimum 30-day period.

    (a) lowest recorded
    (b) highest recorded
    (c) lowest average
    (d) highest average

31. Where shore power accommodations provide two receptacles specifically for an individual boat slip, and these receptacles have different voltages, only the receptacle with the ____ shall be required to be calculated.

    (a) smaller kW demand
    (b) larger kW demand
    (c) higher voltage
    (d) nominal voltage

32. For dwelling unit load calculations in accordance Article 220, the demand factor for a marina service or feeder with 45 shore power receptacles is ____.

    (a) 40 percent
    (b) 50 percent
    (c) 60 percent
    (d) 70 percent

Article 225—Outside Branch Circuits and Feeders

1. In accordance with Article 225—Outside Branch Circuits and Feeders, open individual conductors shall not be smaller than ____ copper for spans up to 50 ft in length and ____ copper for a longer span, unless supported by a messenger wire.
   - (a) 10 AWG, 8 AWG
   - (b) 8 AWG, 8 AWG
   - (c) 6 AWG, 8 AWG
   - (d) 6 AWG, 6 AWG

2. Overhead feeder conductors shall have a minimum vertical clearance of ____ over residential property and driveways, as well as those commercial areas not subject to truck traffic, where the voltage does not exceed 300V to ground.
   - (a) 10 ft
   - (b) 12 ft
   - (c) 15 ft
   - (d) 18 ft

3. The minimum clearance for overhead feeder conductors not exceeding 1,000V that pass over public streets, alleys, roads, and parking areas subject to truck traffic is ____.
   - (a) 10 ft
   - (b) 12 ft
   - (c) 15 ft
   - (d) 18 ft

4. If a set of 120/240V overhead feeder conductors terminates at a through-the-roof raceway or approved support, with not more than 6 ft of these conductors, 4 ft horizontally, passing over the roof overhang, the minimum clearance above the roof for these conductors shall not be less than ____.
   - (a) 12 in.
   - (b) 18 in.
   - (c) 2 ft
   - (d) 5 ft

5. The requirement for maintaining a 3-ft vertical clearance from the edge of the roof shall not apply to the final feeder conductor span where the conductors are attached to ____.
   - (a) a building pole
   - (b) the side of a building
   - (c) an antenna
   - (d) the base of a building

6. Overhead feeder and branch-circuit clearances from chimneys, radio and television antennas, tanks, and other nonbuilding or nonbridge structures, shall not be less than ____.
   - (a) 3 ft
   - (b) 6 ft
   - (c) 8 ft
   - (d) 10 ft

7. The vertical clearance of final spans of overhead conductors above or within ____ measured horizontally of platforms, projections, or surfaces that will permit personal contact shall be maintained in accordance with 225.18.
   - (a) 3 ft
   - (b) 6 ft
   - (c) 8 ft
   - (d) 10 ft

8. Overhead branch-circuit and feeder conductors shall not be installed beneath openings through which materials may be moved, such as openings in farm and commercial buildings, and shall not be installed where they obstruct ____ these openings.
   - (a) entrance to
   - (b) egress from
   - (c) access to
   - (d) a safe descent from

9. In accordance with Article 225—Outside Branch Circuits and Feeders, the disconnecting means for a building supplied by a feeder shall be installed at a(an) ____ location.
   - (a) accessible
   - (b) readily accessible
   - (c) outdoor
   - (d) indoor

10. In accordance with Article 225—Outside Branch Circuits and Feeders, there shall be no more than ____ switches or circuit breakers to serve as the disconnecting means for a building supplied by a feeder.
    - (a) two
    - (b) four
    - (c) six
    - (d) eight

11. In accordance with Article 225—Outside Branch Circuits and Feeders, a building disconnecting means that supplies only limited loads of a single branch circuit shall have a rating of not less than ____.

    (a) 15A
    (b) 20A
    (c) 25A
    (d) 30A

12. For all other installations supplied by a feeder(s) or branch circuit(s) and not specifically identified in 225.39(A) through (C), the feeder or branch-circuit disconnecting means shall have a rating of not less than ____.

    (a) 20A
    (b) 30A
    (c) 40A
    (d) 60A

Article 230—Services

1. A building or structure shall be supplied by a maximum of ____ service(s), unless specifically permitted otherwise.

    (a) one
    (b) two
    (c) three
    (d) four

2. Under special conditions additional services are permitted for a(an) ____.

    (a) fire pump
    (b) emergency system
    (c) optional standby system
    (d) any of these

3. If necessary to meet capacity requirements, additional services are permitted for a single building or other structure by ____.

    (a) the registered design professional
    (b) special permission
    (c) the engineer of record
    (d) master electricians

4. Service conductors shall be considered outside of a building or other structure where installed under not less than ____ of concrete beneath a building or other structure.

    (a) 2 in.
    (b) 4 in.
    (c) 5 in.
    (d) 6 in.

5. Circuit conductors other than service conductors, shall not be installed in the same ____ as the service conductors.

    (a) raceway or cable
    (b) handhole enclosure
    (c) underground box
    (d) all of these

6. ____ or supply-side bonding jumpers or conductors shall be permitted within service raceways.

    (a) Grounding electrode conductors
    (b) Backup supply conductors
    (c) Load management control conductors having overcurrent protection
    (d) none of these

7. The vertical clearance of final spans of overhead service conductors above, or within ____ measured horizontally of platforms, projections, or surfaces that will permit personal contact shall be maintained.

    (a) 3 ft
    (b) 4 ft
    (c) 5 ft
    (d) 6 ft

8. The minimum size service-drop conductor permitted is ____ copper or ____ aluminum or copper-clad aluminum.

    (a) 8 AWG, 8 AWG
    (b) 8 AWG, 6 AWG
    (c) 6 AWG, 8 AWG
    (d) 6 AWG, 6 AWG

9. Overhead service conductors installed over roofs shall have a vertical clearance of not less than ____ above the roof surface.

    (a) 3 ft
    (b) 4 ft
    (c) 5 ft
    (d) 8 ft 6 in.

10. Where the voltage between conductors does not exceed 300 and the roof has a slope of 4 in. in 12 in. or greater, a reduction in clearance to ____ over the roof is permitted.
    (a) 3 ft
    (b) 4 ft
    (c) 5 ft
    (d) 8 ft

11. Where the voltage between conductors does not exceed 300, a reduction in clearance above only the overhanging portion of the roof to not less than ____ shall be permitted if not more than 6 ft of overhead service conductors, pass above the roof overhang 4 ft horizontally.
    (a) 12 in.
    (b) 18 in.
    (c) 2 ft
    (d) 5 ft

12. The requirement to maintain a 3-ft vertical clearance from the edge of a roof does not apply to the final conductor span where the service drop is attached to ____.
    (a) a service pole
    (b) the side of a building
    (c) an antenna
    (d) the base of a building

13. Where the voltage between overhead service conductors does not exceed 300V and the roof area is guarded or isolated, a reduction in clearance to ____ is permitted.
    (a) 1 ft
    (b) 2 ft
    (c) 3 ft
    (d) 6 ft

14. Overhead service conductors shall have a minimum clearance from final grade of ____ above areas or sidewalks accessible only to pedestrians, measured from final grade or other accessible surface where the voltage does not exceed 150V to ground.
    (a) 8 ft
    (b) 10 ft
    (c) 12 ft
    (d) 15 ft

15. Overhead service conductors shall have a minimum vertical clearance of ____ from final grade over residential property and driveways, as well as over commercial areas not subject to truck traffic where the voltage does not exceed 300V to ground.
    (a) 10 ft
    (b) 12 ft
    (c) 15 ft
    (d) 18 ft

16. The minimum clearance for overhead service conductors that pass over public streets, alleys, roads, parking areas subject to truck traffic is ____.
    (a) 10 ft
    (b) 12 ft
    (c) 15 ft
    (d) 18 ft

17. Where conduits are used as service masts, hubs shall be ____ for use with service-entrance equipment.
    (a) identified
    (b) approved
    (c) of a heavy-duty type
    (d) listed

18. Wiring methods permitted for service-entrance conductors include ____.
    (a) IGS cable
    (b) NM cable
    (c) UF cable
    (d) all of these

19. Wiring methods permitted for service-entrance conductors include ____.
    (a) rigid metal conduit
    (b) electrical metallic tubing
    (c) PVC conduit
    (d) all of these

20. Service-entrance cables which are not installed underground, where subject to physical damage, shall be protected by ____.
    (a) rigid metal conduit
    (b) IMC
    (c) Schedule 80 PVC conduit
    (d) any of these

21. Service-entrance cables mounted in contact with a building shall be supported at intervals not exceeding ____.

    (a) 24 in.
    (b) 30 in.
    (c) 3 ft
    (d) 4 ft

22. Barriers shall be placed in service equipment such that no uninsulated, ungrounded service busbar or service ____ is exposed to inadvertent contact by persons or maintenance equipment while servicing load terminations with the service disconnect in the open position.

    (a) phase conductor
    (b) neutral conductor
    (c) terminal
    (d) disconnect

23. The service disconnecting means shall be marked to identify it as being suitable for use as service equipment and shall be ____.

    (a) weatherproof
    (b) listed or field evaluated
    (c) approved
    (d) moisture resistant

24. Where the service equipment for areas of nursing homes and limited care facilities used exclusively as ____ is replaced, a surge-protective device (SPD) shall be installed.

    (a) patient sleeping rooms
    (b) critical care areas
    (c) public areas
    (d) emergency egress

25. A service disconnecting means shall be installed at a(an) ____ location.

    (a) dry
    (b) readily accessible
    (c) outdoor
    (d) indoor

26. A service disconnecting means shall not be installed in ____.

    (a) bathrooms
    (b) hallways
    (c) outside
    (d) electrical rooms

27. Each service disconnecting means shall be permanently ____ to identify it as a service disconnect.

    (a) identified
    (b) positioned
    (c) marked
    (d) arranged

28. When the service contains two to six service disconnecting means, they shall be ____ and marked to indicate the load served.

    (a) the same size
    (b) grouped
    (c) in the same enclosure
    (d) from the same manufacturer

29. The additional service disconnecting means for fire pumps, emergency systems, legally required standby, or optional standby services shall be installed remote from the one to six service disconnecting means for normal service to minimize the possibility of ____ interruption of supply.

    (a) intentional
    (b) accidental
    (c) simultaneous
    (d) prolonged

30. For installations that supply only limited loads of a single branch circuit, the service disconnecting means shall have a rating of not less than ____.

    (a) 15A
    (b) 20A
    (c) 25A
    (d) 30A

31. For installations consisting of not more than two 2-wire branch circuits, the service disconnecting means shall have a rating of not less than ____.

    (a) 15A
    (b) 20A
    (c) 25A
    (d) 30A

32. For a one-family dwelling, the service disconnecting means shall have a rating of not less than ____, 3-wire.

    (a) 90A
    (b) 100A
    (c) 125A
    (d) 200A

33. ____ are permitted to be connected to the supply side of the service disconnecting means.
    (a) Cable limiters
    (b) Meter sockets
    (c) Solar PV systems
    (d) all of these

34. A meter-mounted transfer switch shall be listed and be capable of transferring ____.
    (a) the load served
    (b) 125 percent of the continuous load served
    (c) the maximum short-circuit current
    (d) all of these

35. Ground-fault protection of equipment shall be provided for solidly grounded wye electrical services of more than 150V to ground, but not exceeding 1,000V phase-to-phase for each service disconnecting means rated ____ or more.
    (a) 1,000A
    (b) 1,500A
    (c) 2,000A
    (d) 2,500A

Article 240—Overcurrent Protection

1. If an ____ or less overcurrent protective device is an adjustable trip device installed in accordance with 240.4(B)(1), (B)(2), and (B)(3), it shall be permitted to be set to a value that does not exceed the next higher standard value above the ampacity of the conductors being protected as shown in Table 240.6(A) where restricted access in accordance with 240.6(C) is provided.
    (a) 600A
    (b) 800A
    (c) 1,000A
    (d) 1,200A

2. If the circuit's overcurrent device exceeds ____, the conductor ampacity shall have a rating not less than the rating of the overcurrent device.
    (a) 800A
    (b) 1,000A
    (c) 1,200A
    (d) 2,000A

3. Unless specifically permitted in 240.4(E) or (G), the overcurrent protection for 14 AWG copper-clad aluminum conductors shall not exceed 10A provided that ____.
    (a) continuous loads do not exceed 8A
    (b) circuit breakers are listed and marked for use with 14 AWG copper-clad aluminum conductors
    (c) fuses are listed and marked for use with 14 AWG copper-clad aluminum conductors
    (d) all of these

4. Overcurrent protection shall not exceed ____.
    (a) 15A for 14 AWG copper
    (b) 20A for 12 AWG copper
    (c) 30A for 10 AWG copper
    (d) all of these

5. Fixture wire is permitted to be tapped to the branch-circuit conductor in accordance with which of the following?
    (a) 15A or 20A circuits—18 AWG, up to 50 ft of run length
    (b) 15A or 20A circuits—16 AWG, up to 100 ft of run length
    (c) 20A circuits—14 AWG and larger
    (d) all of these

6. The standard ampere rating(s) for fuses is(are) ____.
    (a) 1A
    (b) 6A
    (c) 601A
    (d) all of these

7. Standard ampere ratings for circuit breakers and fuses do not include ____.
    (a) 10A
    (b) 35A
    (c) 75A
    (d) 225A

8. For adjustable trip circuit breakers, restricted access is defined as ____.
    (a) located behind bolted equipment enclosure doors
    (b) located behind locked doors accessible only to qualified personnel
    (c) password protected, with password accessible only to qualified personnel
    (d) any of these

9. Supplementary overcurrent protective devices are not permitted to be used ____.
   (a) to provide additional overcurrent protection for luminaires
   (b) to provide additional overcurrent protection for appliances
   (c) as the required branch-circuit overcurrent protective device
   (d) none of these

10. Feeder taps are permitted to be located at any point on the ____ side of the feeder overcurrent protective device.
   (a) load
   (b) line
   (c) supply
   (d) end

11. When feeder taps not over 10 ft long leave the enclosure in which the tap is made, the ampacity of the tap conductors cannot be less than ____ of the rating of the device protecting the feeder.
   (a) one-tenth
   (b) one-fifth
   (c) one-half
   (d) two-thirds

12. Tap conductors not over 25 ft in length are permitted, providing the ____.
   (a) ampacity of the tap conductors is not less than one-third the rating of the overcurrent device protecting the feeder conductors being tapped
   (b) tap conductors terminate in a single circuit breaker or set of fuses that limits the load to the ampacity of the tap conductors
   (c) tap conductors are suitably protected from physical damage
   (d) all of these

13. Circuit breakers and switches containing fuses shall be readily accessible and installed so the center of the grip of the operating handle of the switch or circuit breaker, when in its highest position, is not more than ____ above the floor or working platform.
   (a) 6 ft 4 in.
   (b) 6 ft 5 in.
   (c) 6 ft 6 in.
   (d) 6 ft 7 in.

14. Overcurrent protective devices shall not be located ____.
   (a) where exposed to physical damage
   (b) near easily ignitible materials, such as in clothes closets
   (c) in bathrooms, showering facilities, or locker rooms with showering facilities
   (d) all of these

15. ____ shall not be located over the steps of a stairway.
   (a) Disconnect switches
   (b) Overcurrent protective devices
   (c) Knife switches
   (d) Transformers

16. Circuit breaker enclosures shall be permitted to be installed ____ where the circuit breaker is installed in accordance with 240.81
   (a) vertically
   (b) horizontally
   (c) face up
   (d) face down

17. Plug fuses of the Edison-base type shall have a maximum rating of ____.
   (a) 20A at 125V
   (b) 30A at 125V
   (c) 40A at 125V
   (d) 50A at 125V

18. Plug fuses of the Edison-base type shall be used only ____.
   (a) where over fusing is necessary
   (b) for replacement in existing installations
   (c) as a replacement for Type S fuses
   (d) if rated 50A and above

19. Circuit breakers used to switch high-intensity discharge lighting circuits shall be listed and marked as ____.
   (a) SWD
   (b) HID
   (c) SWD or HID
   (d) SWD and HID

Article 242—Overvoltage Protection

1. A surge-protective device shall not be installed in circuits over ____.
    - (a) 480V
    - (b) 600V
    - (c) 1,000V
    - (d) 4,160V

Article 250—Grounding and Bonding

1. For grounded systems, normally noncurrent-carrying conductive materials enclosing electrical conductors or equipment shall be connected to earth so as to limit ____ on these materials.
    - (a) the voltage to ground
    - (b) current
    - (c) arcing
    - (d) resistance

2. For grounded systems, normally noncurrent-carrying conductive materials enclosing electrical conductors shall be connected together and to the ____ to establish an effective ground-fault current path.
    - (a) ground
    - (b) earth
    - (c) electrical supply source
    - (d) enclosure

3. In grounded systems, normally noncurrent-carrying electrically conductive materials that are likely to become energized shall be connected ____ in a manner that establishes an effective ground-fault current path.
    - (a) together
    - (b) to the electrical supply source
    - (c) to the closest grounded conductor
    - (d) together and to the electrical supply source

4. Equipment grounding conductors, grounding electrode conductors, and bonding jumpers shall be connected by ____.
    - (a) listed pressure connectors
    - (b) terminal bars
    - (c) exothermic welding
    - (d) any of these

5. Alternating-current circuits of less than 50V shall be grounded if supplied by a transformer whose supply system exceeds ____.
    - (a) 150V to ground
    - (b) 300V to ground
    - (c) 600V to ground
    - (d) 1,000V to ground

6. The grounding electrode conductor connection shall be made at any accessible point from the load end of the overhead service conductors, ____ to the terminal or bus to which the grounded service conductor is connected at the service disconnecting means.
    - (a) service drop
    - (b) underground service conductors
    - (c) service lateral
    - (d) any of these

7. If the main bonding jumper is a wire or busbar and is installed from the grounded conductor terminal bar to the equipment grounding terminal bar in the service equipment, the ____ is permitted to be connected to the equipment grounding terminal bar to which the main bonding jumper is connected.
    - (a) equipment grounding conductor
    - (b) grounded service conductor
    - (c) grounding electrode conductor
    - (d) system bonding jumper

8. A grounded conductor shall not be connected to normally noncurrent-carrying metal parts of equipment, to equipment grounding conductor(s), or be reconnected to ground on the load side of the ____ except as otherwise permitted.
    - (a) service disconnecting means
    - (b) distribution panel
    - (c) switchgear
    - (d) switchboard

9. For a grounded system, an unspliced ____ shall be used to connect the equipment grounding conductor(s) and the service disconnect enclosure to the grounded conductor of the system within the enclosure for each service disconnect.
    - (a) grounding electrode
    - (b) main bonding jumper
    - (c) busbar
    - (d) insulated copper conductor

10. If an ac system operating at 1,000V or less is grounded at any point, the ____ shall be routed with the ungrounded conductors to each service disconnecting means and shall be connected to each disconnecting means grounded conductor(s) terminal or bus.

    (a) system bonding jumper
    (b) supply-side bonding jumper
    (c) grounded conductor
    (d) equipment grounding conductor

11. The grounded conductor brought to service equipment shall be routed with the phase conductors and shall not be smaller than specified in Table ____ when the service-entrance conductors are 1,100 kcmil copper and smaller.

    (a) 250.102(C)(1)
    (b) 250.122
    (c) 310.16
    (d) 430.52

12. If ungrounded service-entrance conductors are connected in parallel, the size of the grounded conductors in each raceway shall be based on the total circular mil area of the parallel ungrounded service-entrance conductors in the raceway, sized in accordance with 250.24(D)(1), but not smaller than ____.

    (a) 1/0 AWG
    (b) 2/0 AWG
    (c) 3/0 AWG
    (d) 4/0 AWG

13. A main bonding jumper shall be a ____ or similar suitable conductor.

    (a) wire
    (b) bus
    (c) screw
    (d) any of these

14. A grounded conductor shall not be connected to normally non-current carrying metal parts of equipment, be connected to equipment grounding conductors, or be reconnected to ground on the _____ side of the system bonding jumper.

    (a) supply
    (b) grounded
    (c) high voltage
    (d) load

15. The connection of the system bonding jumper for a separately derived system shall be made ____ on the separately derived system from the source to the first system disconnecting means or overcurrent device.

    (a) in at least two locations
    (b) in every location that the grounded conductor is present
    (c) at any single point
    (d) effectively

16. If a building or structure is supplied by a feeder from an outdoor separately derived system, a system bonding jumper at both the source and the first disconnecting means shall be permitted if doing so does not establish a(an) ____ path for the grounded conductor.

    (a) series
    (b) parallel
    (c) conductive
    (d) effective

17. For a single separately derived system, the grounding electrode conductor connects the grounded conductor of the derived system to the grounding electrode at the same point on the separately derived system where the ____ is connected.

    (a) metering equipment
    (b) transfer switch
    (c) system bonding jumper
    (d) largest circuit breaker

18. A grounding electrode system and grounding electrode conductor at a building or structure shall not be required if only a ____ supplies the building or structure.

    (a) 4-wire service
    (b) single or multiwire branch circuit
    (c) 3-wire service
    (d) any of these

19. An equipment grounding conductor shall be run with the supply conductors and be connected to the building or structure ____ and to the grounding electrode.

    (a) rebar
    (b) disconnecting means
    (c) structural steel
    (d) ground rod

20. The frame of a vehicle-mounted generator shall not be required to be connected to a(an) ____ if the generator only supplies equipment mounted on the vehicle, or cord-and-plug-connected equipment through receptacles mounted on the vehicle.

    (a) grounding electrode
    (b) grounded conductor
    (c) ungrounded conductor
    (d) equipment grounding conductor

21. Impedance grounded systems in which a grounding impedance device, typically a resistor, limits the ground-fault current for a 480V up to 1,000V three-phase system are permitted where ____.

    (a) the conditions of maintenance and supervision ensure that only qualified persons service the installation
    (b) ground detectors are installed on the system
    (c) line-to-neutral loads are not served
    (d) all of these

22. In order for a metal underground water pipe to be used as a grounding electrode, it shall be in direct contact with the earth for ____.

    (a) 5 ft
    (b) 10 ft or more
    (c) less than 10 ft
    (d) 20 ft or more

23. One or more metal in-ground support structure(s) in direct contact with the earth vertically for ____ or more, with or without concrete encasement, is permitted to be a grounding electrode in accordance with 250.52.

    (a) 4 ft
    (b) 6 ft
    (c) 8 ft
    (d) 10 ft

24. The minimum length of a 4 AWG concrete-encased electrode is at least ____.

    (a) 10 ft
    (b) 20 ft
    (c) 25 ft
    (d) 50 ft

25. Rebar in multiple pieces used as a concrete-encased electrode shall be connected together by ____ tie wires or other effective means.

    (a) steel
    (b) plastic
    (c) aluminum
    (d) fiber glass

26. An electrode encased by at least 2 in. of concrete, located horizontally near the bottom or vertically and within that portion of a concrete foundation or footing that is in direct contact with the earth, is permitted as a grounding electrode when it consists of a bare copper conductor not smaller than ____.

    (a) 8 AWG
    (b) 6 AWG
    (c) 4 AWG
    (d) 1/0 AWG

27. If multiple concrete-encased electrodes are present at a building or structure, it shall be permissible to bond only ____ into the grounding electrode system.

    (a) one
    (b) two
    (c) three
    (d) four

28. Concrete-encased grounding electrodes that are installed where the concrete is installed with ____ is not considered to be in direct contact with the earth.

    (a) insulation
    (b) vapor barriers
    (c) films
    (d) any of these

29. A ground ring encircling the building or structure can be used as a grounding electrode when the ____.

    (a) ring is in direct contact with the earth
    (b) ring consists of at least 20 ft of bare copper conductor
    (c) bare copper conductor is not smaller than 2 AWG
    (d) all of these

30. Rod and pipe grounding electrodes shall not be less than ____ in length.

    (a) 6 ft
    (b) 8 ft
    (c) 10 ft
    (d) 20 ft

31. Grounding electrodes of the rod type less than _____ in diameter shall be listed.

    (a) ½ in.
    (b) ⅝ in.
    (c) ¾ in.
    (d) 1 in.

32. _____ shall not be used as a grounding electrode(s).

    (a) Metal underground gas piping systems
    (b) Aluminum
    (c) Swimming pool structures and structural rebar
    (d) all of these

33. _____ electrodes shall be free from nonconductive coatings such as paint or enamel.

    (a) Rod
    (b) Pipe
    (c) Plate
    (d) all of these

34. The grounding electrode conductor to a ground rod that serves as a supplemental electrode for the metal water pipe electrode is not required to be larger than _____ copper wire.

    (a) 8 AWG
    (b) 6 AWG
    (c) 4 AWG
    (d) 3 AWG

35. If a single rod, pipe, or plate grounding electrode has a resistance to earth of 25 ohms or less, the _____ electrode shall not be required.

    (a) additional
    (b) supplemental
    (c) auxiliary
    (d) surplus

36. If multiple rod, pipe, or plate electrodes are installed to supplement the water pipe electrode, they shall not be less than _____ apart.

    (a) 3 ft
    (b) 4 ft
    (c) 5 ft
    (d) 6 ft

37. A rod or pipe electrode shall be installed such that at least _____ of length is in contact with the soil.

    (a) 30 in.
    (b) 6 ft
    (c) 8 ft
    (d) 10 ft

38. Where rock bottom is encountered, a rod or pipe electrode shall be driven at an angle not to exceed _____ from the vertical.

    (a) 15 degrees
    (b) 30 degrees
    (c) 45 degrees
    (d) 60 degrees

39. The upper end of the rod electrode shall be _____ ground level unless the aboveground end and the grounding electrode conductor attachment are protected against physical damage as specified in 250.10.

    (a) no more than 1 in. above
    (b) no more than 2 in. above
    (c) no more than 3 in. above
    (d) flush with or below ground level

40. Plate electrodes shall be installed not less than _____ below the surface of the earth.

    (a) 30 in.
    (b) 4 ft
    (c) 5 ft
    (d) 6 ft

41. Where bonding jumper(s) are used to connect the grounding electrodes together to form the grounding electrode system, _____ is not permitted to be used as a conductor to interconnect the electrodes.

    (a) rebar
    (b) structural steel
    (c) a grounding plate
    (d) none of these

42. If the supplemental electrode is a rod, pipe, or plate electrode, that portion of the bonding jumper that is the sole connection to the supplemental grounding electrode is not required to be larger than _____ copper.

    (a) 8 AWG
    (b) 6 AWG
    (c) 4 AWG
    (d) 1 AWG

43. When a ground ring is used as a grounding electrode, it shall be installed at a depth below the earth's surface of not less than ____.

    (a) 18 in.
    (b) 24 in.
    (c) 30 in.
    (d) 8 ft

44. When installing ____ electrodes, the earth shall not be used as an effective ground-fault current path.

    (a) auxiliary
    (b) supplemental
    (c) oversized
    (d) aluminum

45. Bare or covered aluminum or copper-clad aluminum grounding electrode conductors without an extruded polymeric covering shall not be installed where subject to corrosive conditions or be installed in direct contact with ____.

    (a) concrete
    (b) bare copper conductors
    (c) wooden framing members
    (d) all of these

46. Aluminum or copper-clad aluminum grounding electrode conductors external to buildings or equipment enclosures shall not terminate within ____ of the earth.

    (a) 12 in.
    (b) 18 in.
    (c) 20 in.
    (d) 24 in.

47. If ____, a grounding electrode conductor or its enclosure shall be securely fastened to the surface on which it is carried.

    (a) concealed
    (b) exposed
    (c) accessible
    (d) none of these

48. Grounding electrode conductors smaller than ____ shall be protected in rigid metal conduit, IMC, PVC conduit, electrical metallic tubing, or cable armor.

    (a) 10 AWG
    (b) 8 AWG
    (c) 6 AWG
    (d) 4 AWG

49. Grounding electrode conductors in contact with ____ shall not be required to comply with 300.5 but shall be protected if subject to physical damage.

    (a) water
    (b) the earth
    (c) metal
    (d) all of these

50. Grounding electrode conductors shall be installed in one continuous length without a splice or joint, unless spliced by ____.

    (a) connecting together sections of a busbar
    (b) irreversible compression-type connectors listed as grounding and bonding equipment
    (c) the exothermic welding process
    (d) any of these

51. The common grounding electrode conductor shall be sized in accordance with 250.66, based on the sum of the circular mil area of the ____ ungrounded conductor(s) of each set of conductors that supplies the disconnecting means.

    (a) smallest
    (b) largest
    (c) color of the
    (d) material of the

52. Ferrous metal raceways for grounding electrode conductors shall be ____ continuous from the point of attachment to cabinets or equipment to the grounding electrode.

    (a) electrically
    (b) physically
    (c) mechanically
    (d) integrally

53. Ferrous metal raceways for grounding electrode conductors shall be bonded at each end of the raceway or enclosure to the grounding electrode or grounding electrode conductor to create a(an) ____ parallel path.

    (a) mechanically
    (b) electrically
    (c) physically
    (d) effective

54. The grounding electrode conductor is permitted to be run to any ____ available in the grounding electrode system.

    (a) panelboards
    (b) bonding jumper
    (c) switchgear
    (d) convenient grounding electrode

55. Bonding jumpers from grounding electrodes are permitted to be connected to a busbar not less than ____.

    (a) ⅛ in. thick × 1 in. wide
    (b) ⅛ in. thick × 2 in. wide
    (c) ¼ in. thick × 1 in. wide
    (d) ¼ in. thick × 2 in. wide

56. A grounding electrode conductor sized at ____ is required for a service supplied with 400 kcmil parallel conductors in three raceways.

    (a) 1 AWG
    (b) 1/0 AWG
    (c) 2/0 AWG
    (d) 3/0 AWG

57. A grounding electrode conductor sized at ____ is required for a service supplied with 250 kcmil conductors paralleled in two raceways.

    (a) 1 AWG
    (b) 1/0 AWG
    (c) 2/0 AWG
    (d) 3/0 AWG

58. A metal water pipe grounding electrode conductor sized at ____ is required for a 400A service supplied with 500 kcmil conductors.

    (a) 1 AWG
    (b) 1/0 AWG
    (c) 2/0 AWG
    (d) 3/0 AWG

59. The minimum grounding electrode conductor to a rod, pipe, or plate electrode for a 30A service with 10 AWG conductors is ____.

    (a) 8 AWG
    (b) 6 AWG
    (c) 1/0 AWG
    (d) 4/0 AWG

60. A metal water pipe grounding electrode conductor sized at ____ is required for a service supplied with 350 kcmil conductors.

    (a) 6 AWG
    (b) 3 AWG
    (c) 2 AWG
    (d) 1/0 AWG

61. A(An) ____ is the smallest size grounding electrode conductor permitted for a solidly grounded ac system.

    (a) 8 AWG
    (b) 6 AWG
    (c) 1/0 AWG
    (d) 4/0 AWG

62. A service consisting of 12 AWG service-entrance conductors requires a grounding electrode conductor sized no less than ____.

    (a) 10 AWG
    (b) 8 AWG
    (c) 6 AWG
    (d) 4 AWG

63. The largest size copper grounding electrode conductor required based on Table 250.66 is ____.

    (a) 6 AWG
    (b) 1/0 AWG
    (c) 3/0 AWG
    (d) 250 kcmil

64. The largest sized grounding electrode conductor to a rod, pipe, or plate electrode required for a 400A service with 500 kcmil conductors is ____.

    (a) 8 AWG
    (b) 6 AWG
    (c) 1/0 AWG
    (d) 4/0 AWG aluminum

65. If the grounding electrode conductor to a ground rod does not extend on to other types of electrodes, the grounding electrode conductor shall not be required to be larger than ____ copper wire.

    (a) 10 AWG
    (b) 8 AWG
    (c) 6 AWG
    (d) 4 AWG

66. Where necessary to ensure the _____ path for a metal piping system used as a grounding electrode, bonding shall be provided around insulated joints and around any equipment likely to be disconnected for repairs or replacement.

    (a) grounding
    (b) bonding
    (c) connection
    (d) termination

67. Interior metal water piping that is electrically continuous with a metal underground water pipe electrode and is located not more than ____ from the point of entrance to the building, as measured along the water piping, is permitted to extend the connection to an electrode(s).

    (a) 2 ft
    (b) 3 ft
    (c) 4 ft
    (d) 5 ft

68. The metal structural frame of a building is permitted to be used as a conductor to ____ electrodes that are part of the grounding electrode system, or as a grounding electrode conductor.

    (a) interconnect
    (b) identify
    (c) separate
    (d) none of these

69. Metal enclosures and raceways containing ____ conductors shall be connected to the grounded system conductor if the electrical system is grounded.

    (a) service
    (b) feeder
    (c) branch-circuit
    (d) outside feeder or branch-circuit

70. Metal components that are installed in a run of an underground nonmetallic raceway(s) and are isolated from possible contact by a minimum cover of ____ to all parts of the metal components shall not be required to be connected to the grounded conductor, supply-side bonding jumper, or grounding electrode conductor.

    (a) 12 in.
    (b) 18 in.
    (c) 24 in.
    (d) 30 in.

71. The minimum size supply-side bonding jumper for a service raceway containing 4/0 AWG aluminum conductors is ____.

    (a) 6 AWG aluminum
    (b) 4 AWG aluminum
    (c) 4 AWG copper
    (d) 3 AWG copper

72. Where ungrounded supply conductors are paralleled in two or more raceways, the bonding jumper for each raceway shall be based on the size of the ____ in each raceway.

    (a) overcurrent protection for conductors
    (b) grounded conductors
    (c) largest ungrounded supply conductors
    (d) sum of all conductors

73. If service conductors are connected in parallel in three separate metal raceways, with 600 kcmil conductors per phase, the minimum copper supply-side bonding jumper size for each service raceway is _____.

    (a) 1/0 AWG
    (b) 2/0 AWG
    (c) 3/0 AWG
    (d) 4/0 AWG

74. The minimum size copper equipment bonding jumper for a 40A-rated circuit is ____.

    (a) 14 AWG
    (b) 12 AWG
    (c) 10 AWG
    (d) 8 AWG

75. An equipment bonding jumper can be installed on the outside of a raceway, provided the length of the equipment bonding jumper is not more than ____ long and the equipment bonding jumper is routed with the raceway.

    (a) 3 ft
    (b) 4 ft
    (c) 5 ft
    (d) 6 ft

76. Metal water piping systems shall be bonded to the ____, or to one or more grounding electrodes used if the grounding electrode conductor or bonding jumper to the grounding electrode is of sufficient size.

    (a) grounded conductor at the service
    (b) service equipment enclosure
    (c) grounding electrode conductor if of sufficient size
    (d) any of these

77. Bonding jumper(s) for the metal water piping systems shall not be required to be larger than ____ copper.

    (a) 1/0 AWG
    (b) 2/0 AWG
    (c) 3/0 AWG
    (d) 4/0 AWG

78. The metal water piping system(s) installed in or attached to a building or structure [250.104(A)(3)] shall be bonded to ____.

    (a) the building or structure disconnecting means enclosure where located at the building or structure
    (b) the equipment grounding conductor run with the supply conductors
    (c) one or more grounding electrodes
    (d) any of these

79. The bonding jumper(s) required for the metal water piping system(s) installed in or attached to a building or structure supplied by a feeder(s) or branch circuit(s) shall be sized in accordance with ____.

    (a) 250.66
    (b) 250.102(D)
    (c) 250.122
    (d) 310.16

80. If installed ____ a building or structure, a metal piping system that is likely to become energized shall be bonded.

    (a) in
    (b) on
    (c) under
    (d) in or on

81. The building structural steel bonding jumper size for a 400A service supplied with 500 kcmil conductors is ____.

    (a) 6 AWG
    (b) 3 AWG
    (c) 2 AWG
    (d) 1/0 AWG

82. Exposed structural metal that is interconnected to form a metal building frame, not intentionally grounded or bonded, and is likely to become energized shall be bonded to the ____.

    (a) service equipment enclosure
    (b) grounded conductor at the service
    (c) disconnecting means for buildings or structures supplied by a feeder or branch circuit
    (d) any of these

83. A transformer supplies power to a 100A panelboard with 2 AWG THWN-2 conductors. The size of the bonding jumper in copper required to bond the building steel to the secondary grounded conductor is ____.

    (a) 8 AWG
    (b) 6 AWG
    (c) 4 AWG
    (d) 2 AWG

84. A separately derived system supplies power to a 200A panelboard with 3/0 AWG conductors. The minimum size copper bonding jumper required to bond the building steel to the secondary grounded conductor is _____.

    (a) 8 AWG
    (b) 6 AWG
    (c) 4 AWG
    (d) 2 AWG

85. Exposed, normally noncurrent-carrying metal parts of cord-and-plug-connected equipment shall be connected to the equipment grounding conductor if operated at over ____ to ground.

    (a) 24V
    (b) 50V
    (c) 120V
    (d) 150V

86. Flexible metal conduit used as an EGC where flexibility for movement of equipment is required after installation shall ____.

    (a) be provided with a wire type equipment grounding conductor or bonding jumper
    (b) not require a wire-type EGC if less than 6 ft
    (c) not require a wire-type EGC if protected by 20A or less
    (d) none of these

87. FMC can be used as the equipment grounding conductor if the length in any ground return path does not exceed 6 ft and the circuit conductors contained in the conduit are protected by overcurrent devices rated at _____ or less.

    (a) 15A
    (b) 20A
    (c) 30A
    (d) 60A

88. LFMC is acceptable as an equipment grounding conductor when it terminates in _____ and is protected by an overcurrent device rated 20A or less for trade sizes ⅜ through ½.

    (a) labeled fittings
    (b) identified fittings
    (c) approved fittings
    (d) listed fittings

89. A wire-type equipment grounding conductor can be identified by _____.

    (a) a continuous outer finish that is green
    (b) being bare
    (c) a continuous outer finish that is green with one or more yellow stripes
    (d) any of these

90. An insulated or covered conductor _____ and larger is permitted, at the time of installation, to be permanently identified as an equipment grounding conductor at each end and at every point where the conductor is accessible.

    (a) 8 AWG
    (b) 6 AWG
    (c) 4 AWG
    (d) 1/0 AWG

91. A 1,600A feeder that supplies distribution equipment will require a _____ equipment grounding conductor.

    (a) 3/0 copper
    (b) 4/0 copper
    (c) 4/0 aluminum
    (d) 250 kcmil aluminum

92. A 60A feeder supplying an electrically powered irrigation machine will require a(an) _____ equipment grounding conductor.

    (a) 14 AWG
    (b) 12 AWG
    (c) 10 AWG
    (d) 8 AWG

93. A _____ equipment grounding conductor is required for a 15A branch circuit that provides power for a Low-Voltage lighting system.

    (a) 14 AWG
    (b) 14 AWG aluminum
    (c) 12 AWG
    (d) 10 AWG aluminum

94. The equipment grounding conductor for a 70A circuit supplying fixed equipment in the patient care area of a health care facility shall not be smaller than _____.

    (a) 10 AWG
    (b) 8 AWG
    (c) 6 AWG
    (d) 4 AWG

95. Equipment grounding conductors are not required to be _____ than the circuit conductors.

    (a) larger
    (b) smaller
    (c) less
    (d) none of these

96. If the ungrounded conductors are increased in size for any reason other than as required in 310.15(B) or 310.15(C), wire-type equipment grounding conductors shall be increased in size proportionately to the increase in _____ of the ungrounded conductors.

    (a) ampacity
    (b) circular mil area
    (c) diameter
    (d) temperature rating

97. In accordance with 250.134, non-current-carrying metal parts of fastened in place equipment, raceways, and other enclosures, shall be connected to an _____.

    (a) grounded conductor
    (b) equipment grounding conductor
    (c) ungrounded conductor
    (d) none of these

98. Load-side equipment such as the frames of ranges or dryers in existing installations are permitted to be connected to the _____ circuit conductor.

    (a) grounded
    (b) ungrounded
    (c) black
    (d) red

99. It shall be permissible to ground meter enclosures immediately adjacent to the service disconnecting means to the _____ circuit conductor on the load side of the service disconnect.

    (a) grounding
    (b) bonding
    (c) grounded
    (d) phase

REVIEW QUESTIONS

Please use the 2023 *Code* book to answer the following questions.

CHAPTER 3—WIRING METHODS AND MATERIALS

Article 300—General Requirements for Wiring Methods and Materials

1. Conductors for ac and dc circuits under 1,000V ac and 1,500V dc, can occupy the same ____ provided that all conductors have an insulation rating equal to the maximum voltage applied to any conductor.

    (a) equipment wiring enclosure
    (b) cable
    (c) raceway
    (d) any of these

2. Where a cable or raceway-type wiring method is installed through bored holes in joists, rafters, or wood members, the holes shall be bored so that the edge of the hole is ____ the edges of the wood member.

    (a) not less than 1¼ in. from
    (b) immediately adjacent to
    (c) not less than ¹⁄₁₆ in. from
    (d) 90° away from

3. Cables laid in wood notches require protection against nails or screws by using a steel plate at least ____ thick, installed before the building finish is applied.

    (a) ¹⁄₁₆ in.
    (b) ⅛ in.
    (c) ¼ in.
    (d) ½ in.

4. A ¹⁄₁₆-in. steel plate for ____ is not required for protection when installed in wood notches.

    (a) UF cable
    (b) NM cable
    (c) MC cable
    (d) intermediate metal conduit

5. Where cables and nonmetallic raceways are installed parallel to framing members, the nearest outside surface of the cable or raceway shall be ____ the nearest edge of the framing member where nails or screws are likely to penetrate.

    (a) not less than 1¼ in. from
    (b) immediately adjacent to
    (c) not less than ¹⁄₁₆ in. from
    (d) 90 degrees away from

6. A cable, raceway, or box installed under metal-corrugated sheet roof decking shall be supported so the top of the cable, raceway, or box is not less than ____ from the lowest surface of the roof decking to the top of the cable, raceway, or box.

    (a) ½ in.
    (b) 1 in.
    (c) 1½ in.
    (d) 2 in.

7. When installed under metal-corrugated sheet roof decking, ____ and intermediate metal conduit, with listed steel or malleable iron fittings and boxes, shall not be required to comply with 300.4(E).

    (a) rigid metal conduit
    (b) electrical metallic tubing
    (c) Schedule 80 PVC
    (d) all of these

8. Conduit bushings installed to protect insulated conductors ____ or larger contained within raceways that are constructed wholly of insulating material, shall not be used to secure a fitting or raceway.

    (a) 4 AWG
    (b) 6 AWG
    (c) 8 AWG
    (d) 10 AWG

9. The minimum cover requirement for UF cable that supplies a 120V, 30A circuit is ____.

    (a) 6 in.
    (b) 12 in.
    (c) 18 in.
    (d) 24 in.

10. Electrical metallic tubing that is directly buried under a two-family dwelling driveway shall have at least ____ of cover.

    (a) 6 in.
    (b) 12 in.
    (c) 18 in.
    (d) 24 in.

11. Rigid metal conduit that is directly buried outdoors shall have at least ____ of cover.

    (a) 6 in.
    (b) 12 in.
    (c) 18 in.
    (d) 24 in.

12. When installing PVC underground without concrete cover, there shall be a minimum of ____ of cover.

    (a) 6 in.
    (b) 12 in.
    (c) 18 in.
    (d) 22 in.

13. A PVC raceway covered in 2 in. of concrete is required to have a minimal buried depth of ____.

    (a) 6 in.
    (b) 18 in.
    (c) 12 in.
    (d) 24 in.

14. The minimum cover requirement for UF cable that supplies a 120V, 15A GFCI-protected circuit under a driveway of a one-family dwelling is ____.

    (a) 6 in.
    (b) 12 in.
    (c) 16 in.
    (d) 24 in.

15. For a dwelling location, direct buried cables that are GFCI protected at no more than 20A shall have a cover of ____.

    (a) 6 in.
    (b) 12 in.
    (c) 18 in.
    (d) 24 in.

16. UF cable used with a 24V landscape lighting system can have a minimum cover of ____.

    (a) 6 in.
    (b) 12 in.
    (c) 18 in.
    (d) 24 in.

17. ____ shall be defined as the shortest distance measured between a point on the top surface of direct-buried cable and the top surface of finished grade.

    (a) Notched
    (b) Cover
    (c) Gap
    (d) Spacing

18. The interior of underground raceways shall be considered a ____ location.

    (a) wet
    (b) dry
    (c) damp
    (d) corrosive

19. MC Cable ____ for direct burial or concrete encasement shall be permitted under a building without installation in a raceway in accordance with 330.10(A)(5).
    - (a) listed
    - (b) identified
    - (c) tagged
    - (d) labeled

20. Where direct-buried conductors and cables emerge from grade, they shall be protected by enclosures or raceways to a point at least ____ above finished grade.
    - (a) 3 ft
    - (b) 6 ft
    - (c) 8 ft
    - (d) 10 ft

21. Direct-buried service conductors that are not encased in concrete and that are buried 18 in. or more below grade shall have their location identified by a warning ribbon placed in the trench at least ____ above the underground installation.
    - (a) 6 in.
    - (b) 10 in.
    - (c) 12 in.
    - (d) 18 in.

22. Backfill used for underground wiring shall not damage ____ or prevent adequate compaction of fill or contribute to corrosion.
    - (a) raceways
    - (b) cables
    - (c) conductors
    - (d) any of these

23. Direct-buried conductors, cables, or raceways which are subject to movement by settlement or frost shall be arranged to prevent damage to the ____ or to equipment connected to the raceways.
    - (a) cable
    - (b) raceway
    - (c) enclosed conductors
    - (d) expansion fitting

24. Raceways, cable trays, cablebus, auxiliary gutters, cable armor, boxes, cable sheathing, cabinets, enclosures (other than surrounding fences and walls), elbows, couplings, fittings, supports, and support hardware shall be of materials suitable for ____.
    - (a) corrosive locations
    - (b) wet locations
    - (c) the environment in which they are to be installed
    - (d) damp locations

25. Where corrosion protection is necessary and the conduit is threaded anywhere other than at the factory where the product is listed, the threads shall be coated with a(an) ____ electrically conductive, corrosion-resistant compound.
    - (a) marked
    - (b) listed
    - (c) labeled
    - (d) approved

26. Where portions of cable raceways or sleeves are required to be sealed due to different temperatures, sealants shall be identified for use with ____, a bare conductor, a shield, or other components.
    - (a) low temperature conditions
    - (b) high temperature conditions
    - (c) a stranded conductor
    - (d) cable insulation or conductor insulation

27. Raceways shall be provided with expansion, expansion-deflection, or deflection fittings where necessary to compensate for thermal expansion, deflection, and ____.
    - (a) contraction
    - (b) warping
    - (c) bending
    - (d) cracking

28. Where raceways are installed in wet locations above grade, the interior of these raceways shall be considered a ____ location.
    - (a) wet
    - (b) dry
    - (c) damp
    - (d) corrosive

29. Wiring located within the cavity of a fire-rated floor-ceiling or roof-ceiling assembly shall not be secured to, or supported by, the ceiling assembly, including the ceiling support ____.

    (a) wires
    (b) hangers
    (c) rods
    (d) none of these

30. Raceways may be used as a means of support where the raceway contains power-supply conductors for electrically controlled equipment and is used to ____ Class 2 power-limited or Class 3 power-limited circuit conductors or cables that are solely for the purpose of connection to the equipment control circuits.

    (a) support
    (b) secure
    (c) strap
    (d) none of these

31. Raceways, cable armors, and cable sheaths shall be ____ between cabinets, boxes, conduit bodies, fittings, or other enclosures or outlets.

    (a) continuous
    (b) protected
    (c) buried
    (d) encased in concrete

32. In multiwire branch circuits, the continuity of a(an) ____ shall not depend on device connections such as lampholders, receptacles, and so forth.

    (a) ungrounded conductor
    (b) grounded conductor
    (c) grounding electrode
    (d) raceway

33. Where the opening to an outlet, junction, or switch point is less than 8 in. in any dimension, the length of free conductor of each conductor, spliced or unspliced, shall extend at least ____ outside the opening of the enclosure.

    (a) 1 in.
    (b) 3 in.
    (c) 6 in.
    (d) 12 in.

34. A vertical run of 4/0 AWG shall be supported at intervals not exceeding ____.

    (a) 40 ft
    (b) 80 ft
    (c) 100 ft
    (d) 120 ft

35. Size 3/0 AWG conductors installed in vertical raceways shall be supported at least every ____.

    (a) 60 ft
    (b) 80 ft
    (c) 100 ft
    (d) 180 ft

36. Conductors carrying alternating current installed in ferrous metal raceways or enclosures shall be arranged so as to avoid heating the surrounding ferrous metal by induction. To accomplish this, the ____ conductor(s) shall be grouped together.

    (a) phase
    (b) grounded
    (c) equipment grounding
    (d) all of these

37. Electrical installations in hollow spaces, vertical shafts, and ventilation or air-handling ducts shall be made so that the possible spread of fire or products of combustion will not be ____.

    (a) substantially increased
    (b) allowed
    (c) inherent
    (d) possible

38. Electrical installations in hollow spaces shall be made so as to not increase the spread of fire, such as boxes installed in a wall cavity on opposite sides of a fire-rated wall where a minimum horizontal separation of ____ usually applies between boxes.

    (a) 6 in.
    (b) 12 in.
    (c) 18 in.
    (d) 24 in.

39. No wiring of any type shall be installed in ducts used to transport ____.

    (a) dust
    (b) flammable vapors
    (c) loose stock
    (d) all of these

40. Equipment and devices shall only be permitted within ducts to transport environmental air if necessary for their direct action upon, or sensing of, the ____.

    (a) contained air
    (b) air quality
    (c) air temperature
    (d) humidity

Article 310—Conductors for General Wiring

1. The ____ core of a copper-clad aluminum conductor shall be made of an AA-8000 series electrical grade aluminum alloy conductor material.

    (a) aluminum
    (b) copper
    (c) steel
    (d) iron

2. Insulated conductors with the letters HH in their designation have a ____ insulation rating in a dry location.

    (a) 60°C
    (b) 75°C
    (c) 90°C
    (d) 110°C

3. Insulated conductors with letter designation of ____, are permitted in a wet location with a maximum operating temperature of 90°C.

    (a) USE
    (b) RHW
    (c) XHWN
    (d) THWN-2

4. Conductors with TW insulation have a temperature rating of ____.

    (a) 60°C
    (b) 75°C
    (c) 90°C
    (d) 110°C

5. The insulation of USE-2 cable is ____ resistant.

    (a) heat
    (b) moisture
    (c) sunlight
    (d) heat and moisture

6. The conductors described in 310.4 shall be permitted for use in any of the ____ covered in Chapter 3 and as specified in their respective tables or as permitted elsewhere in this *Code*.

    (a) wiring methods
    (b) cables
    (c) conduits
    (d) tubing

7. Insulated conductors and cables used in ____ shall be any of the types identified in this *Code*.

    (a) dry and damp locations
    (b) dry locations
    (c) damp locations
    (d) wet and damp locations

8. Insulated conductors and cables used in ____ shall be Types FEP, FEPB, MTW, PFA, RHH, RHW, RHW-2, SA, THHN, THW, THW-2, THHW, THWN, THWN-2, TW, XHH, XHHW, XHHW-2, XHHN, XHWN, XHWN-2, Z, or ZW.

    (a) dry and damp locations
    (b) dry locations
    (c) damp locations
    (d) wet and damp locations

9. Insulated conductors and cables used in wet locations shall be ____.

    (a) moisture-impervious metal-sheathed
    (b) types MTW, RHW, RHW-2, TW, THW, THW-2, THHW, THWN, THWN-2, XHHW, XHHW-2, XHWN, XHWN-2 or ZW
    (c) of a type listed for use in wet locations
    (d) any of these

10. In general, the minimum size conductor permitted for parallel installations is ____.

    (a) 10 AWG
    (b) 4 AWG
    (c) 1 AWG
    (d) 1/0 AWG

11. Parallel conductors shall have the same ____.

    (a) length
    (b) conductor material
    (c) size in circular mil area
    (d) all of these

12. Where conductors in parallel are run in ____ raceway(s), the raceway(s) shall have the same electrical characteristics.

    (a) separate
    (b) similar
    (c) the same
    (d) different

13. Where there are no adjustment or correction factors required, the service conductors for a rated service of ____ supplying the entire load associated with an individual dwelling unit, Table 310.12(A) shall be permitted to be applied.

    (a) 100A
    (b) 200A
    (c) 400A
    (d) all of these

14. Where there are no adjustment or correction factors required, the feeder conductors rated between 100A and ____ supplying the entire load associated with an individual dwelling unit, Table 310.12(A) shall be permitted to be applied.

    (a) 150A
    (b) 200A
    (c) 300A
    (d) 400A

15. In accordance with Article 310, temperature correction and adjustment factors are permitted to be applied to the ampacity for the temperature rating of the ____, if the corrected and adjusted ampacity does not exceed the ampacity for the temperature rating of the termination in accordance with 110.14(C).

    (a) conductor
    (b) feeder
    (c) service
    (d) termination

16. For raceways exposed to direct sunlight on or above rooftops where the distance above the roof to the bottom of the raceway or cable is less than ____, a temperature adder of 60°F shall be added to the outdoor temperature to determine the ambient temperature correction factor.

    (a) ¼ in.
    (b) ⅓ in.
    (c) ½ in.
    (d) ¾ in.

17. ____ insulated conductors shall not be subject to ampacity adjustment where installed exposed to direct sunlight on a rooftop.

    (a) THW-2
    (b) XHHW-2
    (c) THWN-2
    (d) RHW-2

18. Conductor adjustment factors shall not apply to conductors in raceways having a length not exceeding ____.

    (a) 12 in.
    (b) 24 in.
    (c) 36 in.
    (d) 48 in.

19. Where six current-carrying conductors are run in the same conduit, the ampacity of each conductor shall be adjusted to ____ of its ampacity.

    (a) 40 percent
    (b) 60 percent
    (c) 80 percent
    (d) 90 percent

20. A raceway contains two three-phase, 4-wire circuits where the neutrals carry only the unbalanced current from the other conductors. The ampacity adjustment factor for these conductors is ____.

    (a) 70 percent
    (b) 80 percent
    (c) 90 percent
    (d) 100 percent

21. The minimum size THHN conductor for a 150A noncontinuous load is ____.

    (a) 1 AWG
    (b) 1/0 AWG
    (c) 2/0 AWG
    (d) 3/0 AWG

22. The minimum conductor size required for a 60A load if the terminals are rated 75°C is ____ THW copper.

    (a) 2 AWG
    (b) 4 AWG
    (c) 6 AWG
    (d) 8 AWG

23. The minimum size THW service-entrance conductors for a 200A commercial service is ____.

    (a) 2/0 AWG
    (b) 3/0 AWG
    (c) 4/0 AWG
    (d) 250 KCMIL

24. The maximum allowable ampacity for each of 6 THW conductors in a raceway is ____.

    (a) 55A
    (b) 65A
    (c) 70A
    (d) 80A

25. The ampacities specified in Table 310.16 apply to ____.

    (a) conductors rated 60°C, 75°C, or 90°C
    (b) wiring installed in an ambient temperature of 86°F
    (c) where there is not more than three current-carrying conductors
    (d) all of these

Article 312—Cabinets, Cutout Boxes, And Meter Enclosures

1. Cabinets, cutout boxes, and meter socket enclosures installed in wet locations shall be ____.

    (a) waterproof
    (b) raintight
    (c) weatherproof
    (d) watertight

2. In walls constructed of wood or other ____ material, electrical cabinets shall be flush with the finished surface or project therefrom.

    (a) nonconductive
    (b) porous
    (c) fibrous
    (d) combustible

3. Noncombustible surfaces that are broken or incomplete shall be repaired so there will be no gaps or open spaces greater than ____ at the edge of a cabinet or cutout box employing a flush-type cover.

    (a) $\frac{1}{32}$ in.
    (b) $\frac{1}{16}$ in.
    (c) $\frac{1}{8}$ in.
    (d) $\frac{1}{4}$ in.

4. Nonmetallic-sheathed cables can enter the top of surface-mounted cabinets, cutout boxes, and meter socket enclosures through nonflexible raceways not less than 18 in. and not more than ____ in length if all of the required conditions are met.

    (a) 3 ft
    (b) 10 ft
    (c) 25 ft
    (d) 100 ft

5. The minimum wire-bending space and gutter width at terminals for 4/0 AWG entering an enclosure is ____.

    (a) 4 in.
    (b) 6 in.
    (c) 7 in.
    (d) 8 in.

6. The minimum wire-bending space and gutter width at terminals for 500 kcmil entering an enclosure is ____.

    (a) 4 in.
    (b) 6 in.
    (c) 7 in.
    (d) 8 in.

7. Cabinets, cutout boxes, and meter socket enclosures can be used for conductors feeding through, spliced, or tapping off to other enclosures, switches, or overcurrent devices where ____.

    (a) the total area of the conductors at any cross section does not exceed 40 percent of the cross-sectional area of that space
    (b) the total area of conductors, splices, and taps installed at any cross section does not exceed 75 percent of the cross-sectional area of that space
    (c) a warning label on the enclosure identifies the closest disconnecting means for any feed-through conductors
    (d) all of these

Article 314—Boxes, Conduit Bodies, and Handhole Enclosures

1. Boxes and conduit bodies shall be of an approved size to provide free space for all enclosed ____.

   (a) conductors
   (b) splices
   (c) terminations
   (d) all of these

2. According to the *NEC*, the volume of a 3 in. × 2 in. × 2 in. device box for conductor fill is ____.

   (a) 8 cu in.
   (b) 10 cu in.
   (c) 12 cu in.
   (d) 14 cu in.

3. A metal box sized ____ can accommodate nine 12 AWG conductors.

   (a) 4 in. × 4 in. × 1¼ in.
   (b) 3¾ in. × 2 in. × 3 in.
   (c) 3¾ in.× 2 in.× 3½ in.
   (d) none of these

4. The number of 12 AWG THWN-2 conductors permitted in a 4 in. × 4 in.× 1½ in. box is ____.

   (a) 7
   (b) 9
   (c) 11
   (d) 13

5. The total volume occupied by two internal cable clamps, six 12 AWG conductors, and a single-pole switch is ____.

   (a) 2.00 cu in.
   (b) 4.50 cu in.
   (c) 14.50 cu in.
   (d) 20.25 cu in.

6. When counting the number of conductors in a box, a conductor running through the box with an unbroken loop or coil not less than twice the minimum length required for free conductors shall be counted as ____ double volume(s) allowance.

   (a) one
   (b) two
   (c) three
   (d) four

7. Equipment grounding conductor(s), and not more than ____ fixture wire(s) smaller than 14 AWG is(are) permitted to be omitted from the calculations where they enter the box from a domed luminaire or similar canopy and terminate within that box.

   (a) one
   (b) two
   (c) three
   (d) four

8. Where one or more internal cable clamps are present in the box, a single volume allowance shall be made based on the ____ present in the box.

   (a) largest conductor
   (b) smallest conductor
   (c) average conductor size
   (d) number of devices

9. Where a luminaire stud or hickey is present in the box, ____ volume allowance shall be made for each type of fitting, based on the largest conductor present in the box.

   (a) a single
   (b) a double
   (c) a ¼
   (d) no additional

10. For the purposes of determining box fill, each device or utilization equipment in the box which is wider than a single device box counts as two volume allowances for each ____ required for the mounting.

    (a) in.
    (b) ft
    (c) gang
    (d) box

11. A device or utilization equipment wider than a single 2 in. device box shall have ____ volume allowance provided for each gang required for mounting.

    (a) a single
    (b) a double
    (c) a ¼
    (d) no additional

12. Where up to four equipment grounding conductors enter a box, _____ allowance in accordance with Table 314.16(B) shall be made based on the largest equipment grounding conductor entering the box.

    (a) a single
    (b) a double
    (c) a ¼ inch
    (d) no additional

13. Where nonmetallic sheath cables are used, the sheath shall extend not less than _____ inside the box and beyond any cable clamp.

    (a) ¼ in.
    (b) ⅜ in.
    (c) ½ in.
    (d) ¾ in.

14. In installations within noncombustible walls or ceilings, the front edge of a box, plaster ring, extension ring, or listed extender employing a flush-type cover, shall be set back not more than ____ from the finished surface.

    (a) ⅛ in.
    (b) ¼ in.
    (c) ⅜ in.
    (d) ½ in.

15. In installations within walls or ceilings constructed of wood or other combustible surface material, boxes, plaster rings, extension rings, or listed extenders shall ____.

    (a) extend to the finished surface or project therefrom
    (b) not be permitted
    (c) be fire rated
    (d) be set back no more than ¼ in.

16. Noncombustible surfaces that are broken or incomplete around boxes employing a flush-type cover shall be repaired so there will be no gaps or open spaces larger than ____ at the edge of the box.

    (a) ¹⁄₁₆ in.
    (b) ⅛ in.
    (c) ¼ in.
    (d) ½ in.

17. Enclosures not over 100 cu in. having threaded entries and not containing a device shall be considered to be supported where ____ or more conduits are threaded wrenchtight into the enclosure and each conduit is secured within 3 ft of the enclosure.

    (a) one
    (b) two
    (c) three
    (d) four

18. Two intermediate metal or rigid metal conduits threaded wrenchtight into an enclosure can be used to support an outlet box containing devices or luminaires if each raceway is supported within ____ of the box.

    (a) 12 in.
    (b) 18 in.
    (c) 24 in.
    (d) 36 in.

19. Boxes used at luminaire outlets on a vertical surface shall be marked on the interior of the box to indicate the maximum weight of the luminaire that is permitted to be supported by the box if other than ____.

    (a) 6 lb
    (b) 12 lb
    (c) 35 lb
    (d) 50 lb

20. A vertically mounted luminaire weighing not more than ____ can be supported to a device box or plaster ring with at least two No. 6 or larger screws.

    (a) 4 lb
    (b) 6 lb
    (c) 8 lb
    (d) 10 lb

21. Boxes used at luminaire or lampholder outlets in a ceiling shall be designed so that a luminaire or lampholder can be attached and the boxes shall be required to support a luminaire weighing a minimum of ____.

    (a) 20 lb
    (b) 30 lb
    (c) 40 lb
    (d) 50 lb

22. A luminaire that weighs more than ____ can be supported by an outlet box that is listed for the weight of the luminaire.
    (a) 20 lb
    (b) 30 lb
    (c) 40 lb
    (d) 50 lb

23. Listed outlet boxes to support ceiling-suspended fans that weigh more than ____ shall have the maximum allowable weight marked on the box.
    (a) 35 lb
    (b) 50 lb
    (c) 60 lb
    (d) 70 lb

24. Outlet boxes mounted in the ceilings of habitable rooms ____, in a location acceptable for the future installation of a ceiling-suspended (paddle) fan, shall be listed for the support of ceiling-suspended paddle fans.
    (a) used for childcare
    (b) of guest suites
    (c) of dwelling occupancies
    (d) of apartments

25. In straight pulls of 2-in. raceways, the length of the pull box shall be a minimum of ____ the trade diameter of the 2-in. raceway.
    (a) 2 times
    (b) 4 times
    (c) 5 times
    (d) 8 times

26. The minimum distance from the raceway entry to the opposite wall of a pull or junction box for a U pull with two 3-in. raceways is ____.
    (a) 16 in.
    (b) 15 in.
    (c) 18 in.
    (d) 21 in.

27. Where splices, angle, or U pulls are made, the distance between each raceway entry inside the box and the opposite wall of the box may not be less than ____ the trade size of the largest raceway.
    (a) six times
    (b) eight times
    (c) ten times
    (d) twelve times

28. The minimum depth required for a pull box in a wet location that has a 3½ in. raceway with three 400 kcmil XHHW compact aluminum conductors entering the wall opposite a removable cover is ____.
    (a) 5 in.
    (b) 7 in.
    (c) 9 in.
    (d) 11 in.

29. Where a raceway or cable entry is in the wall of a box or conduit body opposite a removable cover, the distance from that wall to the cover shall be permitted to comply with the distance required for ____ wire(s) per terminal in accordance with Table 312.6(A).
    (a) one
    (b) two
    (c) three
    (d) four

30. Pull boxes or junction boxes with any dimension over ____ shall have all conductors cabled or racked in an approved manner.
    (a) 3 ft
    (b) 6 ft
    (c) 9 ft
    (d) 12 ft

31. Handhole enclosures shall be designed and installed to withstand ____.
    (a) 600 lb of pressure
    (b) 3,000 lb of pressure
    (c) 6,000 lb of pressure
    (d) all loads likely to be imposed on them

32. Handhole enclosure covers shall have an identifying mark or logo that prominently identifies the function of the enclosure, such as ____.
    (a) danger
    (b) utility
    (c) high voltage
    (d) electric

33. Handhole enclosure covers shall require the use of tools to open, or they shall weigh over ____.
    (a) 45 lb
    (b) 70 lb
    (c) 100 lb
    (d) 200 lb

Article 320—Armored Cable (AC)

1. AC cable is permitted in ____.

   (a) wet locations
   (b) corrosive conditions
   (c) damp locations
   (d) cable trays

2. Exposed runs of MC cable, except as provided in 300.11(B), shall closely follow the _____ of the building finish or of running boards.

   (a) surface
   (b) exterior
   (c) inside
   (d) outside

3. Where AC cable is run across the top of a framing member(s) in an attic space not accessible by permanently installed stairs or ladders, guard strip protection shall only be required within ____ of the scuttle hole or attic entrance.

   (a) 3 ft
   (b) 4 ft
   (c) 5 ft
   (d) 6 ft

4. AC cable shall be supported and/or secured by ____.

   (a) staples or straps
   (b) cable ties listed and identified for securement and support
   (c) AC cable fittings
   (d) any of these

5. AC cable shall be secured at intervals not exceeding 4½ ft and within ____ of every outlet box, cabinet, conduit body, or fitting.

   (a) 6 in.
   (b) 8 in.
   (c) 10 in.
   (d) 12 in.

6. Horizontal runs of AC cable installed in wooden or metal framing members or similar supporting means shall be considered supported and secured where such support does not exceed ____ intervals.

   (a) 2-ft
   (b) 3-ft
   (c) 4½-ft
   (d) 6-ft

7. AC cable shall provide an adequate path for ____ to act as an equipment grounding conductor.

   (a) fault current
   (b) short-circuit current
   (c) overcurrent
   (d) arcing current

Article 330—Metal-Clad Cable (MC)

1. Article ____ covers the use, installation, and construction specifications of metal-clad cable, MC.

   (a) 300
   (b) 310
   (c) 320
   (d) 330

2. MC cable containing four or fewer conductors, sized no larger than 10 AWG, shall be secured within ____ of every box, cabinet, fitting, or other cable termination.

   (a) 8 in.
   (b) 12 in.
   (c) 18 in.
   (d) 24 in.

Article 334—Nonmetallic-Sheathed Cable (NM)

1. NM and NMC cables are permitted in ____, except as prohibited in 334.12.

   (a) one- and two-family dwellings and their attached/detached garages and storage buildings
   (b) multifamily dwellings and their detached garages permitted to be of Types III, IV, and V construction
   (c) other structures permitted to be of Types III, IV, and V construction
   (d) any of these

2. NM cable can be installed in multifamily dwellings and their detached garages permitted to be of Type(s) ____ construction.

   (a) III
   (b) IV
   (c) V
   (d) all of these

3. NM cable shall be protected from physical damage by ____.
   (a) EMT
   (b) Schedule 80 PVC conduit
   (c) RMC
   (d) any of these

4. Where conduit or tubing is used for the protection from physical damage of NM cable, it shall be provided with a bushing or adapter that provides protection from abrasion at the point the cable ____ the raceway.
   (a) enters and exits
   (b) leaves and comes into
   (c) begins and ends
   (d) none of these

5. Where NM cable is run at angles with joists in unfinished basements and crawl spaces, it is permissible to secure cables not smaller than ____ conductors directly to the lower edges of the joist.
   (a) three, 6 AWG
   (b) four, 8 AWG
   (c) four, 10 AWG
   (d) two 6 AWG or three 8 AWG

6. NM cable on a wall of an unfinished basement installed in a listed raceway shall have a ____ installed at the point where the cable enters the raceway.
   (a) suitable insulating bushing or adapter
   (b) sealing fitting
   (c) bonding bushing
   (d) junction box

7. When NM cable is run across the top of a floor joist in an attic without permanent ladders or stairs, guard strips within ____ of the scuttle hole or attic entrance shall protect the cable.
   (a) 3 ft
   (b) 4 ft
   (c) 5 ft
   (d) 6 ft

8. The radius of the curve of the inner edge of any bend during or after installation of NM cable shall not be less than ____ the diameter of the cable or the major diameter dimension of the cable for flat cables.
   (a) 5 times
   (b) 6 times
   (c) 7 times
   (d) 8 times

9. Nonmetallic-sheathed cable shall be permitted to be unsupported where the cable is ____.
   (a) fished between access points through concealed spaces in finished buildings or structures
   (b) not more than 6 ft from the last point of cable support to the point of connection to a luminaire within an accessible ceiling in one-, two-, or multifamily dwellings
   (c) between framing members and exterior masonry walls
   (d) where installed in attics

Article 336—Power and Control Tray Cable (TC)

1. TC cable can be used ____.
   (a) for power, lighting, control, and signal circuits
   (b) in cable trays including those with mechanically discontinuous segments up to 1 ft
   (c) for Class 1 control circuits as permitted in Parts II and III of Article 725
   (d) all of these

2. Which of following statements about power and control tray cable is incorrect?
   (a) It may be used in a raceway.
   (b) It may be used for power, lighting, or control circuits.
   (c) It may be installed where it will be exposed to physical damage.
   (d) It may be used in cable trays in hazardous locations where the conditions of maintenance and supervision ensure that only qualified persons will service the installation.

3. TC cable shall not be used where ____.
   (a) it will be exposed to physical damage
   (b) installed outside of a raceway or cable tray system, unless permitted in 336.10(4), 336.10(7), 336.10(9), and 336.10(10)
   (c) exposed to direct rays of the sun, unless identified as sunlight resistant
   (d) all of these

4. Bends in TC cable shall be made so as not to damage the cable. For TC Cable larger than 1 in. and up to 2 in. in diameter, without metal shielding, the minimum bending radius shall be at least ____ times the overall diameter of the cable.
   (a) 2 times
   (b) 3 times
   (c) 5 times
   (d) 7 times

Article 338—Service-Entrance Cable (Types SE and USE)

1. USE cable is not permitted for ____ wiring.
   (a) underground
   (b) interior
   (c) aerial
   (d) aboveground installations

Article 340—Underground Feeder and Branch-Circuit Cable (UF)

1. A permitted wiring method for use in underground installations is ____.
   (a) SE cable
   (b) UF cable
   (c) THHN in PVC conduit
   (d) NM in a raceway

2. UF cable is permitted to be installed as single-conductor cables, when all conductors of the feeder or branch circuit, including the grounded conductor and equipment grounding conductor, if any, are ____.
   (a) run in the same trench
   (b) within a nonmetallic raceway
   (c) within a metallic raceway
   (d) none of these

Article 342—Intermediate Metal Conduit (IMC)

1. Where intermediate metal conduit is threaded in the field, a standard cutting die with a taper of ____ per ft shall be used.
   (a) ½ in.
   (b) ¾ in.
   (c) 1 in.
   (d) 1½ in.

Article 344—Rigid Metal Conduit (RMC)

1. RMC conduit shall be permitted to be installed where subject to ____ physical damage.
   (a) severe
   (b) minor
   (c) minimal
   (d) massive

2. RMC smaller than trade size ____ or larger than trade size ____ shall not be used.
   (a) ¾, 4
   (b) ½, 4
   (c) ½, 6
   (d) ¾, 6

3. Cut ends of RMC shall be ____ or otherwise finished to remove rough edges.
   (a) threaded
   (b) reamed
   (c) painted
   (d) galvanized

4. RMC shall be securely fastened within ____ of each outlet box, junction box, device box, cabinet, conduit body, or other conduit termination.
   (a) 3 ft
   (b) 4 ft
   (c) 5 ft
   (d) 6 ft

5. Where framing members do not readily permit fastening, RMC may be fastened within ____ of each outlet box, junction box, device box, cabinet, conduit body, or other conduit termination.
   (a) 3 ft
   (b) 4 ft
   (c) 5 ft
   (d) 8 ft

6. Where approved, RMC shall not be required to be securely fastened within ____ of the service head for above-the-roof termination of a mast.

   (a) 1 ft
   (b) 2 ft
   (c) 3 ft
   (d) 5 ft

7. Trade size 2 RMC run straight with threaded couplings shall be supported at intervals not exceeding ____.

   (a) 10 ft
   (b) 12 ft
   (c) 14 ft
   (d) 16 ft

8. The maximum distance between supports for a vertical installation of trade size 2 RMC is ____.

   (a) 16 ft
   (b) 10 ft
   (c) 20 ft
   (d) 18 ft

9. Running threads shall not be used on RMC for connection at ____.

   (a) boxes
   (b) cabinets
   (c) couplings
   (d) meter sockets

Article 348—Flexible Metal Conduit (FMC)

1. Flexible metal conduit shall be supported at intervals not exceeding ____.

   (a) 1 ft
   (b) 3 ft
   (c) 4½ ft
   (d) 6 ft

2. Cable ties used to securely fasten flexible metal conduit shall be ____ for securement and support.

   (a) approved
   (b) labeled
   (c) listed
   (d) listed and identified

Article 350—Liquidtight Flexible Metal Conduit (LFMC)

1. The minimum size liquid tight flexible metal conduit is ____.

   (a) trade size ⅜
   (b) trade size ½
   (c) trade size ¾
   (d) trade size 1

Article 352—Rigid Polyvinyl Chloride Conduit (PVC)

1. PVC conduit shall be permitted to be ____.

   (a) encased in concrete
   (b) used for the support of luminaires
   (c) installed in movie theaters
   (d) none of these

2. PVC conduit is permitted in locations subject to severe corrosive influences and where subject to chemicals for which the materials are specifically ____.

   (a) approved
   (b) identified
   (c) listed
   (d) non-hazardous

3. PVC smaller than trade size ____ or larger than trade size ____ shall not be used.

   (a) ½, 4
   (b) ¾, 4
   (c) ½, 6
   (d) ¾, 6

4. PVC conduit shall be securely fastened within ____ of each box.

   (a) ½ ft
   (b) 1 ft
   (c) 2 ft
   (d) 3 ft

5. PVC conduit trade sizes 1¼ to 2 shall be supported no greater than ____ between supports.

   (a) 3 ft
   (b) 4 ft
   (c) 5 ft
   (d) 6 ft

6. Expansion fittings for PVC conduit shall be provided to compensate for thermal expansion and contraction where the length change, in accordance with Table 352.44(A), is expected to be ____ or greater in a straight run between securely mounted items such as boxes, cabinets, elbows, or other conduit terminations.

   (a) 1/16 in.
   (b) 1/8 in.
   (c) 1/4 in.
   (d) 1/2 in.

7. Expansion fittings for underground runs of direct buried PVC conduit emerging from the ground shall be provided above grade when required to compensate for ____.

   (a) earth settling
   (b) earth movement
   (c) frost heave
   (d) all of these

Article 358—Electrical Metallic Tubing (EMT)

1. EMT smaller than trade size ____ or larger than trade size ____ shall not be used.

   (a) 3/4, 4
   (b) 1/2, 4
   (c) 1/2, 6
   (d) 3/4, 6

2. EMT shall be securely fastened in place at intervals not to exceed ____.

   (a) 4 ft
   (b) 5 ft
   (c) 8 ft
   (d) 10 ft

3. EMT run between termination points shall be securely fastened within ____ of each outlet box, junction box, device box, cabinet, conduit body, or other tubing termination.

   (a) 12 in.
   (b) 18 in.
   (c) 2 ft
   (d) 3 ft

Article 362—Electrical Nonmetallic Tubing (ENT)

1. Cut ends of ENT shall be trimmed inside and ____ to remove rough edges.

   (a) outside
   (b) tapered
   (c) filed
   (d) beveled

2. ENT shall be installed as a ____ system in accordance with 300.18 and shall be securely ____ by an approved means and supported in accordance with 362.30(A) and (B).

   (a) complete
   (b) underground
   (c) overhead
   (d) none of these

3. Cable ties used to securely fasten ENT shall be ____ for the application and for securing and supporting.

   (a) identified
   (b) labeled
   (c) listed
   (d) identified and listed

4. Electrical nonmetallic tubing may extend a maximum of ____ from a fixture terminal connection without support for tap connections to lighting fixtures.

   (a) 3 ft
   (b) 5 ft
   (c) 6 ft
   (d) 8 ft

5. Joints between lengths of ENT, couplings, fittings, and boxes shall be made by ____.

   (a) a qualified person
   (b) set screw fittings
   (c) an approved method
   (d) exothermic welding

Article 376—Metal Wireways

1. Metal wireways shall not be permitted for ____.

   (a) exposed work
   (b) hazardous (classified) locations
   (c) wet locations
   (d) severe corrosive environments

2. For metal wireways, where single conductor cables comprising each phase, neutral, or grounded conductor of an alternating-current circuit are connected in parallel, the conductors shall be installed in groups consisting of not more than ____ per phase, neutral, or grounded conductor.

   (a) one conductor
   (b) two conductors
   (c) three conductors
   (d) four conductors

3. The purpose of having all parallel conductor sets installed in metal wireways within the same group, is to prevent ____ imbalance in the paralleled conductors due to inductive reactance.

   (a) current
   (b) voltage
   (c) inductive
   (d) all of these

4. The sum of the cross-sectional areas of all conductors at any cross section of a metal wireway shall not exceed ____ of the interior cross-sectional area of the wireway.

   (a) 50 percent
   (b) 20 percent
   (c) 25 percent
   (d) 80 percent

5. The ampacity adjustment factors in 310.15(C)(1) shall be applied to a metal wireway only where the number of current-carrying conductors in any cross section of the wireway exceeds ____.

   (a) 30
   (b) 40
   (c) 50
   (d) 60

6. Splices and taps are permitted within metal wireways provided they are accessible and shall not fill the wireway to more than ____ of its area at that point.

   (a) 35 percent
   (b) 40 percent
   (c) 55 percent
   (d) 75 percent

Article 386—Surface Metal Raceways

1. Splices and taps in surface metal raceways without removable covers shall be made only in ____.

   (a) boxes
   (b) raceways
   (c) conduit bodies
   (d) none of these

2. Surface metal raceway enclosures providing a transition from other wiring methods shall have a means for connecting a(an) ____ conductor.

   (a) grounded
   (b) ungrounded
   (c) equipment grounding
   (d) all of these

Article 392—Cable Trays

1. Cable trays can be used as a support system for ____.

   (a) service conductors, feeders, and branch circuits
   (b) communications circuits
   (c) control and signaling circuits
   (d) all of these

2. Single conductor cables and single insulated conductors used in cable trays shall be marked on the surface for use in cable trays and shall be no smaller than ____.

   (a) 1 AWG
   (b) 1/0 AWG
   (c) 2/0 AWG
   (d) 4/0 AWG

3. Cable tray systems shall not be used ____.

   (a) in hoistways
   (b) where subject to severe physical damage
   (c) in hazardous (classified) locations
   (d) in hoistways or where subject to severe physical damage

4. Cable tray systems shall be permitted to have mechanically discontinuous ____ between cable tray runs or between cable tray runs and equipment.

   (a) portions
   (b) segments
   (c) pieces
   (d) any of these

5. Each run of cable tray shall be ____ before the installation of cables.

    (a) tested for 25 ohms of resistance
    (b) insulated
    (c) completed
    (d) all of these

6. Cable trays shall be ____ except as permitted by 392.18(D).

    (a) exposed
    (b) accessible
    (c) readily accessible
    (d) exposed and accessible

7. Cable trays shall be supported at ____ in accordance with the installation instructions.

    (a) intervals
    (b) portions
    (c) segments
    (d) any of these

8. A box is not required where conductors or cables in cable tray transition to a raceway wiring method from a ____.

    (a) cable tray
    (b) enclosure
    (c) outlet box
    (d) conduit body

9. Cable ____ made and insulated by approved methods can be located within a cable tray provided they are accessible and do not project above the side rails where the splices may be subject to physical damage.

    (a) connections
    (b) jumpers
    (c) splices
    (d) conductors

10. Metal cable trays containing only nonpower conductors (such as communications, data, and signaling conductors and cables) shall be electrically continuous through approved connections or the use of a(an) ____.

    (a) grounding electrode conductor
    (b) bonding jumper
    (c) equipment grounding conductor
    (d) none of these

11. Steel or aluminum cable tray systems are permitted to be used as an equipment grounding conductor, provided the cable tray sections and fittings are identified as ____, among other requirements.

    (a) an equipment grounding conductor
    (b) special equipment
    (c) industrial grade
    (d) all of these

CHAPTER 4

REVIEW QUESTIONS

Please use the 2023 *Code* book to answer the following questions.

CHAPTER 4—EQUIPMENT FOR GENERAL USE

Article 400—Flexible Cords

1. Article _____ covers general requirements, applications, and construction specifications for flexible cords and flexible cables.
   - (a) 300
   - (b) 310
   - (c) 400
   - (d) 402

2. Flexible cords and flexible cables can be used for _____.
   - (a) wiring of luminaires
   - (b) portable and mobile signs or appliances
   - (c) connection of utilization equipment to facilitate frequent interchange
   - (d) all of these

3. Flexible cord sets and power-supply cords shall not be used as a substitute for _____ wiring of a structure.
   - (a) temporary
   - (b) fixed
   - (c) concealed
   - (d) permanent

4. Flexible cord sets and power-supply cords shall not be used where they are _____.
   - (a) run through holes in walls, ceilings, or floors
   - (b) run through doorways, windows, or similar openings
   - (c) used as a substitute for the fixed wiring of a structure
   - (d) all of these

5. Flexible cords, flexible cables, cord sets (extension cords), and power-supply cords are not permitted to be concealed by walls, floors, or ceilings, or above suspended or dropped ceilings.
   - (a) ceilings
   - (b) suspended or dropped ceilings
   - (c) floors or walls
   - (d) all of these

6. Unless specifically permitted in 400.10, flexible cords, flexible cables, cord sets, and power-supply cords shall not be used where subject to _____ damage.
   - (a) physical
   - (b) severe
   - (c) harsh
   - (d) minor

7. Flexible cords shall be protected by _____ where passing through holes in covers, outlet boxes, or similar enclosures.
   - (a) sleeves
   - (b) grommets
   - (c) raceways
   - (d) bushing or fittings

Article 402—Fixture Wires

1. Thermoplastic covered flexible stranded fixture wire TFF has an operating temperature of _____.
   - (a) 140°F
   - (b) 167°F
   - (c) 194°F
   - (d) 302°F

2. Thermoplastic covered fixture wire TF has an operating temperature of ____.

    (a) 140°F
    (b) 167°F
    (c) 194°F
    (d) 302°F

3. The ampacity of 18 AWG fixture wire is ____.

    (a) 6A
    (b) 8A
    (c) 10A
    (d) 14A

4. The ampacity of 14 AWG fixture wire is ____.

    (a) 6A
    (b) 8A
    (c) 10A
    (d) 17A

5. The ampacity of 12 AWG fixture wire is ____.

    (a) 6A
    (b) 8A
    (c) 10A
    (d) 23A

6. The smallest size fixture wire permitted by the *NEC* is ____.

    (a) 18 AWG
    (b) 16 AWG
    (c) 14 AWG
    (d) 12 AWG

Article 404 —Switches

1. The grounded circuit conductor for the controlled lighting circuit shall be installed at the location where switches control lighting loads that are supplied by a grounded general-purpose branch circuit serving ____.

    (a) habitable rooms or occupiable spaces
    (b) attics
    (c) crawlspaces
    (d) basements

2. All switches and circuit breakers used as switches shall be located so that they can be operated from a readily ____ place.

    (a) accessible
    (b) visible
    (c) operable
    (d) open

3. In general, switches and circuit breakers used as switches, shall be installed such that the center of the grip of the operating handle of the switch or circuit breaker, when in its highest position, is not more than ____ above the floor or working platform.

    (a) 5 ft 6 in.
    (b) 6 ft 7 in.
    (c) 7 ft 6 in.
    (d) 10 ft

4. Snap switches shall not be grouped or ganged in enclosures unless the voltage between adjacent devices does not exceed ____, or unless installed with identified barriers between adjacent devices.

    (a) 100V
    (b) 200V
    (c) 300V
    (d) 400V

5. Metal faceplates for snap switches, including dimmer and similar control switches, shall be connected ____ whether or not a metal faceplate is installed.

    (a) to the grounded electrode
    (b) to the equipment grounding conductor
    (c) to the grounded conductor
    (d) to the ungrounded conductor

6. Alternating-current general-use snap switches shall only be used on ac circuits and may be used for controlling motor loads not exceeding ____ of the ampere rating of the switch at its rated voltage.

    (a) 70 percent
    (b) 80 percent
    (c) 110 percent
    (d) 125 percent

7. Snap switches directly connected to aluminum conductors and rated ____ or less shall be marked CO/ALR.

(a) 15A
(b) 20A
(c) 30A
(d) 50A

Article 406—Receptacles, Attachment Plugs, and Flanged Inlets

1. Receptacles rated 20A or less and designed for the direct connection of aluminum conductors shall be marked ____.

(a) AL
(b) AL/CU
(c) CU
(d) CO/ALR

2. Receptacles incorporating an isolated grounding conductor connection intended for the reduction of electromagnetic interference shall be identified by ____ located on the face of the receptacle.

(a) the letters IG
(b) a green circle
(c) a green square
(d) an orange triangle

3. 15A and 20A receptacles that are controlled by an automatic control device for the purpose of energy management or building automation shall be permanently marked with the word ____.

(a) power
(b) controlled
(c) energy management
(d) any of these

4. When nongrounding-type receptacles are replaced by GFCI-type receptacles where attachment to an equipment grounding conductor does not exist in the receptacle enclosure, ____ shall be marked No Equipment Ground.

(a) the receptacle
(b) the protective device
(c) the branch circuit
(d) these receptacles or their cover plates

5. Weather-resistant receptacles ____ where replacements are made at receptacle outlets that are required to be so protected elsewhere in the *Code*.

(a) shall be provided
(b) are not required
(c) are optional
(d) are not allowed

6. Automatically controlled receptacles shall be replaced with ____ controlled receptacles.

(a) listed
(b) suitably
(c) equivalently
(d) identified

7. Receptacles mounted to and supported by a cover shall be secured by more than ____ screw(s) unless listed and identified for securing by a single screw.

(a) one
(b) two
(c) three
(d) four

8. After installation, receptacle faces shall be flush with or project from faceplates of insulating material and shall project a minimum of ____ from metal faceplates.

(a) 0.015 in.
(b) 0.020 in.
(c) 0.125 in.
(d) 0.250 in.

9. Receptacles shall not be grouped or ganged in enclosures unless the voltage between adjacent devices does not exceed ____.

(a) 100V
(b) 200V
(c) 300V
(d) 400V

10. An outdoor receptacle in a location protected from the weather shall be installed in an enclosure that is weatherproof when the receptacle is ____.

(a) covered
(b) enclosed
(c) protected
(d) recessed in the finished surface

11. A receptacle is considered to be in a location protected from the weather when located under roofed open porches, canopies, marquees, and the like, where it will not be subjected to ____.

    (a) spray from a hose
    (b) a direct lightning hit
    (c) beating rain or water runoff
    (d) falling or wind-blown debris

12. Where required for receptacles in damp or wet locations, ____ covers of outlet box hoods shall be able to open at least 90°, or fully open if the cover is not designed to open 90° from the closed to open position, after installation.

    (a) flush
    (b) hinged
    (c) surface mounted
    (d) any of these

13. Receptacles of ____, 125V and 250V installed in a wet location shall have an enclosure that is weatherproof whether or not the attachment plug cap is inserted.

    (a) 15A and 20A
    (b) 30A and less
    (c) up to 50A
    (d) up to 100A

14. Where 15A and 20A receptacles are installed in a wet location, the outlet box ____ shall be listed and identified as extra-duty use.

    (a) sleeve
    (b) hood
    (c) threaded entry
    (d) mounting

15. Where 15A and 20A receptacles are installed in a wet location, hinged covers of outlet box hoods shall be able to open at least ____, or fully open if the cover is not designed to open 90° from the closed to open position, after installation.

    (a) 90°
    (b) 120°
    (c) 180°
    (d) 360°

16. All 15A and 20A, 125V and 250V nonlocking-type receptacles shall be listed and so identified as the ____ type.

    (a) weatherproof
    (b) weather-resistant
    (c) raintight
    (d) waterproof

17. Receptacles shall not be installed within a zone measured ____ horizontally from any outside edge of the bathtub or shower stall, including the space outside the bathtub or shower stall space below the zone, and 8 ft vertically above the top of the bathtub rim or shower stall threshold.

    (a) 3 ft
    (b) 4 ft
    (c) 5 ft
    (d) 6 ft

18. All nonlocking type 125V and 250V, 15A and 20A receptacles installed in ____ shall be listed as tamper resistant.

    (a) dwelling units
    (b) boathouses
    (c) mobile homes
    (d) all of these

19. Where tamper-resistant receptacles are required, receptacles located more than ____ above the floor shall not be required to be tamper resistant.

    (a) 4 ft
    (b) 5 ft
    (c) 5½ ft
    (d) 6 ft 7 in.

20. Nonlocking-type 15A and 20A, 125V and 250V receptacles in a dwelling unit shall be listed as tamper resistant except ____.

    (a) receptacles located more than 8½ ft above the floor
    (b) receptacles that are part of an appliance
    (c) receptacles that are part of a luminaire
    (d) receptacles that are part of a luminaire or appliance

21. Nonlocking-type 125V and 250V, 15A and 20A receptacles installed in ____ shall be listed as tamper resistant.

    (a) guest rooms and guest suites of hotels and motels
    (b) childcare facilities
    (c) preschools and elementary education facilities
    (d) all of these

Article 408—Switchboards and Panelboards

1. Article 408 covers ____.

   (a) switchboards

   (b) switchgear

   (c) panelboards

   (d) all of these

2. Panelboards supplied by a three-phase, 4-wire, delta-connected system shall have the phase with the higher voltage-to-ground connected to the ____ phase.

   (a) A

   (b) B

   (c) C

   (d) any of these

3. A switchboard, switchgear, or panelboard containing a 4-wire, ____ system where the midpoint of one phase winding is grounded, shall be legibly and permanently field-marked to caution that one phase has a higher voltage-to-ground.

   (a) wye-connected

   (b) delta-connected

   (c) solidly grounded

   (d) ungrounded

4. Every panelboard circuit and circuit ____ shall be provided with a legible and permanent description.

   (a) location

   (b) installation

   (c) manufacturer

   (d) modification

5. Conduits and raceways, including end fittings, shall not rise more than ____ above the bottom of a switchboard enclosure.

   (a) 3 in.

   (b) 4 in.

   (c) 5 in.

   (d) 6 in.

6. For other than a totally enclosed switchboard, a space shall be provided between the top of the switchboard and any combustible ceiling that is not less than ____.

   (a) 3 ft

   (b) 6 ft

   (c) 6 ft 6 in.

   (d) 3 ft 6 in.

7. A panelboard shall be protected by an overcurrent device within the panelboard, or at any point on the ____ side of the panelboard.

   (a) load

   (b) supply

   (c) branch circuit

   (d) any of these

8. Where a panelboard is supplied through a transformer, the overcurrent protection shall be located ____.

   (a) at the main distribution panel

   (b) on the primary side of the transformer

   (c) on the secondary side of the transformer

   (d) on either the primary or secondary side of the transformer

Article 410—Luminaires

1. All luminaires, lampholders, and retrofit kits shall be ____.

   (a) listed

   (b) approved

   (c) labeled

   (d) listed or labeled

2. No parts of cord-connected luminaires, chain-, cable-, or cord-suspended luminaires, lighting track, pendants, or paddle fans with a light kit, shall be located within a zone measured 3 ft horizontally and ____ vertically from the top of the bathtub rim or shower stall threshold.

   (a) 4 ft

   (b) 6 ft

   (c) 8 ft

   (d) 12 ft

3. Luminaires located where subject to bathroom shower spray shall be marked suitable for ____ locations.

   (a) damp

   (b) wet

   (c) outdoor

   (d) wet or outdoor

4. Where luminaires are installed in a clothes closet, the clothes closet storage space shall be the volume bounded by the sides and back closet walls and planes extending from the closet floor vertically to a height of ____ or to the highest clothes' hanging rod.

    (a) 5½ ft
    (b) 6 ft
    (c) 6 ft 7 in.
    (d) 7 ft

5. A ____ type luminaire can be installed in a clothes closet storage space.

    (a) surface-mounted or recessed incandescent luminaire or LED luminaire with completely enclosed light source
    (b) surface-mounted or recessed fluorescent luminaire
    (c) surface-mounted fluorescent or LED luminaire identified as suitable for clothes closets
    (d) any of these

6. Incandescent luminaires with ____ enclosed lamps and pendant luminaires or lampholders shall not be permitted in clothes closet storage spaces.

    (a) open
    (b) partially
    (c) open or partially
    (d) any of these

7. Surface-mounted fluorescent or LED luminaires shall be permitted to be installed within the clothes closet storage space where ____ for this use.

    (a) identified
    (b) listed
    (c) approved
    (d) none of these

8. Surface-mounted fluorescent luminaires in clothes closet storage spaces are permitted on the wall above the door or on the ceiling, provided there is a minimum clearance of ____ from the storage space.

    (a) 3 in.
    (b) 6 in.
    (c) 8 in.
    (d) 12 in.

9. In clothes closet storage spaces, recessed incandescent or LED luminaires with a completely enclosed light source can be installed in the wall or the ceiling, provided there is a minimum clearance of ____ from the storage space.

    (a) 3 in.
    (b) 6 in.
    (c) 8 in.
    (d) 12 in.

10. A pole supporting luminaires shall have a handhole not less than ____ with a cover suitable for use in wet locations to provide access to the supply terminations within the pole or pole base.

    (a) 2 in. × 2 in.
    (b) 2 in. × 4 in.
    (c) 4 in. × 4 in.
    (d) 4 in. × 6 in.

11. Luminaires with exposed conductive ____ shall be connected to an equipment grounding conductor.

    (a) parts
    (b) surfaces
    (c) guards
    (d) any of these

12. Luminaires shall be ____ to an equipment grounding conductor.

    (a) securely connected
    (b) clamped
    (c) mechanically connected
    (d) none of these

13. Replacement luminaires are not required to be connected to an equipment grounding conductor if no equipment grounding conductor exists at the outlet box and the luminaire is ____.

    (a) more than 20 years old
    (b) mounted to the box using nonmetallic fittings and screws
    (c) mounted more than 6 ft above the floor
    (d) GFCI protected

14. An electric-discharge or LED luminaire can be cord connected provided the luminaire is located ____ the outlet, the cord is visible for its entire length except at terminations, and the cord is not subject to strain or physical damage.

    (a) within
    (b) directly below
    (c) directly above
    (d) adjacent to

15. Where recessed luminaires are installed, adjacent combustible materials shall not be subject to temperatures in excess of ____.
    (a) 60°C
    (b) 75°C
    (c) 90°C
    (d) 110°C

16. A recessed luminaire that is not identified for contact with insulation shall have all recessed parts spaced not less than ____ from combustible materials.
    (a) ½ in.
    (b) ⅝ in.
    (c) ¾ in.
    (d) 1 in.

17. Recessed luminaires that are identified to be in contact with insulation are designated ____.
    (a) Type BC
    (b) Type BI
    (c) Type CI
    (d) Type IC

18. Thermal insulation shall not be installed above a recessed luminaire or within ____ of the recessed luminaire's enclosure or wiring compartment unless the luminaire is identified as Type IC.
    (a) 1 in.
    (b) 1¼ in.
    (c) 1½ in.
    (d) 3 in.

Article 411—Low-Voltage Lighting

1. The output circuits of the power system for Low-Voltage lighting systems shall be rated for ____ maximum under all load conditions.
    (a) 15A
    (b) 20A
    (c) 25A
    (d) 30A

2. Low-voltage lighting system transformers shall be supplied from a maximum ____ branch circuit.
    (a) 15A
    (b) 20A
    (c) 25A
    (d) 30A

Article 422—Appliances

1. Appliances such as ____ rated 150V or less to ground and 60A or less shall be provided with GFCI protection.
    (a) tire inflation machines
    (b) vending machines
    (c) dishwashers
    (d) all of these

2. The GFCI device required for appliances shall be readily accessible, listed, and located ____.
    (a) within the branch-circuit overcurrent device
    (b) in a device or outlet within the supply circuit
    (c) in an integral part of the attachment plug
    (d) all of these

3. The ampacities of individual branch-circuit conductors for appliances shall not be less than the marked rating of the ____.
    (a) receptacle outlet
    (b) appliance
    (c) overcurrent protective device
    (d) power cord

4. If a branch circuit supplies a single nonmotor-operated appliance, the rating of overcurrent protection shall not exceed ____ if the overcurrent protection rating is not marked and the appliance is rated 13.30A or less.
    (a) 15A
    (b) 20A
    (c) 25A
    (d) 30A

5. If a branch circuit supplies a single nonmotor-operated appliance, the rating of overcurrent protection shall not exceed _____ of the appliance rated current if the overcurrent protection rating is not marked and the appliance is rated over 13.30A.

   (a) 100 percent
   (b) 125 percent
   (c) 150 percent
   (d) 160 percent

6. An appliance with central heating equipment, other than fixed electric space-heating equipment, shall be supplied by a(an) _____ branch circuit.

   (a) multiwire
   (b) individual
   (c) multipurpose
   (d) small-appliance

7. A waste disposer can be cord-and-plug-connected; the cord shall not be less than 18 in. or more than _____ in length.

   (a) 30 in.
   (b) 36 in.
   (c) 42 in.
   (d) 48 in.

8. Where a waste disposer is cord-and-plug-connected, the receptacles shall be _____ to protect against physical damage to the flexible cord.

   (a) located
   (b) shielded
   (c) guarded
   (d) any of these

9. The flexible cord for a(an) in-sink waste disposer shall have an equipment grounding conductor and terminate with a _____ attachment plug.

   (a) 3-wire
   (b) 4-wire
   (c) nongrounding-type
   (d) grounding-type

10. The length of the flexible cord for a trash compactor shall not be less than 3 ft or exceed _____ in length, measured from the face of the attachment plug to the plane of the rear of the appliance.

    (a) 2 ft
    (b) 4 ft
    (c) 6 ft
    (d) 8 ft

11. The length of the flexible cord for a built-in dishwasher shall not be less than 3 ft or exceed _____ in length, measured from the face of the attachment plug to the plane of the rear of the appliance.

    (a) 6½ ft
    (b) 7 ft
    (c) 7½ ft
    (d) 8 ft

12. Receptacles for built-in dishwashers and trash compactors shall be located so as to protect against physical damage to the _____.

    (a) flexible cord
    (b) cord cap
    (c) appliance
    (d) receptacle

13. Where a built-in trash compactor is to be cord-and-plug connected the receptacle shall be located _____ occupied by the appliance.

    (a) in the space
    (b) adjacent to the space
    (c) directly above the space
    (d) in the space or adjacent to the space

14. Where the flexible cord for a built-in trash compactor or dishwasher passes through an opening, it shall be protected against damage by a(an) _____.

    (a) bushing
    (b) grommet
    (c) approved means
    (d) any of these

15. For permanently connected appliances rated at not over ____ or ⅛ hp, the branch-circuit overcurrent device shall be permitted to serve as the disconnecting means where the switch or circuit breaker is within sight from the appliance or is capable of being locked in the open position.

    (a) 75 VA
    (b) 150 VA
    (c) 225 VA
    (d) 300 VA

16. For permanently connected appliances rated over ____, the branch-circuit switch or circuit breaker can serve as the disconnecting means where the switch or circuit breaker is within sight from the appliance or is capable of being locked in the open position.

    (a) 200 VA
    (b) 300 VA
    (c) 400 VA
    (d) 500 VA

17. For permanently connected motor-operated appliances with motors rated over ____, a switch or circuit breaker located within sight from the motor-operated appliance or capable of being locked in the open position can serve as the appliance disconnect.

    (a) ⅛ hp
    (b) ¼ hp
    (c) 15A
    (d) 1 kW

18. A furnace protected with a circuit breaker accessible to the user does not require a disconnect if provided with a ____.

    (a) unit switch
    (b) fusible disconnect
    (c) circuit breaker disconnect
    (d) pull out disconnect

Article 424—Fixed Electric Space-Heating Equipment

1. The branch-circuit conductor(s) ampacity shall not be less than ____ of the load of the fixed electric space-heating equipment and any associated motor(s).

    (a) 80 percent
    (b) 110 percent
    (c) 125 percent
    (d) 150 percent

2. Means shall be provided to simultaneously disconnect the ____ of all fixed electric space-heating equipment from all ungrounded conductors.

    (a) heater
    (b) motor controller(s)
    (c) supplementary overcurrent device(s)
    (d) all of these

3. GFCI protection must be provided for cables installed in electrically heated floors of ____.

    (a) bathrooms
    (b) hydromassage bathtub locations
    (c) kitchens
    (d) all of these

4. Duct heater controller equipment shall have a disconnecting means installed within ____ the controller except as allowed by 424.19(A).

    (a) 25 ft of
    (b) sight from
    (c) the side of
    (d) none of these

Article 430—Motor Circuits, Controllers, and Adjustable-Speed Drives

1. For general motor applications, separate motor overload protection shall be based on ____.

    (a) *NEC* Tables 430.248 and 430.250
    (b) the manufacturer's instructions
    (c) the motor disconnect current rating
    (d) the motor nameplate current rating

2. Branch-circuit conductors supplying a single continuous-duty motor shall have an ampacity not less than ____ rating.

    (a) 125 percent of the motor's nameplate current
    (b) 125 percent of the motor's full-load current
    (c) 125 percent of the motor's full locked-rotor
    (d) 80 percent of the motor's full-load current

3. Conductors supplying several motors shall have an ampacity not less than ____ of the full-load current rating of the highest rated motor, plus the sum of the full-load current ratings of all other motors in the group.

    (a) 80 percent
    (b) 100 percent
    (c) 125 percent
    (d) 150 percent

4. Overload devices are intended to protect motors, motor control apparatus, and motor branch-circuit conductors against ____.

    (a) excessive heating due to motor overloads
    (b) excessive heating due to failure to start
    (c) short circuits and ground faults
    (d) excessive heating due to motor overloads and excessive heating due to failure to start

5. Each motor used in a continuous-duty application and rated more than 1 hp shall be protected against overload. The overload device for motors with a marked temperature rise of 40°C or less shall be rated at no more than ____ of the motor nameplate full-load current rating.

    (a) 100 percent
    (b) 115 percent
    (c) 125 percent
    (d) 140 percent

6. A separate overload device used to protect continuous-duty motors rated more than 1 hp shall be selected to trip at no more than ____ of the motor nameplate full-load current rating if marked with a service factor of 1.15 or greater.

    (a) 100 percent
    (b) 115 percent
    (c) 125 percent
    (d) 140 percent

7. Short-circuit and ground-fault protection for a branch-circuit to which a motor or motor-operated appliance is connected shall be capable of carrying the ____ current of the motor.

    (a) ampacity
    (b) time delay
    (c) thermal protection
    (d) starting

8. Where the motor short-circuit and ground-fault protection devices determined by Table 430.52(C)(1) do not correspond to the standard sizes or ratings, a ____ rating that does not exceed the next ____ standard ampere rating is permitted.

    (a) higher
    (b) lower
    (c) smaller
    (d) larger

9. The maximum dual-element time-delay fuse branch-circuit protection for a single-phase motor is ____ of the appropriate full-load current rating found in Table 430.248.

    (a) 100 percent
    (b) 115 percent
    (c) 125 percent
    (d) 175 percent

10. The maximum rating or setting of an inverse time breaker used as the motor branch-circuit short-circuit and ground-fault protective device for a single-phase motor is ____ of the full-load current given in Table 430.248.

    (a) 100 percent
    (b) 115 percent
    (c) 125 percent
    (d) 250 percent

11. Motor branch-circuit short-circuit and ground-fault protection and motor overload protection ____ be combined in a single protective device where the rating of the device provides the required overload protection.

    (a) shall be permitted to
    (b) shall not be permitted to
    (c) shall be
    (d) shall not

12. A motor control circuit is tapped from the load side of the motor short-circuit protective device. The control circuit conductors are 14 AWG, the conductors require only short-circuit protection, and do not extend beyond the motor control equipment enclosure. The maximum overcurrent protection permitted for this motor control circuit is ____.

    (a) 15A
    (b) 20A
    (c) 50A
    (d) 100A

13. An 8 AWG motor control circuit conductor that extend beyond the motor control equipment enclosure shall have an overcurrent protective device sized not greater than _____ of the value specified in Table 310.16 for 60°C conductors.

    (a) 100 percent
    (b) 150 percent
    (c) 300 percent
    (d) 450 percent

14. The maximum rating of the overcurrent protective device for 14 AWG motor control wiring that extends beyond the enclosure is ____.

    (a) 15A
    (b) 20A
    (c) 45A
    (d) 100A

15. Motor controllers shall have horsepower ratings at the application voltage ____ the horsepower rating of the motor.

    (a) not lower than
    (b) not higher than
    (c) equal to
    (d) six times

16. A ____ rated in amperes is permitted as a controller for all motors.

    (a) branch-circuit inverse time circuit breaker or molded case switch
    (b) dual-element time-delay fuse
    (c) snap switch
    (d) GFCI-protected device

17. For stationary motors of 2 hp or less and 300V or less on ac circuits, the motor controller can be an ac-rated only general-use snap switch where the motor full-load current rating is not more than ____ of the rating of the switch.

    (a) 50 percent
    (b) 60 percent
    (c) 70 percent
    (d) 80 percent

18. An individual disconnecting means shall be provided for each motor controller and be located ____ from the controller location.

    (a) in sight
    (b) within 3 ft
    (c) within 10 ft
    (d) within 25 ft

19. A ____ shall be located in sight from the motor location and the driven machinery location.

    (a) controller
    (b) protective device
    (c) disconnecting means
    (d) all of these

20. A branch-circuit overcurrent device can serve as the disconnecting means for a stationary motor of ____ or less.

    (a) ⅛ hp
    (b) ¼ hp
    (c) ⅓ hp
    (d) ½ hp

21. A horsepower-rated ____ having a horsepower rating not less than the motor rating is permitted to serve as the disconnecting means.

    (a) attachment plug and receptacle
    (b) flanged surface inlet and cord connector
    (c) attachment plug and cord connector
    (d) any of these

22. The full-load current of a 115V, 1 hp ac motor is ____.

    (a) 12A
    (b) 14A
    (c) 16A
    (d) 20A

23. The full-load current of a 230V, 1.50 hp ac motor is ____.

    (a) 10A
    (b) 12A
    (c) 14A
    (d) 16A

24. The full-load current of a three-phase 208V, 2 hp motor is ____.

    (a) 7.50A
    (b) 12A
    (c) 14A
    (d) 16A

25. The full-load current of a three-phase 208V, 7.50 hp motor is ____.

    (a) 19A
    (b) 22A
    (c) 24.20A
    (d) 38A

26. The full-load current of a three-phase 230V, 10 hp motor is _____.

    (a) 19A
    (b) 22A
    (c) 28A
    (d) 38A

27. The full-load current of a three-phase 460V, 15 hp motor is _____.

    (a) 19A
    (b) 21A
    (c) 29A
    (d) 42A

Article 440—Air-Conditioning Equipment

1. An air-conditioning multi-motor equipment has a nameplate that indicates a minimum circuit ampacity of 30A and a maximum overcurrent protective device of 60A. The smallest THWN-2 conductors permitted are _____.

    (a) 14 AWG
    (b) 12 AWG
    (c) 10 AWG
    (d) 8 AWG

2. An air-conditioning multi-motor equipment nameplate shows that the minimum supply circuit ampacity as 24A and the maximum circuit breaker size as 40A. The smallest conductor contained in NM cable permitted for this circuit is _____.

    (a) 10/2 NM cable
    (b) 12/2 NM cable
    (c) 14/2 NM cable
    (d) 8/2 NM cable

3. The disconnecting means for air-conditioning and refrigerating equipment shall be readily accessible and _____ from the air-conditioning or refrigerating equipment.

    (a) visible
    (b) 10 ft
    (c) 20 ft
    (d) within sight

4. An individual motor-compressor protective device having a rating or setting not exceeding _____ of the motor-compressor rated-load current or branch-circuit selection current, whichever is greater, is permitted.

    (a) 115 percent
    (b) 125 percent
    (c) 175 percent
    (d) 225 percent

Article 445—Generators

1. Nameplates or manufacturer's instructions shall provide information as listed in 445.11(1) through (5) for all generators rated more than _____.

    (a) 12 kW
    (b) 15 kW
    (c) 18 kW
    (d) 20 kW

2. The ampacity of the conductors from the generator output terminals to the overcurrent protection shall not be less than _____ of the nameplate current rating of the generator.

    (a) 75 percent
    (b) 115 percent
    (c) 125 percent
    (d) 140 percent

3. Generators shall have the _____ conductor sized not smaller than required to carry the maximum unbalanced current as determined by 220.61.

    (a) neutral
    (b) grounding
    (c) bonding
    (d) none of these

Article 450—Transformers

1. The primary overcurrent protection for a transformer rated 1,000V, nominal, or less, with no secondary protection and having a primary current rating of _____ shall be set at not more than 125 percent or a higher rating that does not exceed the next higher standard rating shall be permitted.

    (a) 9A or more
    (b) less than 9A
    (c) 2A or more
    (d) less than 2A

2. Where no secondary overcurrent protection is used, a 480V, 50A transformer shall have an individual overcurrent device on the primary side rated at a maximum _____ of the rated primary current of the transformer.

    (a) 115 percent
    (b) 125 percent
    (c) 167 percent
    (d) 250 percent

3. Transformers with ventilating openings shall be installed so that the ventilating openings are _____.

    (a) a minimum 18 in. above the floor
    (b) not blocked by walls or obstructions
    (c) aesthetically located
    (d) vented to the exterior of the building

4. Transformer top surfaces that are horizontal and readily accessible shall be marked _____.

    (a) to warn of high surface temperature(s)
    (b) with the arc-flash boundary
    (c) to prohibit storage
    (d) all of these

5. Transformers, other than Class 2 or Class 3 transformers, shall have a disconnecting means located either in sight of the transformer or in a remote location. Where located in a remote location, the disconnecting means shall be lockable open in accordance with 110.25 and _____.

    (a) its location shall be field marked on the transformer
    (b) accessible only to qualified persons
    (c) placed in supervisory locations
    (d) none of these

CHAPTER 5

REVIEW QUESTIONS

Please use the 2023 *Code* book to answer the following questions.

CHAPTER 5—SPECIAL OCCUPANCIES

Article 500—Hazardous (Classified) Locations

1. Hazardous (classified) locations shall be classified depending on the properties of the _____ that could be present, and the likelihood that a flammable or combustible concentration or quantity is present.

   (a) flammable or combustible liquid-produced vapors
   (b) flammable gases
   (c) combustible dusts or fiber/flyings
   (d) all of these

2. In the layout of electrical installations for hazardous (classified) locations, it is frequently possible to locate much of the equipment in a reduced level of classification or in an _____ location to reduce the amount of special equipment required.

   (a) unclassified
   (b) classified
   (c) Class I
   (d) Class II

3. When determining a Class I, Division 2 location, the _____ is(are) a factor(s) that should be considered in determining the classification and extent of the location.

   (a) quantity of flammable material that might escape in case of an accident
   (b) adequacy of ventilating equipment
   (c) record of the industry or business with respect to explosions or fires
   (d) all of these

4. Class II locations are those that are hazardous because of the presence of _____.

   (a) combustible dust
   (b) easily ignitible fibers/flyings
   (c) flammable gases or vapors
   (d) flammable liquids or gases

5. Locations in which combustible dust is in the air under normal operating conditions in quantities sufficient to produce explosive or ignitible mixtures are classified as _____.

   (a) Class I, Division 2
   (b) Class II, Division 1
   (c) Class II, Division 2
   (d) Class III, Division 1

6. A Class II, Division 2 location is a location _____.

   (a) in which combustible dust due to abnormal operations may be present in the air in quantities sufficient to produce explosive or ignitible mixtures
   (b) where combustible dust accumulations are present but are normally insufficient to interfere with the normal operation of electrical equipment but could as a result of infrequent malfunctioning of handling or processing equipment become suspended in the air
   (c) in which combustible dust accumulations on, in, or in the vicinity of the electrical equipment could be sufficient to interfere with the safe dissipation of heat from electrical equipment
   (d) all of these

7. Class III locations are those that are hazardous (classified) because of the presence of ____.

   (a) combustible dust
   (b) combustible nonmetal fibers/flyings
   (c) flammable gases or vapors
   (d) flammable liquids or gases

8. Hazardous (classified) locations where ignitible fibers/flyings are handled, manufactured, or used shall be classified as ____.

   (a) Class I, Division 3
   (b) Class II, Division 2
   (c) Class III, Division 1
   (d) Class III, Division 2

9. Combustible fibers/flyings that may be found in a Class III, ____ hazardous location include flat platelet-shaped particulates, such as metal flakes, and fibrous board, such as particle board.

   (a) Division 1
   (b) Division 2
   (c) Division 3
   (d) Division 4

10. Ignitible fibers/flyings in Class III, Division 1 locations can include ____.

    (a) rayon
    (b) cotton
    (c) cocoa fiber
    (d) any of these

11. A Class III, Division ____ location is where ignitible fibers/flyings are stored or handled but not manufactured.

    (a) 1
    (b) 2
    (c) 3
    (d) all of these

12. Electrical and electronic equipment in hazardous (classified) locations shall be protected by a(an) ____ technique.

    (a) explosionproof
    (b) dust-ignitionproof
    (c) dusttight
    (d) any of these

13. Suitability of identified equipment for use in a hazardous (classified) location shall be determined by ____.

    (a) equipment listing or labeling
    (b) evidence of equipment evaluation from a qualified testing laboratory or inspection agency concerned with product evaluation
    (c) evidence acceptable to the authority having jurisdiction, such as a manufacturer's self-evaluation or an owner's engineering judgment
    (d) any of these

14. Threaded conduits or fittings installed in hazardous (classified) locations shall be made wrenchtight to ____.

    (a) prevent sparking when a fault current flows through the conduit system
    (b) prevent seepage of gases or fumes
    (c) prevent sag in the conduit runs
    (d) maintain a workmanship like installation

15. In Class I, Division 1 locations, threaded rigid metal conduit entries into explosionproof equipment shall be made up of ____.

    (a) at least five threads fully engaged
    (b) listed pressure fittings
    (c) four threads coated with listed epoxy
    (d) listed threaded bushings

Article 501—Class I Hazardous (Classified) Locations

1. In Class I, Division 1 locations, the use of threaded rigid metal conduit (RMC) or threaded intermediate metal conduit (IMC), shall be permitted, including RMC or IMC conduit systems with supplemental ____ protection coatings.

   (a) rust
   (b) corrosion
   (c) paint
   (d) none of these

2. Where PVC, RTRC, or HDPE is used in Class I, Division 1 underground locations, the concrete encasement shall be permitted to be omitted where RMC or IMC conduit is used for the last ____ of the underground run to emergence or to the point of connection to the aboveground raceway.

   (a) 12 in.
   (b) 18 in.
   (c) 24 in.
   (d) 30 in.

3. If ____ is necessary to minimize the transmission of vibration from equipment during operation or to allow for movement after installation during maintenance in a Class I, Division 1 location, flexible fittings listed for the location or flexible cord in accordance with 501.140, are permitted if terminated with cord connectors listed for the location.

    (a) flexibility
    (b) mobility
    (c) movement
    (d) none of these

4. Boxes and fittings must be ____ for Class I, Division 1 locations.

    (a) designed
    (b) labeled
    (c) marked
    (d) identified

5. In Class I hazardous locations, sealing compound shall be used in MI cable termination fittings to ____.

    (a) prevent the passage of gas or vapor
    (b) exclude moisture and other fluids from the cable insulation
    (c) limit a possible explosion
    (d) prevent the escape of powder

6. Seals are provided in conduit and cable systems to ____ and prevent the passage of flames from one portion of the electrical installation to another through the conduit.

    (a) minimize the passage of gas or vapor
    (b) exclude moisture and other fluids from the cable insulation
    (c) limit a possible explosion
    (d) prevent the escape of powder

7. In Class I, Division 1 locations, conduit seals shall be installed within ____ from the explosionproof enclosure or as required by the enclosure marking.

    (a) 12 in.
    (b) 18 in.
    (c) 20 in.
    (d) 24 in.

8. In Class I, Division 1 locations, seals shall not be required for conduit entering an enclosure if the switch, circuit breaker, fuse, relay, or resistor is ____.

    (a) enclosed within a chamber hermetically sealed against the entrance of gases or vapors
    (b) immersed in oil in accordance with 501.115(B)(1)(2) (c) enclosed within an enclosure, identified for the location, and marked Leads Factory Sealed, Factory Sealed, or Seal not Required, or equivalent
    (c) enclosed within an enclosure, identified for the location, and marked Leads Factory Sealed, Factory Sealed, or Seal not Required, or equivalent
    (d) any of these

9. Class I, Division 1 conduit seals shall be installed if a ____ or larger conduit enters any explosionproof enclosure with splices, terminals, or taps and without a make-and-break contact.

    (a) trade size 1
    (b) trade size 2
    (c) trade size 3
    (d) trade size 4

10. A conduit run between a conduit seal and the point at which the conduit leaves a Class I, Division 1 location shall contain no union, coupling, box, or other fitting except for a listed ____ reducer installed at the conduit seal.

    (a) explosionproof
    (b) fireproof
    (c) vaportight
    (d) dusttight

11. A sealing fitting is permitted to be installed within ____ of either side of the boundary where a conduit leaves a Class I, Division 1 location.

    (a) 5 ft
    (b) 6 ft
    (c) 8 ft
    (d) 10 ft

12. The minimum thickness of sealing compound in Class I locations shall not be less than the trade size of the conduit or sealing fitting and, in no case, shall the thickness of the compound be less than ____.

    (a) ⅛ in.
    (b) ¼ in.
    (c) ⅜ in.
    (d) ⅝ in.

13. Luminaires installed in Class I, Division 1 locations shall be identified as a complete assembly for the Class I, Division 1 location and shall be clearly marked to indicate the ____ for which it is identified.

    (a) maximum wattage of lamps
    (b) minimum conductor size
    (c) maximum overcurrent protection permitted
    (d) all of these

14. Luminaires installed in Class I, Division 1 locations shall be protected from physical damage by a suitable ____.

    (a) warning label
    (b) pendant
    (c) guard or by location
    (d) all of these

Article 502—Class II Hazardous (Classified) Locations

1. In Class II, Division 1 locations, the use of threaded rigid metal conduit (RMC) or threaded intermediate metal conduit (IMC) shall be permitted, including RMC or IMC conduit systems with supplemental ____ protection coatings.

    (a) rust
    (b) corrosion
    (c) paint
    (d) none of these

2. Luminaires for fixed lighting installed in Class II, Division 2 locations shall be protected from physical damage by a suitable ____.

    (a) warning label
    (b) pendant
    (c) guard or by location
    (d) all of these

Article 511—Commercial Repair and Storage Garages

1. In major repair garages where ventilation is not provided, any pit or depression below floor level shall be a Class I, ____ location.

    (a) Division 1
    (b) Division 2
    (c) Division 1 or Division 2
    (d) Division 1 and Division 2

2. For each floor area inside a minor repair garage where ventilation is not provided and Class I liquids or gaseous fuels are not transferred or dispensed, the entire area up to a level of ____ above the floor is considered to be a Class I, Division 2 location.

    (a) 6 in.
    (b) 12 in.
    (c) 18 in.
    (d) 24 in.

3. Any pit for which ventilation is not provided below a minor repair garage floor level is considered to be a Class I, ____ location.

    (a) Division 1
    (b) Division 2
    (c) Division 1 or Division 2
    (d) Division 1 and Division 2

4. Fixed electrical equipment installed in spaces above a hazardous (classified) location in a commercial garage shall be ____.

    (a) well ventilated
    (b) GFPE protected
    (c) GFCI protected
    (d) located above the level of any defined Class I location or identified for the location

5. Fixed lighting in a commercial garage located over lanes on which vehicles are commonly driven shall be located not less than ____ above floor level.

    (a) 10 ft
    (b) 12 ft
    (c) 14 ft
    (d) 16 ft

6. In commercial garages, GFCI protection for personnel shall be provided as required in ____.

    (a) 210.8(A)
    (b) 210.8(B)
    (c) 210.8(C)
    (d) 210.8(D)

Article 514—Motor Fuel Dispensing Facilities

1. In motor fuel dispensing facilities, locations where flammable liquids having a flash point ____, such as gasoline, will not be handled is permitted to be unclassified.
   - (a) above 100°F
   - (b) below 100°F
   - (c) below 86°F
   - (d) above 86°F

2. Wiring within dispenser enclosure and all electrical equipment integral with dispensing hose or nozzle of an overhead gasoline dispensing device at a motor fuel dispensing facility is classified as a ____ location.
   - (a) Class I, Division 1
   - (b) Class I, Division 2
   - (c) Class II, Division 1
   - (d) Class II, Division 2

3. Underground wiring to motor fuel dispensers shall be installed in ____.
   - (a) threaded rigid metal conduit
   - (b) threaded steel IMC
   - (c) PVC conduit, RTRC conduit, and HDPE conduit when buried under not less than 2 ft of cover
   - (d) any of these

4. A listed seal for motor fuel dispensers shall be provided in each conduit run ____.
   - (a) adjacent to a dispenser
   - (b) within 36 in. of a dispenser
   - (c) inside the dispenser equipment
   - (d) entering or leaving a dispenser

5. Fuel dispensing systems shall be provided with one or more clearly identified emergency shutoff devices or electrical disconnects. Such devices or disconnects shall be installed in approved locations but not less than 20 ft or more than ____ from the fuel dispensing devices that they serve.
   - (a) 20 ft
   - (b) 40 ft
   - (c) 50 ft
   - (d) 100 ft

Article 517—Health Care Facilities

1. Wiring methods in healthcare facilities shall comply with Chapters 1 through 4 of the *NEC* except as modified in Article ____.
   - (a) 511
   - (b) 516
   - (c) 517
   - (d) 518

2. In patient care spaces, metal faceplates shall be connected to an effective ground-fault current path by means of ____ securing the faceplate to a metal yoke or strap of a receptacle or to a metal outlet box.
   - (a) ground clips
   - (b) rivets
   - (c) metal mounting screws
   - (d) spot welds

3. In Category 2 spaces, each patient bed location of health care facilities shall be provided with a minimum of ____ receptacles.
   - (a) two
   - (b) four
   - (c) six
   - (d) eight

Article 518—Assembly Occupancies

1. In assembly occupancies, NM cable, ENT, and PVC conduit can be installed in those portions of the building not required to be of ____ construction by the applicable building code.
   - (a) Class I, Division 1
   - (b) fire-rated
   - (c) occupancy-rated
   - (d) aboveground

Article 525—Carnivals, Circuses, Fairs, and Similar Events

1. Overhead wiring outside of tents and concession areas of carnivals and circuses which are accessible to pedestrians shall maintain a ____ clearance in accordance with 225.18.
   - (a) maximum
   - (b) minimum
   - (c) horizontal
   - (d) vertical

Article 555—Marinas, Boatyards, and Docking Facilities

1. In land areas not subject to tidal fluctuation, the electrical datum plane shall be a horizontal plane that is _____ above the highest water level for the area occurring under normal circumstances.

    (a) 1 ft
    (b) 1½ ft
    (c) 2 ft
    (d) 2½ ft

2. Service equipment for a floating building, dock, or marina shall be located on land no closer than _____ horizontally from, and adjacent to, the structure served.

    (a) 3 ft
    (b) 5 ft
    (c) 8 ft
    (d) 10 ft

3. Receptacles that provide shore power for boats in marinas and docking facilities shall be rated not less than _____.

    (a) 15A
    (b) 20A
    (c) 30A
    (d) 60A

Article 590—Temporary Installations

1. Temporary electric power and lighting installations shall be permitted for a period not to exceed 90 days for _____ decorative lighting and similar purposes.

    (a) Christmas
    (b) New Year's
    (c) July 4th
    (d) holiday

2. Type(s) _____ cable(s) can be used for temporary branch-circuit installations in any dwelling, building, or structure without any height limitation or limitation by building construction type and without concealment within walls, floors, or ceilings.

    (a) NM
    (b) NMC
    (c) SE
    (d) any of these

3. Type(s) _____ cable(s) shall be permitted to be installed in a branch-circuit raceway in a temporary underground installation.

    (a) NM
    (b) NMC
    (c) SE
    (d) any of these

4. All lamps for general illumination at temporary installations shall be protected from accidental contact or breakage by a suitable luminaire or lampholder with a(an) _____.

    (a) box
    (b) cable
    (c) enclosure
    (d) guard

5. A(An) _____ with a cover installed shall be required for all splices at temporary installations.

    (a) box
    (b) conduit body
    (c) enclosure
    (d) any of these

6. For temporary installations on construction sites, a box, conduit body, or other enclosure shall not be required if the circuit conductors being spliced are all from _____ terminated in listed fittings that mechanically secure the cable sheath to maintain effective electrical continuity.

    (a) metal-sheathed cable assemblies
    (b) the same power source
    (c) GFCI-protected circuits
    (d) GFPE-protected circuits

7. GFCI protection is required for all temporary wiring used for construction, remodeling, maintenance, repair, or demolition of buildings, structures, or equipment from power derived from a(an) _____ or generator.

    (a) electric utility company
    (b) cable or cord
    (c) feeder
    (d) separately derived system

8. All ____, 125V receptacle outlets that are not part of the permanent wiring of the building or structure and are used by personnel for temporary power shall be GFCI protected.

   (a) 15A
   (b) 20A
   (c) 30A
   (d) all of these

9. When using portable receptacles for temporary wiring installations that are not part of the building or structure, employees shall be protected on construction sites by either ground-fault circuit-interrupters or by the use of a(an) ____.

   (a) insulated conductor program
   (b) double insulated conductor program
   (c) flexible conductor program
   (d) assured equipment grounding conductor program

CHAPTER 6

REVIEW QUESTIONS

Please use the 2023 *Code* book to answer the following questions.

CHAPTER 6—SPECIAL EQUIPMENT

Article 600—Electric Signs

1. Fixed, mobile, or portable electric signs, section signs, outline lighting, photovoltaic powered signs, and retrofit kits shall be ____ and installed in conformance with that listing, unless otherwise approved by special permission.

    (a) marked
    (b) assembled
    (c) identified for the location
    (d) listed and labeled

2. Each commercial building and occupancy accessible to pedestrians shall have at least one sign outlet in an accessible location at each entrance to each tenant space supplied by a branch circuit rated at least ____.

    (a) 15A
    (b) 20A
    (c) 30A
    (d) 40A

3. A sign or outline lighting outlet shall not be required at commercial building or occupancy entrances for ____ that are intended to be used only by service personnel or employees.

    (a) deliveries
    (b) service corridors
    (c) service hallways
    (d) any of these

4. Branch circuits that supply signs shall be considered to be ____ loads for the purposes of calculations.

    (a) continuous
    (b) separate
    (c) combined
    (d) dynamic

5. Metal or nonmetallic poles used to support signs are permitted to enclose ____.

    (a) supply conductors
    (b) surge-protective devices
    (c) lightning arresters
    (d) overcurrent protective devices

6. Each sign and outline lighting system circuit supplying a sign, outline lighting system, or skeleton tubing shall be controlled by an externally operable switch or circuit breaker that opens all ____ conductors and controls no other load.

    (a) ungrounded
    (b) grounded
    (c) equipment grounding
    (d) all of these

7. The disconnect for a sign or outline lighting shall be located at the point the feeder circuit or branch circuits supplying a sign or outline lighting system enters a ____.

    (a) sign enclosure
    (b) sign body
    (c) pole in accordance with 600.5(D)(3)
    (d) any of these

8. Where the disconnecting means is out of the line of sight from any section of a sign or outline lighting able to be energized, the disconnecting means shall be ____ in accordance with 110.25.

    (a) secured
    (b) bolted
    (c) lockable
    (d) visible when installed

9. A permanent field-applied marking identifying the location of the disconnecting means shall be applied to the sign in a location visible during ____.

    (a) installation
    (b) repair
    (c) retrofitting
    (d) servicing

10. Bonding conductors installed outside of a sign or raceway used for the bonding connections of the noncurrent-carrying metal parts of signs shall be protected from physical damage and shall be copper not smaller than ____.

    (a) 14 AWG
    (b) 12 AWG
    (c) 8 AWG
    (d) 6 AWG

11. At least one lighting outlet containing a switch or controlled by a wall switch shall be installed in in attic spaces containing ballasts for electric signs with the ____ located at the usual point of entry to these spaces.

    (a) receptacle
    (b) switch
    (c) point of control
    (d) luminaire

Article 620—Elevators

1. At least ____ 125V, single-phase, 15A or 20A, duplex receptacle(s) shall be provided in each elevator machine room and elevator machinery space.

    (a) one
    (b) two
    (c) three
    (d) four

2. Electrical wiring, raceways, and cables used directly in connection with an elevator shall be permitted inside the hoistway, machine rooms, control rooms, machinery spaces, and control spaces, including wiring for ____.

    (a) communications with the car
    (b) fire detection systems
    (c) pit sump pumps
    (d) any of these

Article 625 Electric—Vehicle Power Transfer System

1. Each outlet installed for the purpose of supplying EVSE (electric vehicle supply equipment) greater than ____ or 120V charging electric vehicles shall be supplied by an individual branch circuit.

    (a) 12A
    (b) 16A
    (c) 18A
    (d) 20A

2. Electric vehicle charging loads shall be considered to be a(an) ____ load.

    (a) noncontinuous
    (b) hard
    (c) extended
    (d) continuous

3. Where the equipment is listed for charging electric vehicles that require ventilation for ____ charging, mechanical ventilation, such as a fan, shall be provided.

    (a) outdoor
    (b) indoor
    (c) exterior
    (d) any of these

Article 630—Electric Welders

1. The ampacity of the supply conductors to an individual electric arc welder shall not be less than the ____ current value of the nameplate rating.

    (a) effective
    (b) instantaneous
    (c) peak
    (d) none of these

Article 640—Audio Signal Amplification and Reproduction Equipment

1. Audio system equipment supplied by branch-circuit power shall not be located within ____ horizontally of the inside wall of a pool, spa, hot tub, fountain, or prevailing tidal high-water mark.

    (a) 18 in.
    (b) 2 ft
    (c) 5 ft
    (d) 10 ft

Article 645—Information Technology Equipment (ITE)

1. Article 645 does not apply unless an information technology equipment room contains ____.

    (a) a disconnecting means complying with 645.10
    (b) a separate heating/ventilating/air-conditioning (HVAC) system
    (c) separation by fire-resistance-rated walls, floors, and ceilings
    (d) all of these

2. Where the area under the floor is accessible and openings minimize the entrance of debris beneath the floor, ____, and receptacles associated with the information technology equipment is permitted.

    (a) power-supply cords and communication cables
    (b) connecting and interconnecting cables
    (c) cord-and-plug connections
    (d) all of these

Article 680—Swimming Pools, Spas, Hot Tubs, Fountains, and Similar Installations

1. Field-installed terminals for swimming pools in damp or wet locations or corrosive environments shall be composed of copper, copper alloy, or stainless steel and shall be ____ for direct burial use.

    (a) identified
    (b) labeled
    (c) listed
    (d) approved

2. Overhead conductors and open overhead wiring not in ____ shall comply with the minimum clearances given in Table 680.9(A).

    (a) tubing
    (b) a conduit
    (c) a cable
    (d) a raceway

3. Underground wiring within 5 ft horizontally from the inside wall of the pool ____.

    (a) shall be permitted
    (b) shall not be permitted
    (c) shall be required
    (d) none of these

4. Rigid metal conduit, intermediate metal conduit, rigid polyvinyl chloride conduit, reinforced thermosetting resin conduit, and liquidtight flexible nonmetallic conduit shall be considered to be resistant to the ____ environments that may be present in or about the areas covered by Article 680.

    (a) dry
    (b) damp
    (c) wet
    (d) corrosive

5. Outlets serving pool motors on branch circuits rated above 150V to ground and 60A or less shall be provided with ____ protection.

    (a) SPGFCI
    (b) GFCI
    (c) shunt-trip
    (d) current-limiting

6. A 125V receptacle shall be installed a minimum of ____ and a maximum of 20 ft from the inside wall of a permanently installed pool.

    (a) 3 ft
    (b) 6 ft
    (c) 8 ft
    (d) 12 ft

7. GFCI-protected receptacles that provide power for water-pump motors related to the circulation and sanitation system of a pool shall be located not less than ____ from the inside walls of the pool.

(a) 3 ft
(b) 6 ft
(c) 8 ft
(d) 12 ft

8. All receptacles rated 125V through 250V, 60A or less, located within ____ of the inside walls of a pool shall have GFCI protection.

(a) 6 ft
(b) 8 ft
(c) 10 ft
(d) 20 ft

9. Luminaires installed above new outdoor pools or the area extending ____ horizontally from the inside walls of the pool shall be installed at a height of not less than 12 ft above the maximum water level of the pool.

(a) 3 ft
(b) 5 ft
(c) 10 ft
(d) 12 ft

10. Transformers and power supplies used for the supply of underwater luminaires for swimming pools, together with the transformer or power-supply enclosure, shall be listed, labeled, and identified for ____ use.

(a) damp location
(b) wet location
(c) outdoor location
(d) swimming pool and spa

11. For permanently installed pools, a GFCI shall be installed in the branch circuit supplying luminaires operating at more than the low-voltage ____.

(a) setting
(b) listing
(c) contact limit
(d) trip limit

12. Wet-niche luminaires shall be installed with the top of the luminaire lens not less than ____ below the normal water level of the pool.

(a) 6 in.
(b) 12 in.
(c) 18 in.
(d) 24 in.

13. When PVC is run from a pool light forming shell to a pool junction box, an 8 AWG ____ bonding jumper shall be installed in the raceway.

(a) solid bare
(b) solid insulated copper
(c) stranded insulated copper
(d) solid or stranded insulated copper

14. A pool light junction box connected to a conduit that extends directly to a forming shell shall be ____ for this use.

(a) listed
(b) identified
(c) labeled
(d) all of these

15. The pool light junction box shall be located not less than ____, measured from the inside of the bottom of the box, above the ground level or pool deck, or not less than 8 in. above the maximum pool water level, whichever provides the greater elevation.

(a) 4 in.
(b) 6 in.
(c) 8 in.
(d) 12 in.

16. The pool light junction box shall be located not less than ____ from the inside wall of the pool, unless separated from the pool by a solid fence, wall, or other permanent barrier

(a) 2 ft
(b) 3 ft
(c) 4 ft
(d) 6 ft

17. The parts specified in 680.26(B)(1) through (B)(7) shall be bonded together using solid copper conductors, insulated, covered, or bare, not smaller than ____.
    (a) 12 AWG
    (b) 10 AWG
    (c) 8 AWG
    (d) 6 AWG

18. All receptacles rated 125V through 250V, 60A or less, located within ____ of the inside walls of a storable pool, storable spa, or storable hot tub shall have GFCI protection or SPGFCI protection in accordance with 680.5(B) or (C) as applicable.
    (a) 8 ft
    (b) 10 ft
    (c) 15 ft
    (d) 20 ft

Article 690—Solar Photovoltaic (PV) Systems

1. For crystalline and multicrystalline silicon modules, the PV system voltage ambient temperature correction is ____ if the ambient temperature is 20°C.
    (a) 1.02
    (b) 1.04
    (c) 1.06
    (d) 1.08

2. The maximum dc voltage for a PV source circuit is permitted to be calculated in accordance with the sum of the PV module-rated open-circuit voltage of the series-connected modules in the PV string circuit ____ for the lowest expected ambient temperature using the open-circuit voltage temperature coefficients in accordance with the instructions included in the listing or labeling of the module.
    (a) corrected
    (b) adjusted
    (c) demanded
    (d) none of these

3. For crystalline and multicrystalline silicon modules, the maximum dc source circuit voltage is equal to the sum of the PV module rated open-circuit voltage of the ____-connected modules in the PV string circuit corrected for the lowest expected ambient temperature using the correction factors provided in Table 690.7(A).
    (a) parallel
    (b) series
    (c) series-parallel
    (d) multiwire

4. For circuit sizing and current calculation of PV systems, the maximum PV source current is equal to the sum of the short-circuit current ratings of the PV modules connected in ____ multiplied by 125 percent.
    (a) series
    (b) parallel
    (c) series-parallel
    (d) multiwire

5. For circuit sizing and current calculation of PV systems, the maximum PV inverter output circuit current is equal to the inverter ____ output current rating.
    (a) average
    (b) peak
    (c) continuous
    (d) intermittent

6. For circuit sizing calculations of PV systems without adjustment and/or correction factors, the minimum conductor size must have an ampacity not less than the maximum currents calculated in 690.8(A) multiplied by ____.
    (a) 75 percent
    (b) 100 percent
    (c) 125 percent
    (d) 150 percent

7. Overcurrent devices for PV source circuits shall be sized not less than ____ of the maximum currents calculated in 690.8(A).
    (a) 80 percent
    (b) 100 percent
    (c) 125 percent
    (d) 250 percent

8. The overcurrent device rating for a PV source circuit assembly that, together with its overcurrent device(s), is listed for continuous operation at 100 percent of its rating shall be permitted to be used at ____ of its rating.

   (a) 100 percent
   (b) 125 percent
   (c) 225 percent
   (d) 150 percent

9. Photovoltaic systems with PV system dc circuits operating at ____ dc or greater between any two conductors shall be protected by a listed PV arc-fault circuit interrupter, or other system components listed to provide equivalent protection.

   (a) 30V
   (b) 50V
   (c) 80V
   (d) 120V

10. PV system dc circuits that utilize metal-clad cables installed ____ shall be permitted without AFCI protection where the circuits are not installed in or on buildings.

    (a) in metal raceways
    (b) in enclosed metal cable trays
    (c) underground
    (d) any of these

11. PV system dc circuits that utilize metal-clad cables installed ____ shall be permitted without AFCI protection where the circuits are located in or on detached structures whose sole purpose is to support or contain PV system equipment.

    (a) in metal raceways
    (b) in enclosed metal cable trays
    (c) underground
    (d) any of these

12. PV system circuits installed on or in buildings shall include ____ to reduce shock hazard for firefighters.

    (a) ground-fault circuit protection
    (b) arc-fault circuit protection
    (c) a rapid shutdown function
    (d) automated power transfer

13. Where not otherwise allowed in an equipment's listing, PV system dc circuits shall not occupy the same equipment wiring enclosure, cable, or raceway as other non-PV systems, or inverter output circuits, unless separated from other circuits by a ____.

    (a) barrier
    (b) partition
    (c) barrier or partition
    (d) none of these

14. PV system dc circuits shall not occupy the same equipment wiring enclosure, cable, or raceway as other non-PV systems, or inverter output circuits, unless the PV system dc circuits are separated from other circuits by a barrier or ____.

    (a) partition
    (b) sleeve
    (c) double insulation
    (d) shield

15. Single-conductor PV system cables with ____ insulation marked sunlight resistant can be used to connect photovoltaic modules in outdoor locations within the PV array.

    (a) THHN
    (b) USE-2
    (c) RHW-2
    (d) USE-2 and RHW-2

16. Mating connectors used in PV source circuits shall be polarized and shall have a configuration that are ____ with receptacles in other electrical systems on the premises.

    (a) noninterchangeable
    (b) interchangeable
    (c) compatible
    (d) none of these

17. Equipment grounding conductors for PV system circuits shall be sized in accordance with ____.

    (a) 250.4
    (b) 250.66
    (c) 250.102
    (d) 250.122

Article 695—Fire Pumps

1. The requirements for _____ are not covered by Article 695.

   (a) the installation of pressure maintenance pumps
   (b) fire pump controllers
   (c) fire pump disconnects
   (d) all of these

2. When a fire pump is supplied by an individual source, the _____ shall be rated to carry indefinitely the sum of the locked-rotor current of the largest fire pump motor and the full-load current of all of the other pump motors and accessory equipment.

   (a) overcurrent protective device(s)
   (b) pump motor conductors
   (c) pump motor controllers
   (d) source supply conductors

3. All wiring from the controllers to the fire pump motors shall be in _____, listed MC cable with an impervious covering, or MI cable.

   (a) rigid or intermediate metal conduit
   (b) electrical metallic tubing (EMT)
   (c) liquidtight flexible metallic or nonmetallic conduit
   (d) any of these

4. A(An) _____ surge protective device shall be installed in or on the fire pump controller.

   (a) listed
   (b) labeled
   (c) identified
   (d) approved

CHAPTER 7

REVIEW QUESTIONS

Please use the 2023 *Code* book to answer the following questions.

CHAPTER 7—SPECIAL CONDITIONS

Article 700—Emergency Systems

1. Article _____ applies to the electrical safety of the installation, operation, and maintenance of emergency systems intended to supply, distribute, and control electricity for illumination, power, or both, to required facilities when the normal electrical supply or system is interrupted.

   (a) 500
   (b) 600
   (c) 700
   (d) 800

2. Emergency systems are generally installed in places of assembly where artificial illumination is required for safe exiting and for panic control in buildings subject to occupancy by large numbers of persons, such as _____ and similar institutions.

   (a) hotels
   (b) theaters and sports arenas
   (c) health care facilities
   (d) all of these

3. The _____ shall conduct or witness a test of the complete emergency system upon installation and periodically afterward.

   (a) electrical engineer
   (b) authority having jurisdiction
   (c) qualified person
   (d) manufacturer's representative

4. Emergency system equipment shall be maintained in accordance with _____.

   (a) the authority having jurisdiction
   (b) UL listing(s)
   (c) manufacturer instructions and industry standards
   (d) OSHA regulations

5. A _____ record shall be kept of required tests and maintenance on emergency systems.

   (a) written
   (b) typed
   (c) emailed
   (d) stored

6. An emergency system shall have adequate _____ in accordance with Article 220 or by another approved method.

   (a) lighting
   (b) capacity
   (c) voltage
   (d) power

7. An emergency system's capacity shall be sufficient for the _____ and transient power and energy requirements associated with any expected loads.

   (a) demand load current
   (b) rapid load changes
   (c) peak-demand current
   (d) shaved-load current

8. The alternate power source shall be permitted to supply emergency, legally required standby, and optional standby system loads where the source has adequate capacity or where load management is provided as needed to ensure adequate power to the ____ in order of priority.

    (a) emergency circuits, legally required standby circuits, optional standby circuits
    (b) legally required standby circuits, emergency circuits, optional standby circuits
    (c) legally required standby circuits, optional standby circuits, emergency circuits
    (d) optional standby circuits, emergency circuits, legally required standby circuits

9. For emergency systems, transfer equipment shall be ____ for emergency use and approved by the authority having jurisdiction.

    (a) automatic
    (b) listed
    (c) marked
    (d) all of these

10. Automatic transfer switches for emergency systems shall be ____.

    (a) able to be remotely operated
    (b) able to be locked in the closed position
    (c) permitted to be reconditioned
    (d) electrically operated and mechanically held

11. An emergency transfer switch for emergency systems shall supply only ____.

    (a) emergency loads
    (b) computer equipment
    (c) UPS equipment
    (d) all of these

12. Where used for emergency systems, the short-circuit current rating of the transfer equipment, based on the specific overcurrent protective device type and settings protecting the transfer equipment, shall be field marked on the ____ of the transfer equipment.

    (a) exterior
    (b) top
    (c) interior
    (d) underside

13. Audible, visual, and facility or network remote annunciation devices shall be provided, where applicable to ____.

    (a) indicate a malfunction of the emergency source
    (b) indicate that the emergency source is carrying load
    (c) indicate a charging malfunction on a battery required for source readiness
    (d) all of these

14. In locations containing an emergency system, a ____ shall be placed at the service-entrance equipment indicating the type and location of each on-site emergency power source.

    (a) sign
    (b) label
    (c) marking
    (d) plaque

15. A listed ____ protective device shall be installed in or on all emergency systems switchgear, switchboards and panelboards.

    (a) surge
    (b) GFCI
    (c) AFCI
    (d) GFPE

16. Emergency circuits shall be permanently marked so they will be readily identified as a ____ of an emergency circuit or system.

    (a) segment
    (b) section
    (c) component
    (d) critical branch

17. All boxes and enclosures (including transfer switches, generators, and power panels) for emergency circuits shall be ____ marked as a component of an emergency circuit or system.

    (a) approved and
    (b) permanently
    (c) legibly
    (d) luminescent and

18. Wiring from an emergency source or emergency source distribution overcurrent protection to emergency loads shall be kept independent of all other wiring and equipment except in ____.

    (a) transfer equipment enclosures
    (b) exit or emergency luminaires supplied from two sources
    (c) listed load control relays supplying exit or emergency luminaires, or a common junction box, attached to exit or emergency luminaires supplied from two sources
    (d) all of these

19. If wiring from an emergency source is used to supply emergency and other loads, then ____ switchgear sections or switchboard sections, with or without a common bus, or individual disconnects mounted in separate enclosures shall be used to separate emergency loads from all other loads.

    (a) separate vertical
    (b) separate horizontal
    (c) combined vertical and horizontal
    (d) identified

20. Emergency circuit wiring power sources, such as a generator or multiple integral overcurrent protective devices shall each be permitted to supply a designated emergency or a designated nonemergency load, provided that there is complete ____ between emergency and nonemergency loads.

    (a) labeling
    (b) distinction
    (c) separation
    (d) identification

21. Wiring from an emergency source to supply emergency and other (nonemergency) loads shall be permitted if the common bus of separate sections of the switchgear, separate sections of the switchboard, or the individual enclosures are supplied by single or multiple feeders with or without ____.

    (a) overcurrent protection at the source
    (b) ground-fault protection at the source
    (c) a current-limiting device at the source
    (d) load-shaving monitoring

22. Emergency systems circuit wiring shall be designed and located to minimize the hazards that might cause failure because of ____.

    (a) flooding
    (b) fire
    (c) icing
    (d) all of these

23. Line voltage supply wiring and installation of ____ emergency lighting control devices shall comply with 700.10 while Class 2 emergency circuits shall comply with 700.11(B) through (D).

    (a) Class 1
    (b) Class 2
    (c) Class 3
    (d) Class 4

24. All boxes and enclosures for ____ emergency circuits shall be permanently marked as a component of an emergency circuit or system unless the intent of such circuits is obvious.

    (a) Class 1
    (b) Class 2
    (c) Class 3
    (d) Class 4

25. Exposed cable, cable tray, or raceway systems shall be permanently marked to be identified as a component of an emergency circuit or system within ____ of each connector.

    (a) 12 in.
    (b) 18 in.
    (c) 2 ft
    (d) 3 ft

26. If installed alongside nonemergency Class 2 circuits that are bundled, Class 2 emergency circuits shall be ____ separately.

    (a) tagged
    (b) color-coded
    (c) bundled
    (d) labeled

27. Wiring of Class 2 emergency circuits shall comply with the requirements of 300.4 and be installed in a(an) ____.

    (a) raceway
    (b) armored-cable or metal-clad cable
    (c) cable tray
    (d) any of these

28. Wiring protection requirements for Class 2 emergency circuits shall not apply to wiring that do not exceed ____ in length and that terminate at an emergency luminaire or an emergency lighting control device

    (a) 2 ft
    (b) 3 ft
    (c) 4 ft
    (d) 6 ft

29. Wiring protection requirements for Class 2 emergency circuits shall not apply to locked rooms or locked enclosures that are accessible only to ____.

    (a) qualified persons
    (b) staff
    (c) maintenance personnel
    (d) licensed individuals

30. Emergency system sources of power shall be such that, in the event of failure of the normal supply to, or within, the building or group of buildings concerned, emergency lighting, emergency power, or both shall be available within the time required for the application but not to exceed _____.

    (a) 5 seconds
    (b) 10 seconds
    (c) 30 seconds
    (d) 60 seconds

31. Emergency equipment for emergency systems shall be _____ and located so as to minimize the hazards that might cause complete failure due to flooding, fires, icing, and vandalism.

    (a) approved
    (b) listed
    (c) installed
    (d) designed

32. The emergency power source shall be of suitable rating and capacity to supply and maintain the total load for the duration determined by the system design and in no case shall the duration be less than _____ of system operation unless used for emergency illumination in 700.12(C)(4) or unit equipment in 700.12(H).

    (a) 1 hour
    (b) 90 minutes
    (c) 2 hours
    (d) 3 hours

33. Storage batteries and UPS used to supply emergency illumination shall maintain the total load for a minimum period of _____, without the voltage applied to the load falling below 87½ percent of nominal voltage.

    (a) 1 hour
    (b) 1½ hours
    (c) 2 hours
    (d) 2½ hours

34. Battery-equipped emergency luminaires shall be on the same branch circuit that serves the normal lighting in the area and connected _____ any local switches.

    (a) with
    (b) ahead of
    (c) after
    (d) downstream of

35. Battery-equipped emergency luminaires shall be on the same or a different branch circuit as that serving the normal lighting in the area if that circuit is equipped with means to _____ the status of that area's normal lighting branch circuit ahead of any local switches.

    (a) alert to
    (b) indicate
    (c) monitor
    (d) react to

36. In emergency systems, no appliances or lamps, other than those specified as required for emergency use, shall be supplied by _____.

    (a) emergency lighting circuits
    (b) multiwire branch circuits
    (c) HID-rated circuit breakers
    (d) only load-shaved circuits

37. Emergency lighting systems shall be designed and _____ so that the failure of any illumination source cannot leave in total darkness any space that requires emergency illumination.

    (a) installed
    (b) listed
    (c) inspected
    (d) labeled

38. Emergency system(s) overcurrent protective devices shall be selectively coordinated with all _____ overcurrent protective devices.

    (a) supply-side
    (b) load-side only
    (c) downstream
    (d) reconditioned

39. Where emergency system(s) OCPDs are replaced, they shall be _____ to ensure selective coordination is maintained with all supply-side and load-side OCPDs.

    (a) inspected
    (b) identified
    (c) re-evaluated
    (d) arranged

40. Where ____ to the emergency system(s) occur, selective coordination of the emergency system(s) OCPDs with all supply-side and load-side OCPDs shall be re-evaluated.

    (a) modifications
    (b) additions
    (c) deletions
    (d) any of these

Article 701—Legally Required Standby Systems

1. Article 701 applies to the electrical safety of the installation, operation, and maintenance of ____ systems.

    (a) emergency
    (b) legally required standby
    (c) optional standby
    (d) dwelling-unit standby

2. The branch-circuit overcurrent devices in legally required standby system circuits shall be accessible only to ____.

    (a) the authority having jurisdiction
    (b) authorized persons
    (c) the general public
    (d) qualified persons

3. The ____ shall conduct or witness the commissioning of the complete legally required standby system upon installation.

    (a) electrical engineer
    (b) authority having jurisdiction
    (c) qualified person
    (d) manufacturer's representative

4. Legally required standby systems shall be tested ____ on a schedule and in a manner approved by the authority having jurisdiction to ensure the systems are maintained in proper operating condition.

    (a) monthly
    (b) quarterly
    (c) annually
    (d) periodically

5. Legally required standby system equipment shall be maintained in accordance with ____.

    (a) UL listing(s)
    (b) local emergency services requirements
    (c) manufacturer instructions and industry standards
    (d) local jurisdictional requirements

6. A ____ record shall be kept of required tests and maintenance on legally required standby systems.

    (a) written
    (b) typed
    (c) emailed
    (d) stored

7. Legally required standby system equipment shall be suitable for ____ at its terminals.

    (a) the available fault current
    (b) the maximum overload current only
    (c) the minimum fault current
    (d) a one-hour rating

8. A legally required standby system shall have adequate capacity in accordance with Article ____ or by another approved method.

    (a) 210
    (b) 220
    (c) 230
    (d) 700

9. Transfer equipment for legally required standby systems shall be ____.

    (a) automatic
    (b) listed
    (c) marked for emergency system or legally required standby use
    (d) all of these

10. Automatic transfer switches on legally required standby systems shall be electrically operated and ____ held.

    (a) electrically
    (b) mechanically
    (c) gravity
    (d) any of these

11. Where used for legally required standby systems, the short-circuit current rating of the transfer equipment, based on the specific overcurrent protective device type and settings protecting the transfer equipment, shall be field marked on the ____ of the transfer equipment.

    (a) exterior
    (b) top
    (c) interior
    (d) underside

12. Audible and visual signal devices shall be provided, where practicable, for legally required standby systems to indicate ____.

    (a) a malfunction of the standby source
    (b) that the standby source is carrying load
    (c) that the battery charger is not functioning
    (d) all of these

13. A sign shall be placed at the service entrance indicating the ____ of each on-site legally required standby power source.

    (a) capacity
    (b) date of last testing
    (c) manufacturer
    (d) type and location

14. Where a legally required standby source of power is installed, the transition time from the instant of failure of the normal power source to the emergency generator source shall not exceed ____.

    (a) 10 seconds
    (b) 20 seconds
    (c) 30 seconds
    (d) 60 seconds

15. Where approved by the authority having jurisdiction, connections ahead of and not within the same cabinet, enclosure, vertical switchgear section, or vertical switchboard section as the ____ disconnecting means shall be permitted for legally required standby systems.

    (a) emergency
    (b) service
    (c) optional
    (d) all of these

16. Legally required standby system overcurrent protective devices (OCPDs) shall be ____ with all supply-side and load-side OCPDs.

    (a) series rated
    (b) selectively coordinated
    (c) installed in parallel
    (d) labeled in accordance

17. Where legally required standby system OCPDs are replaced, they shall be ____ to ensure selective coordination is maintained with all supply-side and load-side OCPDs.

    (a) inspected
    (b) identified
    (c) re-evaluated
    (d) arranged

18. Where ____ to legally required standby systems occur, selective coordination of the legally required standby system OCPDs with all supply-side and load-side OCPDs shall be re-evaluated.

    (a) modifications
    (b) additions
    (c) deletions
    (d) any of these

Article 702—Optional Standby Systems

1. Article 702 applies to ____ optional standby systems.

    (a) temporarily installed
    (b) portable
    (c) readily accessible
    (d) the installation and operation of

2. Optional standby system wiring is permitted to occupy the same ____ with other general wiring.

    (a) raceways
    (b) cables
    (c) boxes and cabinets
    (d) all of these

3. If the connection of load is manual or nonautomatic, an optional standby system shall have adequate ____ for the supply of all equipment intended to be operated at one time.

    (a) ventilation
    (b) supervision
    (c) fuel supply
    (d) capacity and rating

4. Manual and nonautomatic transfer equipment for optional standby systems require ____ intervention.

    (a) human
    (b) animal
    (c) electrician
    (d) inspector

5. Where automatic transfer equipment is used, an optional standby system shall be capable of supplying ____.

    (a) the full load that is automatically connected
    (b) all equipment where life safety is dependent
    (c) all emergency and egress lighting
    (d) all fire and security systems

6. Where an energy management system (EMS) is employed in accordance with 750.30 that will automatically manage the connected load of an optional standby system, the standby source shall have a capacity sufficient to supply ____ that will be connected by the EMS.

    (a) 80 percent of the load
    (b) 100 percent of the load
    (c) 125 percent of the load
    (d) the maximum load

7. Optional standby system interconnection or transfer equipment shall be designed and installed so as to prevent the inadvertent interconnection of ____ of supply in any operation of the equipment.

    (a) the normal source
    (b) the standby source
    (c) all sources
    (d) none of these

8. For optional standby systems, the temporary connection of a portable generator without transfer equipment shall be permitted where conditions of maintenance and supervision ensure that only qualified persons will service the installation, and where the normal supply is physically isolated by ____.

    (a) a lockable disconnecting means
    (b) the disconnection of the normal supply conductors
    (c) an extended power outage
    (d) a lockable disconnecting means or the disconnection of the normal supply conductors

9. Meter-mounted optional standby system transfer switches installed between the ____ and the meter enclosure shall be listed meter-mounted transfer switches.

    (a) service connection point
    (b) utility meter
    (c) utility transformer
    (d) cold sequence disconnect

10. For optional standby systems, meter-mounted ____ transfer switches use human intervention.

    (a) automatic
    (b) manual
    (c) monitoring
    (d) remote

11. Where used for optional standby systems in other than dwelling units, the short-circuit current rating of the transfer equipment, based on the specific overcurrent protective device type and settings protecting the transfer equipment, shall be field marked on the ____ of the transfer equipment.

    (a) exterior
    (b) top
    (c) interior
    (d) underside

12. A sign shall be placed at the service-entrance equipment for other than one- and two-family dwellings that indicates the ____ of each on-site optional standby power source.

    (a) installer
    (b) date of installation
    (c) date of last testing
    (d) type and location

13. For ____ dwelling units, a sign shall be placed at the disconnecting means required in 230.85 that indicates the location of each permanently installed on-site optional standby power source disconnect or means to shut down the prime mover as required in 445.19(C).

    (a) apartment
    (b) guest suite
    (c) multi-family
    (d) one- and two-family

14. Where a power inlet is used for an optional standby system's temporary connection to a portable generator, a warning sign shall be placed near the inlet to indicate the ____ that the system is capable of, based on the wiring of the transfer equipment.

    (a) type of fuel supply
    (b) type of derived system
    (c) type of GFCI protection
    (d) temporary power supply time

15. For optional standby purposes, a portable generator rated 15 kW or less is installed using a flanged inlet or other cord-and-plug-type connection, the flanged inlet or other cord-and-plug-type connection shall be located ____ of a building or structure.

    (a) outside
    (b) inside
    (c) outside or inside
    (d) none of these

Article 705—Interconnected Electric Power Production Sources

1. Article 705 covers the installation of one or more electric power production sources operating in parallel with a(an) _____ source(s) of electricity.

   (a) secondary
   (b) alternate
   (c) primary
   (d) stand-alone

2. The output of interactive electric power production sources equipment shall be _____ disconnected from all ungrounded conductors of the primary source when one or more of the phases of the primary source to which it is connected opens.

   (a) manually
   (b) automatically
   (c) manually or automatically
   (d) manually and automatically

3. Interconnected electric power production sources microgrid systems shall be capable of operating in interactive mode with a primary source of power, or electric utility, or other electric power production and distribution network and shall be permitted to disconnect from other sources and operate in _____ mode.

   (a) automated
   (b) emergency
   (c) isolated
   (d) island

4. Interconnection and interactive equipment intended to connect to or operate in parallel with power production sources shall be listed for the required interactive function or be _____ for the interactive function and have a field label applied, or both.

   (a) tested
   (b) evaluated
   (c) approved
   (d) licensed

5. Installations of one or more interconnected electrical power production sources operating in parallel with a primary source(s) of electricity shall be performed only by _____.

   (a) qualified persons
   (b) utility company persons
   (c) the authority having jurisdiction
   (d) utility company persons or the authority having jurisdiction

6. For interconnected electric power production source(s), a permanent _____, denoting the location of each power source disconnecting means for the building or structure, shall be installed at each service equipment location or at an approved readily visible location.

   (a) label
   (b) plaque
   (c) directory
   (d) any of these

7. Interconnected power production installations with multiple co-located power production sources shall be permitted to be _____ as a group(s).

   (a) identified
   (b) labeled
   (c) marked
   (d) all of these

8. Interconnected electric power production source(s) are permitted to be connected to the _____ side of the service disconnecting means in accordance with 230.82(6).

   (a) line
   (b) supply
   (c) source
   (d) any of these

9. For interconnected electric power production sources connected to a service, the ampacity of the _____ connected to the power production source service disconnecting means shall not be less than the sum of the power production source maximum circuit current in 705.28(A).

   (a) service conductors
   (b) power production source output current
   (c) service disconnect rating
   (d) sum of all overcurrent protective devices

10. For interconnected electric power production source(s) connected to a service, the service conductors connected to the power production source service disconnecting means shall be sized in accordance with 705.28 and not be smaller than _____ copper.

    (a) 8 AWG
    (b) 6 AWG
    (c) 4 AWG
    (d) 3 AWG

11. A disconnecting means in accordance with Parts VI through VIII of Article 230 shall be provided to ____ all ungrounded conductors of an interconnected electric power production source from the conductors of other systems.

    (a) coordinate
    (b) disconnect
    (c) protect
    (d) all of these

12. Interconnected electric power production source metal enclosures, metal wiring methods, and metal parts associated with the service connected to a power production source shall be ____ in accordance with Parts II through V and VIII of Article 250.

    (a) installed
    (b) grounded
    (c) bonded
    (d) protected

13. The rating of the overcurrent protective device of the interconnected electric power production source service disconnecting means shall be used to determine if ____ is required in accordance with 230.95.

    (a) ground-fault protection of equipment
    (b) arc-fault protection
    (c) surge protection
    (d) lightning protection

14. The output of an interconnected electric power source shall be permitted to be connected to the ____ side of the service disconnecting means of the other source(s) at any distribution equipment on the premises.

    (a) load
    (b) bottom
    (c) top
    (d) line

15. Where the interconnected electric power production source output connection is made to a feeder at a location other than the opposite end of the feeder from the primary source overcurrent device, that portion of the feeder on the load side of the power source output connection shall be protected by a(an) ____.

    (a) feeder ampacity not less than the sum of the primary source overcurrent device and 125 percent of the power source output circuit current
    (b) overcurrent device at the load side of the power source connection point rated not greater than the ampacity of the feeder
    (c) feeder ampacity not less than the sum of the primary source overcurrent device and 125 percent of the power source output circuit current, or an overcurrent device at the load side of the power source connection point rated not greater than the ampacity of the feeder
    (d) none of these

16. Where interconnected electric power production source output connections are made at busbars, the sum of ____ of the power source(s) output circuit current and the rating of the overcurrent device protecting the busbar shall not exceed the busbar ampere rating.

    (a) 100 percent
    (b) 110 percent
    (c) 115 percent
    (d) 125 percent

17. Where two interconnected electric power production sources are located at opposite ends of a busbar that contains loads, the sum of 125 percent of the power-source(s) output circuit current and the rating of the overcurrent device protecting the busbar shall not exceed ____ of the busbar ampere rating.

    (a) 100 percent
    (b) 115 percent
    (c) 120 percent
    (d) 125 percent

18. When determining the ampere rating of busbars associated with load-side source connections of interconnected electric power production sources, one can use the sum of the ampere ratings of all overcurrent devices on ____, both load and supply devices, excluding the rating of the overcurrent device protecting the busbar, but shall not exceed the ampacity of the busbar.

    (a) metering equipment
    (b) panelboards
    (c) switchgear
    (d) all of these

19. Where interconnected electric power production source output connections are made at either end of a ____ panelboard in dwellings, it shall be permitted where the sum of 125 percent of the power-source(s) output circuit current and the rating of the overcurrent device protecting the busbar does not exceed 120 percent of the busbar ampere rating.

    (a) front-fed
    (b) back-fed
    (c) center-fed
    (d) none of these

20. Interconnected electric power production source connections shall be permitted on busbars of panelboards that supply ____ connected to feed-through conductors.

    (a) power distribution blocks
    (b) terminals
    (c) lugs
    (d) none of these

21. An emergency management system (EMS), in accordance with 705.30, shall be permitted to limit current and loading on the busbars and conductors supplied by the output of one or more interconnected electric power production sources or ____ sources.

    (a) utility power
    (b) energy storage
    (c) stand-alone power
    (d) all of these

22. A listed power control system (PCS) is a type of EMS that is capable of monitoring multiple interconnected electric power production sources and controlling the current on busbars and conductors to prevent ____.

    (a) overloading
    (b) fault currents
    (c) short-circuits
    (d) power surges

23. Means shall be provided to disconnect power source output circuit conductors of interconnected electric power production source equipment from conductors of other systems. The disconnecting means shall be a ____.

    (a) manually operable switch or circuit breaker
    (b) load-break-rated pull-out switch
    (c) device listed or approved for the intended application
    (d) any of these

24. Wiring methods and fittings ____ for use with interconnected electric power production source systems shall be permitted in addition to the general wiring methods and fittings permitted elsewhere in this *Code*.

    (a) marked
    (b) labeled
    (c) identified
    (d) listed

25. Where not elsewhere required or permitted in this *Code*, the maximum current for interconnected power production sources controlled by an EMS, shall be calculated using ____.

    (a) the peak output current
    (b) a 30-day average output current
    (c) the current setpoint of the EMS
    (d) the main overcurrent device rating

26. Equipment containing overcurrent devices supplied from interconnected electric power production sources shall be marked to indicate the presence of ____.

    (a) leakage current
    (b) all sources
    (c) selective coordination
    (d) emergency loads

27. Fused disconnects at interconnected electric power production source output connections are considered suitable for _____ unless otherwise marked.
    (a) backfeed
    (b) current limiting
    (c) current adjustment
    (d) slash rating

28. Listed plug-in-type circuit breakers backfed from interconnected electric power production sources that are listed and identified as _____ shall not require a fastener as required by 408.36(D).
    (a) interactive
    (b) active
    (c) reactive
    (d) interactive or active

29. In accordance with Article 705, for the purpose of overcurrent protection, the primary side of transformers with sources on each side shall be the side connected to the largest source of _____ current.
    (a) available fault
    (b) short-circuit
    (c) output power source
    (d) available fault current or short-circuit

30. For interconnected electric power production sources systems, risks to personnel and equipment associated with the primary source could occur if an interactive electric power production source can operate as an intentional _____.
    (a) island
    (b) power production system
    (c) primary source of power
    (d) none of these

31. For interconnected electric power production source system(s), single-phase power sources in interactive systems shall be connected to three-phase power systems in order to limit unbalanced voltages at the point of interconnection to not more than _____.
    (a) 2 percent
    (b) 3 percent
    (c) 5 percent
    (d) 10 percent

32. Interconnected electric power sources operating in island mode shall be permitted to supply 120V to single-phase, 3-wire, 120V/240V distribution equipment where there are no 240V outlets and where there are no _____ branch circuits.
    (a) multiwire
    (b) series
    (c) parallel
    (d) all of these

Article 706—Energy Storage Systems

1. Article 706 applies to all energy storage systems (ESS) having a capacity greater than _____ that may be stand-alone or interactive with other electric power production sources.
   (a) 1 kWh
   (b) 2 kWh
   (c) 5 kWh
   (d) 10 kWh

2. The installation and maintenance of energy storage system (ESS) equipment and all associated wiring and interconnections shall be performed only by _____.
   (a) qualified persons
   (b) ESS specialists
   (c) licensed electricians
   (d) maintenance personnel

3. Each energy storage system (ESS) shall be provided with a nameplate plainly visible after installation and marked with the _____.
   (a) rated frequency
   (b) number of phases (if ac)
   (c) rating in kW or kVA
   (d) all of these

4. Energy storage systems shall be _____.
   (a) labeled
   (b) identified for their use
   (c) listed
   (d) classified

5. Energy storage systems for other than one- and two-family dwellings shall be ____ upon installation.

    (a) field evaluated
    (b) commissioned
    (c) documented
    (d) registered

6. The ____ voltage of an energy storage system (ESS) shall be the rated ESS input and output voltage(s) indicated on the ESS nameplate(s) or system listing.

    (a) minimum
    (b) maximum
    (c) sustainable
    (d) operating

7. Means shall be provided to ____ the energy storage system (ESS) from all wiring systems, including other power systems, utilization equipment, and its associated premises wiring

    (a) disconnect
    (b) shut down
    (c) turn off
    (d) eliminate

8. The disconnecting means for energy storage systems (ESS) shall be readily accessible and shall be located within sight and within ____ from the ESS.

    (a) 3 ft
    (b) 5 ft
    (c) 10 ft
    (d) 25 ft

9. Where the disconnecting means for energy storage systems cannot be located within sight of the ESS, the disconnecting means, or the enclosure providing access to the disconnecting means, shall be capable of being ____ in accordance with 110.25.

    (a) locked
    (b) labeled
    (c) installed remotely
    (d) identified

10. In cases where the battery is separate from the energy storage system (ESS) electronics and is subject to field servicing, a disconnecting means shall be readily accessible and located ____ the battery.

    (a) adjacent to
    (b) within 3 ft of
    (c) within sight of
    (d) within 25 ft of

11. Energy storage system (ESS) battery circuits exceeding 240V dc nominal between conductors or to ground shall have provisions to disconnect the series-connected strings into segments not exceeding ____ dc nominal for maintenance by qualified persons.

    (a) 30V
    (b) 60V
    (c) 120V
    (d) 240V

12. For required notification and marking purposes for energy storage systems (ESS) for available fault current derived from the stationary battery system, ____ can provide information about available fault current on any particular battery model.

    (a) UL listings
    (b) battery equipment suppliers
    (c) equipment labeling
    (d) the design engineer

13. Where controls to activate the energy storage system (ESS) battery disconnecting means are used and are not located within sight of the battery, the location of the controls shall be marked ____.

    (a) on the batteries
    (b) adjacent to the batteries
    (c) on the disconnecting means
    (d) in a secure location

14. Energy storage system (ESS) battery disconnecting means shall be legibly marked in the field and shall include the ____.

    (a) nominal battery voltage
    (b) available fault current and arc-flash label
    (c) date the calculation was performed
    (d) all of these

15. Where an energy storage system (ESS) has separate input (charge) and output (discharge) circuits or ratings, these shall be considered ____.
    (a) as continuous loads
    (b) separately
    (c) individually
    (d) none of these

16. The energy storage system (ESS) inverter output circuit maximum current shall be ____.
    (a) the inverter continuous output current rating
    (b) the inverter continuous input current rating
    (c) 110 percent of the inverter continuous output current rating
    (d) 125 percent of the inverter continuous input current rating

17. An energy storage system (ESS) circuit conductor connected at one end to a supply with integral fault protection, and also connected to sources having an available maximum circuit current greater than the ampacity of the conductor, shall be protected from ____ at the point of connection to the higher current source.
    (a) overcurrent
    (b) ground fault
    (c) overload
    (d) short circuit

18. Listed electronic power converter circuits powered by an energy storage system (ESS) have ____ fault protection.
    (a) integral
    (b) exterior
    (c) interior
    (d) internal

19. Overcurrent protective devices, where required, shall be rated in accordance with Article 240 and the rating provided on systems serving the energy storage system (ESS) shall be not less than ____ of the maximum currents calculated in 706.30(A).
    (a) 110 percent
    (b) 115 percent
    (c) 125 percent
    (d) 167 percent

Article 710—Stand-Alone Systems

1. Article 710 covers electric power production systems that operate in ____ and not connected to an electric utility supply.
    (a) island mode
    (b) standby mode
    (c) tandem mode
    (d) generating mode

2. According to the scope of 710.1, stand-alone systems often include a single or a compatible interconnection of sources such as ____.
    (a) engine generators
    (b) solar PV or wind
    (c) ESS or batteries
    (d) all of these

3. All stand-alone power production equipment or systems shall be approved for use ____.
    (a) as legally required standby power
    (b) as optional standby power
    (c) in island mode
    (d) as supplemental power on demand

4. A permanent ____ shall be installed at a building supplied by a stand-alone system at each service equipment location or at an approved readily visible location and shall denote the location of each power source disconnect for the building or be grouped with other plaques or directories for other on-site sources.
    (a) plaque
    (b) label
    (c) directory
    (d) any of these

5. The maximum current shall be the stand-alone continuous inverter ____ rating when the inverter is producing rated power at the lowest input voltage.
    (a) input current
    (b) output current
    (c) wattage
    (d) peak load

6. Power supply to premises wiring systems fed by stand-alone or isolated microgrid power sources is permitted to have _____ than the calculated load.

    (a) less capacity
    (b) greater capacity
    (c) 120 percent greater capacity
    (d) 125 percent greater capacity

7. For general-use loads, the stand-alone system capacity can be calculated using the sum of the capacity of the firm sources, such as _____.

    (a) generators
    (b) energy storage system inverters
    (c) generators and energy storage system inverters
    (d) PV combiners

8. The circuit conductors between a stand-alone source and a _____ shall be sized based on the sum of the output ratings of the stand-alone source(s).

    (a) distribution panel
    (b) building or structure disconnect
    (c) calculated load
    (d) demand load

9. Stand-alone and isolated microgrid systems shall be permitted to supply 120V to single-phase, 3-wire, 120V/240V service equipment or distribution panels where there are no 240V outlets and no _____ branch circuits.

    (a) single
    (b) multiple
    (c) multiwire
    (d) all of these

Article 722—Cables for Power-Limited Circuits

1. Power-limited circuits installed in _____ shall comply with 300.22.

    (a) ducts
    (b) plenums
    (c) other space used for environmental air
    (d) any of these

2. A bushing shall be installed where power-limited cables _____ from raceways used for mechanical support or protection.

    (a) emerge
    (b) enter
    (c) exit
    (d) any of these

3. Nonmetallic _____ and other nonmetallic cable accessories used to secure and support power-limited cables in other spaces used for environmental air (plenums) shall be listed as having low smoke and heat release properties

    (a) wires
    (b) hangars
    (c) straps
    (d) cable ties

4. Power-limited fire alarm cables shall not be strapped, taped, or attached by any means to the exterior of any conduit or other raceway as a means of _____.

    (a) support
    (b) securement
    (c) strapping
    (d) all of these

5. The accessible portion of abandoned power-limited cables shall be _____.

    (a) removed
    (b) replaced
    (c) repaired
    (d) any of these

6. Power-limited cables installed in buildings shall be _____.

    (a) identified
    (b) marked
    (c) labeled
    (d) listed

7. Class 2, Class 3, and PLTC power-limited cables, installed as wiring methods within buildings, shall be listed as resistant to the spread of _____ and other criteria in accordance with 722.179(A)(1) through (A)(16).

    (a) fire
    (b) water
    (c) smoke
    (d) dust

8. Power-limited plenum cable shall be listed as suitable for use in ducts, plenums, and other space for environmental air and shall be listed as having adequate fire-resistant and ____ producing characteristics.

   (a) medium-smoke
   (b) high-smoke
   (c) low-smoke
   (d) no-smoke

9. Riser power-limited cable shall be listed as suitable for use in a vertical run in a shaft or from ____ and shall be listed as having fire-resistant characteristics capable of preventing the carrying of fire from floor to floor.

   (a) floor to wall
   (b) up to bottom
   (c) wall to wall
   (d) floor to floor

10. Cable used in a wet location shall be listed for use in wet locations and be marked wet or wet location or have a moisture-impervious ____ sheath.

    (a) metal
    (b) plastic
    (c) fiberglass
    (d) any of these

Article 724—Class 1 Power-Limited Circuits

1. Article ____ covers Class 1 circuits, including power-limited Class 1 remote-control and signaling circuits that are not an integral part of a device or utilization equipment.

   (a) 722
   (b) 723
   (c) 724
   (d) 725

2. Class 1 power-limited circuits shall be ____ at terminal and junction locations in a manner that prevents unintentional interference with other circuits during testing and servicing.

   (a) grouped
   (b) identified
   (c) taped
   (d) isolated

3. Class 1 circuits installed in ducts, ____, and other spaces used for environmental air shall comply with 300.22.

   (a) plenums
   (b) air-conditioning units
   (c) suspended ceilings
   (d) any of these

4. Bushings shall be installed for Class 1 power-limited circuits where cables emerge from raceways used for ____ support or protection in accordance with 300.15(C).

   (a) mechanical
   (b) electrical
   (c) extra
   (d) none of these

5. Class 1 power-limited circuits shall be supplied from a source with a rated output of not more than ____ and 1,000 VA.

   (a) 12V
   (b) 24V
   (c) 30V
   (d) 50V

6. Class 1 cables and conductors installed exposed on the surfaces of ceilings and sidewalls shall be supported by the ____ such that the cable will not be damaged by normal building use.

   (a) building structure
   (b) raceway
   (c) suspended-ceiling support wires
   (d) hard lid ceiling

7. Class 1 cables shall be supported by straps, staples, hangers, cable ties, or similar fittings that are designed and installed to ____ the cable.

   (a) properly support
   (b) not damage
   (c) not create impedance in
   (d) all of these

8. ____ or other contaminants can result in an undetermined alteration of Class 1 power-limited circuit cable properties.

   (a) Paint and plaster
   (b) Cleaners and abrasives
   (c) Corrosive residues
   (d) all of these

9. Class 1 power-limited circuit overcurrent protection shall not exceed ____ for 18 AWG conductors and ____ for 16 AWG.

    (a) 7A, 10A
    (b) 8A, 10A
    (c) 9A, 12A
    (d) 10A, 15A

10. Power-supply conductors and Class 1 power-limited circuit conductors can occupy the same cable, enclosure, or raceway without a barrier ____.

    (a) only where the equipment powered is functionally associated
    (b) where the circuits involved are not a mixture of ac and dc
    (c) under no circumstances
    (d) only where the equipment is essential for life safety

11. Class 1 circuits and power-supply circuits are permitted to be installed together with the conductors of ____ where separated by a barrier.

    (a) electric light
    (b) power
    (c) nonpower-limited fire alarm
    (d) all of these

Article 725—Class 2 Power-Limited Circuits

1. Article ____ covers power-limited circuits, including power-limited remote-control and signaling circuits, which are not an integral part of a device or of utilization equipment.

    (a) 722
    (b) 724
    (c) 725
    (d) 726

2. Class 2 and Class 3 circuits installed in ____, plenums, or other space used for environmental air shall comply with 300.22.

    (a) ducts
    (b) air-conditioning units
    (c) suspended ceilings
    (d) any of these

3. The listing and installation of cables for Class 2 and Class 3 circuits shall comply with Part I and Part II of Article ____.

    (a) 300
    (b) 722
    (c) 760
    (d) 770

4. Where damage to power-limited circuits can result in a failure of safety-control equipment that would introduce a direct fire or life ____, the power-limited circuits shall be installed in accordance with 724.31.

    (a) hazard
    (b) threat
    (c) situation
    (d) none of these

5. The power source for a Class 2 circuit shall be ____.

    (a) a listed Class 2 transformer
    (b) a listed Class 2 power supply
    (c) other listed equipment marked to identify the Class 2 power source
    (d) any of these

6. ____ audio/video information technology, communications, and industrial equipment limited-power circuits are permitted to be used as the power source for a Class 2 or a Class 3 circuit.

    (a) Listed
    (b) Labeled
    (c) Identified
    (d) Approved

7. Equipment supplying Class 2 or Class 3 circuits shall be durably marked where plainly visible to indicate ____.

    (a) each circuit that is a Class 2 or Class 3 circuit
    (b) the circuit VA rating
    (c) the size of conductors serving each circuit
    (d) all of these

8. Use of ____ wiring methods for Class 2 and Class 3 circuits on the load side of the power source shall be permitted.

    (a) Class 1
    (b) Class 2
    (c) Class 3
    (d) Class 4

9. Conductors of Class 2 and Class 3 circuits on the load side of the power source shall be ____ in accordance with 722.179.

    (a) bare
    (b) covered
    (c) insulated
    (d) all of these

10. Cables and conductors of Class 2 and Class 3 circuits ____ be placed with conductors of electric light, power, Class 1, nonpower-limited fire alarm circuits, and medium power network-powered broadband communications circuits.

    (a) shall be permitted to
    (b) shall not
    (c) shall
    (d) shall be required to

11. As a general rule, open conductors of Class 2 and Class 3 signaling circuits shall be separated by at least ____ from conductors of electric power and light.

    (a) 2 in.
    (b) 4 in.
    (c) 6 in.
    (d) 8 in.

12. Sections 725.144(A) and (B) shall apply to ____ circuits that transmit power and data to a powered device over listed cabling.

    (a) all
    (b) Class 1, 2, and 3
    (c) Class 2 and 3
    (d) low-voltage

13. For the purposes of bundling cables transmitting power and data, the requirements of 300.11 and Parts I and III of Article 725 shall apply to Class 2 and Class 3 circuits that transmit power and data. The conductors that carry power for the data circuits shall be ____.

    (a) copper
    (b) copper-clad aluminum
    (c) aluminum
    (d) any of these

14. For the purposes of bundling cables transmitting power and data, one example of the use of cables for Class 2 or Class 3 circuits that transmit power and data is the connection of ____.

    (a) closed-circuit TV cameras (CCTV)
    (b) antennas
    (c) coaxial cable
    (d) none of these

15. Where the bundling of cables transmitting power and data are concerned, the 8P8C connector is in widespread use with powered communications systems using Class 2 or Class 3 circuits and these connectors are typically rated at ____ maximum.

    (a) 0.50A
    (b) 1.00A
    (c) 1.20A
    (d) 1.30A

16. When using Table 725.144, bundle sizes over ____ cables, or conductor sizes smaller than 26 AWG, ampacities shall be permitted to be determined by qualified personnel under engineering supervision.

    (a) 129
    (b) 178
    (c) 187
    (d) 192

17. Where only half of the conductors in each cable are carrying current, the values in Table 725.144 shall be permitted to be increased by a factor of ____.

    (a) 1
    (b) 1.2
    (c) 1.4
    (d) 1.6

18. Where Types CL3P, CL2P, CL3R, CL2R, CL3, or CL2 transmit power and data, the rated current per conductor of the power source shall not exceed the ampacities in Table 725.144 at an ambient temperature of ____.

    (a) 30°C
    (b) 60°C
    (c) 75°C
    (d) 90°C

19. One example of the use of Class 2 cables is a network of closed-circuit TV cameras using 24 AWG, 60°C rated, ____, Category 5e balanced twisted-pair cabling.

    (a) CL2R
    (b) PLTC
    (c) OCFN
    (d) MC cable

Article 750—Energy Management Systems

1. Article ____ applies to the installation and operation of energy management systems.

   (a) 690
   (b) 724
   (c) 750
   (d) 760

2. Energy management systems shall be permitted to ____ electrical loads and sources in accordance with 750.30(A) through (C).

   (a) monitor
   (b) control
   (c) monitor and control
   (d) none of these

3. Where an EMS is employed to control electrical power through the use of a remote means, a directory identifying the controlled device(s) and circuit(s) shall be posted on the ____.

   (a) enclosure of the controller
   (b) disconnect
   (c) branch-circuit overcurrent device
   (d) any of these

4. Energy management systems shall be listed ____.

   (a) as a complete energy management system
   (b) as a kit for field installation in switch or overcurrent device enclosures
   (c) individual components assembled as a system
   (d) any of these

Article 760—Fire Alarm Systems

1. Article 760 covers the requirements for the installation of wiring and equipment of ____.

   (a) communications systems
   (b) antennas
   (c) fire alarm systems
   (d) fiber optics

2. Fire alarm systems include ____.

   (a) fire detection and alarm notification
   (b) guard's tour
   (c) sprinkler waterflow
   (d) all of these

3. Fire alarm circuits shall be identified at all terminal and junction locations in a manner that helps prevent unintentional signals on fire alarm system circuits during ____ of other systems.

   (a) installation
   (b) testing and servicing
   (c) renovations
   (d) all of these

4. ____ fire alarm cables installed in ducts, plenums, or other spaces used for environmental air shall comply with 300.22.

   (a) Fire rated
   (b) Metal-clad
   (c) Power-limited and nonpower-limited
   (d) Line-voltage

5. ____ fire alarm cables selected in accordance with Table 760.154 and installed in accordance with 722.135 and 300.22(B) Ex, shall be permitted to be installed in ducts specifically fabricated for environmental air.

   (a) Power-limited
   (b) Nonpower-limited
   (c) Power-limited and nonpower-limited
   (d) Line-voltage

6. Where ____ cables are utilized for fire alarm circuits, the cables shall be installed in accordance with Article 770.

   (a) Class 1
   (b) Class 2
   (c) Class 3
   (d) optical fiber

7. The number and ____ of fire alarm cables and conductors shall comply with 300.17.

   (a) cross-sectional area
   (b) diameter
   (c) material
   (d) size

8. Fire alarm circuit cables and conductors installed exposed on the surface of ceilings and sidewalls shall be supported by ____, hangers, or similar fittings designed and installed so as not to damage the cable.

   (a) straps
   (b) staples
   (c) cable ties
   (d) any of these

9. Where abandoned fire alarm cables are identified for future use with a tag, the tag shall be of sufficient durability to withstand ____.

    (a) the environment involved
    (b) heat
    (c) moisture
    (d) sunlight

10. A listed ____ shall be installed on the supply side of a fire alarm control panel in accordance with Part II of Article 242.

    (a) current-limiting device
    (b) selectively coordinated device
    (c) surge-protective device (SPD)
    (d) current transformer

11. The branch circuit supplying power-limited fire alarm equipment shall not be supplied through ____ circuit interrupters.

    (a) ground-fault
    (b) arc-fault
    (c) ground-fault or arc-fault
    (d) none of these

12. The fire alarm circuit disconnecting means for a power-limited fire alarm system shall ____.

    (a) have red identification
    (b) be accessible only to qualified personnel
    (c) be identified as FIRE ALARM CIRCUIT
    (d) all of these

13. A ____ alarm branch-circuit disconnecting means shall be permitted to be secured in the on position.

    (a) fire
    (b) security
    (c) smoke
    (d) all of these

14. ____ protection is not required for receptacles in dwelling-unit unfinished basements that supply power for fire alarm systems.

    (a) SPD
    (b) AFCI
    (c) GFCI
    (d) any of these

15. Fire alarm equipment supplying power-limited fire alarm circuits shall be durably marked where plainly visible to indicate each circuit that is ____.

    (a) supplied by a nonpower-limited fire alarm circuit
    (b) a power-limited fire alarm circuit
    (c) a fire alarm circuit
    (d) supervised

16. The maximum breaker size on the supply side of a fire alarm transformer is ____.

    (a) 5A
    (b) 10A
    (c) 15A
    (d) 20A

17. Cable splices or terminations in power-limited fire alarm systems shall be made in listed ____ or utilization equipment.

    (a) fittings
    (b) boxes or enclosures
    (c) fire alarm devices
    (d) any of these

18. Power-limited fire alarm circuit cables and conductors shall not be placed in any cable, cable tray, compartment, enclosure, manhole, ____, or similar fitting with conductors of electric light, power, Class 1, nonpower-limited fire alarm circuits, and medium-power network-powered broadband communications circuits.

    (a) outlet box
    (b) device box
    (c) raceway
    (d) any of these

19. Power-limited fire alarm circuit conductors are permitted to be ____ to the exterior of any conduit or other raceway as a means of support.

    (a) strapped
    (b) taped
    (c) attached by any means
    (d) none of these

Article 770—Optical Fiber Cables

1. Article 770 covers the installation of optical fiber cables. This article does not cover the construction of ____ cables.

   (a) coaxial
   (b) tray
   (c) optical fiber
   (d) industrial trolley

2. Optical fiber cables shall be permitted to be installed in any raceway included in Chapter 3 if installed in accordance with the requirements of _____.

   (a) Article 90
   (b) Chapter 1
   (c) Chapter 2
   (d) Chapter 3

3. Access to electrical equipment shall not be denied by an accumulation of optical fiber cables that ____ the removal of panels, including suspended-ceiling panels.

   (a) prevent
   (b) hinder
   (c) block
   (d) require

4. Optical fiber cables installed ____ on the surface of ceilings and walls shall be supported by the building structure in such a manner that the cable will not be damaged by normal building use.

   (a) exposed
   (b) in raceways
   (c) hidden
   (d) exposed and concealed

5. Paint, plaster, cleaners, abrasives, corrosive residues, or other contaminants may result in an undetermined alteration of optical fiber cable ____.

   (a) usefulness
   (b) voltage
   (c) properties
   (d) reliability

6. The ____ portion of abandoned optical fiber cables shall be removed.

   (a) accessible
   (b) exposed
   (c) concealed
   (d) salvageable

7. Openings around penetrations of optical fiber cables and communications raceways through fire-resistant-rated walls, partitions, floors, or ceilings shall be ____ using approved methods to maintain the fire-resistance rating.

   (a) closed
   (b) opened
   (c) draft stopped
   (d) firestopped

8. Nonconductive optical fiber cables ____ permitted to occupy the same cabinet, outlet box, panel, or similar enclosure housing the electrical terminations of an electric light, power, Class 1, non-power-limited fire alarm, or medium-power network-powered broadband communications circuit.

   (a) shall be
   (b) shall not be
   (c) any of these
   (d) none of these

9. Nonconductive optical fiber cables shall not be permitted to occupy the same ____ or similar enclosure unless the nonconductive optical fiber cables are functionally associated with the electric circuits.

   (a) cabinet
   (b) outlet box
   (c) panel
   (d) any of these

Please use the 2023 *Code* book to answer the following questions.

CHAPTER 8—COMMUNICATIONS SYSTEMS

Article 800—General Requirements for Communications Systems

1. The Article ____ general requirements apply to communications circuits, community antenna television and radio distribution systems, network-powered broadband communications systems, and premises-powered broadband communications systems, unless modified by Articles 805, 820, 830, or 840.

    (a) 110
    (b) 300
    (c) 700
    (d) 800

2. Only those sections of ____ referenced in Chapter 8 shall apply to Chapter 8.

    (a) Chapters 1 through 4
    (b) Chapters 2 and 3
    (c) Chapters 1 through 7
    (d) the Annexes

3. For communications circuit wiring in ____, the requirements of 300.22(A) shall apply.

    (a) underfloor spaces
    (b) suspended-ceiling spaces
    (c) plenums
    (d) ducts for dust or loose stock, or for vapor removal

4. For communications circuit wiring in ____, the requirements of 300.22(C)(3) shall apply.

    (a) spaces used for environmental air
    (b) ducts for dust
    (c) ducts for loose stock
    (d) ducts for vapor removal

5. Where ____ cable is used to provide a communications circuit within a building, Article 770 shall apply

    (a) coaxial
    (b) fire alarm
    (c) low-voltage
    (d) optical fiber

6. Communications cable ties intended for use in other space used for environmental air (plenums) shall be ____ as having low smoke and heat release properties.

    (a) listed
    (b) labeled
    (c) identified
    (d) approved

7. For communications systems, access to electrical equipment shall not be denied by an accumulation of ____ that prevent(s) the removal of suspended-ceiling panels.

    (a) routers
    (b) amplifiers
    (c) ductwork
    (d) wires and cables

8. Communications cables installed ____ on the surface of ceilings and sidewalls shall be supported by the building structure in such a manner that the cable will not be damaged by normal building use.

   (a) in raceways
   (b) in conduit
   (c) hidden
   (d) exposed

9. For communications systems, plenum ____ and other nonmetallic cable accessories used to secure and support cables in other spaces used for environmental air (plenums) shall be listed as having low smoke and heat release properties in accordance with 800.17.

   (a) fittings
   (b) hangars
   (c) straps
   (d) cable ties

10. The ____ portions of abandoned communications cables shall be removed.

    (a) accessible
    (b) exposed
    (c) concealed
    (d) damaged

11. Openings around penetrations of communications cables, communications raceways, and cable routing assemblies through fire-resistant-rated walls, partitions, floors, or ceilings shall be ____ using approved methods to maintain the fire resistance rating.

    (a) closed
    (b) opened
    (c) draft stopped
    (d) firestopped

12. Where practicable on buildings, a separation of at least ____ shall be maintained between lightning protection conductors and all communications wires and cables and CATV-type coaxial cables.

    (a) 1 ft
    (b) 2 ft
    (c) 3 ft
    (d) 6 ft

13. Wires and cables for communications systems shall be permitted to be installed in any raceway included in ____.

    (a) Chapter 3
    (b) Chapter 8
    (c) Article 300
    (d) Article 800

14. The raceway fill requirements of Chapters 3 and 9 shall apply to ____-power network-powered broadband communications cables.

    (a) low
    (b) medium
    (c) high
    (d) multiconductor

15. Cables used for communications circuits, communications wires, cable routing assemblies, and communications raceways installed in buildings shall be ____ and installed in accordance with the limitations of the listing.

    (a) marked
    (b) labeled
    (c) identified
    (d) listed

16. Communications wires and cables and CATV-type ____ cables shall not be strapped, taped, or attached by any means to the exterior of any raceway as a means of support.

    (a) camera
    (b) coaxial
    (c) internet
    (d) telephone

17. ____ communications plenum cables shall be listed as being suitable for use in ducts, plenums, and other spaces used for environmental air.

    (a) CMR
    (b) CMG
    (c) CMX
    (d) CMP

Article 810—Antenna Systems

1. Article _____ covers antenna systems for radio and television receiving equipment, amateur and citizen band radio transmitting and receiving equipment, and certain features of transmitter safety.
   - (a) 680
   - (b) 700
   - (c) 810
   - (d) 840

2. _____ that connect antennas to equipment shall comply with the appropriate article of Chapter 8.
   - (a) Equipment grounding conductors
   - (b) Coaxial cables
   - (c) Power conductors
   - (d) Tuning cables

3. Masts and metal structures supporting antennas shall be grounded or bonded in accordance with 810.21, unless the antenna and its related supporting mast or structure are within a zone of protection defined by a _____ radius rolling sphere.
   - (a) 75-ft
   - (b) 100-ft
   - (c) 125-ft
   - (d) 150-ft

4. NFPA 780, *Standard for the Installation of Lightning Protection Systems*, provides information for the application of the term _____ as used in 810.15.
   - (a) air terminals
   - (b) zone protection
   - (c) rolling sphere
   - (d) copper rod

5. Underground antenna conductors for radio and television receiving station equipment shall be separated at least _____ from any light, power, or Class 1 circuit conductors.
   - (a) 12 in.
   - (b) 18 in.
   - (c) 5 ft
   - (d) 6 ft

6. Indoor antennas and indoor lead-ins shall not be run nearer than _____ to conductors of other wiring systems in the premise.
   - (a) 2 in.
   - (b) 3 in.
   - (c) 4 in.
   - (d) 6 in.

7. Indoor antennas and indoor lead-ins shall be permitted to occupy the same box or enclosure with conductors of other wiring systems where separated from such other conductors by _____.
   - (a) insulation rated at the highest voltage present
   - (b) an effective permanently installed barrier
   - (c) at least 2 in of separation
   - (d) at least 4 in of separation

8. Receiving station antenna discharge units shall be located outside the building or inside the building between the point of entrance of the lead-in and the radio set or transformers and as near as practicable to the _____.
   - (a) entrance of the conductors to the building
   - (b) intersystem bonding termination
   - (c) grounding electrode system
   - (d) any of these

9. The bonding conductor or grounding electrode conductor for a radio/television receiving station antenna system shall be protected where subject to physical damage, and where installed in a metal raceway, both ends of the raceway shall be bonded to the _____ conductor.
   - (a) contained
   - (b) grounded
   - (c) ungrounded
   - (d) largest

10. The bonding conductor or grounding electrode conductor for an antenna mast or antenna discharge unit for radio and television equipment shall be run to the _____ in as straight a line as practicable.
    - (a) lightning arrester
    - (b) surge-protective device
    - (c) grounding electrode
    - (d) main electrical disconnect enclosure

11. If the building or structure served has an intersystem bonding termination, the bonding conductor for the radio and television equipment antenna mast or antenna discharge unit, shall be connected to the ____.

    (a) main electrical disconnect enclosure
    (b) grounding electrode
    (c) surge protective device
    (d) intersystem bonding termination

12. For antenna systems, an intersystem bonding termination device shall not be mounted on a door or cover even if the door or cover is ____.

    (a) plastic
    (b) removable
    (c) nonremovable
    (d) fiberglass

13. The bonding conductor or grounding electrode conductor for radio and television receiving station antenna discharge units shall not be smaller than ____.

    (a) 10 AWG copper
    (b) 8 AWG aluminum
    (c) 17 AWG copper-clad steel or bronze
    (d) any of these

14. If a separate grounding electrode is installed for the radio and television receiving station equipment, it shall be bonded to the building's electrical power grounding electrode system with a bonding jumper not smaller than ____.

    (a) 10 AWG
    (b) 8 AWG
    (c) 6 AWG
    (d) 1/0 AWG

Article 820—Community Antenna Television and Radio Distribution Systems

1. Coaxial cable is permitted to deliver power to equipment that is directly associated with the radio frequency distribution system if the voltage is not over ____.

    (a) 12V
    (b) 30V
    (c) 60V
    (d) 90V

2. Coaxial cable can have a maximum voltage of ____.

    (a) 60V
    (b) 70V
    (c) 80V
    (d) 90V

3. A coaxial feed is installed in a trench containing a residential 240V service. What is the minimum separation?

    (a) 12 inches
    (b) 18 inches
    (c) 6 inches
    (d) 10 inches

4. In installations where the coaxial cable enters the building, the outer conductive shield shall be grounded in accordance with 820.100. The grounding shall be as close as practicable to the point of entrance not to exceed ____ in length.

    (a) 8 ft
    (b) 12 ft
    (c) 15 ft
    (d) 20 ft

5. Where installed, a ____ primary protector shall be applied on each community antenna and radio distribution (CATV) cable external to the premises.

    (a) listed
    (b) approved
    (c) identified
    (d) suitable

6. For communications systems using coaxial cable completely contained within the building or the exterior zone of protection defined by a ____ radius rolling sphere and isolated from outside cable plant, the shield is permitted to be grounded by a connection to an equipment grounding conductor as described in 250.118.

    (a) 75 ft
    (b) 100 ft
    (c) 125 ft
    (d) 150 ft

7. Unpowered equipment and enclosures or equipment powered by coaxial cable shall be considered ____ where connected to the metallic cable shield.

    (a) grounded
    (b) bonded
    (c) grounded and bonded
    (d) none of these

8. Coaxial cable(s) marked ____ is(are) plenum rated.

    (a) CATVX
    (b) CATVR
    (c) CATVP
    (d) any of these

9. Permitted substitutions for CATV cable include ____.

    (a) CATVP
    (b) CMP
    (c) CATVR
    (d) any of these

10. CATVR coaxial cable may be substituted with Types BMR, BLR, or BLP for installation in ____.

    (a) risers
    (b) plenums
    (c) dwellings
    (d) any of these

11. The coaxial cable voltage rating shall not be marked on the ____.

    (a) cable
    (b) box
    (c) manufacture specs
    (d) cut sheets

Article 830—Network-Powered Broadband Communications Systems

1. Overhead network powered broadband communications cable shall have a minimum vertical clearance of ____ over areas subject to truck traffic, where the voltage does not exceed 300V-to-ground.

    (a) 10 ft
    (b) 12 ft
    (c) 15.5 ft
    (d) 18 ft

2. Overhead network powered broadband communications cable shall have a minimum clearance of ____ from windows that are designed to be opened, doors, porches, balconies, ladders, stairs, fire escapes, or similar locations.

    (a) 3 ft
    (b) 4 ft
    (c) 6 ft
    (d) 10 ft

NEC REVIEW QUESTIONS— PRACTICE EXAM

The following 100-question random order Practice Exam will help you assess your knowledge of the *National Electrical Code*.

Please use the 2023 *Code* book to answer the questions.

Want to practice online? Scan the QR code to access these questions online to get familiar with the online environment in which you'll most likely be taking your exam.

1. Article ____ covers use and application, arrangement, and enforcement of the *National Electrical Code*.

    (a) 90
    (b) 110
    (c) 200
    (d) 300

2. A surge-protective device shall not be installed in circuits over ____.

    (a) 480V
    (b) 600V
    (c) 1,000V
    (d) 4,160V

3. USE cable is not permitted for ____ wiring.

    (a) underground
    (b) interior
    (c) aerial
    (d) aboveground installations

4. Splices and taps in surface metal raceways without removable covers shall be made only in ____.

    (a) boxes
    (b) raceways
    (c) conduit bodies
    (d) none of these

5. The branch-circuit conductor(s) ampacity shall not be less than ____ of the load of the fixed electric space-heating equipment and any associated motor(s).

    (a) 80 percent
    (b) 110 percent
    (c) 125 percent
    (d) 150 percent

6. Article 645 does not apply unless an information technology equipment room contains ____.

    (a) a disconnecting means complying with 645.10
    (b) a separate heating/ventilating/air-conditioning (HVAC) system
    (c) separation by fire-resistance-rated walls, floors, and ceilings
    (d) all of these

7. Power-limited circuits installed in ____ shall comply with 300.22.

    (a) ducts
    (b) plenums
    (c) other space used for environmental air
    (d) any of these

8. The purpose of the *NEC* is for ____.

    (a) it to be used as a design manual
    (b) use as an instruction guide for untrained persons
    (c) the practical safeguarding of persons and property
    (d) interacting with inspectors

9. For grounded systems, normally noncurrent-carrying conductive materials enclosing electrical conductors shall be connected together and to the ____ to establish an effective ground-fault current path.

   (a) ground
   (b) earth
   (c) electrical supply source
   (d) enclosure

10. RMC smaller than trade size ____ or larger than trade size ____ shall not be used.

    (a) ¾, 4
    (b) ½, 4
    (c) ½, 6
    (d) ¾, 6

11. All switches and circuit breakers used as switches shall be located so that they can be operated from a readily ____ place.

    (a) accessible
    (b) visible
    (c) operable
    (d) open

12. Where no secondary overcurrent protection is used, a 480V, 50A transformer shall have an individual overcurrent device on the primary side rated at a maximum ____ of the rated primary current of the transformer.

    (a) 115 percent
    (b) 125 percent
    (c) 167 percent
    (d) 250 percent

13. Electrical wiring, raceways, and cables used directly in connection with an elevator shall be permitted inside the hoistway, machine rooms, control rooms, machinery spaces, and control spaces, including wiring for ____.

    (a) communications with the car
    (b) fire detection systems
    (c) pit sump pumps
    (d) any of these

14. The installation and maintenance of energy storage system (ESS) equipment and all associated wiring and interconnections shall be performed only by ____.

    (a) qualified persons
    (b) ESS specialists
    (c) licensed electricians
    (d) maintenance personnel

15. Coaxial cable can have a maximum voltage of ____.

    (a) 60V
    (b) 70V
    (c) 80V
    (d) 90V

16. Unless specifically permitted in 240.4(E) or (G), the overcurrent protection for 14 AWG copper-clad aluminum conductors shall not exceed 10A provided that ____.

    (a) continuous loads do not exceed 8A
    (b) circuit breakers are listed and marked for use with 14 AWG copper-clad aluminum conductors
    (c) fuses are listed and marked for use with 14 AWG copper-clad aluminum conductors
    (d) all of these

17. PVC smaller than trade size ____ or larger than trade size ____ shall not be used.

    (a) ½, 4
    (b) ¾, 4
    (c) ½, 6
    (d) ¾, 6

18. Luminaires located where subject to bathroom shower spray shall be marked suitable for ____ locations.

    (a) damp
    (b) wet
    (c) outdoor
    (d) wet or outdoor

19. For each floor area inside a minor repair garage where ventilation is not provided and Class I liquids or gaseous fuels are not transferred or dispensed, the entire area up to a level of ____ above the floor is considered to be a Class I, Division 2 location.

    (a) 6 in.
    (b) 12 in.
    (c) 18 in.
    (d) 24 in.

20. All wiring from the controllers to the fire pump motors shall be in ____, listed MC cable with an impervious covering, or MI cable.

    (a) rigid or intermediate metal conduit
    (b) electrical metallic tubing (EMT)
    (c) liquidtight flexible metallic or nonmetallic conduit
    (d) any of these

21. Where an EMS is employed to control electrical power through the use of a remote means, a directory identifying the controlled device(s) and circuit(s) shall be posted on the ____.

    (a) enclosure of the controller
    (b) disconnect
    (c) branch-circuit overcurrent device
    (d) any of these

22. In dwelling units and guest rooms or guest suites, voltage shall not exceed 120V for cord and plug equipment connected to loads rated ____.

    (a) 1,440 VA
    (b) 1,500 VA
    (c) 1,800 VA
    (d) 2,400 VA

23. Snap switches shall not be grouped or ganged in enclosures unless the voltage between adjacent devices does not exceed ____, or unless installed with identified barriers between adjacent devices.

    (a) 100V
    (b) 200V
    (c) 300V
    (d) 400V

24. Boxes and fittings must be ____ for Class I, Division 1 locations.

    (a) designed
    (b) labeled
    (c) marked
    (d) identified

25. Manual and nonautomatic transfer equipment for optional standby systems require ____ intervention.

    (a) human
    (b) animal
    (c) electrician
    (d) inspector

26. For communications circuit wiring in ____, the requirements of 300.22(C)(3) shall apply.

    (a) spaces used for environmental air
    (b) ducts for dust
    (c) ducts for loose stock
    (d) ducts for vapor removal

27. Circuit conductors other than service conductors, shall not be installed in the same ____ as the service conductors.

    (a) raceway or cable
    (b) handhole enclosure
    (c) underground box
    (d) all of these

28. PVC conduit trade sizes 1¼ to 2 shall be supported no greater than ____ between supports.

    (a) 3 ft
    (b) 4 ft
    (c) 5 ft
    (d) 6 ft

29. If a branch circuit supplies a single nonmotor-operated appliance, the rating of overcurrent protection shall not exceed ____ of the appliance rated current if the overcurrent protection rating is not marked and the appliance is rated over 13.30A.

    (a) 100 percent
    (b) 125 percent
    (c) 150 percent
    (d) 160 percent

30. For circuit sizing and current calculation of PV systems, the maximum PV inverter output circuit current is equal to the inverter ____ output current rating.

    (a) average
    (b) peak
    (c) continuous
    (d) intermittent

31. ____ fire alarm cables selected in accordance with Table 760.154 and installed in accordance with 722.135 and 300.22(B) Ex, shall be permitted to be installed in ducts specifically fabricated for environmental air.

    (a) Power-limited
    (b) Nonpower-limited
    (c) Power-limited and nonpower-limited
    (d) Line-voltage

32. The lighting load unit values of Table 220.42(A) are based on minimum load conditions and ____ power factor and might not provide sufficient capacity for the installation contemplated.

    (a) 80 percent
    (b) 85 percent
    (c) 90 percent
    (d) 92 percent

33. NM cable on a wall of an unfinished basement installed in a listed raceway shall have a ____ installed at the point where the cable enters the raceway.

    (a) suitable insulating bushing or adapter
    (b) sealing fitting
    (c) bonding bushing
    (d) junction box

34. Incandescent luminaires with ____ enclosed lamps and pendant luminaires or lampholders shall not be permitted in clothes closet storage spaces.

    (a) open
    (b) partially
    (c) open or partially
    (d) any of these

35. An emergency system shall have adequate ____ in accordance with Article 220 or by another approved method.

    (a) lighting
    (b) capacity
    (c) voltage
    (d) power

36. The ____ portion of abandoned optical fiber cables shall be removed.

    (a) accessible
    (b) exposed
    (c) concealed
    (d) salvageable

37. The vertical clearance of final spans of overhead conductors above or within ____ measured horizontally of platforms, projections, or surfaces that will permit personal contact shall be maintained in accordance with 225.18.

    (a) 3 ft
    (b) 6 ft
    (c) 8 ft
    (d) 10 ft

38. Trade size 2 RMC run straight with threaded couplings shall be supported at intervals not exceeding ____.

    (a) 10 ft
    (b) 12 ft
    (c) 14 ft
    (d) 16 ft

39. Class III locations are those that are hazardous (classified) because of the presence of ____.

    (a) combustible dust
    (b) combustible nonmetal fibers/flyings
    (c) flammable gases or vapors
    (d) flammable liquids or gases

40. Interconnected power production installations with multiple co-located power production sources shall be permitted to be ____ as a group(s).

    (a) identified
    (b) labeled
    (c) marked
    (d) all of these

41. Unpowered equipment and enclosures or equipment powered by coaxial cable shall be considered ____ where connected to the metallic cable shield.

    (a) grounded
    (b) bonded
    (c) grounded and bonded
    (d) none of these

42. A grounded conductor shall not be connected to normally noncurrent-carrying metal parts of equipment, to equipment grounding conductor(s), or be reconnected to ground on the load side of the ____ except as otherwise permitted.

    (a) service disconnecting means
    (b) distribution panel
    (c) switchgear
    (d) switchboard

43. Where a waste disposer is cord-and-plug-connected, the receptacles shall be ____ to protect against physical damage to the flexible cord.

    (a) located
    (b) shielded
    (c) guarded
    (d) any of these

44. A legally required standby system shall have adequate capacity in accordance with Article ____ or by another approved method.

    (a) 210
    (b) 220
    (c) 230
    (d) 700

45. Communications cables installed ____ on the surface of ceilings and sidewalls shall be supported by the building structure in such a manner that the cable will not be damaged by normal building use.

    (a) in raceways
    (b) in conduit
    (c) hidden
    (d) exposed

46. Supplementary overcurrent protective devices are not permitted to be used ____.

    (a) to provide additional overcurrent protection for luminaires
    (b) to provide additional overcurrent protection for appliances
    (c) as the required branch-circuit overcurrent protective device
    (d) none of these

47. The flexible cord for a(an) in-sink waste disposer shall have an equipment grounding conductor and terminate with a ____ attachment plug.

    (a) 3-wire
    (b) 4-wire
    (c) nongrounding-type
    (d) grounding-type

48. Meter-mounted optional standby system transfer switches installed between the ____ and the meter enclosure shall be listed meter-mounted transfer switches.

    (a) service connection point
    (b) utility meter
    (c) utility transformer
    (d) cold sequence disconnect

49. The bonding conductor or grounding electrode conductor for a radio/television receiving station antenna system shall be protected where subject to physical damage, and where installed in a metal raceway, both ends of the raceway shall be bonded to the ____ conductor.

    (a) contained
    (b) grounded
    (c) ungrounded
    (d) largest

50. If an ac system operating at 1,000V or less is grounded at any point, the ____ shall be routed with the ungrounded conductors to each service disconnecting means and shall be connected to each disconnecting means grounded conductor(s) terminal or bus.

    (a) system bonding jumper
    (b) supply-side bonding jumper
    (c) grounded conductor
    (d) equipment grounding conductor

51. A conduit run between a conduit seal and the point at which the conduit leaves a Class I, Division 1 location shall contain no union, coupling, box, or other fitting except for a listed ____ reducer installed at the conduit seal.

    (a) explosionproof
    (b) fireproof
    (c) vaportight
    (d) dusttight

52. Cable used in a wet location shall be listed for use in wet locations and be marked wet or wet location or have a moisture-impervious ____ sheath.

    (a) metal
    (b) plastic
    (c) fiberglass
    (d) any of these

53. There shall be a minimum of one additional ____ branch circuit for dwelling unit laundry receptacle outlet(s).

    (a) 15A
    (b) 20A
    (c) auxiliary
    (d) supplemental

54. A receptacle is considered to be in a location protected from the weather when located under roofed open porches, canopies, marquees, and the like, where it will not be subjected to ____.

    (a) spray from a hose
    (b) a direct lightning hit
    (c) beating rain or water runoff
    (d) falling or wind-blown debris

55. Where used for legally required standby systems, the short-circuit current rating of the transfer equipment, based on the specific overcurrent protective device type and settings protecting the transfer equipment, shall be field marked on the ____ of the transfer equipment.

    (a) exterior
    (b) top
    (c) interior
    (d) underside

56. Nonmandatory information relative to the use of the *NEC* is provided in informative annexes and are ____.

    (a) included for information purposes only
    (b) not enforceable requirements of the *Code*
    (c) enforceable as a requirement of the *Code*
    (d) included for information purposes only and are not enforceable requirements of the *Code*

57. Where conductors in parallel are run in ____ raceway(s), the raceway(s) shall have the same electrical characteristics.

    (a) separate
    (b) similar
    (c) the same
    (d) different

58. Where used for emergency systems, the short-circuit current rating of the transfer equipment, based on the specific overcurrent protective device type and settings protecting the transfer equipment, shall be field marked on the ____ of the transfer equipment.

    (a) exterior
    (b) top
    (c) interior
    (d) underside

59. A fountain is defined as an ornamental structure or recreational water feature from which one or more jets or streams of water are discharged into the air, including splash pads, and ____ pools.

    (a) ornamental
    (b) wading
    (c) seasonal
    (d) permanently installed

60. Receptacles of ____, 125V and 250V installed in a wet location shall have an enclosure that is weatherproof whether or not the attachment plug cap is inserted.

    (a) 15A and 20A
    (b) 30A and less
    (c) up to 50A
    (d) up to 100A

61. For ____ dwelling units, a sign shall be placed at the disconnecting means required in 230.85 that indicates the location of each permanently installed on-site optional standby power source disconnect or means to shut down the prime mover as required in 445.19(C).

    (a) apartment
    (b) guest suite
    (c) multi-family
    (d) one- and two-family

62. When sizing a service or feeder for fixed appliances in dwelling units, a demand factor of 75 percent of the total nameplate ratings can be applied if there are ____ or more appliances fastened in place.

    (a) two
    (b) three
    (c) four
    (d) five

63. The maximum rating of the overcurrent protective device for 14 AWG motor control wiring that extends beyond the enclosure is ____.

    (a) 15A
    (b) 20A
    (c) 45A
    (d) 100A

64. For the purposes of bundling cables transmitting power and data, one example of the use of cables for Class 2 or Class 3 circuits that transmit power and data is the connection of ____.

    (a) closed-circuit TV cameras (CCTV)
    (b) antennas
    (c) coaxial cable
    (d) none of these

65. The connection of the system bonding jumper for a separately derived system shall be made ____ on the separately derived system from the source to the first system disconnecting means or overcurrent device.

    (a) in at least two locations
    (b) in every location that the grounded conductor is present
    (c) at any single point
    (d) effectively

66. Single-conductor PV system cables with ____ insulation marked sunlight resistant can be used to connect photovoltaic modules in outdoor locations within the PV array.

    (a) THHN
    (b) USE-2
    (c) RHW-2
    (d) USE-2 and RHW-2

67. When modifications to the electrical installation occur that affect the available fault current at the service, the available fault current shall be verified or ____ as necessary to ensure the service equipment ratings are sufficient for the available fault current at the line terminals of the equipment.

    (a) recalculated
    (b) increased
    (c) decreased
    (d) adjusted

68. A recessed luminaire that is not identified for contact with insulation shall have all recessed parts spaced not less than ____ from combustible materials.

    (a) ½ in.
    (b) ⅝ in.
    (c) ¾ in.
    (d) 1 in.

69. The maximum breaker size on the supply side of a fire alarm transformer is ____.

    (a) 5A
    (b) 10A
    (c) 15A
    (d) 20A

70. ____ insulated conductors shall not be subject to ampacity adjustment where installed exposed to direct sunlight on a rooftop.

    (a) THW-2
    (b) XHHW-2
    (c) THWN-2
    (d) RHW-2

71. Where two interconnected electric power production sources are located at opposite ends of a busbar that contains loads, the sum of 125 percent of the power-source(s) output circuit current and the rating of the overcurrent device protecting the busbar shall not exceed ____ of the busbar ampere rating.

    (a) 100 percent
    (b) 115 percent
    (c) 120 percent
    (d) 125 percent

72. Plug fuses of the Edison-base type shall be used only ____.

    (a) where over fusing is necessary
    (b) for replacement in existing installations
    (c) as a replacement for Type S fuses
    (d) if rated 50A and above

73. Wiring from an emergency source or emergency source distribution overcurrent protection to emergency loads shall be kept independent of all other wiring and equipment except in ____.

    (a) transfer equipment enclosures
    (b) exit or emergency luminaires supplied from two sources
    (c) listed load control relays supplying exit or emergency luminaires, or a common junction box, attached to exit or emergency luminaires supplied from two sources
    (d) all of these

74. Wiring methods permitted for service-entrance conductors include ____.

    (a) rigid metal conduit
    (b) electrical metallic tubing
    (c) PVC conduit
    (d) all of these

75. Where interconnected electric power production source output connections are made at either end of a ____ panelboard in dwellings, it shall be permitted where the sum of 125 percent of the power-source(s) output circuit current and the rating of the overcurrent device protecting the busbar does not exceed 120 percent of the busbar ampere rating.

    (a) front-fed
    (b) back-fed
    (c) center-fed
    (d) none of these

76. Where direct-buried conductors and cables emerge from grade, they shall be protected by enclosures or raceways to a point at least ____ above finished grade.

    (a) 3 ft
    (b) 6 ft
    (c) 8 ft
    (d) 10 ft

77. The rating of any one cord-and plug-connected utilization equipment on a 15A, 120V branch circuit shall not exceed ____.

    (a) 12A
    (b) 15A
    (c) 16A
    (d) 20A

78. An emergency management system (EMS), in accordance with 705.30, shall be permitted to limit current and loading on the busbars and conductors supplied by the output of one or more interconnected electric power production sources or ____ sources.

    (a) utility power
    (b) energy storage
    (c) stand-alone power
    (d) all of these

79. Direct-buried conductors, cables, or raceways which are subject to movement by settlement or frost shall be arranged to prevent damage to the ____ or to equipment connected to the raceways.

    (a) cable
    (b) raceway
    (c) enclosed conductors
    (d) expansion fitting

80. Where the service equipment for areas of nursing homes and limited care facilities used exclusively as ____ is replaced, a surge-protective device (SPD) shall be installed.

    (a) patient sleeping rooms
    (b) critical care areas
    (c) public areas
    (d) emergency egress

81. An appliance receptacle outlet installed for a specific appliance shall be installed within ____ of the intended location of the appliance.

    (a) sight
    (b) 3 ft
    (c) 6 ft
    (d) the length of the cord

82. A(An) ____ is a point on the wiring system at which current is taken to supply utilization equipment.

    (a) box
    (b) receptacle
    (c) outlet
    (d) device

83. Equipment containing overcurrent devices supplied from interconnected electric power production sources shall be marked to indicate the presence of ____.

    (a) leakage current
    (b) all sources
    (c) selective coordination
    (d) emergency loads

84. Wiring of Class 2 emergency circuits shall comply with the requirements of 300.4 and be installed in a(an) ____.

    (a) raceway
    (b) armored-cable or metal-clad cable
    (c) cable tray
    (d) any of these

85. Wiring protection requirements for Class 2 emergency circuits shall not apply to wiring that do not exceed ____ in length and that terminate at an emergency luminaire or an emergency lighting control device

    (a) 2 ft
    (b) 3 ft
    (c) 4 ft
    (d) 6 ft

86. Wiring protection requirements for Class 2 emergency circuits shall not apply to locked rooms or locked enclosures that are accessible only to ____.

    (a) qualified persons
    (b) staff
    (c) maintenance personnel
    (d) licensed individuals

87. Emergency system sources of power shall be such that, in the event of failure of the normal supply to, or within, the building or group of buildings concerned, emergency lighting, emergency power, or both shall be available within the time required for the application but not to exceed ____.

    (a) 5 seconds
    (b) 10 seconds
    (c) 30 seconds
    (d) 60 seconds

88. Emergency equipment for emergency systems shall be ____ and located so as to minimize the hazards that might cause complete failure due to flooding, fires, icing, and vandalism.

    (a) approved
    (b) listed
    (c) installed
    (d) designed

89. The emergency power source shall be of suitable rating and capacity to supply and maintain the total load for the duration determined by the system design and in no case shall the duration be less than ____ of system operation unless used for emergency illumination in 700.12(C)(4) or unit equipment in 700.12(H).

    (a) 1 hour
    (b) 90 minutes
    (c) 2 hours
    (d) 3 hours

90. ____ is, for grounded circuits, the voltage between the given conductor and that point or conductor of the circuit that is grounded; for ungrounded circuits, the greatest voltage between the given conductor and any other conductor of the circuit.

    (a) Line-to-line voltage
    (b) voltage to ground
    (c) Phase-to-phase voltage
    (d) Neutral to ground voltage

91. Ground-fault protection of equipment shall be provided for solidly grounded wye electrical services of more than 150V to ground, but not exceeding 1,000V phase-to-phase for each service disconnecting means rated ____ or more.

    (a) 1,000A
    (b) 1,500A
    (c) 2,000A
    (d) 2,500A

92. Kitchen and dining room countertop receptacle outlets in dwelling units shall be installed on or above the countertop or work surface, but not more than ____ above the countertop or work surface.

    (a) 12 in.
    (b) 18 in.
    (c) 20 in.
    (d) 24 in.

93. No wiring of any type shall be installed in ducts used to transport ____.

    (a) dust
    (b) flammable vapors
    (c) loose stock
    (d) all of these

94. If the supplemental electrode is a rod, pipe, or plate electrode, that portion of the bonding jumper that is the sole connection to the supplemental grounding electrode is not required to be larger than ____ copper.

    (a) 8 AWG
    (b) 6 AWG
    (c) 4 AWG
    (d) 1 AWG

95. If ____, a grounding electrode conductor or its enclosure shall be securely fastened to the surface on which it is carried.

    (a) concealed
    (b) exposed
    (c) accessible
    (d) none of these

96. Ferrous metal raceways for grounding electrode conductors shall be bonded at each end of the raceway or enclosure to the grounding electrode or grounding electrode conductor to create a(an) _____ parallel path.

    (a) mechanically
    (b) electrically
    (c) physically
    (d) effective

97. The largest size copper grounding electrode conductor required based on Table 250.66 is _____.

    (a) 6 AWG
    (b) 1/0 AWG
    (c) 3/0 AWG
    (d) 250 kcmil

98. If service conductors are connected in parallel in three separate metal raceways, with 600 kcmil conductors per phase, the supply-side bonding jumper size for each service raceway is _____.

    (a) 1/0 AWG
    (b) 3/0 AWG
    (c) 250 kcmil
    (d) 500 kcmil

99. A transformer supplies power to a 100A panelboard with 2 AWG THWN-2 conductors. The size of the bonding jumper in copper required to bond the building steel to the secondary grounded conductor is _____.

    (a) 8 AWG
    (b) 6 AWG
    (c) 4 AWG
    (d) 2 AWG

100. A _____ equipment grounding conductor is required for a 15A branch circuit that provides power for a low-voltage lighting system.

    (a) 14 AWG
    (b) 14 AWG aluminum
    (c) 12 AWG
    (d) 10 AWG aluminum

MODULE 11

NEC REVIEW QUESTIONS *CODE* RULE INDEX

The following is a reference index for topics in the *National Electrical Code*. It displays the *Code* rule so you can go to that content in the *2023 NEC* edition for additional review. This is an excellent reference to help you become more comfortable with your *Code* book.

MODULE

III

NEC CALCULATIONS

Introduction to Module III—*NEC* Calculations

In this module you will cover the calculations topics and questions typically included in journeyman exams. This module will walk you through each of these topics, step-by-step, one example, and one calculation at a time. You will learn to consider the conditions necessary for the types of questions you will be required to answer on most electrical exams. So, get out your *Code* book, calculator, highlighters, ruler, and sharpen your pencils!

Module III includes the units titled:

▶ **Unit 1—Raceway Calculations**

▶ **Unit 2—Box Calculations**

▶ **Unit 3—Conductor Sizing and Protection Calculations**

▶ **Unit 4—Motor, Air-Conditioning, and Transformer Calculations**

▶ **Unit 5—Voltage-Drop Calculations**

▶ **Unit 6—Dwelling Unit Calculations**

Carefully studying the information, examples, and graphics in this module will help you gain the confidence to be able to answer those important exam calculation questions.

UNIT 1

RACEWAY CALCULATIONS

Introduction to Unit 1—Raceway Calculations

Raceways must be large enough to avoid damaging the insulation when conductors are pulled into them. Before we can even begin to properly size the raceways that protect electrical conductors, we need a thorough understanding of *NEC* Chapter 9, and how and when to apply the information contained in the Tables located here. There are 24 Tables contained in Chapter 9 and a "Notes to Tables" section that applies to various tables and their applications.

Chapter 9 and Annex C of the *NEC* are the primary references for determining allowable conductor fill in raceways. For the most common condition, where multiple conductors of the same size are installed together in a raceway, the maximum number of conductors permitted can be determined from the tables in Annex C.

For situations where conductors of different sizes are mixed in a raceway, Chapter 9 contains the information necessary to calculate the required raceway size. Because different conductor types (THWN-2, THHW, USE, and so forth) have different insulation thicknesses, they occupy varying amounts of a raceway's cross-sectional area. The number and size of conductors permitted in any raceway depends on the conductor type to be installed and the raceway type.

Metal wireways must be sized using the requirements of Article 376 based on the maximum conductor fill permitted and wire-bending space. Cable trays must be sized using the requirements of Article 392 and Annex C depending on the cable tray type, the cable type, and the conductor type.

1.1 Conductor Cross-Sectional Area—Chapter 9, Tables 5 and 8

Chapter 9, Table 5—Cross-sectional Areas of Insulated Conductors

Chapter 9, Table 5, lists the approximate conductor cross-sectional area of insulated conductors based on worst-case scenarios for round concentric-lay-stranded conductors.

▶ **Chapter 9, Table 5—THWN-2, Example 1**

Question: What is the cross-sectional area of one 10 THWN-2 conductor? ▶Figure 1–1

(a) 0.0097 sq in.   (b) 0.0172 sq in.
(c) 0.0211 sq in.   (d) 0.0366 sq in.

Answer: (c) 0.0211 sq in.

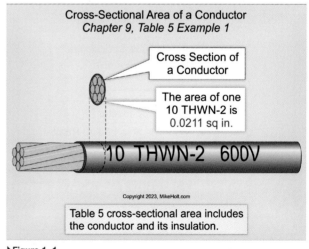

Cross-Sectional Area of a Conductor
Chapter 9, Table 5 Example 1

Cross Section of a Conductor

The area of one 10 THWN-2 is 0.0211 sq in.

10 THWN-2 600V

Copyright 2023, MikeHolt.com

Table 5 cross-sectional area includes the conductor and its insulation.

▶Figure 1–1

▶ **Chapter 9, Table 5—THWN-2, Example 2**

Question: What is the cross-sectional area of one 8 THWN-2 conductor? ▶**Figure 1–2**

(a) 0.0097 sq in.   (b) 0.0172 sq in.
(c) 0.0211 sq in.   (d) 0.0366 sq in.

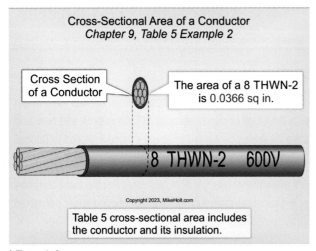

▶Figure 1–2

Answer: (d) 0.0366 sq in.

▶ **Chapter 9, Table 5—RHW With an Outer Cover, Example 3**

Question: What is the cross-sectional area of one 10 RHW conductor with an outer cover? ▶**Figure 1–3**

(a) 0.0172 sq in.   (b) 0.0437 sq in.
(c) 0.0278 sq in.   (d) 0.0835 sq in.

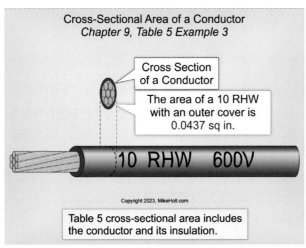

▶Figure 1–3

Solution:

The note at the end of Table 5 states that conductor Types RHH, RHW, and RHW-2 without outer coverings are identified on the table with an asterisk (*).

Answer: (b) 0.0437 sq in.

▶ **Chapter 9, Table 5—RHH With an Outer Cover, Example 4**

Question: What is the cross-sectional area of one 8 RHH conductor with an outer cover? ▶**Figure 1–4**

(a) 0.0172 sq in.   (b) 0.0206 sq in.
(c) 0.0278 sq in.   (d) 0.0835 sq in.

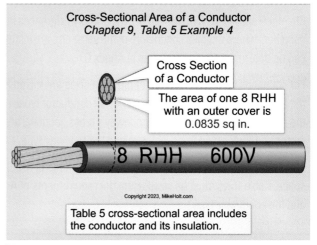

▶Figure 1–4

Answer: (d) 0.0835 sq in.

▶ **Chapter 9, Table 5—RHH Without an Outer Cover, Example 5**

Question: What is the cross-sectional area of one 10 RHH conductor without an outer cover? ▶**Figure 1–5**

(a) 0.0117 sq in.   (b) 0.0333 sq in.
(c) 0.0278 sq in.   (d) 0.0556 sq in.

Answer: (b) 0.0333 sq in.

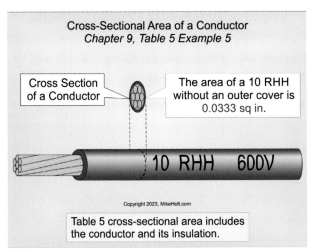

▶Figure 1–5

▶ **Chapter 9, Table 5—RHW Without an Outer Cover, Example 6**

Question: *What is the cross-sectional area of one 8 RHW conductor without an outer cover?* ▶Figure 1–6

(a) 0.0117 sq in.   (b) 0.0252 sq in.
(c) 0.0278 sq in.   (d) 0.0556 sq in.

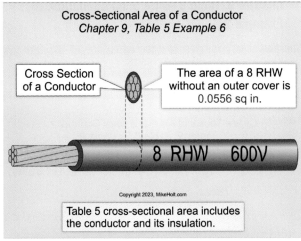

▶Figure 1–6

Answer: *(d) 0.0556 sq in.*

Chapter 9, Table 5A—Cross-sectional Areas of Compact Insulated Conductors

Chapter 9, Table 5A, lists the approximate conductor area based on worst-case scenarios for round compact stranded copper and aluminum conductors.

Compact stranding is the result of a manufacturing process where each strand of the conductor is shaped to the extent that the space between the strands is virtually eliminated. ▶Figure 1–7

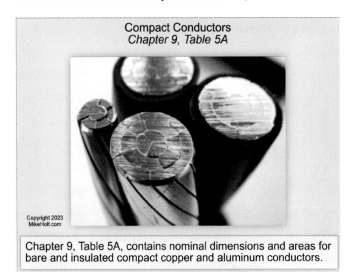

Chapter 9, Table 5A, contains nominal dimensions and areas for bare and insulated compact copper and aluminum conductors.

▶Figure 1–7

▶ **Chapter 9, Table 5A—XHHW Compact Conductors, Example 1**

Question: *What is the cross-sectional area of one 1 XHHW compact conductor?* ▶Figure 1–8

(a) 0.0117 sq in.   (b) 0.1352 sq in.
(c) 0.2733 sq in.   (d) 0.5216 sq in.

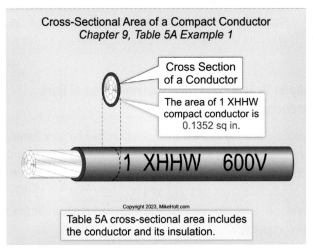

▶Figure 1–8

Answer: *(b) 0.1352 sq in.*

▶ **Chapter 9, Table 5A—THHW Compact Conductors, Example 2**

Question: What is the cross-sectional area of one 4/0 THHW compact conductor? ▶Figure 1–9

(a) 0.0117 sq in.

(b) 0.1352 sq in.

(c) 0.3267 sq in.

(d) 0.5216 sq in.

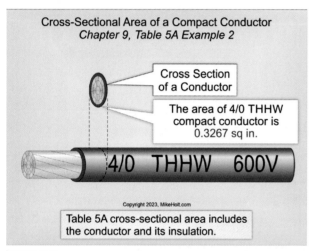

▶Figure 1–9

Answer: (c) 0.3267 sq in.

Author's Comment:

▶ Although the ampacity of copper and aluminum for the same size conductor is different, the cross-sectional areas of copper and aluminum compact conductors are the same.

Chapter 9, Table 8—Cross-Sectional Area of Bare Conductors

Chapter 9, Table 8, lists the approximate conductor area based on worst-case scenarios for round uninsulated concentric-lay-stranded conductors. It contains conductor property information such as the conductor's cross-sectional area in circular mils, the number of strands per conductor, the cross-sectional area in square inches for bare conductors.

The number of strands in a conductor is found in the 4th column under "Stranding," then "Quantity." A "1" denotes a solid conductor.

▶ **Chapter 9, Table 8—Bare Stranded Conductor, Example 1**

Question: What is the cross-sectional area of one 10 AWG bare stranded conductor? ▶Figure 1–10

(a) 0.008 sq in. (b) 0.011 sq in. (c) 0.038 sq in. (d) 0.015 sq in.

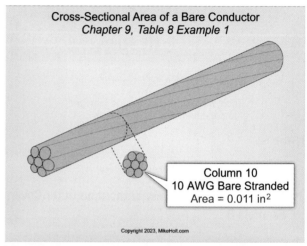

▶Figure 1–10

Answer: (b) 0.011 sq in. [Chapter 9, Table 8, Column 10]

▶ **Chapter 9, Table 8—Bare Solid Conductor, Example 2**

Question: What is the cross-sectional area of one 10 AWG bare solid conductor? ▶Figure 1–11

(a) 0.008 sq in. (b) 0.011 sq in. (c) 0.038 sq in. (d) 0.015 sq in.

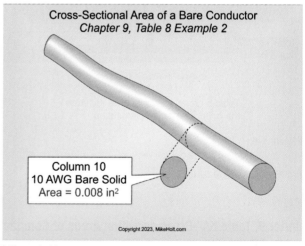

▶Figure 1–11

Answer: (a) 0.008 sq in. [Chapter 9, Table 8, Column 10]

1.2 Raceway Properties

Raceways must be large enough to avoid damage to the insulation of the conductor (or even the conductor itself) due to abrasion and/or friction that might occur when conductors are pulled into the raceway [300.17]. For situations where conductors of varied sizes are mixed in a raceway, Chapter 9 contains the information necessary to calculate their cumulative area which is required for appropriately sizing the raceway. Because different conductor types (THHN, THHW, THWN-2, and so forth) have different insulation thicknesses, the number and size of conductors permitted in each raceway will often vary depending on the conductor type used.

Chapter 9, Table 1—Conductor Fill

Table 1 of Chapter 9 lists the maximum percent of the cross-sectional area of a raceway permitted for the installation of conductors and cables. ▶Figure 1–12

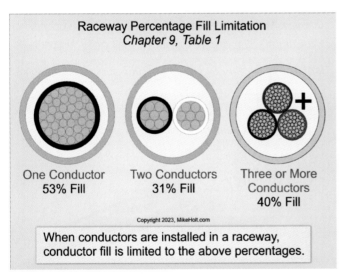

▶Figure 1–12

Notes to Chapter 9 Tables

Note (1) to Chapter 9 Tables—Conductors all the Same Size. When all conductors are the same size and the same insulation, raceways can be sized using Annex C. ▶Figure 1–13

Note (3) to Chapter 9 Tables—Equipment Grounding Conductors. When equipment grounding or bonding conductors are installed, the actual area of the conductor must be used when calculating raceway fill. ▶Figure 1–14

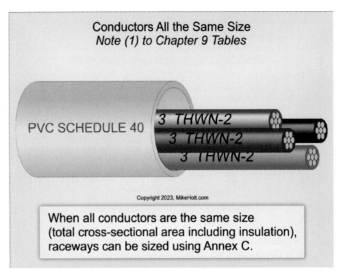

▶Figure 1–13

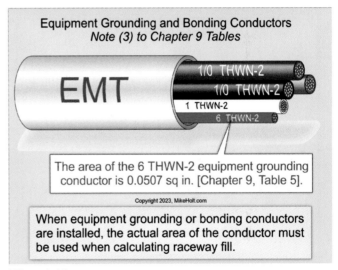

▶Figure 1–14

Note (4) to Chapter 9 Tables—Raceways not Exceeding 24 Inches in Length. When a raceway doesn't exceed 24 in. in length, it's permitted to be filled to 60 percent of its total cross-sectional area in accordance with Table 4 of Chapter 9. ▶Figure 1–15

Chapter 9, Table 4, Raceway Cross-Sectional Area (sq in.)

The total cross-sectional area and percent area for fill for all raceways are contained in Table 4 of Chapter 9. ▶Figure 1–16

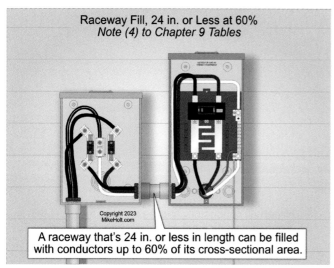

▶Figure 1–15

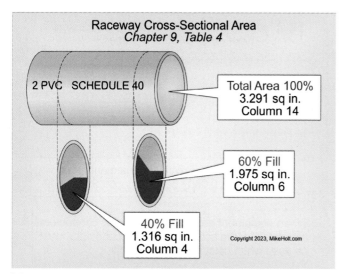

▶Figure 1–16

▶ Chapter 9, Table 4—40% Raceway Conductor Fill, Example 1

Question: What is the cross-sectional area of permitted conductor fill for 1 in. EMT that's 30 in. long and contains four conductors? ▶**Figure 1–17**

(a) 0.346 sq in.   (b) 1.013 sq in.   (c) 2.067 sq in.   (d) 3.356 sq in.

Answer: (a) 0.346 sq in. [Chapter 9, Table 1, and Table 4, 40% column]

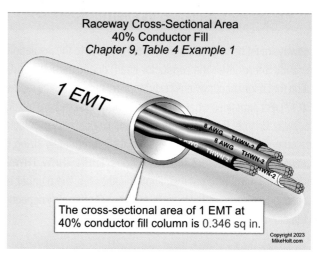

▶Figure 1–17

▶ Chapter 9, Table 4—40% Raceway Conductor Fill, Example 2

Question: What is the cross-sectional area of permitted conductor fill for 2 in. EMT that's 30 in. long and contains four conductors? ▶**Figure 1–18**

(a) 1.342 sq in.   (b) 2.013 sq in.   (c) 2.067 sq in.   (d) 3.356 sq in.

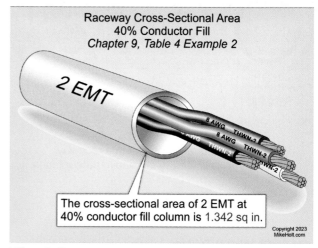

▶Figure 1–18

Answer: (a) 1.342 sq in. [Chapter 9, Table 1, and Table 4, 40% column]

► **Chapter 9, Table 4—60% Raceway Conductor Fill, Example 3**

Question: What is the cross-sectional area of permitted conductor fill for a 2 in. EMT nipple? ►Figure 1–19

(a) 1.342 sq in.   (b) 2.013 sq in.   (c) 2.067 sq in.   (d) 3.356 sq in.

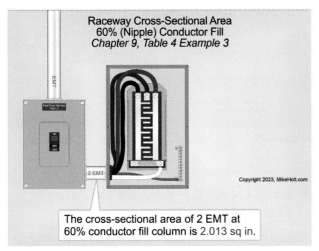

▶Figure 1–19

Solution:

Reminder: For a raceway 24 in. and shorter (often called nipple), use the 60% column [Chapter 9, Notes to Tables Note (4) and Table 4, 60% column].

Answer: (b) 2.013 sq in.

► **Chapter 9, Table 4—Raceway Trade Size, Example 1**

Question: What is the minimum EMT required for three conductors having a total area of 1.25 sq in.?

(a) Trade Size ½ *(b) Trade Size 1½*
(c) Trade Size 2 *(d) Trade Size 3*

Answer: (c) Trade Size 2 (1.342 sq in.) [Chapter 9, Table 1, and Table 4, 40% column]

► **Chapter 9, Table 4—Raceway Trade Size, Example 2**

Question: What is the minimum PVC Schedule 80 required for three conductors having a total area of 0.35 sq in.?

(a) Trade Size ½ *(b) Trade Size 1*
(c) Trade Size 1¼ *(d) Trade Size 1½*

Answer: (c) Trade Size 1¼ (0.495 sq in.) [Chapter 9, Table 1, and Table 4, 40% column]

1.3 Sizing Raceways, Conductors all the Same Size—Annex C

When all conductors in a conduit or tubing are the same size (total cross-sectional area including insulation), the number of conductors permitted in a raceway can be determined by simply looking at the tables located in Annex C—Raceway Fill Tables for Conductors and Fixture Wires of the Same Size.

The Annex C.1 through C.13(A) tables cannot be used to determine raceway sizing when conductors of different sizes are installed in the same raceway. For situations where conductors of varied sizes are mixed in a raceway, Chapter 9 contains the information necessary to calculate the required raceway size. Because different conductor types (THW, TW, THWN-2, and so forth) have different insulation thicknesses, the number and size of conductors permitted in each raceway often depend on the conductor type used.

▶ **Annex C, Table C.1—Conductors in EMT, Example 1**

Question: How many 14 RHH conductors (with cover) can be installed in trade size 1 EMT? ▶Figure 1–20

(a) 13 conductors (b) 11 conductors
(c) 19 conductors (d) 25 conductors

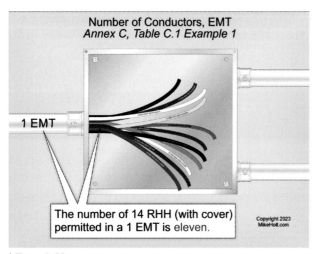

The number of 14 RHH (with cover) permitted in a 1 EMT is eleven.

▶Figure 1–20

Answer: (b) 11 conductors [Annex C, Table C.1]

The asterisk (*) note at the end of Annex C, Table C.1 indicates that conductor insulation types "RHH*," "RHW*," and "RHW-2*" means that these types of conductors do not have an outer covering. Insulation types "RHH," "RHW," and "RHW-2" (without the asterisk) do have an outer cover. This is a cover (which may be a fibrous material) that increases the cross-sectional area of the conductor more than the thin nylon cover encountered with conductors such as THWN-2.

▶ **Annex C, Table C.1—Conductors in EMT, Example 2**

Question: How many 8 THWN-2 conductors can be installed in trade size ¾ EMT? ▶Figure 1–21

(a) 3 conductors (b) 5 conductors
(c) 6 conductors (d) 8 conductors

Answer: (c) 6 conductors [Annex C, Table C.1]

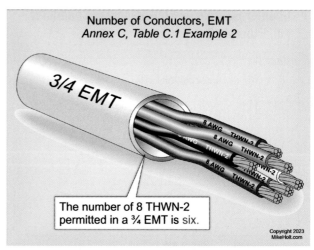

The number of 8 THWN-2 permitted in a ¾ EMT is six.

▶Figure 1–21

▶ **Annex C, Table C.1—Conductors in EMT, Example 3**

Question: How many 12 THWN-2 conductors can be installed in trade size 1 EMT? ▶Figure 1–22

(a) 13 conductors (b) 15 conductors
(c) 18 conductors (d) 26 conductors

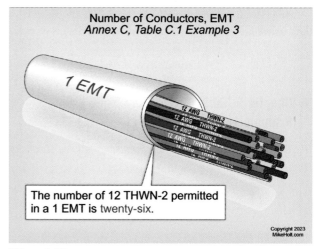

The number of 12 THWN-2 permitted in a 1 EMT is twenty-six.

▶Figure 1–22

Answer: (d) 26 conductors [Annex C, Table C.1]

▶ **Annex C, Table C.2—Conductors in ENT, Example 4**

Question: How many 6 XHHW conductors can be installed in trade size 1 ENT? ▶Figure 1–23

(a) 4 conductors
(b) 5 conductors
(c) 6 conductors
(d) 7 conductors

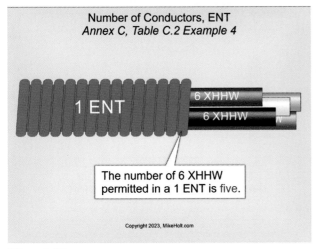

Number of Conductors, ENT
Annex C, Table C.2 Example 4

1 ENT
6 XHHW
6 XHHW

The number of 6 XHHW permitted in a 1 ENT is five.

Copyright 2023, MikeHolt.com

▶Figure 1–23

Answer: (b) 5 conductors [Annex C, Table C.2]

▶ **Annex C, Table C.3—Conductors in FMC, Example 5**

Question: If trade size 1¼ FMC has three THWN-2 conductors (not compact), what is the largest conductor permitted to be installed? ▶Figure 1–24

(a) 1 THWN-2
(b) 1/0 THWN-2
(c) 2/0 THWN-2
(d) 3/0 THWN-2

Answer: (a) 1 THWN-2 [Annex C, Table C.3]

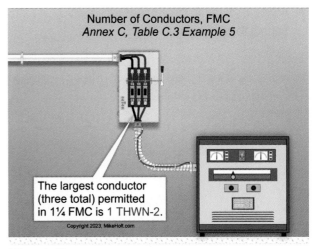

Number of Conductors, FMC
Annex C, Table C.3 Example 5

The largest conductor (three total) permitted in 1¼ FMC is 1 THWN-2.

Copyright 2023, MikeHolt.com

▶Figure 1–24

▶ **Annex C, Table C.8—Fixture Wire in LFMC, Example 6**

Question: How many 18 TFFN conductors can be installed in trade size ¾ LFMC? ▶Figure 1–25

(a) 14 conductors
(b) 26 conductors
(c) 30 conductors
(d) 39 conductors

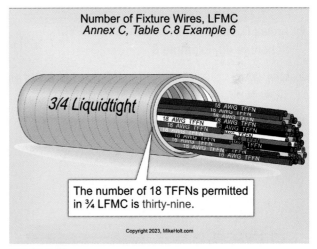

Number of Fixture Wires, LFMC
Annex C, Table C.8 Example 6

3/4 Liquidtight

The number of 18 TFFNs permitted in ¾ LFMC is thirty-nine.

Copyright 2023, MikeHolt.com

▶Figure 1–25

Answer: (d) 39 conductors [Annex C, Table C.8]

▶ **Annex C, Table C.10—Conductors in PVC Schedule 80, Example 7**

Question: *What is the smallest trade size PVC Schedule 80 that can be used for the installation of a single 3/0 THWN-2 as a grounding electrode conductor?* ▶Figure 1–26

(a) ½   (b) ¾   (c) 1   (d) 1¼

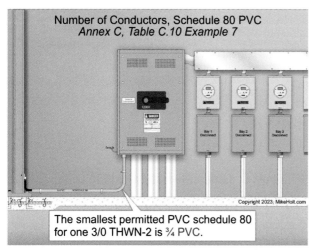

The smallest permitted PVC schedule 80 for one 3/0 THWN-2 is ¾ PVC.

▶Figure 1–26

Answer: *(b) ¾ [Annex C, Table C.10]*

▶ **Annex C, Table C.11—Conductors in PVC Schedule 40, Example 8**

Question: *What is the smallest trade size PVC Schedule 40 that can be used for five 6 THWN-2 conductors?* ▶Figure 1–27

(a) ½   (b) ¾   (c) 1   (d) 1¼

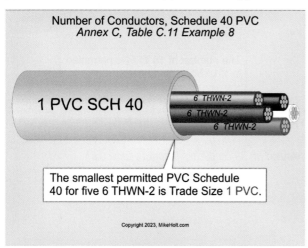

The smallest permitted PVC Schedule 40 for five 6 THWN-2 is Trade Size 1 PVC.

▶Figure 1–27

Answer: *(c) 1 [Annex C, Table C.11]*

Compact Insulated Conductors

▶ **Annex C, Table C.10(A)—Compact Conductors in PVC Schedule 80, Example 9**

Question: *What minimum trade size PVC Schedule 80 is suitable for four 4/0 THWN-2 compact conductors?* ▶Figure 1–28

(a) 1   (b) 1½   (c) 2   (d) 2½

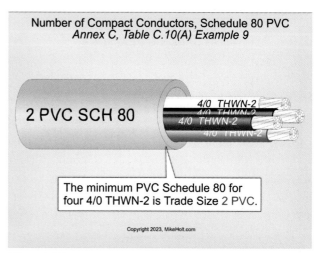

The minimum PVC Schedule 80 for four 4/0 THWN-2 is Trade Size 2 PVC.

▶Figure 1–28

Answer: *(c) 2 [Annex C, Table C.10(A)]*

▶ **Annex C, Table C.11(A)—Compact Conductors in PVC Schedule 40, Example 10**

Question: *If a trade size 2 PVC Schedule 40 has four THWN-2 compact conductors, what is the largest compact conductor permitted to be installed?* ▶Figure 1–29

(a) 1/0 AWG   (b) 2/0 AWG   (c) 3/0 AWG   (d) 4/0 AWG

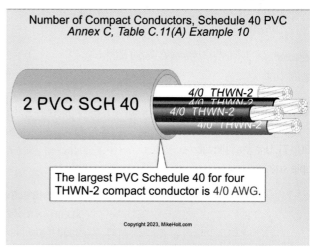

The largest PVC Schedule 40 for four THWN-2 compact conductor is 4/0 AWG.

▶Figure 1–29

Answer: *(d) 4/0 THWN-2 [Annex C, Table C.11(A)]*

Author's Comment:

▶ Compact stranding is the result of a manufacturing process where the conductor strands are shaped and compressed to the extent that the voids between the strands are virtually eliminated [Annex C, Table C.11(A) Definition]. Unless the question specifically states compact conductors, assume the conductors are not the compact type.

1.4 Raceways Sizing with Different Size Conductors

According to Note 6 to Chapter 9, we are to use Tables 4, 5, and 5A when sizing raceways for conductors of varied sizes. Table 4 provides the cross-sectional area of raceways, while Tables 5 and 5A give the cross-sectional areas of conductors. This is also the method to use when doing calculations for raceways that are 24 in. and shorter, as Annex C does not account for the 60 percent fill allowance provided by Table 4. ▶Figure 1–30

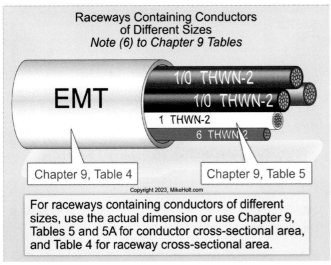

Raceways Containing Conductors of Different Sizes
Note (6) to Chapter 9 Tables

EMT — 1/0 THWN-2, 1/0 THWN-2, 1 THWN-2, 6 THWN-2

Chapter 9, Table 4 | Chapter 9, Table 5

Copyright 2023, MikeHolt.com

For raceways containing conductors of different sizes, use the actual dimension or use Chapter 9, Tables 5 and 5A for conductor cross-sectional area, and Table 4 for raceway cross-sectional area.

▶Figure 1–30

Raceway Sizing Steps. Raceways must be large enough to avoid damaging the insulation when conductors are pulled into the raceway [300.17]. Use the following steps to determine the raceway size and nipple size:

Step 1: Determine the cross-sectional area. Determine the cross-sectional area (in square inches) for each conductor from Chapter 9, Table 5 for insulated conductors and from Chapter 9, Table 8 for bare conductors.

Step 2: Determine the total cross-sectional area for all conductors.

Step 3: Size the raceway according to the percent fill as listed in Chapter 9, Table 1.

Chapter 9, Table 4 includes the distinct types of raceways with columns representing the allowable percentage fills such as 40 percent for three or more conductors, and 60 percent for raceways 24 in. or less in length. Be careful when selecting the raceway from Chapter 9, Table 4 as it is divided into numerous tables for each raceway type, and you must choose the correct one for the type of raceway for which you are performing the calculations.

▶ Raceway Sizing 40 Percent Fill, Example 1

Question: *What's the minimum size trade size PVC Schedule 40 required for three 500 kcmil THWN-2 conductors, one 250 kcmil THWN-2 conductor, and one 3 THWN-2 conductor?* ▶**Figure 1–31**

(a) 2 *(b) 2½* *(c) 3* *(d) 3½*

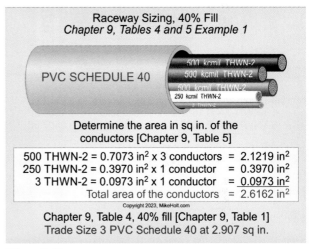

Raceway Sizing, 40% Fill
Chapter 9, Tables 4 and 5 Example 1

PVC SCHEDULE 40 — 500 kcmil THWN-2, 500 kcmil THWN-2, 500 kcmil THWN-2, 250 kcmil THWN-2, 3 THWN-2

Determine the area in sq in. of the conductors [Chapter 9, Table 5]

500 THWN-2 = 0.7073 in² x 3 conductors	= 2.1219 in²
250 THWN-2 = 0.3970 in² x 1 conductor	= 0.3970 in²
3 THWN-2 = 0.0973 in² x 1 conductor	= 0.0973 in²
Total area of the conductors	= 2.6162 in²

Copyright 2023, MikeHolt.com

Chapter 9, Table 4, 40% fill [Chapter 9, Table 1]
Trade Size 3 PVC Schedule 40 at 2.907 sq in.

▶Figure 1–31

Solution:

Step 1: *Determine the cross-sectional area of the conductors [Chapter 9, Table 5].*

500 THWN-2	*0.7073 sq in. × 3 conductors*	*2.1219 sq in.*
250 THWN-2	*0.3970 sq in. × 1 conductor*	*0.3970 sq in.*
3 THWN-2	*0.0973 sq in. × 1 conductor*	*0.0973 sq in.*

Step 2: *Determine the total cross-sectional area for all conductors.*

Total Cross-Sectional Area of all Conductors = 2.6162 sq in.

Step 3: *Size the raceway according to the percent fill as listed in Chapter 9, Table 1.*

• • •

Size the conduit at 40 percent fill [Chapter 9, Table 1] using Chapter 9, Table 4 (be sure to select the table for PVC Schedule 40). Trade Size 3 PVC Schedule 40 has an allowable cross-sectional area of 2.907 sq in. for over two conductors in the 40 percent column.

Answer: *(c) 3*

▶ Raceway Sizing 40 Percent Fill, Example 2

Question: *What is the minimum trade size EMT required for three 3/0 THWN-2 conductors, one 1 THWN-2 conductor, and one 6 THWN-2 conductor?* ▶**Figure 1–32**

(a) 2   *(b) 2½*   *(c) 3*   *(d) 3½*

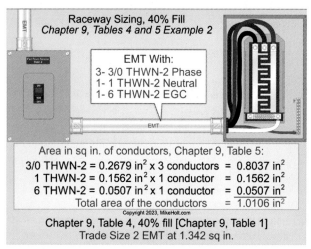

▶Figure 1–32

Solution:

Step 1: *Determine the cross-sectional area of the conductors [Chapter 9, Table 5].*

3/0 THWN-2	*0.2679 sq in. × 3 conductors*	*0.8037 sq in.*
1 THWN-2	*0.1562 sq in. × 1 conductor*	*0.1562 sq in.*
6 THWN-2	*0.0507 sq in. × 1 conductor*	*0.0507 sq in.*

Step 2: *Determine the total cross-sectional area for all conductors.*

Total Cross-Sectional Area of all Conductors = 1.0106 sq in.

Step 3: *Size the raceway according to the percent fill as listed in Chapter 9, Table 1.*

Size the tubing at 40 percent fill [Chapter 9, Table 1] using Chapter 9, Table 4. A trade size 2 EMT has an allowable cross-sectional area of 1.342 sq in. for over two conductors in the 40 percent column.

Answer: *(a) 2*

▶ Raceway Sizing 60 Percent Fill, Example 3

Question: *What is the minimum trade size PVC nipple required for three 500 kcmil THWN-2 conductors, one 250 kcmil THWN-2 conductor, and one 3 THWN-2 conductor?* ▶**Figure 1–33**

(a) 2   *(b) 2½*   *(c) 3*   *(d) 3½*

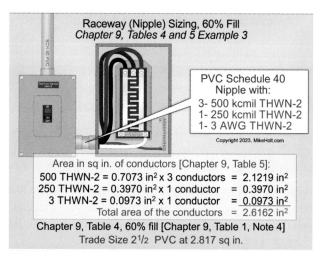

▶Figure 1–33

Solution:

Step 1: *Determine the cross-sectional area of the conductors [Chapter 9, Table 5].*

500 THWN-2	*0.7073 sq in. × 3 conductors*	*2.1219 sq in.*
250 THWN-2	*0.3970 sq in. × 1 conductor*	*0.3970 sq in.*
3 THWN-2	*0.0973 sq in. × 1 conductor*	*0.0973 sq in.*

Step 2: *Determine the total cross-sectional area for all conductors.*

Total Cross-Sectional Area of all Conductors = 2.6162 sq in.

Step 3: *Size the raceway according to the percent fill as listed in Chapter 9, Table 1 and Note (4) to the Chapter 9 Tables.*

Size the conduit at 60 percent fill [Chapter 9, Table 1] using Chapter 9, Table 4 (be sure to select the table for PVC Schedule 40). Trade size 2½ PVC Schedule 40 has an allowable cross-sectional area of 2.817 sq in. for over two conductors in the 60 percent column.

Answer: *(b) 2½*

▶ Raceway Sizing 60 Percent Fill, Example 4

Question: What is the minimum trade size RMC nipple required for three 3/0 THWN-2 conductors, one 1 THWN-2 conductor, and one 6 THWN-2 conductor? ▶Figure 1–34

(a) 1½   (b) 3½   (c) 2½   (d) 4½

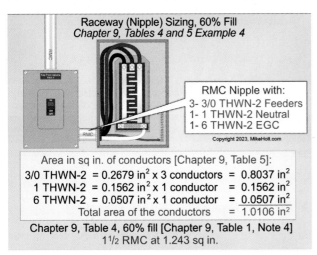

▶Figure 1–34

Solution:

Step 1: Determine the cross-sectional area of the conductors [Chapter 9, Table 5].

3/0 THWN-2	0.2679 sq in. × 3 conductors	0.8037 sq in.
1 THWN-2	0.1562 sq in. × 1 conductor	0.1562 sq in.
6 THWN-2	0.0507 sq in. × 1 conductor	0.0507 sq in.

Step 2: Determine the total cross-sectional area for all conductors.

Total Cross-Sectional Area of all Conductors = 1.0106 sq in.

Step 3: Size the raceway according to the percent fill as listed in Chapter 9, Table 1 and Note (4) to the Chapter 9 Tables.

Size the conduit at 60 percent fill [Chapter 9, Table 1] using Chapter 9, Table 4 (be sure to select the table for RMC). Trade size 1½ RMC has an allowable cross-sectional area of 1.243 sq in. for over two conductors in the 60 percent column.

Answer: (a) 1½

1.5 Multiconductor and Optical Fiber Cables— Chapter 9, Note (5) and Note (9)

Note (5) and Note (9) to Chapter 9 Tables— Multiconductor Cable and Optical Fiber Cables

For multiconductor and optical fiber cables not included in Chapter 9; use the actual diameter from the manufacturer for raceway sizing. Multiconductor and optical fiber cables are treated as a single conductor for raceway sizing. For cables with elliptical cross sections, the cable cross-sectional area in sq in. is based on the major diameter of the ellipse as the circle's diameter.

If only the cable diameter is given, you must determine the conductor sq in. area using the following formula: **Area = 3.14 x (Diameter x ½)²**

▶ Note (5) and Note (9) to Chapter 9 Tables, Example

Question: What trade size EMT is required for one NM cable having a major diameter (elliptical) of 0.44 inches? ▶Figure 1–35

(a) ½   (b) 3/4   (c) 1   (d) 1¼

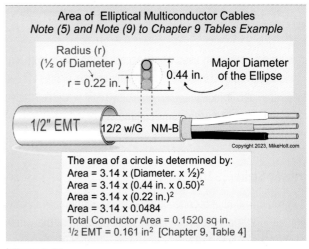

▶Figure 1–35

Solution:

Area = 3.14 × (Diameter ×½)²

Area = 3.14 × (0.44 in. × 0.50)²

Area = 3.14 × (0.22 in.)²

Area = 3.14 × 0.0484

Area = 0.1520 in.²

Trade Size ½ Area = 0.161 in.² [Chapter 9, Table 4]

Answer: (a) ½

1.6 Wireways and Cable Tray Systems

Wireways

According to Article 100, a "Metal Wireway" is a sheet metal trough with hinged or removable covers for housing and protecting electric conductors and cable, and in which conductors are placed after the raceway has been installed [376.2]. ▶**Figure 1–36**

A sheet metal trough with hinged or removable covers for housing and protecting electric wires and cable, and in which conductors are placed after the raceway has been installed.

▶Figure 1–36

Wireways are commonly used where access to the conductors within the raceway is required to make terminations, splices, or taps to several devices at a specific location. Their prohibitive cost precludes their use for long distances, except in some commercial or industrial occupancies where the wiring is frequently altered, maintained, or updated.

Wireway Sizing [376.22(A)]

The maximum number of conductors or cables permitted in a wireway is limited to 20 percent of the cross-sectional area of the wireway [376.22(A)]. ▶**Figure 1–37**

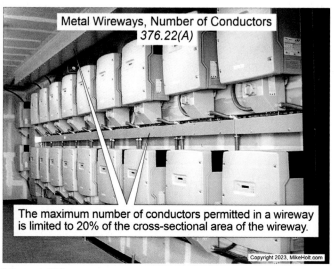

The maximum number of conductors permitted in a wireway is limited to 20% of the cross-sectional area of the wireway.

▶Figure 1–37

▶ Wireway Sizing [376.22(A)], Example 1

Question: *What is the cross-sectional area of a 6 in. × 6 in. wireway?* ▶Figure 1–38

(a) 6 sq in.   *(b) 16 sq in.*   *(c) 36 sq in.*   *(d) 66 sq in.*

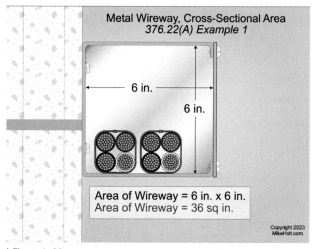

Metal Wireway, Cross-Sectional Area
376.22(A) Example 1

6 in.

6 in.

Area of Wireway = 6 in. x 6 in.
Area of Wireway = 36 sq in.

▶Figure 1–38

Solution:

The cross-sectional area is found by multiplying height by depth:
6 in. × 6 in. = 36 sq in.

Answer: *(c) 36 sq in.*

▶ Wireway Sizing [376.22(A)], Example 2

Question: What is the maximum allowable conductor fill in sq in. for a 6 in. × 6 in. wireway? ▶Figure 1–39

(a) 5 sq in.   (b) 6.50 sq in.   (c) 7.20 sq in.   (d) 8.90 sq in.

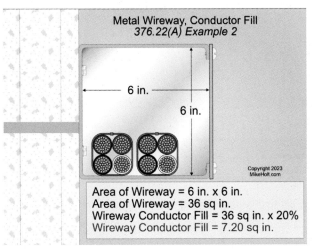

Metal Wireway, Conductor Fill
376.22(A) Example 2

6 in.
6 in.

Area of Wireway = 6 in. x 6 in.
Area of Wireway = 36 sq in.
Wireway Conductor Fill = 36 sq in. x 20%
Wireway Conductor Fill = 7.20 sq in.

▶Figure 1–39

Solution:

Wireway Area = 6 in. × 6 in.
Wireway Area = 36 sq in.

Wireway Conductor Fill = 36 sq in. × 20%
Wireway Conductor Fill = 7.20 sq in. [376.22(A)]

Answer: (c) 7.20 sq in.

▶ Wireway Sizing [376.22(A)], Example 3

Question: What is the maximum number of 3/0 THWN-2 conductors that can be installed in a 6 in. × 6 in. wireway? ▶Figure 1–40

(a) 14 conductors   (b) 16 conductors
(c) 20 conductors   (d) 26 conductors

Solution:

Wireway Area = 6 in. × 6 in.
Wireway Area = 36 sq in.

Wireway Conductor Fill = 36 sq in. × 20%
Wireway Conductor Fill = 7.20 sq in. [376.22(A)]

Area of 3/0 THWN-2 = 0.2679 sq in. [Chapter 9, Table 5]

Number 3/0 THWN-2 Conductors in Wireway =
  7.20 sq in./0.2679 sq in.
Number 3/0 THWN-2 Conductors in Wireway =
  26.88 conductors

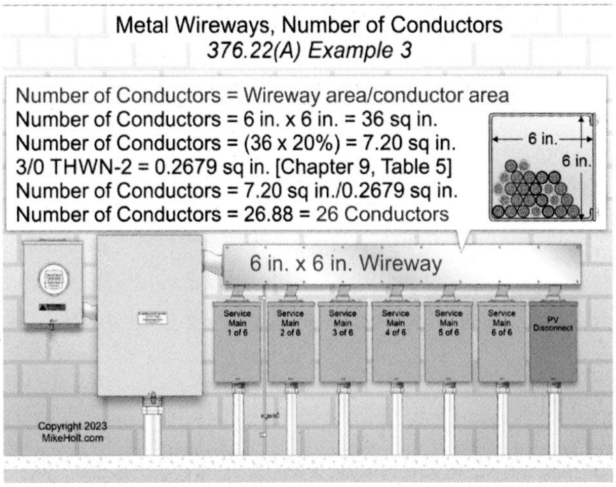

Metal Wireways, Number of Conductors
376.22(A) Example 3

Number of Conductors = Wireway area/conductor area
Number of Conductors = 6 in. x 6 in. = 36 sq in.
Number of Conductors = (36 x 20%) = 7.20 sq in.
3/0 THWN-2 = 0.2679 sq in. [Chapter 9, Table 5]
Number of Conductors = 7.20 sq in./0.2679 sq in.
Number of Conductors = 26.88 = 26 Conductors

6 in.
6 in.

6 in. x 6 in. Wireway

Service Main 1 of 6 | Service Main 2 of 6 | Service Main 3 of 6 | Service Main 4 of 6 | Service Main 5 of 6 | Service Main 6 of 6 | PV Disconnect

▶Figure 1–40

Answer: (d) 26 conductors

Author's Comment:

▶ The 0.80 or larger rounding up rule of Note (7) to the Chapter 9 Tables only applies to circular raceways such as conduit or tubing.

▶ Wireway Sizing [376.22(A)], Example 4

Question: What is the maximum number of 500 kcmil THWN-2 conductors that can be installed in a 6 in. × 6 in. wireway? ▶Figure 1–41

(a) 4 conductors   (b) 6 conductors
(c) 10 conductors   (d) 20 conductors

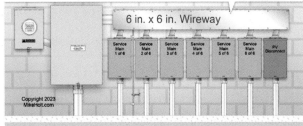

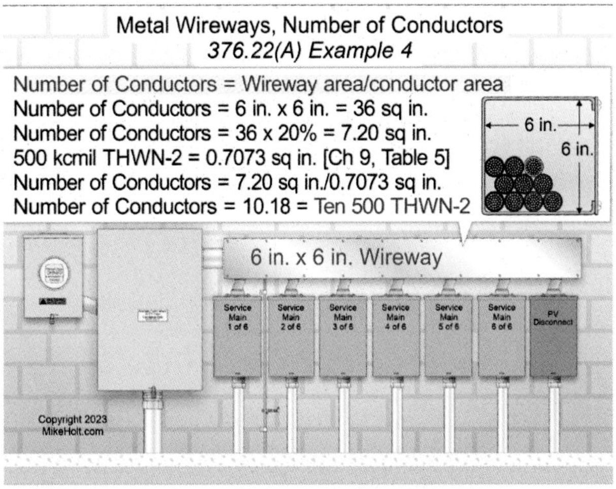

Metal Wireways, Number of Conductors
376.22(A) Example 4

Number of Conductors = Wireway area/conductor area
Number of Conductors = 6 in. x 6 in. = 36 sq in.
Number of Conductors = 36 x 20% = 7.20 sq in.
500 kcmil THWN-2 = 0.7073 sq in. [Ch 9, Table 5]
Number of Conductors = 7.20 sq in./0.7073 sq in.
Number of Conductors = 10.18 = Ten 500 THWN-2

6 in.
6 in.

6 in. x 6 in. Wireway

Service Main 1 of 6 | Service Main 2 of 6 | Service Main 3 of 6 | Service Main 4 of 6 | Service Main 5 of 6 | Service Main 6 of 6 | PV Disconnect

▶Figure 1–41

• • •

Solution:

Wireway Area = 6 in. × 6 in.
Wireway Area = 36 sq in.

Wireway Conductor Fill = 36 sq in. × 20%
Wireway Conductor Fill = 7.20 sq in. [376.22(A)]

Area of 500 kcmil THWN-2 = 0.7073 sq in. [Chapter 9, Table 5]

Number 500 kcmil Conductors in Wireway = 7.20 sq in./0.7073 sq in.
Number 500 kcmil Conductors in Wireway = 10.18 conductors

Answer: (c) 10 conductors

▶ Wireway Sizing [376.22(A)44], Example 5

Question: What minimum size wireway is suitable for three 500 kcmil THWN-2, one 250 kcmil THWN-2, and four 4/0 THWN-2 conductors?

(a) 4 in. × 4 in. (16 sq in.)   *(b) 6 in. × 6 in. (36 sq in.)*
(c) 8 in. × 8 in. (64 sq in.)   *(d) 10 in. × 10 in. (100 sq in.)*

Solution:

Find the conductor area [Chapter 9, Table 5].

500 kcmil THWN-2 = 0.7073 sq in. × 3
500 kcmil THWN-2 = 2.1219 sq in.
250 kcmil THWN-2 = 0.3970 sq in.

4/0 THWN-2 = 0.3237 sq in. × 4
4/0 THWN-2 = 1.2948 sq in.

Total Conductor Area = 3.8137 sq in.

The wireway must not be filled to over 20 percent of its cross-sectional area [376.22(A)]. Twenty percent is equal to one-fifth, so we can multiply the required conductor area by five to find the minimum square inch area required.

Conductor Area × 5 = Required Wireway Minimum Area
3.8137 sq in. × 5 = 19.07 sq in.

A 6 in. × 6 in. wireway has a cross-sectional area of 36 sq in. and will be large enough.

Answer: (b) 6 in. × 6 in. (36 sq in.)

Cable Tray Systems

According to Article 100, a "Cable Tray System" is a unit or assembly of units or sections with associated fittings forming a rigid structural system used to securely fasten or support cables and raceways. ▶Figure 1–42

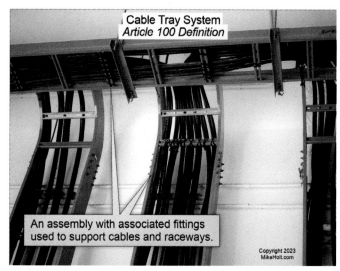

▶Figure 1–42

A cable tray system is a unit or assembly of units or sections with associated fittings forming a structural system used to securely fasten or support cables and raceways. A cable tray is not a raceway. It is a support system for raceways, cables, and enclosures. Cable trays can be used as a support system for wiring methods containing branch circuits, feeders, service conductors, and Chapters 7 and 8 wiring methods.

Cable Tray Sizing

The inside width of a cable tray can be sized in accordance with 392.22(B)(1) or Annex C.18 and C.20.

▶ Cable Tray Sizing, 392.22(B)(1)(d), Example 1

Qiestion: What is the minimum inside width cable tray needed to accommodate ten 1/0 THWN-2 conductors?

(a) 2 in.   *(b) 4 in.*   *(c) 6 in.*   *(d) 8 in.*

Solution:

Cable Tray Inside Width = Conductor Diameter* × Number of Conductors
Cable Tray Width = 0.486 in.* × 10 conductors
Cable Tray Width = 4.86 in.
Cable Tray Width = 6 in. [Table 392.22(B)(1)]
*Chapter 9, Table 5 for 1/0 THWN-2

Answer: (d) 8 in., 392.22(B)(1)(d)

▶ **Cable Tray Sizing, 392.22(B)(1)(d), Example 2**

Qiestion: *What is the minimum inside width cable tray needed to accommodate ten 2/0 THWN-2 conductors?*

(a) 10 in.   *(b) 12 in.*   *(c) 14 in.*   *(d) 16 in.*

Solution:

Cable Tray Inside Width = Conductor Diameter* × Number of Conductors

Cable Tray Width = 0.532 in. × 10 conductors*
Cable Tray Width = 5.32 in.
Cable Tray Width = 6 in. [Table 392.22(B)(1)]
*Chapter 9, Table 5, for 2/0 THWN-2

Answer: *(b) 12 in., 392.22(B)(1)(d)*

▶ **Cable Tray Sizing, Annex C Table C.18, Example 1**

Question: *What is the minimum width cable tray needed to accommodate thirty-two 250 kcmil THHN conductors?* ▶*Figure 1–43*

(a) 12 in.   *(b) 18 in.*   *(c) 24 in.*   *(d) 30 in.*

Cable Tray Width Sizing
Single-Conductor Cables
Annex C, Table C.18 Example 1

Thirty-two 250 kcmil THHN single-conductor cables require a 12 in. wide cable tray.

Copyright 2023, MikeHolt.com

▶Figure 1–43

Answer: *(a) 12 in.*

▶ **Cable Tray Sizing, Annex C Table C.18, Example 2**

Question:: *What is the minimum width cable tray needed to accommodate forty 350 kcmil THHN conductors?* ▶*Figure 1–44*

(a) 12 in.   *(b) 18 in.*   *(c) 20 in.*   *(d) 24 in.*

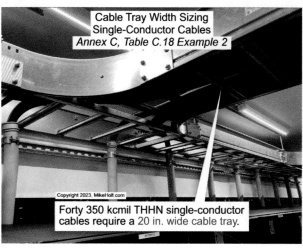

Cable Tray Width Sizing
Single-Conductor Cables
Annex C, Table C.18 Example 2

Copyright 2023, MikeHolt.com

Forty 350 kcmil THHN single-conductor cables require a 20 in. wide cable tray.

▶Figure 1–44

Answer: *(c) 20 in.*

▶ **Cable Tray Sizing, Annex C Table C.19, Example 1**

Question: *What is the minimum width cable tray needed to accommodate forty 350 kcmil XHHW conductors?* ▶*Figure 1–45*

(a) 12 in.   *(b) 18 in.*   *(c) 20 in.*   *(d) 30 in.*

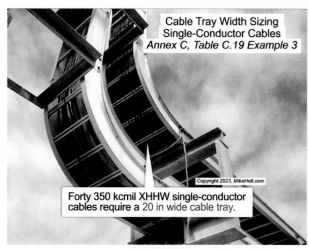

Cable Tray Width Sizing
Single-Conductor Cables
Annex C, Table C.19 Example 3

Copyright 2023, MikeHolt.com

Forty 350 kcmil XHHW single-conductor cables require a 20 in wide cable tray.

▶Figure 1–45

Answer: *(c) 20 in.*

▶ **Cable Tray Sizing, Annex C Table C.19, Example 2**

Question: What is the minimum width cable tray needed to accommodate forty 500 kcmil XHHW conductors? ▶Figure 1–46

(a) 12 in. (b) 18 in. (c) 24 in. (d) 30 in.

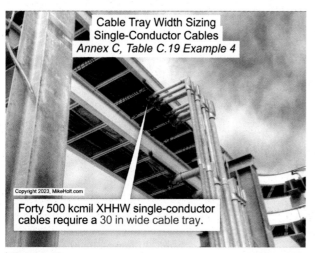

Cable Tray Width Sizing
Single-Conductor Cables
Annex C, Table C.19 Example 4

Copyright 2023, MikeHolt.com

Forty 500 kcmil XHHW single-conductor cables require a 30 in wide cable tray.

▶Figure 1–46

Answer: (d) 30 in.

1.7 Tips for Raceway Calculations

Tip 1: Take your time.

Tip 2: Use a ruler or a straightedge when using tables and highlight key words and important sections.

Tip 3: Watch for distinct types of raceways and conductor insulations, particularly RHH/RHW/RHW-2 with or without an outer cover.

Tip 4: Watch for the difference between conductors and compact conductors.

Unit 1—Conclusion

The importance of protecting conductor insulation during installation must be understood by every electrician. The principles covered in this unit have focused on helping you achieve that goal.

You have learned how to use the tables in Chapter 9 of the *NEC* when performing raceway fill calculations. First, the area of the conductor is found using Chapter 9, Table 5 for insulated conductors, or Chapter 9, Table 8 for bare conductors. Then after totaling the cross-sectional areas of all the conductors, the raceway trade size from Chapter 9, Table 4 is selected using the available cross-sectional area of the raceway. Take your time when working out these calculations to select the correct insulation type and the correct raceway for your problem.

Annex C provides a faster method of sizing raceways than using the Chapter 9 Tables when the conductors are all the same AWG/kcmil size, and the same size in cross-sectional area (including the insulation). There are numerous tables in Annex C (based on the raceway type) that can be used to reduce the time spent on calculations, so once again be sure to take your time and be certain you are using the correct table.

Metal wireways must be sized using the requirements of Article 376. The maximum fill for wireways isn't just how much you can squeeze into them. There are specific limits on conductor cross-sectional area, number of conductors, and wire-bending space. Following the rules of Article 376 will provide a better installation and take the mystery out of sizing wireways.

Cable trays must be sized using the requirements of Article 392 and Annex C. Sizing a cable tray can be incredibly difficult; it depends on the cable tray type, the cable type, and the conductor type. In this textbook, we demonstrated the method to size a cable tray for the same size single conductor cable in accordance with Annex C and 392.22(D)(b).

REVIEW QUESTIONS

Please use the 2023 *Code* book and this textbook to answer the following questions.

1.1 Conductor Cross-Sectional Area—Chapter 9, Tables 5 and 8

Chapter 9, Table 5—Cross-sectional Areas of Insulated Conductors

1. What is the cross-sectional area in square inches for 14 RHW (without an outer cover)?
   - (a) 0.0172 sq in.
   - (b) 0.0209 sq in.
   - (c) 0.0252 sq in.
   - (d) 0.0278 sq in.

2. What is the cross-sectional area in square inches for 12 RHH (with an outer cover)?
   - (a) 0.0117 sq in.
   - (b) 0.0252 sq in.
   - (c) 0.0327 sq in.
   - (d) 0.0353 sq in.

3. What is the cross-sectional area in square inches for 12 THHN?
   - (a) 0.0133 sq in.
   - (b) 0.0147 sq in.
   - (c) 0.0233 sq in.
   - (d) 0.0321 sq in.

4. What is the cross-sectional area in square inches for 10 THW?
   - (a) 0.0172 sq in.
   - (b) 0.0243 sq in.
   - (c) 0.0252 sq in.
   - (d) 0.0278 sq in.

5. What is the cross-sectional area in square inches for 10 THHN conductor?
   - (a) 0.0117 sq in.
   - (b) 0.0172 sq in.
   - (c) 0.0211 sq in.
   - (d) 0.0252 sq in.

Chapter 9, Table 5A—Cross-sectional Areas of Compact Insulated Conductors

6. What is the cross-sectional area in square inches for a 8 RHH compact conductor without an outer cover?
   - (a) 0.0531 sq in.
   - (b) 0.0683 sq in.
   - (c) 0.0881 sq in.
   - (d) 0.1194 sq in.

7. What is the cross-sectional area in square inches for a 6 RHH compact conductor without an outer cover?
   - (a) 0.0531 sq in.
   - (b) 0.0683 sq in.
   - (c) 0.0881 sq in.
   - (d) 0.1194 sq in.

8. What is the cross-sectional area in square inches for a 1 THHW aluminum compact conductor?
   - (a) 0.1698 sq in.
   - (b) 0.1963 sq in.
   - (c) 0.2332 sq in.
   - (d) 0.2733 sq in.

9. What is the cross-sectional area in square inches for a 1/0 THHN aluminum compact conductor?

    (a) 0.1352 sq in.
    (b) 0.1590 sq in.
    (c) 0.1924 sq in.
    (d) 0.2290 sq in.

10. What is the cross-sectional area in square inches for a 2/0 XHHW aluminum compact conductor?

    (a) 0.1352 sq in.
    (b) 0.1590 sq in.
    (c) 0.1885 sq in.
    (d) 0.2290 sq in.

Chapter 9, Table 8—Cross-Sectional Area of Bare Conductors

11. What is the cross-sectional area in square inches for a 10 AWG stranded?

    (a) 0.007 sq in.
    (b) 0.011 sq in.
    (c) 0.012 sq in.
    (d) 0.106 sq in.

12. What is the cross-sectional area in square inches for a 10 AWG having a single strand?

    (a) 0.008 sq in.
    (b) 0.012 sq in.
    (c) 0.101 sq in.
    (d) 0.106 sq in.

13. What is the cross-sectional area in square inches for a 8 AWG solid conductor?

    (a) 0.013 sq in.
    (b) 0.027 sq in.
    (c) 0.038 sq in.
    (d) 0.045 sq in.

14. What is the cross-sectional area in square inches for a 1/0 AWG aluminum?

    (a) 0.087 sq in.
    (b) 0.109 sq in.
    (c) 0.137 sq in.
    (d) 0.173 sq in.

15. What is the cross-sectional area in square inches for a 4/0 AWG aluminum?

    (a) 0.187 sq in.
    (b) 0.219 sq in.
    (c) 0.337 sq in.
    (d) 0.473 sq in.

1.2 Raceway Properties

Chapter 9, Table 1—Conductor Fill

16. The permitted raceway fill for two conductors is ___.

    (a) 30 percent
    (b) 31 percent
    (c) 40 percent
    (d) 53 percent

17. The permitted raceway fill for five conductors is ___.

    (a) 35 percent
    (b) 40 percent
    (c) 55 percent
    (d) 60 percent

Notes to Chapter 9 Tables

18. When calculating raceway conductor fill, equipment grounding conductors shall ___.

    (a) not be required to be counted
    (b) have the actual dimensions used
    (c) not be counted if in a nipple
    (d) not be counted if for a wye three-phase balanced load

19. What is the maximum length of a raceway nipple?

    (a) 1 ft
    (b) 2 ft
    (c) 3 ft
    (d) 4 ft

20. Where raceway nipples having a maximum length not to exceed 24 in. are installed between boxes, cabinets, and similar enclosures, the nipples is permitted to be filled to _____ of their total cross-sectional area.

    (a) 30 percent
    (b) 40 percent
    (c) 60 percent
    (d) 70 percent

21. When the calculated number of conductors or cables, all the same size, installed in a conduit or in tubing includes a decimal, the next higher whole number shall be used when this decimal is _____ or larger.
    (a) 0.40
    (b) 0.60
    (c) 0.70
    (d) 0.80

22. For the purposes of conduit fill, a multiconductor cable is considered _____ conductor(s) for calculating percentage conduit or tubing fill area.
    (a) one
    (b) two
    (c) three
    (d) four

Chapter 9, Table 4, Raceway Cross-Sectional Area (sq in.)

23. The cross-sectional area of trade size 1 IMC is approximately ____.
    (a) 0.62 sq in.
    (b) 0.96 sq in.
    (c) 1.22 sq in.
    (d) 2.13 sq in.

24. What is the cross-sectional area of permitted conductor fill for trade size 1 EMT containing four conductors?
    (a) 0.346 sq in.
    (b) 1.013 sq in.
    (c) 2.067 sq in.
    (d) 3.356 sq in.

25. What is the cross-sectional area of permitted conductor fill for trade size 2 EMT containing four conductors?
    (a) 1.342 sq in.
    (b) 2.013 sq in.
    (c) 2.067 sq in.
    (d) 3.356 sq in.

26. What is the cross-sectional area of permitted conductor fill for a 2 in. EMT nipple?
    (a) 1.342 sq in.
    (b) 2.013 sq in.
    (c) 2.067 sq in.
    (d) 3.356 sq in.

27. What is the cross-sectional area of permitted conductor fill for a 1½ RMC nipple?
    (a) 0.882 sq in.
    (b) 1.072 sq in.
    (c) 1.243 sq in.
    (d) 1.343 sq in.

Chapter 9, Table 4, Raceway Trade Size

28. What is the minimum size EMT required for three conductors having a total area of 1.25 sq in.?
    (a) Trade size ½
    (b) Trade size 1½
    (c) Trade size 1¼
    (d) Trade size 2

29. What is the minimum size for PVC Schedule 80 for three conductors having a total area of 0.35 sq in.?
    (a) Trade size ½
    (b) Trade size 1
    (c) Trade size 1¼
    (d) Trade size 1½

30. What is the minimum size for PVC Schedule 80 nipple for a conductor area of.836 sq in.?
    (a) Trade size 1
    (b) Trade size 1¼
    (c) Trade size 1½
    (d) Trade size 1¾

1.3 Sizing Raceways, Conductors all the Same Size—Annex C

31. How many 18 TFFN conductors can be installed in trade size ¾ EMT?
    (a) 24 conductors
    (b) 29 conductors
    (c) 30 conductors
    (d) 38 conductors

32. How many 16 TFFN conductors can be installed in trade size ¾ EMT?

    (a) 26 conductors
    (b) 29 conductors
    (c) 30 conductors
    (d) 40 conductors

33. How many 12 THWN-2 conductors can be installed in trade size 1 EMT?

    (a) 13 conductors
    (b) 16 conductors
    (c) 26 conductors
    (d) 35 conductors

34. How many 10 THWN-2 conductors can be installed in trade size ¾ EMT?

    (a) 10 conductors
    (b) 11 conductors
    (c) 15 conductors
    (d) 16 conductors

35. How many 6 RHH conductors (without outer cover) are permitted in trade size 1¼ ENT?

    (a) 7 conductors
    (b) 8 conductors
    (c) 9 conductors
    (d) 10 conductors

36. How many 8 THW conductors are permitted in trade size ¾ FMC?

    (a) 4 conductors
    (b) 5 conductors
    (c) 6 conductors
    (d) 7 conductors

37. How many 1/0 XHHW conductors are permitted in trade size 2 FMC?

    (a) 6 conductors
    (b) 7 conductors
    (c) 13 conductors
    (d) 16 conductors

38. How many 8 AWG THW compact conductors are permitted in trade size ¾ FMC?

    (a) 4 conductors
    (b) 5 conductors
    (c) 7 conductors
    (d) 11 conductors

39. How many 12 RHH conductors (with outer cover) can be installed in a trade size 1 IMC?

    (a) 5 conductors
    (b) 7 conductors
    (c) 9 conductors
    (d) 11 conductors

40. How many 8 RHH with outer cover conductors are permitted in trade size 1½ RMC?

    (a) 10 conductors
    (b) 14 conductors
    (c) 16 conductors
    (d) 20 conductors

41. How many 8 RHH without outer cover conductors are permitted in trade size 1½ RMC?

    (a) 10 conductors
    (b) 14 conductors
    (c) 15 conductors
    (d) 20 conductors

Compact Insulated Conductors

42. How many 6 THW-2 compact conductors can be installed in trade size 1 EMT?

    (a) 3 conductors
    (b) 5 conductors
    (c) 6 conductors
    (d) 9 conductors

43. How many 8 THW compact conductors are permitted in trade size 1½ RMC?

    (a) 12 conductors
    (b) 14 conductors
    (c) 16 conductors
    (d) 20 conductors

44. How many 1/0 THW-2 compact conductors can be installed in trade size 2 RMC?

    (a) 6 conductors
    (b) 7 conductors
    (c) 8 conductors
    (d) 9 conductors

45. How many 4/0 THW-2 compact conductors can be installed in trade size 3 PVC?

    (a) 6 conductors
    (b) 7 conductors
    (c) 8 conductors
    (d) 9 conductors

1.4 Raceways Sizing with Different Size Conductors

46. What's the minimum size PVC required for three 500 kcmil THWN-2 conductors, one 250 kcmil THWN-2 conductor, and one 3 AWG THWN-2 conductor?

    (a) Trade size 2
    (b) Trade size 2½
    (c) Trade size 3
    (d) Trade size 3½

47. What's the minimum size EMT required for three 3/0 AWG THWN-2 conductors, one 1 AWG THWN-2 conductor, and one 6 AWG THWN-2 conductor?

    (a) Trade size 2
    (b) Trade size 2½
    (c) Trade size 3
    (d) Trade size 3½

48. What's the minimum size PVC nipple required for three 500 kcmil THWN-2 conductors, one 250 kcmil THWN-2 conductor, and one 3 AWG THWN-2 conductor?

    (a) Trade size 2
    (b) Trade size 2½
    (c) Trade size 3
    (d) Trade size 3½

49. What's the minimum RMC nipple required for three 3/0 AWG THWN-2 conductors, one 1 AWG THWN-2 conductor, and one 6 AWG THWN-2 conductor?

    (a) Trade size 1½
    (b) Trade size 3½
    (c) Trade size 2½
    (d) Trade size 4½

1.5 Multiconductor and Optical Fiber Cables—Chapter 9, Note (5) and Note (9)

50. What trade size ENT raceway is required for four Cat 6 cables having a diameter of 0.22 inches?

    (a) Trade size ½
    (b) Trade size ¾
    (c) Trade size 1
    (d) Trade size 1¼

51. What trade size ENT is required for three fiber optic cables having a diameter of 0.20 inches?

    (a) Trade size ½
    (b) Trade size ¾
    (c) Trade size 1
    (d) Trade size 1¼

52. What trade size ENT is required for four fiber optic cables having a diameter of 0.30 inches?

    (a) Trade size ½
    (b) Trade size ¾
    (c) Trade size 1
    (d) Trade size 1¼

1.6 Wireways and Cable Tray Systems

Wireway Sizing

53. What is the cross-sectional area of a 4 in. × 4 in. wireway?

    (a) 10 sq in.
    (b) 16 sq in.
    (c) 36 sq in.
    (d) 66 sq in.

54. What is the maximum allowable sq in. of conductor fill for a 4 in. × 4 in. wireway?

    (a) 2.4 sq in.
    (b) 3.2 sq in.
    (c) 5.3 sq in.
    (d) 12.4 sq in.

55. What is the maximum number of 400 kcmil THHN conductors that can be installed in a 4 in. × 4 in. wireway?

    (a) 4 conductors
    (b) 5 conductors
    (c) 6 conductors
    (d) 7 conductors

Cable Tray Sizing—Annex C.18

56. What is the minimum width cable tray size needed to accommodate fifteen 1/0 THHN conductors?

    (a) 2 in.
    (b) 4 in.
    (c) 6 in.
    (d) 8 in.

57. What is the minimum width cable tray size needed to accommodate twenty 2/0 THHN conductors?

    (a) 10 in.
    (b) 12 in.
    (c) 14 in.
    (d) 16 in.

Cable Tray Sizing—Annex C.19

58. What is the maximum number of 1/0 XHHW conductors permitted in a 16 in. wide cable tray?

    (a) 22 conductors
    (b) 24 conductors
    (c) 26 conductors
    (d) 32 conductors

59. What is the maximum number of 2/0 XHHW conductors permitted in an 18 in. wide cable tray?

    (a) 22 conductors
    (b) 24 conductors
    (c) 26 conductors
    (d) 33 conductors

UNIT

2

BOX CALCULATIONS

Introduction to Unit 2—Box Calculations

Boxes containing 6 AWG and smaller conductors must be sized so that in no case can the volume of the box, as shown in Table 314.16(A), be less than the volume requirement as calculated in 314.16(B). Pay close attention to the details on applying the proper volume allowance per conductor based on the rules of 314.16(B)(1) through (5).

For conductors 4 AWG and larger, pull and junction boxes must be sized to allow conductors to be installed so the conductor insulation is not damaged. Pull and junction boxes are sized based on the trade size of the raceways terminating at the box and whether the conductors are pulled straight, at an angle, or a U pull in accordance with 314.28. In addition, we will cover how to calculate the minimum distance between raceways in a pull and junction box.

The following are the Parts covered in this unit:

▸ Part A—Outlet Box Sizing

▸ Part B— Pull and Junction Boxes

These types of questions require you to draw out the problem, so do not rush and try to be as neat as possible.

Part A—Outlet Box Sizing

Introduction

Boxes containing 6 AWG and smaller conductors must be sized in an approved manner to provide free space for all conductors. In no case can the volume of the box, as calculated in 314.16(A), be less than the volume requirement as calculated in 314.16(B). ▸Figure 2–1

Author's Comment:

▸ The requirements for sizing boxes containing conductors 4 AWG and larger are 314.28, and those for sizing hand-hole enclosures are contained in 314.30(A). An outlet box is used for the attachment of devices and luminaires and has a specific amount of space (volume) for conductors, devices, and fittings. The volume taken up by conductors, devices, and fittings in a box must not exceed the box fill capacity. ▸Figure 2–2

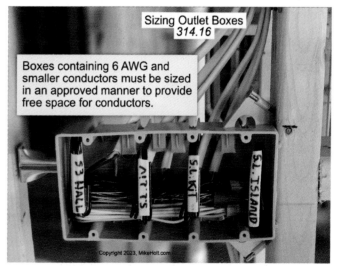

Sizing Outlet Boxes
314.16

Boxes containing 6 AWG and smaller conductors must be sized in an approved manner to provide free space for conductors.

Copyright 2023, MikeHolt.com

▸Figure 2–1

The volume taken up by conductors, devices, and fittings in a box must not exceed the box fill capacity.

▶Figure 2–2

Box Volume [314.16(A)]

The volume of a box is the total volume of its assembled parts, including plaster rings, raised covers, and extension rings. The total volume includes only those parts that are marked with their volumes in cubic inches [314.16(A)] or included in Table 314.16(A). ▶Figure 2–3

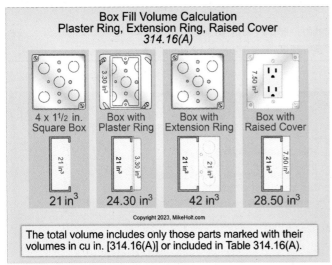

▶Figure 2–3

▶ Box Volume [314.16(A)], Example

Question: What is the total volume of a 4 in. × 4 in. × 1½ in. outlet box with a 4 in. × 4 in. × 1½ in. extension ring, and a raised cover stamped with a volume of 7.50 in.³? ▶Figure 2–4

(a) 40.90 in.³   (b) 49.50 in.³   (c) 44.50 in.³   (d) 50.90 in.³

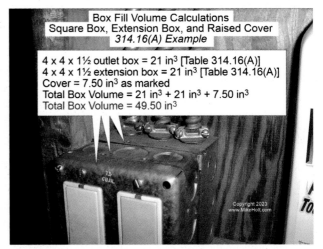

▶Figure 2–4

Solution:

Outlet Box	4 × 4 × 1½	21.00 in.³
Extension Ring	4 × 4 × 1½	21.00 in.³
Cover		+ 7.50 in.³
Total Volume of Assembled Parts		49.50 in.³

Answer: (b) 49.50 in.³

2.1 Box Sizing—Conductors All the Same Size [Table 314.16(A)]

When all the conductors in an outlet box are the same size (insulation does not matter), Table 314.16(A) can be used to determine the:

(1) Number of conductors permitted in the outlet box, or

(2) Outlet box size required for the given number of conductors

> **Author's Comment:**
>
> ▸ If the outlet box contains switches, receptacles, luminaire studs, luminaire hickeys, cable clamps, or equipment grounding conductors, then we must make an allowance for these items, which are not reflected in Table 314.16(A).

Table 314.16(A) Metal Boxes								
Box Trade Size		Min. Volume	Maximum Number of Conductors (arranged by AWG size)					
in.	Box Shape	in.³	18	16	14	12	10	8
(4 × 1¼)	round/ octagonal	12.50	8	7	6	5	5	5
(4 × 1½)	round/ octagonal	15.50	10	8	7	6	6	5
(4 × 2⅛)	round/ octagonal	21.50	14	12	10	9	8	7
(4 × 1¼)	square	18.00	12	10	9	8	7	6
(4 × 1½)	square	21.00	14	12	10	9	8	7
(4 × 2⅛)	square	30.30	20	17	15	13	12	10

▶ **Box Sizing—Same Size Conductors [Table 314.16(A)], Example 1**

Question: What is the minimum depth 4 in. square outlet box for three 12 THW and six 12 THWN-2 conductors?

(a) 4 × 1¼ in. square
(b) 4 × 1½ in. square
(c) 4 × 2⅛ in. square
(d) 4 × 2⅛ in. with extension

Solution:

Table 314.16(A) permits nine 12 AWG conductors; the insulation type is not a factor when calculating box fill.

Answer: (b) 4 × 1½ in. square

▶ **Box Sizing—Same Size Conductors [Table 314.16(A)], Example 2**

Question: How many 14 THWN-2 conductors are permitted to be installed in a 4 in. × 1½ in. round box?

(a) 7 conductors
(b) 9 conductors
(c) 10 conductors
(d) 11 conductors

Answer: (a) 7 conductors [Table 314.16(A)]

Table 314.16(A) does not consider switches, receptacles, luminaire studs, luminaire hickeys, cable clamps, or equipment grounding conductors. The calculated conductor volumes determined by 314.16(B)(1) through (B)(5) are added together to determine the total volume of the conductors, devices, and fittings. ▶Figure 2–5

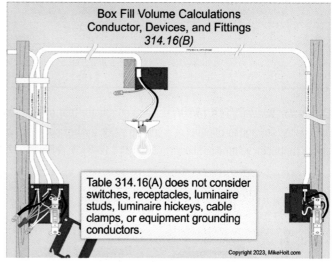

Box Fill Volume Calculations
Conductor, Devices, and Fittings
314.16(B)

Table 314.16(A) does not consider switches, receptacles, luminaire studs, luminaire hickeys, cable clamps, or equipment grounding conductors.

Copyright 2023, MikeHolt.com

▶Figure 2–5

Raceway and cable fittings, including locknuts and bushings, are not counted for box fill calculations. ▶Figure 2–6

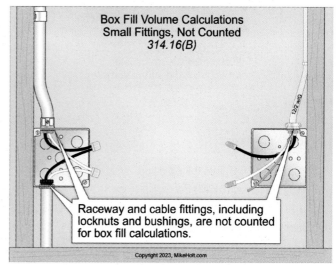

Box Fill Volume Calculations
Small Fittings, Not Counted
314.16(B)

Raceway and cable fittings, including locknuts and bushings, are not counted for box fill calculations.

Copyright 2023, MikeHolt.com

▶Figure 2–6

Table 314.16(B) Volume Allowance Required per Conductor	
Conductor AWG	Volume Cu In.
18	1.50
16	1.75
14	2.00
12	2.25
10	2.50
8	3.00
6	5.00

Conductor Volume [314.16(B)(1)]. Each conductor that originates outside the box and terminates or is spliced inside the box counts as a single conductor volume as shown in Table 314.16(B)(1). ▶Figure 2–7

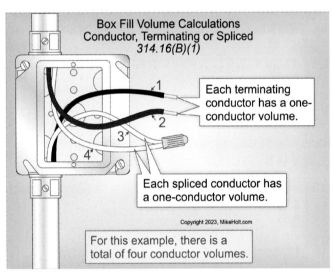

Box Fill Volume Calculations
Conductor, Terminating or Spliced
314.16(B)(1)

Each terminating conductor has a one-conductor volume.

Each spliced conductor has a one-conductor volume.

Copyright 2023, MikeHolt.com

For this example, there is a total of four conductor volumes.

▶Figure 2–7

Author's Comment:

▶ Table 314.16(B) lists the conductor cubic inch volumes for 18 AWG through 6 AWG. For example, one 14 AWG conductor has a volume of 2 cu in. If a box has four 14 AWG conductors, the conductor volume is 8 cu in.

▶ Conductor insulation is not a factor for box fill calculations.

Each conductor loop having a total length of less than 12 in. is considered a single conductor volume, and each conductor loop having a length of at least 12 in. is considered as two conductor volumes in accordance with Table 314.16(B)(1) [300.14]. ▶Figure 2–8

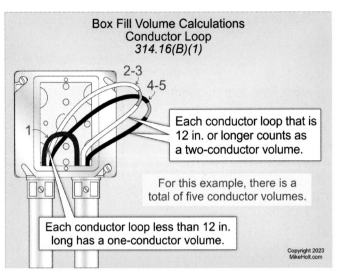

Box Fill Volume Calculations
Conductor Loop
314.16(B)(1)

Each conductor loop that is 12 in. or longer counts as a two-conductor volume.

For this example, there is a total of five conductor volumes.

Each conductor loop less than 12 in. long has a one-conductor volume.

Copyright 2023 MikeHolt.com

▶Figure 2–8

At least 6 in. of conductor, measured from the point in the box where the conductors enter the enclosure, must be available at each point for conductor splices or terminations. ▶Figure 2–9

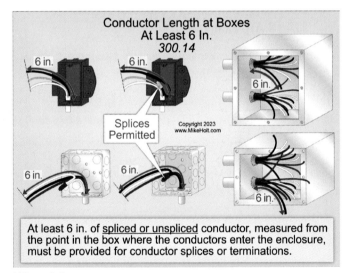

Conductor Length at Boxes
At Least 6 In.
300.14

6 in.

6 in.

6 in.

Splices Permitted

Copyright 2023 www.MikeHolt.com

6 in.

6 in.

6 in.

At least 6 in. of <u>spliced or unspliced</u> conductor, measured from the point in the box where the conductors enter the enclosure, must be provided for conductor splices or terminations.

▶Figure 2–9

Boxes that have openings of less than 8 in. in any dimension, must have at least 6 in. of conductor, measured from the point where the conductors enter the box, and at least 3 in. of conductor outside the box. ▶Figure 2–10

Conductors that originate and terminate within the box, such as pigtails, are not counted at all. ▶Figure 2–11

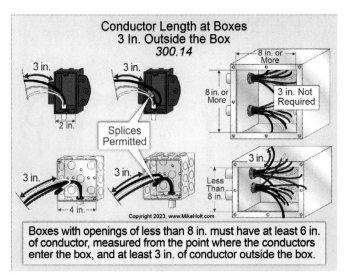

▶Figure 2–10

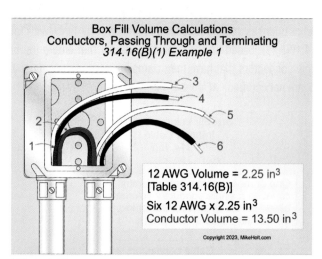

▶Figure 2–12

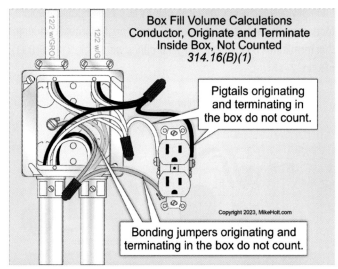

▶Figure 2–11

▶ Conductor Volume [314.16(B)(1)], Example 1

Question: *What is the cubic inch volume for four 12 AWG conductors terminating in a box and two 12 AWG conductors passing through?* ▶Figure 2–12

(a) 10.50 in.³   (b) 11.50 in.³   (c) 12.50 in.³   (d) 13.50 in.³

Solution:

Table 314.16(B) 12 AWG Volume = 2.25 in.³

Conductor Volume = 6 conductors × 2.25
Conductor Volume = 13.50 in.³

Answer: *(d) 13.50 in.³*

▶ Conductor Volume [314.16(B)(1)], Example 2

Question: *What is the cubic inch volume for two 12 AWG conductors passing through a box without a loop and two 12 AWG conductors passing through with a loop for device termination?* ▶Figure 2–13

(a) 10.50 in.³   (b) 11.50 in.³   (c) 12.50 in.³   (d) 13.50 in.³

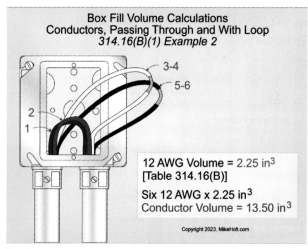

▶Figure 2–13

Solution:

Table 314.16(B) 12 AWG Volume = 2.25 in.³

Conductor Volume = 6 conductors × 2.25
Conductor Volume = 13.50 in.³

Answer: *(d) 13.50 in.³*

Cable Clamp Volume [314.16(B)(2)]. One or more internal cable clamps count as a single conductor volume in accordance with Table 314.16(B)(1), based on the largest conductor that enters the box. Cable connectors that have their clamping mechanism outside the box are not counted. ▶Figure 2–14

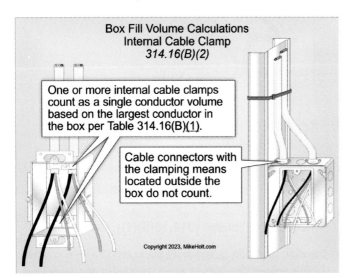

▶Figure 2–14

Support Fitting Volume [314.16(B)(3)]. Each luminaire stud or luminaire hickey counts as a single conductor volume in accordance with Table 314.16(B)(1), based on the largest conductor that enters the box. ▶Figure 2–15

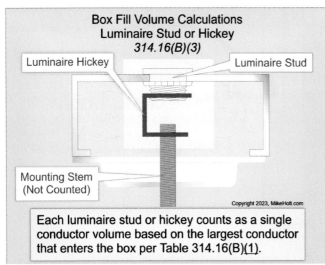

▶Figure 2–15

Device Yoke Volume [314.16(B)(4)]. Each single-gang device yoke (regardless of the physical size of the device) counts as two conductor volumes based on the largest conductor that terminates on the device in accordance with Table 314.16(B)(1). ▶Figure 2–16

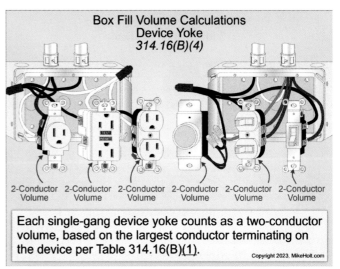

▶Figure 2–16

Each device yoke wider than 2 in. counts as a two-conductor volume for each gang required for mounting, based on the largest conductor that terminates on the device in accordance with Table 314.16(B)(1). ▶Figure 2–17

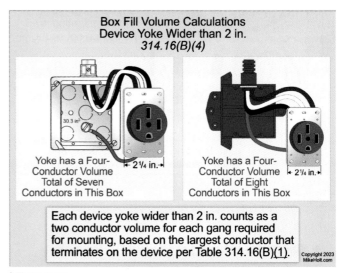

▶Figure 2–17

Equipment Grounding Conductor Volume [314.16(B)(5)]. Up to four equipment grounding conductors count as a single conductor volume based on the largest equipment grounding conductor that enters the box in accordance with Table 314.16(B)(1).

A ¼ volume allowance applies for each additional equipment grounding conductor or equipment bonding jumper that enters the box, based on the largest equipment grounding or bonding conductor.

Equipment grounding conductors for isolated ground receptacles count as an additional single conductor volume in accordance with Table 314.16(B). ▶Figure 2–18

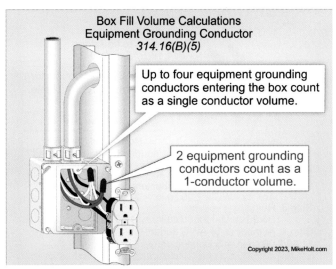

▶Figure 2–18

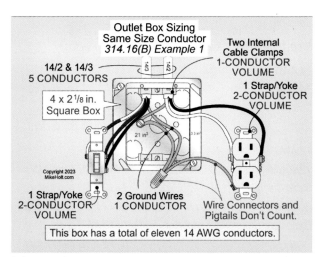

▶Figure 2–19

Answer: (d) 11 conductors

2.3 Outlet Box Sizing, Examples [314.16(B)]

To determine the size of the outlet box when the conductors are of varied sizes (insulation is not a factor), follow these steps:

Step 1: Determine the number and size of conductor equivalents in the box.

Step 2: Determine the volume of the conductor equivalents from Table 314.16(B).

Step 3: Size the box by using Table 314.16(A).

▶ **Outlet Box Sizing [314.16(B)], Example 1**

Question: What is the total number of conductors used for the box fill calculations in ▶Figure 2–19?

(a) 5 conductors
(b) 7 conductors
(c) 9 conductors
(d) 11 conductors

Solution:

Switch and Conductors	5–14 AWG conductors[†]
Receptacles and Conductors	4–14 AWG conductors[††]
Equipment Grounding Conductor	1–14 AWG conductors
Cable Clamps	+1–14 AWG conductors
Total	11–14 AWG conductors

[†]Two conductors for the device and three conductors terminating.

[††]Two conductors for the device and two conductors terminating.

Each 14 AWG conductor counts as 2 cu in. [Table 314.16(B)(1)].

11 conductors × 2 cu in. = 22 cu in.

▶ **Outlet Box Sizing [314.16(B)], Example 2**

Question: Which minimum depth, 4 in. square outlet box is required for one 14/3 with ground NM cable that terminates on a 3-way switch, and one 12/2 w/G NM cable that terminates on a receptacle? The box has internally installed cable clamps. ▶Figure 2–20

(a) 4 × 1¼ square
(b) 4 × 1½ square
(c) 4 × 2⅛ square
(d) 4 × 3 square

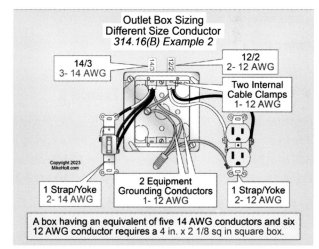

▶Figure 2–20

• • •

Solution:

Step 1: *Determine the number of each size conductor.*

14 AWG

14/3 NM	*3–14 AWG conductors*
Switch	*+2–14 AWG conductors*
Total	*5–14 AWG conductors*

12 AWG

12/2 NM	*2–12 AWG conductors*
Cable Clamp	*1–12 AWG conductors*
Receptacle	*2–12 AWG conductors*
Equipment Grounding Conductor	*+1–12 AWG conductors*
Total	*6–12 AWG conductors*

All equipment grounding conductors count as one conductor, based on the largest equipment grounding conductor entering the box [314.16(B)(5)].

Step 2: *Determine the volume of the conductors [Table 314.16(B)(1)].*

14 AWG

2 cu in. each	*2 cu in. × 5 conductors*	*10.00 cu in.*

12 AWG

2.25 cu in. each	*2.25 cu in. × 6 conductors*	*+13.50 cu in.*
Total Volume		*23.50 cu in.*

Step 3: *Select the outlet box from Table 314.16(A).*

A 4 in. × 2⅛ sq in., 30.30 cu in. box meets the minimum cu in. requirements.

Answer: *(c) 4 × 2⅛ sq in.*

▶ Outlet Box Sizing [314.16(B)], Example 3

Question: *How many 14 AWG conductors can be pulled through a 4 in. square × 2⅛ in. deep box with a plaster ring with a marking of 3.60 cu in.? The box contains two receptacles, five 12 AWG conductors, and two 12 AWG equipment grounding conductors.* ▶Figure 2–21

(a) 4 conductors	*(b) 5 conductors*
(c) 6 conductors	*(d) 7 conductors*

Solution:

Step 1: *Determine the volume of the box assembly [300.14].*

Box Assembly Volume = Box 30.30 cu in. + 3.60 cu in. plaster ring
Box Assembly Volume = 33.90 cu in.

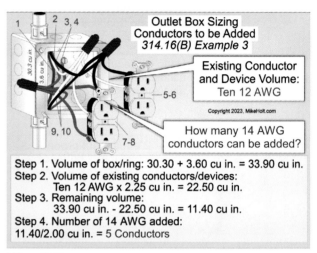

Outlet Box Sizing
Conductors to be Added
314.16(B) Example 3

Existing Conductor
and Device Volume:
Ten 12 AWG

Copyright 2023, MikeHolt.com

How many 14 AWG
conductors can be added?

Step 1. Volume of box/ring: 30.30 + 3.60 cu in. = 33.90 cu in.
Step 2. Volume of existing conductors/devices:
    Ten 12 AWG x 2.25 cu in. = 22.50 cu in.
Step 3. Remaining volume:
    33.90 cu in. - 22.50 cu in. = 11.40 cu in.
Step 4. Number of 14 AWG added:
11.40/2.00 cu in. = 5 Conductors

▶Figure 2–21

Step 2: *Determine the volume of the devices and conductors in the box:*

Two Receptacles	*4–12 AWG*
Five 12 AWG Conductors	*5–12 AWG*
Two 12 AWG Equipment Grounding Conductors	*1–12 AWG*

Total Device Volume and Conductors = Ten–12 AWG × 2.25 cu in.
Total Device Volume and Conductors = 22.50 cu in.

Step 3: *Determine the remaining volume permitted for the 14 AWG conductors (volume of the box minus the volume of the existing devices and conductors).*

Remaining Volume = 33.90 cu in. – 22.50 cu in.
Remaining Volume = 11.40 cu in.

Step 4: *Determine the number of 14 AWG conductors (at 2.00 cu in. each) permitted in the remaining volume of 11.40 cu in.:*

14 AWG = 2.00 cu in. each [Table 314.16(B)(1)]

11.40 cu in./2.00 cu in. = 5 conductors

Five 14 AWG conductors can be pulled through.

Answer: *(b) 5 conductors*

2.4 Tips for Outlet Box Sizing

Tip 1: If conductors are the same size, add them together and size the box using the AWG size columns of Table 314.16(A).

Tip 2: If the box contains different size of conductors, use Table 314.16(B)(1) to find the area of each conductor, add them up, and then size the box from Table 314.16(A) using the cu in. column.

Part B—Pull and Junction Boxes

Introduction

Pull and junction boxes must be sized to allow conductors to be installed so the conductor insulation is not damaged. For conductors 4 AWG and larger, pull and junction boxes are sized based on the trade size of the raceways terminating at the box in accordance with 314.28. ▶Figure 2–22

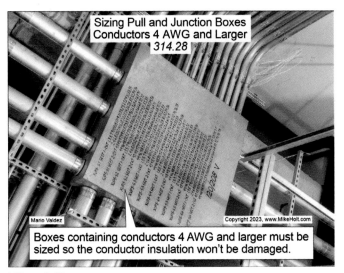

Boxes containing conductors 4 AWG and larger must be sized so the conductor insulation won't be damaged.

▶Figure 2–22

Author's Comment:

▶ The requirements for sizing boxes containing conductors 6 AWG and smaller are contained in 314.16.

▶ If conductors 4 AWG and larger enter a box or other enclosure, a fitting that provides a smooth, rounded, insulating surface (such as a bushing or adapter) is required to protect the conductors from abrasion during and after installation [300.4(G)].

2.5 Pull/Junction Box Sizing Requirements

Boxes for Conductors 4 AWG and Larger [314.28]

Boxes containing conductors 4 AWG and larger that are required to be insulated must be sized so the conductor insulation will not be damaged. Boxes covered by this section include straight pulls, U pulls, and angle pulls. ▶Figure 2–23

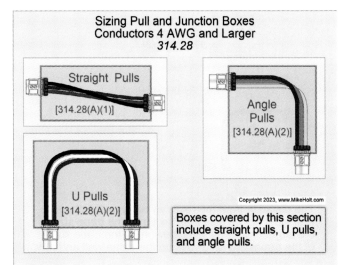

Boxes covered by this section include straight pulls, U pulls, and angle pulls.

▶Figure 2–23

Straight Pulls [314.28(A)(1)]. The minimum distance from where the conductors enter to the opposite wall must not be less than eight times the trade size of the largest raceway. A straight-pull calculation applies when conductors enter one side of a box and leave through the opposite wall of the box. ▶Figure 2–24

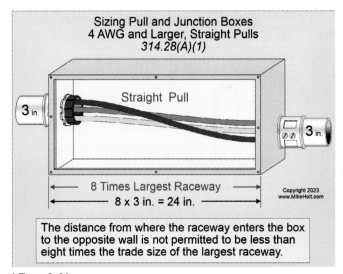

The distance from where the raceway enters the box to the opposite wall is not permitted to be less than eight times the trade size of the largest raceway.

▶Figure 2–24

Angle Pulls [314.28(A)(2)]. These occur when conductors enter a wall and leave through one that is located 90 degrees from the entry wall. The distance from the raceway entry to the opposite wall must not be less than six times the trade size of the largest raceway, plus the sum of the trade sizes of the remaining raceways on the same wall and row. ▶Figure 2–25

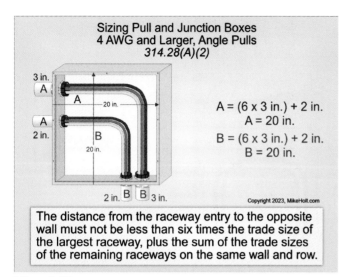

▶Figure 2–25

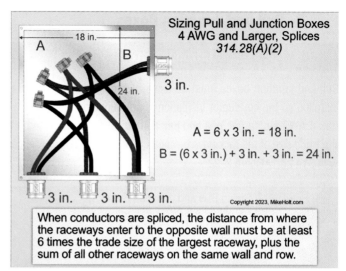

▶Figure 2–27

U Pulls [314.28(A)(2)]. A conductor that enters and leaves from the same wall is a U pull. The distance from where the raceways enter to the opposite wall must not be less than six times the trade size of the largest raceway, plus the sum of the trade sizes of the remaining raceways on the same wall and row. ▶Figure 2–26

Distance Between Raceway Entries [314.28(A)(2)]. The distance between raceway entries enclosing the same conductor must not be less than six times the trade size of the largest raceway, measured from the raceways' opening nearest edge to nearest edge. ▶Figure 2–28 and ▶Figure 2–29

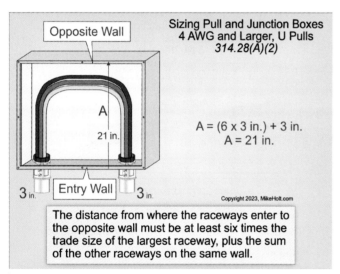

▶Figure 2–26

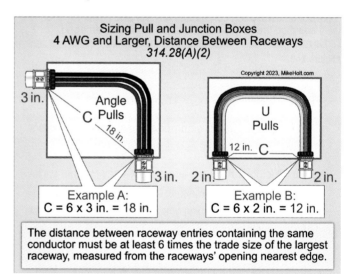

▶Figure 2–28

Splices [314.28(A)(2)]. When conductors are spliced, the distance from where the raceways enter to the opposite wall must not be less than six times the trade size of the largest raceway, plus the sum of the trade sizes of the remaining raceways on the same wall and row. ▶Figure 2–27

Author's Comment:

▶ The measurement between raceway entries is taken from the actual raceway entry, not the locknuts or bushings used to terminate the raceways.

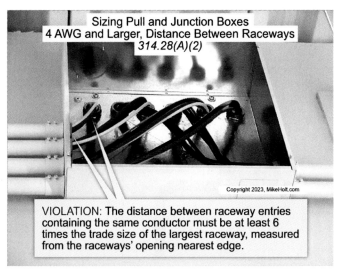

Sizing Pull and Junction Boxes
4 AWG and Larger, Distance Between Raceways
314.28(A)(2)

VIOLATION: The distance between raceway entries containing the same conductor must be at least 6 times the trade size of the largest raceway, measured from the raceways' opening nearest edge.

▶Figure 2–29

314.28(A)(2) Ex: When conductors enter an enclosure with a removable cover, such as a conduit body or wireway, the distance from where the conductors enter to the removable cover must not be less than the bending distance listed in Table 312.6(A) for one conductor per terminal. ▶Figure 2–30

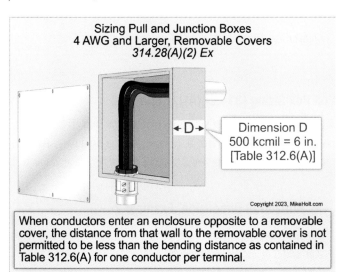

Sizing Pull and Junction Boxes
4 AWG and Larger, Removable Covers
314.28(A)(2) Ex

←D→

Dimension D
500 kcmil = 6 in.
[Table 312.6(A)]

When conductors enter an enclosure opposite to a removable cover, the distance from that wall to the removable cover is not permitted to be less than the bending distance as contained in Table 312.6(A) for one conductor per terminal.

▶Figure 2–30

2.6 How to Size Pull/Junction Boxes

When sizing pull and junction boxes, follow these suggestions:

Tip 1: Always draw out the problem.

Tip 2: Calculate the HORIZONTAL distance(s):

- ▶ Left to right straight calculation
- ▶ Right to left straight calculation
- ▶ Left to right angle or U pull calculation
- ▶ Right to left angle or U pull calculation

Tip 3: Calculate the VERTICAL distance(s):

- ▶ Top to bottom straight calculation
- ▶ Bottom to top straight calculation
- ▶ Top to bottom angle or U pull calculation
- ▶ Bottom to top angle or U pull calculation

Tip 4: Calculate the distance between raceways enclosing the same conductors.

2.7 Pull Box Sizing Examples

Pull Box Sizing [314.28(A)], Example 1

A junction box contains two 3 in. raceways on the left side and one 3 in. raceway on the right side. The conductors from one of the 3 in. raceways on the left wall are pulled through the 3 in. raceway on the right wall. The conductors from the other 3 in. raceway on the left wall are pulled through a 3 in. raceway at the bottom of the pull box.

▶ **Horizontal Dimension, Example 1**

Question: What is the horizontal dimension of this box? ▶Figure 2–31

(a) 18 in.　　(b) 21 in.　　(c) 24 in.　　(d) 30 in.

Solution:

Left to Right Straight Pull = 8 × 3 in. = 24 in.
Right to Left Straight Pull = 8 × 3 in. = 24 in.

Left to Right Angle Pull = (6 × 3 in.) + 3 in.
Left to Right Angle Pull = 21 in.

Right to Left Angle Pull = no calculation

Answer: (c) 24 in. [314.28(A)]

• • •

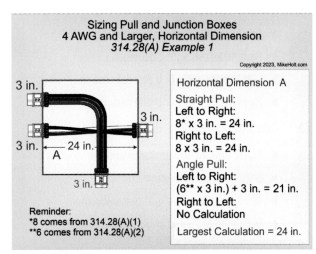

▶Figure 2–31

▶ Vertical Dimension, Example 1

Question: *What is the vertical dimension of a junction box having a 3 in. raceway on the bottom wall of the junction box with no raceways on the top wall of the box?* ▶**Figure 2–32**

(a) 18 in.   (b) 21 in.   (c) 24 in.   (d) 30 in.

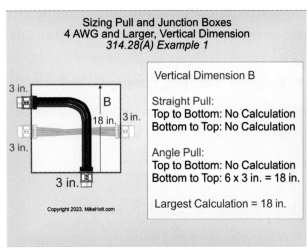

▶Figure 2–32

Solution:

Top to Bottom Straight = no calculation

Bottom to Top Straight = no calculation

Top to Bottom Angle = no calculation

Bottom to Top Angle = 6 × 3 in.
Bottom to Top Angle = 18 in.

Answer: *(a) 18 in. [314.28(A)]*

▶ Distance Between Raceway Entries, Example 1

Question: *What is the minimum distance between the two 3 in. raceways containing the same conductors?* ▶**Figure 2–33**

(a) 18 in.   (b) 21 in.   (c) 24 in.   (d) 30 in.

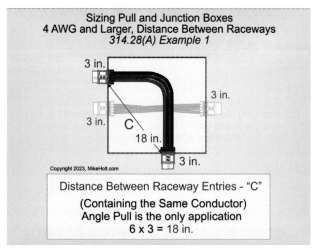

▶Figure 2–33

Solution:

6 × 3 in. = 18 in.

Answer: *(a) 18 in. [314.28(A)(2)]*

Pull Box Sizing [314.28(A)], Example 2

A pull box contains a 2 in. and 3 in. raceway on the left side, a 3 in. raceway on the top, and a 2 in. raceway on the right side. The 2 in. raceways are a straight pull and the 3 in. raceways are an angle pull.

▶ Horizontal Dimension, Example 2

Question: *What is the horizontal dimension of a junction box having 2 in. and 3 in. raceways on the left wall, and a 2 in. raceway on the right wall of the box?* ▶**Figure 2–34**

(a) 20 in.   (b) 24 in.   (c) 28 in.   (d) 30 in.

Solution:

Left to Right Straight Pull = 8 × 2 in. = 16 in.
Right to Left Straight Pull = 8 × 2 in. = 16 in.

Left to Right Angle Pull = (6 × 3 in.) + 2 in.
Left to Right Angle Pull = 20 in.

Right to Left Angle Pull = no calculation

Answer: *(a) 20 in. [314.28(A)(2)]*

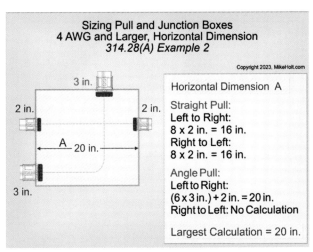

▶Figure 2-34

▶ Vertical Dimension, Example 2

Question: What is the vertical dimension of a junction box having a 3 in. raceway on the top with no raceways on the bottom wall of the box? ▶Figure 2-35

(a) 14 in.   (b) 18 in.   (c) 21 in.   (d) 26 in.

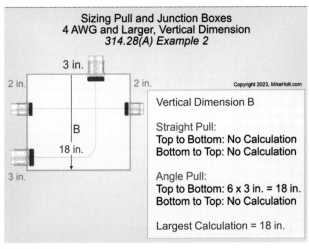

▶Figure 2-35

Solution:

Top to Bottom Straight = no calculation

Bottom to Top Straight = no calculation

Top to Bottom Angle = 6 × 3 in.
Top to Bottom Angle = 18 in.

Bottom to Top Angle = no calculation

Answer: (b) 18 in. [314.28(A)(2)]

▶ Distance Between Raceways, Example 2

Question: If the two 3 in. raceways contain the same conductors, what is the minimum distance between these raceways? ▶Figure 2-36

(a) 18 in.   (b) 21 in.   (c) 24 in.   (d) 30 in.

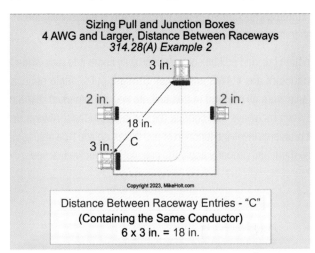

▶Figure 2-36

Solution:

6 × 3 in. = 18 in.

Answer: (a) 18 in. [314.28(A)(2)]

2.8 Tips for Pull Box Sizing

Tip 1: Slow down and take your time on these calculations. It is easy to make simple mistakes.

Tip 2: Pull box calculations can be tricky—remember which wall you are working on.

Tip 3: Box calculations become easier with more practice. Use practical field examples to practice calculations.

Tip 4: Draw up some sample pull boxes and calculate them for practice.

Unit 2—Conclusion

When sizing outlet boxes if they contain all the same size conductors simply take a look at Table 314.16(A) to size the box. Several details for determining the correct size outlet box to be used were covered. They will be important for an exam. Be sure to remember what items are counted in box fill calculations and review the information if necessary.

Junction box and pull box calculations only come into play when the conductors are 4 AWG and larger. Straight pulls, angle pulls, and U pulls were all covered in this unit, as well as minimum distances between raceways that contain the same conductors. Always draw out problems involving junction or pull boxes, so you'll be able to visualize them and properly apply the calculations you've learned.

UNIT
2

REVIEW QUESTIONS

Please use the 2023 *Code* book and this textbook to answer the following questions.

PART A—OUTLET BOX SIZING

2.1 Box Sizing—Conductors All the Same Size [314.16(A)]

1. What size outlet box is the minimum required for six 14 TW conductors and three 14 THW conductors?

   (a) 4 in. × 1¼ in. square box
   (b) 4 in. × 1½ in. round box
   (c) 4 in. × 1¼ in. round box
   (d) 4 in. × 2⅛ in. square box

2. How many 10 TW conductors are permitted in a 4 in. × 1½ in. square deep box?

   (a) 8 conductors
   (b) 9 conductors
   (c) 10 conductors
   (d) 11 conductors

3. How many 14 AWG conductors are permitted to be installed in a 4 in. × 1½ in. round box?

   (a) 7 conductors
   (b) 9 conductors
   (c) 10 conductors
   (d) 11 conductors

4. What size outlet box is the minimum required for three 12 AWG and six 12 AWG conductors?

   (a) 4 × 1¼ in. square
   (b) 4 × 1½ in. square
   (c) 4 × 2⅛ in. square
   (d) any of these

2.3 Outlet Box Sizing Examples [314.16(B)]

5. Each luminaire stud or luminaire hickey counts as a _____ volume in accordance with Table 314.16(B), based on the largest conductor that enters the box.

   (a) zero conductor
   (b) single conductor
   (c) double conductor
   (d) triple conductor

6. What is the 14 AWG conductor count for outlet box sizing containing three current carrying conductors, three grounded conductors, and three equipment grounding conductors?

   (a) 7 conductors
   (b) 8 conductors
   (c) 9 conductors
   (d) 10 conductors

7. What is the cubic inch volume required for four 14/2 NM cables entering an outlet box?

   (a) 12 cu. in.
   (b) 14 cu. in.
   (c) 16 cu. in.
   (d) 18 cu. in.

8. What is the cubic inch volume required for six 14 AWG conductors and a single-pole switch at an outlet box?

   (a) 10 cu. in.
   (b) 12 cu. in.
   (c) 14 cu. in.
   (d) 16 cu. in.

9. What size outlet box is required for six 12 AWG conductors terminating to one switch and two receptacles?

   (a) 4 in. × 1¼ in. square box
   (b) 4 in. × 1½ in. square box
   (c) 4 in. × 2⅛ in. square box
   (d) 3 in. × 2 in. × 3½ in. device box

10. What size outlet box is required for two 12 AWG conductors terminated to a dimmer and two 12 AWG conductors terminated to a receptacle?

    (a) 4 in. × 1¼ in. square
    (b) 4 in. × 1½ in. square
    (c) 4 in. × 2⅛ in. square
    (d) 3 in. × 2 in. × 3½ in. device

11. What size outlet box is required for two 14/2 NM Cables terminating to one switch? The box has two internal cable clamps.

    (a) 4 in. × 1¼ in. square box
    (b) 4 in. × 1½ in. square box
    (c) 4 in. × 2⅛ in. square box
    (d) 3 in. × 2 in. × 3½ in. device box

12. What size outlet box is required for one 12/2 NM cable that terminates on a switch and one 12/3 NM cable that terminates on a receptacle? The box has two internal cable clamps.

    (a) 4 in. × 1¼ in. square box
    (b) 4 in. × 1½ in. square box
    (c) 4 in. × 2⅛ in. square box
    (d) 3 in. × 2 in. × 3½ in. device box

PART B—PULL AND JUNCTION BOXES

2.7 Pull Box Sizing Examples

The following information applies to the next three questions. A junction box contains two trade size 2½ raceways on the left side and one trade size 2½ raceway on the right side. The conductors from one trade size 2½ raceway (on the left wall) are pulled through the raceway on the right wall. The other trade size 2½ raceway conductors (on the left wall) are pulled through a trade size 2½ raceway at the bottom of the pull box.

13. What is the minimum distance from the left wall to the right wall (the A measurement)?

    (a) 18 in.
    (b) 20 in.
    (c) 21 in.
    (d) 24 in.

14. What is the minimum distance from the bottom wall to the top wall (the B measurement)?

    (a) 15 in.
    (b) 18 in.
    (c) 21 in.
    (d) 24 in.

15. What is the minimum distance between the raceways of the angle pull?

    (a) 15 in.
    (b) 18 in.
    (c) 21 in.
    (d) 24 in.

The following information applies to the next three questions. A junction box contains two trade size 2 raceways on the left side, and two trade size 2 raceways on the top.

16. What is the minimum distance from the left wall to the right wall?

    (a) 14 in.
    (b) 21 in.
    (c) 24 in.
    (d) 28 in.

17. What is the minimum distance from the bottom wall to the top wall?

    (a) 14 in.
    (b) 18 in.
    (c) 21 in.
    (d) 24 in.

18. What is the minimum distance between the trade size 2 raceways that contain the same conductors?

    (a) 12 in.
    (b) 18 in.
    (c) 21 in.
    (d) 24 in.

19. The minimum horizontal dimension for the junction box shown in the diagram in ▶Figure 2–37 is ____.

    (a) 18 in.
    (b) 20 in.
    (c) 21 in.
    (d) 24 in.

20. The minimum vertical dimension for the junction box shown in ▶Figure 2–37 is ____.

    (a) 16 in.
    (b) 18 in.
    (c) 20 in.
    (d) 24 in.

21. The minimum distance between the two trade size 2 raceways that contain the same Conductor C as illustrated in ▶Figure 2–37 is ____.

    (a) 12 in.
    (b) 18 in.
    (c) 24 in.
    (d) 30 in.

22. If a trade size 3 raceway entry (250 kcmil) is in the wall opposite a removable cover, the distance from that wall to the cover must not be less than ____.

    (a) 4 in.
    (b) 4½ in.
    (c) 5 in.
    (d) 6 in.

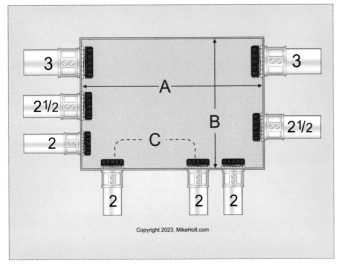

Copyright 2023, MikeHolt.com

▶Figure 2–37

UNIT 3

CONDUCTOR SIZING AND PROTECTION CALCULATIONS

Introduction to Unit 3—Conductor Sizing and Protection Calculations

Every conductor has a certain amount of resistance. Any time current flows through a conductor there's resistance, and heat is generated. The amount of heat produced is directly proportional to the resistance of the wire and the square of the current flow. The amount of current you allow a conductor to carry must be limited to a level that will not cause it to overheat. To make sure the amount of current in a conductor is kept within the proper limits, overcurrent protection is used to open the circuit if necessary. This protection is provided by installing a fuse or circuit breaker, of a size based on the conductor's ampacity.

The following are the Parts covered in this unit:

▶ Part A—Conductor Insulation, Terminals, and Overcurrent Protection

▶ Part B— Conductor Ampacity and Protection

Some specific overcurrent applications and tap rules will be discussed to help you become familiar with the rules for sizing overcurrent protective devices in this unit. Motor, air-conditioning, and transformer circuits will be covered in more depth in Unit 4. Be sure to study this unit carefully to learn how to make the right conductor sizing and protection decisions.

Part A—Conductor Insulation, Terminals, and Overcurrent Protection

Introduction

The insulation temperature rating of a conductor must be limited to an operating temperature that prevents damage to the conductor's insulation. If the conductor carries excessive current, the I^2R heating within it from the current flow could raise the temperature to a level where the insulation could be destroyed. Part A of this unit covers the general rules for overcurrent protection and how to select the proper conductor based on the temperature rating of the equipment terminals.

3.1 Conductor Insulation [Table 310.4(1)]

Table 310.4(1) provides information on conductor insulation properties such as letter type, maximum operating temperature, application, insulation, and outer cover properties. Only conductors in Table 310.4(1) can be installed for the application identified in the table.

Author's Comment:

▶ It's common to see conductors with multiple insulation ratings, such as THHN/THWN. This type of conductor can be used in a dry location at the THHN 90°C ampacity. If it's used in a wet location, you must adhere to the THWN ampacity rating of the 75°C column of Table 310.16 for THWN insulation types. ▶Figure 3–1

▶ When a "–2" is at the end of an insulation (such as THWN-2), the conductor has a maximum operating temperature of 90°C and is suitable to be installed in a dry or wet location. ▶Figure 3–2

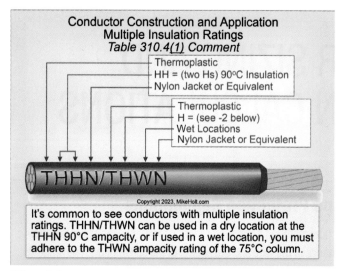

It's common to see conductors with multiple insulation ratings. THHN/THWN can be used in a dry location at the THHN 90°C ampacity, or if used in a wet location, you must adhere to the THWN ampacity rating of the 75°C column.

▶Figure 3–1

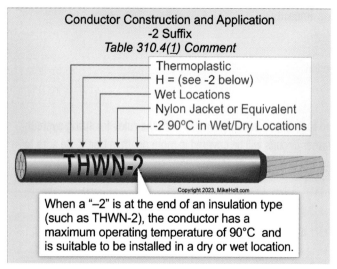

When a "–2" is at the end of an insulation type (such as THWN-2), the conductor has a maximum operating temperature of 90°C and is suitable to be installed in a dry or wet location.

▶Figure 3–2

▶ **Table 310.4(1) Conductor Insulation, Example**

Question: Which of the following describe(s) THHN insulation? ▶Figure 3–3

(a) Thermoplastic insulation

(b) Suitable for dry or damp locations

(c) A maximum operating temperature of 90°C

(d) all of these

Answer: (d) all of these

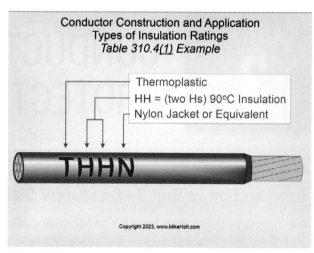

▶Figure 3–3

3.2 Conductor Sizes

Conductor sizes are expressed in American Wire Gauge (AWG), typically from 18 AWG up to 4/0 AWG. Conductor sizes larger than 4/0 AWG are expressed in kcmil (thousand circular mils) [110.6]. ▶Figure 3–4

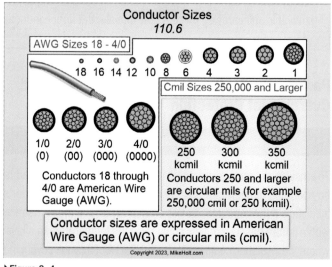

▶Figure 3–4

Table 310.4(1) Conductor Applications and Insulations

Type Letter	Column 2 Insulation	Column 3 Max. Operating Temperature	Column 4 Application	Column 5 Sizes Available AWG or kcmil	Column 6 Outer Covering
RHH	Flame-retardant thermoset	90°C	Dry and damp locations	14–2000	Moisture-resistant, flame-retardant, nonmetallic
RHW	Flame-retardant, moisture-resistant thermoset	75°C	Dry and wet locations	14–2000	Moisture-resistant, flame-retardant, nonmetallic
RHW-2	Flame-retardant, moisture-resistant thermoset	90°C	Dry and wet locations	14–2000	Moisture-resistant, flame-retardant, nonmetallic
THHN	Flame-retardant, heat-resistant thermoplastic	90°C	Dry and damp locations	14–1000	Nylon jacket or equivalent
THHW	Flame-retardant, moisture- and heat-resistant thermoplastic	75°C 90°C	Wet locations Dry locations	14–1000	None
THW	Flame-retardant, moisture- and heat-resistant thermoplastic	75°C	Dry, damp, and wet locations	14–2000	None
THW-2	Flame-retardant, moisture- and heat-resistant thermoplastic	90°C	Dry, damp, and wet locations	14–1000	None
THWN	Flame-retardant, moisture- and heat-resistant thermoplastic	75°C	Dry, damp, and wet locations	14–1000	Nylon jacket or equivalent
THWN-2	Flame-retardant, moisture- and heat-resistant thermoplastic	90°C	Dry, damp, and wet locations	14–1000	Nylon jacket or equivalent
TW	Flame-retardant, moisture-resistant thermoplastic	60°C	Dry, damp, and wet locations	14–2000	None
USE	Heat- and moisture-resistant	75°C	See Article 338	14–2000	Moisture-resistant nonmetallic
USE-2	Heat- and moisture-resistant	90°C	See Article 338	14–2000	Moisture-resistant nonmetallic

3.3 Conductor Size—Equipment Terminal Rating [110.14(C)]

Conductors terminating on equipment must be sized to the lowest terminal temperature rating in accordance with 110.14(C)(1) and (2).

(1) Equipment Terminals. Unless equipment is listed and marked otherwise, conductors are sized based on Table 310.16 in accordance with (a) or (b) as follows:

(a) Equipment Rated 100A or Less. Conductors terminating on equipment for circuits rated 100A or less must be sized as follows:

(2) Conductors rated 90°C can be used but they must be sized to the 60°C temperature column of Table 310.16. ▸Figure 3–5

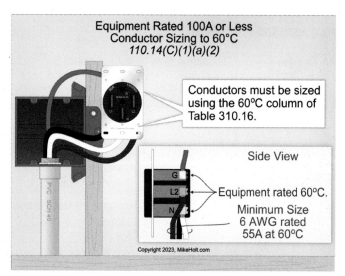

▶Figure 3–5

▶ Conductor Size—Less than 100A [110.14(C)(1) (a)(2)], Example

Question: What size THWN-2 conductor is required for a 50A circuit?
▶Figure 3–6

(a) 10 AWG   (b) 8 AWG   (c) 6 AWG   (d) 4 AWG

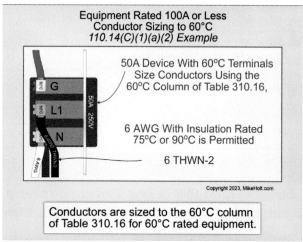

▶Figure 3–6

Answer: (c) 6 AWG rated 55A at 60°C [110.14(C)(1)(a)(2) and Table 310.16]

Equipment Rated 75°C, 110.14(C)(1)(a)(3)

Conductors terminating on equipment rated 75°C can be sized in accordance with the ampacities in the 75°C temperature column of Table 310.16. ▶Figure 3–7

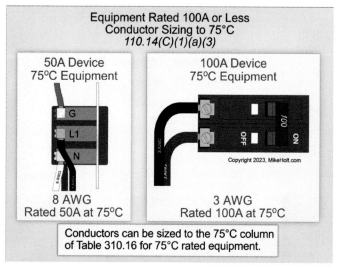

▶Figure 3–7

Author's Comment:

▶ Much of today's equipment has terminals rated 75°C and most of today's conductors have insulation ratings 90°C. If the equipment terminal is rated 75°C, the conductor size must be selected from the 75°C column of Table 310.16 to reduce the chance of the terminal overheating. ▶Figure 3–8

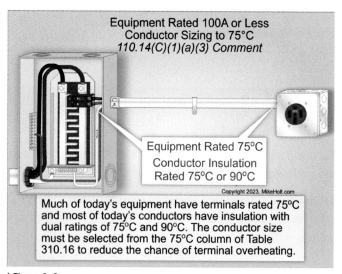

▶Figure 3–8

▶ Conductor Size—Less than 100A [110.14(C)(1)(a)(3)], Example

Question: *What size THWN-2 conductor is required for a 50A circuit where the equipment is rated for 75°C conductors?* ▶**Figure 3–9**

(a) 10 AWG   *(b) 8 AWG*   *(c) 6 AWG*   *(d) 4 AWG*

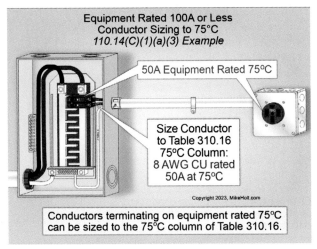

▶Figure 3–9

Answer: *(b) 8 AWG rated 50A at 75°C [110.14(C)(1)(a)(3) and Table 310.16]*

▶ Conductor Size—Over 100A [110.14(C)(1)(b)(2)], Example

Question: *What size THWN-2 aluminum conductor is required to supply a 200A feeder?* ▶**Figure 3–11**

(a) 2/0 AWG   *(b) 3/0 AWG*   *(c) 4/0 AWG*   *(d) 250 kcmil*

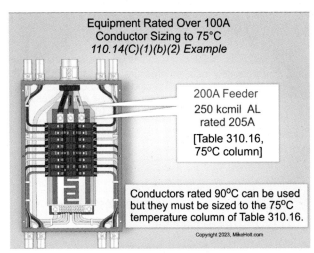

▶Figure 3–11

Answer: *(d) 250 kcmil rated 205A at 75°C [110.14(C)(1)(b)(2) and Table 310.16]*

Equipment Rated Over 100A 110.14(C)(1)(b)

Conductors terminating on equipment for circuits rated over 100A must be sized to the 75°C temperature column of Table 310.16. ▶**Figure 3–10**

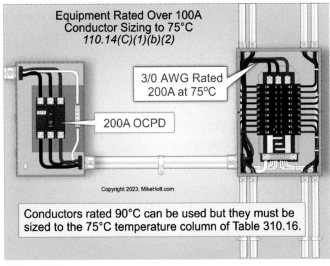

▶Figure 3–10

Separate Connectors [110.14(C)(2)]

Separately installed pressure connectors rated 90°C or more and not connected to electrical equipment, can have the conductors sized in accordance with the 90°C temperature column ampacities of Table 310.16. ▶**Figure 3–12**

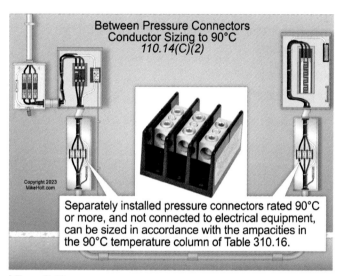

Separately installed pressure connectors rated 90°C or more, and not connected to electrical equipment, can be sized in accordance with the ampacities in the 90°C temperature column of Table 310.16.

▶Figure 3–12

▶ **Conductor Size—Separate Connectors [110.14(C)(2)], Example**

Question: What size THWN-2 aluminum conductor can be used between power distribution blocks rated 90°C for a circuit supplying a 200A noncontinuous load where the circuit overcurrent protection is 200A? ▶**Figure 3–13**

(a) 1/0 AWG   (b) 2/0 AWG   (c) 3/0 AWG   (d) 4/0 AWG

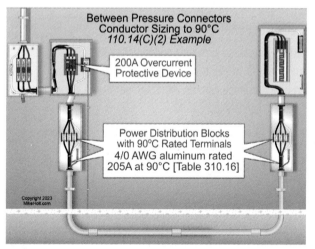

▶Figure 3–13

Answer: (d) 4/0 AWG aluminum rated 205A at 90°C [110.14(C)(2) and Table 310.16]

3.4 Overcurrent Protection of Conductors [240.4]

Overcurrent protection for conductors is required in accordance with their ampacities as specified in 310.14, except as permitted by (A) through (H). ▶Figure 3–14

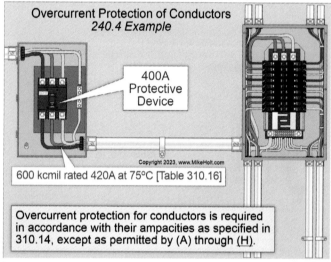

▶Figure 3–14

Overcurrent Protective Devices Rated 800A or Less [240.4(B)]. The next higher standard rating of overcurrent protective device in 240.6 (above the ampacity of the phase conductors being protected) is permitted to be used, provided all the following conditions are met:

(1) The conductors are not part of a branch circuit supplying more than one receptacle for cord-and-plug-connected loads.

(2) The ampacity of a conductor, after the application of ambient temperature correction [310.15(B)(1)], conductor bundling adjustment [310.15(C)(1)], or both, doesn't correspond with the standard rating of a fuse or circuit breaker in 240.6(A).

(3) The next higher standard overcurrent protective device rating from 240.6(A) doesn't exceed 800A.

▶ **Overcurrent Protective Devices 800A or Less [240.4(B)], Example 1**

Question: What's the maximum size overcurrent protective device that can be used to protect 500 kcmil conductors where each conductor has an ampacity of 380A? ▶**Figure 3–15**

(a) 300A   (b) 350A   (c) 400A   (d) 500A

Answer: (c) 400A [240.6(A)]

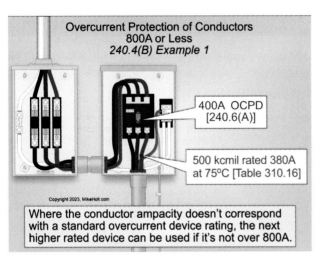

▶Figure 3–15

▶ Overcurrent Protective Devices 800A or Less [240.4(B)], Example 2

Question: What is the maximum size overcurrent protective device that can be used to protect two sets of 500 kcmil conductors in parallel raceways where each conductor has an ampacity of 380A? ▶Figure 3–16

(a) 400A   (b) 500A   (c) 600A   (d) 800A

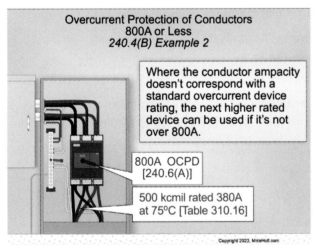

▶Figure 3–16

Conductor Ampacity = 380A × 2 sets
Conductor Ampacity = 760A, maximum OCPD is 800A [240.6(A)]

Answer: *(d) 800A [240.6(A)]*

Overcurrent Protective Devices Over 800A [240.4(C)]. If the circuit's overcurrent protective device exceeds 800A, the conductor ampacity, after the application of ambient temperature correction [310.15(B)(1)], conductor bundling adjustment [310.15(C)(1)], or both, must have a rating of not less than the rating of the overcurrent protective device defined in 240.6.

▶ Overcurrent Protective Devices Over 800A [240.4(C)], Example

Question: What is the minimum size of conductors (paralleled in three sets of conductors per phase) allowed to be protected by a 1,200A overcurrent protective device? ▶Figure 3–17

(a) 400 kcmil   (b) 500 kcmil   (c) 600 kcmil   (d) 750 kcmil

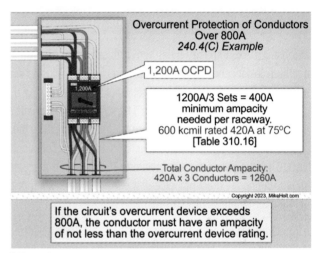

▶Figure 3–17

Solution:

The total ampacity of the three parallel conductor sets must be equal to or greater than 1,200A [240.4(C)]. The ampacity for each conductor within the parallel set must be equal to or greater than 400A (1,200A/3 raceways).

Conductor Size = 600 kcmil conductors per phase rated 420A at 75°C [110.14(C)(1) and Table 310.16]

Total Conductor Ampacity = 420A × 3 conductors
Total Conductor Ampacity = 1,260A

Answer: *(c) 600 kcmil*

Part B—Conductor Ampacity and Protection

Introduction

To determine what size conductor is needed to carry a certain amount of current, the heat that will be generated must be taken into consideration. The number of conductors in the same raceway that are carrying current can affect this decision, as can the ambient temperature.

Factors that impact conductor sizing include conductor ampacity, equipment terminal temperature rating, continuous load factors, overcurrent protection requirements, conductor insulation temperature rating, ambient temperature conductor ampacity correction, and conductor bundling conductor ampacity adjustment.

3.5 Conductor Ampacity Table [310.15(A)]

The Table 310.16 ampacity must be corrected when the ambient temperature is not between 78°F and 86°F and must be adjusted when more than three current-carrying conductors are bundled together. The temperature correction multiplier [310.15(B)(1)] and adjustment multiplier [310.15(C)(1)] are applied to the conductor ampacity based on the temperature rating of the conductor insulation as contained in Table 310.16 (typically in the 90°C column). The corrected or adjusted conductor ampacity must not exceed the temperature rating of the equipment terminations of 110.14(C).

The temperature ampacity correction [310.15(B)(1)] and adjustment ampacity factors [310.15(C)(1)] are applied to the ampacities listed in Table 310.16, based on the conductor's insulation temperature rating.

> **Author's Comment:**
>
> ▸ When correcting or adjusting conductor ampacity, the ampacity is based on the conductor material and its insulation temperature rating as listed in the appropriate column of Table 310.16. It is not based on the temperature rating of the terminal [110.14(C)].
>
> ▸ The neutral conductor might be a current-carrying conductor, but only under the conditions specified in 310.15(E). Equipment grounding conductors are never considered current carrying [310.15(F)].

3.6 Conductor Ampacity Correction [310.15(B)(1)]

Conductor ampacities must be corrected in accordance with Table 310.15(B)(1)(1) when the ambient temperature is greater than 86°F or less than 78°F. ▸Figure 3–18

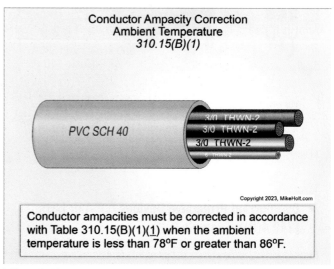

Conductor Ampacity Correction
Ambient Temperature
310.15(B)(1)

PVC SCH 40

3/0 THWN-2
3/0 THWN-2
3/0 THWN-2

Copyright 2023, MikeHolt.com

Conductor ampacities must be corrected in accordance with Table 310.15(B)(1)(1) when the ambient temperature is less than 78°F or greater than 86°F.

▸Figure 3–18

Corrected Conductor Ampacity—Ambient Temperature Correction Formula:

Corrected Ampacity = Table 310.16 Ampacity × Ambient Correction Factor

> ▶ **Conductor Ampacity Correction [Table 310.15(B)(1)(1)], Example 1**
>
> **Question:** *What is the ampacity of a 12 THWN-2 conductor when installed in an ambient temperature of 50°F?* ▸Figure 3–19
>
> (a) 20A   (b) 25A   (c) 31A   (d) 35A
>
> **Solution:**
>
> *The conductor ampacity for 12 THWN-2 is 30A at 90°C [Table 310.16].*
>
> *The correction factor for a 90°C conductor installed in an ambient temperature of 50°F is 1.15 [Table 310.15(B)(1)(1)].*
>
> *Corrected Ampacity = 30A × 115%*
> *Corrected Ampacity = 34.50A, round to 35A*
>
> **Note:** *Ampacity increases when the ambient temperature is less than 86°F.*
>
> **Answer:** *(d) 35A*

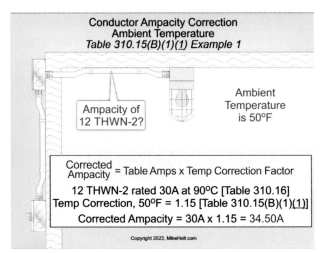

▶Figure 3–19

▶ Conductor Ampacity Correction [Table 310.15(B)(1)(1)], Example 2

Question: What is the ampacity of a 6 THWN-2 conductor installed in an ambient temperature of 122°F? ▶**Figure 3–20**

(a) 35A   (b) 53A   (c) 62A   (d) 75A

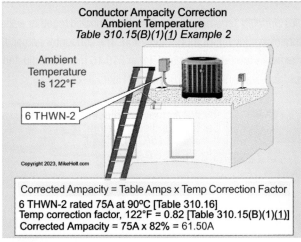

▶Figure 3–20

Solution:

The conductor ampacity for 6 THWN-2 is 75A at 90°C [Table 310.16].

The correction factor for a 90°C conductor installed in an ambient temperature of 122°F is 0.82 [Table 310.15(B)(1)(1)].

Corrected Ampacity = 75A × 82%
Corrected Ampacity = 61.50A, round to 62A

Answer: (c) 62A

Conductor Ampacity Correction Raceways on Rooftops [310.15(B)(2)]

Where raceways are exposed to direct sunlight and located less than ¾ in. above the roof, a temperature of 60°F (33°C) must be added to the outdoor ambient temperature to determine the ambient temperature correction in accordance with Table 310.15(B)(1)(1). ▶**Figure 3–21**

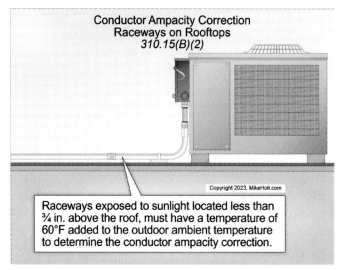

▶Figure 3–21

Author's Comment:

▶ The reason for the temperature adder is because the air inside raceways and cables that are in direct sunlight is significantly hotter than the surrounding air.

▶ Conductor Ampacity Correction Rooftops [310.15(B)(2)], Example

Question: What is the ampacity of a 6 THWN-2 in a raceway ½ in. above the roof, where the ambient temperature is 90°F? ▶**Figure 3–22**

(a) 40A   (b) 41A   (c) 42A   (d) 44A

Solution:

Corrected Temperature = 90°F + 60°F adder [310.15(B)(2)]
Corrected Temperature = 150°F

The temperature correction factor for 150°F = 0.58
* [Table 310.15(B)(1)(1)]*

6 THWN-2 is rated 75A at 90°C [Table 310.16].

Corrected Ampacity = 75A × 58%
Corrected Ampacity = 43.50A, round to 44A

• • •

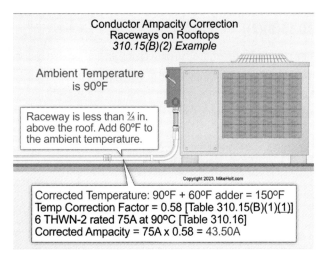

▶Figure 3–22

Answer: (d) 44A

Ex: XHHW-2 insulated conductors are not subject to the rooftop temperature adder.

Note 1: The *ASHRAE Handbook–Fundamentals* (www.ashrae.org) is one source for the ambient temperatures in various locations.

3.7 Conductor Ampacity Adjustment [310.15(C)(1)]

Conductors in Raceways or Cables. Where four or more current-carrying conductors are within a raceway or cable, the conductor ampacities contained in the 90°C column of Table 310.16 must be adjusted in accordance with Table 310.15(C)(1). ▶Figure 3–23

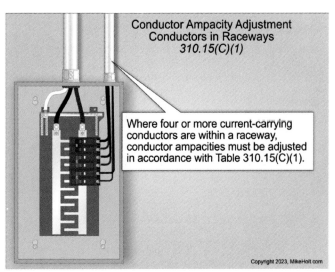

▶Figure 3–23

Author's Comment:

▶ Conductor ampacity reduction is required when four or more current-carrying conductors are bundled together because heat generated by current flow is not able to dissipate as quickly as when there are fewer current-carrying conductors. ▶Figure 3–24

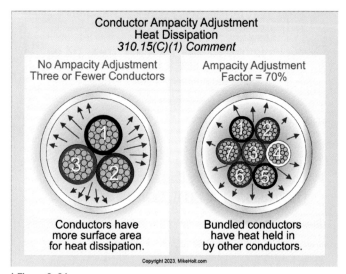

▶Figure 3–24

Cables Bundled Together. Where cables are bundled together without maintaining spacing for more than 24 in., the conductor ampacities contained in the 90°C column of Table 310.16 must be adjusted in accordance with Table 310.15(C)(1). ▶Figure 3–25

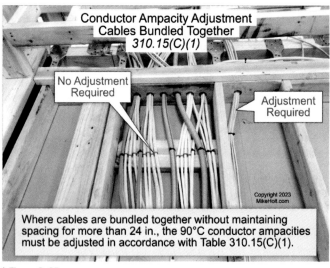

▶Figure 3–25

▶ The neutral conductor is not considered a current-carrying conductor for the purposes of conductor ampacity adjustment [310.15(C)(1)] under the conditions specified in 310.15(E)(1).

▶ Conductor Ampacity Adjustment [310.15(C)(1)], Example 1

Question: What is the adjusted ampacity of four current-carrying 12 THWN-2 conductors in a raceway? ▶Figure 3–26

(a) 20A   (b) 24A   (c) 29A   (d) 32A

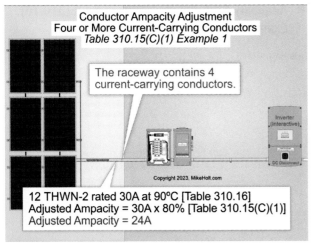

▶Figure 3–26

Solution:

Adjusted Ampacity = Table 310.16 Ampacity × Bundled Ampacity Adjustment Factor from Table 310.15(C)(1)

12 THWN-2 is rated 30A at 90°C [Table 310.16].

The adjustment factor for four current-carrying conductors is 80 percent [Table 310.15(C)(1)].

Adjusted Ampacity = 30A × 80%
Adjusted Ampacity = 24A

Answer: (b) 24A

▶ Conductor Ampacity Adjustment [310.15(C)(1)], Example 2

Question: What is the adjusted ampacity of eight current-carrying 12 THWN-2 conductors in a raceway? ▶Figure 3–27

(a) 16A   (b) 21A   (c) 35A   (d) 43A

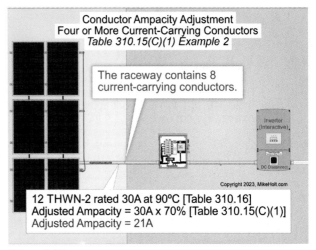

▶Figure 3–27

Solution:

Adjusted Ampacity = Table 310.16 Ampacity × Bundled Ampacity Adjustment Factor from Table 310.15(C)(1)

12 THWN-2 is rated 30A at 90°C [Table 310.16].

The adjustment factor for eight current-carrying conductors is 70 percent [Table 310.15(C)(1)].

Adjusted Ampacity = 30A × 70%
Adjusted Ampacity = 21A

Answer: (b) 21A

Raceways Not Longer than 24 inches [310.15(C)(1)(b)]. Conductor ampacity adjustment from Table 310.15(C)(1) does not apply to conductors in raceways not exceeding 24 in. in length. ▶Figure 3–28

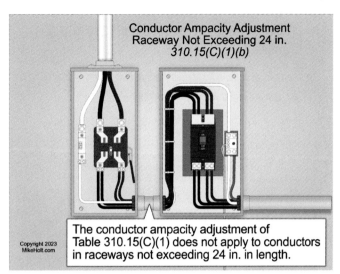

The conductor ampacity adjustment of Table 310.15(C)(1) does not apply to conductors in raceways not exceeding 24 in. in length.

▶Figure 3–28

▶ Raceway Not Exceeding 24 In. [310.15(C)(1)(b)], Example

Question: What is the ampacity of five 3/0 THWN-2 conductors in a raceway that does not exceed 24 in. in length? ▶Figure 3–29

(a) 150A   (b) 195A   (c) 205A   (d) 225A

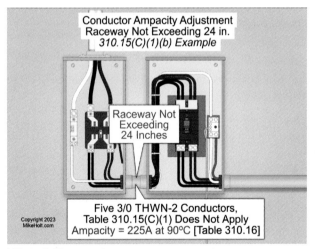

▶Figure 3–29

Solution:

3/0 THWN-2 is rated 225A at 90°C [Table 310.16].

Answer: (d) 225A

3.8 Ampacity Correction and Adjustment [310.15]

When conductors are installed in an ambient temperature is less than 78°F or greater than 86°F and where there are four our more conductors bundled together for more than 24 in., the *NEC* requires the ampacity of a conductors to be corrected and adjusted [310.15].

The higher insulation temperature rating of 90°C rated conductors provide a greater conductor ampacity for use in ampacity correction and adjustment, even though conductors must be sized based on the column that corresponds to the temperature listing of the terminals [110.14(C)(1)].

▶ Ampacity Correction and Adjustment [310.15], Example 1

Question: What is the ampacity of four current-carrying 12 THWN-2 conductors installed in a raceway located ½ in. above a rooftop with an ambient temperature of 94°F? ▶Figure 3–30

(a) 14A   (b) 15A   (c) 16A   (d) 17A

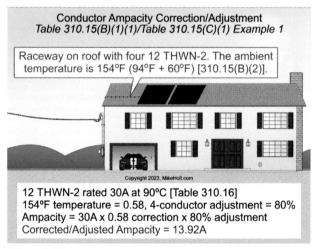

12 THWN-2 rated 30A at 90°C [Table 310.16]
154°F temperature = 0.58, 4-conductor adjustment = 80%
Ampacity = 30A x 0.58 correction x 80% adjustment
Corrected/Adjusted Ampacity = 13.92A

▶Figure 3–30

Solution:

Adjusted/Corrected Ampacity = Table 310.16 Ampacity × Temperature Factor × Bundled Adjustment Factor

The ambient temperature includes the rooftop temperature adder for raceways located less than ¾ above a roof [310.15(B)(2)].

94°F Ambient + 60°F Rooftop Adder = 154°F

The ambient temperature correction factor for 154°F is 0.58 [Table 310.15(B)(1)].

12 THWN-2 is rated 30A at 90°C [Table 310.16].

The adjustment factor for four current-carrying conductors is 80 percent [Table 310.15(C)(1)].

Adjusted/Corrected Ampacity = 30A × 0.58 × 80%
Adjusted/Corrected Ampacity = 13.92A

Answer: *(a) 14A*

▶ **Ampacity Correction and Adjustment [310.15], Example 2**

Question: *What is the ampacity of eight current-carrying 12 XHHW-2 conductors installed in a raceway ½ in. above a rooftop with an ambient temperature of 94°F?* ▶Figure 3–31

(a) 18A   *(b) 20A*   *(c) 22A*   *(d) 24A*

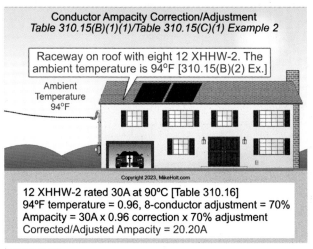

Conductor Ampacity Correction/Adjustment
Table 310.15(B)(1)(1)/Table 310.15(C)(1) Example 2

Raceway on roof with eight 12 XHHW-2. The ambient temperature is 94°F [310.15(B)(2) Ex.]

Ambient Temperature 94°F

Copyright 2023, MikeHolt.com

12 XHHW-2 rated 30A at 90°C [Table 310.16]
94°F temperature = 0.96, 8-conductor adjustment = 70%
Ampacity = 30A x 0.96 correction x 70% adjustment
Corrected/Adjusted Ampacity = 20.20A

▶Figure 3–31

Solution:

Adjusted/Corrected Ampacity = Table 310.16 Ampacity × Temperature Factor × Bundled Adjustment Factor

Note: Roof top ambient temperature adder does not apply to XHHW-2 conductors [310.15(B)(2) Ex.]

The ambient temperature correction factor for 94°F is 0.96 [Table 310.15(B)(1)]. 12 XHHW-2 is rated 30A at 90°C [Table 310.16].

The adjustment factor for eight current-carrying conductors is 70 percent [Table 310.15(C)(1)].

Adjusted/Corrected Ampacity = 30A × 0.96 × 70%
Adjusted/Corrected Ampacity = 20.16A

Answer: *(b) 20A*

3.9 Neutral Current-Carrying Conductor [310.15(E)]

Neutral Not Considered Current Carrying [310.15(E)(1)]. The neutral conductor of a 3-wire, single-phase, 120/240V system, or a 4-wire, three-phase, 208Y/120V or 480Y/277V wye-connected system, supplying linear loads is not considered a current-carrying conductor for the application of conductor ampacity adjustments in accordance with Table 310.15(C)(1). ▶Figure 3–32

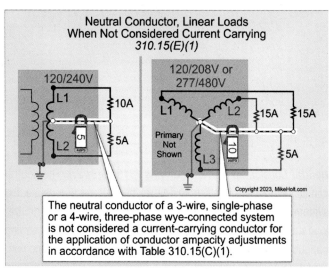

Neutral Conductor, Linear Loads When Not Considered Current Carrying
310.15(E)(1)

120/240V
L1
L2
10A
5A

120/208V or 277/480V
L1 L2
L3
Primary Not Shown
15A 15A
5A

Copyright 2023, MikeHolt.com

The neutral conductor of a 3-wire, single-phase or a 4-wire, three-phase wye-connected system is not considered a current-carrying conductor for the application of conductor ampacity adjustments in accordance with Table 310.15(C)(1).

▶Figure 3–32

▶ **Neutral Not Considered Current Carrying, Example 1**

Question: *What is the neutral current for 120V/240V, where line 1 has 10A and Line 2 has 5A.*

(a) 5A   *(b) 10A*   *(c) 15A*   *(d) 20A*

Solution:

$I_{Neutral}$ = *Line 1 – Line 2*
$I_{Neutral}$ = *10A – 5A*
$I_{Neutral}$ = *5A*

Answer: *(a) 5A*

▶ **Neutral Not Considered Current Carrying, Example 2**

Question: What is the neutral current for a 208Y/120V, three-phase 4-wire system, where line 1 has 15A, line 2 has 15A, line 3 has 5A?

(a) 5A   (b) 10A   (c) 15A   (d) 20A

Solution:

$$I_{Neutral} = \sqrt{(I_{L1}^2 + I_{L2}^2 + I_{L3}^2) - (I_{L1} \times I_{L2}) - (I_{L2} \times I_{L3}) - (I_{L1} \times I_{L3})}$$

$I_{Neutral} = \sqrt{(15A^2 + 15A^2 + 5A^2) - (15A \times 15A) - (15A \times 5A) - (15A \times 5A)}$

$I_{Neutral} = \sqrt{(225 + 225 + 25) - (225) - (75) - (75)}$

$I_{Neutral} = \sqrt{(475) - (225) - (75) - (75)}$

$I_{Neutral} = \sqrt{(475) - (375)}$

$I_{Neutral} = \sqrt{100}$

$I_{Neutral} = 10A$

Answer: (b) 10A

Neutral Considered Current Carrying [310.15(E)(2)]. The neutral conductor of a 3-wire circuit from a 4-wire, three-phase, wye-connected system carries approximately the same current as the line-to-neutral load currents of the other conductors. It is considered a current-carrying conductor for conductor ampacity adjustments in accordance with Table 310.15(C)(1). ▶Figure 3–33

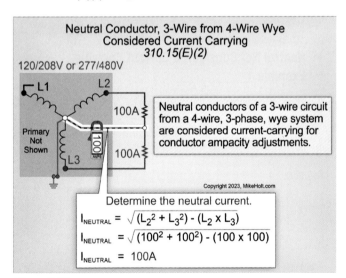

Neutral Conductor, 3-Wire from 4-Wire Wye Considered Current Carrying 310.15(E)(2)

120/208V or 277/480V

Neutral conductors of a 3-wire circuit from a 4-wire, 3-phase, wye system are considered current-carrying for conductor ampacity adjustments.

Copyright 2023, MikeHolt.com

Determine the neutral current.

$I_{NEUTRAL} = \sqrt{(L_2^2 + L_3^2) - (L_2 \times L_3)}$

$I_{NEUTRAL} = \sqrt{(100^2 + 100^2) - (100 \times 100)}$

$I_{NEUTRAL} = 100A$

▶Figure 3–33

▶ **3-Wire Wye Secondary Neutral Current, Example**

Question: What is the neutral current for two 16A, 120V circuits connected to a 208Y/120V, three-phase 4-wire system. ▶Figure 3–34

(a) 8A   (b) 16A   (c) 32A   (d) 40A

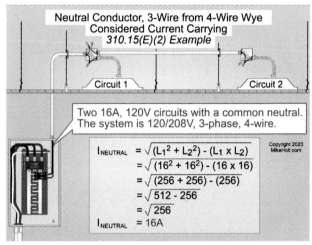

Neutral Conductor, 3-Wire from 4-Wire Wye Considered Current Carrying 310.15(E)(2) Example

Circuit 1   Circuit 2

Two 16A, 120V circuits with a common neutral. The system is 120/208V, 3-phase, 4-wire.

Copyright 2023 MikeHolt.com

$I_{NEUTRAL} = \sqrt{(L_1^2 + L_2^2) - (L_1 \times L_2)}$

$= \sqrt{(16^2 + 16^2) - (16 \times 16)}$

$= \sqrt{(256 + 256) - (256)}$

$= \sqrt{512 - 256}$

$= \sqrt{256}$

$I_{NEUTRAL} = 16A$

▶Figure 3–34

Solution:

$$I_{Neutral} = \sqrt{(I_{Line1}^2 + I_{Line2}^2) - (I_{Line1} \times I_{Line2})}$$

$I_{Neutral} = \sqrt{(16^2 + 16^2) - (16 \times 16)}$

$I_{Neutral} = \sqrt{(512 - 256)}$

$I_{Neutral} = \sqrt{256}$

$I_{Neutral} = 16A$

Answer: (b) 16A

Neutral Nonlinear Loads [310.15(E)(3)]. On a 4-wire, three-phase, wye circuit where the major portion of the load consists of nonlinear loads, the neutral conductor is considered a current-carrying conductor for conductor ampacity adjustments in accordance with Table 310.15(C)(1). ▶Figure 3–35

According to Article 100, a "Nonlinear Load" is a load where the shape of the current waveform does not follow the shape of the applied voltage waveform. ▶Figure 3–36 and ▶Figure 3–37

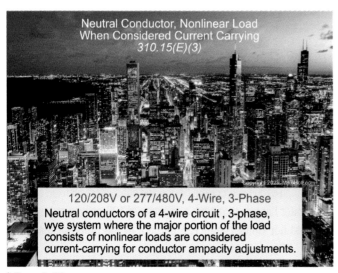

▶Figure 3–35

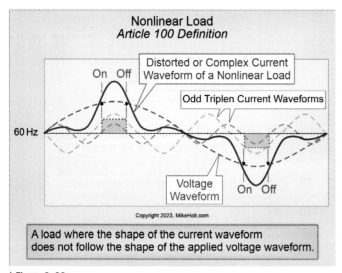

▶Figure 3–36

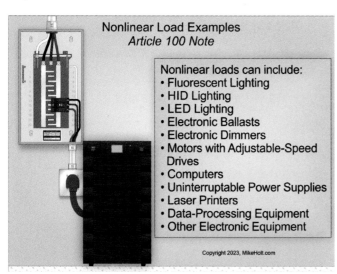

▶Figure 3–37

3.10 Branch Circuit Conductor Sizing [210.19(A)(1)]

Branch circuit conductors must be sized to have an ampacity of not less than 125 percent of the continuous loads, plus 100 percent of the noncontinuous loads, based on the temperature rating of equipment in accordance with 110.14(C)(1) and Table 310.16, prior to conductor ampacity correction and/or adjustment. ▶Figure 3–38

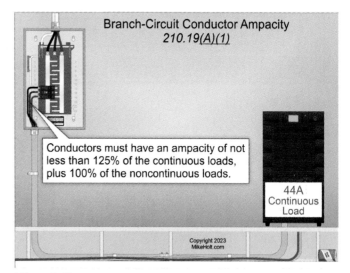

▶Figure 3–38

▶ **Branch Circuit Conductor Sizing [210.19(A)(1)], Example 1**

Question: What size conductors rated 90°C are required for a circuit supplying a 44A continuous load where the equipment is rated for 75°C conductors? ▶Figure 3–39

(a) 8 AWG   (b) 6 AWG   (c) 4 AWG   (d) 3 AWG

Solution:

Step 1: Conductor Ampacity. The conductor must have an ampacity of not less than 55A (44A × 125%).

Step 2: Size conductors in accordance with 110.14(C)(1)(a)(3) and Table 310.16.

6 AWG rated 65A at 75°C is suitable [Table 310.16].

Answer: (b) 6 AWG

• • •

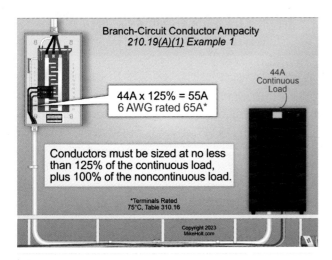

▶Figure 3–39

▶ **Branch Circuit Conductor Sizing [210.19(A)(1)], Example 2**

Question: What size conductor is required for EV charger rated 40A continuous where the equipment is rated for 75°C conductors? ▶Figure 3–40

(a) 8 AWG   (b) 6 AWG   (c) 4 AWG   (d) 3 AWG

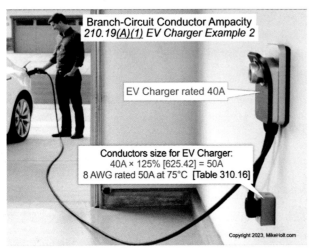

▶Figure 3–40

Solution:

Step 1: *Size the conductor ampacity at 125% of the nameplate rating of the EV [625.42].*

Conductor Ampacity = 40A × 125%
Conductor Ampacity = 50A

Step 2: *Size the conductor [Table 310.16].*

8 AWG rated 50A at 75°C

Answer: (a) 8 AWG

3.11 Branch Circuit Conductor Sizing—Loads

Storage Water Heater Conductor Sizing [422.13]

The branch-circuit overcurrent device and conductors for fixed storage-type water heaters that have a capacity of 120 gallons or less must be sized not smaller than 125 percent of the rating of the water heater. ▶Figure 3–41

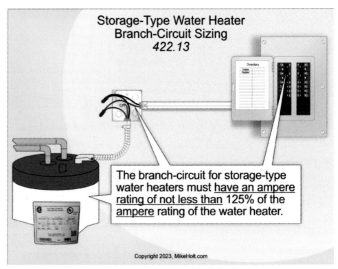

▶Figure 3–41

▶ **Storage Water Heater Conductor Sizing [422.13], Example**

Question: What size conductor is required for a 4,500W, 240V storage water heater? ▶Figure 3–42

(a) 12 AWG   (b) 10 AWG   (c) 8 AWG   (d) 6 AWG

Solution:

Determine the branch-circuit rating [210.19(A)(1) and 422.13].

Circuit Current = 4,500W/240V
Circuit Current = 18.75A

Circuit Rating = 18.75A × 125%
Circuit Rating = 23.44A

Circuit Conductor = 10 AWG rated 30A at 60°C [110.14)(C)(1)(a)(2) and Table 310.16]

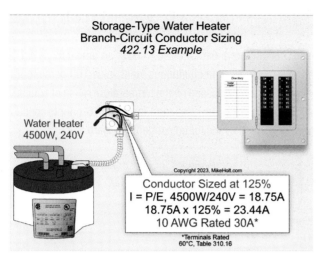

▶Figure 3–42

Answer: (b) 10 AWG

Space-Heating Equipment Conductor Sizing [424.4(B)]

The branch-circuit conductors for fixed electric space-heating equipment and any associated motors must be sized not smaller than 125 percent of the load. ▶Figure 3–43

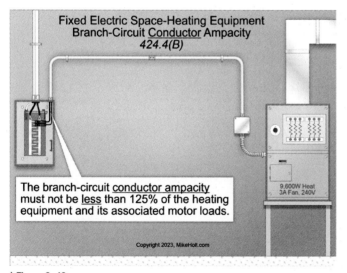

▶Figure 3–43

Author's Comment:

▶ The branch-circuit conductors and overcurrent protection for fixed electric space-heating equipment must have an ampacity of not less than 125 percent of the total heating load [210.19(A)(1) and 210.20(A)].

▶ **Space-Heating Equipment Conductor Sizing [424.4(B)], Example**

Question: What size NM cable is required for a 9,600W, 240V fixed electric space heater that has a 3A, 240V blower motor? ▶Figure 3–44

(a) 12 AWG   (b) 10 AWG   (c) 8 AWG   (d) 6 AWG

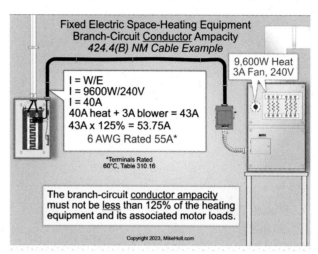

▶Figure 3–44

Solution:

Step 1: Determine the total load.

I = Watts/Volts

I = 9,600W/240V

I = 40A

Total Amperes = 40A (heat) + 3A (blower)
Total Amperes = 43A

Step 2: Size the conductors at 125 percent of the total current load [210.19(A)(1)].

Conductor = 43A × 125%
Conductor = 53.75A; use 6 AWG rated 55A at 60°C [110.14(C)(1)(a)(2), 334.80, and Table 310.16].

Answer: (d) 6 AWG

3.12 Branch Circuit Overcurrent Protection Sizing [210.20(A)]

Branch-circuit overcurrent devices must have a rating of not less than 125 percent of the continuous loads, plus 100 percent of the noncontinuous loads. ▶Figure 3–45

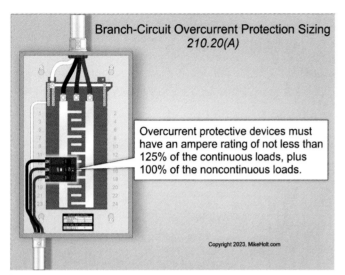

▶Figure 3–45

▶ Branch Circuit Overcurrent Protection Sizing [210.20(A)], Example

Question: What size circuit breaker is required for a 44A continuous load? ▶Figure 3–46

(a) 20A　　　(b) 30A　　　(c) 50A　　　(d) 60A

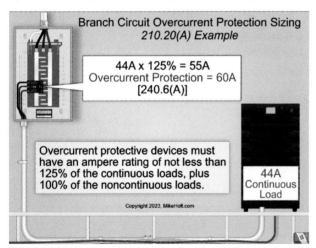

▶Figure 3–46

Solution:

Protection Rating = 44A × 125%

Protection Rating = 55A, the next size up is permitted [240.4(B)] and 240.6(A)

Answer: (d) 60A

3.13 Feeder Conductor Sizing [215.2(A)(1)]

Feeder conductors must be sized to have an ampacity of not less than 125 percent of the continuous loads, plus 100 percent of the noncontinuous loads, based on the temperature rating of equipment in accordance with 110.14(C)(1) and Table 310.16, prior to conductor ampacity correction and/or adjustment. ▶Figure 3–47

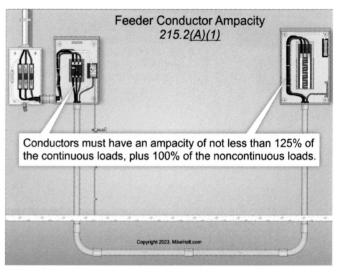

▶Figure 3–47

▶ Feeder Conductor Sizing [215.2(A)(1)], Example 1

Question: What size conductors are required for a 100A continuous load and 100A noncontinuous load? ▶Figure 3–48

(a) 1/0 AWG　　(b) 2/0 AWG　　(c) 3/0 AWG　　(d) 4/0 AWG

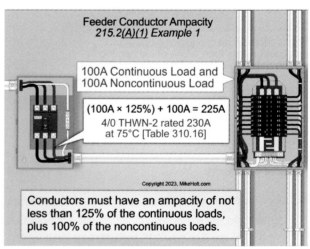

▶Figure 3–48

Step 1: *Determine the minimum conductor ampacity.*

Minimum Conductor Ampacity = (100A × 125%) × 100A
Minimum Conductor Ampacity = 225A

Step 2: *Determine the conductor size.*

4/0 THWN-2, rated 230A [Table 310.16, 75°C column]

Answer: *(d) 4/0 AWG*

▶ **Feeder Conductor Sizing [215.2(A)(1)], Example 2**

Question: *What size conductors are required for a 180A continuous load?* ▶**Figure 3–49**

(a) 1/0 AWG   (b) 2/0 AWG   (c) 3/0 AWG   (d) 4/0 AWG

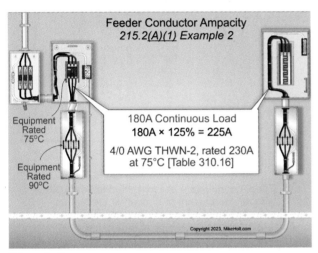

Feeder Conductor Ampacity
215.2(A)(1) Example 2

Equipment Rated 75°C
Equipment Rated 90°C

180A Continuous Load
180A × 125% = 225A

4/0 AWG THWN-2, rated 230A at 75°C [Table 310.16]

Copyright 2023, MikeHolt.com

▶Figure 3–49

Solution:

Step 1: *Determine the minimum conductor ampacity.*

Minimum Conductor Ampacity = 180A × 125%
Minimum Conductor Ampacity = 225A

Step 2: *Determine the conductor size.*

4/0 THWN-2, rated 230A [Table 310.16, 75°C column]

Answer: *(d) 4/0 AWG*

3.14 Feeder Neutral Conductor Size [215.2(A)(1) Ex 3]

Ex 3: Neutral conductors are permitted to have an ampacity of 100 percent of the continuous and noncontinuous loads. ▶Figure 3–50

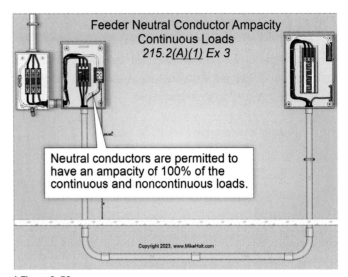

Feeder Neutral Conductor Ampacity
Continuous Loads
215.2(A)(1) Ex 3

Neutral conductors are permitted to have an ampacity of 100% of the continuous and noncontinuous loads.

Copyright 2023, www.MikeHolt.com

▶Figure 3–50

▶ **Feeder Neutral Conductor Size [215.2(A)(1) Ex 3], Example**

Question: *What size neutral conductor is required for a 125A continuous neutral load?* ▶**Figure 3–51**

(a) 1 AWG   (b) 2 AWG   (c) 3 AWG   (d) 4 AWG

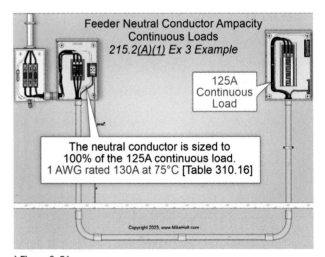

Feeder Neutral Conductor Ampacity
Continuous Loads
215.2(A)(1) Ex 3 Example

125A Continuous Load

The neutral conductor is sized to 100% of the 125A continuous load.
1 AWG rated 130A at 75°C [Table 310.16]

Copyright 2023, www.MikeHolt.com

▶Figure 3–51

Solution:

Step 1: *The neutral conductor is sized to the 125A continuous load at 100 percent [215.2(A)(1) Ex 3].*

Step 2: *Size the conductors in accordance with 110.14(C)(1)(b)(2) and Table 310.16.*

1 AWG has an ampacity of 130A [Table 310.16, 75°C column].

Answer: *(a) 1 AWG*

3.15 Feeder Overcurrent Protection Sizing [215.3]

Feeder overcurrent protective devices must have an ampere rating of not less than 125 percent of the continuous loads, plus 100 percent of the noncontinuous loads. ▶Figure 3–52

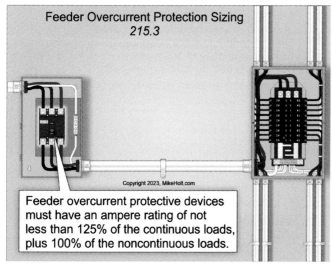

Feeder overcurrent protective devices must have an ampere rating of not less than 125% of the continuous loads, plus 100% of the noncontinuous loads.

▶Figure 3–52

▶ **Feeder Overcurrent Protection Sizing [215.3], Example**

Question: *What size feeder overcurrent protection is required for a 100A continuous load and a 100A noncontinuous load?* ▶Figure 3–53

(a) 200A (b) 225A (c) 250A (d) 300A

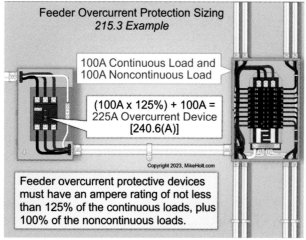

100A Continuous Load and 100A Noncontinuous Load

(100A x 125%) + 100A = 225A Overcurrent Device [240.6(A)]

Feeder overcurrent protective devices must have an ampere rating of not less than 125% of the continuous loads, plus 100% of the noncontinuous loads.

▶Figure 3–53

Solution:

100A Continuous Load × 125 percent continuous load + 100A Noncontinuous Load = 225A [240.6(A)]

Answer: *(b) 225A*

3.16 Feeder Tap Rules [240.21(B)]

Feeder conductors are permitted to be tapped, without overcurrent protection at the tap, as specified in 240.21(B)(1) through (B)(5). ▶Figure 3–54

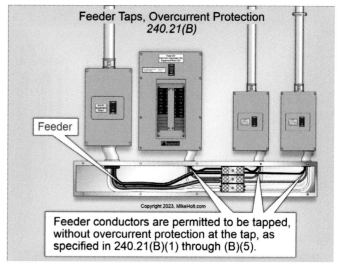

Feeder

Feeder conductors are permitted to be tapped, without overcurrent protection at the tap, as specified in 240.21(B)(1) through (B)(5).

▶Figure 3–54

According to Article 100, "Tap Conductor" is a conductor, other than a service conductor, with overcurrent protection rated more than the ampacity of the conductor. ▶Figure 3–55

The feeder tap is permitted to be made at any point on the load side of the feeder overcurrent protective device, including the load terminals of the overcurrent protective device. ▶Figure 3–56

Feeder Tap Not Over 10 Feet [240.21(B)(1)]. Tap conductors up to 10 ft long are permitted when they comply with the following:

(1) Tap conductors have an ampacity of not less than: ▶Figure 3–57

    a. The calculated load in accordance with Article 220, and

    b. The rating of the equipment frame or the overcurrent protective device where the tap conductors terminate

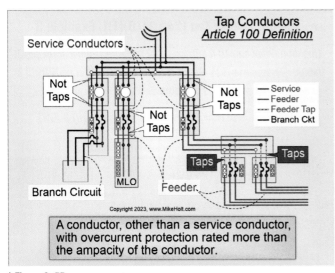

▶Figure 3-55

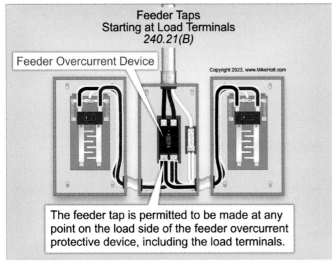

▶Figure 3-56

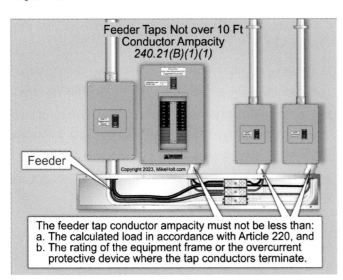

▶Figure 3-57

(2) The tap conductors do not extend beyond the equipment they supply.

(3) Except at the point of connection, tap conductors must be installed within a raceway.

(4) Tap conductors that leave the enclosure where the tap is made must have an ampacity of not less than 10 percent of the rating of the feeder overcurrent protective device. ▶Figure 3-58

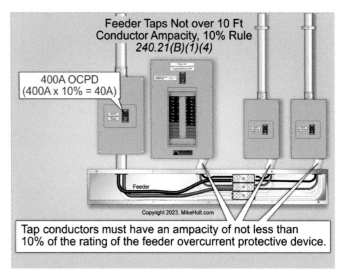

▶Figure 3-58

10-Foot Feeder Tap [240.21(B)(1)]

▶ 10-Foot Feeder Tap [240.21(B)(1)], Example 1

Question: What size 10-ft tap conductor is needed from a 400A circuit breaker to supply a 200A panelboard? ▶Figure 3-59

(a) 1/0 AWG   (b) 2/0 AWG   (c) 3/0 AWG   (d) 4/0 AWG

Solution:

10% of 400A = 40A minimum conductor ampacity

3/0 AWG is rated 200A at 75°C [110.14(C)(1)(b)(2) and Table 310.16] which is greater than 10 percent of the rating of the 400A overcurrent protective device.

Answer: (c) 3/0 AWG

• • •

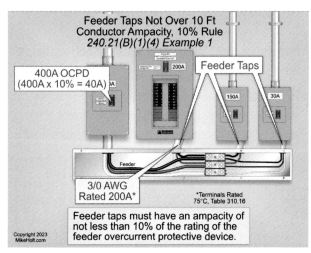

▶Figure 3–59

▶ **10-Foot Feeder Tap [240.21(B)(1)], Example 2**

Question: *What size 10-ft tap conductor is needed from a 400A circuit breaker to supply a 150A feeder disconnect?* ▶Figure 3–60

(a) 1/0 AWG　　(b) 2/0 AWG　　(c) 3/0 AWG　　(d) 4/0 AWG

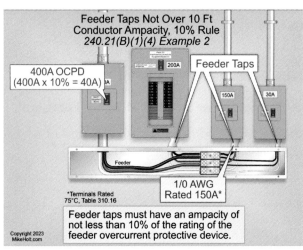

▶Figure 3–60

Solution:

10% of 400A = 40A minimum conductor ampacity

1/0 AWG is rated 150A at 75°C [110.14(C)(1)(b)(2) and Table 310.16] which is greater than 10 percent of the rating of the 400A overcurrent protective device.

Answer: *(a) 1/0 AWG*

▶ **10-Foot Feeder Tap [240.21(B)(1)], Example 3**

Question: *What size 10-ft tap conductor is needed from a 400A circuit breaker to supply a 30A feeder disconnect where the equipment is rated for 75°C conductor?* ▶Figure 3–61

(a) 8 AWG　　(b) 6 AWG　　(c) 4 AWG　　(d) 3 AWG

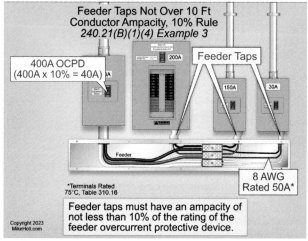

▶Figure 3–61

Solution:

10% of 400A = 40A minimum conductor ampacity

8 AWG is rated 50A at 75°C [110.14(C)(1)(a)(3) and Table 310.16] which is greater than 10 percent of the rating of the 400A overcurrent protective device.

Answer: *(a) 8 AWG*

Feeder Tap Not Over 25 Feet [240.21(B)(2)]. Tap conductors up to 25 ft long are permitted when they comply with the following: ▶Figure 3–62

(1) The tap conductors must have an ampacity not less than 33 percent of the rating of the feeder overcurrent protective device.

(2) The tap conductors terminate in a circuit breaker or set of fuses and have an ampacity no less than the rating of the circuit breaker or fuse.

(3) The tap conductors must be installed in a raceway or other means approved by the authority having jurisdiction.

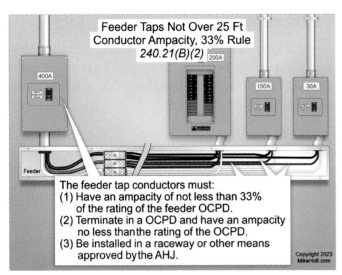

▶Figure 3-62

25-Foot Feeder Tap [240.21(B)(2)]

▶ 25-Foot Feeder Tap [240.21(B)(2)], Example 1

Question: *What size 25-ft tap conductor is needed from a 400A circuit breaker to supply a 200A panelboard?* ▶**Figure 3-63**

(a) 1/0 AWG   (b) 2/0 AWG   (c) 3/0 AWG   (d) 4/0 AWG

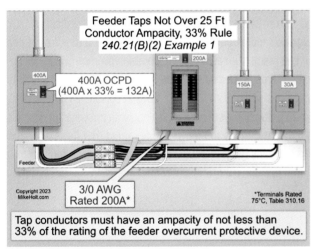

▶Figure 3-63

Solution:

The tap conductor must have a minimum rating of no less than 133A (33 percent of the rating of the 400A overcurrent protective device).

3/0 AWG is rated 200A at 75°C [110.14(C)(1)(b) and Table 310.16] which is greater than 133A (⅓ the rating of the 400A overcurrent protective device) and equal to the 200A disconnect.

Answer: *(c) 3/0 AWG*

▶ 25-Foot Feeder Tap [240.21(B)(2)], Example 2

Question: *What size 25-ft tap conductor is needed from a 400A circuit breaker to supply a 150A feeder disconnect?* ▶**Figure 3-64**

(a) 1/0 AWG   (b) 2/0 AWG   (c) 3/0 AWG   (d) 4/0 AWG

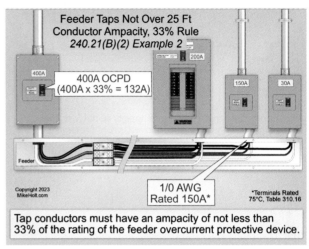

▶Figure 3-64

Solution:

The tap conductor must have a minimum rating of no less than 133A (33 percent of the rating of the 400A overcurrent protective device).

1/0 AWG is rated 150A at 75°C [110.14(C)(1)(b) and Table 310.16] which is greater than 133A (⅓ the rating of the 400A overcurrent protective device) and equal to the 150A disconnect.

Answer: *(a) 1/0 AWG*

▶ 25-Foot Feeder Tap [240.21(B)(2)], Example 3

Question: *What size 25-ft tap conductor is needed from a 400A circuit breaker to supply a 30A feeder disconnect where the equipment is rated for 75°C conductor?* ▶**Figure 3-65**

(a) 3 AWG   (b) 2 AWG   (c) 1 AWG   (d) 1/0 AWG

Solution:

The tap conductor must have a minimum rating of no less than 133A (33 percent of the rating of the 400A overcurrent protective device).

1/0 AWG is rated 150A at 75°C [110.14(C)(1)(a) and Table 310.16] which is greater than 133A (⅓ the rating of the 400A overcurrent protective device) and greater than the 30A disconnect main breaker.

Answer: *(d) 1/0 AWG*

• • •

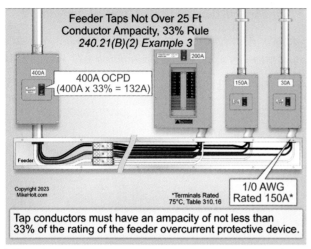

Feeder Taps Not Over 25 Ft
Conductor Ampacity, 33% Rule
240.21(B)(2) Example 3

400A

200A

400A OCPD
(400A x 33% = 132A)

150A

30A

Feeder

Copyright 2023
MikeHolt.com

*Terminals Rated
75°C, Table 310.16

1/0 AWG
Rated 150A*

Tap conductors must have an ampacity of not less than
33% of the rating of the feeder overcurrent protective device.

▶Figure 3–65

Unit 3—Conclusion

Sizing conductors and overcurrent protection is much more compli-cated than it appears at first. This unit has provided an insight into the numerous factors that must be considered to properly size conduc-tors and provide for their protection.

Temperature is a key component in the resistance of a conductor, and consequently, temperature affects a conductor's current-carrying capacity. Elevated temperatures on conductors can lead to the break-down of conductor insulation and damage to equipment. Therefore, when sizing conductors, the ampacity values given in the *NEC* tables must be corrected for ambient temperatures that differ from the 86°F on which the *Code* tables are based. A bundle of current-carrying conductors will have increased operating temperatures, so the *NEC* also requires an adjustment to be made when bundling more than three current-carrying conductors together.

This unit covered at length the fact that conductors must not be sized to a higher temperature column of the ampacity table than the rating the equipment terminals allow. This means that even though you install a 90°C rated conductor such as THWN-2, a lower ampacity column must be used to match the terminal rating. This confusing require-ment results in calculation mistakes, so review this part of the unit again if you are not sure how to apply Section 110.14(C) of the *Code*.

Overcurrent protection must be sized correctly to protect the circuit wiring and equipment, as well as the building structure, from damage that can result from overheating. Common overcurrent device sizing requirements were discussed as well as some of the exceptions to the general rules of Article 240. Several specific examples of over-current protection were explained along with examples of how to size overcurrent devices to help you understand that there are specific rules for many types of equipment or situations that don't follow the general overcurrent protection requirements.

UNIT
3

REVIEW QUESTIONS

Please use the 2023 *Code* book and this textbook to answer the following questions.

Part A—Conductor Insulation, Terminals, and Overcurrent Protection

3.3 Conductor Size—Equipment Terminal Rating [110.14(C)]

Equipment Terminations Rated 100A and Less, Conductor Sized to 60°C [110.14(C)(1)(a)]

1. What is the minimum size conductor permitted to terminate on a 70A circuit breaker or fuse?
    (a) 8 AWG
    (b) 6 AWG
    (c) 4 AWG
    (d) 2 AWG

2. What's the minimum size conductor permitted to terminate on a 50A circuit breaker or fuse?
    (a) 8 AWG
    (b) 6 AWG
    (c) 4 AWG
    (d) 2 AWG

3. What is the minimum size THW conductor permitted to terminate on a 50A circuit breaker if the circuit breaker terminals are listed for 75°C conductor sizing?
    (a) 8 AWG
    (b) 6 AWG
    (c) 4 AWG
    (d) 2 AWG

4. What size THW conductor is required for an air-conditioning-unit if the nameplate requires a minimum conductor ampacity of 34A and the terminals of all the equipment are rated for 75°C conductor sizing?
    (a) 14 AWG
    (b) 12 AWG
    (c) 10 AWG
    (d) 8 AWG

Equipment Terminations Greater than 100A, Conductor Sized to 75°C [110.14(C)(1)(b)]

5. What is the minimum size THW conductor required for a 150A circuit breaker?
    (a) 1/0 AWG
    (b) 2/0 AWG
    (c) 3/0 AWG
    (d) 4/0 AWG

6. What is the minimum size THW conductor required for a 200A circuit breaker?
    (a) 1/0 AWG
    (b) 2/0 AWG
    (c) 3/0 AWG
    (d) 4/0 AWG

7. What is the minimum size THW aluminum conductor required for a 250A feeder supplying a panelboard?
    (a) 250 kcmil
    (b) 300 kcmil
    (c) 350 kcmil
    (d) 400 kcmil

8. What is the minimum size THW aluminum conductor required for a 350A feeder supplying a panelboard?

    (a) 500 kcmil

    (b) 600 kcmil

    (c) 700 kcmil

    (d) 750 kcmil

3.4 Overcurrent Protection of Conductors [240.4]

9. What is the maximum size overcurrent protective device that can be used to protect 4/0 AWG conductors where each conductor has an ampacity of 230A at 75°C?

    (a) 250A

    (b) 300A

    (c) 350A

    (d) 400A

10. What is the maximum size overcurrent protective device that can be used to protect 250 kcmil aluminum conductors where each conductor has an ampacity of 205A at 75°C?

    (a) 200A

    (b) 225A

    (c) 250A

    (d) 275A

11. What is the minimum size of conductors (paralleled in four sets of conductors per phase) allowed to be protected by a 1,600A overcurrent protective device?

    (a) 500 kcmil

    (b) 600 kcmil

    (c) 700 kcmil

    (d) 750 kcmil

12. What is the minimum size of aluminum conductors (paralleled in six sets of conductors per phase) allowed to be protected by a 2,000A overcurrent protective device?

    (a) 500 kcmil

    (b) 600 kcmil

    (c) 700 kcmil

    (d) 750 kcmil

PART B—CONDUCTOR AMPACITY AND PROTECTION

3.6 Conductor Ampacity Correction [310.15(B)(1)]

13. What is the corrected ampacity of three 10 TW conductors in an ambient temperature of 120°F?

    (a) 13.5A

    (b) 17.4A

    (c) 18.4A

    (d) 32.8A

14. What is the corrected ampacity of three 8 THW aluminum in an ambient temperature of 105°F?

    (a) 13.5A

    (b) 17.4A

    (c) 18.4A

    (d) 32.8A

15. What is the corrected ampacity of three 4 THW in an ambient temperature of 50°C?

    (a) 53A

    (b) 57A

    (c) 61A

    (d) 64A

16. What is the corrected ampacity of three 4 XHHW-2 compact aluminum in an ambient temperature of 108°F?

    (a) 63A

    (b) 65A

    (c) 67A

    (d) 69A

17. What is the corrected ampacity of three 1 THW conductors in an ambient temperature of 85°F?

    (a) 122A

    (b) 130A

    (c) 139A

    (d) 142A

18. What is the corrected ampacity of three 1/0 XHHW-2 conductors in an ambient temperature of 154°F?

    (a) 88A

    (b) 99A

    (c) 109A

    (d) 119A

19. What is the corrected ampacity of three 1/0 XHHW-2 aluminum conductors in an ambient temperature of 154°F?

    (a) 78A
    (b) 94A
    (c) 115A
    (d) 126A

20. What is the corrected ampacity of three 250 kcmil THW in an ambient temperature of 40°C?

    (a) 204A
    (b) 214A
    (c) 224A
    (d) 234A

21. What is the corrected ampacity of Type NM 12/3 cable in an ambient temperature of 110°F?

    (a) 22A
    (b) 24A
    (c) 26A
    (d) 28A

22. What is the corrected ampacity of Type UF 10/3 cable in an ambient temperature of 120°F?

    (a) 17A
    (b) 19A
    (c) 21A
    (d) 23A

23. What is the corrected ampacity of a 12 THWN-2 in a raceway ½ in. above the roof, where the ambient temperature is 110°F?

    (a) 12A
    (b) 15A
    (c) 16A
    (d) 17A

24. What is the corrected ampacity of a 10 THWN-2 in a raceway less than ¾ in. above the roof, where the ambient temperature is 120°F?

    (a) 10.6A
    (b) 11.6A
    (c) 12.6A
    (d) 13.6A

3.7 Conductor Ampacity Adjustment [310.15(C)(1)]

25. What is the adjusted ampacity of four 10 THHN conductors in a raceway?

    (a) 20A
    (b) 28A
    (c) 29A
    (d) 32A

26. What is the adjusted ampacity of nine 10 THHN conductors in a raceway?

    (a) 20A
    (b) 28A
    (c) 29A
    (d) 32A

27. What is the adjusted ampacity of seven 8 THW conductors in a raceway?

    (a) 32A
    (b) 35A
    (c) 42A
    (d) 45A

28. What is the adjusted ampacity of nine 8 XHHW-2 compact aluminum conductors in a raceway?

    (a) 32A
    (b) 36A
    (c) 40A
    (d) 45A

29. What is the adjusted ampacity of four 1/0 THWN-2 conductors in a raceway?

    (a) 116A
    (b) 120A
    (c) 136A
    (d) 150A

30. What is the adjusted ampacity of eight 250 kcmil XHHW-2 aluminum conductors in a raceway?

    (a) 160A
    (b) 180A
    (c) 200A
    (d) 205A

31. What is the adjusted ampacity of six 3/0 THWN-2 conductors in a raceway?
    - (a) 160A
    - (b) 180A
    - (c) 200A
    - (d) 205A

32. What is the adjusted ampacity of ten 12 THWN-2 conductors in a raceway?
    - (a) 15A
    - (b) 20A
    - (c) 25A
    - (d) 30A

3.8 Ampacity Correction and Adjustment [310.15]

33. What is the ampacity of eight 12 THW conductors in a raceway at an ambient temperature of 85°F?
    - (a) 17.5A
    - (b) 19.5A
    - (c) 21.5A
    - (d) 22.5A

34. What is the ampacity of nine 10 THW conductors in a raceway at an ambient temperature of 46°C?
    - (a) 13.5A
    - (b) 17.4A
    - (c) 18.4A
    - (d) 27.4A

35. What is the ampacity of four 8 THHN conductors in a raceway at an ambient temperature of 90°F?
    - (a) 40A
    - (b) 42A
    - (c) 44A
    - (d) 46A

36. What is the ampacity of eight 8 THHN conductors in a raceway at an ambient temperature of 100°F?
    - (a) 31A
    - (b) 35A
    - (c) 41A
    - (d) 44A

37. What is the ampacity of eleven RHW 10 aluminum conductors in a raceway at an ambient temperature of 75°F?
    - (a) 14A
    - (b) 16A
    - (c) 18A
    - (d) 20A

38. What is the ampacity of eleven 1/0 THWN conductors in a raceway at an ambient temperature of 90°F?
    - (a) 67A
    - (b) 69A
    - (c) 71A
    - (d) 73A

39. What is the ampacity of fifteen 350 kcmil THWN aluminum conductors in a raceway at an ambient temperature 125°F?
    - (a) 84A
    - (b) 86A
    - (c) 88A
    - (d) 91A

3.9 Neutral Current-Carrying Conductor [310.15(E)]

40. What is the neutral current for 120V/240V, where line 1 has 25A and Line 2 has 15A?
    - (a) 5A
    - (b) 10A
    - (c) 15A
    - (d) 20A

41. What is the neutral current for a 208Y/120V, three-phase 4-wire system, where line 1 has 150A, line 2 has 150A, line 3 has 50A?
    - (a) 50A
    - (b) 100A
    - (c) 150A
    - (d) 200A

42. What is the neutral current for a 208Y/120V, three-phase 4-wire system, where line 1 has 75A, line 2 has 85A, line 3 has 100A?
    - (a) 21.80A
    - (b) 31.80A
    - (c) 41.80A
    - (d) 51.80A

43. What is the neutral current for two 18A, 120V circuits connected to a 208Y/120V, three-phase 4-wire system.

    (a) 16A
    (b) 18A
    (c) 32A
    (d) 40A

3.10 Branch Circuit Conductor Sizing [210.19(A)(1)]

44. What size conductor is required to supply a 22A continuous load?

    (a) 12 AWG
    (b) 10 AWG
    (c) 8 AWG
    (d) 6 AWG

45. What size conductor is required to supply a 32A continuous load?

    (a) 12 AWG
    (b) 10 AWG
    (c) 8 AWG
    (d) 6 AWG

46. What size conductor is required to supply a 55A continuous load?

    (a) 4 AWG
    (b) 3 AWG
    (c) 2 AWG
    (d) 1 AWG

47. What size THW conductor is required to supply a 30 kVA/240V noncontinuous load?

    (a) 4 AWG
    (b) 3 AWG
    (c) 2 AWG
    (d) 1 AWG

48. What size THW conductor is required to supply a 50 kVA/240V noncontinuous load?

    (a) 1/0 AWG
    (b) 2/0 AWG
    (c) 3/0 AWG
    (d) 4/0 AWG

3.11 Branch Circuit Conductor Sizing—Loads

49. What size conductor is required to supply a storage type water heater rated 2.5 kW/240V?

    (a) 14 AWG
    (b) 12 AWG
    (c) 10 AWG
    (d) 8 AWG

50. What size conductor is required to supply a storage type water heater rated 5.5 kW/240V?

    (a) 10 AWG
    (b) 8 AWG
    (c) 6 AWG
    (d) 4 AWG

51. What size SE cable is required to supply a 9 kW electric furnace with a fan motor rated 1 kVA, each rated 240V with 75°C terminals.

    (a) 10 AWG
    (b) 8 AWG
    (c) 6 AWG
    (d) 4 AWG

3.12 Branch Circuit Overcurrent Protection Sizing [210.20(A)]

52. What size circuit breaker is required for a 65A noncontinuous load?

    (a) 60A
    (b) 65A
    (c) 70A
    (d) 75A

53. What size circuit breaker is required for an 85A noncontinuous load?

    (a) 80A
    (b) 85A
    (c) 90A
    (d) 95A

54. What size circuit breaker is required for a 55A continuous load?

    (a) 60A
    (b) 65A
    (c) 70A
    (d) 75A

55. What size circuit breaker is required for a 34A continuous load?

    (a) 30A
    (b) 35A
    (c) 40A
    (d) 45A

56. What size circuit breaker is required for a 25A continuous load and a 25A noncontinuous load?

    (a) 45A
    (b) 50A
    (c) 60A
    (d) 65A

3.13 Feeder Conductor Sizing [215.2(A)(1)]

57. What size THW feeder is required to supply a 150A load?

    (a) 1/0 AWG
    (b) 2/0 AWG
    (c) 3/0 AWG
    (d) 4/0 AWG

58. What size THW feeder is required to supply a 150A continuous load?

    (a) 1/0 AWG
    (b) 2/0 AWG
    (c) 3/0 AWG
    (d) 4/0 AWG

59. What size THW feeder is required to supply a 200A load?

    (a) 1/0 AWG
    (b) 2/0 AWG
    (c) 3/0 AWG
    (d) 4/0 AWG

60. What size THW feeder is required to supply a 200A continuous loads?

    (a) 150 kcmil
    (b) 200 kcmil
    (c) 250 kcmil
    (d) 300 kcmil

61. What size THW feeder is required to supply a 225A continuous loads?

    (a) 150 kcmil
    (b) 200 kcmil
    (c) 250 kcmil
    (d) 300 kcmil

62. What size THW feeder is required to supply 20 kVA/240V continuous loads?

    (a) 1 AWG
    (b) 2 AWG
    (c) 3 AWG
    (d) 4 AWG

63. What size THW feeder is required to supply a 40 kVA/240V noncontinuous load?

    (a) 2/0 AWG
    (b) 3/0 AWG
    (c) 4/0 AWG
    (d) 300 kcmil

64. What size THW aluminum feeder is required to supply a 100A continuous and a 100A noncontinuous load?

    (a) 2/0 AWG
    (b) 3/0 AWG
    (c) 4/0 AWG
    (d) 300 kcmil

3.14 Feeder Neutral Conductor Size [215.2(A)(1) Ex 3]

65. What size feeder neutral is required to supply a 100A line-to-neutral continuous loads, terminals rated 75°C?

    (a) 1 AWG
    (b) 2 AWG
    (c) 3 AWG
    (d) 4 AWG

66. What size feeder neutral is required to supply a 150A line-to-neutral continuous loads?

    (a) 1/0 AWG
    (b) 2/0 AWG
    (c) 3/0 AWG
    (d) 4/0 AWG

67. What size feeder neutral is required to supply a 200A line-to-neutral continuous loads?

    (a) 1 AWG
    (b) 2/0 AWG
    (c) 3/0 AWG
    (d) 4/0 AWG

68. What size feeder neutral is required to supply a dwelling unit with a demand load of 175A, of which 100A are line-to-line, terminals rated 75°C?

    (a) 1 AWG
    (b) 2 AWG
    (c) 3 AWG
    (d) 4 AWG

3.15 Feeder Overcurrent Protection Sizing [215.3]

69. What size feeder overcurrent protective device is required for a 125A continuous load?

    (a) 150A
    (b) 175A
    (c) 200A
    (d) 225A

70. What size feeder overcurrent protective device is required for a 150A continuous load?

    (a) 150A
    (b) 175A
    (c) 200A
    (d) 225A

71. What size feeder overcurrent protective device is required for a 200A continuous load?

    (a) 150A
    (b) 200A
    (c) 225A
    (d) 250A

72. What size feeder overcurrent protective device is required for a 100A of continuous loads and 50A of noncontinuous loads?

    (a) 150A
    (b) 175A
    (c) 200A
    (d) 225A

3.16 Feeder Tap Rules [240.21(B)]

73. What size 10 ft feeder tap conductor is required where the feeder overcurrent protective device is rated 150A with 1/0 THW conductors, the 10 ft feeder tap conductor will be terminating in a 30A breaker?

    (a) 12 AWG
    (b) 10 AWG
    (c) 8 AWG
    (d) 6 AWG

74. What size 10 ft feeder tap conductor is required where the feeder overcurrent protective device is rated 225A with 3/0 THW conductors, the 10 ft feeder tap conductor will be terminating in a 30A breaker?

    (a) 12 AWG
    (b) 10 AWG
    (c) 8 AWG
    (d) 6 AWG

75. What size 10 ft feeder tap conductor is required where the feeder overcurrent protective device is rated 400A with 500 kcmil THW feeder conductors, the 10 ft feeder tap conductor will be terminating in a 60A breaker?

    (a) 12 AWG
    (b) 10 AWG
    (c) 8 AWG
    (d) 6 AWG

76. What 10 ft size feeder tap THW conductor is required where the feeder overcurrent protective device is rated 800A with two sets of 500 kcmil THW feeder conductors per phase, the 10 ft feeder tap conductor will be terminating in a 100A breaker?

    (a) 6 AWG
    (b) 4 AWG
    (c) 3 AWG
    (d) 2 AWG

77. What size THW 25 ft tap THW conductor is required where the feeder overcurrent protective device is rated 400A with 500 kcmil THW feeder conductors, the 25 ft feeder tap conductor will be terminating in a 200A breaker?

    (a) 2 AWG
    (b) 1 AWG
    (c) 2/0 AWG
    (d) 3/0 AWG

78. What size THW 25 ft tap THW conductor is required where the feeder overcurrent protective device is rated 800A with two sets of 500 kcmil THW feeder conductors per phase, the 25 ft feeder tap conductor will be terminating in a 200A breaker?

    (a) 300 kcmil
    (b) 350 kcmil
    (c) 400 kcmil
    (d) 500 kcmil

MOTOR, AIR-CONDITIONING, AND TRANSFORMER CALCULATIONS

Introduction to Unit 4—Motor, Air-Conditioning, and Transformer Calculations

Motor circuits have specific requirements that affect how the overcurrent protective device is sized and installed. Motors typically draw about six times as much current at start-up as they draw during normal operation. Article 430 provides guidance on how to properly protect a motor from overcurrent. Similar rules are included in Article 440 for air conditioners. Careful study of this unit will help you understand the sometimes-confusing requirements of these two articles.

Transformers are essential to electric power distribution. They are at the very core of our ability to manipulate alternating-current voltage allowing for the transmission, distribution, and use of electrical power. It is essential for you to understand transformers, their capabilities, and how they interact with electricity. Article 450 provides the requirements on how to protect the transformer winding and section 240.21 tells us the rules on how to properly size transformer secondary conductors.

The following are the Parts covered in this unit:

▸ Part A—Motor Calculations

▸ Part B— Air-Conditioning Calculations

▸ Part C— Transformers

This unit expands on unit 3 with more unique requirements for overcurrent protection and conductor sizing depending on whether you are dealing with motors, air conditioners, or transformers. Pay close attention to the rules and their specific allowances.

Part A—Motor Calculations

Introduction

Part A covers motors, motor branch-circuit and feeder conductors and their short-circuit and ground-fault protection, and motor overload protection. There are many tables involved in selecting the motor FLC's so be careful to read the question slowly and make sure you know what is being asked.

Understanding when to use the *NEC* table FLC's versus the actual motor nameplate is a crucial component to solving motor calculations for conductor sizing. Another helpful tip in sizing the motor overload protection versus the short-circuit and ground-fault protective device is understanding the rules on when your allowed to use the next size up device rating or when you're not allowed to exceed the rating that was calculated.

4.1 Motor Full-Load Current (FLC)

The motor full-load currents listed in Tables 430.248 and 430.250 are used to determine the conductor size [430.22 and 430.24], and the motor short-circuit and ground-fault overcurrent protective device size [430.52(C)] for continuous duty applications. The full-load currents listed in Table 430.248 can be used for 120V, 208V, and 240V nominal system voltage single-phase ac motors, and the full-load currents listed in Table 430.250 can be used for 120V, 208V, 240V, and 480V nominal system voltages three-phase ac motors.

▶ Direct-Current Motor FLC, Example 1

Question: *What is the full-load current (FLC) of a 2 hp, 120V, dc motor?*

(a) 15A   *(b) 17A*   *(c) 19A*   *(d) 21A*

Solution:

The FLC for a 2 hp, 120V, dc motor is 17A [Table 430.247].

Answer: (b) 17A

▶ Direct-Current Motor FLC, Example 2

Question: *What is the full-load current (FLC) of a 5 hp, 240V, dc motor?*

(a) 20A   *(b) 30A*   *(c) 40A*   *(d) 50A*

Solution:

The FLC for a 2 hp, 240V, motor is 20A [Table 430.247].

Answer: (a) 20A

Single-Phase FLC [Table 430.248]

▶ Single-Phase FLC, Example 1

Question: *What is the full-load current (FLC) of a 2 hp, 240V, motor?* ▶Figure 4–1

(a) 12A   *(b) 13A*   *(c) 14A*   *(d) 16A*

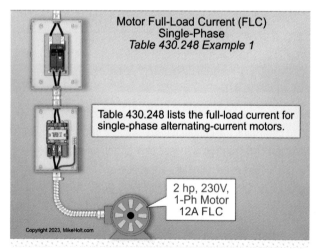

Motor Full-Load Current (FLC)
Single-Phase
Table 430.248 Example 1

Table 430.248 lists the full-load current for single-phase alternating-current motors.

2 hp, 230V, 1-Ph Motor 12A FLC

Copyright 2023, MikeHolt.com

▶Figure 4–1

Solution:

The FLC for a 2 hp, 240V, motor is 12A [Table 430.248].

Answer: (a) 12A

▶ Single-Phase FLC, Example 2

Question: *What is the FLC for a 5 hp, 208V, motor?* ▶Figure 4–2

(a) 30.80A   *(b) 32.20A*   *(c) 40A*   *(d) 56A*

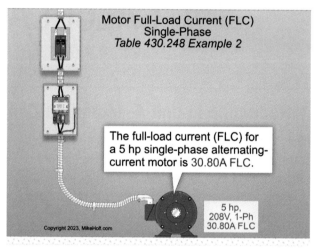

Motor Full-Load Current (FLC)
Single-Phase
Table 430.248 Example 2

The full-load current (FLC) for a 5 hp single-phase alternating-current motor is 30.80A FLC.

5 hp, 208V, 1-Ph 30.80A FLC

Copyright 2023, MikeHolt.com

▶Figure 4–2

Solution:

The FLC for a 5 hp, 208V, motor is 30.80A [Table 430.248].

Answer: (a) 30.80A

▶ Single-Phase FLC, Example 3

Question: *What is the FLC for a 5 hp, 230V, motor?*

(a) 28A   *(b) 31A*   *(c) 39A*   *(d) 52A*

Solution:

The FLC for a 5 hp, 230V, motor is 28A [Table 430.248].

Answer: (a) 28A

Three-Phase FLC [Table 430.250]

▶ Three-Phase FLC, Example 1

Question: *What is the FLC for a 10 hp, 208V, three-phase motor?* ▶Figure 4–3

(a) 21A   *(b) 24.20A*   *(c) 30.80A*   *(d) 46A*

Solution:

The FLC for a 10 hp, 208V, three-phase motor is 30.80A [Table 430.250].

Answer: (c) 30.80A

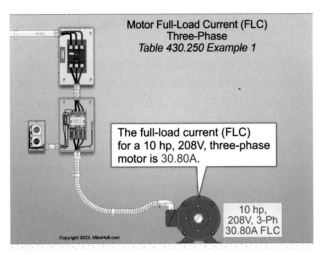

▶Figure 4–3

▶ Three-Phase FLC, Example 2

Question: *What is the FLC for a 20 hp, 230V, three-phase motor?*
▶Figure 4–4

(a) 21A   (b) 24.20A   (c) 30.80A   (d) 54A

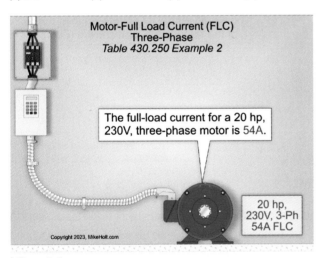

▶Figure 4–4

Solution:

The FLC for a 20 hp, 230V, three-phase motor is 54A [Table 430.250].

Answer: *(d) 54A*

▶ Three-Phase FLC, Example 3

Question: *What is the FLC for a 50 hp, 460V, three-phase motor?*

(a) 35A   (b) 45A   (c) 55A   (d) 65A

Solution:

The FLC for a 50 hp, 460V, three-phase motor is 65A [Table 430.250].

Answer: *(d) 65A*

4.2 Motor Full-Load Current and Motor Nameplate Current Rating [430.6(A)]

Motor current ratings used for the application of Article 430 are determined by (A)(1) and (A)(2). ▶Figure 4–5

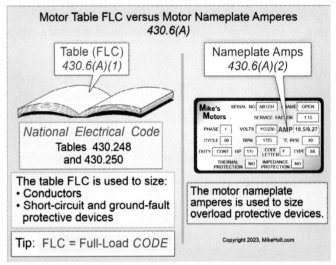

▶Figure 4–5

(1) Table Full-Load Current (FLC). The motor full-load current ratings contained in Tables 430.248 and 430.250 are used to determine conductor sizing [430.22] and the size of the short-circuit and ground-fault overcurrent protection [430.52 and 430.62]. ▶Figure 4–6

Author's Comment:

▸ The motor full-load amperes (FLA) identified on the motor nameplate [430.6(A)(2)] is not permitted to be used to determine the conductor size and the motor short-circuit and ground-fault overcurrent protective device, except for other than continuous duty motor applications as covered in 430.22(E).

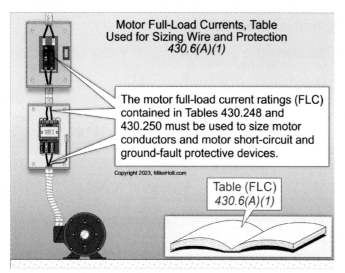

▶Figure 4–6

(2) Motor Nameplate Current Rating (FLA). Overload devices [430.32] and conductor sizing for intermittent duty motors [430.22(E)] must be sized based on the motor nameplate full-load ampere (FLA) rating.

Author's Comment:

▸ The motor nameplate current rating is identified as full-load amperes (FLA). The FLA rating is the current in amperes the motor draws while producing its rated horsepower load at its rated voltage, based on its rated efficiency and power factor. ▶Figure 4–7

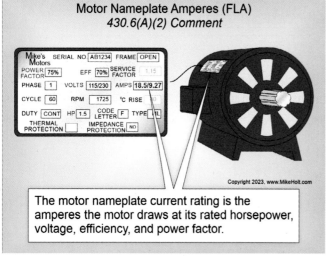

▶Figure 4–7

Author's Comment:

▸ The actual current drawn by the motor's FLA depends on the load on the motor and the actual operating voltage at the motor terminals. If the load increases, the current also increases; or if the motor operates at a voltage below its nameplate rating, the operating current will increase.

4.3 Branch-Circuit Conductor Sizing Continuous Duty Application [430.22]

Branch-circuit conductors to a single motor used for continuous duty must have an ampacity of not less than 125 percent of the motor's full-load current (FLC) as listed in Tables 430.247 through 430.250 [430.6(A)(1) and 430.22]. ▶Figure 4–8

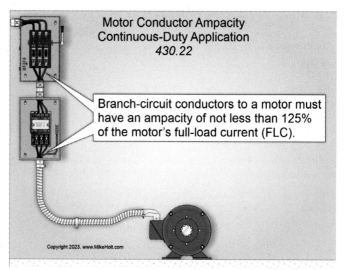

▶Figure 4–8

When selecting motor current from one of these tables, note that the last sentence above each table allows us to use the ampacity columns for a range of system voltages without any adjustment. The actual conductor size must be selected from Table 310.16 according to the terminal temperature rating (60°C or 75°C) of the equipment [110.14(C)(1)].

Motor applications are considered continuous duty unless the nature of the apparatus the motor drives is designed so the motor will not operate continuously under load [Table 430.22(E) Note]. When a motor is not continuous duty because of this type of application, the conductors are sized using the percentages of Table 430.22(E). If a motor must stop when performing its function, such as in the case of an elevator motor, that's a good sign the motor is intermittent duty.

▶ Conductors Sized for Continuous Duty Application [430.22], Single-Phase Example 1

Question: What size conductors are required for a 1 hp, 115V motor?
▶Figure 4–9

(a) 14 AWG   (b) 12 AWG   (c) 10 AWG   (d) 8 AWG

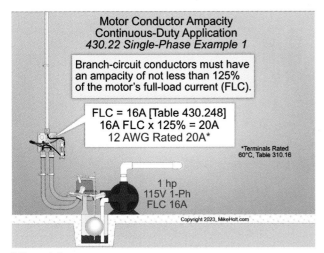

▶Figure 4–9

Solution:

Motor FLC [Table 430.248]: 1 hp, 115V, FLC is 16A.

The conductor is sized no less than 125 percent of the motor FLC:

Conductor Ampacity = 16A × 125%
Conductor Ampacity = 20A

Use 12 AWG conductors rated 20A at 60°C [110.14(C)(1)(a)(2) and Table 310.16].

Note: Any motor application must be considered as continuous duty unless the nature of the apparatus it drives is such that the motor will not operate continuously under any condition of use [Table 430.22(E) Note].

Answer: (b) 12 AWG

▶ Conductors Sized for Continuous Duty Application [430.22], Single-Phase Example 2

Question: What size conductors are required for a 5 hp, 208V motor?
▶Figure 4–10

(a) 14 AWG   (b) 12 AWG   (c) 10 AWG   (d) 8 AWG

Solution:

Motor FLC [Table 430.248]: 5 hp, 208V, FLC = 30.80A

The conductor is sized no less than 125 percent of the motor FLC:

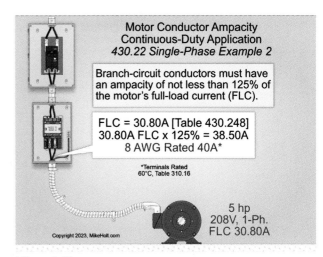

▶Figure 4–10

Conductor Ampacity = 30.80A × 125%
Conductor Ampacity = 38.50A

8 AWG conductors is rated 40A at 60°C [110.14(C)(1)(a)(2) and Table 310.16].

Answer: (d) 8 AWG

▶ Conductors Sized for Continuous Duty Application [430.22], Single-Phase Example 3

Question: What size conductors are required for a 5 hp, 230V motor with terminals rated 75°C? ▶Figure 4–11

(a) 14 AWG   (b) 12 AWG   (c) 10 AWG   (d) 8 AWG

Solution:

Motor FLC [Table 430.248]: 5 hp, 230V, FLC = 28A

The conductor is sized no less than 125 percent of the motor FLC:

Conductor Ampacity = 28A × 125%
Conductor Ampacity = 35A

10 AWG conductors is rated 35A at 75°C [110.14(C)(1)(a)(3) and Table 310.16].

Answer: (c) 10 AWG

• • •

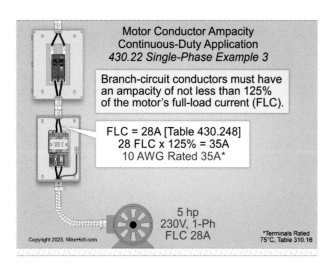

▶Figure 4–11

▶ ## Conductors Sized for Continuous Duty Application [430.22], Three-Phase Example 1

Question: *What size branch-circuit conductors are required for a 5 hp, three-phase, 208V motor?* ▶Figure 4–12

(a) 14 AWG   (b) 12 AWG   (c) 10 AWG   (d) 8 AWG

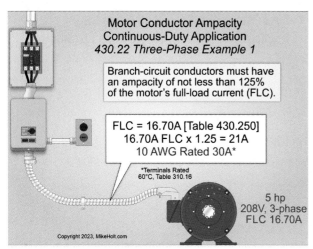

▶Figure 4–12

Solution:

Motor FLC [Table 430.250]: 5 hp, 208V, three-phase FLC = 16.70A.

The conductor is sized no less than 125 percent of the motor FLC:

Conductor Ampacity = 16.70A × 125%
Conductor Ampacity = 22A

10 AWG conductors is rated 30A at 60°C [110.14(C)(1)(a)(2) and Table 310.16].

Answer: (c) 10 AWG

▶ ## Conductors Sized for Continuous Duty Application [430.22], Three-Phase Example 2

Question: *What size branch-circuit conductors are required for a 7½ hp, three-phase, 230V motor with terminals rated 75°C?* ▶Figure 4–13

(a) 14 AWG   (b) 12 AWG   (c) 10 AWG   (d) 8 AWG

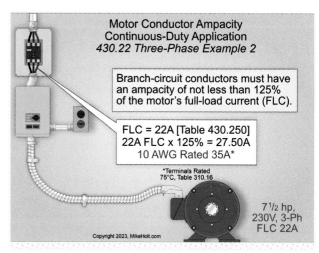

▶Figure 4–13

Solution:

Motor FLC [Table 430.250]: 7½ hp, 230V, three-phase FLC = 22A.

The conductor is sized no less than 125 percent of the motor FLC.

Conductor Ampacity = 22A × 125%
Conductor Ampacity = 27.50A

10 AWG conductors is rated 30A at 60°C [Table 310.16 and 110.14(C)(1)(a)(2)].

Answer: (c) 10 AWG

▶ ## Conductors Sized for Continuous Duty Application [430.22], Three-Phase Example 3

Question: *What size branch-circuit conductors are required for a 25 hp, three-phase, 460V motor with terminals rated 75°C?* ▶Figure 4–14

(a) 12 AWG   (b) 10 AWG   (c) 8 AWG   (d) 6 AWG

Solution:

Motor FLC [Table 430.250]: 25 hp, 460V, three-phase FLC = 34A.

The conductor is sized no less than 125 percent of the motor FLC.

Conductor Ampacity = 34A × 125%
Conductor Ampacity = 42.50A

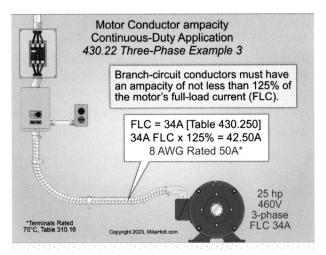

▶Figure 4–14

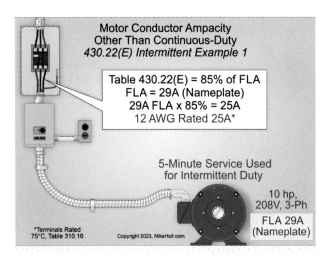

▶Figure 4–15

8 AWG conductors is rated 50A at 75°C [110.14(C)(1)(a)(3) and Table 310.16].

Answer: *(c) 8 AWG*

12 AWG is rated 25A at 75°C [110.14(C)(1)(a)(3) and Table 310.16].

Answer: *(b) 12 AWG*

4.4 Branch-Circuit Conductor Sizing for Duty-Cycle Application [430.22(E)]

Conductors for a motor used in a short-time, intermittent, periodic, or varying duty application must have an ampacity of not less than the percentage of the motor nameplate full-load ampere (FLA) rating shown in Table 430.22(E).

▶ Conductor Sizing for Duty-Cycle Application [430.22(E)], Three-Phase Example 1

Question: *What size branch-circuit conductors are required for a 10 hp, three-phase, 208V motor with a nameplate FLA of 29A, rated for 5-minute service, used for intermittent duty, with terminals rated 75°C?* ▶Figure 4–15

(a) 14 AWG   (b) 12 AWG   (c) 10 AWG   (d) 8 AWG

Solution:

The motor nameplate FLA is used for duty-cycle service. The conductor must be sized no less than 85 percent of the motor FLA [Table 430.22(E)].

Conductor Ampacity = 29A × 85%
Conductor Ampacity = 25A

▶ Conductor Sizing for Duty-Cycle Application [430.22(E)], Three-Phase Example 2

Question: *What size branch-circuit conductors are required for a 20 hp, three-phase, 230V motor with a nameplate FLA of 48A, rated for 30-minute service, used for short-time duty, with terminals rated 75°C?*
▶Figure 4–16

(a) 8 AWG   (b) 6 AWG   (c) 4 AWG   (d) 2 AWG

Solution:

The motor nameplate FLA is used for duty-cycle service. The conductor must be sized no less than 150 percent of the motor FLA [Table 430.22(E)].

Conductor Ampacity = 48A × 150%
Conductor Ampacity = 72A

4 AWG is rated 85A at 75°C [110.14(C)(1)(a)(3) and Table 310.16].

Answer: *(c) 4 AWG*

• • •

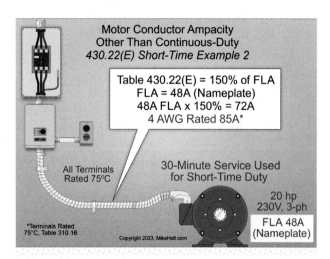

▶Figure 4-16

4.5 Overcurrent Protection

Overcurrent is current in amperes that is greater than the rated current of the equipment or conductors resulting from an overload, short circuit, or ground fault. ▶Figure 4-17

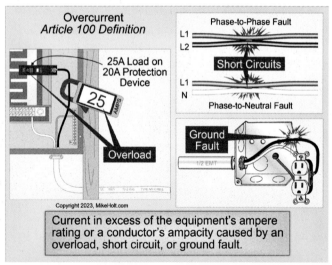

▶Figure 4-17

In motor circuits, the overcurrent protection function is commonly divided into two separate components; one provides overload protection [Article 430, Part III] and the other provides short-circuit and ground-fault protection [430.52 and 430.63]. Short circuits and ground faults are the result of faults which can cause a much higher current flow (Fault current).

Overload Protection

An overload condition is not a short circuit or ground fault. It is a condition where there's current flowing in the motor circuit that's significantly higher than the circuit rating. An overload condition is present when the current flow on the circuit exceeds the equipment ampere rating, which can result in equipment damage due to over-heating [Article 100]. ▶Figure 4-18

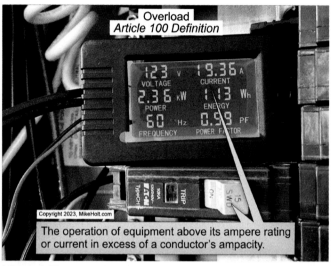

▶Figure 4-18

Overload protective devices, sometimes called "heaters" are intended to protect the motor, the motor control equipment, and the branch-circuit conductors from excessive heating due to motor overload [430.31]. Overload protection is not intended to protect against short circuits or ground-fault currents. It's possible for a motor to become so hot it will burn out or start a fire.

Some of the causes of overload are:

▸ Low voltage to the motor

▸ A locked rotor

▸ The motor too small for the workload

▸ Bad bearings

▸ Single-phasing, meaning one conductor of a three-phase circuit fails causing it to run on two phases

Overload protective devices respond slowly to the rise in current flow so they will allow the motor to start during the short high starting current yet protect the motor from a prolonged overload.

Short-Circuit and Ground-Fault Protection

Branch-circuit short-circuit and ground-fault protective devices are intended to protect the motor, the motor control apparatus, and the conductors against short circuits or ground faults, but they are not intended to protect against an overload [430.51]. Short-circuit or ground-fault protection is designed for fast current rise, short duration, and fast response time. ▸Figure 4–19 and ▸Figure 4–20

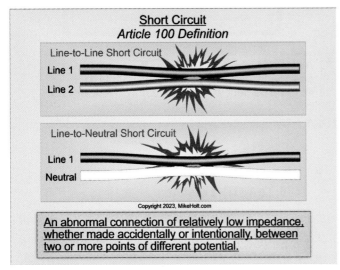

▸Figure 4–19

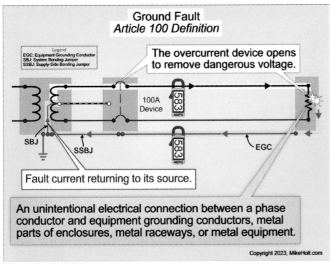

▸Figure 4–20

4.6 Motor Overload Protection

430.31 Overload

Part III of Article 430 contains the requirements for overload devices, which are intended to protect motors, motor control equipment, and motor branch-circuit conductors against excessive heating due to motor overloads and failure to start, but not against short circuits or ground faults. ▸Figure 4–21

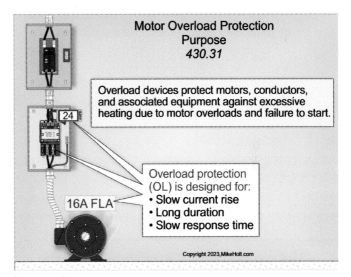

▸Figure 4–21

Author's Comment:

▸ Overload devices can be: ▸Figure 4–22

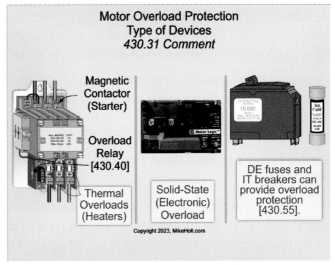

▸Figure 4–22

▸ **Thermal Overloads.** Thermal overloads (heaters) located in an overload relay of a motor contactor (starter). These heater units are selected using a chart or size given by the manufacturer.

▸ **Solid-State (Electronic) Overloads.** Solid-state overload devices have an adjustment dial that can be used to set the trip level. They are installed in an overload relay of a motor contactor (starter).

▸ **Inverse Time Circuit Breaker and Dual-Element Fuses.** Inverse time circuit breakers and dual-element (DE) fuses are permitted to serve as both motor overload protection and the motor short-circuit ground-fault protection if the requirements of 430.32 are met [430.55].

▸ **Fuses.** Fuses can be used for overload protection when sized in accordance with 430.32(A) [430.36].

Note 2: An overload is a condition where equipment is operated above its current rating, or where the current exceeds the conductor ampacity. When an overload condition persists for a long time, equipment failure or a fire from damaging or dangerous overheating can result. A fault, such as a short circuit or ground fault, isn't an overload [Article 100].

Overload protection isn't required where it might introduce additional or increased hazards, as in the case of fire pumps [Article 695].

Note: See 695.7 for the overcurrent protection requirements for fire pump supply conductors.

430.32 Motor Overload Sizing for Continuous-Duty Motors

(A) Motors Rated More Than One Horsepower. Motors rated more than 1 hp, used in a continuous-duty application without integral thermal protection, must have the overload device(s) sized as follows:

(1) Separate Overload Device. An overload device must be selected to open at no more than the following percent of the motor nameplate full-load current (FLA) rating:

Service Factor 1.15 and Greater Overload Sized 125% [430.32(A)(1)]

Motor service factors are safety factors; they indicate how much the motor capacity can be exceeded for short periods without overheating. For example, a motor with a service factor of 1.15 can operate for a brief time at 15 percent more than its rated output without overheating. This is important for motors where loads vary and may peak slightly above the rated torque. ▸**Figure 4–23**

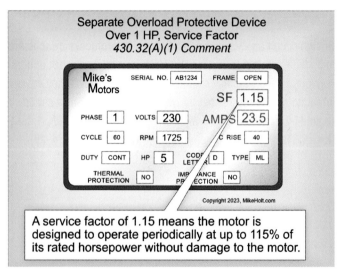

▸Figure 4–23

▸ **Service Factor—Overload Sized at 125% [430.32(A)(1)], Example**

Question: If a dual-element time-delay fuse is used for overload protection, what size fuse is required for a 5 hp, 230V, motor, with a service factor of 1.15, if the motor nameplate current rating is 27A?
▸Figure 4–24

(a) 25A   (b) 30A   (c) 35A   (d) 40A

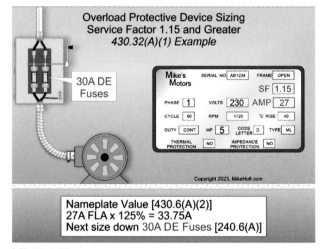

▸Figure 4–24

Solution:

Overload protection is sized to the motor nameplate current rating [430.6(A), 430.32(A)(1), and 430.55].

Overload Protection = 27A × 125%
Overload Protection = 33.75A; use 30A *

*The overload protection is not to exceed 125% of the motor name-plate current, so we must round down to the next smaller overload protection device listed in 240.6(A).

Answer: (b) 30A

Service Factor 1.15 and Greater Overload Sized 140% [430.32(C)]

In a case where the sensing element or setting, or the sizing of the motor overload device, isn't sufficient to allow the motor to start or to carry the load, the overload element setting or sizing can be increased; but not greater than 140 percent of the motor nameplate current rating for motors with a marked service factor of 1.15 or greater [430.32(C)].

▶ **Service Factor 1.15 and Greater Overload Sized 140% [430.32(C)], Example**

Question: A 30A dual-element time-delay fuse is used for the overload protection of a 5 hp, 230V, motor, with a service factor of 1.15, and the motor nameplate current rating is 27A. If the motor is unable to start, what is the maximum size overload protective device allowed?
▶Figure 4–25

(a) 25A   (b) 30A   (c) 35A   (d) 40A

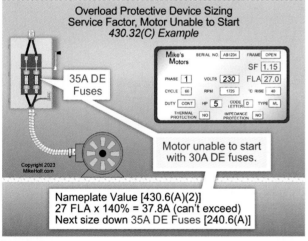

▶Figure 4–25

Solution:

Overload protection is sized according to the motor nameplate current rating, not the motor FLC rating from the Code book tables.

Overload Protection = 27A × 140% [430.32(C)]
Overload Protection = 37.80A; use a 35A*

*The overload protection is not to exceed 140% of the motor name-plate current, so we must round down to the next smaller overload protection device listed in 240.6(A).

Answer: (c) 35A

Temperature 40°C or Less Overload Sized 125% [430.32(A)(1)]

Motors with a nameplate temperature rise rating not over 40°C must have an overload protective device sized no more than 125 percent of the motor nameplate current rating.

A motor with a nameplate temperature rise of 40°C means the motor is designed to operate so it won't heat up more than 40°C above its rated ambient temperature when operated at its rated load and voltage. Studies have shown that when the operating temperature of a motor is increased 10°C, the motor winding insulating material's anticipated life is reduced by 50 percent. ▶Figure 4–26

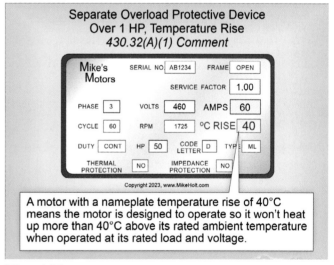

▶Figure 4–26

▶ **Temperature Rise—Overload Sized at 125% [430.32(A)(1)], Example**

Question: If a dual-element time-delay fuse is used for the overload protection, what size fuse is required for a 50 hp, 460V, three-phase motor, with a temperature rise of 39°C, and a motor nameplate current rating of 60A (FLA)? ▶Figure 4-27

(a) 40A   (b) 50A   (c) 60A   (d) 70A

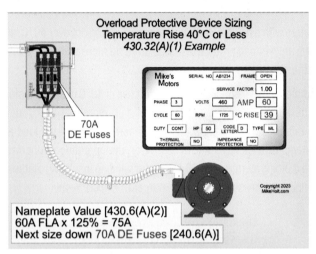

▶Figure 4-27

Solution:

Overload protection is sized according to the motor nameplate current rating, not the motor FLC rating from the Code book tables.

Overload Protection = 60A × 125% [430.32(A)(1)]
Overload Protection = 75A; use a 70A *

*The overload protection is not to exceed 125% of the motor nameplate current, so we must round down to the next smaller overload protection device listed in 240.6(A).

Answer: (d) 70A

Temperature 40°C or Less Overload Sized 140% [430.32(C)]

In a case where the motor overload is not of sufficient size to allow the motor to start, the overload size can be increased; but it cannot exceed 140 percent for motors with a marked temperature rise of 40°C or less [430.32(C)].

▶ **Temperature Rise—Overload Sized at 140% [430.32(C)], Example**

Question: A 70A dual-element time-delay fuse is used for overload protection for a 50 hp, 460V, three-phase motor with a temperature rise of 39°C, and a motor nameplate current rating of 60A (FLA). If the motor is unable to start, what's the maximum size overload protective device allowed? ▶Figure 4-28

(a) 50A   (b) 60A   (c) 70A   (d) 80A

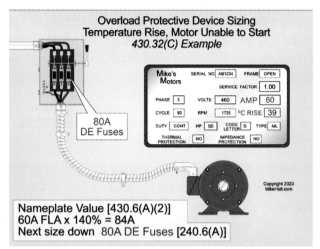

▶Figure 4-28

Solution:

Overload Protection = 60A × 140% [430.32(C)]
Overload Protection = 84A; use an 80A *

*The overload protection is not to exceed 140% of the motor nameplate current, so we must round down to the next smaller overload protection device listed in 240.6(A).

Answer: (d) 80A

Overload Sized at 115% [430.32(A)]

Motors that don't have a service factor rating of 1.15 and up, or a temperature rise rating of 40°C and less, must have the overload protective device sized at not greater than 115 percent of the motor nameplate ampere rating [430.32(A)(1)].

▶ **Other Motors—Overload Sized at 115% [430.32(A)(1)], Example**

Question: *A motor has a nameplate that specifies the following: The service factor is 1.00, with a temperature rise of 41°C, and a nameplate current rating of 25A. What size dual-element time-delay fuse is required when used for the overload protection of this motor?* ▶**Figure 4–29**

(a) 20A   *(b) 25A*   *(c) 30A*   *(d) 40A*

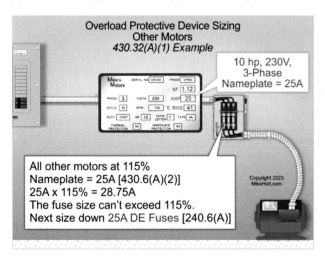

▶Figure 4–29

Solution:

Since the service factor of 1.12 is less than 1.15, and the temperature rise of 41°C is over 40°C, the overload protection is sized to 115 percent of the motor nameplate ampere rating [430.6(A)(2)].

Overload Protection = 25A × 115% [430.32(A)(1)]
Overload Protection = 28.75A; use a 25A*

*The overload protection is not to exceed 115% of the motor nameplate current, so we must round down to the next smaller overload protection device listed in 240.6(A).

Answer: (b) 25A

Other Motors—Overload Sized at 130%, Unable to Start [430.32(C)]

In a case where the motor overload is not of sufficient size to allow the motor to start or to carry the motor running load, the overload size can be increased; but not greater than 130 percent for motors with a service factor of less than 1.15 and a marked temperature rise of over 40°C [430.32(C)].

▶ **Overload Sized at 130%, Unable to Start [430.32(C)], Example**

Question: *A 25A dual-element time-delay fuse is used for the overload protection of a 10 hp, 230V, three-phase motor with a temperature rise of 41°C, a service factor of 1.00, and a motor nameplate current rating of 25A (FLA). If the motor is unable to start, what is the maximum size overload protection allowed?* ▶**Figure 4–30**

(a) 20A   *(b) 25A*   *(c) 30A*   *(d) 40A*

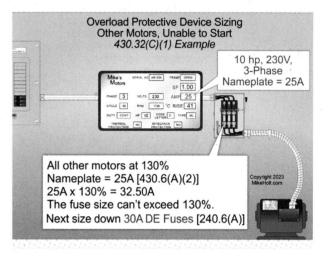

▶Figure 4–30

Solution:

Overload Protection = 25A × 130% [430.32(C)]
Overload Protection = 32.50A; use a 30A*

*The overload protection is not to exceed 115% of the motor nameplate current, so we must round down to the next smaller overload protection device listed in 240.6(A).

Answer: (c) 30A

4.7 Branch-Circuit Short-Circuit and Ground-Fault Protection [430.52]

Motor Starting Current [430.52(B)]

A motor branch-circuit short-circuit and ground-fault protective device must be capable of carrying the motor's starting current. ▶**Figure 4–31**

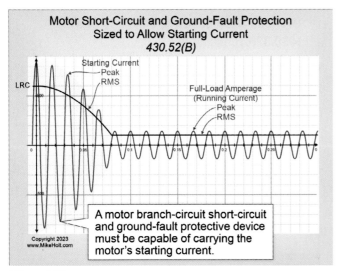

**Motor Short-Circuit and Ground-Fault Protection
Sized to Allow Starting Current
430.52(B)**

A motor branch-circuit short-circuit and ground-fault protective device must be capable of carrying the motor's starting current.

▶Figure 4–31

Author's Comment:

▶ **Motor-Starting Current.** When voltage is first applied to the field winding of an induction motor, only the motor winding resistance opposes the flow of current during start-up. Since the only resistance during motor start-up is the winding resistance, the motor will typically have a starting current of six times the motor nameplate running amperes. ▶Figure 4–32

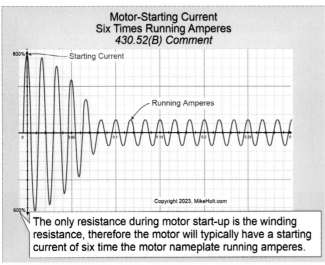

**Motor-Starting Current
Six Times Running Amperes
430.52(B) Comment**

The only resistance during motor start-up is the winding resistance, therefore the motor will typically have a starting current of six time the motor nameplate running amperes.

▶Figure 4–32

▶ **Motor-Running Current.** Once the rotor reaches its rated speed, the starting current reduces to running current due to the counter-electromotive force induced in the motor winding. This is caused by the stator's electromagnetic fields cutting across the armature (rotor) motor windings. This

increases the inductive reactance (X_L) in the rotor windings and results in decreasing the motor's starting current to its running current. ▶Figure 4–33

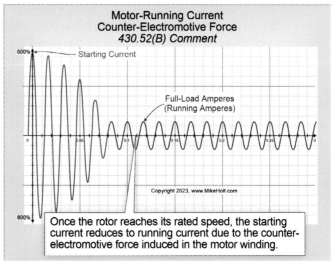

**Motor-Running Current
Counter-Electromotive Force
430.52(B) Comment**

Once the rotor reaches its rated speed, the starting current reduces to running current due to the counter-electromotive force induced in the motor winding.

▶Figure 4–33

Branch-Circuit Short-Circuit and Ground-Fault Protection [430.52(C)(1)]

The motor branch circuit must be protected against short circuits and ground faults by a protective device rating no greater than the percentages contained in Table 430.52(C)(1), unless permitted in 430.52(C)(1)(a). ▶Figure 4–34

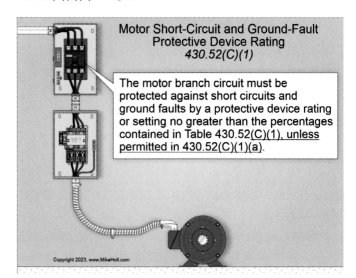

**Motor Short-Circuit and Ground-Fault
Protective Device Rating
430.52(C)(1)**

The motor branch circuit must be protected against short circuits and ground faults by a protective device rating or setting no greater than the percentages contained in Table 430.52(C)(1), unless permitted in 430.52(C)(1)(a).

▶Figure 4–34

Author's Comment:

▸ The motor nameplate full-load amperes (FLA) rating [430.6(A)(2)] is not permitted to be used to determine the motor short-circuit and ground-fault overcurrent protective device.

Table 430.52(C)(1) Maximum Rating or Setting of Motor Branch-Circuit Short-Circuit and Ground-Fault Protective Devices

Motor Type	Nontime Delay Fuse	Dual-Element (Time-Delay) Fuse	Inverse Time Breaker
Wound Rotor	150%	150%	150%
Direct Current	150%	150%	150%
Other Motors	300%	175%	250%

▶ Rating or Setting for Individual Motor Circuit, Example 1

Question: *What is the maximum size inverse time circuit breaker for a 1 hp, 115V, motor?* ▸**Figure 4–35**

(a) 30A   (b) 35A   (c) 40A   (d) 45A

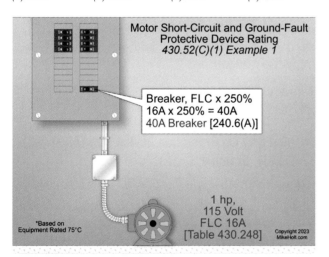

Motor Short-Circuit and Ground-Fault Protective Device Rating
430.52(C)(1) Example 1

Breaker, FLC x 250%
16A x 250% = 40A
40A Breaker [240.6(A)]

*Based on Equipment Rated 75°C

1 hp, 115 Volt FLC 16A [Table 430.248]

Copyright 2023 MikeHolt.com

▸Figure 4–35

Solution:

Determine the branch-circuit protection at 250 percent of the motor's FLC (inverse time breaker) [430.52(C)(1) and Table 430.248].

Branch-Circuit Protection = 16A × 250%
Branch-Circuit Protection = 40A [240.6(A)]

Answer: *(c) 40A breaker*

▶ Rating or Setting for Individual Motor Circuit, Example 2

Question: *What is the maximum size inverse time circuit breaker for a 5 hp, 240V, dc motor?*

(a) 30A   (b) 40A   (c) 50A   (d) 60A

Solution:

Determine the branch-circuit protection at 250 percent of the dc motor's FLC (inverse time breaker) [430.52(C)(1) and Table 430.247].

Branch-Circuit Protection = 20A × 150%
Branch-Circuit Protection = 30A [240.6(A)]

Answer: *(a) 30A breaker*

Next Size Up Overcurrent Protection Device Size [430.52(C)(1)(a)]

If the motor short-circuit and ground-fault protective device values from Table 430.52(C)(1) do not correspond with a standard overcurrent protective device ampere ratings or adjustable settings in 240.6(A), the next higher overcurrent protective device ampere rating or setting can be used. ▸Figure 4–36

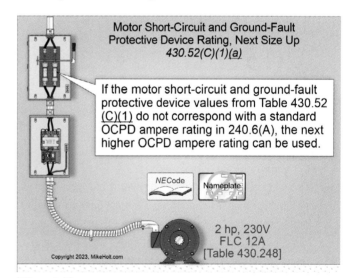

Motor Short-Circuit and Ground-Fault Protective Device Rating, Next Size Up
430.52(C)(1)(a)

If the motor short-circuit and ground-fault protective device values from Table 430.52 (C)(1) do not correspond with a standard OCPD ampere rating in 240.6(A), the next higher OCPD ampere rating can be used.

NECode   Nameplate

2 hp, 230V FLC 12A [Table 430.248]

Copyright 2023, MikeHolt.com

▸Figure 4–36

▶ **Next Size Up Protection Device Size [430.52(C)(1)(a)], Example 1**

Question: What is the maximum size inverse time circuit breaker for a 5 hp, 208V, motor? ▶**Figure 4–37**

(a) 35A   (b) 40A   (c) 60A   (d) 80A

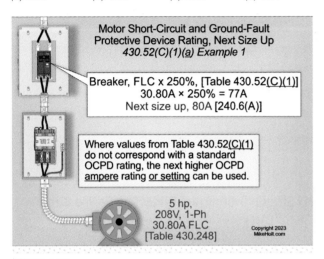

▶Figure 4–37

Solution:

Determine the branch-circuit protection at 250 percent of the motor's FLC [430.52(C)(1) and Table 430.248].

Branch-Circuit Protection = 30.80A × 250%
Branch-Circuit Protection = 77A; use the next size up 80A circuit breaker [240.6(A)]

Answer: *(d) 80A*

Author's Comment:

▶ Remember that the 80A circuit breaker is providing short-circuit and ground-fault protection, and the motor overload protective device (set at 125 percent or 115 percent of the motor's FLA) will protect the motor, motor equipment, and motor circuit conductors against overloads.

▶ **Next Size Up Protection Device Size [430.52(C)(1)(a)], Example 2**

Question: What is the maximum size dual-element fuse for a 5 hp, 230V, three-phase squirrel-cage motor? ▶**Figure 4–38**

(a) 20A   (b) 25A   (c) 30A   (d) 35A

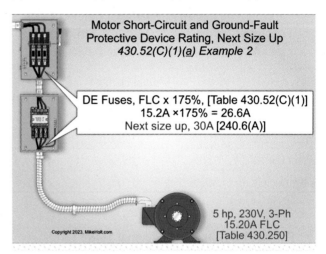

▶Figure 4–38

Solution:

Determine the branch-circuit protection at 175 percent of the motor's FLC [430.52(C)(1) and Table 430.250].

Branch-Circuit Protection = 15.2A × 175%
Branch-Circuit Protection = 26.6A; use the next size up 30A time delay fuser [240.6(A)]

Answer: *(c) 30A*

▶ **Next Size Up Protection Device Size [430.52(C)(1)(a)], Example 3**

Question: What is the maximum size non-time delay fuse for a 20 hp, 460V three-phase squirrel cage resistor starting Design B motor?

(a) 65A   (b) 70A   (c) 85A   (d) 90A

Solution:

Determine the branch-circuit protection at 300 percent of the motor's FLC [430.52(C)(1) and Table 430.250].

Branch-Circuit Protection = 27A × 300%
Branch-Circuit Protection = 81A; use the next size up 90A nontime delay fuse [240.6(A)]

Answer: *(d) 90A*

4.8 Branch-Circuit Summary

Branch-Circuit Conductors [430.22]

Branch-circuit conductors that supply a single motor must have an ampacity of not less than 125 percent of the motor's FLC as listed in Tables 430.247 through 430.250 [430.6(A)]. ▶Figure 4–39

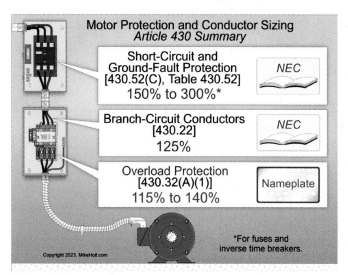

▶Figure 4–39

Branch-Circuit Short-Circuit and Ground-Fault Protection [430.52(C)(1)]

The branch-circuit short-circuit and ground-fault protective device protects the motor, the motor control apparatus, and the conductors against overcurrent due to short circuits or ground faults; but not against overloads [430.51]. Branch-circuit short-circuit and ground-fault protective devices are sized by considering the type of motor and the type of protective device, then applying the percentage of the motor's FLC as listed in Table 430.52. When the protective device values determined from Table 430.52 do not correspond with the standard rating of overcurrent devices as listed in 240.6(A), the next higher overcurrent device can be installed [430.52(C)(1) Ex 1]. See ▶Figure 4–39.

Overload Protection [430.32(A)]

Overload protection is sized based on the motor nameplate rating. See ▶Figure 4–39.

▶ Branch-Circuit Summary, Example

Question: If an inverse time circuit breaker is used for short-circuit and ground-fault protection, what size circuit breaker and conductor is required for a 5 hp, 230V, motor having a nameplate current rating of 26A with terminals rated 75°C? ▶Figure 4–40

(a) 10 AWG, 50A breaker   (b) 10 AWG, 60A breaker
(c) 10 AWG, 70A breaker   (d) 8 AWG, 70A breaker

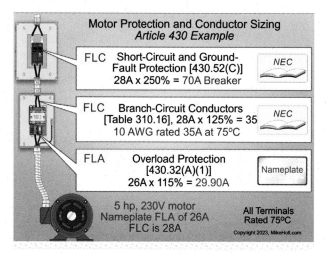

▶Figure 4–40

Solution:

Step 1: Determine the branch-circuit conductor at 125 percent of the motor's FLC [430.22 and Table 430.250].

Branch-Circuit Conductor = 28A × 125%
Branch-Circuit Conductor = 35A

Use 10 AWG rated 35A at 75°C [Table 110.14(C)(1)(a)(3) and Table 310.16].

Step 2: Determine the branch-circuit protection at 250% of motor's FLC [430.52(C)(1) and Table 430.248].

Branch Circuit Protection = 28A × 250%
Branch Circuit Protection = 70A [240.6(A)]

Answer: (c) 10 AWG, 70A breaker

4.9 Motor Circuit Equipment Grounding Conductor Size [250.122(D)(1)]

The equipment grounding conductor for a motor is sized in accordance with 250.122(A), based on the rating of the motor circuit branch-circuit short-circuit and ground-fault protective device. ▶Figure 4–41

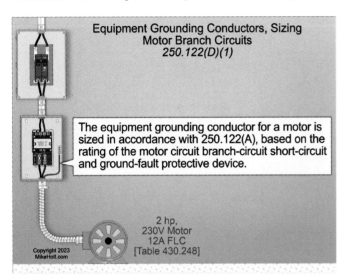

Equipment Grounding Conductors, Sizing
Motor Branch Circuits
250.122(D)(1)

The equipment grounding conductor for a motor is sized in accordance with 250.122(A), based on the rating of the motor circuit branch-circuit short-circuit and ground-fault protective device.

2 hp,
230V Motor
12A FLC
[Table 430.248]

Copyright 2023
MikeHolt.com

▶Figure 4–41

Author's Comment:

▸ The equipment grounding conductor is not required to be larger than the motor circuit conductors. See 250.122(A).

▶ Motor Circuit Equipment Grounding Conductor [250.122(D)(1)], Example 1

Question: What size equipment grounding conductor is required for a 14 AWG motor branch circuit, protected with a 2-pole, 30A circuit breaker in accordance with 430.22 and 430.52(C)(1)? ▶Figure 4–42

(a) 14 AWG   (b) 12 AWG   (c) 8 AWG   (d) 6 AWG

Solution:

The equipment grounding conductor sized to 250.122 is 10 AWG [250.122(D)(1)], however it is not required to be larger than the 14 AWG motor branch-circuit conductors [250.122(A)].

Answer: (a) 14 AWG

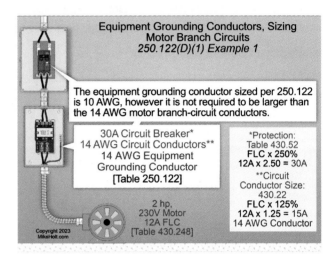

Equipment Grounding Conductors, Sizing
Motor Branch Circuits
250.122(D)(1) Example 1

The equipment grounding conductor sized per 250.122 is 10 AWG, however it is not required to be larger than the 14 AWG motor branch-circuit conductors.

30A Circuit Breaker*
14 AWG Circuit Conductors**
14 AWG Equipment
Grounding Conductor
[Table 250.122]

*Protection:
Table 430.52
FLC x 250%
12A x 2.50 = 30A
**Circuit
Conductor Size:
430.22
FLC x 125%
12A x 1.25 = 15A
14 AWG Conductor

2 hp,
230V Motor
12A FLC
[Table 430.248]

Copyright 2023
MikeHolt.com

▶Figure 4–42

▶ Motor Circuit Equipment Grounding Conductor [250.122(D)(1)], Example 2

Question: What size equipment grounding conductor is required for a 12 AWG motor branch circuit, protected with a 2-pole, 40A circuit breaker in accordance with 430.22 and 430.52(C)(1)?

(a) 14 AWG   (b) 12 AWG   (c) 8 AWG   (d) 6 AWG

Solution:

The equipment grounding conductor sized to 250.122 is 10 AWG [250.122(D)(1)], however it is not required to be larger than the 12 AWG motor branch-circuit conductors [250.122(A)].

Answer: (b) 12 AWG

4.10 Feeder Conductor Sizing [430.24]

Conductors that supply several motors must be sized not smaller than the sum of the following: ▶Figure 4–43

(1) 125 percent of the motor's full-load current (FLC) as listed in Tables 430.248 and 430.250 of the highest rated motor.

(2) The full-load current (FLC) as listed in Tables 430.248 and 430.250 of the other motors.

Author's Comment:

▸ The motor nameplate full-load ampere (FLA) rating [430.6(A)(2)] is not permitted to be used to determine the motor conductor size.

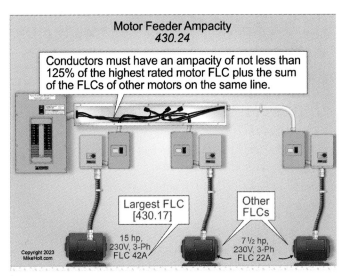

Motor Feeder Ampacity
430.24

Conductors must have an ampacity of not less than 125% of the highest rated motor FLC plus the sum of the FLCs of other motors on the same line.

Largest FLC [430.17]

Other FLCs

15 hp, 230V, 3-Ph FLC 42A

7 ½ hp, 230V, 3-Ph FLC 22A

Copyright 2023 MikeHolt.com

▶Figure 4–43

▶ Feeder Conductors Sized [430.24], Example 1

Question: What size feeder conductors are required for a 2 hp, 230V motor and a 5 hp, 230V motor with terminals rated 75°C? ▶Figure 4–44

(a) 10 AWG   (b) 8 AWG   (c) 6 AWG   (d) 4 AWG

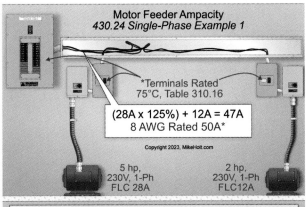

Motor Feeder Ampacity
430.24 Single-Phase Example 1

*Terminals Rated 75°C, Table 310.16

(28A x 125%) + 12A = 47A
8 AWG Rated 50A*

Copyright 2023, MikeHolt.com

5 hp, 230V, 1-Ph FLC 28A

2 hp, 230V, 1-Ph FLC12A

Conductors must have an ampacity of not less than 125% of the highest rated motor FLC plus the sum of the other motors' FLCs.

▶Figure 4–44

Solution:

2 hp FLC = 12A [Table 430.248]

5 hp FLC = 28A [Table 430.248]

Feeder Size = The conductor ampacity must not be less than 125 percent of the highest rated motor's FLC, plus the sum of the FLCs of the other motors.

Feeder Size = (28A × 125%) + 12A

Feeder Size = 35A + 12A

Feeder Size = 47A

Use 8 AWG rated 50A at 75°C [110.14(C)(1)(a)(3) and Table 310.16].

Answer: *(b) 8 AWG*

▶ Feeder Conductors Sized—Three-Phase [430.24], Example 2

Question: What size feeder conductor is required for a 5 hp, three-phase, 230V motor and a 10 hp, three-phase, 230V motor with terminals rated 75°C? ▶Figure 4–45

(a) 10 AWG   (b) 8 AWG   (c) 6 AWG   (d) 4 AWG

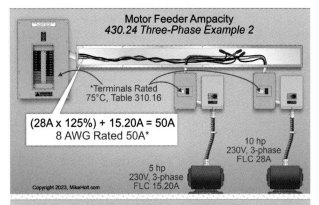

Motor Feeder Ampacity
430.24 Three-Phase Example 2

*Terminals Rated 75°C, Table 310.16

(28A x 125%) + 15.20A = 50A
8 AWG Rated 50A*

10 hp 230V, 3-phase FLC 28A

5 hp 230V, 3-phase FLC 15.20A

Copyright 2023, MikeHolt.com

Conductors must be sized not less than 125% of the largest FLC [430.24(1)] plus the sum of the other FLCs [430.24(2)].

▶Figure 4–45

Solution:

5 hp FLC = 15.20A [Table 430.250]

10 hp FLC = 28A [Table 430.250]

Feeder Size = The conductor ampacity must not be less than 125 percent of the highest rated motor's FLC, plus the sum of the FLCs of the other motors.

Feeder Size = (28A × 125%) + 15.20A

Feeder Size = 35A + 15.20A

Feeder Size = 50.20A

Use 8 AWG rated 50A at 75°C [110.14(C)(1)(a)(3) and Table 310.16].

Answer: *(b) 8 AWG*

Author's Comment:

▶ Calculations that end with a fraction of an ampere of 0.50 or larger can be rounded to the nearest whole number. Decimal fractions smaller than 0.50 can be dropped [220.5(B)]. For example, 50.20A can be rounded down to 50A.

▶ Feeder Conductors Sized [430.24]—Three-Phase, Example 3

Question: *What size feeder conductor is required for a 7½ hp, three-phase, 208V motor; three 5 hp single-phase, 208V motors; and three 1 hp single-phase, 115V motors?* ▶**Figure 4–46** *and* ▶**Figure 4–47**

(a) 6 AWG   (b) 4 AWG   (c) 3 AWG   (d) 2 AWG

Motor Feeder Ampacity
Determine and Balance Largest Group
430.24 Example 3

Motors on Feeder	Phase A (Line 1)	Phase B (Line 2)	Phase C (Line 3)
7½ hp 3-ph on Phase A, B, and C	24.20 ----	24.20 ----	24.20
5 hp 1-ph on Phase A and B	30.80 ---	30.80	
5 hp 1-ph on Phase B and C		30.80 ----	30.80
5 hp 1-ph on Phase A and C	30.80 ----		30.80
1 hp 1-ph on Phase A	16.00		
1 hp 1-ph on Phase B		16.00	
1 hp 1-ph on Phase C			16.00

Motors of the same group (phase) with largest FLC

Copyright 2023, MikeHolt.com

The motors must be balanced to determine the group of motors on the same phase (line).

▶Figure 4–46

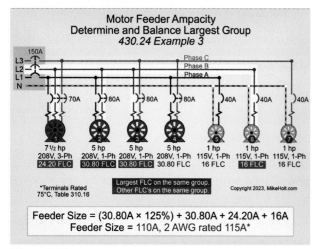

Motor Feeder Ampacity
Determine and Balance Largest Group
430.24 Example 3

*Terminals Rated 75°C, Table 310.16

Largest FLC on the same group.
Other FLC's on the same group.

Copyright 2023, MikeHolt.com

Feeder Size = (30.80A × 125%) + 30.80A + 24.20A + 16A
Feeder Size = 110A, 2 AWG rated 115A*

▶Figure 4–47

Solution:

7½ hp Three-Phase, 208V FLC = 24.20A [Table 430.250]
5 hp Single-Phase, 208V FLC = 30.80A [Table 430.248]
1 hp Single-Phase, 115V = 16A [Table 430.248]

Determine the feeder size. The ampacity must not be less than 125 percent of the highest rated motor's FLC, plus the sum of the FLCs of the other motors. The highest rated motor is based on the motor with the highest full-load current [430.17]. The "other motors in the group" value (on the same line) is determined by balancing the motors'

FLCs on the feeder being sized, then selecting the line that has the highest rated motor on it.

7½ hp Three-Phase, 24.20A FLC with 70A Protection on Phases A, B, and C
5 hp Single-Phase, 30.80A FLC with 80A Protection on Phases A and B
5 hp Single-Phase, 30.80A FLC with 80A Protection on Phases B and C
5 hp Single-Phase, 30.80A FLC with 80A Protection on Phases A and C

1 hp Single-Phase, 16A FLC with 40A protection on Phase A
1 hp Single-Phase, 16A FLC with 40A protection on Phase B
1 hp Single-Phase, 16A FLC with 40A protection on Phase C

	Phase A	Phase B	Phase C
7½ hp Three-Phase	*24.20A*	*24.20A*	*24.20A*
5 hp Single-Phase	*30.80A*	*30.80A*	
5 hp Single-Phase		*30.80A*	*30.80A*
5 hp Single-Phase	*30.80A*		*30.80A*
1 hp Single-Phase	*16.00A*		
1 hp Single-Phase		*16.00A*	
1 hp Single-Phase			*16.00A*

Feeder Size = (30.80A × 125%) + 30.80A + 24.20A + 16A
Feeder Size = 38.50A + 30.80A + 24.20A + 16A
Feeder Size = 109.50A

Use 2 AWG rated 115A at 75°C [110.14(C)(1)(b)(2) and Table 310.16].

Answer: *(d) 2 AWG*

4.11 Feeder Short-Circuit and Ground-Fault Protection [430.62(A)]

Feeder conductors must be protected against short circuits and ground faults by a protective device sized not greater than the largest rating of the branch-circuit short-circuit and ground-fault protective device for any motor, plus the sum of the full-load currents (FLC) of the other motors in the group as listed in Tables 430.248 and 430.250. ▶**Figure 4–48**

Largest Motor with Same Rating. Where two or more motors are supplied by a feeder have the same branch-circuit short-circuit and ground-fault protective device settings, one of the motors must be selected as the largest for the calculation.

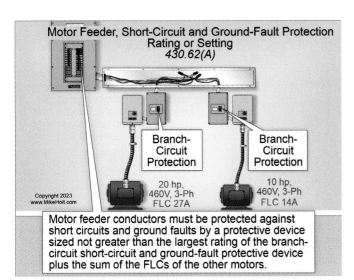

▶Figure 4–48

▶ Feeder Short-Circuit and Ground-Fault Protection [430.62(A)], Example 1

Question: What size feeder overcurrent protection (inverse time breaker) is required for the following two motors? ▶Figure 4–49

* Motor 1–20 hp, 460V, Three-Phase
* Motor 2–10 hp, 460V, Three-Phase

(a) 30A   (b) 40A   (c) 50A   (d) 80A

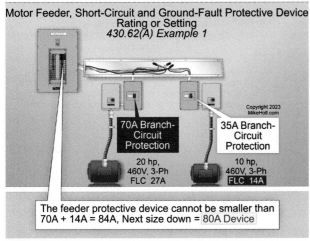

▶Figure 4–49

Solution:

The feeder protective device [430.62(A)] must not be greater than the largest branch-circuit ground-fault and short-circuit protective device plus the other motors' FLC.

Determine the largest branch-circuit ground-fault and short-circuit protective device [240.6(A) and 430.52(C)(1)(a)].

Motor FLCs—Table 430.250

20 hp Motor = 27A × 250%
20 hp Motor = 68; use the next size up, 70A

10 hp Motor = 14A × 250%
10 hp Motor = 35A

Feeder Protection = Not more than 70A + 14A
Feeder Protection = 84A; use the next size down, 80A [240.6(A)]

Answer: *(d) 80A*

Author's Comment:

▶ The "next size up protection" rule for branch circuits [430.52(C)(1)(a)] does not apply to motor feeder overcurrent protective devices.

▶ Feeder Short-Circuit and Ground-Fault Protection [430.62(A)], Example 2

Question: What size feeder overcurrent protective device (inverse time breaker) is required for the following three motors, where the equipment is rated for 75°C conductor? ▶Figure 4–50

* Motor 1–7½ hp, 208V, Three-Phase = 24.20A FLC [Table 430.250]
* Motor 2–5 hp, 208V, Single-Phase = 30.80A FLC [Table 430.248]
* Motor 3–1 hp, 115V, Single-Phase = 16.00A FLC [Table 430.248]

(a) 100A   (b) 110A   (c) 125A   (d) 150A

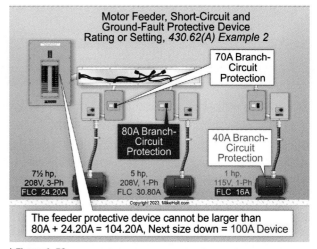

▶Figure 4–50

• • •

Solution:

Step 1: *Feeder overcurrent protection [430.62(A)] is not greater than the largest branch-circuit ground-fault and short-circuit protective device plus the other motors' FLCs.*

Determine the largest branch-circuit ground-fault and short-circuit protective device [240.6(A) and 430.52(C)(1)(a)].

5 hp Motor = 30.80A × 250%
5 hp Motor = 77A; use the next size up, 80A

1 hp Motor = does not apply after balancing

Step 2: *Determine the feeder protection size.*

Feeder Protection = Not more than 80A + 24.20A
Feeder Protection = 104.20A; use the next size down, 100A [240.6(A)]

Answer: *(a) 100A*

Part B—Air-Conditioning Calculations

Introduction

In Part B we will cover how to size the maximum overcurrent protection device and minimum circuit ampacity based on the air-conditioning equipment nameplate. However, if on an exam the air-conditioning equipment nameplate is not given then you will learn how to calculate the short-circuit and ground-fault device as well as the minimum conductor size.

4.12 Air-Conditioning Equipment Nameplate [440.4(B)]

Multimotor air-conditioning equipment must have a visible nameplate marked with the manufacturer's name, rating in volts, number of phases, minimum conductor ampacity, and the maximum rating of the branch-circuit short-circuit and ground-fault protective device. ▶Figure 4–51

Author's Comment:

▸ Hermetic refrigerant motor compressors typically have an integral thermal device that provides overload protection [440.51]. The branch-circuit short-circuit and ground-fault protection is provided with a circuit breaker or fuse which must be installed by the electrician in accordance with the manufacturer's nameplate marking.

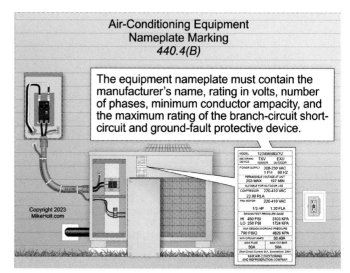

▶Figure 4–51

▶ Air-Conditioning Equipment Nameplate Example

Question: *What size conductor and short-circuit and ground-fault protective device is required for a multimotor air-conditioning compressor? The nameplate minimum circuit ampacity is 31.40A, the maximum circuit breaker rating is 50A, where the equipment is rated for 75°C conductor.* ▶Figure 4–52

(a) 10 AWG, 50A breaker   *(b) 10 AWG, 30A breaker*
(c) 8 AWG, 50A breaker   *(d) 8 AWG, 20A breaker*

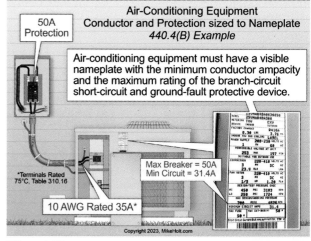

▶Figure 4–52

Solution:

Conductor: Since the terminals are rated 75°C, we can use 10 AWG rated 35A at 75°C [110.14(C)(1)(a)(3) and Table 310.16].

The circuit breaker protection for air-conditioning compressor equipment must have an ampere rating of not more than the 50A marked on the nameplate [440.4(B)]. Use a maximum 50A breaker in accordance with 240.6(A).

Answer: (a) 10 AWG, 50A breaker

4.13 Air-Conditioning Equipment, Short-Circuit and Ground-Fault Protection [440.22]

(A) Individual Motor Compressor. The branch-circuit short-circuit and ground-fault protective device must be capable of carrying the starting current of the motor. The rating or setting must not exceed 175 percent of the rated load current.

Ex 1: If the values for branch-circuit short-circuit and ground-fault protection in accordance with 440.22(A) do not correspond to the standard sizes or ratings of fuses, nonadjustable circuit breakers, thermal protective devices, or available settings of adjustable circuit breakers, a higher size, rating, or available setting that does not exceed the next higher standard ampere rating is permitted.

▶ **Air-Conditioning Equipment Protection Size [440.22(A) Ex 1], Example**

Question: What size branch-circuit short-circuit and ground-fault protective device is required for a 17.60A a/c motor-compressor? ▶Figure 4–53

(a) 35A   (b) 40A   (c) 45A   (d) 50A

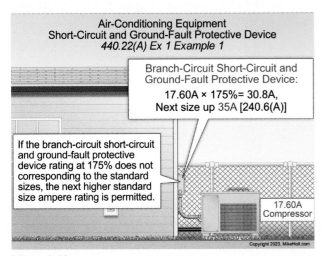

▶Figure 4–53

Solution:

Branch-Circuit Short-Circuit and Ground-Fault Protective Device =
(17.60A × 175%)
Branch-Circuit Short-Circuit and Ground-Fault Protective
Device = 30.8A
Branch-Circuit Short-Circuit and Ground-Fault Protective Device =
35A; use the next size up [240.6(A) and 440.22(A) Ex 1]

Answer: (a) 35A

Ex 2: If the values for branch-circuit short-circuit and ground-fault protection in accordance with 440.22(A) or the rating modified by Ex 1 is not sufficient for the starting current of the motor, the rating or setting is permitted to be increased up to 225 percent of the motor rated-load current or branch-circuit selection current, whichever is greater.

▶ **Air-Conditioning Equipment Protection Size [440.22(A) Ex 2], Example**

Question: What size branch-circuit short-circuit and ground-fault protective device is required for a 21A a/c motor-compressor, where the 175% protective device rating is not sufficient for the starting current of the motor? ▶Figure 4–54

(a) 35A   (b) 40A   (c) 45A   (d) 50A

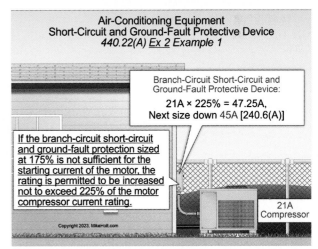

▶Figure 4–54

• • •

Solution:

Branch-Circuit Short-Circuit and Ground-Fault Protective Device =
(21A × 225%)

Branch-Circuit Short-Circuit and Ground-Fault Protective Device
= 47.25A

Branch-Circuit Short-Circuit and Ground-Fault Protective Device =
45A; use the next size down [240.6(A) and 440.22(A) Ex 2]

Answer: *(c) 45A*

(B) Rating or Setting for Equipment. The equipment branch-circuit short-circuit and ground-fault protective device must be capable of carrying the starting current of the equipment. Where the equipment incorporates more than one hermetic refrigerant motor-compressor or a hermetic refrigerant motor-compressor and other motors, the equipment branch-circuit short-circuit and ground-fault protection must comply with 440.22(B)(1).

(1) Motor-Compressor Largest Load. Where a hermetic refrigerant motor-compressor is the largest load connected to the circuit with other loads, the rating or setting of the branch-circuit short-circuit and ground-fault protective device is not permitted to exceed the value specified in 440.22(A) for the largest refrigerant motor-compressor plus the sum of the nameplate current ratings of the other motor loads.

▶ **Air-Conditioning Equipment Protection Size [440.22(B)(1)], Example 1**

Question: What size branch-circuit short-circuit and ground-fault protective device is required for a 17.60A a/c motor-compressor with a 1.20A fan? ▶**Figure 4–55**

(a) 35A   (b) 40A   (c) 45A   (d) 50A

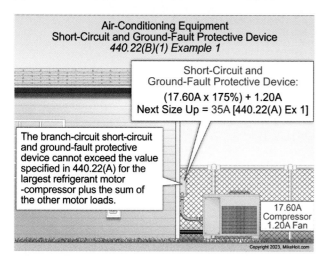

▶Figure 4–55

Solution:

Branch-Circuit Short-Circuit and Ground-Fault Protective Device =
(17.60A × 175%) + 1.20A

Branch-Circuit Short-Circuit and Ground-Fault Protective Device =
30.8A + 1.20A

Branch-Circuit Short-Circuit and Ground-Fault Protective Device = 32A,
use the next size up [440.22(A) Ex 1]

Branch-Circuit Short-Circuit and Ground-Fault Protective Device =
35A, [240.6(A)]

Answer: *(a) 35A*

▶ **Air-Conditioning Equipment Protection Size [440.22(B)(1)], Example 2**

Question: What size branch-circuit short-circuit and ground-fault protective device is required for a 21A a/c motor-compressor with a 1.20A fan, where the 175% protective device rating is not sufficient for the starting current of the motor? ▶**Figure 4–56**

(a) 35A   (b) 40A   (c) 45A   (d) 50A

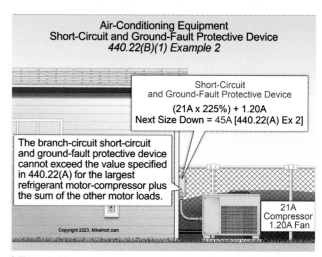

▶Figure 4–56

Solution:

Branch-Circuit Short-Circuit and Ground-Fault Protective Device =
(21A × 225%) + 1.20A

Branch-Circuit Short-Circuit and Ground-Fault Protective Device =
47.25A + 1.20A

Branch-Circuit Short-Circuit and Ground-Fault Protective Device =
48.45A, use the next size down [440.22(A) Ex 2]

Branch-Circuit Short-Circuit and Ground-Fault Protective Device =
45A, [240.6(A)]

Answer: *(c) 45A*

4.14 Air-Conditioning Equipment, Conductor Ampacity [440.33]

Conductors supplying hermetic refrigerant motor-compressors with other motors must have an ampacity of not less than the sum of the following: ▶Figure 4–57

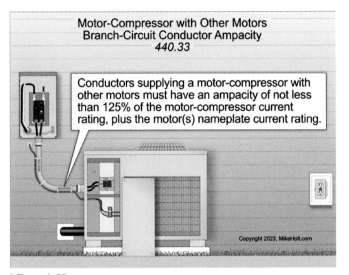

▶Figure 4–57

(1) The hermetic refrigerant motor-compressor nameplate current rating.

(2) The motor(s) nameplate current rating.

(3) 25 percent of the hermetic refrigerant motor-compressor current rating.

▶ A/C Equipment Conductor Size [440.33], Example 1

Question: *What size conductor is required for a 16.70A a/c motor-compressor?* ▶Figure 4–58

(a) 12 AWG   (b) 10 AWG   (c) 8 AWG   (d) 6 AWG

Solution:

Conductor Size = (16.70A × 125%)

Conductor Size = 20.88A

Use 10 AWG rated 30A at 60°C [Table 310.16].

Answer: *(b) 10 AWG*

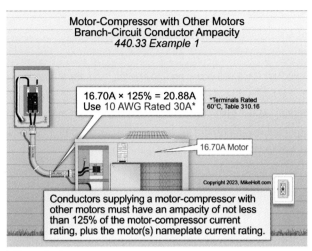

▶Figure 4–58

▶ A/C Equipment Conductor Size [440.33], Example 2

Question: *What size conductor is required for a 21A a/c motor-compressor; terminals are rated 75°C?* ▶Figure 4–59

(a) 12 AWG   (b) 10 AWG   (c) 8 AWG   (d) 6 AWG

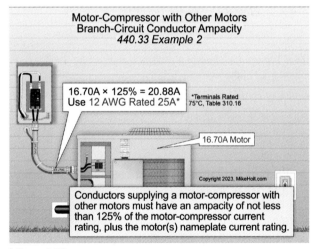

▶Figure 4–59

Solution:

Conductor Size = 21A × 125%

Conductor Size = 26.25A

Use 10 AWG rated 35A at 75°C [240.4(G), 110.14(C)(1)(a)(3) and Table 310.16].

Answer: *(b) 10 AWG*

Part C—Transformers

Introduction

In this Part C we will cover how to size the primary protection only of a transformer using Table 450.3(B) and the applicable notes. In addition, we will also cover how to size the transformer secondary conductors based on the secondary overcurrent protective device they terminate into in accordance with 240.21(C).

4.15 Transformer Primary Only Overcurrent Protection [450.3(B)]

Transformers having a secondary voltage not exceeding 1000V, with primary overcurrent protection only, must have the primary overcurrent protective device sized in accordance with the percentages contained in Table 450.3(B) and its applicable notes.

Table 450.3(B) Primary Protection Only

Primary Current Rating	Maximum Protection
Less than 2A	300%
2A to 9A	167%
More Than 9A	125%, Note 1

Note 1: Transformers having a primary current rating of 9A, or more are permitted to use the "next size up" rule when 125 percent of the primary current does not correspond to the standard rating of a fuse or nonadjustable circuit breaker listed in 240.6(A).

▶ **Primary Protection Current Less than 2A [Table 430.3(B)], Example**

Question: What is the maximum primary only overcurrent device size permitted for a 750 VA, 480V to 240V transformer? ▶Figure 4–60

(a) 3.21A   (b) 4.68A   (c) 5.80A   (d) 6.10A

Solution:

Primary Current = Transformer VA Rating/Primary Voltage
Primary Current = 750 VA/480V
Primary Current = 1.56A

Primary Protection = Primary Current × Table 450.3(B) Percentage
Primary Protection = 1.56A × 300%
Primary Protection = 4.68A

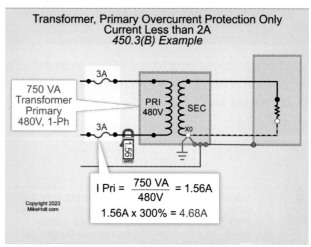

▶Figure 4–60

Table 450.3(B) Note 1 for rounding only applies to primary currents of 9A or more.

Answer: (b) 4.68A

▶ **Primary Protection Current 2A to 9A [Table 430.3(B)], Example**

Question: What is the maximum primary only overcurrent device size permitted for a 2 kVA, 240V to 120V transformer? ▶Figure 4–61

(a) 9.81A   (b) 11.31A   (c) 13.92A   (d) 15.12A

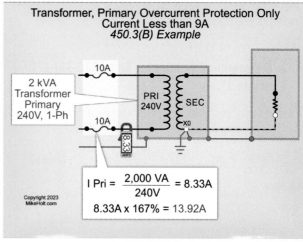

▶Figure 4–61

Solution:

Primary Current = Transformer VA Rating/Primary Voltage
Primary Current = 2,000 VA/240V
Primary Current = 8.33A

Primary Protection = Primary Current × Table 450.3(B) Percentage

Primary Protection = 8.33A × 167%

Primary Protection = 13.92A

Table 450.3(B) Note 1 for rounding only applies to primary currents of 9A or more.

Answer: (c) 13.92A

▶ **Primary Protection Current Greater than 9A [Table 430.3(B)], Example**

Question: What is the maximum primary overcurrent device size permitted for a 30 kVA, three-phase, 480V to 208Y/120V transformer?
▶Figure 4–62

(a) 40A   (b) 45A   (c) 50A   (d) 60A

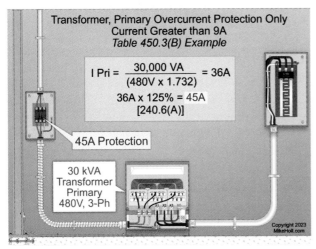

▶Figure 4–62

Solution:

Primary Current = Transformer VA Rating/ (Primary Voltage × 1.732)

Primary Current = 30,000 VA/(480V × 1.732)

Primary Current = 30,000 VA/831.36V

Primary Current = 36A

Primary Protection = Primary Current × Table 450.3(B) Percentage

Primary Protection = 36A × 125%

Primary Protection = 45A

Use a 45A overcurrent device [240.6(A) and Table 450.3(B)].

Answer: (b) 45A

▶ **Primary Protection Current Greater than 9A [Table 430.3(B) Note 1], Example 1**

Question: What is the maximum primary only overcurrent device size permitted for a 45 kVA, three-phase, 480V to 208Y/120V transformer?
▶Figure 4–63

(a) 50A   (b) 60A   (c) 70A   (d) 90A

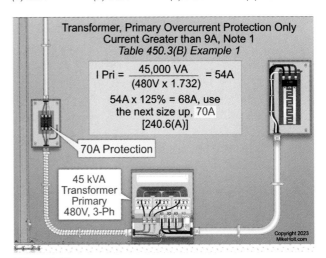

▶Figure 4–63

Solution:

Primary Current = Transformer VA Rating/ (Primary Voltage × 1.732)

Primary Current = 45,000 VA/(480V × 1.732)

Primary Current = 45,000 VA/831.36V

Primary Current = 54A

Primary Protection = Primary Current × Table 450.3(B) Percentage

Primary Protection = 54A × 125%

Primary Protection = 68A

Primary Protection = 70A [240.6(A) and Table 450.3(B), Note 1]

Answer: (c) 70A

▶ **Primary Protection Current Greater than 9A [Table 430.3(B) Note 1], Example 2**

Question: *What is the maximum primary only overcurrent device size permitted for a 75 kVA, three-phase, 480V to 208Y/120V transformer?* ▶Figure 4–64

(a) 100A   (b) 110A   (c) 125A   (d) 175A

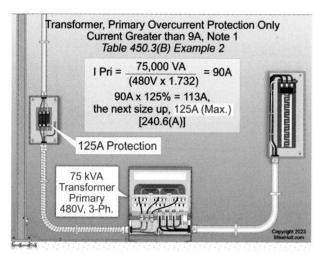

Transformer, Primary Overcurrent Protection Only
Current Greater than 9A, Note 1
Table 450.3(B) Example 2

$$I\ Pri = \frac{75,000\ VA}{(480V \times 1.732)} = 90A$$

90A x 125% = 113A,
the next size up, 125A (Max.)
[240.6(A)]

125A Protection

75 kVA
Transformer
Primary
480V, 3-Ph.

Copyright 2023
MikeHolt.com

▶Figure 4–64

Solution:

Primary Current = Transformer VA Rating/ (Primary Voltage × 1.732)

Primary Current = 75,000 VA/(480V × 1.732)

Primary Current = 75,000 VA/831.36V

Primary Current = 90A

Primary Protection = Primary Current × Table 450.3(B) Percentage

Primary Protection = 90A × 125%

Primary Protection = 113A

Primary Protection = 125A [240.6(A) and Table 450.3(B), Note 1]

Answer: *(c) 125A*

▶ **Primary Protection Current Greater than 9A [Table 430.3(B) Note 1], Example 3**

Question: *What is the maximum primary only overcurrent device size permitted for a 112.50 kVA, three-phase, 480V to 208Y/120V transformer?* ▶Figure 4–65

(a) 125A   (b) 150A   (c) 175A   (d) 225A

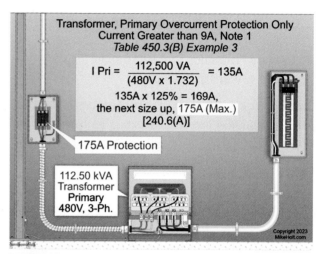

Transformer, Primary Overcurrent Protection Only
Current Greater than 9A, Note 1
Table 450.3(B) Example 3

$$I\ Pri = \frac{112,500\ VA}{(480V \times 1.732)} = 135A$$

135A x 125% = 169A,
the next size up, 175A (Max.)
[240.6(A)]

175A Protection

112.50 kVA
Transformer
Primary
480V, 3-Ph.

Copyright 2023
MikeHolt.com

▶Figure 4–65

Solution:

Primary Current = Transformer VA Rating/ (Primary Voltage × 1.732)

Primary Current = 112,500 VA/(480V × 1.732)

Primary Current = 112,500 VA/831.36V

Primary Current = 135A

Primary Protection = Primary Current × Table 450.3(B) Percentage

Primary Protection = 135A × 125%

Primary Protection = 169A

Primary Protection = 175A [240.6(A) and Table 450.3(B), Note 1]

Answer: *(c) 175A*

4.16 Transformer Secondary Conductor Sizing [240.21(C)]

The next size up rule in 240.4(B) is not permitted for transformer secondary conductors.

(2) Secondary Conductors Not Over 10 Feet. Secondary conductors up to 10 ft long are permitted when they comply with the following:

(1) The secondary conductors must have an ampacity of not less than: ▶Figure 4–66

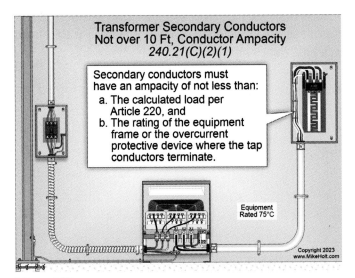

▶Figure 4–66

a. The calculated load in accordance with Article 220, and

b. The rating of the secondary overcurrent protective device where the secondary conductors terminate

▶ Secondary Conductor Sizing Example 1

Question: What size secondary conductor not over 10 ft is required for a 30 kVA, three-phase, 480V to 120/208V transformer that terminates in a 110A main breaker? ▶Figure 4–67

(a) 3 AWG   (b) 2 AWG   (c) 1 AWG   (d) 1/0 AWG

Solution:

2 AWG rated for 115A at 75°C [Table 310.16 and 240.21(C)(2)(1)]

Answer: *(b) 2 AWG*

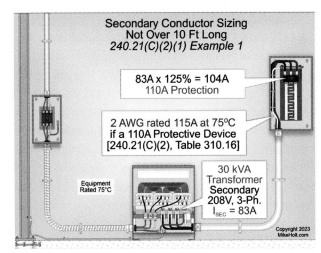

▶Figure 4–67

▶ Secondary Conductor Sizing Example 2

Question: What size secondary conductor not over 10 ft is required for a 75 kVA, three-phase, 480V to 120/208V transformer that terminates in a 300A main breaker? ▶Figure 4–68

(a) 4/0 AWG   (b) 250 kcmil   (c) 300 kcmil   (d) 350 kcmil

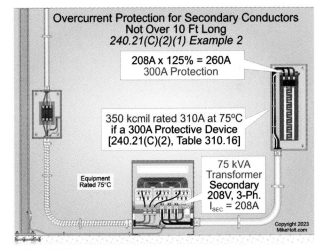

▶Figure 4–68

Solution:

350 kcmil is rated 310A at 75°C [Table 310.16 and 240.21(C)(2)(1)]

Answer: *(d) 350 kcmil*

Unit 4—Conclusion

Articles 430 and 440 can be intimidating and confusing because they seem to "break all the rules" and provisions for motor circuits since they differ from the general *NEC* requirements. This unit explained that the overload protection for motors is treated separately from the short-circuit and ground-fault protection. Motor circuits must accommodate increased starting current and still provide satisfactory running current protection. For this reason, the overcurrent protection rules you learned in Article 240 do not apply to motor circuits. Articles 430 and 440 contain the requirements used to size protection as well as sizing conductors for their respective equipment, branch circuits, and feeders.

A common mistake made in motor circuits is the use of the motor nameplate ampere rating for calculations that should be made using the full-load current rating from the Article 430 tables. The nameplate full-load amperes (FLA) is only used for overload protection; Tables 430.248, 430.249, and 430.250 are used for sizing conductors, and short-circuit and ground-fault protection.

When sizing the primary protection only for transformers 1000V or less make sure to use Table 450.3(B). Calculate the primary current and then determine which column to use in Table 450.3(B). Sizing the transformer secondary conductors couldn't be any easier, simply select the secondary conductor with an ampacity equal to or greater than the secondary protective device ampere rating in accordance with 240.21(C).

UNIT

4

REVIEW QUESTIONS

Please use the 2023 *Code* book and this textbook to answer the following questions.

PART A—MOTOR CALCULATIONS

4.1 Motor Full-Load Current (FLC)

1. What is the FLC for a 5 hp, 115V, direct-current motor?

    (a) 28A
    (b) 32A
    (c) 40A
    (d) 56A

2. What is the FLC for a 5 hp, 115V, motor?

    (a) 28A
    (b) 32A
    (c) 40A
    (d) 56A

3. What is the FLC for a 5 hp, 200V motor?

    (a) 30.2A
    (b) 32.2A
    (c) 34.2A
    (d) 36.2A

4. What is the FLC for a 10 hp, 208V, three-phase motor?

    (a) 28.5A
    (b) 30.8A
    (c) 40.5A
    (d) 68.5A

5. What is the FLC for a 25 hp, 230V, three-phase motor?

    (a) 28A
    (b) 35A
    (c) 40A
    (d) 68A

6. What is the FLC for a 25 hp, 480V, three-phase motor?

    (a) 28A
    (b) 34A
    (c) 40A
    (d) 68A

4.3 Branch-Circuit Conductor Sizing Continuous Duty Application [430.22]

Single-Phase Application

7. What size conductor is required for a 1 hp, 115V motor?

    (a) 14 AWG
    (b) 12 AWG
    (c) 10 AWG
    (d) 8 AWG

8. What size conductor is required for a 2 hp, 230V motor?

    (a) 14 AWG
    (b) 12 AWG
    (c) 10 AWG
    (d) 8 AWG

9. What size conductor is required for a 5 hp, 208V motor?

    (a) 14 AWG
    (b) 12 AWG
    (c) 10 AWG
    (d) 8 AWG

10. What size conductor is required for a 5 hp, 230V motor?

    (a) 14 AWG
    (b) 12 AWG
    (c) 10 AWG
    (d) 8 AWG

Three-Phase Application

11. What size conductor is required for a 5 hp, 208V, three-phase motor?

    (a) 14 AWG
    (b) 12 AWG
    (c) 10 AWG
    (d) 8 AWG

12. What size conductor is required for a 7½ hp, 230V, three-phase motor?

    (a) 14 AWG
    (b) 12 AWG
    (c) 10 AWG
    (d) 8 AWG

13. What size conductor is required for a 10 hp, 230V three-phase motor?

    (a) 14 AWG
    (b) 12 AWG
    (c) 10 AWG
    (d) 8 AWG

14. What size THW conductor is required for a 15 hp, 200V, three-phase motor, terminals rated 75°C?

    (a) 10 AWG
    (b) 8 AWG
    (c) 6 AWG
    (d) 4 AWG

15. What size THW conductor is required for a 15 hp, 208V, three-phase induction type motor, terminals rated 75°C?

    (a) 8 AWG
    (b) 6 AWG
    (c) 4 AWG
    (d) 3 AWG

16. What size THW conductor is required for a 15 hp, 230V, three-phase motor, terminals rated 75°C?

    (a) 8 AWG
    (b) 6 AWG
    (c) 4 AWG
    (d) 3 AWG

17. What size THW conductor is required for a 25 hp, 460V, three-phase Design B motor, terminals rated 75°C?

    (a) 12 AWG
    (b) 10 AWG
    (c) 8 AWG
    (d) 6 AWG

4.4 Branch-Circuit Conductor Sizing for Duty-Cycle Application [430.22(E)]

18. What size branch-circuit conductors are required for a 10 hp, three-phase, 208V motor with a nameplate FLA of 29A, rated for 5-minute service, used for intermittent duty, with terminals rated 75°C?

    (a) 14 AWG
    (b) 12 AWG
    (c) 10 AWG
    (d) 8 AWG

19. What size branch-circuit conductors are required for a 20 hp, three-phase, 230V motor with a nameplate FLA of 48A, rated for 30-minute service, used for short-time duty, with terminals rated 75°C?

    (a) 8 AWG
    (b) 6 AWG
    (c) 4 AWG
    (d) 2 AWG

4.6 Motor Overload Protection

20. Motors with a nameplate service factor (SF) rating of 1.15 or more must have the overload protective device sized at no more than ____ of the motor nameplate current rating.

    (a) 100 percent
    (b) 115 percent
    (c) 125 percent
    (d) 135 percent

21. Motors with a nameplate temperature rise rating not over 40°C must have the overload protective device sized at no more than ____ of the motor nameplate current rating.

    (a) 100 percent
    (b) 115 percent
    (c) 125 percent
    (d) 135 percent

22. Motors that have a service factor rating of 1.10 must have the overload protective device sized at not more than ____ of the motor nameplate ampere rating.

    (a) 100 percent
    (b) 115 percent
    (c) 125 percent
    (d) 135 percent

23. What is the maximum overload setting for a continuous duty motor, with a nameplate current of 20A and service factor of 1.15?

    (a) 20A
    (b) 22A
    (c) 25A
    (d) 30A

24. What is the maximum overload setting for a three-phase motor, with a nameplate current of 30A, service factor of 1.15 and temperature rise of 40°C?

    (a) 31.50A
    (b) 35.70A
    (c) 37.50A
    (d) 39.50A

25. What is the maximum overload setting for an induction type motor, with a nameplate current of 30A and temperature rise of 50°C?

    (a) 31.5A
    (b) 34.5A
    (c) 37.5A
    (d) 39.5A

26. What is the maximum overload setting for a three-phase motor, with a nameplate current of 40A, service factor of 1.15 and temperature rise of 40°C?

    (a) 45A
    (b) 47A
    (c) 48A
    (d) 50A

27. If a dual-element time-delay fuse is used for overload protection, what size fuse is required for a 3 hp, 230V, motor, with a service factor of 1.15, if the motor nameplate current rating is 15A?

    (a) 15A
    (b) 20A
    (c) 25A
    (d) 30A

28. If a dual-element time-delay fuse is used for the overload protection, what size fuse is required for a 15 hp, 460V, three-phase motor, with a temperature rise of 40°C, and a motor nameplate current rating of 18A (FLA)?

    (a) 15A
    (b) 20A
    (c) 25A
    (d) 30A

4.7 Branch-Circuit Short-Circuit and Ground-Fault Protection [430.52(C)(1)]

29. The maximum rating or setting for the branch-circuit short-circuit and ground-fault protective device is ____ of the FLC on a motor if an inverse time breaker is used.

    (a) 150 percent
    (b) 175 percent
    (c) 250 percent
    (d) 300 percent

30. The maximum rating or setting for the branch-circuit short-circuit and ground-fault protective device is ____ of the FLC on a squirrel cage motor if a nontime delay fuse is used.

    (a) 150 percent
    (b) 175 percent
    (c) 250 percent
    (d) 300 percent

31. The maximum rating or setting for the branch-circuit short-circuit and ground-fault protective device is ____ of the FLC on Design-B motor if a dual element fuse is used.

    (a) 150 percent
    (b) 175 percent
    (c) 250 percent
    (d) 300 percent

32. What is the maximum size nontime delay fuses required for a 2 hp, 230V motor?

    (a) 30A
    (b) 35A
    (c) 40A
    (d) 45A

33. What is the maximum size dual-element time-delay fuses required for a 2 hp, 230V motor?

    (a) 25A
    (b) 30A
    (c) 35A
    (d) 40A

34. What is the maximum size inverse time circuit breaker required for a 5 hp, 208V motor?

    (a) 35A
    (b) 40A
    (c) 60A
    (d) 80A

35. What is the maximum size dual-element fuse for a 5 hp, 230V, three-phase squirrel-cage motor?

    (a) 20A
    (b) 25A
    (c) 30A
    (d) 35A

36. What is the maximum size dual-element fuse for a 20 hp, 460V three-phase motor?

    (a) 35A
    (b) 40A
    (c) 45A
    (d) 50A

37. What is the maximum size non-time delay fuse for a 20 hp, 460V three-phase squirrel cage resistor starting Design B motor?

    (a) 65A
    (b) 70A
    (c) 85A
    (d) 90A

4.9 Motor Circuit Equipment Grounding Conductor Size [250.122(D)(1)]

38. What size equipment grounding conductor is required for a 5 hp, 208V three-phase motor protected with an 80A breaker?

    (a) 12 AWG
    (b) 10 AWG
    (c) 8 AWG
    (d) 6 AWG

39. What size equipment grounding conductor is required for a 10 hp 230V three-phase motor protected with a 70A breaker?

    (a) 8 AWG
    (b) 6 AWG
    (c) 4 AWG
    (d) 3 AWG

4.10 Feeder Conductor Sizing [430.24]

40. What size feeder is required for a 3 hp and 5 hp, 230V motors?

    (a) 10 AWG
    (b) 8 AWG
    (c) 6 AWG
    (d) 4 AWG

41. What size THW feeder is required for two 7½ hp, 240V, dc motors, terminals rated 75°C?

    (a) 10 AWG
    (b) 8 AWG
    (c) 6 AWG
    (d) 4 AWG

42. What size THW feeder is required for two 10 hp and one 20 hp, 208V, three-phase motors?

    (a) 1/0 AWG
    (b) 2/0 AWG
    (c) 3/0 AWG
    (d) 4/0 AWG

43. What size THW feeder is required for two 7½ hp and two 15 hp, 230V three-phase motors, terminals rated 75°C?

    (a) 1 AWG
    (b) 1/0 AWG
    (c) 2/0 AWG
    (d) 3/0 AWG

4.11 Feeder Short-Circuit and Ground-Fault Protection [430.62(A)]

44. What is the maximum size inverse time breaker (ITB) required for a 3 hp and 5 hp, 230V three-phase motors?

(a) 40A
(b) 45A
(c) 55A
(d) 60A

45. What is the maximum size dual-element fuse (DE) is required for a 7½ hp and 10 hp, 240V dc motors?

(a) 80A
(b) 90A
(c) 100A
(d) 110A

46. What is the maximum size inverse time breaker (ITB) protection required for two 10 hp and one 20 hp, 208V, three-phase motors?

(a) 125A
(b) 150A
(c) 175A
(d) 200A

47. What is the maximum size non-time delay fuse is required for two 7½ hp and one 15 hp, 230V three-phase motors?

(a) 125A
(b) 150A
(c) 175A
(d) 200A

48. What size inverse time circuit breaker is required for the feeder supplying the three motors?

- One 25 hp, 460V, 3-phase, squirrel-cage motor, nameplate full-load current 32A, Design B, Service Factor 1.15
- Two 30 hp, 460V, 3-phase, wound-rotor motors, primary current 38A, secondary current 65A

(a) 100A
(b) 125A
(c) 150A
(d) 175A

PART B—AIR-CONDITIONING CALCULATIONS

4.12 Air-Conditioning Equipment Nameplate [440.4(B)]

49. What size conductor is permitted for an air-conditioning unit, where the nameplate states minimum circuit ampacity 30A, with maximum overcurrent protection of 50A?

(a) 18 AWG
(b) 16 AWG
(c) 12 AWG
(d) 10 AWG

50. What size conductor is permitted for an air-conditioning unit, where the nameplate states minimum circuit ampacity 45A, with maximum overcurrent protection of 80A?

(a) 12 AWG
(b) 10 AWG
(c) 8 AWG
(d) 6 AWG

4.13 Air-Conditioning Equipment, Short-Circuit and Ground-Fault Protection [440.22]

51. What size branch-circuit short-circuit and ground-fault protective device is required for an 18.6A refrigerant motor-compressor with a 1.5A fan?

(a) 35A
(b) 40A
(c) 45A
(d) 50A

52. What size branch-circuit short-circuit and ground-fault protective device is required for an 18.6A refrigerant motor-compressor with a 1.5A fan, where the 175% protective device rating is not sufficient for the starting current of the motor?

(a) 35A
(b) 40A
(c) 45A
(d) 50A

4.14 Air-Conditioning Equipment, Conductor Ampacity [440.33]

53. What size minimum branch-circuit conductor is required for a 16A refrigerant motor-compressor with a 2A fan?

(a) 14 AWG
(b) 12 AWG
(c) 10 AWG
(d) 8 AWG

54. What size minimum branch-circuit conductor is required for a 25A refrigerant motor-compressor with a 2A fan, terminals rated 75°C?

(a) 14 AWG
(b) 12 AWG
(c) 10 AWG
(d) 8 AWG

PART C—TRANSFORMERS

4.15 Transformer Primary Only Overcurrent Protection [450.3(B)]

55. What is the maximum primary overcurrent device rating for a 25 kVA, 240V transformer with no secondary overcurrent protection?

(a) 90A
(b) 100A
(c) 125A
(d) 150A

56. What is the maximum primary overcurrent device rating for a 45 kVA, 208V three-phase transformer with no secondary overcurrent protection?

(a) 175A
(b) 200A
(c) 225A
(d) 250A

57. What is the maximum primary overcurrent device rating for a 75 kVA, 208V three-phase transformer with no secondary overcurrent protection?

(a) 250A
(b) 300A
(c) 350A
(d) 400A

58. What is the maximum primary overcurrent device rating for a 112.5 kVA, 480V, three-phase transformer with no secondary overcurrent protection?

(a) 175A
(b) 200A
(c) 225A
(d) 250A

59. What is the maximum primary overcurrent protective device for a 40A autotransformer with no secondary overcurrent protection?

(a) 50A
(b) 60A
(c) 70A
(d) 80A

60. What is the maximum primary overcurrent protective device for a 60A autotransformer with no secondary overcurrent protection?

(a) 60A
(b) 70A
(c) 80A
(d) 90A

4.16 Transformer Secondary Conductor Sizing [240.21(C)]

61. What size secondary conductor not over 10 ft is required for a 75 kVA, three-phase, 480V to 120/208V transformer that terminates in a 300A main breaker?

(a) 350 kcmil
(b) 400 kcmil
(c) 500 kcmil
(d) 600 kcmil

62. What size secondary conductor not over 10 ft is required for a 112.5 kVA, three-phase, 480V to 120/208V transformer that terminates in a 400A main breaker?

(a) 350 kcmil
(b) 400 kcmil
(c) 500 kcmil
(d) 600 kcmil

UNIT 5

VOLTAGE-DROP CALCULATIONS

Introduction to Unit 5—Voltage-Drop Calculations

When electrical current flows through a conductor, there is a certain amount of voltage drop in the conductor due to its inherent resistance. Excessive voltage drop can also result in delivering a voltage to the load that's less than the rated voltage of the equipment. The equipment manufacturer's nameplate, instruction manual, or industry standards should be consulted to determine the acceptable operating voltage range.

Ohm's Law shows that the amount of voltage drop present in any electrical circuit is directly proportional to the amount of current flow and resistance in the circuit. The resistance of a circuit is determined by its conductor material (copper or aluminum), cross-sectional area, length, and conductor temperature.

The following are the Parts covered in this unit:

▸ Part A—Conductor Resistance Calculations

▸ Part B— Voltage-Drop Calculations

In this unit, we will show you how to find all the information necessary to make accurate voltage-drop calculations for both single- and three-phase circuits.

Part A—Conductor Resistance Calculations

Introduction

For most everyday purposes, resistance is ignored in the *Code*. However, all conductor materials oppose current flow, and understanding voltage-drop calculations requires knowledge of the factors related to physics of electricity. The total opposition to current flow is called "resistance" in electrical circuits. In Part A we will be using Chapter 9 Table 8 for both alternating-current circuits and direct-current circuits because that is sufficient for most exams.

5.1 Conductor Cross-Sectional Area in Circular Mills [Chapter 9, Table 8]

Bare conductor cross-sectional area Chapter 9, Table 8. The cross-sectional area of a conductor is commonly expressed in circular mils (cmil) and the values are found in Chapter 9, Table 8, regardless of whether direct current or alternating current is in use. Notice that the circular mil area is the same for a specific size conductor regardless of whether it is solid or stranded, or its type of insulation. ▸Figure 5–1

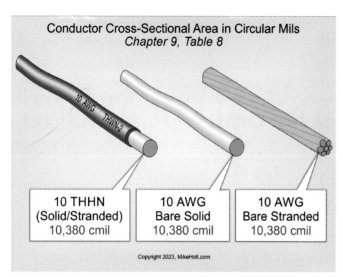

▶Figure 5–1

▶ **Cross-Sectional Area in Circular Mills, Example 1**

Question: What is the cross-sectional area in circular mils for a 14 THWN-2 conductor? ▶Figure 5–2

(a) 4,110 cmil   *(b) 6,530 cmil*   *(c) 10,380 cmil* *(d) 16,510 cmil*

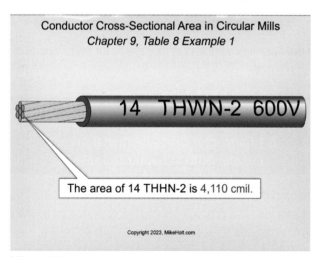

▶Figure 5–2

Answer: (a) 4,110 cmil

▶ **Cross-Sectional Area in Circular Mills, Example 2**

Question: What is the cross-sectional area in circular mils for a 10 RHH conductor? ▶Figure 5–3

(a) 4,100 cmil   *(b) 6,530 cmil*   *(c) 10,380 cmil (d) 16,510 cmil*

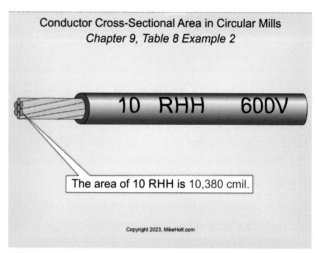

▶Figure 5–3

Answer: (c) 10,380 cmil

▶ **Cross-Sectional Area in Circular Mills, Example 3**

Question: What is the cross-sectional area in circular mils for an 8 RHW conductor? ▶Figure 5–4

(a) 4,100 cmil   *(b) 6,530 cmil*   *(c) 10,380 cmil (d) 16,510 cmil*

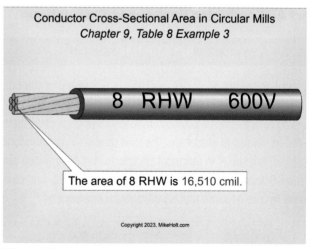

▶Figure 5–4

Answer: (d) 16,510 cmil

▶ Cross-Sectional Area in Circular Mills, Example 4

Question: *What is the cross-sectional area in circular mils for an 8 THHN conductor?* ▶Figure 5–5

(a) 4,100 cmil   (b) 6,530 cmil   (c) 10,380 cmil (d) 16,510 cmil

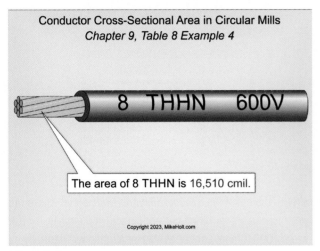

Conductor Cross-Sectional Area in Circular Mills
Chapter 9, Table 8 Example 4

8 THHN 600V

The area of 8 THHN is 16,510 cmil.

Copyright 2023, MikeHolt.com

▶Figure 5–5

Answer: *(d) 16,510 cmil*

▶ Cross-Sectional Area in Circular Mills, Example 5

Question: *What's the cross-sectional area in circular mils for a 1 THWN-2 aluminum compact conductor?* ▶Figure 5–6

(a) 4,100 cmil   (b) 6,530 cmil   (c) 10,380 cmil (d) 83,690 cmil

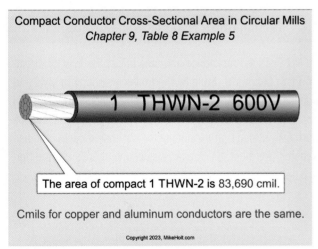

Compact Conductor Cross-Sectional Area in Circular Mills
Chapter 9, Table 8 Example 5

1 THWN-2 600V

The area of compact 1 THWN-2 is 83,690 cmil.

Cmils for copper and aluminum conductors are the same.

Copyright 2023, MikeHolt.com

▶Figure 5–6

Answer: *(d) 83,690 cmil*

5.2 Conductor Resistance

Voltage drop is the loss of potential that results when current is affected by the resistance/impedance of a conductor in a circuit. To calculate the voltage-drop of a circuit, it is essential to know its load and the resistance of the conductors. Metals intended to carry electrical current are called "conductors" or "wires" and, by their nature, they oppose the flow of electrons. Conductors for applications covered by the *NEC* can be solid or stranded and are most often made from copper or aluminum. All materials oppose the flow of electrons. This opposition to electron movement is known as "resistance." All conductors offer some degree of resistance to electron movement.

A conductor's opposition to the flow of direct current depends on the conductor's:

▶ Material (copper or aluminum)

▶ Cross-sectional area (wire size)

▶ Length

▶ Operating temperature

Material

Wire resistance varies with the material from which it is made. A copper wire has a lower resistance compared to an equivalent size aluminum wire. ▶Figure 5–7

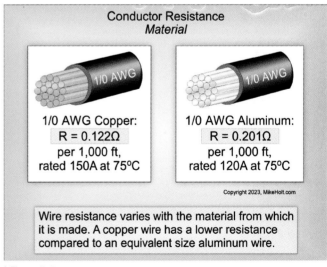

Conductor Resistance
Material

1/0 AWG Copper:
R = 0.122Ω
per 1,000 ft,
rated 150A at 75°C

1/0 AWG Aluminum:
R = 0.201Ω
per 1,000 ft,
rated 120A at 75°C

Copyright 2023, MikeHolt.com

Wire resistance varies with the material from which it is made. A copper wire has a lower resistance compared to an equivalent size aluminum wire.

▶Figure 5–7

Conductor Cross-Sectional Area

The greater the conductor cross-sectional area (the larger the conductor), the greater the number of available electron paths and the lower the conductor resistance. ▶Figure 5–8

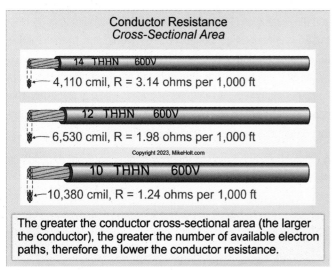

Conductor Resistance
Cross-Sectional Area

14 THHN 600V
4,110 cmil, R = 3.14 ohms per 1,000 ft

12 THHN 600V
6,530 cmil, R = 1.98 ohms per 1,000 ft

10 THHN 600V
10,380 cmil, R = 1.24 ohms per 1,000 ft

The greater the conductor cross-sectional area (the larger the conductor), the greater the number of available electron paths, therefore the lower the conductor resistance.

▶Figure 5–8

Conductor resistance varies inversely with the conductor's size, the smaller the wire size, the greater the resistance. The larger the wire size, the lower the resistance. ▶Figure 5–9

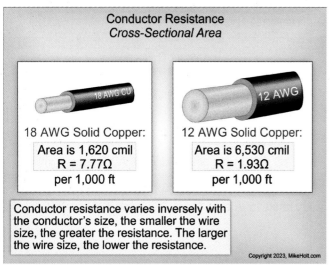

Conductor Resistance
Cross-Sectional Area

18 AWG Solid Copper:
Area is 1,620 cmil
R = 7.77Ω
per 1,000 ft

12 AWG Solid Copper:
Area is 6,530 cmil
R = 1.93Ω
per 1,000 ft

Conductor resistance varies inversely with the conductor's size, the smaller the wire size, the greater the resistance. The larger the wire size, the lower the resistance.

▶Figure 5–9

Conductor Length

The resistance of a conductor is directly proportional to its length—the longer the conductor, the greater the resistance. ▶Figure 5–10

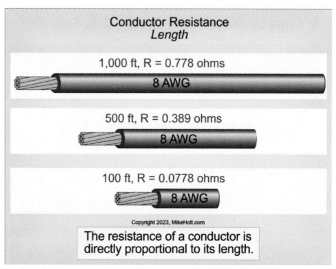

Conductor Resistance
Length

1,000 ft, R = 0.778 ohms
8 AWG

500 ft, R = 0.389 ohms
8 AWG

100 ft, R = 0.0778 ohms
8 AWG

The resistance of a conductor is directly proportional to its length.

▶Figure 5–10

Chapter 9, Table 8 of the *National Electrical Code* provides examples of wire resistances for direct-current circuits and circular mil areas for wires 1000 ft long. Longer or shorter lengths will naturally have different wire resistances.

Temperature

The resistance of a conductor changes with temperature. The amount of change per degree is called the "temperature coefficient." Positive temperature coefficient indicates that as the temperature rises, the conductor resistance also rises. Copper and aluminum conductors have a positive temperature coefficient.

5.3 Conductor Resistance [Chapter 9, Table 8]

The *NEC* lists the resistance and area in circular mils for direct-current in Chapter 9, Table 8. The tables include both solid and stranded conductors. Table 8 lists both coated copper and uncoated copper. Uncoated copper is the most used conductor; unless specifically stated that the conductor is a coated conductor, use uncoated (for most resistance calculations, there's slight difference between the two).

▶ Conductor Resistance, Example 1

Question: *What's the dc resistance of 200 ft of a 12 AWG stranded conductor?* ▶Figure 5–11

(a) 0.21Ω   *(b) 0.29Ω*   *(c) 0.396Ω*   *(d) 0.72Ω*

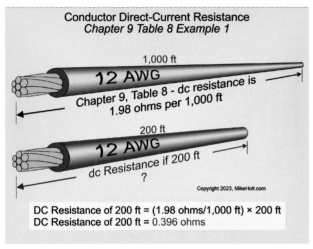

▶Figure 5–11

Solution:

The dc resistance of 12 AWG 1,000 ft long is 1.98Ω [Chapter 9, Table 8].

DC Resistance of 200 ft = (1.98Ω/1,000 ft) × 200 ft
DC Resistance of 200 ft = 0.396Ω

Answer: *(c) 0.396Ω*

▶ Conductor Resistance, Example 2

Question: *What's the dc resistance of 200 ft of a 6 AWG conductor?* ▶Figure 5–12

(a) 0.021Ω   *(b) 0.029Ω*   *(c) 0.049Ω*   *(d) 0.098Ω*

Solution:

The dc resistance of 6 AWG 1,000 ft long is 0.491Ω [Chapter 9, Table 8].

DC Resistance of 200 ft = (0.491Ω/1,000 ft) × 200 ft
DC Resistance of 200 ft = 0.0982Ω

Answer: *(d) 0.098Ω*

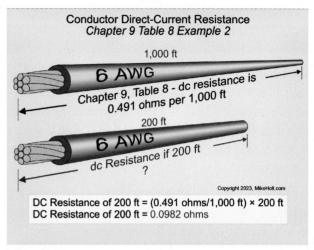

▶Figure 5–12

▶ Conductor Resistance, Example 3

Question: *What's the dc resistance of 200 ft of a 1/0 AWG aluminum conductor?* ▶Figure 5–13

(a) 0.04Ω   *(b) 0.29Ω*   *(c) 0.60Ω*   *(d) 0.72Ω*

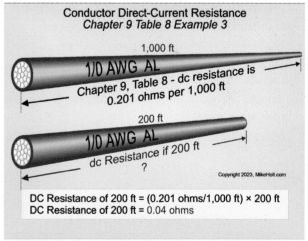

▶Figure 5–13

Solution:

The dc resistance of 1/0 AWG aluminum 1,000 ft long is 0.201Ω [Chapter 9, Table 8].

DC Resistance of 200 ft = (0.201Ω/1,000 ft) × 200 ft
DC Resistance of 200 ft = 0.04Ω

Answer: *(a) 0.04Ω*

Part B—Voltage-Drop Calculations

Introduction

When it comes to sizing conductors to accommodate conductor voltage drop, many factors must be considered. Part B will cover the Ohm's Law method and the KID formula method for calculating voltage drop. On exams they will ask questions relating to sizing the conductor to not exceed the recommended voltage drop percentage, this is also covered here.

A helpful tip for these calculations is to identify each variable in the question and then its just a matter of plugging in the number on the formula to work out the solution for each problem.

5.4 Conductors' Voltage Drop—Ohm's Law Method

The voltage drop of a circuit conductor is in direct proportion to the conductor's resistance and magnitude (amount) of current. A longer conductor results in greater conductor resistance and greater conductor voltage drop. Increased current flow will also result in greater conductor voltage drop. The voltage drop of the circuit conductors for single-phase systems can be determined by the Ohm's Law method or by the formula method.

$$E_{VD} = I \times R$$

E_{VD} = Conductor voltage drop expressed in volts.
I = The load in amperes at 100 percent (not at 125 percent for motors or continuous loads).
R = Conductor resistance; see Chapter 9, Table 8 for dc resistance.

> **Author's Comment:**
>
> ▸ For conductors 1/0 AWG and smaller, the difference in resistance between dc and alternating-current circuits is so minor it can be ignored. In addition, you can ignore the slight differences in resistance between stranded and solid conductors, and between coated or uncoated copper conductors.

▶ Ohm's Law Voltage Drop, Example 1

Question: What is the operating voltage of a 16A, 115V rated load wired with 12 AWG if it is located 150 ft from the power supply, and has a nominal circuit voltage of 120V? ▸Figure 5–14

(a) 110.5V   (b) 116.5V   (c) 117.6V   (d) 118.8V

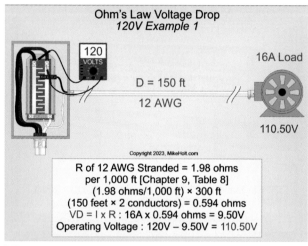

Ohm's Law Voltage Drop
120V Example 1

120 VOLTS

16A Load

D = 150 ft
12 AWG

110.50V

Copyright 2023, MikeHolt.com

R of 12 AWG Stranded = 1.98 ohms
per 1,000 ft [Chapter 9, Table 8]
(1.98 ohms/1,000 ft) × 300 ft
(150 feet × 2 conductors) = 0.594 ohms
VD = I x R : 16A x 0.594 ohms = 9.50V
Operating Voltage : 120V – 9.50V = 110.50V

▸Figure 5–14

Solution:

I = 16A Load

R of 12 AWG Stranded = 1.98Ω per 1,000 ft [Chapter 9, Table 8]

R = (1.98Ω per 1,000 ft/1,000 ft) × 300 ft (150 feet × two conductors)

R = 0.594Ω

Circuit Voltage Drop (E_{VD}) = I × R
E_{VD} = 16A × 0.594Ω
E_{VD} = 9.50V

Equipment Operating Voltage = Nominal Voltage—Circuit Voltage Drop
Equipment Operating Voltage = 120V–9.50V
Equipment Operating Voltage = 110.50

Answer: (a) 110.5V

▶ Ohm's Law Voltage Drop, Example 2

Question: What is the operating voltage of a 24A, 230V rated load wired with 10 AWG if it is located 200 ft from the power supply, and has a nominal circuit voltage of 240V? ▶Figure 5–15

(a) 228V   (b) 229V   (c) 230V   (d) 231V

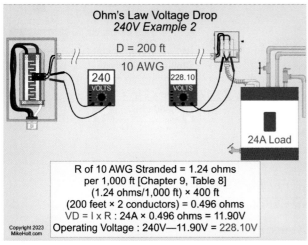

Ohm's Law Voltage Drop
240V Example 2

D = 200 ft
10 AWG

240 VOLTS   228.10 VOLTS

24A Load

R of 10 AWG Stranded = 1.24 ohms
per 1,000 ft [Chapter 9, Table 8]
(1.24 ohms/1,000 ft) × 400 ft
(200 feet × 2 conductors) = 0.496 ohms
VD = I x R : 24A × 0.496 ohms = 11.90V
Operating Voltage : 240V—11.90V = 228.10V

Copyright 2023
MikeHolt.com

▶Figure 5–15

Solution:

I = 24A Load

R of 10 AWG Stranded = 1.24Ω per 1,000 ft [Chapter 9, Table 8]

R = (1.24Ω per 1,000 ft/1,000 ft) × 400 ft (200 feet × two conductors)
R = 0.496Ω

Circuit Voltage Drop (E_{VD}) = I × R
E_{VD} = 24A × 0.496Ω
E_{VD} = 11.90V

Equipment Operating Voltage = Nominal Voltage—Circuit Voltage Drop
Equipment Operating Voltage = 240V–11.90V
Equipment Operating Voltage = 228.10V, round to 228V to match answer options

Answer: (a) 228V

5.5 Single-Phase Circuit Voltage Drop—Formula Method

The *NEC* [210.19 Note] recommends that branch-circuit conductors be sized to prevent a voltage drop of not more than 3 percent. In addition, it recommends that the total voltage drop on both feeders and branch circuits should not exceed 5 percent. ▶Figure 5–16

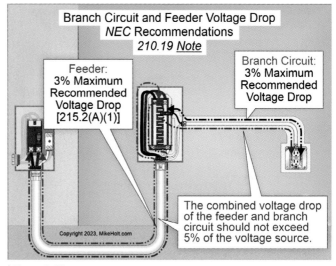

Branch Circuit and Feeder Voltage Drop
NEC Recommendations
210.19 Note

Feeder:
3% Maximum
Recommended
Voltage Drop
[215.2(A)(1)]

Branch Circuit:
3% Maximum
Recommended
Voltage Drop

The combined voltage drop
of the feeder and branch
circuit should not exceed
5% of the voltage source.

Copyright 2023, MikeHolt.com

▶Figure 5–16

The following formula can be used to determine conductor voltage drop for single-phase circuits:

VD = (2 × K × I × D)/Cmil

VD = Voltage Drop. The voltage-drop of the circuit.

2 = Two conductors.

K = Constant. One foot of 1 circular mill copper is 12.90 ohms and one foot of 1 circular mill aluminum is 21.20.

I = Amperes. The load in amperes is at 100 percent (not 125 percent for motors or continuous loads).

D = Distance. The distance of the load is from the power supply. Use the length of one of the wires to the load (not the length of the wire to the load and back) for this formula.

Cmil = Circular Mils. The circular mil area of the circuit conductor is listed in the *NEC* Chapter 9, Table 8.

▶ Voltage Drop—Single-Phase, Example 1

Question: A 16A, 120V, load is located 100 ft from a panelboard and wired with 12 AWG conductors. What is the approximate voltage drop of the branch-circuit conductors? ▶Figure 5–17

(a) 4.25V   *(b) 5.97V*   *(c) 6.32V*   *(d) 7.41V*

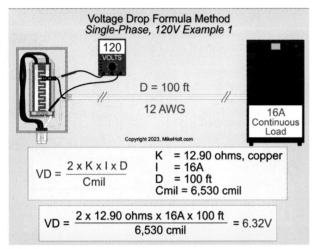

▶Figure 5–17

Solution:

VD = (2 × K × I × D)/Cmil

K = 12.90Ω

I = 16A

D = 100 ft

Cmil = 6,530 cmil [Chapter 9, Table 8]

VD = (2 × 12.90Ω × 16A × 100 ft)/6,530 cmil

VD = 41,280/6,530 cmil

VD = 6.32V

Answer: (c) 6.32V

▶ Voltage Drop—Single-Phase, Example 2

Question: A 24A, 240V, load is located 100 ft from a panelboard and wired with 10 AWG conductors. What is the approximate voltage drop of the branch-circuit conductors? ▶Figure 5–18

(a) 4.25V   *(b) 5.97V*   *(c) 6.32V*   *(d) 7.41V*

Solution:

VD = (2 × K × I × D)/Cmil

K = 12.90Ω

I = 24A

D = 100 ft

Cmil = 10,380 cmil [Chapter 9, Table 8]

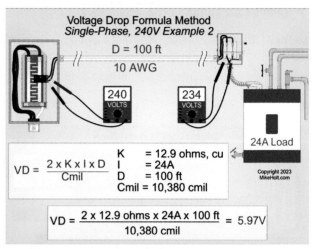

▶Figure 5–18

VD = (2 × 12.90Ω × 24A × 100 ft)/10,380 cmil

VD = 61,920/10,380 cmil

VD = 5.97V

Answer: (b) 5.97V

▶ Voltage Drop—Single-Phase, Example 3

Question: A 24A, 240V, load is located 100 ft from a panelboard and is wired with 8 AWG aluminum conductors. What is the approximate voltage drop of the branch-circuit conductors? ▶Figure 5–19

(a) 4.25V   *(b) 5.97V*   *(c) 6.16V*   *(d) 7.41V*

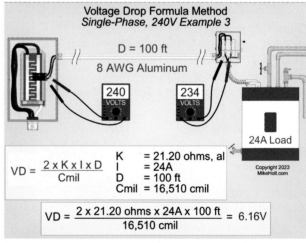

▶Figure 5–19

Solution:

VD = (2 × K × I × D)/Cmil

K = 21.20Ω (aluminum)

I = 24A

D = 100 ft

Cmil = 16,510 cmil [Chapter 9, Table 8]

VD = (2 × 21.20Ω × 24A × 100 ft)/16,510 cmil

VD = 101,760/16,510 cmil

VD = 6.16V

Answer: *(c) 6.16V*

5.6 Three-Phase Circuit Voltage Drop—Formula Method

The following formula can be used to determine conductor voltage drop for three-phase circuits:

Three-Phase: VD = (1.732 × K × I × D)/Cmil

VD = Voltage Drop. The voltage-drop of the circuit.

K = Direct-Current Constant. This constant "K" represents the dc resistance for a 1000 circular mils conductor that's 1000 ft long, at an operating temperature of 75°C. The constant K value is 12.90 ohms for copper and 21.20 ohms for aluminum.

I = Amperes. The load in amperes is at 100 percent (not 125 percent for motors or continuous loads).

D = Distance. The distance of the load is from the power supply. Use the length of one of the wires to the load (not the length of the wire to the load and back) for this formula.

Cmil = Circular Mils. The circular mil area of the circuit conductor as listed in the *NEC* Chapter 9, Table 8 since.

▶ Voltage Drop—Three-Phase, Example 1

Question: *What is the voltage drop of 3/0 AWG conductors that supply a 160A, 208V, three-phase load located 100 ft from the power supply?* ▶Figure 5–20

(a) 2.13V   (b) 3.15V   (c) 4.35V   (d) 5.37V

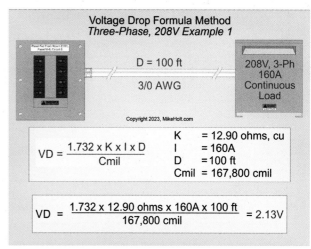

▶Figure 5–20

Solution:

VD = (1.732 × K × I × D)/Cmil

K = 12.90Ω

I = 160A

D = 100 ft

Cmil = 167,800 cmil [Chapter 9, Table 8]

VD = (1.732 × 12.90Ω × 160A × 100 ft)/167,800 cmil

VD = 357,484.80/167,800 cmil

VD = 2.13V

Answer: *(a) 2.13V*

▶ Voltage Drop—Three-Phase, Example 2

Question: What is the voltage drop of 4/0 AWG aluminum conductors that supply a 160A, 208V, three-phase load located 100 ft from the power supply? ▶Figure 5–21

(a) 2.78V   (b) 3.15V   (c) 4.35V   (d) 5.37V

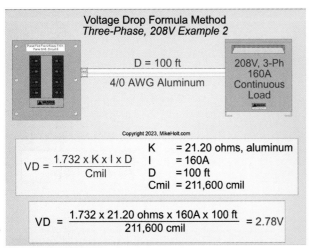

▶Figure 5–21

Solution:

VD = (1.732 × K × I × D)/Cmil

K = 21.20Ω (aluminum)

I = 160A

D = 100 ft

Cmil = 211,600 cmil [Chapter 9, Table 8]

VD = (1.732 × 21.20Ω × 160A × 100 ft)/211,600 cmil

VD = 587,494.40/211,600 cmil

VD = 2.78V

Answer: *(a) 2.78V*

5.7 Sizing Conductor Single-Phase Circuit Voltage Drop—Formula Method

The size of a conductor (its resistance) affects the voltage drop of the conductors. If a lower circuit voltage drop is desired, simply increase the cross-sectional area of the conductor (reduce its resistance).

To size a conductor for a single-phase circuit to accommodate voltage drop, use the following formula:

Cmil = (2 × K × I × D)/VD

Cmil = Circular Mils. The circular mil area of the circuit conductor as listed in the *NEC* Chapter 9, Table 8 since.

2 = Two conductors.

K = Constant. One foot of 1 circular mill copper is 12.90 ohms and one foot of 1 circular mill aluminum is 21.20.

I = Amperes. The load in amperes is at 100 percent (not 125 percent for motors or continuous loads).

D = Distance. The distance of the load is from the power supply. Use the length of one of the wires to the load (not the length of the wire to the load and back) for this formula.

VD = Voltage Drop. Three percent of the voltage source.

▶ Size Conductor Single-Phase, Example 1

Question: What size conductor should be used to limit the voltage drop to no more than three percent if the load of 16A at 120V is located 100 ft from the power supply? ▶Figure 5–22

(a) 12 AWG   (b) 8 AWG   (c) 6 AWG   (d) 4 AWG

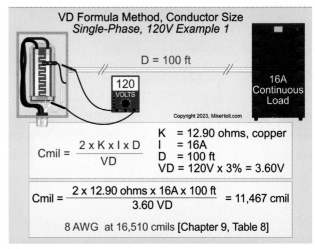

▶Figure 5–22

Solution:

Cmil = (2 × K × I × D)/VD

K = 12.90Ω

I = 16A, loads are always at 100%

D = 100 ft

VD = 120V × 3%

VD = 3.60V

Cmil = (2 × 12.90Ω × 16A × 100 ft)/3.60V

Cmil = 41,280/3.60V

Cmil = 11,466.67

Cmil = Use 8 AWG (16,410 cmil) [Chapter 9, Table 8]

Answer: *(b) 8 AWG*

► Size Conductor Single-Phase, Example 2

Question: *What size conductor should be used to limit the voltage drop to no more than three percent if the load of 24A at 240V is located 100 ft from the power supply?* ►**Figure 5–23**

(a) 12 AWG   (b) 10 AWG   (c) 6 AWG   (d) 4 AWG

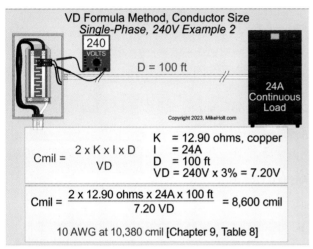

VD Formula Method, Conductor Size
Single-Phase, 240V Example 2

240 VOLTS

D = 100 ft

24A Continuous Load

Copyright 2023, MikeHolt.com

$$Cmil = \frac{2 \times K \times I \times D}{VD}$$

K = 12.90 ohms, copper
I = 24A
D = 100 ft
VD = 240V x 3% = 7.20V

$$Cmil = \frac{2 \times 12.90 \text{ ohms} \times 24A \times 100 \text{ ft}}{7.20 \text{ VD}} = 8,600 \text{ cmil}$$

10 AWG at 10,380 cmil [Chapter 9, Table 8]

►Figure 5–23

Solution:

Cmil = (2 × K × I × D)/VD

K = 12.90Ω

I = 24A, loads are always at 100%

D = 100 ft

VD = 240V × 3%

VD = 7.20V

Cmil = (2 × 12.90Ω × 24A × 100 ft)/7.20V

Cmil = 61,920I/7.20V

Cmil = 8,600

Cmil = Use 10 AWG (10,380 cmil) [Chapter 9, Table 8]

Answer: *(b) 10 AWG*

► Size Conductor Single-Phase, Example 3

Question: *What size aluminum conductor should be used to limit the voltage drop to no more than three percent if the load of 24A at 240V is located 100 ft from the power supply?* ►**Figure 5–24**

(a) 12 AWG   (b) 8 AWG   (c) 6 AWG   (d) 4 AWG

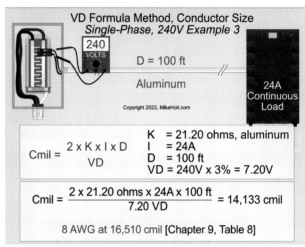

VD Formula Method, Conductor Size
Single-Phase, 240V Example 3

240 VOLTS

D = 100 ft

Aluminum

24A Continuous Load

Copyright 2023, MikeHolt.com

$$Cmil = \frac{2 \times K \times I \times D}{VD}$$

K = 21.20 ohms, aluminum
I = 24A
D = 100 ft
VD = 240V x 3% = 7.20V

$$Cmil = \frac{2 \times 21.20 \text{ ohms} \times 24A \times 100 \text{ ft}}{7.20 \text{ VD}} = 14,133 \text{ cmil}$$

8 AWG at 16,510 cmil [Chapter 9, Table 8]

►Figure 5–24

Solution:

Cmil = (2 × K × I × D)/VD

K = 21.20Ω (aluminum)

I = 24A

D = 100 ft

VD = 240V × 3%

VD = 7.20V

Cmil = (2 × 21.20Ω × 24A × 100 ft)/7.20V

Cmil = 101,760/7.20V

Cmil = 14,133.33

Cmil = Use 8 AWG (16,510 cmil) [Chapter 9, Table 8]

Answer: *(b) 8 AWG*

5.8 Sizing Conductor Three-Phase Circuit Voltage Drop—Formula Method

The size of a conductor (its resistance) affects the voltage drop of the conductors. If a lower circuit voltage drop is desired, simply increase the cross-sectional area of the conductor (reduce its resistance).

To size a conductor for a three-phase circuit to accommodate voltage drop, use the following formula:

Cmil = (1.732 × K × I × D)/VD

Cmil = Circular Mils. The circular mil area of the circuit conductor as listed in the *NEC* Chapter 9, Table 8 since.

K = Constant. One foot of 1 circular mill copper is 12.90 ohms and one foot of 1 circular mill aluminum is 21.20.

I = Amperes. The load in amperes is at 100 percent (not 125 percent for motors or continuous loads).

D = Distance. The distance of the load is from the power supply. Use the length of one of the wires to the load (not the length of the wire to the load and back) for this formula.

VD = Voltage Drop. Three percent of the voltage source.

▶ Size Conductor Three-Phase, Example 1

Question: What size conductor should be used to limit voltage drop from exceeding three percent if the equipment nameplate indicates a 160A continuous load at 208V, three-phase and it is located 100 ft from the power supply? ▶**Figure 5–25**

(a) 8 AWG   (b) 6 AWG   (c) 4 AWG   (d) 2 AWG

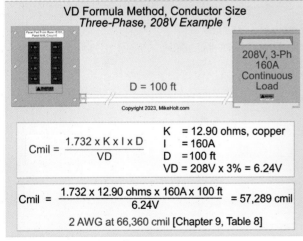

VD Formula Method, Conductor Size
Three-Phase, 208V Example 1

$$Cmil = \frac{1.732 \times K \times I \times D}{VD} \quad \begin{array}{l} K = 12.90 \text{ ohms, copper} \\ I = 160A \\ D = 100 \text{ ft} \\ VD = 208V \times 3\% = 6.24V \end{array}$$

$$Cmil = \frac{1.732 \times 12.90 \text{ ohms} \times 160A \times 100 \text{ ft}}{6.24V} = 57,289 \text{ cmil}$$

2 AWG at 66,360 cmil [Chapter 9, Table 8]

▶Figure 5–25

Solution:

Cmil = (1.732 × K × I × D)/VD

K = 12.90Ω

I = 160A

D = 100 ft

VD = 208V × 3%

VD = 6.240V

Cmil = (1.732 × 12.90Ω × 160A × 100 ft)/6.24V

Cmil = 357,484.80/6.24V

Cmil = 57,289.23

Cmil = Use 2 AWG (66,360 cmil) [Chapter 9, Table 8]

Note: Minimum circuit conductor to supply 160A continuous load (160A × 125% = 200A) would be 3/0 AWG rated 200A at 75°C [310.16].

Answer: (d) 2 AWG

▶ Size Conductor Three-Phase, Example 2

Question: What size aluminum compact conductor should be used to limit voltage drop from exceeding three percent if the equipment nameplate indicates a 160A continuous load at 208V, three-phase and it is located 100 ft from the power supply? ▶**Figure 5–26**

(a) 2 AWG   (b) 1/0 AWG   (c) 4/0 AWG   (d) 250 kcmil

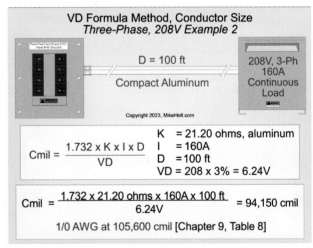

VD Formula Method, Conductor Size
Three-Phase, 208V Example 2

$$Cmil = \frac{1.732 \times K \times I \times D}{VD} \quad \begin{array}{l} K = 21.20 \text{ ohms, aluminum} \\ I = 160A \\ D = 100 \text{ ft} \\ VD = 208 \times 3\% = 6.24V \end{array}$$

$$Cmil = \frac{1.732 \times 21.20 \text{ ohms} \times 160A \times 100 \text{ ft}}{6.24V} = 94,150 \text{ cmil}$$

1/0 AWG at 105,600 cmil [Chapter 9, Table 8]

▶Figure 5–26

Solution:

Cmil = (1.732 × K × I × D)/VD

K = 21.20Ω (aluminum)

I = 160A

D = 100 ft

VD = 208V × 3%

VD = 6.240V

Cmil = (1.732 × 21.20Ω × 160A × 100 ft)/6.24V

Cmil = 587,494.40/6.24V

Cmil = 94,149.74

Cmil = Use 1/0 AWG (105,600 cmil) [Chapter 9, Table 8]

Note: *Minimum circuit conductor to supply 160A continuous load (160A × 125% = 200A) would be 3/0 AWG rated 200A at 75°C [310.16].*

Answer: *(b) 1/0 AWG*

Unit 5—Conclusion

This unit explained that voltage drop is at issue anytime there's current flow and resistance. Every conductor has resistance (opposition to the flow of electrons), which is determined by factors such as the conductor material, cross-sectional area, length, and operating temperature. Excessive voltage drop results in power losses and undervoltage for electrical equipment. Operating equipment at less than the recommended (or required) voltage range can cause irreparable damage, void a warranty, and/or create an electrical hazard.

In this unit, you learned how to correctly size conductors to stay within the requirements or recommendations for voltage drop. Variations of voltage-drop formulas were also reviewed so you will be able to apply the proper formula to use for specific circumstances.

If you're not yet fully comfortable with voltage-drop calculations and the formula variations as you answer the following questions, go back and review this unit carefully to increase your confidence in selecting and applying the correct formula. You'll see how each voltage-drop formula relates to Ohm's Law and that it can all be traced back to the basics!

UNIT
5

REVIEW QUESTIONS

Please use the 2023 *Code* book and this textbook to answer the following questions.

PART A—CONDUCTOR RESISTANCE CALCULATIONS

5.1 Conductor Cross-Sectional Area in Circular Mills [Chapter 9, Table 8]

1. The circular mil area of a 12 AWG conductor is ____.

    (a) 6,530 cmils
    (b) 10,380 cmils
    (c) 16,510 cmils
    (d) 26,240 cmils

2. The circular mil area of a 10 AWG conductor is ____.

    (a) 6,530 cmils
    (b) 10,380 cmils
    (c) 16,510 cmils
    (d) 26,240 cmils

3. The circular mil area of an 8 AWG conductor is ____.

    (a) 6,530 cmils
    (b) 10,380 cmils
    (c) 16,510 cmils
    (d) 26,240 cmils

4. The circular mil area of a 6 AWG conductor is ____.

    (a) 6,530 cmils
    (b) 10,380 cmils
    (c) 16,510 cmils
    (d) 26,240 cmils

5. What's the cross-sectional area in circular mils for a 4 AWG conductor?

    (a) 41,740 cmil
    (b) 43,360 cmil
    (c) 45,380 cmil
    (d) 47,510 cmil

6. What's the cross-sectional area in circular mils for a 2 AWG conductor?

    (a) 64,740 cmil
    (b) 66,360 cmil
    (c) 68,380 cmil
    (d) 70,690 cmil

7. What is the cross-sectional area in circular mils for a 1 AWG conductor?

    (a) 77,740 cmil
    (b) 79,360 cmil
    (c) 81,380 cmil
    (d) 83,690 cmil

8. What is the cross-sectional area in circular mils for a 1/0 AWG conductor?

    (a) 103,690 cmil
    (b) 105,600 cmil
    (c) 107,800 cmil
    (d) 111,600 cmil

9. What is the cross-sectional area in circular mils for a 3/0 AWG aluminum conductor?

   (a) 163,690 cmil
   (b) 165,600 cmil
   (c) 167,800 cmil
   (d) 169,600 cmil

5.2 Conductor Resistance

10. The resistance per 1,000 ft of 10 AWG solid conductor is approximately ____.

    (a) 0.2Ω
    (b) 0.5Ω
    (c) 0.8Ω
    (d) 1.2Ω

11. The resistance per 1,000 ft of 8 AWG conductor is approximately ____.

    (a) 0.2Ω
    (b) 0.5Ω
    (c) 0.8Ω
    (d) 1.2Ω

12. The resistance per 1,000 ft of 6 AWG conductor is approximately ____.

    (a) 0.2Ω
    (b) 0.5Ω
    (c) 0.8Ω
    (d) 1.2Ω

13. The resistance per 1,000 ft of 2 AWG conductor is approximately ____.

    (a) 0.2Ω
    (b) 0.5Ω
    (c) 0.8Ω
    (d) 1.2Ω

14. What is the resistance of 200 ft of 10 AWG solid?

    (a) 0.242Ω
    (b) 0.362Ω
    (c) 0.472Ω
    (d) 0.522Ω

15. What is the resistance of 400 ft of 6 AWG?

    (a) 0.1964Ω
    (b) 0.2163Ω
    (c) 0.2341Ω
    (d) 0.2531Ω

16. What is the resistance of 600 ft of 4 AWG?

    (a) 0.1848Ω
    (b) 0.1937Ω
    (c) 0.2126Ω
    (d) 0.2536Ω

17. What's the resistance of 500 ft of 3 AWG aluminum?

    (a) 0.0231Ω
    (b) 0.1614Ω
    (c) 0.2015Ω
    (d) 0.2330Ω

18. What is the resistance of 100 ft of 1 AWG?

    (a) 0.0154Ω
    (b) 0.1620Ω
    (c) 0.2330Ω
    (d) 0.5610Ω

19. What is the resistance of 400 ft of 1 AWG aluminum?

    (a) 0.0908Ω
    (b) 0.1012Ω
    (c) 0.1423Ω
    (d) 0.1564Ω

20. What is the resistance of 400 ft of 1/0 AWG?

    (a) 0.0488Ω
    (b) 0.0513Ω
    (c) 0.0612Ω
    (d) 0.0738Ω

21. What is the resistance of 800 ft of 1/0 AWG aluminum?

    (a) 0.1588Ω
    (b) 0.1608Ω
    (c) 0.1723Ω
    (d) 0.1856Ω

PART B—VOLTAGE-DROP CALCULATIONS

5.4 Circuit Conductors' Voltage Drop—Ohm's Law Method

22. What is the conductor voltage drop for a 10A continuous load using 12 AWG stranded wire located 100 ft from the power supply?

    (a) 3V
    (b) 4V
    (c) 5V
    (d) 6V

23. What's the conductor voltage drop for a 12A continuous load using 12 AWG stranded wire located 100 ft from the power supply?

    (a) 4.20V
    (b) 4.40V
    (c) 4.75V
    (d) 4.85V

24. What's the conductor voltage drop for a 20A load using 10 AWG stranded wire located 100 ft from the panelboard.

    (a) 4V
    (b) 5V
    (c) 6V
    (d) 7V

5.5 Single-Phase Circuit Voltage Drop—Formula Method

25. What is the voltage drop of 14 AWG supplying a 6A load located 100 ft from the panel?

    (a) 3.77V
    (b) 5.59V
    (c) 5.63V
    (d) 5.66V

26. What is the voltage drop of 10 AWG aluminum supplying a 16A load located 100 ft from the panel?

    (a) 6.54V
    (b) 6.59V
    (c) 6.63V
    (d) 6.66V

27. What is the voltage drop of 10 AWG supplying a 24A load located 100 ft from the panel?

    (a) 5.58V
    (b) 5.69V
    (c) 5763V
    (d) 5.97V

28. What is the voltage drop of 8 AWG supplying a 24A load located 150 ft from the panel?

    (a) 5.55V
    (b) 5.59V
    (c) 5.63V
    (d) 5.66V

29. What is the voltage drop of 6 AWG aluminum supplying a 35A load located 100 ft from the panel?

    (a) 5.55V
    (b) 5.59V
    (c) 5.61V
    (d) 5.66V

30. What's the voltage drop of 10 AWG supplying an 18A motor load located 125 ft from the panel?

    (a) 5.41V
    (b) 5.59V
    (c) 5.63V
    (d) 5.66V

5.6 Three-Phase Circuit Voltage Drop—Formula Method

31. What is the voltage drop of a 16A, 208V, three-phase load located 252 ft from the service using 10 AWG conductors?

    (a) 7.20V
    (b) 7.25V
    (c) 7.90V
    (d) 8.70V

32. What is the voltage drop of a 26A, 208V, three-phase load located 200 ft from the panel, if wired with 8 AWG?

    (a) 5V
    (b) 6V
    (c) 7V
    (d) 8V

33. What is the voltage drop of a 30A, 208V three-phase load located 125 ft from the panel, if wired with 6 AWG aluminum?

    (a) 5.05V
    (b) 5.15V
    (c) 5.25V
    (d) 5.70V

34. What is the voltage drop of a 100A, 208V, three-phase load located 100 ft from the service using 2 AWG conductors?

    (a) 3.37V
    (b) 3.45V
    (c) 3.54V
    (d) 3.60V

35. What is the voltage drop of a 150A, 208V, three-phase load located 150 ft from the service using 250 kcmil compact aluminum conductors?

    (a) 3.30V
    (b) 3.55V
    (c) 3.64V
    (d) 3.70V

5.7 Sizing Conductor Single-Phase Circuit Voltage Drop—Formula Method

36. What size wire is required for a 16A, 120V load located 100 ft from the panel?

    (a) 10 AWG
    (b) 8 AWG
    (c) 6 AWG
    (d) 4 AWG

37. What size aluminum wire is required for a 50A/240V load located 200 ft from the panel?

    (a) 6 AWG
    (b) 4 AWG
    (c) 3 AWG
    (d) 2 AWG

38. What size wire is required for a 5 hp, 240V motor located 125 ft from a panelboard?

    (a) 10 AWG
    (b) 8 AWG
    (c) 6 AWG
    (d) 4 AWG

5.8 Sizing Conductor Three-Phase Circuit Voltage Drop—Formula Method

39. What size wire is required for a 18A, 480V three-phase continuous located 300 ft from a panelboard?

    (a) 12 AWG
    (b) 10 AWG
    (c) 8 AWG
    (d) 6 AWG

40. What size wire is required for a 28A, 480V, three-phase continuous located 300 ft from a panelboard?

    (a) 10 AWG
    (b) 8 AWG
    (c) 6 AWG
    (d) 4 AWG

DWELLING UNIT CALCULATIONS

Introduction to Unit 6—Dwelling Unit Calculations

Sizing the service load for a dwelling unit is not simply a matter of adding up the individual loads or the rated current for all the breaker sizes. The *Code* recognizes there's load diversity and that not all loads will be in use simultaneously. Therefore, it provides various "demand factors" which are to be applied to calculate the "demand load."

The *Code* provides two different load calculation methods—optional and standard; both methods are explained in this unit. Be sure to review the material as many times as needed, paying attention to the examples given, and completing the questions at the end of this unit to further solidify your understanding of these *NEC* requirements.

The following are the Parts covered in this unit:

▶ Part A—Optional Method Load Calculations

▶ Part B—Standard Method Load Calculations

▶ Part C—Neutral Load Calculations

Unit 6 focuses on sizing the service load for a dwelling unit. The *NEC* defines a dwelling unit as a space that provides living facilities with permanent provisions for living, sleeping, cooking and sanitation. ▶Figure 6–1

Dwelling Unit
Article 100 Definition

A unit that contains permanent provisions for living, sleeping, cooking, and sanitation.

▶Figure 6–1

Part A—Optional Method Load Calculations [Article 220, Part IV]

Introduction

Part A covers calculating the service demand load using the optional method contained in Article 220, Part IV. The optional method can only be used for dwelling units served by a single 120/240V or 208Y/120V, 3-wire set of service or feeder conductors with an ampacity of 100A or larger [220.82(A)]. The total service demand load is determined by a combination of 220.82(B) and 220.82(C).

6.1 Dwelling Unit Optional Load Calculations [220.82]

The following steps can be used to determine the demand load on the service conductors for a dwelling unit using the optional method contained in Article 220, Part IV.

Step 1: Determine the total connected load, less air-conditioning and heating [220.82(B)].

The first step is to determine the total connected load for the general lighting and general-use receptacles, small-appliance circuits, laundry circuit, fixed appliances, and motors; except air-conditioning and electric heating as follows: ▶Figure 6–2

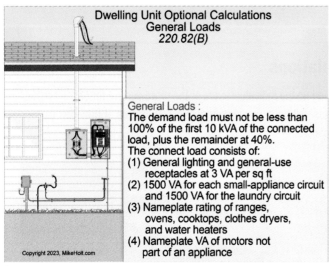

**Dwelling Unit Optional Calculations
General Loads
220.82(B)**

General Loads :
The demand load must not be less than 100% of the first 10 kVA of the connected load, plus the remainder at 40%.
The connect load consists of:
(1) General lighting and general-use receptacles at 3 VA per sq ft
(2) 1500 VA for each small-appliance circuit and 1500 VA for the laundry circuit
(3) Nameplate rating of ranges, ovens, cooktops, clothes dryers, and water heaters
(4) Nameplate VA of motors not part of an appliance

Copyright 2023, MikeHolt.com

▶Figure 6–2

(1) General Lighting. The total connected load must include a 3 VA per sq ft load for general lighting and general-use receptacles. The total square feet are based on the outside dimensions of the dwelling unit, but does not include open porches, garages, or unused or unfinished spaces not adaptable for future use.

(2) Small-Appliance and Laundry Circuits. Two 20A, 120V small-appliance circuits, and one 20A, 120V circuit for the laundry area [210.11(C)(1) and 210.11(C)(2)] are required for each dwelling unit. The load for each of these circuits is based on 1500 VA.

Where a dwelling unit is in a multifamily building that includes laundry facilities for the use of all building occupants, a laundry circuit is not required in each dwelling unit [210.52(F) Ex].

(3) Fixed Appliances. The nameplate VA rating of appliances fastened in place, permanently connected, or located to be on a specific circuit such as dishwashers, waste disposals, microwaves, trash compactors, and water heaters. In addition, the load ratings for dryers, cooking equipment, and special-purpose circuits for ironing stations, elevators, electric vehicle chargers, RVs, welders, and so forth must all be included.

(4) Motor VA. The VA nameplate rating of motors not part of an appliance used for irrigation, boat lifts, wells, and so on must be included at 100%.

Step 2: Determine the demand load for the Step 1 loads [220.82(B)].

Step 2 is to determine the demand load for the loads contained in Step 1. This is accomplished by applying a 100 percent demand load to the first 10 kVA of the total connected load, then a 40 percent demand to the remainder of the total connected load.

Step 3: Determine the air-conditioning versus heating demand load [220.82(C)].

Next, determine the largest of the following loads and add it to the demand load value determined in Step 2. ▶Figure 6–3

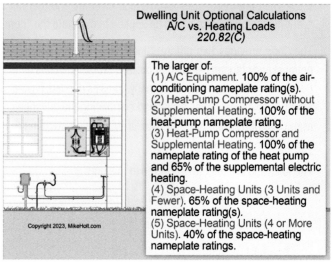

**Dwelling Unit Optional Calculations
A/C vs. Heating Loads
220.82(C)**

The larger of:
(1) A/C Equipment. 100% of the air-conditioning nameplate rating(s).
(2) Heat-Pump Compressor without Supplemental Heating. 100% of the heat-pump nameplate rating.
(3) Heat-Pump Compressor and Supplemental Heating. 100% of the nameplate rating of the heat pump and 65% of the supplemental electric heating.
(4) Space-Heating Units (3 Units and Fewer). 65% of the space-heating nameplate rating(s).
(5) Space-Heating Units (4 or More Units). 40% of the space-heating nameplate ratings.

Copyright 2023, MikeHolt.com

▶Figure 6–3

(1) Air-Conditioning. 100 percent of the air-conditioning nameplate rating.

(2) Heat-Pump Compressor without Supplemental Heating. 100 percent of the heat-pump nameplate rating.

(3) Heat-Pump Compressor and Supplemental Heating. 100 percent of the nameplate rating of the heat pump and 65 percent of the supplemental electric heat rating.

(4) Space-Heating, Three Units and Less. 65 percent of the space-electric heating nameplate rating.

(5) Space-Heating, Four or More Units. 40 percent of the space-electric heating nameplate rating.

Step 4: Determine the service disconnect and conductor sizing.

The last step is to determine the total service demand load in amperes for the dwelling unit by adding the values of Step 2 and Step 3 together, then dividing the sum by the nominal voltage (208V or 240V). Once the service demand load in amperes is known, the service disconnect can be sized in accordance with the standard size overcurrent protective device contained in 240.6(A).

Dwelling unit service conductors supplied by a 120/240V systems can be sized in accordance with 310.12(A) for service conductors.

6.2 Dwelling Unit Optional Load Calculation [220.82]

▶ Dwelling Unit Optional Load Calculation [220.82], Example

Question: What size aluminum service conductors are required for a 6,000 sq ft dwelling unit containing the following loads? ▶Figure 6–4

- Dishwasher, 12A at 120V
- Disposal (Waste), 10A at 120V
- Trash Compactor, 8A at 120V
- Water Heater, 4,500W at 240V
- Microwave, 16A at 120V
- Vent Fan ½ hp at 120V
- Dryer, 4,000W at 120/240V
- Range, 14,000W at 120/240V
- A/C Condenser, 30A at 240V
- Electric Heating, 9.6 kW

(a) 1/0 AWG   (b) 2/0 AWG   (c) 3/0 AWG   (d) 4/0 AWG

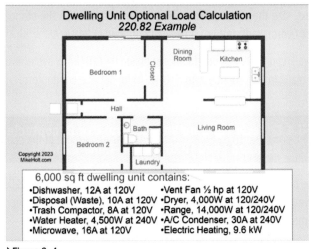

▶Figure 6–4

Solution:

Step 1: Determine the total connected load, less air-conditioning and electric heating [220.82(B)].

General Lighting	6,000 sq ft × 3 VA	18,000 VA
Small-Appliance Circuits	1,500 VA × 2 circuits	3,000 VA
Laundry Circuit		1,500 VA

Fixed Appliances and Equipment:

Dishwasher	120V × 12A	1,440 VA
Disposal (Waste)	120 × 10A	1,200 VA
Trash Compactor	120V × 8A	960 VA
Water Heater	4,500W	4,500 W
Microwave	120V × 16A	1,920 VA
Vent Fan ½ hp	120V × 9.8A	1,176 VA
Dryer	4,000W	5,000 W
Cooking, Range	14,000 W	+14,000 W
Total Connected Load		52,696 VA

Step 2: Determine the demand load for Step 1 loads [220.82(B)].

Connected Load	52,696 VA	
First 10 kW at 100%	−10,000 VA × 100%	10,000 VA
Remainder at 40%	42,696 VA × 40%	+ 17,078 VA
Demand Load		27,078 VA

Step 3: Determine the air-conditioning versus electric heating demand load [220.82(C)]; air-conditioning at 100 percent [220.82(C)(1)] versus electric heating at 65 percent [220.82(C)(4)].

Air-Conditioning = Volts × Amperes
A/C Condenser = 240V × 30A
A/C Condenser = 7,200 VA

Electric Heating at 65%:
Electric Heating Zone = 9,600 W

Space Heating Demand Load = 9,600W × 65%
Space Heating Demand Load = 6,240W, omit since it is smaller
  a/c 220.60

Step 4: Determine the service disconnect and conductor sizing.

Step 1. Demand Load	27,078 VA
Step 2. Air-Conditioning Load	+7,200 VA
Total Demand Load	34,278 VA

Service Size in Amperes = VA Demand Load/System Volts
Service Size in Amperes = 34,278 VA/240V
Service Size in Amperes = 143A
Service Disconnect Size = 150A

2/0 AWG aluminum [Table 310.12(A)]

Answer: (b) 2/0 AWG

Part B—Standard Method Load Calculations [Article 220, Part III]

Introduction

Part B covers calculating the service demand load using the standard method contained in Article 220, Part III. It is important to be familiar with the requirements of Article 220 so the proper demand factors are correctly applied. To keep your calculations organized and more importantly accurate, the standard calculation method should be worked in the following order:

▸ Step 1: General Lighting Load

▸ Step 2: Appliances

▸ Step 3: Clothes Dryers

▸ Step 4: Cooking Equipment

▸ Step 5: Air-Conditioning versus Heating

▸ Step 6: Service Size

6.3 Dwelling Unit Standard Load Calculation

The following steps can be used to determine the demand load on the service conductors for a dwelling unit using the standard method contained in Article 220, Part III.

Step 1: Determine the load for general lighting and general-use receptacles, and the small-appliance and laundry circuits [220.41 and Table 220.45].

The first step is to determine the total connected load for the general lighting and general-use receptacles, small-appliance circuits, laundry circuit, and fixed appliances as follows:

(1) General Lighting. The total connected load must include a 3 VA per sq ft load for general lighting and general-use receptacles. The total square feet are based on the outside dimensions of the dwelling unit, but does not include open porches or unused or unfinished spaces not adaptable for future use.

(2) Small-Appliance and Laundry Circuits. Two 20A, 120V small-appliance circuits and one 20A, 120V circuit for the laundry area [210.11(C)(1) and 210.11(C)(2)] are required for each dwelling unit. The load for each of these circuits is based on 1500 VA.

Step 2: Determine the appliance demand load [220.53].

Appliances include disposals (waste), dishwashers, trash compactors, water heaters, and so forth. The demand load is determined by applying a 75 percent demand factor to the nameplate rating when there are four or more appliances. There's no demand factor applied to appliances when there are three or less.

Step 3: Determine the clothes dryer demand load [220.54].

When a dryer is to be installed, the greater of the nameplate rating or 5000W must be used.

Step 4: Determine the electric cooking equipment demand load [220.55].

The demand load for electric cooking equipment is determined in accordance with 220.55.

Step 5: Determine the air-conditioning versus heating demand load [220.60].

Select the larger of 125 percent of the air-conditioning load plus 100 percent for the other air-conditioning loads [220.50] and compare it to 100 percent of the electric heating load [220.51] if they're not both likely to be on at the same time.

Step 6: Determine the service disconnect and conductor sizing [310.12(A)].

First, add up the demand loads for the general lighting, small-appliance circuits, fixed appliances, dryers, cooking equipment, other loads, air-conditioning, heat, and motor loads, and then divide the total by the nominal system voltage.

Next, size the service disconnect in accordance with the standard size overcurrent protective device contained in 240.6(A).

Dwelling unit service conductors supplied by 120/240V systems can be sized in accordance with 310.12(A) for service conductors.

6.4 General Lighting and General-Use Receptacle Demand Load [220.41 and Table 220.45]

Due to "load diversity," the *Code* permits the application of Table 220.45 demand factors to the total connected load. To determine the feeder demand load for these circuits, use the following steps:

Step 1: Determine the total connected load for the following [220.41]:

(1) General lighting and general-use receptacles at 3 VA per sq ft. ▶Figure 6–5

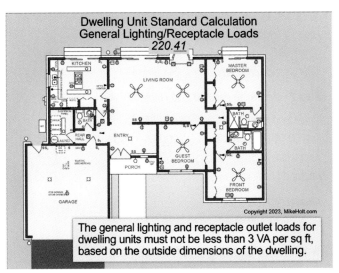

▶Figure 6–5

The dimensions for determining the area are based on the outside dimensions of the building and do not include open porches or spaces not adaptable for future use [220.5(C)]. ▶Figure 6–6

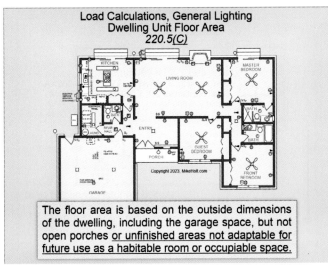

▶Figure 6–6

(2) Two small-appliance circuits each at 1500 VA [210.11(C)(1), 210.52(B), and 220.52(A)].

(3) One laundry circuit at 1500 VA [210.11(C)(2) and 210.52(F), and 220.52(B)]. ▶Figure 6–7

Step 2: Determine the general lighting and general-use demand load by applying the Table 220.45 demand factors to the total connected load (from Step 1) by the following factors:

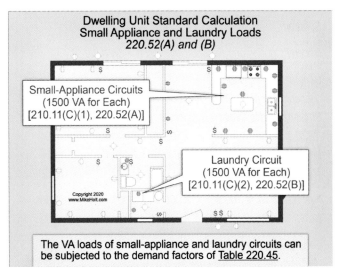

▶Figure 6–7

(1) First 3000 VA of Step 1 at a 100 percent demand factor.

(2) The remaining VA of Step 1 at a 35 percent demand factor.

▶ General Lighting Load, Example 1

Question: What is the general lighting and general-use receptacle, small-appliance, and laundry circuit demand load for a 40 ft × 50 ft dwelling unit? ▶Figure 6–8

(a) 4,500 VA   (b) 5,625 VA   (c) 5,825 VA   (d) 6,225 VA

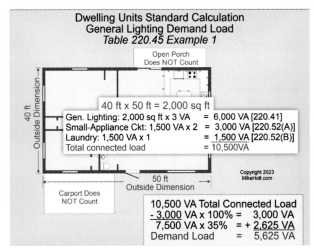

▶Figure 6–8

• • •

Solution:

General Lighting and Receptacles = 40 ft × 50 ft

General Lighting and Receptacles [220.41]	*2,000 sq ft × 3 VA per sq ft*	*6,000 VA*
Small-Appliance Circuit [220.52(A)]	*1,500 VA × 2 circuits*	*3,000 VA*
Laundry Circuit [220.52(B)]	*1,500 VA × 1 circuit*	*+1,500 VA*
Total General Lighting		*10,500 VA*
First 3,000 VA at 100%	*3,000 VA × 100%*	*3,000 VA*
Next 117,000* VA at 35%	*7,500 VA × 35%*	*+2,625 VA*
General Lighting and General-Use Receptacles Calculated Load =		*5,625 VA*

*Note: Remember to subtract 3,000 VA from 120,000 VA when using Table 220.45 since the 35 percent only applies to the 3,001 VA to 120,000 VA range.

Answer: (b) 5,625 VA

▶ General Lighting Load, Example 2

Question: What is the general lighting and general-use receptacle, small-appliance, and laundry circuit demand load for a 4,000 sq ft dwelling unit? ▶*Figure 6–9*

(a) 2,700 VA   (b) 8,100 VA   (c) 7,725 VA   (d) 12,600 VA

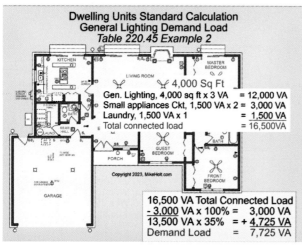

▶Figure 6–9

Solution:

Step 1: *Determine the general lighting, general-use receptacles, small-appliance, and laundry circuit connected load [220.41].*

General Lighting	*4,000 sq ft × 3 VA =*	*12,000 VA*
Small-Appliance Circuits [210.52(B)]	*1,500 VA × 2 =*	*3,000 VA*
Laundry Circuit [210.52(F)]	*1,500 VA × 1 =*	*+1,500 VA*
Total Connected Load		*16,500 VA*

Step 2: *Determine demand load [Table 220.42].*

Total Connected Load	*16,500 VA*	
First 3,000 VA at 100%	*−3,000 VA × 100%*	*3,000 VA*
Remainder at 35%	*13,500 VA × 35%*	*+4,725 VA*
Demand Load		*7,725 VA*

Answer: (c) 7,725 VA

▶ General Lighting Load, Example 3

Question: What is the general lighting and general-use receptacle, small-appliance, and laundry circuit demand load for a 6,000 sq ft dwelling unit? ▶*Figure 6–10*

(a) 2,700 VA   (b) 5,625 VA   (c) 8,100 VA   (d) 9,825 VA

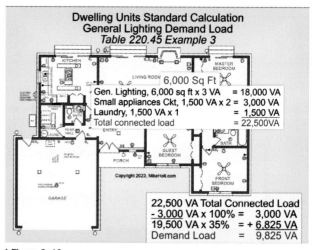

▶Figure 6–10

Solution:

Step 1: *Determine the general lighting, general-use receptacles, small-appliance, and laundry circuit connected load [220.41].*

General Lighting	*6,000 sq ft × 3 VA*	*18,000 VA*
Small-Appliance Circuits [210.52(B)]	*1,500 VA × 2*	*3,000 VA*
Laundry Circuit [210.52(F)]	*1,500 VA × 1*	*+1,500 VA*
Total Connected Load		*22,500 VA*

Step 2: *Determine demand load [Table 220.42].*

Total Connected Load	22,500 VA	
First 3,000 VA at 100%	–3,000 VA × 100% =	3,000 VA
Remainder at 35%	19,500 VA × 35% =	+6,825 VA
Demand Load		9,825 VA

Answer: *(d) 9,825 VA*

6.5 Fixed Appliance Demand Load [220.53]

Fixed appliances include waste disposals, dishwashers, trash compactors and so forth. The demand load is determined by adding the nameplate ratings of the appliances together and applying a 75 percent demand factor when there are four or more appliances. There is no demand factor applied to fixed appliances when there are three or less. ▶Figure 6–11

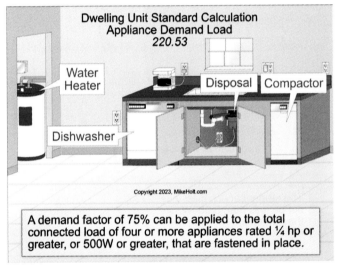

A demand factor of 75% can be applied to the total connected load of four or more appliances rated ¼ hp or greater, or 500W or greater, that are fastened in place.

▶Figure 6–11

Heating and air-conditioning equipment, cooking appliances, clothes dryers, motors, and other loads are not considered fixed appliances for the purposes of the 75 percent demand factor contained in 220.53.

▶ Fixed Appliance Demand Load, Example 1

Question: *What's the service demand load for a dishwasher (1,500 VA), Disposal (Waste) (1,000 VA), and a water heater (4,500 W)?* ▶Figure 6–12

(a) 5,000 VA   (b) 6,000 VA   (c) 7,000 VA   (d) 8,000 VA

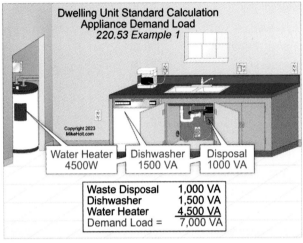

▶Figure 6–12

Solution:

Dishwasher	1,500 VA
Disposal (Waste)	1,000 VA
Water Heater	+4,500 W
Demand Load	7,000 VA

The demand factor of 75% does not apply since there are only three fixed appliances.

Answer: *(c) 7,000 VA*

▶ Fixed Appliance Demand Load, Example 2

Question: *What's the service demand load for a dishwasher (1,200 VA), Disposal (Waste) (900 VA), a water heater (4,500 W) and a microwave (1,500 VA)?* ▶Figure 6–13

(a) 3,015 VA   (b) 4,020 VA   (c) 6,075 VA   (d) 8,363 VA

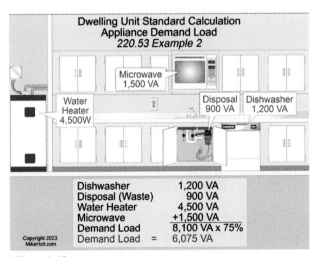

▶Figure 6–13

Solution:

Dishwasher	1,200 VA
Disposal (Waste)	900 VA
Water Heater	4,500 VA
Microwave	+1,500 VA
Demand Load	8,100 VA

Demand Load = 8,100 VA × 75%

Demand Load = 6,075 VA

Answer: *(c) 6,075 VA*

6.6 Dryer Demand Load [220.54]

When a dryer is to be installed, the larger of the nameplate rating or 5000W must be used. ▶Figure 6–14

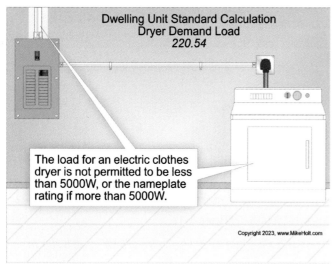

▶Figure 6–14

▶ Dryer Demand Load, Example 1

Question: *What is the service demand load for a 5.50 kW clothes dryer?* ▶Figure 6–15

(a) 5.50 kW   (b) 5.60 kW   (c) 5.70 kW   (d) 5.80 kW

Answer: *(a) 5.50 kW*

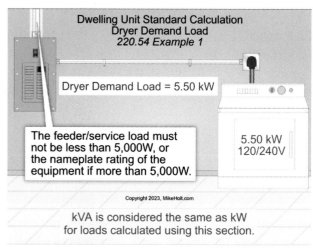

▶Figure 6–15

▶ Dryer Demand Load, Example 2

Question: *What is the service demand load for a 4.50 kW clothes dryer?* ▶Figure 6–16

(a) 4.50 kW   (b) 5 kW   (c) 5.70 kW   (d) 5.80 kW

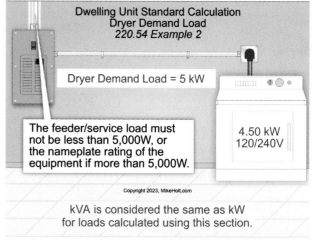

▶Figure 6–16

Answer: *(b) 5 kW*

6.8 Electric Cooking Equipment Demand Load [220.55]

The demand load for electric cooking equipment is determined in accordance with 220.55 and Table 220.55, including Table Notes.

▶ **Table 220.55 Column C—Over 8¾ kW to 12 kW, Example**

Question: *What is the service demand load for one 12 kW range?*
▶Figure 6–17

(a) 6 kW *(b) 8 kW* *(c) 10 kW* *(d) 12 kW*

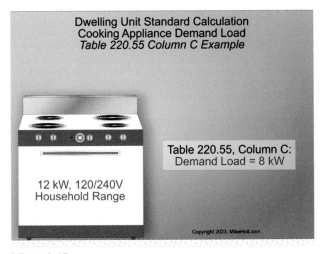

▶Figure 6–17

Solution:

Column C Calculated Load = 8 kW

Answer: *(b) 8 kW [Table 220.55, Column C]*

▶ **Table 220.55 Column C Note 1 —Over 12 kW, Example**

Question: *What is the service demand load for one 14 kW range?*
▶Figure 6–18

(a) 6.6 kW *(b) 8.8 kW* *(c) 11 kW* *(d) 12 kW*

Step 1: *Determine the Table 220.55, Column C demand load for one 14 kW range.*

Step 2: *Because the range is 14 kW, it exceeds 12 kW by 2 kW. Column C demand load must be increased by 5 percent for each kW or major fraction of a kW that exceeds 12 kW.*

Step 3: *Increase the Column C: 8 kW by 10 percent.*

8 kW × 110% = 8.8 kW

Answer: *(b) 8.8 kW [Table 220.55 Note 1]*

For ranges rated more than 12 kW, the maximum demand in Column C must be increased 5 percent for each additional kilowatt of rating, or major fraction thereof, by which the rating of individual ranges exceeds 12 kW.

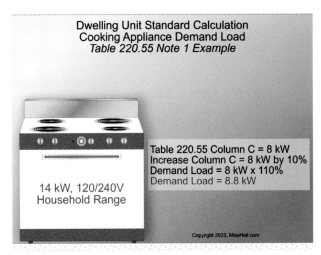

▶Figure 6–18

▶ **Table 220.55 Note 4, Example**

Question: *What is the load for branch circuit conductor sizing for a 12 kW range?* ▶Figure 6–19

(a) 6 kW *(b) 8 kW* *(c) 10 kW* *(d) 12 kW*

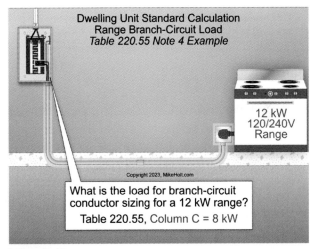

▶Figure 6–19

Solution:

Column C Calculated Load = 8 kW

Branch-Circuit Load in Amperes = I = P/E

P = 8,000W

Answer: *(b) 8 kW*

Table 220.55 Note 5. The branch-circuit load for one wall-mounted oven or one counter-mounted cooking unit must not be less than the nameplate rating (100 percent) of the appliance.

▶ Table 220.55 Note 5, Example

Question: What is the branch circuit load for a 6 kW wall-mounted oven? ▶Figure 6–20

(a) 4 kW   *(b) 4.5 kW*   *(c) 5 kW*   *(d) 6 kW*

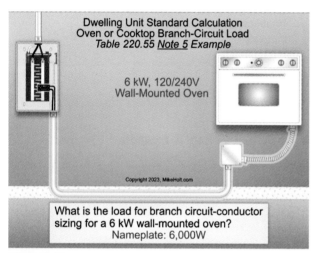

Dwelling Unit Standard Calculation
Oven or Cooktop Branch-Circuit Load
Table 220.55 *Note 5* Example

6 kW, 120/240V
Wall-Mounted Oven

Copyright 2023, MikeHolt.com

What is the load for branch circuit-conductor sizing for a 6 kW wall-mounted oven?
Nameplate: 6,000W

▶Figure 6–20

Answer: (d) 6 kW

Table 220.55 Note 6. The branch-circuit load for one counter-mounted cooking unit and up to two wall-mounted ovens is determined by adding the nameplate ratings together and treating that value as a single range to determine the load in accordance with Table 220.55 and Notes.

▶ Table 220.55 Note 6, Example

Question: What is the branch circuit load for a 6 kW counter-mounted cooking unit and two 3 kW wall-mounted ovens connected on a circuit? ▶Figure 6–21

(a) 6 kW   *(b) 8 kW*   *(c) 10 kW*   *(d) 12 kW*

Solution:

Step 1: Determine the total connected load.

Total Connected Load = 6 kW + 3 kW + 3 kW
Total Connected Load = 12 kW

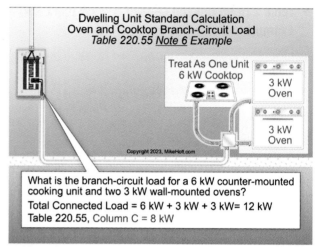

Dwelling Unit Standard Calculation
Oven and Cooktop Branch-Circuit Load
Table 220.55 *Note 6* Example

Treat As One Unit
6 kW Cooktop

3 kW Oven

3 kW Oven

Copyright 2023, MikeHolt.com

What is the branch-circuit load for a 6 kW counter-mounted cooking unit and two 3 kW wall-mounted ovens?
Total Connected Load = 6 kW + 3 kW + 3 kW= 12 kW
Table 220.55, Column C = 8 kW

▶Figure 6–21

Step 2: Determine the calculated kW load as a single 12 kW range.

Table 220.55, Column C = 8 kW

Answer: (b) 8 kW

6.10 Electric Vehicle [220.57]

The electric vehicle supply equipment is calculated at the larger of 7200 watts/VA or the nameplate rating of the equipment. ▶Figure 6–22

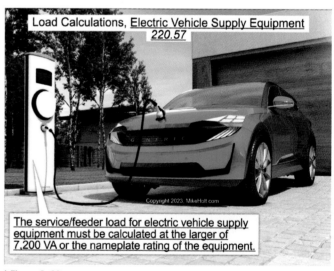

Load Calculations, Electric Vehicle Supply Equipment
220.57

Copyright 2023, MikeHolt.com

The service/feeder load for electric vehicle supply equipment must be calculated at the larger of 7,200 VA or the nameplate rating of the equipment.

▶Figure 6–22

6.11 Air-Conditioning Versus Heating [220.50, 220.51, and 220.60]

Air-Conditioning Loads [220.50(B)]

Conductors supplying air-conditioning equipment must have an ampacity of not less than 125 percent of the largest air-conditioning load [440.33].

Fixed Electric Space-Heating Load [220.51]

The load for fixed electric space-heating equipment must be calculated at 100 percent of the total connected load.

Noncoincident Loads [220.60]

Select the larger of 125 percent of the air-conditioning load (if it is the largest motor-type load in the dwelling unit) plus 100 percent for the other air-conditioning loads [220.50] and compare it to 100 percent of the electric heating load [220.51] if they are not both likely to be on at the same time [220.60].

▶ Air-Conditioning versus Heating, Example 1

Question: What is the demand load for a 16.70A, 240V air-conditioning unit and a 6 kW, 240V electric space heater? ▶Figure 6–23

(a) 5 kW   (b) 6 kW   (c) 11 kW   (d) 15 kW

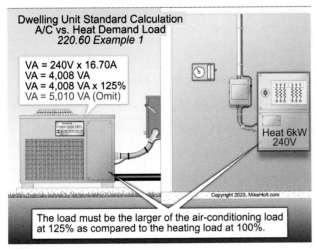

▶Figure 6–23

Solution:

Step 1: *Determine the air-conditioning load at 125 percent in accordance with 220.50(B).*

Air-Conditioning VA Load = 240V × 16.70A
Air-Conditioning VA Load = 4,008 VA
Air-Conditioning VA Load = 4,008 VA × 125%
Air-Conditioning VA Load = 5,010 VA

Step 2: *Determine the electric space-heating load at 100 percent in accordance with 220.51.*

Electric Space-Heating Load = 6,000W

Step 3: *Determine the larger of air-conditioning load at 125 percent as compared to the electric space-heating load at 100 percent in accordance with 220.60.*

Electric Space-Heating Load = 6,000 W

Answer: (b) 6 kW

▶ Air-Conditioning versus Heating, Example 2

Question: What is the service demand load for a dwelling unit with an air conditioner rated 30A at 240V versus electric heating of 9.6 kW. ▶Figure 6–24

(a) 7.6 kVA   (b) 9.6 kW   (c) 11.6 kVA   (d) 13.6 kVA

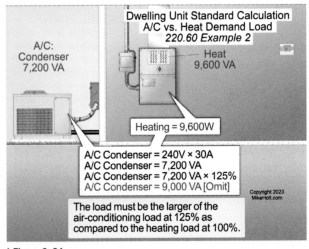

▶Figure 6–24

Solution:

Air-Conditioning = Volts × Amperes
A/C Condenser = 240V × 30A
A/C Condenser = 7,200 VA
A/C Condenser = 7,200 VA × 125%
A/C Condenser = 9,000 VA, omit [220.60]

Heating = 9,600W

Answer: (b) 9.6 kW [220.50, 220.51, and 220.60]

▶ Air-Conditioning versus Heating, Example 3

Question: What is the service demand load for a dwelling unit with an air conditioner rated 20A at 240V versus electric heating of 7.5 kW. ▶Figure 6–25

(a) 7 kVA   (b) 7.5 kW   (c) 8 kVA   (d) 9 kVA

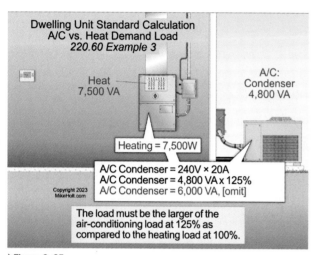

Dwelling Unit Standard Calculation
A/C vs. Heat Demand Load
220.60 Example 3

Heat
7,500 VA

A/C:
Condenser
4,800 VA

Heating = 7,500W

A/C Condenser = 240V × 20A
A/C Condenser = 4,800 VA x 125%
A/C Condenser = 6,000 VA, [omit]

Copyright 2023
MikeHolt.com

The load must be the larger of the air-conditioning load at 125% as compared to the heating load at 100%.

▶Figure 6–25

Solution:

Air-Conditioning = Volts × Amperes
A/C Condenser = 240V × 20A
A/C Condenser = 4,800 VA × 125%
A/C Condenser = 6,000 VA, omit [220.60]

Heating = 7,500W

Answer: (b) 7.5 kW

6.12 Service Conductor Size [Table 310.12(A)]

(A) Services. Service conductors supplying the entire load associated with a dwelling unit can be sized in accordance with Table 310.12(A) where there is no conductor ampacity adjustment or correction as required by 310.14.

Step 1: Add up the demand loads for general-lighting, fixed appliances, dryers, cooking equipment, air-conditioning, heat, and motors. Divide this sum by the nominal system voltage.

Step 2: Next, size the service disconnect in accordance with the standard size overcurrent protective device contained in 240.6(A).

Step 3: Size the service conductor ampacity for one-family dwellings and individual dwelling units of two-family and multifamily dwellings in accordance with Table 310.12(A) where the calculated demand load does not exceed 400A.

When the calculated demand load exceeds 400A, the service conductor must be sized in accordance with Table 310.16.

▶ Service Conductor Size, Example 1

Question: What size service conductors are required for a dwelling unit that has a 200A service disconnect? ▶Figure 6–26

(a) 1/0 AWG   (b) 2/0 AWG   (c) 3/0 AWG   (d) 4/0 AWG

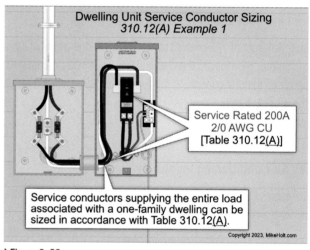

Dwelling Unit Service Conductor Sizing
310.12(A) Example 1

Service Rated 200A
2/0 AWG CU
[Table 310.12(A)]

Service conductors supplying the entire load associated with a one-family dwelling can be sized in accordance with Table 310.12(A).

Copyright 2023, MikeHolt.com

▶Figure 6–26

Answer: (b) 2/0 AWG [Table 310.12(A)]

▶ Service Conductor Size, Example 2

Question: What size aluminum service conductors are required for a dwelling unit that has a 200A service disconnect? ▶Figure 6–27

(a) 1/0 AWG   (b) 2/0 AWG   (c) 3/0 AWG   (d) 4/0 AWG

Answer: (d) 4/0 AWG [Table 310.12(A)]

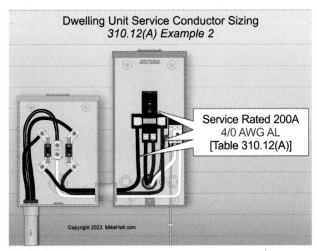

Dwelling Unit Service Conductor Sizing
310.12(A) Example 2

Service Rated 200A
4/0 AWG AL
[Table 310.12(A)]

Copyright 2023, MikeHolt.com

▶Figure 6–27

6.13 Standard Method Load Calculations [Article 220, Part III]

▶ **Standard Method Load Calculations, Example [Article 220, Part III]**

Question: What size service aluminum conductors are required for a dwelling unit of 6,000 sq ft having the following loads?

- *Dishwasher, 12A at 120V*
- *Disposal (Waste), 10A at 120V*
- *Trash Compactor, 8A at 120V*
- *Water Heater, 4,500W at 240V*
- *Microwave, 16A at 120V*
- *Vent Fan 7.2A at 120V*
- *Dryer, 4,000W at 120/240V*
- *Cooking, Range, 14,000W at 120/240V*
- *Electric Vehicle, 40A at 240V*
- *A/C Condenser, 30A at 240V*
- *Electric Heating, 9.6 kW*

(a) 250 kcmil   (b) 300 kcmil   (c) 350 kcmil   (d) 400 kcmil

Solution:

Step 1: *Determine the general lighting, general-use receptacles, small-appliance circuit, and laundry circuit demand load.*

General Lighting and Receptacles		
Load [220.41]	6,000 sq ft × 3 VA	18,000 VA
Small-Appliance Circuits		
[210.52(B)]	1,500 VA × 2	3,000 VA
Laundry Circuit		
[210.52(F)]	1,500 VA × 1	+1,500 VA
Total Connected Load		22,500 VA
Total Connected Load	22,500 VA	
First 3,000 VA at 100%	−3,000 VA × 100%	3,000 VA
Remainder at 35%	19,500 VA × 35%	+6,825 VA
Demand Load		9,825 VA

Step 2: *Determine the fixed appliance demand load [220.53].*

Dishwasher	12A × 120V	1,440 VA
Disposal (Waste)	10A × 120V	1,200 VA
Trash Compactor	8A × 120V	960 VA
Water Heater		4,500 W
Microwave	16A × 120V	1,920 VA
Vent Fan	7.2A × 120V	+ 864 VA
Total Connected Load		10,884 VA

Demand Load = Connected Load × Demand Factor [220.53]

Demand Load = 10,884 VA × 75%

Demand Load = 8,163 VA

Step 3: *Determine the dryer demand Load [220.54].*

The dryer nameplate is 4,000W, but the dryer load cannot be less than 5,000W.

Step 4: *Determine the cooking equipment demand load [220.55].*

Column C Calculated = 8 kW × 110%

Column C Calculated = 8.8 kW*

*14 kW exceeds 12 kW by 2 kW. The Column C value (8 kW) must be increased 5 percent for each kW over 12 kW [Table 220.55, Note 1].

2 × 5% is a 10 percent increase of the Column C value resulting in 110 percent.

Step 5: *Determine the electric vehicle demand load [220.57].*

EV Demand Load = 240V × 40A

EV Demand Load = 9,600 VA

• • •

Step 6: *Determine air-conditioning versus electric heating demand load [220.50, 220.51, 220.60, and 430.22].*

Select the larger of 125 percent of the air-conditioning load (if it is the largest motor-type load) in the dwelling unit, plus 100 percent for the other air-conditioning loads [220.50] and compare it to 100 percent of the electric heating load [220.51] if they are not both likely to be on at the same time [220.60].

Air-Conditioning = Volts × Amperes
A/C Condenser = 240V × 30A
A/C Condenser = 7,200 VA

Air-Conditioning Total = 7,200 VA × 125%
Air-Conditioning Total = 9,000 VA

Electric Heating at 100%:
Electric Heating Unit 1 = 9,600W

Step 7: *Determine the service demand load VA.*

Step 1: General Lighting,	
Receptacles, and Laundry	9,825 VA
Step 2: Fixed Appliances	8,163 VA
Step 3: Dryer	5,000 VA
Step 4: Cooking Equipment	8,800 VA
Step 5: Electric Vehicle	9,600 VA
Step 6: Heating	9,600 VA
Total Demand Load	50,988 VA

Step 8: *Determine the service demand load in amperes.*

Service Load in Amperes = VA/Volts
Service Load in Amperes = 50,988 VA/240V
Service Load in Amperes = 212A

Step 9: *Determine the service rating in amperes.*

Use a 225A service [240.6(A)].
250 kcmil aluminum [Table 310.12(A)].

Answer: *(a) 250 kcmil*

6.14 Number of General Lighting and General-Purpose Receptacle Circuits [210.11(A)]

The number of branch circuits required is determined by dividing the total calculated general lighting load in amperes by the ampere rating of the circuit. See Annex D, Example D1(a) for details.

▶ Number of General Lighting Circuits, Example 1

Question: *How many 15A, 120V circuits are required for the general lighting and general-use receptacles for a dwelling having a floor area of 2,400 sq ft?* ▶Figure 6–28

(a) Three   (b) Four   (c) Five   (d) Six

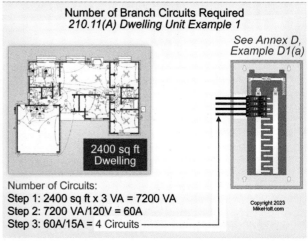

Number of Branch Circuits Required
210.11(A) Dwelling Unit Example 1

See Annex D, Example D1(a)

2400 sq ft Dwelling

Number of Circuits:
Step 1: 2400 sq ft x 3 VA = 7200 VA
Step 2: 7200 VA/120V = 60A
Step 3: 60A/15A = 4 Circuits

Copyright 2023 MikeHolt.com

▶Figure 6–28

Solution:

Step 1: *Determine the total VA load.*

VA = 2,400 sq ft × 3 VA per sq ft [Table 220.41]
VA = 7,200 VA

Step 2: *Determine the amperes.*

I = Volt-Ampere/Volts
I = 7,200 VA/120V
I = 60A

Step 3: *Determine the number of circuits.*

Number of 15A Circuits = 60A/15A
Number of 15A Circuits = Four

Answer: *(b) Four*

▶ Number of General Lighting Circuits, Example 2

Question: How many 20A, 120V circuits are required for the general lighting and general-use receptacles for a dwelling having a floor area of 2,400 sq ft? ▶Figure 6-29

(a) Three (b) Four (c) Five (d) Six

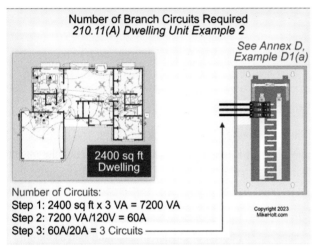

Number of Branch Circuits Required
210.11(A) Dwelling Unit Example 2

See Annex D, Example D1(a)

2400 sq ft
Dwelling

Number of Circuits:
Step 1: 2400 sq ft x 3 VA = 7200 VA
Step 2: 7200 VA/120V = 60A
Step 3: 60A/20A = 3 Circuits

Copyright 2023
MikeHolt.com

▶Figure 6-29

Solution:

Step 1: *Determine the total VA load.*

VA = 2,400 sq ft × 3 VA per sq ft [Table 220.41]
VA = 7,200 VA

Step 2: *Determine the amperes.*

I = Volt-Ampere/Volts
I = 7,200 VA/120V
I = 60A

Step 3: *Determine the number of circuits.*

Number of 20A Circuits = 60A/20A
Number of 20A Circuits = Three

Answer: (a) Three

Part C—Neutral Load Calculations

Introduction

Thus far we have covered both optional and standard methods for calculating the total service demand load in a single-family dwelling, however the neutral must be calculated using the standard method in Article 220, Part III only! In accordance with 220.61 the neutral demand load must include 100 percent of the line to neutral loads and 70 percent of the dryer and range loads for a single-family dwelling.

6.15 Neutral Calculations— Dryers and Ranges [220.61]

Dryer Neutral Load [220.61(B)(1)]

The service neutral load for electric clothes dryers can be based on 70 percent of the demand load as determined by 220.54.

▶ Neutral Load—Dryer, Example

Question: What is the neutral load for one 5.5 kW dryer? ▶Figure 6-30

(a) 3.85 kW (b) 4.6 kW (c) 5 kW (d) 5.5 kW

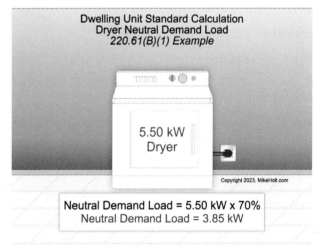

Dwelling Unit Standard Calculation
Dryer Neutral Demand Load
220.61(B)(1) Example

5.50 kW
Dryer

Copyright 2023, MikeHolt.com

Neutral Demand Load = 5.50 kW x 70%
Neutral Demand Load = 3.85 kW

▶Figure 6-30

Solution:

Neutral Calculated Demand Load = 5.5 kW × 70 % [220.61(B)(1)]
Neutral Calculated Demand Load = 3.85 kW

See Annex D, Examples D1(a) and D1(b) for more neutral calculations.

Answer: (a) 3.85 kW

Cooking Equipment Neutral Load [220.61(B)(1)]

The neutral load for household cooking appliances, such as electric ranges, wall-mounted ovens, or counter-mounted cooking units, is calculated at 70 percent of the demand load as determined by 220.55.

▶ Neutral Load—Cooking Equipment, Example

Question: What is the neutral load for one 14 kW range? ▶Figure 6–31

(a) 3,510W   *(b) 4,910W*   *(c) 5,710W*   *(d) 6,160W*

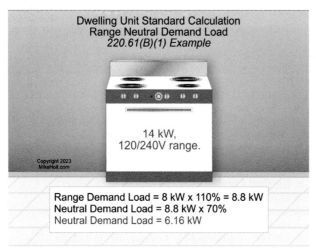

Dwelling Unit Standard Calculation
Range Neutral Demand Load
220.61(B)(1) Example

14 kW,
120/240V range.

Copyright 2023
MikeHolt.com

Range Demand Load = 8 kW x 110% = 8.8 kW
Neutral Demand Load = 8.8 kW x 70%
Neutral Demand Load = 6.16 kW

▶Figure 6–31

Solution:

Step 1: *Since the range exceeds 12 kW, we must comply with Note 1 of Table 220.55. The first step is to determine the demand load as listed in Column C of Table 220.55 for one unit which is 8 kW.*

Step 2: *The Column C value (8 kW) must be increased by 5 percent for each kVA that the range exceeds 12 kW [Table 220.55, Note 1]: 14 kW – 12 kW = 2 kW.*

2 × 5% = 10 percent increase of the Column C value resulting in 110 percent

Cooking Equipment Demand Load = 8 kW × 110%
Cooking Equipment Demand Load = 8.8 kW

Neutral Demand Load = 8,800W × 70% [220.61(B)(1)]
Neutral Demand Load = 6,160W

Answer: *(d) 6,160W*

6.16 Service Neutral Calculation [220.61]

(A) Neutral Calculated Load. The neutral calculated load for feeders or services is the maximum calculated load between the neutral conductor and any one phase conductor.

> **Author's Comment:**
>
> ▸ Line-to-line loads do not place any load on the neutral conductor, therefore line-to-line loads are not considered in the neutral calculation.

(B) Neutral Calculated Load Reductions.

(1) Electric Ranges, Ovens, Cooking Units. The neutral load for household electric ranges, wall-mounted ovens, or counter-mounted cooking units can be calculated at 70 percent of the cooking equipment demand load as determined in accordance with Table 220.55.

(1) Dryer Load. The neutral load for household electric dryers can be calculated at 70 percent of the dryer calculated load as determined in accordance with Table 220.54.

▶ Example

Question: What is the service neutral load for 6,000 sq ft. dwelling unit containing the following loads?

- *Dishwasher, 12A at 120V*
- *Disposal (Waste), 10A at 120V*
- *Microwave, 16A at 120V*
- *Water Heater (Tankless), 40A at 240V*
- *Dryer, 4,000W at 120/240V*
- *Cooking, Range, 14,000W at 120/240V*
- *Trash Compactor, 8A at 120V*
- *A/C Condenser, 30A at 240V (no neutral)*
- *Electric Heating, 9.6 kW at 240V (no neutral)*

(a) 68A   *(b) 78A*   *(c) 88A*   *(d) 98A*

Solution:

Step 1: *Determine the general lighting and general-use receptacles, and the laundry circuit demand load [Table 220.45].*

General Lighting and Receptacles

Load [220.41]	6,000 sq ft × 3 VA	18,000 VA
Small-Appliance Circuits		
[210.52(B)]	1,500 VA × 2	3,000 VA
Laundry Circuit [210.52(F)]	1,500 VA × 1	+1,500 VA
Total Connected Load		22,500 VA

Total Connected Load	22,500 VA	
First 3,000 VA at 100%	−3,000 VA × 100%	3,000 VA
Remainder at 35%	19,500 VA × 35%	+6,825 VA
Demand Load		9,825 VA

Step 2: *Determine the fixed appliance demand load [220.53].*

Dishwasher	12A × 120V	1,440 VA
Disposal (Waste)	10A × 120V	1,200 VA
Trash Compactor	8A × 120V	960 VA
Microwave	16A × 120V	1,920 VA
Water Heater (Tankless)		+ 0 VA*
Total Connected Load		5,520 VA

*Water heaters do not have neutrals.

Demand Load = Connected Load × Demand Factor [220.53]
Demand Load = 5,520 VA × 75%
Demand Load = 4,140 VA

Step 3: *Determine the dryer demand load [220.54].*

Dryer (Nameplate) 4,000W = 5,000W* × 70% [220.61(B)]
Dryer (Nameplate) 4,000W = 3,500W
*The dryer load cannot be less than 5,000W.

Step 4: *Determine the cooking equipment demand load [Table 220.55].*

Column C Calculated = 8 kW × 110%*
Column C Calculated = 8.8 kW

Neutral Load = 8,800 W × 70% [220.61(B)(1)]
Neutral Load = 6,160 W

*14 kW exceeds 12 kW by 2 kW. The Column C value (8 kW) must be increased 5 percent for each kW over 12 kW [Table 220.55, Note 1].

2 × 5% = 10 percent increase of the Column C value

Step 5: *Determine the service neutral size [310.12(D)].*

Step 1: General Lighting, Receptacles, and Laundry	9,825 VA
Step 2: Fixed Appliances	4,140 VA
Step 3: Dryer	3,500 VA
Step 4: Cooking Equipment	+6,160 VA
Total Demand Load	23,625 VA

Step 6: *Determine the service neutral size in amperes.*

Service Neutral Load in Amperes = VA/Volts
Service Neutral Load in Amperes = 23,625 VA/240V
Service Neutral Load in Amperes = 98A

Answer: *(d) 98A*

Unit 6—Conclusion

The residential service calculations covered in this unit required you to understand and apply many different demand factors. Since not all loads are used simultaneously in a home, the service is sized on a percentage of the total connected load, based on what the *NEC* calls "demand factors."

The *Code* doesn't explain how demand factors were derived, and it's not necessary for you to understand this in order to apply them correctly. Be sure to work on some practice calculations so you understand how to apply the various demand factors to a dwelling unit calculation. It's important to have a good working knowledge of this before going on to Unit 7—Multifamily Dwelling Calculations which will build on the concepts developed in this unit.

Both the standard and the optional service calculation methods were discussed in this unit. Remember that these are two distinctly different calculation methods so be sure not to mix them together. On an exam, you'll likely be told which one to use on a specific question, but if the question doesn't specify the method, use the standard calculation.

Remember the different *Code* sections and Tables necessary to correctly answer the practice and challenge questions. Your goal should be to remember where in the *NEC* you need to look for the information you need rather than trying to memorize the information in every *Code* section and Table.

REVIEW QUESTIONS

Please use the 2023 *Code* book and this textbook to answer the following questions.

PART A—OPTIONAL METHOD LOAD CALCULATIONS [ARTICLE 220, PART IV]

6.2 Dwelling Unit Optional Load Calculation [220.82] Example

The following information applies to the next two questions. Using the optional method for a 1500 sq ft dwelling unit containing the following loads:

- Disposal, waste (1 kVA)
- Dishwasher (1.50 kVA)
- Water heater (5 kW)
- Dryer (5.50 kW)
- Cooktop (6 kW)
- Two ovens (each 3 kW)
- Two separately controlled 5 kW space-electric heating-units
- Air-conditioning (17A/240V)

1. What is the service disconnecting rating?
   - (a) 90A
   - (b) 100A
   - (c) 110A
   - (d) 125A

2. What size aluminum conductor is required for the service disconnect?
   - (a) 1 AWG
   - (b) 1/0 AWG
   - (c) 2/0 AWG
   - (d) 3/0 AWG

The following information applies to the next two questions. Using the optional method for a 3,000 sq ft dwelling unit plus 900 sq ft porch and 400 sq ft carport (not a garage) with the following loads:

- Dishwasher, 1.50 kW
- Disposal, waste (1 kVA)
- Trash compactor (1.50 kVA)
- Hot tub (40A/240V)
- RV outlet (50A/240V)
- Two A/C heat-pumps (each at 21A/240V)
- Radiant heating (totaling 50A/240V with six separately controlled units)

3. What is the service disconnecting rating?
   - (a) 125A
   - (b) 150A
   - (c) 175A
   - (d) 200A

4. What size aluminum conductor is required for the service disconnect?
   - (a) 1/0 AWG
   - (b) 2/0 AWG
   - (c) 3/0 AWG
   - (d) 4/0 AWG

The following information applies to the next two questions. The dwelling has a floor area of 1,500 ft², exclusive of an unfinished cellar not adaptable for future use, unfinished attic, and open porches. It has a:

- Range (12 kW)
- Water heater (2.5 kW)
- Dishwasher (1.2 kW)
- Electric space heating installed in five rooms (9 kW)
- Clothes dryer (5 kW)
- Room air-conditioning unit (6A, 230V)

5. Using the optional method, what size service is required?

    (a) 81A
    (b) 85A
    (c) 88A
    (d) 90A

6. What size neutral is required

    (a) 45A
    (b) 57A
    (c) 64A
    (d) 73A

The following information applies to the next two questions. The dwelling has a floor area of 1,500 ft², exclusive of an unfinished cellar not adaptable for future use, unfinished attic, and open porches. It has:

- Two wall-mounted ovens (4 kW)
- One counter-mounted cooking unit (5.1 kW)
- Water heater (4.5 kW)
- Dishwasher (1.2 kW)
- Combination clothes washer and dryer (5 kW)
- Six room air-conditioning units (7A, 230V)
- Permanently installed bathroom space heater (1.5 kW)

7. Using the optional method, what size service is required?

    (a) 109A
    (b) 111A
    (c) 115A
    (d) 122A

8. What size neutral is required

    (a) 45A
    (b) 62A
    (c) 64A
    (d) 73A

The following information applies to the next question. The dwelling has a floor area of 2,000 ft², exclusive of an unfinished cellar not adaptable for future use, unfinished attic, and open porches. It has a:

- Range (12 kW)
- Water heater (4.5 kW)
- Dishwasher (1.2 kW)
- Clothes dryer (5 kW)
- Heat pump (24A) with 15 kW of backup heat

9. Using the optional method, what size service is required?

    (a) 139A
    (b) 145A
    (c) 147A
    (d) 152A

PART B—STANDARD METHOD LOAD CALCULATIONS [ARTICLE 220, PART III]

6.4 General Lighting and General-Use Receptacle Demand Load [220.41 and Table 220.45]

10. What is the general lighting demand load for a 2,500 sq ft dwelling unit, with a 1,000 sq ft open porch and 500 sq ft garage?

    (a) 5,275 VA
    (b) 6,150 VA
    (c) 6,275 VA
    (d) 6,725 VA

11. What is the general lighting demand load for a 4,000 sq ft dwelling unit, with a 1,000 sq ft open porch and 1,000 sq ft garage?

    (a) 4,625 VA
    (b) 5,135 kVA
    (c) 6,500 VA
    (d) 7,725 VA

12. What is the general lighting demand load for a 5,000 sq ft dwelling unit, with a 1,000 sq ft open porch and 1,000 sq ft garage?

    (a) 5,600 VA
    (b) 6,500 VA
    (c) 7,625 VA
    (d) 8,775 VA

The following information applies to the next two questions. The dwelling has a floor area of 1,500 ft², exclusive of an unfinished cellar not adaptable for future use, unfinished attic, and open porches. Appliances are a 12 kW range and a 5.5 kW, 240V dryer.

13. Using the standard method, what size service is required?
    - (a) 55A
    - (b) 67A
    - (c) 78A
    - (d) 93A

14. What size neutral is required?
    - (a) 45A
    - (b) 57A
    - (c) 61A
    - (d) 73A

6.5 Fixed Appliance Demand Load [220.53]

15. What is the demand load for a dishwasher (1.2 kW) and water heater (4 kW)?
    - (a) 4.8 kVA
    - (b) 4.9 kVA
    - (c) 5.1 kVA
    - (d) 5.2 kVA

16. What is the demand load for a disposal (940 VA), a dishwasher (1,250 VA), and a water heater (4,500W)?
    - (a) 5,018 VA
    - (b) 6,272 VA
    - (c) 6,690 VA
    - (d) 8,363 VA

17. What is the demand load for a disposal (940 VA), a dishwasher (1,250 VA), a trash compactor (1,100 VA), and a water heater (4,500W)?
    - (a) 5,843 VA
    - (b) 7,303 VA
    - (c) 7,490 VA
    - (d) 9,738 VA

6.6 Dryer Demand Load [220.54]

18. What is the demand load for a 4 kW dryer?
    - (a) 3 kW
    - (b) 4 kW
    - (c) 5 kW
    - (d) 6 kW

19. What is the demand load for a 5 kW dryer?
    - (a) 3 kW
    - (b) 4 kW
    - (c) 5 kW
    - (d) 6 kW

20. What is the demand load for a 5.5 kW dryer?
    - (a) 3 kW
    - (b) 4 kW
    - (c) 5 kW
    - (d) 5.5 kW

6.8 Electric Cooking Equipment Demand Load [220.55]

Service Demand Load

21. What is the demand load for a 9 kW range?
    - (a) 7 kW
    - (b) 8 kW
    - (c) 9 kW
    - (d) 1 kW

22. What is the demand load for an 11.5 kW range?
    - (a) 7 kW
    - (b) 8 kW
    - (c) 9 kW
    - (d) 1 kW

23. What is the demand load for a 13.6 kW range?
    - (a) 6 kW
    - (b) 8 kW
    - (c) 8.8 kW
    - (d) 9.2 kW

24. What is the demand load for a 15 kW range?
    - (a) 8.2 kW
    - (b) 9.2 kW
    - (c) 10.2 kW
    - (d) 11.2 kW

25. What is the demand load for a 15.5 kW range?

    (a) 9.6 kW
    (b) 112 kW
    (c) 13.2 kW
    (d) 15.6 kW

26. What is the demand load for a 16 kW range?

    (a) 9.6 kW
    (b) 11,2 kW
    (c) 13.2 kW
    (d) 15.6 kW

27. What is the demand load for a 19 kW range?

    (a) 10.2 kW
    (b) 10.8 kW
    (c) 11.2 kW
    (d) 11.5 kW

28. What is the demand load for a 24 kW range?

    (a) 12.8 kW
    (b) 13.2 kW
    (c) 14.3 kW
    (d) 14.8 kW

Branch Circuit Demand Load

29. What is the branch-circuit load for a 3 kW oven?

    (a) 3 kW
    (b) 4 kW
    (c) 5 kW
    (d) 6 kW

30. What is the branch-circuit demand load for a 6 kW counter-mounted cooking unit?

    (a) 3 kW
    (b) 4 kW
    (c) 5 kW
    (d) 6 kW

31. What is the branch-circuit demand load for two 3 kW ovens and one 6 kW cooktop connected to the same branch circuit in the same room?

    (a) 5 kW
    (b) 6 kW
    (c) 7 kW
    (d) 8 kW

6.11 Air-Conditioning Versus Heating [220.50, 220.51, and 220.60]

32. What is the demand load for a 28A/240V air conditioner versus three baseboard heaters (3 kW each)?

    (a) 6 kW
    (b) 7 kW
    (c) 8 kW
    (d) 9 kW

33. What is the demand load for a 17A/240V air conditioner versus 8 kW of space electric heating?

    (a) 4 kW
    (b) 5 kW
    (c) 6 kW
    (d) 8 kW

34. What is the demand load for a 28A/240V air conditioner versus 8 kW of space electric heating?

    (a) 8.1 kVA
    (b) 8.2 kVA
    (c) 8.4 kVA
    (d) 8.6 kVA

35. What is the demand load for a 15A/240V heat-pump air conditioner with 6 kW of supplemental space electric heating?

    (a) 10.1 kVA
    (b) 10.2 kVA
    (c) 10.3 kVA
    (d) 10.5 kVA

36. What is the demand load for a 20A/240V air conditioner versus 8 kW of space electric heating?

    (a) 4 kW
    (b) 5 kW
    (c) 6 kW
    (d) 8 kW

37. What is the demand load for a 25A/240V air conditioner versus 8 kW of space electric heating?

    (a) 5 kW
    (b) 6 kW
    (c) 7 kW
    (d) 8 kW

6.12 Service Conductor Size [Table 310.12(A)]

38. What size service conductor is required if the demand load for a dwelling unit is 120A?

    (a) 2 AWG
    (b) 2/0 AWG
    (c) 3/0 AWG
    (d) 4/0 AWG

39. What size service conductor is required if the demand load for a dwelling unit is 140A?

    (a) 1 AWG
    (b) 2/0 AWG
    (c) 3/0 AWG
    (d) 4/0 AWG

40. What size aluminum feeder conductor is required if the demand load for a dwelling unit is 170A?

    (a) 2 AWG
    (b) 1 AWG
    (c) 1/0 AWG
    (d) 3/0 AWG

41. What size feeder conductor is required if the demand load for a dwelling unit is 220A?

    (a) 2 AWG
    (b) 1 AWG
    (c) 2/0 AWG
    (d) 3/0 AWG

42. What size service conductor is required if the demand load for a dwelling unit is 300A?

    (a) 2 AWG
    (b) 1 AWG
    (c) 2/0 AWG
    (d) 250 kcmil

6.13 Standard Method Load Calculations [Article 220, Part III]

43. What is the general lighting demand load for a 1,500 sq ft dwelling unit?

    (a) 4,700 VA
    (b) 4,900 VA
    (c) 5,100 VA
    (d) 5,300 VA

44. What is the demand load for one dishwasher (1.5 kVA) and one water heater (4 kW)?

    (a) 5.1 kVA
    (b) 5.3 kVA
    (c) 5.5 kVA
    (d) 5.7 kVA

45. What is the demand load for a 4.5 kW dryer?

    (a) 4 kW
    (b) 5 kW
    (c) 6 kW
    (d) 7 kW

46. What is the demand load for a 14 kW range?

    (a) 8.5 kW
    (b) 8.6 kW
    (c) 8.8 kW
    (d) 8.9 kW

47. What is the demand load for a 18A/240V air conditioner versus 6 kW electric heating?

    (a) 3 kW
    (b) 4 kW
    (c) 5 kW
    (d) 6 kW

48. What is the minimum demand load for an electric vehicle outlet?

    (a) 6,900 VA
    (b) 7,000 VA
    (c) 7,200 VA
    (d) 7,400 VA

49. What size service conductor is required for a dwelling unit having a total demand load of 30 kVA?

    (a) 4 AWG
    (b) 2 AWG
    (c) 1/0 AWG
    (d) 3/0 AWG

6.14 Number of General Lighting and General-Purpose Receptacle Circuits [210.11(A)]

50. How many 15A, 120V general purpose circuits are required for a 2,000 sq ft dwelling unit?

    (a) 1 circuit
    (b) 2 circuits
    (c) 3 circuits
    (d) 4 circuits

51. How many 15A, 120V general purpose circuits are required for a 4,000 sq ft dwelling unit?

    (a) 4 circuits
    (b) 5 circuits
    (c) 6 circuits
    (d) 7 circuits

52. How many 20A, 120V general purpose circuits are required for a 2,000 sq ft dwelling unit?

    (a) 1 circuit
    (b) 2 circuits
    (c) 3 circuits
    (d) 4 circuits

53. How many 20 A, 120V general purpose circuits are required for a 4,000 sq ft dwelling unit?

    (a) 3 circuits
    (b) 4 circuits
    (c) 5 circuits
    (d) 6 circuits

PART C—NEUTRAL LOAD CALCULATIONS

6.15 Neutral Calculations—Dryers and Ranges [220.61]

54. The neutral load for household cooking appliances, such as electric ranges, wall-mounted ovens, or counter-mounted cooking units, is permitted to be calculated at ____ of the load as determined by 220.55.

    (a) 50 percent
    (b) 60 percent
    (c) 70 percent
    (d) 80 percent

55. The neutral load for household electric clothes dryers is permitted to be calculated at ____ of the load as determined by 220.54.

    (a) 50 percent
    (b) 60 percent
    (c) 70 percent
    (d) 80 percent

56. What is the neutral load for one 6 kW household dryer?

    (a) 4.2 kW
    (b) 4.7 kW
    (c) 5.4 kW
    (d) 6.6 kW

57. What is the neutral load for one 9 kW range?

    (a) 5.4 kW
    (b) 5.6 kW
    (c) 5.8 kW
    (d) 5.9 kW

NEC CALCULATIONS— PRACTICE EXAM

The following 50-question random order Practice Exam will test your knowledge of Module III—*NEC* Calculations.

Please use the 2023 *Code* book and this textbook to answer the following questions.

Want to practice online? Scan the QR code to access these questions online to get familiar with the online environment in which you'll most likely be taking your exam.

UNIT 1—RACEWAY CALCULATIONS

1.3 Sizing Raceways, Conductors all the Same Size—Annex C

1. How many 8 RHH with outer cover conductors are permitted in trade size 1½ RMC?

    (a) 10 conductors
    (b) 14 conductors
    (c) 16 conductors
    (d) 20 conductors

Compact Insulated Conductors

2. How many 8 THW compact conductors are permitted in trade size 1½ RMC?

    (a) 12 conductors
    (b) 14 conductors
    (c) 16 conductors
    (d) 20 conductors

1.4 Raceways Sizing with Different Size Conductors

3. What's the minimum size PVC nipple required for three 500 kcmil THWN-2 conductors, one 250 kcmil THWN-2 conductor, and one 3 AWG THWN-2 conductor?

    (a) Trade size 2
    (b) Trade size 2½
    (c) Trade size 3
    (d) Trade size 3½

1.5 Multiconductor and Optical Fiber Cables—Chapter 9, Note (5) and Note (9)

4. What trade size ENT is required for four fiber optic cables having a diameter of 0.30 inches?

    (a) Trade size ½
    (b) Trade size ¾
    (c) Trade size 1
    (d) Trade size 1¼

1.6 Wireways and Cable Tray Systems

Wireway Sizing

5. 55 What is the maximum number of 400 kcmil THHN conductors that can be installed in a 4 in. × 4 in. wireway?

    (a) 4 conductors
    (b) 5 conductors
    (c) 6 conductors
    (d) 7 conductors

Cable Tray Sizing—Annex C

6. What is the minimum size cable tray needed to accommodate twenty 2/0 THWN-2/TC conductors?

    (a) 10 in.
    (b) 12 in.
    (c) 14 in.
    (d) 16 in.

UNIT 2—BOX CALCULATIONS

PART A—OUTLET BOX SIZING

2.3 Outlet Box Sizing Examples [314.16(B)]

7. What size outlet box is required for one 12/2 NM cable that terminates on a switch and one 12/3 NM cable that terminates on a receptacle? The box has two internal cable clamps.

    (a) 4 in. × 1¼ in. square box
    (b) 4 in. × 1½ in. square box
    (c) 4 in. × 2⅛ in. square box
    (d) 3 in. × 2 in. × 3½ in. device box

PART B—PULL AND JUNCTION BOXES

2.7 Pull Box Sizing Examples

The following information applies to the next three questions. A junction box contains two trade size 2 raceways on the left side, and two trade size 2 raceways on the top.

8. What is the minimum distance from the left wall to the right wall?

    (a) 14 in.
    (b) 21 in.
    (c) 24 in.
    (d) 28 in.

9. What is the minimum distance from the bottom wall to the top wall?

    (a) 14 in.
    (b) 18 in.
    (c) 21 in.
    (d) 24 in.

UNIT 3—CONDUCTOR SIZING AND PROTEXTION

PART A—CONDUCTOR INSULATION, TERMINALS, AND OVERCURRENT PROTECTION

3.3 Conductor Size—Equipment Terminal Rating [110.14(C)]

Equipment Terminations Rated 100A and Less, Conductor Sized to 60°C [110.14(C)(1)(a)]

10. What is the minimum size THW conductor permitted to terminate on a 50A circuit breaker if the circuit breaker terminals are listed for 75°C conductor sizing?

    (a) 8 AWG
    (b) 6 AWG
    (c) 4 AWG
    (d) 2 AWG

Equipment Terminations Greater than 100A, Conductor Sized to 75°C [110.14(C)(1)(b)]

11. What is the minimum size THW aluminum conductor required for a 250A feeder supplying a panelboard?

    (a) 250 kcmil
    (b) 300 kcmil
    (c) 350 kcmil
    (d) 400 kcmil

3.4 Overcurrent Protection of Conductors [240.4]

12. What is the minimum size of conductors (paralleled in four sets of conductors per phase) allowed to be protected by a 1,600A overcurrent protective device?

    (a) 500 kcmil
    (b) 600 kcmil
    (c) 700 kcmil
    (d) 750 kcmil

PART B—CONDUCTOR AMPACITY AND PROTECTION

3.6 Conductor Ampacity Correction [310.15(B)(1)]

13. What is the ampacity of three 250 kcmil THW in an ambient temperature of 40°C?

    (a) 204A
    (b) 214A
    (c) 224A
    (d) 234A

3.7 Conductor Ampacity Adjustment [310.15(C)(1)]

14. What is the ampacity of eight 250 kcmil XHHW-2 aluminum conductors in a raceway?

    (a) 160A
    (b) 180A
    (c) 200A
    (d) 205A

3.9 Neutral Current-Carrying Conductor [310.15(E)]

15. What is the neutral current for a 208Y/120V, three-phase 4-wire system, where line 1 has 75A, line 2 has 85A, line 3 has 100A?

    (a) 21.80A
    (b) 31.80A
    (c) 41.80A
    (d) 51.80A

3.10 Branch Circuit Conductor Sizing [210.19(A)(1)]

16. What size THW conductor is required to supply a 50 kVA/240V noncontinuous load?

    (a) 1/0 AWG
    (b) 2/0 AWG
    (c) 3/0 AWG
    (d) 4/0 AWG

3.12 Branch Circuit Overcurrent Protection Sizing [210.20(A)]

17. What size circuit breaker is required for a branch circuit that has a 25A continuous load and a 25A noncontinuous load?

    (a) 45A
    (b) 50A
    (c) 60A
    (d) 65A

3.13 Feeder Conductor Sizing [215.2(A)(1)]

18. What size THW aluminum feeder is required to supply a 100A continuous and a 100A noncontinuous load?

    (a) 2/0 AWG
    (b) 3/0 AWG
    (c) 4/0 AWG
    (d) 300 kcmil

3.14 Feeder Neutral Conductor Size [215.2(A)(1) Ex 3]

19. What size feeder neutral is required to supply a dwelling unit with a demand load of 175A, of which 100A are line-to-line, terminals rated 75°C?

    (a) 1 AWG
    (b) 2 AWG
    (c) 3 AWG
    (d) 4 AWG

3.15 Feeder Overcurrent Protection Sizing [215.3]

20. What size feeder overcurrent protective device is required for a 100A of continuous loads and 50A of noncontinuous loads?

    (a) 150A
    (b) 175A
    (c) 200A
    (d) 225A

3.16 Feeder Tap Rules [240.21(B)]

21. What size THW 25 ft tap THW conductor is required where the feeder overcurrent protective device is rated 800A with two sets of 500 kcmil THW feeder conductors per phase, the 25 ft feeder tap conductor will be terminating in a 200A breaker?

    (a) 300 kcmil
    (b) 350 kcmil
    (c) 400 kcmil
    (d) 500 kcmil

UNIT 4—MOTOR, AIR-CONDITIONING, AND TRANSFORMER CALCULATIONS

PART A—MOTOR CALCULATIONS

4.3 Branch-Circuit Conductor Sizing Continuous Duty Application [430.22]

Three-Phase Application

22. What size THW conductor is required for a 15 hp, 230V, three-phase motor, terminals rated 75°C?

    (a) 8 AWG
    (b) 6 AWG
    (c) 4 AWG
    (d) 3 AWG

4.4 Branch-Circuit Conductor Sizing for Duty-Cycle Application [430.22(E)]

23. What size branch-circuit conductors are required for a 20 hp, three-phase, 230V motor with a nameplate FLA of 48A, rated for 30-minute service, used for short-time duty, with terminals rated 75°C?

    (a) 8 AWG
    (b) 6 AWG
    (c) 4 AWG
    (d) 2 AWG

4.6 Motor Overload Protection

24. If a dual-element time-delay fuse is used for overload protection, what size fuse is required for a 3 hp, 230V, motor, with a service factor of 1.15, if the motor nameplate current rating is 15A?

    (a) 15A
    (b) 20A
    (c) 25A
    (d) 30A
    (d) 30A

4.7 Branch-Circuit Short-Circuit and Ground-Fault Protection [430.52(C)(1)]

25. What is the maximum size non-time delay fuse for a 20 hp, 460V three-phase squirrel cage resistor starting Design B motor?

    (a) 65A
    (b) 70A
    (c) 85A
    (d) 90A

4.9 Motor Circuit Equipment Grounding Conductor Size [250.122(D)(1)]

26. What size equipment grounding conductor is required for a 10 hp 230V three-phase motor protected with a 70A breaker?

    (a) 8 AWG
    (b) 6 AWG
    (c) 4 AWG
    (d) 3 AWG

4.10 Feeder Conductor Sizing [430.24]

27. What size THW feeder is required for two 7½ hp, 240V, dc motors, terminals rated 75°C?

    (a) 10 AWG
    (b) 8 AWG
    (c) 6 AWG
    (d) 4 AWG

4.11 Feeder Short-Circuit and Ground-Fault Protection [430.62(A)]

28. What size inverse time circuit breaker is required for the feeder supplying the three motors?

    • One 25 hp, 460V, 3-phase, squirrel-cage motor, nameplate full-load current 32A, Design B, Service Factor 1.15
    • Two 30 hp, 460V, 3-phase, wound-rotor motors, primary current 38A, secondary current 65A

    (a) 100A
    (b) 125A
    (c) 150A
    (d) 175A

PART B—AIR-CONDITIONING CALCULATIONS

4.12 Air-Conditioning Equipment Nameplate [440.4(B)]

29.   What size conductor is permitted for an air-conditioning unit, where the nameplate states minimum circuit ampacity 45A, with maximum overcurrent protection of 80A?

(a) 12 AWG
(b) 10 AWG
(c) 8 AWG
(d) 6 AWG

4.13 Air-Conditioning Equipment, Short-Circuit and Ground-Fault Protection [440.22]

30.   What size maximum branch-circuit short-circuit and ground-fault protective device is required for an 18.6A refrigerant motor-compressor with a 1.5A fan?

(a) 35A
(b) 40A
(c) 45A
(d) 50A

4.14 Air-Conditioning Equipment, Conductor Ampacity [440.33]

31.   What size minimum branch-circuit conductor is required for a 25A refrigerant motor-compressor with a 2A fan, terminals rated 75°C?

(a) 14 AWG
(b) 12 AWG
(c) 10 AWG
(d) 8 AWG

PART C—TRANSFORMERS

4.15 Transformer Primary Only Overcurrent Protection [450.3(B)]

32.   What is the maximum primary overcurrent device rating for a 75 kVA, 208V three-phase transformer with no secondary overcurrent protection?

(a) 250A
(b) 300A
(c) 350A
(d) 400A

4.16 Transformer Secondary Conductor Sizing [240.21(C)]

33.   What size secondary conductor is required for a 112.5 kVA, three-phase, 480V to 120/208V transformer that terminates in a 400A main breaker?

(a) 350 kcmil
(b) 400 kcmil
(c) 500 kcmil
(d) 600 kcmil

UNIT 5—VOLTAGE-DROP CALCULATIONS

PART A—CONDUCTOR RESISTANCE CALCULATIONS

5.2 Conductor Resistance

34.   What is the resistance of 400 ft of 1 AWG aluminum?

(a) 0.0908Ω
(b) 0.1012Ω
(c) 0.1423Ω
(d) 0.1564Ω

PART B—VOLTAGE-DROP CALCULATIONS

5.4 Circuit Conductors' Voltage Drop—Ohm's Law Method

35.   What's the conductor voltage drop for a 12A continuous load using 12 AWG stranded wire located 100 ft from the power supply?

(a) 4.20V
(b) 4.40V
(c) 4.75V
(d) 4.85V

5.5 Single-Phase Circuit Voltage Drop—Formula Method

36.   What is the voltage drop of 6 AWG aluminum supplying a 35A load located 100 ft from the panel?

(a) 5.55V
(b) 5.59V
(c) 5.61V
(d) 5.66V

5.6 Three-Phase Circuit Voltage Drop—Formula Method

37. What is the voltage drop of a 150A, 208V, three-phase load located 150 ft from the service using 250 kcmil compact aluminum conductors?

    (a) 3.30V
    (b) 3.55V
    (c) 3.64V
    (d) 3.70V

5.7 Sizing Conductor Single-Phase Circuit Voltage Drop—Formula Method

38. 38 What size wire is required for a 5 hp, 240V motor located 125 ft from a panelboard?

    (a) 10 AWG
    (b) 8 AWG
    (c) 6 AWG
    (d) 4 AWG

5.8 Sizing Conductor Three-Phase Circuit Voltage Drop—Formula Method

39. What size wire is required for a 28A, 480V, three-phase contin-uous located 300 ft from a panelboard?

    (a) 10 AWG
    (b) 8 AWG
    (c) 6 AWG
    (d) 4 AWG

UNIT 6—DWELLING UNIT CALCULATIONS

PART A—OPTIONAL METHOD LOAD CALCULATIONS [ARTICLE 220, PART IV]

6.2 Dwelling Unit Optional Load Calculation [220.82] Example

The following information applies to the next question. The dwelling has a floor area of 2,000 ft², exclusive of an unfinished cellar not adaptable for future use, unfinished attic, and open porches. It has a:

- Range (12 kW)
- Water heater (4.5 kW)
- Dishwasher (1.2 kW)
- Clothes dryer (5 kW)
- Heat pump (24A) with 15 kW of backup heat

40. Using the optional method, what size service is required?

    (a) 139A
    (b) 145A
    (c) 145A
    (d) 152A

PART B—STANDARD METHOD LOAD CALCULATIONS [ARTICLE 220, PART III]

6.4 General Lighting and General-Use Receptacle Demand Load [220.41 and Table 220.45]

The following information applies to the next two questions. The dwelling has a floor area of 1,500 ft², exclusive of an unfinished cellar not adaptable for future use, unfinished attic, and open porches. Appliances are a 12 kW range and a 5.5 kW, 240V dryer.

41. Using the standard method, what size service is required?

    (a) 55A
    (b) 67A
    (c) 78A
    (d) 93A

42. What size neutral is required?

    (a) 45A
    (b) 57A
    (c) 61A
    (d) 73A

6.5 Fixed Appliance Demand Load [220.53]

43. What is the demand load for a disposal (940 VA), a dishwasher (1,250 VA), and a water heater (4,500W)?

    (a) 5,018 VA
    (b) 6,272 VA
    (c) 6,690 VA
    (d) 8,363 VA

6.6 Dryer Demand Load [220.54]

44. What is the demand load for a 5.5 kW dryer?

    (a) 3 kW
    (b) 4 kW
    (c) 5 kW
    (d) 5.5 kW

6.8 Electric Cooking Equipment Demand Load [220.55]

Service Demand Load

45. What is the demand load for a 13.6 kW range?

    (a) 6 kW
    (b) 8 kW
    (c) 8.8 kW
    (d) 9.2 kW

Branch Circuit Demand Load

46. What is the branch-circuit demand load for a 6 kW counter-mounted cooking unit?

    (a) 3 kW
    (b) 4 kW
    (c) 5 kW
    (d) 6 kW

6.11 Air-Conditioning Versus Heating [220.50, 220.51, and 220.60]

47. What is the demand load for a 15A/240V heat-pump air conditioner with 6 kW of supplemental space electric heating?

    (a) 10.1 kVA
    (b) 10.2 kVA
    (c) 10.3 kVA
    (d) 10.5 kW

6.12 Service Conductor Size [Table 310.12(A)]

48. What size aluminum feeder conductor is required if the demand load for a dwelling unit is 170A?

    (a) 2 AWG
    (b) 1 AWG
    (c) 1/0 AWG
    (d) 3/0 AWG

6.14 Number of General Lighting and General-Purpose Receptacle Circuits [210.11(A)]

49. How many 20A, 120V general purpose circuits are required for a 2,000 sq ft dwelling unit?

    (a) 1 circuit
    (b) 2 circuits
    (c) 3 circuits
    (d) 4 circuits

PART C—NEUTRAL LOAD CALCULATIONS

6.15 Neutral Calculations—Dryers and Ranges [220.61]

50. What is the neutral load for one 6 kW household dryer?

    (a) 4.2 kW
    (b) 4.7 kW
    (c) 5.4 kW
    (d) 6.6 kW

Introduction to Module IV—Advanced *NEC* Calculations

Journeyman exams do not typically include questions regarding the material covered in this module, but master's and contractor's exams do! The advanced calculations covered in Module IV are the most time-consuming questions you will encounter in an exam, so it's important to become proficient at completing these correctly.

Module IV includes the units titled:

▸ **Unit 7—Multifamily Dwelling Calculations**

▸ **Unit 8—Commercial Calculations**

Spend the time you need on the material covered in this module to build confidence in these topics, and make sure to complete all the practice questions.

MULTIFAMILY DWELLING CALCULATIONS

Introduction to Unit 7—Multifamily Dwelling Calculations

There are many similarities in the electrical requirements for multifamily and single-family dwellings, many of the principles explained in Unit 6 will still be used for multifamily dwellings here in Unit 7. One key difference is that demand factors are allowed for multifamily dwellings because diversity in usage is expected, so the maximum connected load isn't likely to be in use simultaneously.

Article 220 allows two distinctly different methods of calculating the service load for a dwelling unit—the standard method in Part III and the optional method in Part IV. The two methods are different and have certain conditions as to when which one should be applied. This in turn will often result in two different service load totals.

The following are the Parts covered in this unit:

▸ Part A—Optional Method Load Calculations

▸ Part B—Standard Method Load Calculations

▸ Part C—Service Neutral Load Calculations

Remember that the *Code* defines a "Dwelling Unit" as a single unit providing complete and independent living facilities for one or more persons, including permanent provisions for living, sleeping, cooking, and sanitation. A multifamily dwelling is a building with three or more dwelling units. ▸Figure 7–1

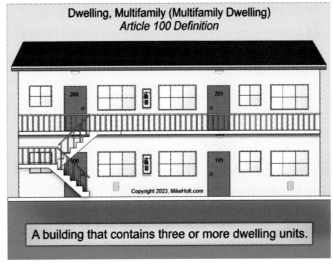

Dwelling, Multifamily (Multifamily Dwelling)
Article 100 Definition

Copyright 2023, MikeHolt.com

A building that contains three or more dwelling units.

▸Figure 7–1

Part A—Optional Method Load Calculations [Article 220, Part IV]

Introduction

In Part A of unit 7 you will use Article 220, Part IV which covers the "optional method" for calculating the service demand load for a multi-family dwelling. In unit 6 we covered single-family dwelling optional load calculations but here we will focus on the multifamily dwelling which allows demand factors in Table 220.84 based on the number of units in the multifamily dwelling because of load diversity.

7.1 Multifamily Dwelling Optional Load Calculations [220.84]

The following steps can be used to determine service sizes for a multifamily dwelling using the optional method contained in Article 220, Part IV.

Step 1: Determine the connected load [220.84(C)].

The first step is to determine the total connected load for the general lighting and general-use receptacles, small-appliance circuits, laundry circuit, appliances and equipment, and motors; except air-conditioning and heating as follows:

(1) General Lighting and General-Use Receptacles. The total connected load must include A 3 VA per sq ft load for general lighting and general-use receptacles. The total square feet are based on the outside dimensions of the dwelling unit, but does not include open porches, garages, or unused or unfinished spaces not adaptable for future use.

(2) Small-Appliance and Laundry Circuits. Two 20A, 120V small-appliance circuits, and one 20A, 120V circuit the laundry area [210.11(C)(1) and 210.11(C)(2)] are required for each dwelling unit. The load for each of these circuits is based on 1500 VA.

Where a dwelling unit is in a multifamily building that includes laundry facilities for the use of all building occupants, a laundry circuit is not required in each dwelling unit [210.52(F) Ex].

(3) Appliances and Equipment. The nameplate VA rating of appliances fastened in place, permanently connected, or located to be on a specific circuit such as dishwashers, waste disposals, microwaves, trash compactors, and water heaters. In addition, the load ratings for dryers, cooking equipment, and special-purpose circuits equipment (such as ironing stations) must all be included.

(4) Motor VA. The nameplate VA rating of motors not part of an appliance used for irrigation, boat lifts, wells, and so on must be included at 100%.

(5) Air-Conditioning versus Heating. The larger of the air-conditioning load or the space-heating load.

Step 2: Determine the demand load.

The demand load is determined by applying the demand factor from Table 220.84 to the total connected load (Step 1).

Step 3: Determine the size of the service disconnect and conductors.

Next, determine the total service demand load in amperes for the dwelling unit by adding the values of Step 2 and Step 3 together, then dividing the sum by 240V. Once the service demand load in amperes is known, the service disconnect can be sized in accordance with the standard size overcurrent protective device contained in 240.6(A).

The last step in the process is to determine the size of service conductors in accordance with 310.16.

7.2 Multifamily Dwelling Optional Method, Example [220.84]

▶ **Parallel Service and Service Conductors Sizing— Single-Phase, Example**

Question: *What size aluminum service conductor (paralleled in two raceways) is required for a ten-unit multifamily building with the following loads in each 1,000 sq ft unit? The system voltage is 120/240V single-phase.* ▶Figure 7–2

Note: *Laundry facilities are provided on the premises for all tenants [210.52(F) Ex 1].*

* *Dishwasher, 1,200 VA at 120V*
* *Disposal, 900 VA at 120V*
* *Water Heater, 4,500W at 240V*
* *Dryer, 4,000W at 120/240V*
* *Range, 12,000W at 120/240V*
* *Air-Conditioning, 4,008 VA at 240V*
* *Electric Heating, 6,000W at 240V*

(a) 300 kcmil (b) 350 kcmil (c) 400 kcmil (d) 500 kcmil

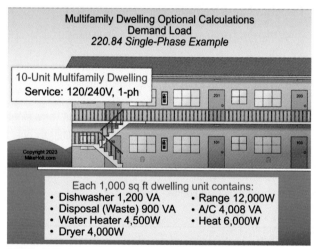

Multifamily Dwelling Optional Calculations
Demand Load
220.84 Single-Phase Example

10-Unit Multifamily Dwelling
Service: 120/240V, 1-ph

Each 1,000 sq ft dwelling unit contains:
* Dishwasher 1,200 VA
* Disposal (Waste) 900 VA
* Water Heater 4,500W
* Dryer 4,000W
* Range 12,000W
* A/C 4,008 VA
* Heat 6,000W

▶Figure 7–2

Solution:

Step 1: *Determine the total connected load.*

General Lighting and General-Use Receptacles	1,000 sq ft × 3 VA	3,000 VA
Small-Appliance Circuits	2 circuits × 1,500 VA	3,000 VA
Dishwasher		1,200 VA
Disposal		900 VA
Water Heater		4,500 W
Dryer (Nameplate)		4,000 W
Range (Nameplate)		12,000 W

Heat	*6,000 W*
Air-Conditioning (4,008 VA), omit 220.60	*+ 0 VA*
Total Connected Load	*34,600 VA*

Step 2: *Determine the demand load.*

Demand Load = Connected Load × Table 220.84 Demand Factor

Demand Load = 34,600 VA × 10 Units × 43%

Demand Load = 148,780 VA

Step 3: *Determine the size of the service disconnect and conductors.*
▶Figure 7–3

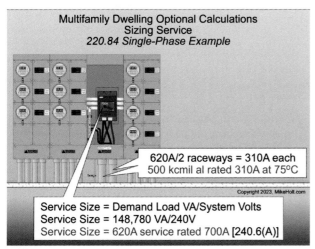

▶Figure 7–3

Service Size = Demand Load VA/System Volts

Service Size = 148,780 VA/240V

Service Size = 620A

Service Conductor Per Raceway = 620A/2 raceways

Service Conductor Per Raceway = 310A

Use 500 kcmil aluminum rated 310A at 75°C [110.14(C)(1)(b)(2) and Table 310.16].

Answer: *(d) 500 kcmil*

Part B—Standard Method Load Calculations [Article 220, Part III]

Introduction

In Part B of unit 7 you will use Article 220, Part III which covers the "standard method" for calculating the service demand load for a multifamily dwelling. The calculations for individual dwelling units in multifamily dwellings are the same as the single-family dwellings calculations you covered in Unit 6 but includes adding the number of units to each step to determine the total service demand load.

To keep your calculations organized and more importantly accurate, the standard calculation method should be worked in the following order:

- ▶ Step 1: General Lighting Load
- ▶ Step 2: Appliances
- ▶ Step 3: Clothes Dryers
- ▶ Step 4: Cooking Equipment
- ▶ Step 5: Air-Conditioning versus Heating
- ▶ Step 6: Service Size

Each step is explained in detail in this textbook and following them will allow you to determine the correct service load for a multifamily dwelling unit.

Step 1: General lighting and general-use receptacles, and small-appliance and laundry circuits [Table 220.42].

The first step is to determine the total connected load for the general lighting and general-use receptacles, small-appliance circuits, and laundry circuit as follows:

(1) General Lighting. The total connected load must include a 3 VA per sq ft load for general lighting and general-use receptacles. The total square feet is based on the outside dimensions of the dwelling unit, but doesn't include open porches or unused or unfinished spaces not adaptable for future use.

(2) Small-Appliance and Laundry Circuits. Two 20A, 120V small-appliance circuits and one 20A, 120V circuit for the laundry area is required for each dwelling unit [210.11(C)(1) and 210.11(C)(2)]. The load for each of these circuits is based on 1500 VA.

Where a dwelling unit is within a multifamily building that includes laundry facilities for the use of all building occupants, then a laundry circuit is not required in each dwelling unit [210.52(F) Ex].

Step 2: Appliances [220.53].

Appliances within the scope of 220.53 include disposals, dishwashers, trash compactors, water heaters, and so forth. The demand load is determined by applying a 75 percent demand factor to the nameplate rating when there is four or more appliances. There is no demand factor applied to appliances when there is three or less.

Step 3: Dryers [220.54].

When a dryer is to be installed, the greater of the nameplate rating or 5000W must be used.

Step 4: Electric cooking equipment [220.55].

The demand load for electric cooking equipment is determined in accordance with 220.55 and Table 220.55, including Table 220.55 Heading and Notes 1, 2, and 3.

Step 5: Air-conditioning versus Heating.

Select the larger of 125 percent of the air-conditioning load (if it is the largest motor-type load in the dwelling unit) plus 100 percent for the other air-conditioning loads [220.50] and compare it to 100 percent of the heating load [220.51] if they are not both likely to be on at the same time [220.60].

Step 6: Service Conductors Size.

The first step in determining the rated service and conductor sizes is to add up the demand loads for the general-lighting and small-appliance circuits, appliances, dryers, cooking equipment, air-conditioning, heat, and motor loads, and then dividing the total by the nominal system voltage.

Next, size the service disconnect in accordance with the standard size overcurrent protective device contained in 240.6(A).

7.3 General Lighting and General-Use Receptacle Demand Load [220.41 and 220.45]

The *NEC* recognizes that the general lighting and receptacle, small appliance, and laundry circuits will not all be on at full load at the same time. This is called "load diversity," and it allows a demand factor to be applied to the total connected load [220.45]. To determine the service demand load for these circuits, use the following steps:

Step 1: Determine the total connected load for the following:

(1) General lighting and general-use receptacles at 3 VA per sq ft [220.41]. The dimensions for determining the area is based on the outside dimensions of the building and do not include open porches or spaces not adaptable for future use [220.5(C)].

(2) Two small-appliance circuits each at 1500 VA [210.11(C)(1) and 210.52(B)].

(3) One laundry circuit at 1500 VA [210.11(C)(2) and 210.52(F)].

Step 2: Determine the general lighting and general-use demand load by applying the Table 220.45 demand factors to the total connected load (from Step 1 by) the following factors:

(1) First 3000 VA of Step 1 at a 100 percent demand factor

(2) The next 117,000 VA of Step 1 at a 35 percent demand factor

(3) The remainder at 25 percent demand factor

▶ General Lighting Demand Load, Example 1

Question: What is the general lighting and receptacle demand load for a ten-unit apartment building? Each unit is 1,000 sq ft. ▶Figure 7–4

(a) 21,300 VA   (b) 24,700 VA   (c) 25,600 VA   (d) 28,200 VA

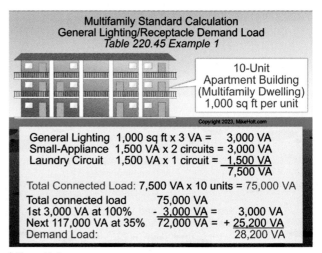

▶Figure 7–4

Solution:

Step 1: Determine general lighting and general-use receptacles, small-appliance and laundry circuit connected load.

General Lighting	1,000 sq ft × 3 VA	3,000 VA
Small-Appliance Circuits	1,500 VA × 2 circuits	3,000 VA
Laundry Circuit		+1,500 VA
Connected Load for One Unit		7,500 VA

Step 2: Determine general lighting and general-use, small-appliance, and laundry circuit demand load [Table 220.42].

Connected Load = 7,500 VA × 10 units
Connected Load = 75,000 VA

Connected Load	75,000 VA	
First 3,000 VA at 100%	−3,000 VA × 100%	3,000 VA
Remainder at 35%	72,000 VA × 35%	+25,200 VA
Total Demand Load		28,200 VA

Answer: (d) 28,200 VA

▶ General Lighting Demand Load, Example 2

Question: What is the general lighting and receptacle (including the small-appliance circuits) demand load for an apartment building that contains 20 units? Each apartment is 1,500 sq ft. ▶**Figure 7–5**

Note: Laundry facilities are provided on the premises for all tenants [210.52(F) Ex 1].

(a) 30,200 VA   (b) 35,500 VA   (c) 40,590 VA   (d) 51,450 VA

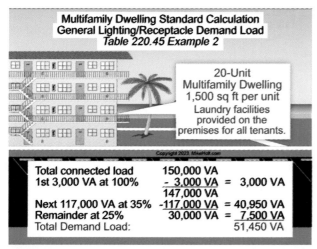

Multifamily Dwelling Standard Calculation
General Lighting/Receptacle Demand Load
Table 220.45 Example 2

20-Unit
Multifamily Dwelling
1,500 sq ft per unit
Laundry facilities
provided on the
premises for all tenants.

Copyright 2023, MikeHolt.com

Total connected load	150,000 VA	
1st 3,000 VA at 100%	- 3,000 VA	= 3,000 VA
	147,000 VA	
Next 117,000 VA at 35%	-117,000 VA	= 40,950 VA
Remainder at 25%	30,000 VA	= 7,500 VA
Total Demand Load:		51,450 VA

▶Figure 7–5

Solution:

Step 1: *Determine general lighting and general-use receptacles, small-appliance and laundry circuit connected load.*

General Lighting	1,500 sq ft × 3 VA	4,500 VA
Small-Appliance Circuits	1,500 VA × 2 Circuits	3,000 VA
Laundry Circuit,		
omit [210.52(F) Ex 1]		+ 0 VA
Connected Load for One Unit		7,500 VA

Step 2: *Determine general lighting and general-use, small-appliance, and laundry circuit demand load [Table 220.42].*

Connected Load	7,500 VA × 20 Units	150,000 VA
First 3,000 VA at 100%	3,000 VA × 100%	– 3,000 VA
Demand Load		147,000 VA
Demand Load	147,000 VA	
Next 117,000 VA* at 35%	–117,000 VA × 35%	40,950 VA
Remainder at 25%	30,000 VA × 25%	+ 7,500 VA
Total Demand Load		51,450 VA

*Remember to subtract 3,000 VA from 120,000 VA when using Table 220.45 since 35 percent only applies to 3,001 VA to 120,000 VA.

Answer: (d) 51,450 VA

7.4 Appliance Demand Load [220.53]

The appliance demand load is determined by applying a 75 percent demand factor to the nameplate rating of four or more appliances that are fastened in place, such as a disposal, dishwasher, trash compactor, water heater, and so forth. The appliance demand load for three or less appliances is 100 percent factor.

▶ Appliance Demand Load, Example 1

Question: What is the appliance demand load for the service to a ten-unit multifamily building that contains a 1,200 VA dishwasher, a 900 VA disposal, and a 4,500W water heater in each unit? ▶**Figure 7–6**

(a) 45,000 VA   (b) 50,000 VA   (c) 49,500 VA   (d) 60,000 VA

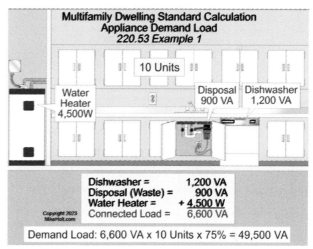

Multifamily Dwelling Standard Calculation
Appliance Demand Load
220.53 Example 1

10 Units

Water
Heater
4,500W

Disposal | Dishwasher
900 VA | 1,200 VA

Copyright 2023
MikeHolt.com

Dishwasher =	1,200 VA
Disposal (Waste) =	900 VA
Water Heater =	+ 4,500 W
Connected Load =	6,600 VA

Demand Load: 6,600 VA x 10 Units x 75% = 49,500 VA

▶Figure 7–6

Solution:

Dishwasher	1,200 VA
Disposal	900 VA
Water Heater	+4,500 W
Connected Load per Unit	6,600 VA

Connected Load = 6,600 VA × 10 Units
Total Connected Load = 66,000 VA

Demand Load = Connected Load × Demand Factor [220.53]
Demand Load = 66,000 VA × 75%*
Total Demand Load = 49,500 VA

*Use the total number of appliances to determine if the 75 percent demand factor applies. In this case, there is 30 appliances on the service conductors [220.53].

Answer: (c) 49,500 VA

▶ Appliance Demand Load, Example 2

Question: What is the appliance demand load for the service to a twenty-unit multifamily building that contains a 1,200 VA dishwasher, a 900 VA disposal, and a 4,500W water heater in each unit? ▶**Figure 7–7**

(a) 61,000 VA   (b) 77,000 VA   (c) 86,000 VA   (d) 99,000 VA

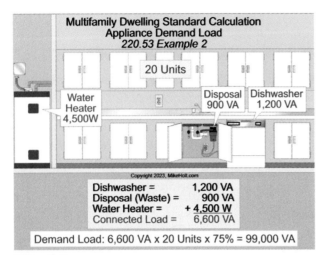

Multifamily Dwelling Standard Calculation
Appliance Demand Load
220.53 Example 2

Water Heater 4,500W   Disposal 900 VA   Dishwasher 1,200 VA

Dishwasher =	1,200 VA
Disposal (Waste) =	900 VA
Water Heater =	+ 4,500 W
Connected Load =	6,600 VA

Demand Load: 6,600 VA x 20 Units x 75% = 99,000 VA

▶Figure 7–7

Solution:

Dishwasher	*1,200 VA*
Disposal	*900 VA*
Water Heater	*+4,500 W*
Connected Load per Unit	*6,600 VA*

Connected Load = 6,600 VA × 20 units
Total Connected Load = 132,000 VA

Demand Load = Connected Load × Demand Factor [220.53]
Demand Load = 132,000 VA × 75%*
Total Demand Load = 99,000 VA

*Use the total number of appliances to determine if the 75 percent demand factor applies. In this case, there is 60 appliances on the service conductors [220.53].

Answer: (d) 99,000 VA

7.5 Dryer Demand Load [220.54]

When a dryer is to be installed, the larger of the nameplate rating or 5000W must be used. Depending on the number of units, the total demand load must be in accordance with Table 220.54, including the application of any demand factors. ▶**Figure 7–8**

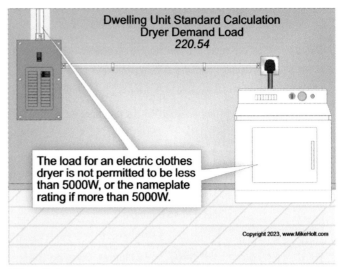

Dwelling Unit Standard Calculation
Dryer Demand Load
220.54

The load for an electric clothes dryer is not permitted to be less than 5000W, or the nameplate rating if more than 5000W.

▶Figure 7–8

▶ Dryer Demand Load [220.54], Example 1

Question: What is the service demand load for ten 4 kW dryers? ▶**Figure 7–9**

(a) 5 kW   (b) 25 kW   (c) 45 kW   (d) 60 kW

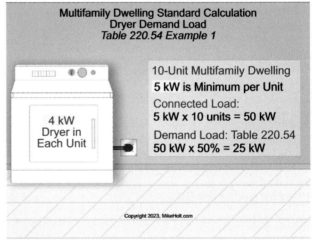

Multifamily Dwelling Standard Calculation
Dryer Demand Load
Table 220.54 Example 1

4 kW Dryer in Each Unit

10-Unit Multifamily Dwelling
5 kW is Minimum per Unit
Connected Load:
5 kW x 10 units = 50 kW
Demand Load: Table 220.54
50 kW x 50% = 25 kW

▶Figure 7–9

Solution:

The question gave a nameplate rating of 4 kW, however the minimum load for a dryer is 5 kW [220.54].

5 kW is the minimum load for calculation [220.54].

Connected Load = 5 kW × 10 units
Total Connected Load = 50 kW

Demand Load = 50 kW × 50% [Table 220.54]
Total Demand Load = 25 kW

Answer: (b) 25 kW

▶ Dryer Demand Load [220.54], Example 2

Question: What is the service demand load for ten 5.5 kW dryers?
▶Figure 7–10

(a) 15 kW (b) 27.5 kW (c) 45 kW (d) 60 kW

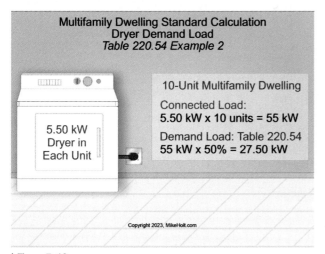

▶Figure 7–10

Solution:

Connected Load = 5.5 kW × 10 units
Total Connected Load = 55 kW

Demand Load = 55 kW × 50% [Table 220.54]
Total Demand Load = 27.5 kW

Answer: (b) 27.5 kW

▶ Dryer Demand Load [220.54], Example 3

Question: What is the service demand load for twenty 5.5 kW dryers?
▶Figure 7–11

(a) 23 kW (b) 37 kW (c) 42 kW (d) 60 kW

Solution:

*For 20 dryers, the demand factor percent is 47 percent minus
1 percent for each dryer over 11 units [Table 220.54].*

Percent = 47% – [1% × (number of dryers exceeding 11)]
Percent = 47% – [1% × (20 dryers–11 dryers)]
Percent = 47% – [1% × 9 dryers]
Percent = 47% – 9%
Percent = 38%

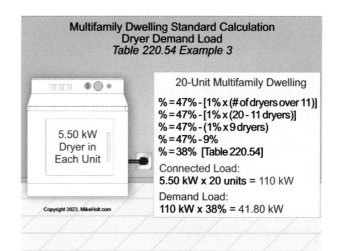

▶Figure 7–11

Connected Load = 5.5 kW × 20 units
Total Connected Load = 110 kW

Demand Load = 110 kW × 38%
Total Demand Load = 41.8 kW, round to 42 kW

Answer: (c) 42 kW

▶ Dryer Demand Load [220.54], Example 4

Question: What is the service demand load for forty 5 kW dryers?
▶Figure 7–12

(a) 15 kW (b) 27 kW (c) 39.9 kW (d) 53 kW

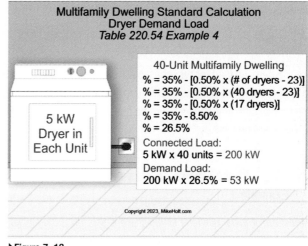

▶Figure 7–12

• • •

Solution:

For 40 dryers, the demand factor percent is 35 percent minus 0.50 percent for each dryer over 23 units [Table 220.54].

Demand Factor (Percent) = 35% – [0.50% × (Number of Dryers Exceeding 23)]

Demand Factor (Percent) = 35% – [0.50% × (40 dryers – 23 dryers)]

Demand Factor (Percent) = 35% – [0.50% × 17 dryers]

Demand Factor (Percent) = 35% – 8.50%

Demand Factor (Percent) = 26.50%

Connected Load = 5 kW × 40 units

Total Connected Load = 200 kW

Demand Load = 200 kW × 26.5%

Demand Load = 53 kW

Answer: *(d) 53 kW*

7.6 Single-Phase Dryers on Three-Phase Service [220.54]

Where single-phase dryers are supplied by a three-phase, 4-wire service, the total load is based on twice the maximum number of dryers connected between any two phases [220.54].

What does "based on twice the maximum number of dryers between any two phases mean"? The single-phase dryers on a three-phase system must be balanced to determine the maximum number of dryers on any phase. The demand factor for this condition is then applied to determine the demand load for two phases.

Once the demand load for two phases is known, divide the value by two to determine the demand load for one phase of the three phases. Next, multiply the demand load for one phase by three to determine the total demand load.

▶ Single-Phase Dryers on Three-Phase Service, Example 1

Question: *If there is fifteen single-phase dryers on a three-phase service, What is the maximum number of dryers between any two phases?* ▶Figure 7–13

(a) 5   (b) 10   (c) 15   (d) 20

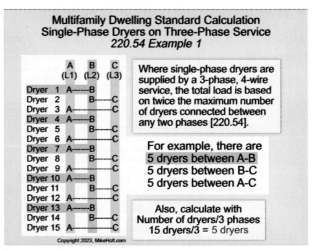

▶Figure 7–13

Solution:

If fifteen single-phase dryers are balanced on all three phases (A–B, B–C, and A–C), there will be five single-phase dryers between any two phases.

Answer: *(a) 5*

▶ Single-Phase Dryers on Three-Phase Service, Example 2

Question: *If there is fifteen single-phase dryers on a three-phase service, What is the maximum number of dryers counted for the demand load on any phase?* ▶Figure 7–14

(a) 10   (b) 14   (c) 21   (d) 28

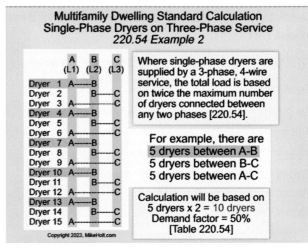

▶Figure 7–14

Solution:

Step 1: *Determine the maximum number of dryers between any two phases.*

15 Dryers/3 Three-Phases = 5 dryers (units) between any two phases

There are five dryers between A–B, five dryers between B–C, and five dryers between A–C.

Step 2: *The demand factor is based on twice the maximum number of dryers between any two phases.*

Number of Dryers Between Two Phases = 5 dryers × 2 phases
Number of Dryers Between Two Phases = 10 dryers

Answer: (a) 10

▶ **Single-Phase Dryers on Three-Phase Service, Example 3**

Question: *What is the service demand load for fifteen single-phase dryers on a three-phase service?* ▶**Figure 7–15**

(a) 25.5 kW   *(b) 30.5 kW*   *(c) 34.5 kW*   *(d) 37.5 kW*

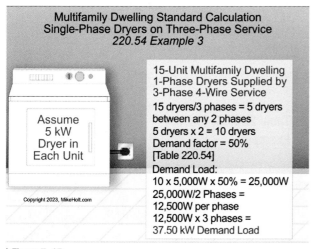

Multifamily Dwelling Standard Calculation
Single-Phase Dryers on Three-Phase Service
220.54 Example 3

Assume 5 kW Dryer in Each Unit

15-Unit Multifamily Dwelling
1-Phase Dryers Supplied by
3-Phase 4-Wire Service
15 dryers/3 phases = 5 dryers
between any 2 phases
5 dryers x 2 = 10 dryers
Demand factor = 50%
[Table 220.54]
Demand Load:
10 x 5,000W x 50% = 25,000W
25,000W/2 Phases =
12,500W per phase
12,500W x 3 phases =
37.50 kW Demand Load

Copyright 2023, MikeHolt.com

▶Figure 7–15

Solution:

Step 1: *Determine the maximum number of dryers between any two phases.*

15 Dryers/3 Three-Phases = 5 dryers between any two phases

There are 5 dryers between A–B, 5 dryers between B–C, and 5 dryers between A–C.

Step 2: *Apply the Table 220.54 demand factor for twice the maximum number of dryers between any two phases.*

5 Units × 2 Phases = 10 units
Table 220.54 for 10 Units = 50%

Since the kW rating was not given in the question, assume 5 kW (5,000W).

Demand Load = 10 × 5,000W × 50%
Demand Load = 50,000W × 50%
Demand Load = 25,000W

Step 3: *Determine the demand load per phase.*

25,000W/2 Phases = 12,500W for one phase

Step 4: *Determine the demand load for three phases.*

Demand Load for Three Phases = 12,500W × 3 phases
Demand Load for Three Phases = 37,500W for three phases
Demand Load for Three Phases = 37,500W/1,000
Demand Load for Three Phases = 37.5 kW

Answer: (d) 37.5 kW

▶ **Single-Phase Dryers on Three-Phase Service, Example 4**

Question: *What is the service demand load for twenty 5.5 kW single-phase dryers on a three-phase service?* ▶**Figure 7–16**

(a) 35 kW   *(b) 40 kW*   *(c) 45 kW*   *(d) 51 kW*

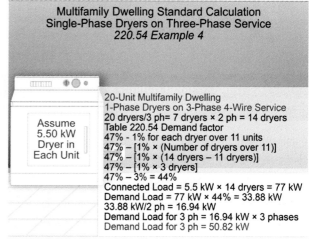

Multifamily Dwelling Standard Calculation
Single-Phase Dryers on Three-Phase Service
220.54 Example 4

Assume 5.50 kW Dryer in Each Unit

20-Unit Multifamily Dwelling
1-Phase Dryers on 3-Phase 4-Wire Service
20 dryers/3 ph = 7 dryers × 2 ph = 14 dryers
Table 220.54 Demand factor
47% - 1% for each dryer over 11 units
47% – [1% × (Number of dryers over 11)]
47% – [1% × (14 dryers – 11 dryers)]
47% – [1% × 3 dryers]
47% – 3% = 44%
Connected Load = 5.5 kW × 14 dryers = 77 kW
Demand Load = 77 kW × 44% = 33.88 kW
33.88 kW/2 ph = 16.94 kW
Demand Load for 3 ph = 16.94 kW × 3 phases
Demand Load for 3 ph = 50.82 kW

▶Figure 7–16

• • •

Solution:

Step 1: *Determine the maximum number of dryers between any two phases.*

20 Dryers/3 Three-Phases = 7 dryers between A–B, 7 dryers between B–C, and 6 dryers between A–C

Step 2: *Apply the Table 220.54 demand factor for twice the maximum number of dryers between any two phases.*

7 Dryers × 2 = 14 dryers

For 14 dryers, the demand factor is 47 percent minus one percent for each dryer over 11 units [Table 220.54].

Percent = 47% – [1% × (number of dryers exceeding 11)]
Percent = 47% – [1% × (14 dryers – 11 dryers)]
Percent = 47% – [1% × 3 dryers]
Percent = 47% – 3%
Percent = 44%

Connected Load = 5.5 kW × 14 units
Connected Load = 77 kW

Demand Load = 77 kW × 44%
Demand Load = 33.88 kW

Step 3: *Determine the demand load per phase.*

33.88 kW/2 Phases = 16.94 kW for one phase

Step 4: *Determine the demand load for three phases.*

Demand Load for Three Phases = 16.94 kW × 3 phases
Demand Load for Three Phases = 50.82 kW, round to 51 kW

Answer: *(d) 51 kW*

7.7 Single-Phase Ranges on Single-Phase Service [220.55]

The demand load for electric cooking equipment is determined in accordance with 220.55 and Table 220.55 Column C to be used in all cases except as otherwise permitted in Note 3 to Table 220.55.

▶ **Table 220.55, Column C—Over 8¾ kW to 12 kW, Example 1**

Question: What is the service demand load for twenty 9 kW ranges?
▶Figure 7–17

(a) 28 kW   *(b) 30 kW*   *(c) 35 kW*   *(d) 42 kW*

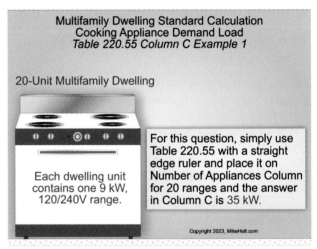

Multifamily Dwelling Standard Calculation
Cooking Appliance Demand Load
Table 220.55 Column C Example 1

20-Unit Multifamily Dwelling

Each dwelling unit contains one 9 kW, 120/240V range.

For this question, simply use Table 220.55 with a straight edge ruler and place it on Number of Appliances Column for 20 ranges and the answer in Column C is 35 kW.

Copyright 2023, MikeHolt.com

▶Figure 7–17

Solution:

Table 220.55, Column C maximum demand load for twenty units is 35 kW.

Answer: *(c) 35 kW [Table 220.55, Column C]*

▶ **Table 220.55, Column C—Over 8¾ kW to 12 kW, Example 2**

Question: What is the service demand load for forty 10 kW ranges?
▶Figure 7–18

(a) 28 kW   *(b) 30 kW*   *(c) 35 kW*   *(d) 55 kW*

Solution:

Table 220.55, Column C maximum demand load for forty units is 15 kW + 1 kW for each range 26–40.

Demand Load = Table 220.55 Column C
Demand Load = 15 kW + 1 kW for each range 26-40
Demand Load = 40 kW +15 kW (1 kW × 15 ranges)
Demand Load = 55 kW

Answer: *(d) 55 kW [Table 220.55, Column C]*

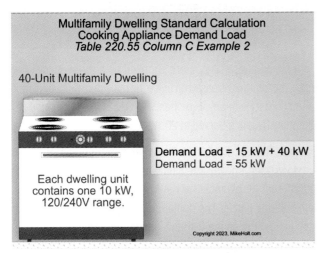

▶Figure 7–18

▶ **Table 220.55, Note 1—Over 12 kW with Equal Ratings, Example 1**

Question: What is the service demand load for twenty 14 kW ranges?
▶Figure 7–19

(a) 28 kW   (b) 30 kW   (c) 38.5 kW   (d) 42 kW

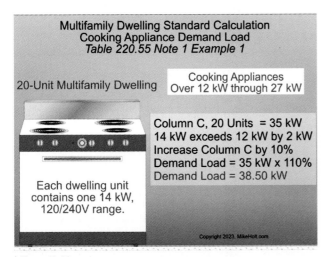

▶Figure 7–19

Solution:

Step 1: The Table 220.55, Column C maximum demand load is 35 kW.

Step 2: A 14 kW range exceeds 12 kW by 2 kW. Increase the Column C maximum demand load by five percent for each kW more than 12 kW.

Increase Column C = 2 × 5%
Increase Column C = 10%

Step 3: Determine the demand load.

Demand Load = Column C Value × Multiplier
Demand Load = 35 kW × 110%
Demand Load = 38.5 kW

Answer: (c) 38.5 kW

▶ **Table 220.55, Note 1—Over 12 kW with Equal Ratings, Example 2**

Question: What is the service demand load for forty 14 kW ranges?
▶Figure 7–20

(a) 28 kW   (b) 30 kW   (c) 38 kW   (d) 61 kW

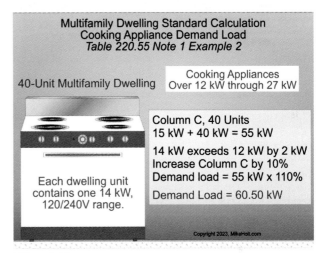

▶Figure 7–20

Solution:

Step 1: The Table 220.55, Column C maximum demand load for forty units is 15 kW + 1 kW for each range 26–40.

Demand Load = 40 kW +15 kW (1 kW for each range 26–40)
Demand Load = 55 kW

Step 2: Determine the multiplier. A 14 kW range exceeds 12 kW by 2 kW. Increase the Column C maximum demand load by five percent for each kW more than 12 kW [Table 220.55 note 1].

Increase Column C = 2 × 5%
Increase Column C = 10%

Step 3: Determine the demand load.

Demand Load = 55 kW × 110%
Demand Load = 60.5 kW, round to 61 kW

Answer: (d) 61 kW

▶ **Table 220.55, Column B versus Column C—Less than 8¾ kW, Note 3 Example**

Question: *What is the service demand load for ten 8 kW ranges?* ▶**Figure 7-21**

(a) 9 kW   *(b) 20 kW*   *(c) 25 kW*   *(d) 45 kW*

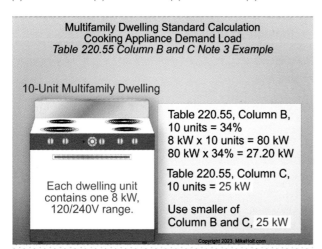

▶Figure 7-21

Solution:

According to the title *of Table 220.55, the demand load for ranges are to be based on Column C values, except as permitted by Note 3 to Table 220.55 which 'permits' the use Column B value when the ranges are less than 8¾. When you get a question for ranges that are less than 8¾ kW, complete the following steps.*

Step 1: Determine the demand load using the Table 220.55 Column B demand factor as permitted by Note 3.

Demand Load = Connected Load × Table 220.55 Column B Demand Factor
Demand Load = (8 kW × 10 units) × 34%
Demand Load = 80 kW × 34%
Demand Load = 27.2 kW

Step 2: Determine the demand load using the Table 220.55 Column C demand load as specified in the title of Table 220.55.

Demand Load = Table 220.55 Column C Demand Load
Demand Load for 10 Unit 8 kW Units = 25 kW

Step 3: Select the smaller of Column B value vs Column C value [Table 220.55 Heading, Note 3 to Table 220.55, and Example D4(b)].

Column C Demand Load 25 kW (based on 12 kW ranges) is smaller than the Column B Demand Load (based on 8 kW ranges)] of 27.2 kW.

Answer: (c) 25 kW

7.8 Single-Phase Ranges on Three-Phase Service [220.55]

Where single-phase ranges are supplied by a three-phase, 4-wire service, the total load is based on twice the maximum number of ranges connected between any two phases [220.55]. See, Example D5(a) Multifamily Dwelling Served at 208Y/120V, Three-Phase in Annex D.

What does "based on twice the maximum number of ranges between any two phases" mean? The single-phase ranges on a three-phase system must be balanced to determine the maximum number of ranges on any phase. The demand factor for this condition is then applied to determine the demand load for two phases.

Once the demand load for two phases is known, divide the value by two to determine the demand load for one phase of the three phases. Next, multiply the demand load for one phase by three to determine the total demand load.

▶ **Single-Phase Ranges on Three-Phase Service, Number of Ranges Example 1**

Question: *If there is fifteen single-phase ranges on a three-phase service, What is the maximum number of ranges between any two phases?* ▶**Figure 7-22**

(a) 5   *(b) 10*   *(c) 15*   *(d) 20*

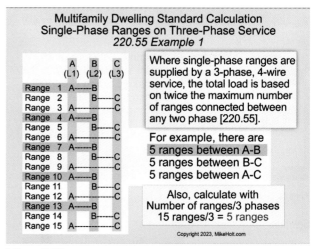

▶Figure 7-22

Solution:

Determine the maximum number of ranges between any two phases.

15 Ranges/3 Three-Phases = 5 ranges between A–B, 5 ranges between B–C, and 5 ranges between A–C.

Answer: (a) 5

▶ **Single-Phase Ranges on Three-Phase Service, Number of Ranges Example 2**

Question: If there is fifteen single-phase ranges on a three-phase service, What is the number of ranges used to determine the range demand load? ▶Figure 7–23

(a) 10   (b) 14   (c) 21   (d) 28

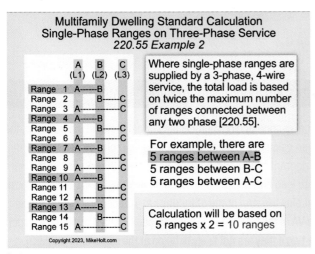

▶Figure 7–23

Solution:

Step 1: Determine the maximum number of ranges between any two phases.

15 Ranges/3 Three-Phases = 5 ranges between A–B, 5 ranges between B–C, and 5 ranges between A–C

Step 2: Calculate twice the maximum number of ranges between any two phases [220.55].

5 Ranges × 2 = 10 ranges

The service demand load in table 220.55 applies to twice the number of ranges between any two phases.

Answer: (a) 10

▶ **Single-Phase Ranges on Three-Phase Service, Demand Load Example**

Question: What is the service demand load for fifteen single-phase, 12 kW ranges on a three-phase service? ▶Figure 7–24

(a) 28.5 kW   (b) 30.5 kW   (c) 34.5 kW   (d) 37.5 kW

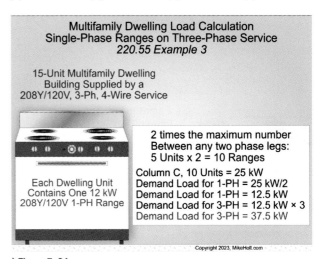

▶Figure 7–24

Solution:

Step 1: Determine the maximum number of ranges between any two phases.

15 Ranges/3 Three-Phases = 5 ranges between A–B, 5 ranges between B–C, and 5 ranges between A–C

Step 2: Calculate twice the maximum number of ranges between any two phases [220.55].

5 Ranges × 2 = 10 ranges

The service demand load in table 220.55 applies to twice the number of ranges between any two phases so apply the Table 220.55 demand factor to ten rangers.

Step 3: Apply the Table 220.55 demand factor for twice the maximum number of ranges between any two phases.

Column C Demand Load for 10 Units = 25 kW [Table 220.55]

Step 4: Determine the demand load.

Demand Load for One Phase = 25 kW/2 phases
Demand Load for One Phase = 12.5 kW

Demand Load for Three Phases = 12.5 kW × 3 phases
Demand Load for Three Phases = 37.5 kW

Answer: (d) 37.5 kW

▶ Single-Phase Ranges on Three-Phase Service, Demand Load Note 1 Example

Question: What is the service demand load for twenty single-phase 14 kW ranges on a three-phase service? ▶Figure 7–25

(a) 28.5 kW   (b) 30.5 kW   (c) 34.5 kW   (d) 47.85 kW

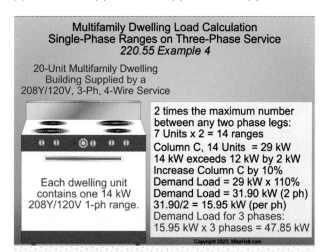

Multifamily Dwelling Load Calculation
Single-Phase Ranges on Three-Phase Service
220.55 Example 4

20-Unit Multifamily Dwelling
Building Supplied by a
208Y/120V, 3-Ph, 4-Wire Service

Each dwelling unit
contains one 14 kW
208Y/120V 1-ph range.

2 times the maximum number
between any two phase legs:
7 Units x 2 = 14 ranges
Column C, 14 Units = 29 kW
14 kW exceeds 12 kW by 2 kW
Increase Column C by 10%
Demand Load = 29 kW x 110%
Demand Load = 31.90 kW (2 ph)
31.90/2 = 15.95 kW (per ph)
Demand Load for 3 phases:
15.95 kW x 3 phases = 47.85 kW

Copyright 2023, MikeHolt.com

▶Figure 7–25

Solution:

Step 1: *Determine the maximum number of ranges between any two phases.*

20 Ranges/3 Three-Phases = 7 ranges between A–B, 7 ranges between B–C, and 6 ranges between A–C

Step 2: *Calculate twice the maximum number of ranges between any two phases [220.55].*

Number of Ranges (between two phases) = 7 units × 2
Number of Ranges (between two phases) = 14 ranges

The service demand load in Table 220.55 applies to twice the number of ranges between any two phases so apply the Table 220.55 demand factor to 14 rangers.

Step 3: *Apply the Table 220.55 demand factor for twice the maximum number of ranges between any two phases.*

Demand Factor = 29 kW (based on 14 ranges)

14 kW range exceeds 12 kW by 2 kW.

Step 4: *Determine the multiplier.*

Increase the Column C maximum demand load (29 kW) by five percent for each kW more than 12 kW.

Demand Load = 29 kW × 110%
Demand Load = 31.9 kW for two phases

Step 5: *Determine the demand load.*

Demand Load for Two Phases = 31.9 kW/two phases
Demand Load for Two Phases = 15.95 kW

Demand Load for Three Phases = 15.95 kW × 3 phases
Demand Load for Three Phases = 47.85 kW

Answer: (d) 47.85 kW

7.9 Air-Conditioning and Heating Demand Load

If the air-conditioning motor is the largest motor in the question, then, when calculating the air-conditioning load of a multimotor hermetic refrigerant motor-compressor, compare 125 percent of the name-plate load current of the air-conditioning load in VA [220.50] for one unit plus the sum of the other units at 100 percent to 100 percent of the VA of the fixed electric heating load [220.51]. Select the larger of the two if they are not likely to be on at the same time [220.60]. If the air-conditioning and electric heating load is to be used at the same time, such as a heat pump, then the air-conditioning at 125 percent and heating load at 100 percent must be added together.

▶ Air-Conditioning versus Heating Demand Load, Example 1

Question: What is the service demand load for a ten-unit multifamily building where each unit has 16.7A, 240V air-conditioning as compared to 6 kW electric heat? ▶Figure 7–26

(a) 50 kVA   (b) 60 kW   (c) 160 kVA   (d) 250 kVA

Solution:

Step 1: *Determine the air-conditioning load.*

Air-Conditioning Unit VA = Volts × Amperes
Air-Conditioning = 240V × 16.70A
Air-Conditioning = 4,008 VA
Air-Conditioning = (4,008 VA × 125% × 1 unit) + (4,008 VA × 9 units)
Air-Conditioning = 5,010 VA + 36,072 VA
Air-Conditioning = 41,082 VA
Air-Conditioning = 41,082 VA/1,000
Air-Conditioning = 41.08 kVA, omit since it is smaller than heat 220.60

Step 2: *Determine the electric heating load.*

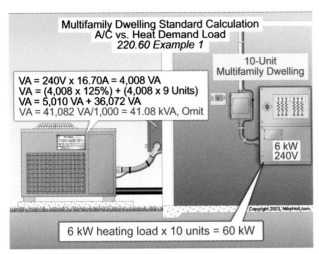

▶Figure 7–26

Heating Load = 6 kW × 10 units
Heating Load = 60 kW [220.51]

Answer: (b) 60 kW

▶ **Air-Conditioning versus Heating Demand Load, Example 2**

Question: What is the service demand load for a twenty-unit multifamily building where each unit has 208V motor-compressor air-conditioning rated 23.10A as compared to 6 kW electric heat? ▶**Figure 7–27**

(a) 105 kVA   (b) 116 kVA   (c) 123 kVA   (d) 120 kW

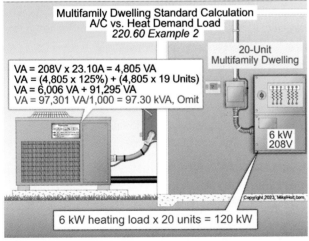

▶Figure 7–27

Solution:

Step 1: *Determine the air-conditioning load.*

Air-Conditioning = Volts × Amperes
Air-Conditioning = 208V × 23.10A

Air-Conditioning = 4,805 VA
Air-Conditioning = (4,805 VA × 125% × 1 unit) + (4,805 VA × 19 units)
Air-Conditioning = 6,006 VA + 91,295 VA
Air-Conditioning = 97,301 VA
Air-Conditioning = 97,301 VA/1,000
Air-Conditioning = 97.30 kVA, omit since it is smaller than heat 220.60

Step 2: *Determine the electric heating load.*

Heating Load = 6 kW × 20 units
Heating Load = 120 kW [220.51]

Answer: (d) 120 kW

7.10 Service Conductor Sizing [Table 310.16]

After applying the demand load factors as permitted in Article 220 and calculating the total demand load, service conductors are sized in accordance with Table 310.16. The *NEC* permits conductors to be run in parallel, which means smaller conductors in multiple sets (instead of just one conductor) can be used [310.10(G)].

▶ **Service Conductor Size—Single-Phase, Example**

Question: What size service conductor paralleled in three raceways is required for a ten-unit multifamily building having a demand load of 187,700 VA? The system is 120/240V, single-phase. ▶**Figure 7–28**　.

(a) 300 kcmil   (b) 350 kcmil aluminum
(c) 400 kcmil   (d) 500 kcmil

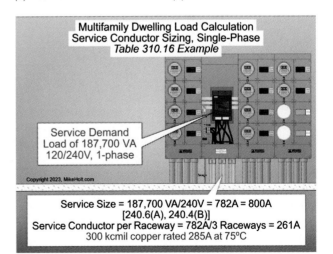

▶Figure 7–28

• • •

Solution:

Step 1: *Determine the service size.*

Service Size = Demand Load VA/System Volts

Service Size = 187,700 VA/240V

Service Size = No less than 782A

Service Size = 800A [240.6(A)]

Step 2: *Determine the service conductor size per raceway.*

Service conductors must have an ampacity of no less than 782A, protected by an 800A overcurrent protective device in accordance with 240.4(B).

Service Conductor per Raceway = 782A/3 raceways
Service Conductor per Raceway = 261A

Use 300 kcmil rated 285A at 75°C [110.14(C)(1)(b)(2) and Table 310.16].

Answer: *(a) 300 kcmil*

▶ Service Conductor Size—Three-Phase, Example

Question: *What size aluminum service conductor paralleled in three raceways is required for a twenty-unit multifamily building having a demand load of 314 kVA? The system is 208Y/120V, three-phase.*
▶Figure 7–29

(a) 300 kcmil   (b) 400 kcmil   (c) 500 kcmil   (d) 600 kcmil

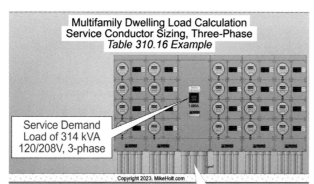

Multifamily Dwelling Load Calculation
Service Conductor Sizing, Three-Phase
Table 310.16 Example

Service Demand Load of 314 kVA 120/208V, 3-phase

Copyright 2023, MikeHolt.com

Service Size = 314,000 VA/(208V x 1.732) = 872A = 1,000A
[240.6(A), 240.4(C)]
Service Conductor per Raceway = 1,000A/3 Raceways = 333A
600 kcmil aluminum rated 340A at 75°C

▶Figure 7–29

Solution:

Step 1: *Determine the service size.*

Service Size = Demand Load VA/(System Volts × 1.732)

Service Size = 314,000 VA/(208V × 1.732)

Service Size = 314,000 VA/360.26

Service Size = 872A

Service Size = 1000A [240.6(A)]

Step 2: *Determine the service conductor size per raceway.*

Service conductors must have an ampacity of no less than 1,000A, protected by a 1,000A overcurrent protective device in accordance with 240.4(C).

Service Conductor per Raceway = 1,000A/3 raceways*
Service Conductor per Raceway = 333A

Use 600 kcmil aluminum rated 340A at 75°C [110.14(C)(1)(b)(2) and Table 310.16].

*Conductors on overcurrent devices rated over 800A must have a rating of not less than the rating of the overcurrent device [240.6(C)].

Answer: *(d) 600 kcmil*

7.11 Multifamily Dwelling Calculations— Standard Method, Examples

The following examples demonstrate the steps used to determine service sizes for a multifamily dwelling using the standard method contained in Article 220, Part III:

▶ Standard Method Service Load Calculations— Single-Phase, Example

Question: *What size service and service conductor (paralleled three raceways) is required for a ten-unit multifamily building having the following loads in each 1,000 sq ft unit? The system is 120/240V, single-phase.* ▶Figure 7–30

- *Dishwasher, 1,200 VA at 120V*
- *Disposal (Waste), 900 VA at 120V*
- *Water Heater, 4,500W at 240V*
- *Dryer, 4,000W at 120/240V*
- *Range, 8,000W at 120/240V*
- *Air-Conditioning, 16.70A at 240V*
- *Electric Heating, 6,000W*

(a) 300 kcmil   (b) 400 kcmil aluminum
(c) 500 kcmil aluminum   (d) a or c

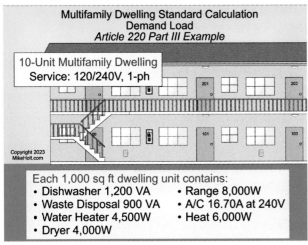

▶Figure 7–30

Solution:

Step 1: *Determine the general lighting and general-use receptacles, and the small-appliance and laundry circuits demand [Table 220.45].*

General Lighting [220.42(A)]	1,000 sq ft × 3 VA	3,000 VA
Small-Appliance Circuits		
[210.52(B)]	1,500 VA × 2 circuits	3,000 VA
Laundry Circuit [210.52(F)]		+1,500 VA
Connected Load per Unit		7,500 VA
Connected Load for 10 Units	7,500 VA × 10 units	75,000 VA
First 3,000 VA at 100%	−3,000 VA × 100%	3,000 VA
Remainder at 35%	72,000 VA × 35%	+25,200 VA
Demand Load		28,200 VA

Step 2: *Determine the appliance demand load [220.53].* ▶**Figure 7–31**

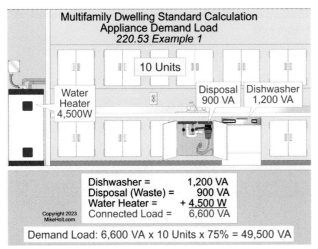

▶Figure 7–31

Dishwasher	1,200 VA
Disposal (Waste)	900 VA
Water Heater	+4,500 W
Connected Load per Unit	6,600 VA

Connected Load for 10 Units = 6,000 × 10 units
Connected Load for 10 Units = 66,000 VA

Demand Load = 66,000 VA × 75%*
Demand Load = 49,500 VA

*Use the total number of appliances to determine if the 75 percent demand factor applies. In this case, there are 30 appliances on the service conductors.

Step 3: *Determine the dryer demand load [220.54].*

Dryers must be calculated at a minimum of 5,000W or the nameplate, whichever is larger. ▶**Figure 7–32**

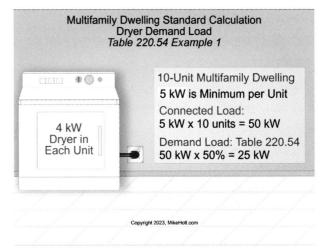

▶Figure 7–32

Connected Load = 5,000W × 10 units
Connected Load = 50,000W

Dryer Demand Factor for 10 Dryers (Percent) = 50%

Dryer Demand Load = 50,000W × 50%
Dryer Demand Load = 25,000W

Step 4: *Determine the electric cooking equipment demand load [220.55].*

When you get a question for ranges that fall in Column B, complete the following steps. See Note 1 of Table 220.55 and the introduction text contained in Annex D.

The Table 220.55, Column B demand factor for ten units is 34%. ▶**Figure 7–33**

• • •

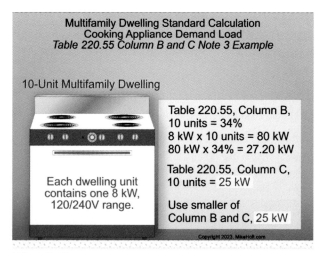

▶Figure 7–33

Demand Load = (8 kW × 10 units) × 34%

Demand Load = 80 kW × 34%

Demand Load = 27.20 kW

Use Table 220.55, Column C maximum demand load of 25 kW for ten units.

Demand Load = 25 kW

Note: *Always select the smaller of Column B versus Column C.*

Step 5: *Determine the air-conditioning versus heating demand load [220.60].* ▶Figure 7–34

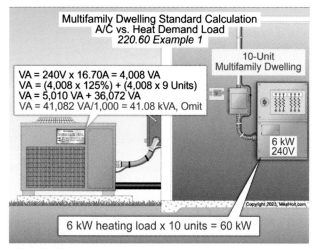

▶Figure 7–34

Air-Conditioning = Volts × Amperes

Air-Conditioning = 240V × 16.70A

Air-Conditioning = 4,008 VA

Air-Conditioning = (4,008 VA × 125% × 1 unit) + (4,008 VA × 9 units)

Air-Conditioning = 5,010 VA + 36,072 VA

Air-Conditioning = 41,082 VA, omit since it is smaller than heat 220.60

Heating = kW × Number of Units [220.51]

Heating = 6 kW × 10 units

Heating = 60 kW

Step 6: *Determine 25% of the largest motor type load.*

Air-Conditioning = 4,005 VA × 25%

Air-Conditioning = 1,002 VA

Step 7: *Determine the service and service conductor sizes [310.16].*

Step 1. General Lighting Demand Load	*28,200 VA*
Step 2. Appliance Demand Load	*49,500 VA*
Step 3. Dryer Demand Load	*25,000 W*
Step 4. Electric Cooking Equipment Demand Load	*25,000 W*
Step 5. Heating Demand Load [220.51]	*60,000 W*
Step 6. AC 25%	*+ 1,002 W*
Total Demand Load	*188,702 VA*

Service Size = Demand Load VA/System Volts ▶Figure 7–35

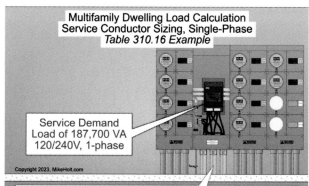

▶Figure 7–35

Service Size = 188,702 VA/240V

Service Size = 786A, round up to 800A [240.6(A)]

Service Conductor per Raceway = 786A/3 raceways

Service Conductor per Raceway = 262A

Use 300 kcmil rated 285A at 75°C [110.14(C)(1)(b)(1) and Table 310.16].

Answer: *(a) 300 kcmil*

7.12 Two-Family (Duplex) Dwelling Units Load Calculations [220.85]

The demand load is the smaller of:

▶ The standard calculation method for two units [Article 220, Part III].

▶ The optional calculation method for three in accordance with 220.84. ▶Figure 7–36

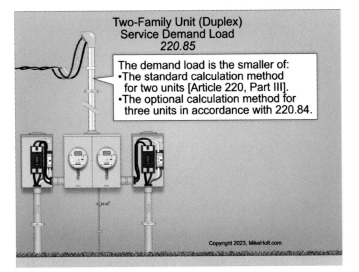

▶Figure 7–36

▶ Standard Calculation for a Two-Family Dwelling, Part II of Article 220, Example

Question: Using the standard method, what size service conductors will be required for a two-family dwelling where each unit is 1,600 sq ft and contains the following loads? ▶Figure 7–37

- Dishwasher, 1,200 VA at 120V
- Disposal (Waste), 900 VA at 120V
- Water Heater, 4,500 VA at 240V
- Dryer, 5,000W at 120/240V
- Range, 9,000W at 120/240V
- Air-Conditioning, 16.70A at 240V
- Heating, 9,600W

(a) 250 kcmil
(b) 300 kcmil
(c) 350 kcmil
(d) a or c

Solution:

Step 1: Determine general lighting and general-use receptacles, and the small-appliance and laundry circuits demand loads.

General Lighting [220.42(A)]	1,600 sq ft × 3 VA	4,800 VA
Small-Appliance [210.52(B)]	1,500 VA × 2 VA	3,000 VA
Laundry Circuit [210.52(F)]	1,500 VA × 1 VA	+1,500 VA
Unit Connected Load	9,300 VA × 2 units	18,600 VA
Demand Factors of Table 220.42	18,600 VA	
First 3,000 VA at 100%	–3,000 VA × 100%	3,000 VA
Remainder at 35%	15,600 VA × 35%	+5,460 VA
Demand Load		8,460 VA

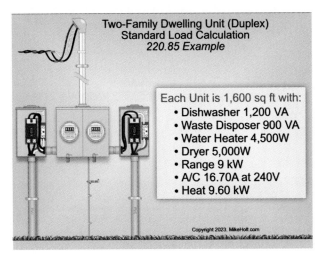

▶Figure 7–37

Step 2: Determine the appliance demand load [220.53].

Dishwashers	1,200 VA × 2	2,400 VA
Disposals	900 VA × 2	1,800 VA
Water Heaters	4,500W × 2	+9,000 W
Connected Load		13,200 VA

Demand Load [220.53] = 13,200 VA × 75%
Demand Load [220.53] = 9,900 VA

Step 3: Determine the dryer demand load [220.54].

5,000W × 2 Dryers = 10,000W

Step 4: Determine the electric cooking equipment demand load [220.55].

Range: The Column C demand load for ranges for two units is 11,000W.

• • •

Step 5: *Determine the air-conditioning versus heating [220.51].*

Air-Conditioning = Volts × Amperes

Air-Conditioning = 240V × 16.70A

Air-Conditioning = 4,008 VA

Air-Conditioning = (4,008 VA × 125%) + 4,008 VA

Air-Conditioning = 5,010 VA + 4,008 VA

Air-Conditioning = 9,018 VA, omit since it is smaller than heat 220.60

Heating = 9.60 kW × 2 Units

Heating = 19,200W

Step 6: *Determine the service and service conductor sizes.* ▶**Figure 7-38**

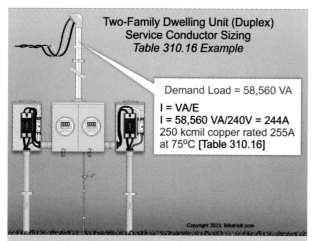

▶Figure 7-38

Step 1. General Lighting, Receptacles, Small-Appliance,

and Laundry Demand Load	*8,460 VA*
Step 2. Appliance Demand Load	*9,900 VA*
Step 3. Dryer Demand Load	*10,000 W*
Step 4. Electric Cooking Equipment Demand Load	*11,000 W*
Step 5. Heating Demand Load	*19,200 W*
Total Demand Load	*58,560 VA*

Service Size = Demand Load VA/System Volts

Service Size = 58,560 VA/240V

Service Size = 244A

Use 250 kcmil rated 255A at 75°C [110.14(C)(1)(b)(2) and Table 310.16].

Answer: *(a) 250 kcmil*

▶ **Two-Family Dwelling (Duplex), Optional Method, Three Units, 220.85, Example**

Question: *Using the multifamily optional method, what size service conductor is required for a two-family dwelling (based on three units), where each unit is 1,600 sq ft and contains the following loads?*
▶Figure 7-39

• *Dishwasher, 1,200 VA at 120V*

• *Disposal (Waste), 900 VA at 120V*

• *Water Heater, 4,500W at 240V*

• *Dryer, 5,000W at 120/240V*

• *Range, 9,000W at 120/240V*

• *Air-Conditioning, 16.70A at 240V*

• *Heating, 9,600W*

(a) 4/0 AWG	*(b) 300 kcmil*
(c) 350 kcmil	*(d) a or b*

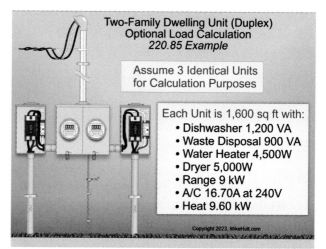

▶Figure 7-39

Solution:

Step 1: *Determine the total connected load [220.84(C)].*

General Lighting		
[220.84(C)(1)]	*1,600 sq ft × 3 VA*	*4,800 VA*
Small-Appliance		
[220.84(C)(2)]	*1,500 VA × 2 circuits*	*3,000 VA*
Laundry Circuit		
[220.84(C)(2)]	*1,500 VA × 1 circuit*	*1,500 VA*
Dishwasher		*1,200 VA*
Disposal (Waste)		*900 VA*
Water Heater		*4,500 VA*
Dryer		*5,000 W*
Range		*9,000 VA*

Air-Conditioning (4,008 VA), omit since it is
  smaller than heat 220.60   *0 VA*
Heating   *+9,600 VA*
Connected Load per Unit   *39,500 VA*

Connected Load for Three Units = 39,500 VA × 3 units
Connected Load for Three Units = 118,500 VA

Step 2: *Determine the total demand load.*

Demand Load = Connected Load × Table 220.84 Demand Factor
Demand Load = 118,500 VA × 45%
Demand Load = 53,325 VA

Step 3: *Determine the size of the service disconnect and conductors.*
▶Figure 7–40

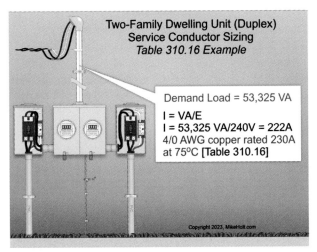

▶Figure 7–40

Service Size = Demand Load VA/System Volts
Service Size = 53,325 VA/240V
Service Size = 222A

Use 4/0 AWG rated 230A at 75°C [110.14(C)(1)(b)(2) and Table 310.16].

Answer: *(a) 4/0 AWG*

Part C—Neutral Load Calculations

Introduction

Thus far we have covered both optional and standard methods for calculating the total service demand load in a multifamily dwelling, however the neutral must be calculated using the standard method in Article 220, Part IV only! In accordance with 220.61 the neutral demand load must include 100 percent of the line to neutral loads, 70 percent of the dryer and range loads, and 70 percent of all the neutral load exceeding 200A for a multifamily dwelling.

7.13 Neutral Demand Load— Dryers and Ranges [220.61]

Dryer Neutral Demand Load

The neutral demand load for dryers is calculated at 70 percent of the demand load as determined by 220.54.

▶ Dryers Neutral Demand Load, Example

Question: *What is the neutral demand load for ten 5.5 kW dryers?*
▶Figure 7–41

(a) 19.25 kW   *(b) 27.5 kW*   *(c) 45 kW*   *(d) 60 kW*

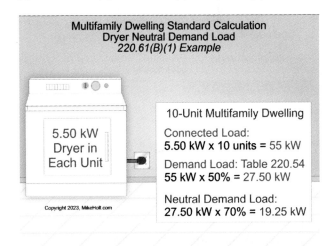

▶Figure 7–41

Solution:

Connected Load = 5.5 kW × 10 dryers
Connected Load = 55 kW

Service Demand Load = Connected Load × Table 220.54 Demand Factor
Service Demand Load = 55 kW × 50%
Service Demand Load = 27.5 kW

Neutral Demand Load = Service Demand Load × 70%
Neutral Demand Load = 27.5 kW × 70%
Neutral Demand Load = 19.25 kW

Answer: *(a) 19.25 kW*

Range Neutral Demand Load

The neutral demand load for ranges is calculated at 70 percent of the demand load as determined by 220.55.

▶ Ranges Neutral Demand Load, Example

Question: *What is the neutral demand load for twenty 14 kW ranges?*
▶Figure 7–42

(a) 27 kW   *(b) 30 kW*   *(c) 38 kW*   *(d) 42 kW*

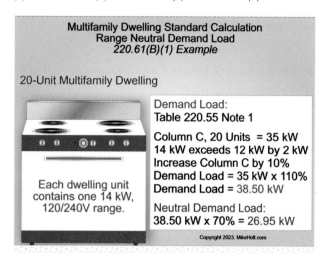

Multifamily Dwelling Standard Calculation
Range Neutral Demand Load
220.61(B)(1) Example

20-Unit Multifamily Dwelling

Each dwelling unit contains one 14 kW, 120/240V range.

Demand Load:
Table 220.55 Note 1

Column C, 20 Units = 35 kW
14 kW exceeds 12 kW by 2 kW
Increase Column C by 10%
Demand Load = 35 kW x 110%
Demand Load = 38.50 kW

Neutral Demand Load:
38.50 kW x 70% = 26.95 kW

Copyright 2023, MikeHolt.com

▶Figure 7–42

Solution:

Step 1: *Determine the service demand load.*

Table 220.55, Column C Demand Load is 35 kW.

Step 2: *A 14 kW range exceeds 12 kW by 2 kW. Increase the Column C demand load by five percent for each kW more than 12 kW.*

Step 3: *Increase the Column C value by 10 percent.*

Demand Load = 35 kW × 110%
Demand Load = 38.5 kW

Neutral Demand Load = Service Demand Load × 70%
Neutral Demand Load = 38.5 kW × 70%
Neutral Demand Load = 26.95 kW, round to 27 kW

Answer: (a) 27 kW

7.14 Service Neutral Demand Load [220.61(B)]

The neutral load is the maximum unbalanced calculated load between the neutral conductor and any phase conductor as determined by Article 220 Part III and adjusted in accordance with 220.61(B).

Neutral Reduction Over 200A [220.61(B)(2)]

If the neutral load, after applying the 70 percent adjustment in accordance with 220.61(A), still exceeds 200A then the "over 200A 70 percent factor" can be applied. See Annex D, Example D4(a) Multifamily Dwelling. ▶Figure 7–43

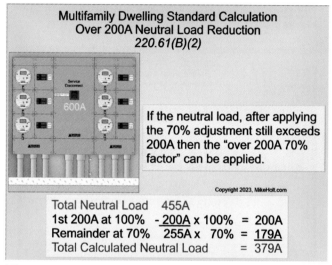

Multifamily Dwelling Standard Calculation
Over 200A Neutral Load Reduction
220.61(B)(2)

600A

If the neutral load, after applying the 70% adjustment still exceeds 200A then the "over 200A 70% factor" can be applied.

Copyright 2023, MikeHolt.com

Total Neutral Load   455A
1st 200A at 100%   - 200A x 100% = 200A
Remainder at 70%   255A x 70% = 179A
Total Calculated Neutral Load   = 379A

▶Figure 7–43

▶ Service Neutral—Single-Phase, Example

Question: *What is the service neutral demand load for a ten-unit multifamily building having the following loads in each 1,000 sq ft unit?* ▶Figure 7–44

- *Dishwasher, 1,200 VA at 120V*
- *Disposal, 900 VA at 120V*
- *Water Heater, 4,500W at 240V*
- *Dryer, 4,000W at 120/240V*
- *Range, 8,000W at 120/240V*
- *Air-Conditioning, 16.70A at 240V*
- *Electric Heating, 6,000W at 240V*

(a) 250A   *(b) 270A*   *(c) 290A*   *(d) 310A*

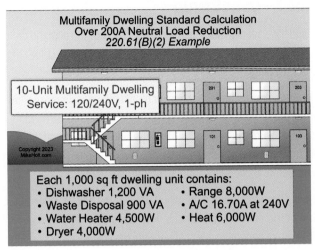

Multifamily Dwelling Standard Calculation Over 200A Neutral Load Reduction 220.61(B)(2) Example

10-Unit Multifamily Dwelling
Service: 120/240V, 1-ph

201   203

101   103

Copyright 2023
MikeHolt.com

Each 1,000 sq ft dwelling unit contains:
- Dishwasher 1,200 VA
- Waste Disposal 900 VA
- Water Heater 4,500W
- Dryer 4,000W
- Range 8,000W
- A/C 16.70A at 240V
- Heat 6,000W

▶Figure 7–44

Solution:

Step 1: *Determine the general lighting, general-use receptacles, and the small-appliance and laundry circuits demand [Table 220.42].*

General Lighting		
[220.42(A)]	1,000 sq ft × 3 VA	3,000 VA
Small-Appliance Circuits		
[210.52(B)]	1,500 VA × 2 circuits	3,000 VA
Laundry Circuit [210.52(F)]		+1,500 VA
Connected Load for One Unit		7,500 VA
Connected Load 10 units	7,500 VA × 10 units	75,000 VA
First 3,000 VA at 100%		
[Table 220.42]	–3,000 VA × 100%	3,000 VA
Remainder at 35%	72,000 VA × 35%	+25,200 VA
Demand Load		28,200 VA

Step 2: *Determine the appliance demand load [220.53].*

Dishwasher	1,200 VA
Disposal (Waste)	+ 900 VA
Connected Load per Unit	2,100 VA

Connected Load for 10 Units = 2,100 VA × 10 units
Connected Load for 10 Units = 21,000 VA

Demand Load = 21,000 VA × 75%*
Demand Load = 15,750 VA

Use the total number of appliances to determine if the 75 percent demand factor applies. In this case, there are 20 appliances on the service conductors [220.53]. The water heaters are not included in the neutral calculation because they are line-to-line loads.

Step 3: *Determine the dryer demand load [220.54]. Dryers must be calculated at a minimum of 5,000W or the nameplate, whichever is larger [220.54].*

Connected Load = 5 kW × 10 units
Connected Load = 50 kVA

Dryer Demand Factor for 10 Dryers (Percent) = 50%

Dryer Demand Load = 50 kVA × 50%
Dryer Demand Load = 25 kVA

Neutral Demand Load = 25 kVA × 70% [220.61(B)(1)]
Neutral Demand Load = 17.50 kVA

Step 4: *Determine the electric cooking equipment demand load [220.55].*

When you get a question for ranges that fall in Column B, complete the following steps. See Note 1 of Table 220.55 and the introduction text contained in Annex D.

Table 220.55, Column B demand factor for ten units is 34 percent.

Range Demand Load = (8 kW × 10 Units) × 34%
Range Demand Load = 80 kW × 34%
Range Demand Load = 27.2 kW

The Table 220.55, Column C maximum demand load for ten units is 25kW.

Neutral Demand Load = Range Demand Load × 70%
Neutral Demand Load = 25 kW × 70% [220.61(B)(1)]
Neutral Demand Load = 17.5 kW

Step 5: *Determine the service neutral demand load.*

Step 1. General Lighting, Receptacles, Small-Appliance, and Laundry Neutral	28,200 VA
Step 2. Appliance Neutral	15,750 VA
Step 3. Dryer Neutral	17,500 W
Step 4. Electric Cooking Equipment	+17,500 W
Total Neutral Demand Load	78,950 VA

Neutral Load = 78,950 VA/240V
Neutral Load = 329A

Step 6: *Determine the neutral reduction over 200A [220.61(B)(2)].*

In addition to the 70 percent demand factor contained in 220.61(B)(1), a further demand factor of 70 percent is permitted to be applied to that portion of the unbalanced load more than 200A. ▶Figure 7–45

• • •

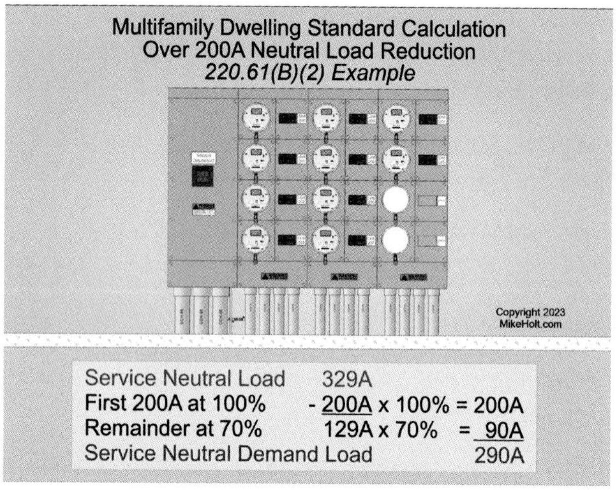

Multifamily Dwelling Standard Calculation
Over 200A Neutral Load Reduction
220.61(B)(2) Example

Service Neutral Load	329A	
First 200A at 100%	-200A x 100%	= 200A
Remainder at 70%	129A x 70%	= 90A
Service Neutral Demand Load		290A

▶Figure 7–45

Service Neutral Demand Load	329A	
First 200A at 100%	−200A × 100%	200A
Remainder at 70%	129A × 70%	+ 90A
Service Neutral Size		290A

Answer: (c) 290A

Unit 7—Conclusion

As you have seen in this unit, the process for applying demand factors for the service of multifamily dwellings is like doing so for single-family dwellings.

Some additional demand factors for multifamily dwellings are allowed on the presumption that there will be significantly less simultaneous power consumption among the various units. The demand factors of Table 220.54 can be applied to dryers, but there must be five units or more before there's less than a 100 percent demand.

One of the single most confusing tables in the *NEC* is Table 220.55 for electric cooking appliances. Pay close attention to that table while you're becoming adept at applying the column values and Table Notes correctly. What might be especially confusing is that the first two columns are percentage multipliers, while the third one is the maximum demand kW value.

Be sure to make (and take) the time necessary to thoroughly study all of Unit 6 so you can confidently complete the calculations using Table 220.55 as well as applying the other factors for sizing the main service for a multifamily dwelling.

UNIT
7

REVIEW QUESTIONS

Please use the 2023 *Code* book and this textbook to answer the following questions.

PART A—OPTIONAL METHOD LOAD CALCULATIONS [ARTICLE 220, PART IV]

7.2 Multifamily Dwelling Optional Method [220.84] Examples

1. Using the optional method, What is the demand load for a five-unit multifamily dwelling where the total connected load is 40 kVA/120/240V, for each unit?

   (a) 361A
   (b) 368A
   (c) 375A
   (d) 393A

2. Using the optional method, What is the demand load for an eight-unit multifamily dwelling where the total connected load is 25 kVA/120/240V, for each unit?

   (a) 349A
   (b) 358A
   (c) 365A
   (d) 375A

3. Using the optional method, What is the demand load for a ten-unit multifamily dwelling where the total connected load is 20 kVA/120/240V, for each unit?

   (a) 346A
   (b) 358A
   (c) 365A
   (d) 375A

4. Using the optional method, What is the demand load for a fifteen-unit multifamily dwelling where the total connected load is 30 kVA/120/240V, for each unit?

   (a) 675A
   (b) 700A
   (c) 725A
   (d) 750A

Use the following information for the next four questions. A multifamily dwelling equipped with electric cooking and space heating or air conditioning has 40 dwelling units. The area of each dwelling unit is 840 ft². A common laundry facility is available to all tenants.

Each dwelling unit is equipped with:

- Electric range, 8 kW at 120/240V
- Four electric space heaters, 1.5 kW at 240V
- Electric water heater, 2.5 kW at 240V

5. Using the standard method, what size feeder is required for each dwelling unit?

   (a) 55A
   (b) 67A
   (c) 78A
   (d) 93A

6. Using the standard method, what size neutral is required to each dwelling unit?

   (a) 35A
   (b) 57A
   (c) 64A
   (d) 73A

7. Using the optional method, what size service is required for the 40 dwelling units?

(a) 735A

(b) 857A

(c) 964A

(d) 1,028A

8. Using the standard method, what size service neutral is required for the 40 dwelling units?

(a) 374A

(b) 457A

(c) 564A

(d) 673A

PART B—STANDARD METHOD LOAD CALCULATIONS [ARTICLE 220, PART III]

7.3 General Lighting and General-Use Receptacle Demand Load [220.41 and 220.45]

9. What is the general lighting, general-use receptacle, small-appliance, and laundry circuit demand load for a 10-unit apartment building, each 2,000 sq ft?

(a) 35.6 kVA

(b) 36.7 kVA

(c) 37.6 kVA

(d) 38.7 kVA

10. What is the general lighting, general-use receptacle, small-appliance, and laundry circuit demand load for a 15-unit apartment building, each 1,000 sq ft?

(a) 37 kVA

(b) 39 kVA

(c) 41 kVA

(d) 44 kVA

11. What is the general lighting and general-use receptacle, and small-appliance circuit demand load for a 20-unit apartment building, each 840 sq ft? **Note:** Common laundry facilities are provided for all units.

(a) 40.1 kVA

(b) 40.6 kVA

(c) 43.4 kVA

(d) 44.5 kVA

7.4 Appliance Demand Load [220.53]

12. Using the standard method, what is the appliance demand load for ten 7.5 kW water heaters?

(a) 52 kVA

(b) 54 kVA

(c) 56 kVA

(d) 59 kVA

13. Using the standard method, what is the appliance demand load for a 16-unit multifamily building, each unit contains a disposal (940 VA), a dishwasher (1,250 VA), and a water heater (4,500 VA)?

(a) 78 kVA

(b) 80 kVA

(c) 84 kVA

(d) 88 kVA

14. Using the standard method, what is the appliance demand load for a 28-unit apartment building contains a disposal (900 VA), a dishwasher (1,200 VA), and a water heater (5 kVA)?

(a) 141 kVA

(b) 145 kVA

(c) 149 kVA

(d) 154 kVA

7.5 Dryer Demand Load [220.54]

15. Using the standard load calculation method, what is the service demand factor for five dryers?

(a) 19 kW

(b) 21 kW

(c) 23 kW

(d) 25 kW

16. Using the standard load calculation method, what is the service demand factor for ten 4 kW dryers?

(a) 25 kW

(b) 29 kW

(c) 31 kW

(d) 33 kW

17. Using the standard load calculation method, what is the service demand factor for ten 5.25 kW dryers?

(a) 23 kW

(b) 26 kW

(c) 27 kW

(d) 28 kW

18. Using the standard load calculation method, what is the service demand factor for eleven dryers?

    (a) 23 kW
    (b) 26 kW
    (c) 27 kW
    (d) 28 kW

7.6 Single-Phase Dryers on Three-Phase Service [220.54]

19. What is the demand load for nine 5 kW dryers on a 208Y/120V three-phase service?

    (a) 29.52 kW
    (b) 30.54 kW
    (c) 33.75 kW
    (d) 36.55 kW

20. What is the demand load for twelve 4 kW dryers on a 208Y/120V three-phase service?

    (a) 32 kW
    (b) 34 kW
    (c) 36 kW
    (d) 38 kW

21. What is the demand load for fifteen 5.5 kW dryers on a 208Y/120V three-phase service?

    (a) 38.52 kW
    (b) 39.55 kW
    (c) 41.25 kW
    (d) 43.52 kW

7.7 Single-Phase Ranges on Single-Phase Service [220.55]

Table 220.55, Column C—Over 8¾ kW to 12 kW

22. What is the demand load for nine 9 kW ranges?

    (a) 24 kW
    (b) 28 kW
    (c) 31 kW
    (d) 33 kW

23. What is the demand load for twenty 12 kW ranges?

    (a) 35 kW
    (b) 37 kW
    (c) 41 kW
    (d) 43 kW

Table 220.55, Note 1—Over 12 kW with Equal Ratings

24. What is the demand load for five 12.4 kW ranges?

    (a) 18 kW
    (b) 20 kW
    (c) 24 kW
    (d) 28 kW

25. What is the demand load for two 13 kW ranges?

    (a) 10.25 kW
    (b) 10.25 kW
    (c) 11.55 kW
    (d) 12.25 kW

26. What is the demand load for three 15.5 kW ranges?

    (a) 14.6 kW
    (b) 15.4 kW
    (c) 16.8 kW
    (d) 17.2 kW

27. What is the demand load for thirty 16 kW ranges?

    (a) 46 kW
    (b) 48 kW
    (c) 50 kW
    (d) 54 kW

Table 220.55, Column B—Less than 8¾ kW, Note 3

28. What is the demand load for fifteen 8 kW cooking units?

    (a) 30 kW
    (b) 32 kW
    (c) 34 kW
    (d) 36 kW

7.8 Single-Phase Ranges on Three-Phase Service [220.55]

29. What is the demand load for nine 12 kW ranges on a 208Y/120V three-phase service?

    (a) 29.5 kW
    (b) 30.5 kW
    (c) 31.5 kW
    (d) 32.5 kW

30. What is the demand load for twelve 12 kW ranges on a 208Y/120V three-phase service?

    (a) 32.5 kW
    (b) 34.5 kW
    (c) 36.5 kW
    (d) 38.5 kW

31. What is the demand load for twenty-one 12 kW ranges on a 208Y/120V three-phase service?

    (a) 38.5 kW
    (b) 39.5 kW
    (c) 41.5 kW
    (d) 43.5 kW

32. What is the demand load for 24 ranges rated 16 kW on a 208Y/120V three-phase service?

    (a) 55.8 kW
    (b) 57.2 kW
    (c) 64.4 kW
    (d) 73.3 kW

7.9 Air-Conditioning and Heating Demand Load

33. What is the demand load for a 10-unit multifamily building using the standard method? Each unit has air-conditioning of 18.8A/240V and 9.6 kW electric heat?

    (a) 86 kW
    (b) 88 kW
    (c) 90 kW
    (d) 96 kW

34. What is the demand load for a 20-unit multifamily building using the standard method? Each unit has air-conditioning of 23.7A/240V and 7.5 kW electric heat?

    (a) 120 kW
    (b) 130 kW
    (c) 140 kW
    (d) 150 kW

35. What is the demand load for a 25-unit multifamily building using the standard method? Each unit has air-conditioning of 17A/240V and 5 kW electric heat?

    (a) 105 kW
    (b) 115 kW
    (c) 125 kW
    (d) 135 kW

36. What is the demand load for a 40-unit multifamily building using the standard method? Each unit has air-conditioning of 17A/240V and two 3 kW baseboard heaters?

    (a) 210 kW
    (b) 220 kW
    (c) 230 kW
    (d) 240 kW

37. What is the demand load for a 25-unit multifamily building using the standard method? Each unit has air-conditioning of 12A/240V containing 6 kW supplemental electric heating.

    (a) 200 kVA
    (b) 210 kVA
    (c) 215 kVA
    (d) 223 kVA

7.10 Service Conductor Sizing [Table 310.16]

38. What size aluminum service conductor is required for a 120/240V, multifamily building that has a total demand load of 90 kW?

    (a) 500 kcmil
    (b) 600 kcmil
    (c) 700 kcmil
    (d) 800 kcmil

39. What size service conductor is required for a 120/240V, multifamily building that has a total demand load of 90 kW?

    (a) 500 kcmil
    (b) 600 kcmil
    (c) 700 kcmil
    (d) 800 kcmil

40. What size service conductor is required for a multifamily building that has a total demand load of 260 kW for a 208Y/120V, three-phase system? The conductors are paralleled in two raceways.

    (a) Two—300 kcmil
    (b) Two—350 kcmil
    (c) Two—500 kcmil
    (d) Two—700 kcmil

41. What size aluminum service conductor is required for a multifamily building that has a total demand load of 260 kW for a 208Y/120V, three-phase system? The conductors are paralleled in three raceways.

    (a) Three–300 kcmil AL
    (b) Three–350 kcmil AL
    (c) Three–500 kcmil AL
    (d) Three–700 kcmil AL

7.11 Multifamily Dwelling Calculations—Standard Method, Examples

The following information applies to the next seven questions. A multifamily building 120/240V single phase service has 12-units, each 1,500 sq ft with:

- Dishwasher, 1.5 kVA at 120V
- Water heater, 4 kW at 240V
- Dryer, 4.5 kW at 120/240V
- Washing machine, 1.2 kVA at 120V
- Range, 14.2 kW at 120/240V
- Air-conditioning, 3 hp at 240V
- Heat, 5 kW at 240V

42. What is the demand load for the general lighting, general-use receptacles, and the small-appliance and laundry circuits?

    (a) 40 kVA
    (b) 45 kVA
    (c) 50 kVA
    (d) 55 kVA

43. What is the demand load for the appliances?

    (a) 41 kVA
    (b) 46 kVA
    (c) 50 kVA
    (d) 55 kVA

44. What is the demand load for the 4.5 kW dryers?

    (a) 27.6 kW
    (b) 29.7 kW
    (c) 31.3 kW
    (d) 33.4 kW

45. What is the demand load for the 14.2 kW ranges?

    (a) 27 kW
    (b) 30 kW
    (c) 35 kW
    (d) 38 kW

46. What is the demand load for the air-conditioning versus electric heating?

    (a) 50 kW
    (b) 55 kW
    (c) 60 kW
    (d) 65 kW

47. What is the total demand load for the dwelling unit?

    (a) 180 kVA
    (b) 190 kVA
    (c) 200 kVA
    (d) 207 kVA

48. What is the minimum ampere rating of the service disconnect?

    (a) 861A
    (b) 871A
    (c) 881A
    (d) 891A

7.12 Two-Family (Duplex) Dwelling Units Load Calculations [220.85]

49. Using the standard method, What is the demand load in amperes (120/240V single-phase service) for a duplex where each-unit is 1,100 sq ft and contains:

    - Dishwasher, 11A at 120V
    - Disposal, 8A at 120V
    - Water Heater, 3.5 kW at 240V
    - Refrigerator, 1.1 kVA at 120V
    - Range, 9 kW at 120/240V
    - Air-Conditioning, 1 hp at 120V
    - Heating, 5 kW at 240V

    (a) 147A
    (b) 157A
    (c) 167A
    (d) 177A

50. Using the standard method, What is the demand load in amperes (120/240V single-phase service) for a duplex where each-unit is 1,400 sq ft and contains:

    - Dishwasher, 11A at 120V
    - Disposal, 8A at 120V
    - Water heater 3 kW at 240V
    - Refrigerator, 1.1 kVA at 120V
    - Dryer, 4 kW at 120/240V
    - Range, 9 kW at 120/240V
    - Air-Conditioning, 15A at 120V
    - Electric Heating, 5 kW at 240V

    (a) 163A
    (b) 173A
    (c) 183A
    (d) 198A

51. Using the standard method, What is the demand load in amperes (120/240V single-phase service) for a duplex where each-unit is 1,500 sq ft and contains:

    - Dishwasher, 10A at 120V
    - Disposal, 5A at 120V
    - Water Heater, 3 kW at 240V
    - Refrigerator, 1.1 kVA at 120V
    - Dryer, 4 kW at 120/240V
    - Range, 9 KW at 120/240V
    - Air-Conditioning, 21A at 240V
    - Electric Heating, 5 KW at 240V

    (a) 184A
    (b) 194A
    (c) 200A
    (d) 214A

52. Using the standard method, what size service and conductors will be required for a two-family dwelling (120/240V single-phase service) where each-unit is 1,000 sq ft and contains the following loads:

    - Dishwasher, 1.1 kVA at 120V
    - Disposal, 900 VA at 120V
    - Water Heater, 4.5 kW at 240V
    - Dryer, 4.5 kW at 120/240V
    - Range, 12 kW at 120/240V
    - Air-Conditioning, 13.80A at 240V
    - Heating, 7.5 kW at 240V

    (a) 200A service with 3/0 AWG conductors
    (b) 225A service with 4/0 AWG conductors
    (c) 250A service with 250 kcmil conductors
    (d) 250A service with 300 kcmil conductors

53. Using the optional method, What is the demand load in amperes (120/240V single-phase service) for a duplex where each-unit is 1,100 sq ft and contains:

    - Dishwasher, 11A at 120V
    - Disposal, 8A at 120V
    - Water Heater, 3.5 kW at 240V
    - Range, 9 kW at 120/240V
    - Air-Conditioning, 1 hp at 120V
    - Heating, 5 kW at 240V

    (a) 147A
    (b) 155A
    (c) 167A
    (d) 177A

54. Using the optional method, What is the demand load in amperes (120/240V single-phase service) for a duplex where each-unit is 1,400 sq ft and contains:

    - Dishwasher, 11A at 120V
    - Disposal, 5A at 120V
    - Water Heater, 3 kW at 240V
    - Dryer, 4 kW at 120/240V
    - Range, 9 kW at 120/240V
    - Air-Conditioning, 15A at 120V
    - Electric Heating, 5 kW at 240V

    (a) 163A
    (b) 173A
    (c) 178A
    (d) 193A

55. Using the optional method, What is the demand load in amperes (120/240V single-phase service) for a duplex where each-unit is 1,500 sq ft and contains:

- Dishwasher, 10A at 120V
- Disposal, 5A at 120V
- Water Heater, 3 kW at 240V
- Dryer, 4 kW at 120/240V
- Range, 9 kW at 120/240V
- Air-Conditioning, 21A at 240V
- Electric Heating, 5 kW at 240V

(a) 179A
(b) 194A
(c) 204A
(d) 214A

56. Using the optional method, what size service and conductor will be required for a two-family dwelling (120/240V single-phase service) where each-unit is 1,000 sq ft and contains the following loads:

- Dishwasher, 1.1 kVA at 120V
- Disposal, 900 VA at 120V
- Water Heater, 4.5 kW at 240V
- Dryer, 4.5 kW at 120/240V
- Range, 12 kW at 120/240V
- Air-Conditioning, 13.8A at 240V
- Heating, 7.5 kW at 240V

(a) 200A service with 3/0 AWG conductors
(b) 225A service with 4/0 AWG conductors
(c) 250A service with 250 kcmil conductors
(d) 250A service with 300 kcmil conductors

PART C—NEUTRAL LOAD CALCULATIONS

7.13 Neutral Demand Load—Dryers and Ranges [220.61]

Dryer Neutral Demand Load

57. What is the neutral demand load for ten 5 kW dryers?

(a) 16.5 kW
(b) 17.5 kW
(c) 18.5 kW
(d) 19.5 kW

58. What is the neutral load for ten 6 kW dryers?

(a) 20 kW
(b) 21 kW
(c) 22 kW
(d) 23 kW

59. What is the neutral load for fifty 4 kW dryers?

(a) 38 kW
(b) 41 kW
(c) 44 kW
(d) 47 kW

60. What is the neutral load for fifty 6 kW dryers?

(a) 53 kW
(b) 56 kW
(c) 59 kW
(d) 61 kW

Range Neutral Demand Load

61. What is the dwelling unit neutral load for ten 9 kW ranges?

(a) 18 kW
(b) 19 kW
(c) 20 kW
(d) 21 kW

62. What is the neutral demand load for fifteen 12 kW ranges?

(a) 21 kW
(b) 30 kW
(c) 38 kW
(d) 40 kW

63. What is the neutral demand load for twenty 15 kW ranges?

(a) 28 kW
(b) 30 kW
(c) 32 kW
(d) 34 kW

UNIT

8

COMMERCIAL CALCULATIONS

Introduction to Unit 8—Commercial Calculations

Commercial buildings have different use patterns than dwellings. In a commercial building, certain loads (such as store lighting) are used for extended periods of time (continuous loads). Homes have a diversity of usage as discussed in Units 6 and 7, which allow us to apply demand factors to many of the loads used in them. There are some demand factors for commercial buildings, but they are different from those used in dwelling unit calculations. Commercial occupancies include many distinct types of businesses and uses.

The following are the Parts covered in this unit:

▶ Part A—General Commercial Demand Loads

▶ Part B— Office, Mobile Home, Kitchen, Restaurants, and School Examples

▶ Part C—Welder Calculations

▶ Part D—Light Industrial Calculations

As you study this unit, pay careful attention to when demand factors can be applied and when a load must be considered a "continuous-duty load" for proper conductor sizing.

Part A—General Commercial Demand Loads

Introduction

In commercial occupancies the service demand load is broken up into different components depending on the type of load present. In Part A of Unit 8 we will focus on some common general loads that are typically found in commercial buildings. Some examples of the demand loads include general lighting loads [Table 220.42(A)], sign circuit load [220.14(F)], multioutlet assembly load [220.14(H)], receptacle load [220.14(I)], and air-conditioning versus heating load [220.60].

8.1 General Lighting Load [Table 220.42(A)]

The general lighting load specified in Table 220.42(A) based on the outside dimensions of the building or area involved [220.5(C)] must be used to calculate the general lighting load. ▶Figure 8–1 and ▶Figure 8–2

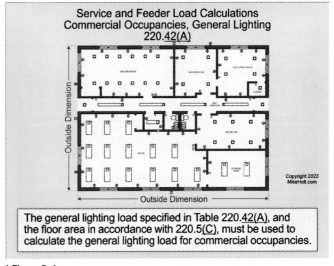

The general lighting load specified in Table 220.42(A), and the floor area in accordance with 220.5(C), must be used to calculate the general lighting load for commercial occupancies.

▶Figure 8–1

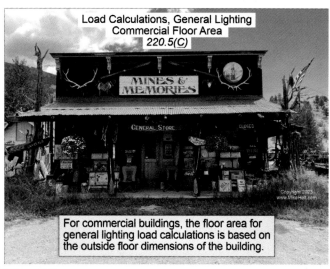

For commercial buildings, the floor area for general lighting load calculations is based on the outside floor dimensions of the building.

▶Figure 8–2

8.2 General Lighting Load, Examples [Table 220.42(A)]

▶ Office Lighting, Example

Question: What is the general lighting demand load for a 100,000 sq ft office building? ▶Figure 8–3

(a) 130 kVA   (b) 180 kVA   (c) 225 kVA   (d) 254 kVA

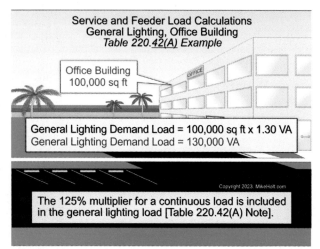

▶Figure 8–3

Solution:

General Lighting Demand Load = 100,000 sq ft × 1.30 VA
General Lighting Demand Load = 130,000 VA, or 130 kVA

Answer: (a) 130 kVA [Table 220.42(A)]

▶ Restaurant Lighting, Example

Question: What is the general lighting demand load for a 10,000 sq ft restaurant? ▶Figure 8–4

(a) 15 kVA   (b) 17 kVA   (c) 19 kVA   (d) 25 kVA

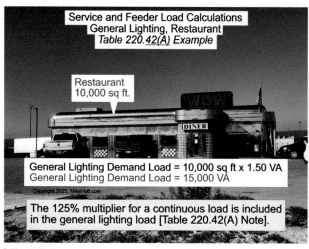

▶Figure 8–4

Solution:

General Lighting Demand Load = 10,000 sq ft × 1.50 VA
General Lighting Demand Load = 15,000 VA, or 15 kVA

Answer: (a) 15 kVA [Table 220.42(A)]

▶ School Lighting, Example

Question: What is the general lighting demand load for a 50,000 sq ft school? ▶Figure 8–5

(a) 65 kVA   (b) 70 kVA   (c) 75 kVA   (d) 80 kVA

Solution:

General Lighting Demand Load = 50,000 sq ft × 1.5 VA
General Lighting Demand Load = 75,000 VA, or 75 kVA

Answer: (c) 75 kVA [Table 220.42(A)]

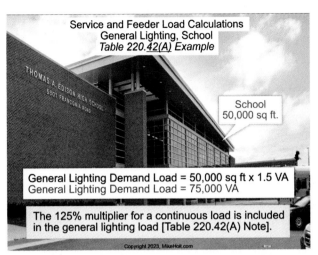

▶Figure 8–5

▶ Store (Retail) Lighting, Example

Question: *What is the general lighting demand load for a 21,000 sq ft store?* ▶Figure 8–6

(a) 40 kVA   *(b) 50 kVA*   *(c) 60 kVA*   *(d) 70 kVA*

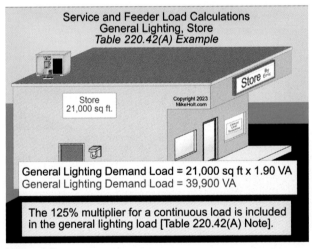

▶Figure 8–6

Solution:

General Lighting Demand Load = 21,000 sq ft × 1.90 VA

General Lighting Demand Load = 39,900 VA, or 39.9 kVA, round to 40 kVA

Answer: *(a) 40 kVA [Table 220.42(A)]*

8.3 General Lighting Load Demand Factors [Table 220.45]

The *Code* recognizes that not all luminaires will be on at the same time, and it permits the demand factors of Table 220.45 to be applied to the general lighting load.

Hotel and Motel General Lighting Demand Factors

▶ First 20,000 VA at 60 percent demand factor

▶ Next 80,000 VA at 50 percent demand factor

▶ Remaining VA at 35 percent demand factor

▶ Hotel General Lighting Demand Load, Example 1

Question: *What is the general lighting demand load for a 260,000 sq ft hotel?* ▶Figure 8–7

(a) 142 kVA   *(b) 157 kVA*   *(c) 167 kVA*   *(d) 172 kVA*

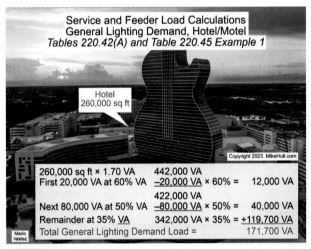

▶Figure 8–7

Solution:

260,000 sq ft × 1.70 VA	*442,000 VA*	
First 20,000 VA at 60%	*−20,000 VA × 60%*	*12,000 VA*
	422,000 VA	
Next 80,000 VA at 50%	*−80,000 VA × 50%*	*40,000 VA*
Remainder at 35%	*342,000 VA × 35%*	*+119,700 VA*
General Lighting Demand Load		*171,700 VA*

Answer: *(d) 172 kVA [Tables 220.42(A) and 220.45]*

▶ Hotel General Lighting Demand Load, Example 2

Question: What is the general lighting demand load for a 40-room hotel? Each unit contains 600 sq ft of area. ▶Figure 8–8

(a) 22 kVA   (b) 23 kVA   (c) 24 kVA   (d) 25 kVA

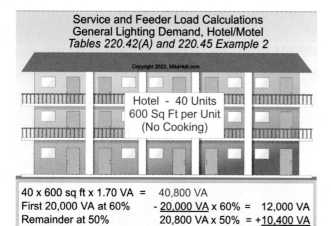

Service and Feeder Load Calculations
General Lighting Demand, Hotel/Motel
Tables 220.42(A) and 220.45 Example 2

Copyright 2023, MikeHolt.com

Hotel - 40 Units
600 Sq Ft per Unit
(No Cooking)

40 x 600 sq ft x 1.70 VA =	40,800 VA	
First 20,000 VA at 60%	- 20,000 VA x 60% =	12,000 VA
Remainder at 50%	20,800 VA x 50% =	+10,400 VA
General Lighting Demand Load		22,400 VA

▶Figure 8–8

Solution:

40 units × 600 sq ft		
× 1.70 VA	40,800 VA	
First 20,000 VA at 60%	−20,000 VA × 60%	12,000 VA
Remainder at 50%	20,800 VA × 50%	+10,400 VA
Total General Lighting Demand Load		22,400 VA

Answer: (a) 22 kVA [Tables 220.42(A) and 220.45]

8.4 Number of General Lighting Circuits

The number of general lighting branch circuits required is determined by dividing the total calculated general lighting load in amperes by the ampere rating of the circuit, see Annex D, Example D3.

▶ Number of General Lighting Circuits—Office Lighting, Example

Question: How many 20A, 120V general lighting branch circuit are required for a 100,000 sq ft office building?

(a) 54 circuits   (b) 60 circuits   (c) 66 circuits   (d) 72 circuits

Solution:

Step 1: Determine the general lighting load [Table 220.42(A)].

General Lighting Demand Load = 100,000 sq ft × 1.30 VA
General Lighting Demand Load = 130,000 VA

Step 2: Determine the number of circuits [220.11(A)].

Circuits = 130,000 VA/(120V × 20A)
Circuits = 130,000 VA/2,400 VA
Circuits = 54 circuits

Answer: (a) 54 circuits

*Includes the 125% continuous load factor [Table 220.42(A) Note].

▶ Number of General Lighting Circuits—Store (Retail) Lighting, Example

Question: How many 20A, 120V general lighting branch circuit are required for a 21,000 sq ft store building? ▶Figure 8–9

(a) 16 circuits   (b) 17 circuits   (c) 18 circuits   (d) 19 circuits

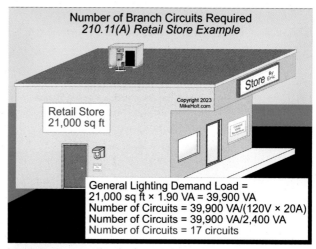

Number of Branch Circuits Required
210.11(A) Retail Store Example

Store By Eric

Copyright 2023 MikeHolt.com

Retail Store
21,000 sq ft

General Lighting Demand Load =
21,000 sq ft × 1.90 VA = 39,900 VA
Number of Circuits = 39,900 VA/(120V × 20A)
Number of Circuits = 39,900 VA/2,400 VA
Number of Circuits = 17 circuits

▶Figure 8–9

Solution:

Step 1: Determine the general lighting load [Table 220.42(A)].

General Lighting Demand Load = 21,000 sq ft × 1.90 VA
General Lighting Demand Load = 39,900 VA

Step 2: Determine the number of circuits [220.11(A)].

Circuits = 39,900 VA/(120V × 20A)
Circuits = 39,900 VA/2,400 VA
Circuits = 17 circuits

Answer: (b) 17 circuits

8.5 Sign Circuit [220.14(F)]

Each commercial occupancy accessible to pedestrians must have one 20A branch circuit for a sign [600.5(A)]. The load for a commercial sign circuit supplying a sign outlet must be calculated at a minimum of 1200 VA [220.14(F)]. ▶Figure 8–10

Branch-Circuit Load Calculations
Sign Outlets
220.14(F)

Each commercial occupancy accessible to pedestrians must have one 20A branch circuit for a sign [600.5(A)]. The calculated load must be a minimum of 1,200 VA.

Copyright 2023, MikeHolt.com

▶Figure 8–10

Branch Circuit. For conductor sizing, the sign circuit is considered a continuous load and the circuit must be sized at 125 percent of 1200 VA in accordance with 210.19(A)(1) in accordance with 600.5(C).

Feeder/Service. For conductor sizing, the sign circuit is considered a continuous load in accordance with 600.5(C) and the circuit must be sized at 125 percent of 1200 VA in accordance with 215.2(A)(1)(1) for feeders and 230.42(A)(1) for services [Example D3, Annex D].

▶ **Sign Load, Example**

Question: For service/feeder conductor sizing, what is the demand load for an electric sign? ▶Figure 8–11

(a) 1,200 VA   (b) 1,500 VA   (c) 1,920 VA   (d) 2,400 VA

Solution:

Determine the sign circuit demand load [220.14(F) and 230.42(A)(1)].

Sign Demand Load = 1,200 VA × 125%
Sign Demand Load = 1,500 VA

Answer: (b) 1,500 VA

Load Calculations, Sign Outlets
220.14(F) Example

Sign Demand Load = 1,200 VA × 125% [230.42(A)(1)]
Sign Demand Load = 1,500 VA

Copyright 2023, MikeHolt.com

▶Figure 8–11

8.6 Multioutlet Assemblies [220.14(H)]

Fixed multioutlet assemblies in commercial occupancies must be calculated in accordance with (1) or (2).

(1) For each 5 ft, or fraction thereof, of a multioutlet assembly where it is unlikely utilization equipment will be used simultaneously, has a demand of 180 VA for service calculations. ▶Figure 8–12

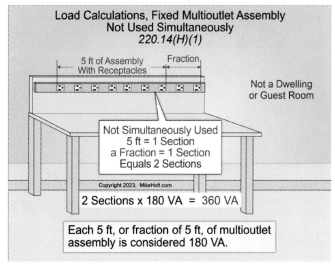

Load Calculations, Fixed Multioutlet Assembly
Not Used Simultaneously
220.14(H)(1)

5 ft of Assembly With Receptacles — Fraction

Not a Dwelling or Guest Room

Not Simultaneously Used
5 ft = 1 Section
a Fraction = 1 Section
Equals 2 Sections

Copyright 2023, MikeHolt.com

2 Sections x 180 VA = 360 VA

Each 5 ft, or fraction of 5 ft, of multioutlet assembly is considered 180 VA.

▶Figure 8–12

(2) If the equipment is expected to be used simultaneously, then each 1 ft or fraction of a foot places a demand of 180 VA for service calculations. ▶Figure 8–13

Note: Do not apply a 125 percent continuous load multiplier to multioutlet assemblies. See Annex D, Example D3 for details.

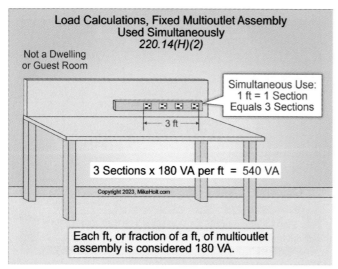

▶Figure 8–13

▶ Multioutlet Assembly, Example

Question: For service conductor sizing, What is the service demand load for 10 workstations; each has 6 ft of multioutlet assembly not used simultaneously and 3 ft of multioutlet assembly simultaneously used? ▶**Figure 8–14**

(a) 5 kVA   (b) 6 kVA   (c) 7 kVA   (d) 9 kVA

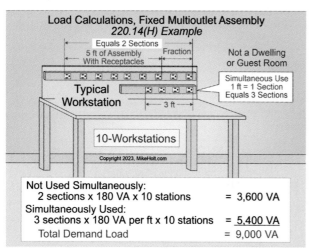

▶Figure 8–14

Solution:

Step 1: Each 6-ft length of multioutlet assembly not used simultaneously.

Equals two 180 VA allowances per station (5-ft length of multioutlet assembly plus one fraction of a 5-ft length).

Step 2: Each 3-length of multioutlet receptacle assembly used simultaneously.

Equals three 180 VA allowances per station (one for each 1-ft length of multioutlet assembly).

Not Simultaneously Used		
2 sections × 180 VA × 10 stations		3,600 VA
Used Simultaneously		
3 sections × 180 VA × 10 stations		+5,400 VA
Total Load		9,000 VA

Answer: (d) 9 kVA [220.14(H)]

8.7 Receptacle Demand Load [220.14(I) and 220.47]

The load for general-use receptacle outlets in a nondwelling occupancy is 180 VA [220.14(I)].

Number of Receptacle Outlets Permitted on a Circuit

The number of receptacle outlets per circuit is calculated by dividing the VA rating of the circuit by 180 VA for each receptacle outlet.

▶ Receptacles Outlets per 20A Circuit [220.14(I)], Example

Question: How many receptacle outlets are allowed on a 20A, 120V circuit in a nondwelling occupancy? ▶**Figure 8–15**

(a) 11   (b) 13   (c) 15   (d) 17

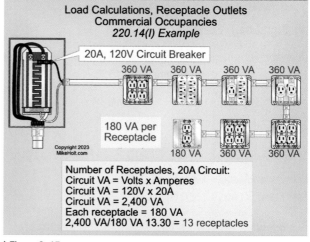

▶Figure 8–15

Solution:

Circuit VA = Volts × Amperes
Circuit VA = 120V × 20A
Circuit VA = 2,400 VA

Number of Receptacle Outlets = 2,400 VA/180 VA
Number of Receptacle Outlets = 13

Answer: (b) 13

Receptacle Outlet Demand Load [220.47]

The receptacle demand load for a service is determined in accordance with 220.14(I) at 180 VA per receptacle outlet as adjusted by the demand factor contained in Table 220.47.

Step 1: First 10,000 VA of receptacle outlet load at 100%

Step 2: Remainder of receptacle outlet load at 50%

Step 3: Total Step 1 and Step 2

Note: Receptacles are not considered continuous loads, see Annex D, Example D(3) for details.

▶ **Receptacle Demand Load—Table 220.47, Example 1**

Question: For service conductor sizing, What is the demand load for one hundred duplex receptacles in a nondwelling occupancy?
▶Figure 8–16

(a) 10 kVA   *(b) 14 kVA*   *(c) 19 kVA*   *(d) 27 kVA*

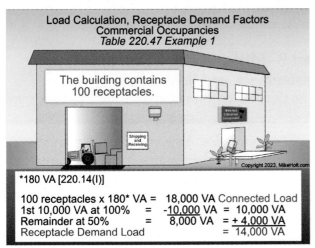

▶Figure 8–16

Solution:

100 Receptacles × 180 VA	*18,000 VA*	
First 10 kVA at 100%	*−10,000 VA × 100%*	*10,000 VA*
Remainder at 50%	*8,000 VA × 50%*	*+ 4,000 VA*
Receptacle Demand Load		*14,000 VA*

Answer: (b) 14 kVA

▶ **Receptacle Demand Load—Table 220.47, Example 2**

Question: For service conductor sizing, What is the demand load for one hundred fifty duplex receptacles in a nondwelling occupancy?
▶Figure 8–17

(a) 10 kVA   *(b) 14 kVA*   *(c) 18.50 kVA*   *(d) 27 kVA*

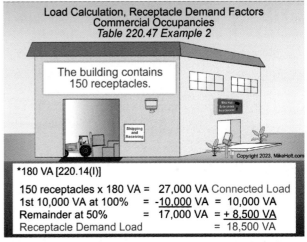

▶Figure 8–17

Solution:

150 Receptacles × 180 VA	*27,000 VA*	
First 10 kVA at 100%	*−10,000 VA × 100%*	*10,000 VA*
Remainder at 50%	*17,000 VA × 50%*	*+8,500 VA*
Receptacle Demand Load		*18,500 VA*

Answer: (c) 18.50 kVA

8.8 Air-Conditioning versus Heating Demand Load [220.60]

If the air-conditioning motor is the largest motor in the question, then, when calculating the air-conditioning load of a multimotor hermetic refrigerant motor-compressor, compare 125 percent of the nameplate marked rated load current of the air-conditioning load in VA [220.50] to 100 percent of the VA of the fixed electric heating load [220.51]. Then select the larger of the two if they are not likely to be on at the same time [220.60].

▶ **Air-Conditioning versus Heating, Example 1**

Question: What is the service demand load for a building with an air-conditioning unit rated 16.70A at 240V compared to 6 kW heat? ▶Figure 8–18

(a) 5 kVA   *(b) 6 kW*   *(c) 7 kVA*   *(d) 8 kVA*

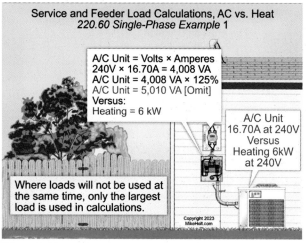

Service and Feeder Load Calculations, AC vs. Heat
220.60 Single-Phase Example 1

A/C Unit = Volts × Amperes
240V × 16.70A = 4,008 VA
A/C Unit = 4,008 VA × 125%
A/C Unit = 5,010 VA [Omit]
Versus:
Heating = 6 kW

A/C Unit 16.70A at 240V Versus Heating 6kW at 240V

Where loads will not be used at the same time, only the largest load is used in calculations.

Copyright 2023
MikeHolt.com

▶Figure 8–18

Solution:

Air-Conditioning = Volts × Amperes

Air-Conditioning = 240V × 16.70A

Air-Conditioning = 4,008 VA

Air-Conditioning = 4,008 VA × 125%

Air-Conditioning = 5,010 VA/1,000

Air-Conditioning = 5.01 kVA, omit since it is smaller than heat 220.60

Heating = 6 kW

Answer: (b) 6 kW

▶ **Air-Conditioning versus Heating, Example 2**

Question: What is the service demand load for a building with an air-conditioning unit rated 23.10A, 208V, three-phase compared to 6 kW heat? ▶Figure 8–19

(a) 7.30 kVA   *(b) 8.20 kVA*   *(c) 9.30 kVA*   *(d) 10.40 kVA*

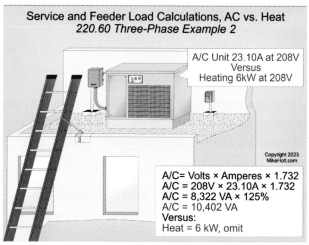

Service and Feeder Load Calculations, AC vs. Heat
220.60 Three-Phase Example 2

A/C Unit 23.10A at 208V
Versus
Heating 6kW at 208V

A/C= Volts × Amperes × 1.732
A/C = 208V × 23.10A × 1.732
A/C = 8,322 VA × 125%
A/C = 10,402 VA
Versus:
Heat = 6 kW, omit

Copyright 2023
MikeHolt.com

▶Figure 8–19

Solution:

Air-Conditioning = Volts × Amperes × 1.732

Air-Conditioning = 208V × 23.10A × 1.732

Air-Conditioning = 8,322 VA

Air-Conditioning = 8,322 VA × 125%

Air-Conditioning = 10,402 VA/1,000

Air-Conditioning = 10.40 kVA

Heating = 6 kW, omit since it is smaller than a/c 220.60

Answer: (d) 10.40 kVA

Part B—Office, Mobile Home, Kitchen, Restaurants, and School Examples

Introduction

The *NEC* contains detailed requirements for calculating service loads for many types of occupancies. Although most of these rules are in Article 220, others affecting service loads are scattered in individually titled articles in Chapters 5 through 8 of the *Code*. Commercial load calculations can be a challenging subject because there are many diverse types of commercial occupancies and some have extremely specific and unique rules for calculating the service loads. In Part B of Unit 8 we will cover commercial load calculation examples of office buildings, mobile home parks, commercial kitchens, restaurants, and school buildings.

8.9 Office Building, Example

Office Building, Example Calculation Steps

▶ Office Building, Example

Question: *For conductor sizing, What is the service demand load for a 30,000 sq ft. office building with a single-phase, 120/240V service? The building has the following loads:*

- *Actual Lighting Load: LED luminaires, 200 each rated at 1.65A at 120V used continuously*
- *Receptacles, 400 each at 120V*
- *Air-Conditioning, 50A at 240V*
- *Heat, 15 kW at 240V*
- *Irrigation Pump Motors, 5 hp at 240V*
- *Sign, 1,200 VA at 120V*

(a) 500A   (b) 600A   (c) 700A   (d) 800A

Solution:

Step 1: *Determine the lighting demand load.*

Step 1a: *Determine the general lighting demand load [Table 220.42(A)].*

Use the larger of the actual lighting load listed or the VA per sq ft from Table 220.42(A). See Annex D, Example D3.

General Lighting Demand Load = 30,000 sq ft × 1.30 VA
General Lighting Demand Load = 39,600 VA (omit)

Step 1b: *Determine the actual lighting connected load.*

Actual Lighting Connected Load = 200 units × 120V × 1.65A × 125%
Actual Lighting Connected Load = 49,500 VA

Step 2: *Determine the actual receptacle demand load [220.14(I) and 220.47].*

400 Receptacle Yokes
  × 180 VA [220.14(I)]   72,000 VA
First 10 kVA at 100%   −10,000 VA × 100%   10,000 VA
Remainder at 50%   62,000 VA × 50%   +31,000 VA
Receptacle Demand Load   41,000 VA

Step 3: *Determine the sign circuit demand load [220.14(F) and 230.42(A)(1)].*

1,200 VA × 125% = 1,500 VA

Step 4: *Determine the air-conditioning versus heating demand load.*

Air-Conditioning = Volts × Amperes
Air-Conditioning = 240V × 50A
Air-Conditioning = 12,000 VA
Air-Conditioning = 12,000 VA × 125%
Air-Conditioning = 15,000 VA/1,000
Air-Conditioning = 15 kVA

Heating = 14,000 VA, omit it is smaller than a/c load [220.51 and 220.60]

Step 5: *Determine the irrigation pump motor (5 hp, single-phase) load [220.50 and 430.24].*

240V FLC = 28A [Table 430.248]

VA = Volts × Amperes
VA = 240V × 28A
VA = 6,720 VA × 125%
VA = 8,400 VA

Step 6: *Determine the service demand load:*

- *A connected load column which is the total load calculated following the Article 220 requirements.*
- *A demand load column which includes continuous loads and noncontinuous loads.*
- *A neutral load column which provides the neutral loading for sizing the neutral conductor*.*

Conductor	Connected Load	Demand Load	Neutral Load*
Step 1. Lighting	49,500 VA	49,500 VA	31,200 VA
Step 2. Receptacles	41,000 VA	41,000 VA	41,000 VA
Step 3. Sign	1,200 VA	1,500 VA	1,200 VA
Step 4. A/C	15,000 VA	15,000 VA	0 VA
Step 5. Irrigation Pump	+ 6,720 VA	+ 8,400 VA	+ 0 VA
	113,420 VA	115,450 VA	73,400 VA

The neutral conductor is sized at 100 percent of the continuous load [215.2(A)(1) Ex 3].

Step 7: *Determine service size.*

Service Size = Demand Load VA/System Volts
Service Size = 115,450 VA/240V
Service Size = 481A; use a 500A service [240.6(A)]

Answer: *(a) 500A*

8.10 Mobile Home Parks [550.31]

The demand factors for mobile home parks provided in Table 550.31 is based on a minimum of 16,000 VA for each mobile home lot.

▶ Manufactured Home Park, Example

Question: For conductor sizing, What is the demand load for a mobile home park with facilities for 35 sites? The system is 120/240V, single-phase. ▶Figure 8–20

(a) 400A   *(b) 560A*   *(c) 800A*   *(d) 1,000A*

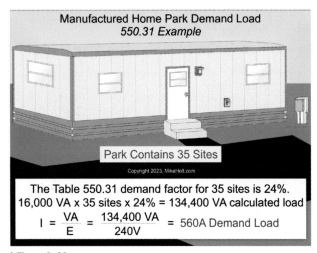

Manufactured Home Park Demand Load
550.31 Example

Park Contains 35 Sites

Copyright 2023, MikeHolt.com

The Table 550.31 demand factor for 35 sites is 24%.
16,000 VA x 35 sites x 24% = 134,400 VA calculated load
$$I = \frac{VA}{E} = \frac{134,400\ VA}{240V} = 560A\ \text{Demand Load}$$

▶Figure 8–20

Solution:

Since no calculated load in accordance with 550.18 is given, use 16,000 VA per site and calculate in accordance with the demand factor percentages in Table 550.31.

Demand Load = VA × Sites × Demand Factor

35 Sites = 0.24 demand factor [Table 550.31]

Demand Load = 16,000 VA × 35 sites × 24%
Demand Load = 134,400 VA

I = VA/E

I = 134,000 VA/240V
I = 560A

Answer: (b) 560A

8.11 Kitchen Equipment and Restaurants

Kitchen Equipment Load, Commercial [220.56]

Table 220.56 can be used to calculate the demand load for thermostat-controlled or intermittently used commercial kitchen equipment such as electric cooking equipment, dishwasher booster heaters, water heaters, and other similar kitchen loads. The kitchen equipment feeder/service calculated load must not be less than the sum of the two largest kitchen equipment loads. Table 220.56 demand factors do not apply to space-heating, ventilating, or air-conditioning equipment. ▶Figure 8–21

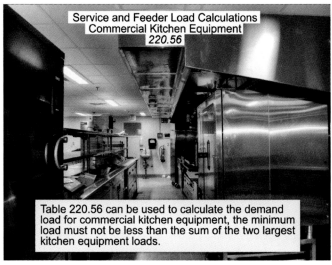

Service and Feeder Load Calculations
Commercial Kitchen Equipment
220.56

Table 220.56 can be used to calculate the demand load for commercial kitchen equipment, the minimum load must not be less than the sum of the two largest kitchen equipment loads.

▶Figure 8–21

▶ Kitchen Equipment, Example 1

Question: What is the service demand load for one 15 kW water heater, one 15 kW booster water heater, one 3 kW oven, and one 2 kW deep fryer in a commercial kitchen? ▶Figure 8–22

(a) 20 kW   *(b) 30 kW*   *(c) 40 kW*   *(d) 50 kW*

Solution:

Step 1: Determine the total connected load.

Total Connected Load = 15 kW + 15 kW + 3 kW + 2 kW
Total Connected Load = 35 kW

Step 2: Determine the feeder/service calculated load based on four units [Table 220.56].

Feeder/Service Calculated Load = 35 kW × 80%
Feeder/Service Calculated Load = 28 kW

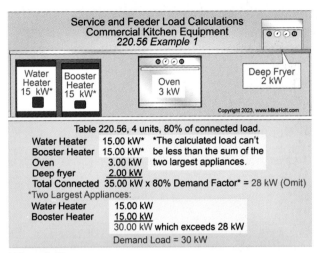

▶Figure 8–22

Check the size of the two largest appliances. The 15 kW water heater plus the 15 kW booster heater is 30 kW. The feeder/service calculated load is 30 kW because it cannot be less than the sum of the two largest appliances.

Answer: (b) 30 kW

▶ Kitchen Equipment, Example 2

Question: What is the service demand load for one 15 kW water heater, one 15 kW booster water heater, two 10 kW oven, and two 5 kW deep fryer in a commercial kitchen? ▶Figure 8–23

(a) 20 kW   (b) 30 kW   (c) 40 kW   (d) 50 kW

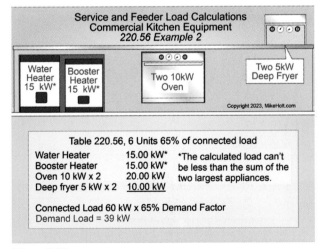

▶Figure 8–23

Solution:

Step 1: Determine the total connected load.

Total Connected Load = 15 kW + 15 kW + 10 kW + 10 kW + 5 kW + 5 kW

Total Connected Load = 60 kW

Step 2: Determine the feeder/service calculated load based on four units [Table 220.56].

Feeder/Service Calculated Load = 60 kW × 65%

Feeder/Service Calculated Load = 39 kW, round to 40 kW to match answer choices

Check the size of the two largest appliances. The 15 kW water heater plus the 15 kW booster heater is 30 kW.

Answer: (c) 40 kW

Restaurant—Optional Method [220.88]

The following steps can be used to determine the service conductor size for a restaurant using the optional method described in 220.88:

Step 1:   Add the nameplate rating of all loads at 100 percent and include both the air-conditioning and heating loads [Table 220.88 Note].

Step 2:   Apply the demand factors from Table 220.88 to the total connected load (include the air-conditioning and heating loads in the total) [Note to Table 220.88].

▶ All-Electric Restaurant, Example 1

Question: What size service conductor paralleled in two raceways is required for a 208Y/120V, three-phase restaurant that all-electric and has a total connected load of 300 kVA? ▶Figure 8–24

(a) 250 kcmil   (b) 300 kcmil   (c) 350 kcmil   (d) 400 kcmil

Solution:

Table 220.88
Total Connected Load = 300 kVA

First 200 kVA at 80%	160 kVA
Remainder at 10%	+10 kVA
Demand Load	170 kVA

$I = VA/(E × 1.732)$

$I = 170,000 VA/(208V × 1.732)$

$I = 472A$

• • •

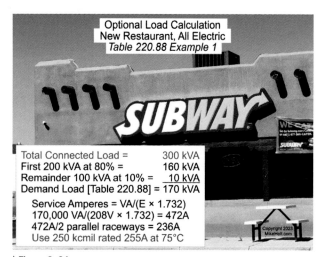

Total Connected Load = 300 kVA
First 200 kVA at 80% = 160 kVA
Remainder 100 kVA at 10% = 10 kVA
Demand Load [Table 220.88] = 170 kVA

Service Amperes = VA/(E × 1.732)
170,000 VA/(208V × 1.732) = 472A
472A/2 parallel raceways = 236A
Use 250 kcmil rated 255A at 75°C

▶Figure 8–24

Amperes per Parallel Conductor = 472A/2 raceways
Amperes per Parallel Conductor = 236A

Use 250 kcmil rated 255A at 75°C [110.14(C)(1)(b)(2) and Table 310.16].

250 kcmil Rated 255A × 2 Conductors = 510A

Answer: *(a) 250 kcmil*

▶ All-Electric Restaurant, Example 2

Question: *What size service conductor paralleled in two raceways is required for a 208Y/120V, three-phase all-electric restaurant with a total connected load of 400 kVA?*

(a) 250 kcmil   (b) 300 kcmil   (c) 350 kcmil   (d) 400 kcmil

Solution:

Table 220.88
Total Connected Load = 400 kVA

First 325 kVA	*172.5 kVA*
Remainder 75 kVA at 50%	*+ 37.5 kVA*
Demand Load	*210.0 kVA*

I = VA/(E × 1.732)

I = 210,000 VA/(208V × 1.732)
I = 210,000 VA/360V
I = 583A

Amperes per Parallel Conductor = 583A/2 raceways
Amperes per Parallel Conductor = 292A

Use 350 kcmil rated 310A at 75°C [110.14(C)(1(b)(2) and Table 310.16].

350 kcmil Rated 310A × 2 Conductors = 620A

Answer: *(c) 350 kcmil*

▶ Not All-Electric Restaurant, Example 1

Question: *What size service conductor paralleled in three raceways is required for a 208Y/120V, three-phase restaurant that is not all-electric and has a total connected load of 300 kVA?* ▶Figure 8–25

(a) 250 kcmil   (b) 300 kcmil   (c) 400 kcmil   (d) 500 kcmil

Total Connected Load = 300 kVA
First 200 kVA = 200 kVA
Remainder 100 kVA at 50% = 50 kVA
Demand Load [Table 220.88] 250 kVA

Service Amperes = VA/(E × 1.732)
250,000 VA/(208V × 1.732) = 694A
694A/3 parallel raceways = 231A
Use 250 kcmil rated 255A at 75°C

▶Figure 8–25

Solution:

Table 220.88
Total Connected Load = 300 kVA

First 200 kVA	*200 kVA*
Remainder 100 kVA at 50%	*+ 50 kVA*
Demand Load	*250 kVA*

I = VA/(E × 1.732)
I = 250,000 VA/(208V × 1.732)
I = 694A

Amperes per Parallel Conductor = 694A/3 raceways
Amperes per Parallel Conductor = 231A

Use 250 kcmil rated 255A at 75°C [110.14(C)(1)(b)(2) and Table 310.16].

250 kcmil Rated 255A × 3 Conductors = 765A

Answer: *(a) 250 kcmil*

▶ Not All-Electric Restaurant, Example 2

Question: Question: What size aluminum service conductor paralleled in three raceways is required for a 208Y/120V, three-phase restaurant that is not all-electric and has a total connected load of 400 kVA?

(a) 300 kcmil   (b) 400 kcmil   (c) 500 kcmil   (d) 600 kcmil

Solution:

Table 220.88
Total Connected Load = 400 kVA

First 325 kVA	262.50 kVA
Remainder 75 kVA at 45%	+33.75 kVA
Demand Load	295.75 kVA

$I = VA/(E \times 1.732)$

$I = 295.75 \, VA/(208V \times 1.732)$

$I = 822A$

This will require a minimum of a 1,000A overcurrent device [240.6(A)].

Service Conductor per Raceway = 1,000A*/3 raceways
Service Conductor per Raceway = 333A

Use 600 kcmil aluminum rated 340A at 75°C [110.14(C)(1)(b)(2) and Table 310.16].

*Conductors on overcurrent devices rated over 800A must have a rating of no less than the rating of the overcurrent device [240.6(C)].

Answer: (d) 600 kcmil

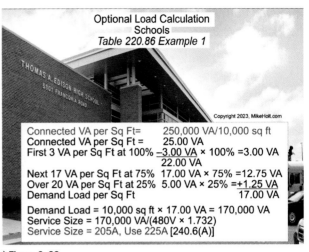

▶Figure 8–26

Solution:

Step 1: Determine the connected load per sq ft.

Connected VA = 250,000 VA
Sq Ft of School = 10,000 sq ft

Connected VA per Sq Ft = 250,000 VA/10,000 sq ft
Connected VA per Sq Ft = 25.00 VA

Step 2: Determine the demand load per sq ft.

Connected VA per Sq Ft	25.00 VA	
First 3 VA per Sq Ft at 100%	–3.00 VA × 100% 22.00 VA	3.00 VA
Next 17 VA per Sq Ft at 75%	17.00 VA × 75%	12.75 VA
Over 20 VA per Sq Ft at 25%	5.00 VA × 25%	+1.25 VA
Demand Load per Sq Ft		17.00 VA

Step 3: Determine the total demand load.

Total Demand Load = 10,000 sq ft × 17.00 VA
Total Demand Load = 170,000 VA

Step 4: Determine the service disconnect size.

Service Disconnect Size = 170,000 VA/(480V × 1.732)
Service Disconnect Size = 170,000 VA/831.36V
Service Disconnect Size = 205A
Service Disconnect Size = 225A [240.6(A)]

Answer: (b) 225A

8.12 School Optional Method Load Calculations [220.86]

The service load for schools is permitted to be calculated in accordance with Table 220.86. The connected load includes interior and exterior lighting, power, water heating, cooking, other loads, and the larger of the air-conditioning or space-heating loads.

▶ School Optional Method Load Calculations, Example 1

Question: What size service disconnect is required for a 10,000 sq ft school with a total connected load of 250 kVA, 480V, three-phase? ▶Figure 8–26

(a) 200A   (b) 225A   (c) 250A   (d) 300A

▶ **School Optional Method Load Calculations, Example 2**

Question: What size service conductor is required for an 8,000 sq ft school with a total connected load of 175 kVA, 480V, three-phase?

(a) 156A   *(b) 164A*   *(c) 174A*   *(d) 187A*

Solution:

Step 1: *Determine the connected load per sq ft.*

Connected VA = 175,000 VA

Sq Ft of School = 8,000 sq ft

Connected VA per Sq Ft = 175,000 VA/8,000 sq ft
Connected VA per Sq Ft = 21.88 VA

Step 2: *Determine the demand load per sq ft.*

Connected VA per Sq Ft	21.88 VA	
First 3 VA per Sq Ft at 100%	–3.00 VA × 100%	3.00 VA
	18.88 VA	
Next 17 VA per Sq Ft at 75%	17.00 VA × 75%	12.75 VA
Over 20 VA per Sq Ft at 25%	1.88 VA × 25%	+0.47 VA
Demand VA Load per Sq Ft		16.22 VA

Step 3: *Determine the total demand load.*

Total Demand Load = 8,000 sq ft × 16.22 VA
Total Demand Load = 129,750 VA

Step 4: *Determine the service conductor size.*

Service Conductor Size = 129,750 VA/(480V × 1.732)
Service Conductor Size = 129,750 VA/831.36V
Service Conductor Size = 156A

Answer: (a) 156A

Part C—Welder Calculations

Introduction

Electric welding equipment is a very specialized load that is calculated using the nameplate current and duty cycle of the specific type of welder. In Part C of unit 8 we will cover two types of electric welders, the first one is arcing welders which operate by creating an electric arc between two surfaces. The second is resistance welders which operate by heating a metal rod until it melts. Both types of welders result in high momentary current draws. Article 630 of the *NEC* requires information about current rating and duty cycle to be marked on the nameplate of the equipment. ▶Figure 8–27

Article 630 covers electric arc welding and resistance welding equipment.

▶Figure 8–27

8.13 Arc Welders

Branch-Circuit Conductors—Arc Welders [630.11(A)]

The branch circuit conductors for arc welders must have an ampacity of not less than the rated primary current multiplied by the factor contained in Table 630.11(A) based on the duty cycle of the arc welder.

▶ **Nonmotor-Generator Arc Welder, Example 1**

Question: What is the minimum branch circuit for a nonmotor-generator arc welder that has a primary current rating of 30A with a duty cycle of 30 percent? ▶Figure 8–28

(a) 16.50A   *(b) 17.50A*   *(c) 18.50A*   *(d) 19.50A*

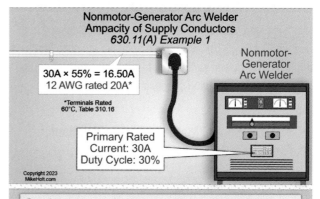

Conductors must have an ampacity of not less than the rated primary current multiplied by Table 630.11(A) factor based on the duty cycle of the arc welder.

▶Figure 8–28

Solution:

Demand Load = Primary Rating × Multiplier [Table 630.11(A)]

Demand Load = 30A × 55%

Demand Load = 16.50A

Answer: (a) 16.50A

▶ Nonmotor-Generator Arc Welder, Example 2

Question: What is the minimum branch circuit for a nonmotor-generator arc welder that has a primary current rating of 40A with a duty cycle of 50 percent? ▶**Figure 8–29**

(a) 26.40A   (b) 27.40A   (c) 28.40A   (d) 29.40A

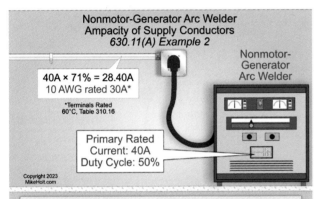

▶Figure 8–29

Solution:

Demand Load = Primary Rating × Multiplier [Table 630.11(A)]

Demand Load = 40A × 71%

Demand Load = 28.40A

Answer: (c) 28.40A

▶ Motor-Generator Arc Welder, Example 1

Question: What is the minimum branch circuit for a motor-generator arc welder that has a primary current rating of 30A with a duty cycle of 30 percent? ▶**Figure 8–30**

(a) 18.60A   (b) 20.60A   (c) 25.60A   (d) 30.60A

Solution:

Demand Load = Primary Rating × Multiplier [Table 630.11(A)]

Demand Load = 30A × 62%

Demand Load = 18.60A

Answer: (a) 18.60A

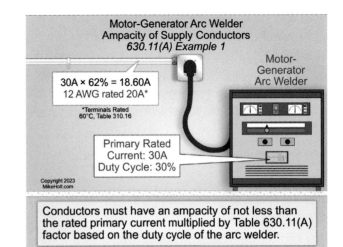

▶Figure 8–30

▶ Motor-Generator Arc Welder, Example 2

Question: What is the minimum branch circuit for a motor-generator arc welder that has a primary current rating of 40A with a duty cycle of 50 percent? ▶**Figure 8–31**

(a) 20A   (b) 25A   (c) 30A   (d) 35A

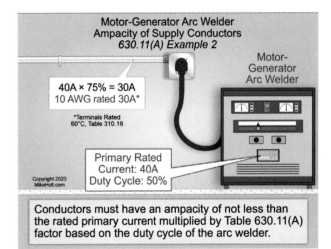

▶Figure 8–31

Solution:

Demand Load = Primary Rating × Multiplier [Table 630.11(A)]

Demand Load = 40A × 75%

Demand Load = 30A

Answer: (c) 30A

Feeder Conductors—Arc Welders [630.11(B)]

Feeder conductors that supply a group of arc welders must have a minimum ampacity of not less than the sum of the currents as determined in 630.11(A) based on 100 percent of the two largest arc welders, 85 percent for the third largest arc welder, 70 percent for the fourth largest arc welder, and 60 percent for all remaining arc welders.

▶ Feeder Nonmotor-Generator Arc Welders, Example

Question: What is the minimum feeder conductor size for five 30A nonmotor-generator arc welders with a duty cycle of 30 percent?

(a) 4 AWG   (b) 1 AWG   (c) 1/0 AWG   (d) 2/0 AWG

Solution:

Demand Load = Primary Rating × Multiplier [Table 630.11(A)] × Arc Welder Percentage [630.11(B)]

Welder 1	30A × 55% = 16.50A × 100%	16.50A
Welder 2	30A × 55% = 16.50A × 100%	16.50A
Welder 3	30A × 55% = 16.50A × 85%	14.03A
Welder 4	30A × 55% = 16.50A × 70%	11.55A
Welder 5	30A × 55% = 16.50A × 60%	+ 9.90A
Total Demand Load		68.61A

Minimum Conductor Size = 4 AWG rated 70A at 60°C [110.14(C)(1)(a)(2) and Table 310.16]

Answer: (a) 4 AWG

▶ Motor-Generator Arc Welders, Example

Question: What is the minimum feeder conductor size for five 30A motor-generator arc welders with a duty cycle of 30 percent?

(a) 4 AWG   (b) 3 AWG   (c) 2 AWG   (d) 1 AWG

Solution:

Demand Load = Primary Rating × Multiplier [Table 630.11(A)] × Arc Welder Percentage [630.11(B)]

Welder 1	30A × 62% = 18.60A × 100%	18.60A
Welder 2	30A × 62% = 18.60A × 100%	18.60A
Welder 3	30A × 62% = 18.60A × 85%	15.81A
Welder 4	30A × 62% = 18.60A × 70%	13.02A
Welder 5	30A × 62% = 18.60A × 60%	+11.60A
Total Demand Load		77.63A

Minimum Conductor Size = 4 AWG rated 85A at 75°C [110.14(C)(1)(b)(2) and Table 310.16]

Answer: (a) 4 AWG

8.14 Resistance Welders

Branch-Circuit Conductors—Resistance Welders [630.31(A)(2)]

The supply conductors for resistance welders with a specific duty cycle and nonvarying current levels must have an ampacity of not less than the rated primary current multiplied by the factors in Table 630.31(A), based on the duty cycle of the resistance welder.

▶ Resistance Welders, Example 1

Question: What is the minimum branch-circuit required for a 30A resistance welder having a duty cycle of 30 percent? ▶Figure 8–32

(a) 16.50A   (b) 17.50A   (c) 18.50A   (d) 20.50A

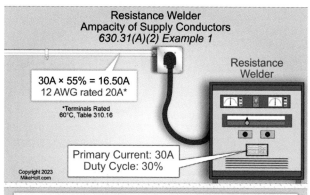

Resistance Welder
Ampacity of Supply Conductors
630.31(A)(2) Example 1

30A × 55% = 16.50A
12 AWG rated 20A*

*Terminals Rated 60°C, Table 310.16

Resistance Welder

Primary Current: 30A
Duty Cycle: 30%

Copyright 2023
MikeHolt.com

Conductors must have an ampacity of not less than the rated primary current multiplied by Table 630.31(A)(2) factor based on the duty cycle of the resistance welder.

▶Figure 8–32

Solution:

Demand Load = Primary Rating × Multiplier [Table 630.31(A)(2)]
Demand Load = 30A × 55%
Demand Load = 16.50A

Answer: (a) 16.50A

▶ **Resistance Welders, Example 2**

Question: *What is the minimum branch-circuit required for a 50A resistance welder having a duty cycle of 50 percent?* ▶**Figure 8–33**

(a) 35.50A　　*(b) 45.50A*　　*(c) 55.50A*　　*(d) 65.50A*

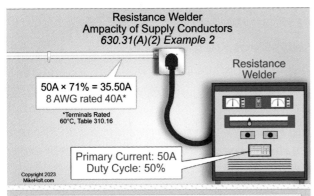

Resistance Welder
Ampacity of Supply Conductors
630.31(A)(2) Example 2

50A × 71% = 35.50A
8 AWG rated 40A*

*Terminals Rated
60°C, Table 310.16

Primary Current: 50A
Duty Cycle: 50%

Copyright 2023
MikeHolt.com

Conductors must have an ampacity of not less than the rated primary current multiplied by Table 630.31(A)(2) factor based on the duty cycle of the resistance welder.

▶Figure 8–33

Solution:

Demand Load = Primary Rating × Multiplier [Table 630.31(A)(2)]
Demand Load = 50A × 71%
Demand Load = 35.50A

Answer: *(a) 35.50A*

Feeder Conductors—Resistance Welders [630.31(B)]

Feeder conductors must have an ampacity of not less than the sum of the value determined using 630.31(A)(2) for the largest resistance welder, plus 60 percent of the values determined for all remaining resistance welders.

▶ **Resistance Welders, Example 1**

Question: *What is the minimum feeder conductor size for five 30A resistance welders with a duty cycle of 30 percent?*

(a) 4 AWG　　*(b) 3 AWG*　　*(c) 2 AWG*　　*(d) 1 AWG*

Solution:

Demand Load = Primary Rating × Multiplier [Table 630.31(A)(2)]
× Resistance Welder Percentage [630.31(B)]

Welder 1	30A × 55% = 16.50A × 100%	16.50A
Welder 2	30A × 55% = 16.50A × 60%	9.90A
Welder 3	30A × 55% = 16.50A × 60%	9.90A
Welder 4	30A × 55% = 16.50A × 60%	9.90A
Welder 5	30A × 55% = 16.50A × 60%	+ 9.90A
Total Demand Load		56.10A

Minimum Conductor Size = 4 AWG rated 70A at 60°C
[110.14(C)(1)(a)(2) and Table 310.16]

Answer: *(a) 4 AWG*

▶ **Resistance Welders, Example 2**

Question: *What is the minimum feeder conductor size for five 50A resistance welders with a duty cycle of 50 percent?*

(a) 4 AWG　　*(b) 3 AWG*　　*(c) 2 AWG*　　*(d) 1 AWG*

Solution:

Demand Load = Primary Rating × Multiplier [Table 630.31(A)(2)]
× Resistance Welder Percentage [630.31(B)]

Welder 1	50A × 71% = 35.50A × 100%	35.50A
Welder 2	50A × 71% = 35.50A × 60%	21.30A
Welder 3	50A × 71% = 35.50A × 60%	21.30A
Welder 4	50A × 71% = 35.50A × 60%	21.30A
Welder 5	50A × 71% = 35.50A × 60%	+21.30A
Total Demand Load		120.70A

Minimum Conductor Size = 1 AWG rated 130A at 75°C
[110.14(C)(1)(b)(2) and Table 310.16]

Answer: *(d) 1 AWG*

Part D—Light Industrial Calculations

Introduction

In Part D of unit 8 we will combine everything we learned in Parts A, B, and C to calculate unique industrial buildings. These calculations require a high level of focus and attention to detail.

8.15 Light Industrial Calculations

▶ Light Industrial Calculations, Example 1

Question: What is the service demand load for a light industrial manufacturing building with the following loads?

- Lighting, 11,600 VA at 277V used continuously
- Twenty-two receptacle outlets, 20A at 120V
- Three arc welders of the nonmotor-generator type, 23A at 480V, at 60% duty cycle
- Air compressor, 5 hp at 480V, three-phase
- Grinder, 1½ hp at 480V, three-phase
- Three continuous use industrial process dryers, 15 kVA, at 480V, three-phase

(a) 102A   (b) 120A   (c) 122A   (d) 132A

Solution:

Step 1: Determine the noncontinuous loads and motor loads. The noncontinuous and motor loads can be combined [430.24].

(1) Noncontinuous Loads:

(a) Receptacle Load [220.47]:

Receptacle Load = 22 Receptacles × 180 VA
Receptacle Load = 3,960 VA

(b) Welder Load [630.11(A) and Table 630.11(A)]:

A multiplier of 0.78 is allowed for 60% duty cycle welders:

Each Welder = 480V × 23A × 78%
Each Welder = 8,611 VA

Welder Demand Factors for 3 Welders: [630.11(B)]:

First Welder, 100%	8,611 VA × 100%	8,611 VA
Second Welder, 100%	8,611 VA × 100%	8,611 VA
Third Welder, 85%	8,611 VA × 85%	+7,320 VA
Welder Demand Load		24,542 VA

(2) Motor Loads [430.24 and Table 430.250]:

(a) Air Compressor, 5 hp	480V × 7.60A × 1.732	6,310 VA
(b) Grinder, 1½ hp	480V × 3A × 1.732	2,490 VA
(c) Largest Motor 25%	6,310 VA × 25%	+1,580 VA
Motor Loads		10,400 VA
Noncontinuous Loads and Motor Loads [430.24]		38,860 VA

Step 2: Determine the continuous loads.

(1) General Lighting (given)	11,600 VA × 125%	14,500 VA
(2) Industrial Dryers	15 kVA × 3 × 125%	+56,250 VA
Continuous Loads		70,750 VA

Step 3: Determine the overcurrent protection [215.3]. The overcurrent protection device must be sized at 125 percent of the continuous loads, plus the noncontinuous loads:

(1) Noncontinuous and Motor Loads		38,860 VA
(2) Continuous Loads	56,600 VA × 125%	+70,750 VA
		109,610 VA

Step 4: Convert VA to amperes to size the overcurrent device.

$I = VA/(E × 1.732)$

I = 109,610 VA/(480V × 1.732)

I = 109,610 VA/831V

I = 132A

Note: Conductor and overcurrent protection is as follows:

Overcurrent Device = 150A [240.6]

Use 1/0 AWG rated 150A at 75°C [110.14(C)(1)(b)(1) and Table 310.16].

Answer: (d) 132A

▶ Light Industrial Calculations, Example 2

Question: What is the service demand load for a light industrial manufacturing building with the following loads?

- Lighting, 20,000 VA at 277V used continuously
- One hundred and fifty receptacle outlets, 20A at 120V
- Five welders, nonmotor-generator arc type, 50A at 480V, 50% duty cycle
- Air compressor, 10 hp at 480V, three-phase
- Grinder, 2 hp at 480V, three-phase
- Three continuous use industrial process dryers, 10 kVA at 480V, three-phase

(a) 155A   (b) 195A   (c) 203A   (d) 215A

Solution:

Step 1: *Determine the noncontinuous loads and motor loads. The noncontinuous and motor loads can be combined [430.24].*

(1) Noncontinuous Loads:

(a) Receptacle Load [220.47]:

150 Receptacles × 180 VA	27,000 VA	
First 10 kVA at 100%	−10,000 VA × 100%	10,000 VA
Remainder at 50%	17,000 VA × 50%	+8,500 VA
Receptacle Demand Load		18,500 VA

(b) Welder Load [630.11(A) and Table 630.11(A)].

A multiplier of 0.71 is allowed for 50% duty cycle welders.

Each Welder = 480V × 50A × 71%

Each Welder = 17,040 VA

Welder Demand Factors for 5 Welders: [630.11(B)]:

Welder 1	17,040 VA × 100%	17,040 VA
Welder 2	17,040 VA × 100%	17,040 VA
Welder 3	17,040 VA × 85%	14,484 VA
Welder 4	17,040 VA × 70%	11,928 VA
Welder 5	17,040 VA × 60%	+10,224 VA
Welder Demand Load	70,716 VA	+70,716 VA

Noncontinuous Loads:	89,212 VA

(2) Motor Loads [430.24 and Table 430.250]:

(a) Air Compressor 10 hp	480V × 14A × 1.732	11,639 VA
(b) Grinder 2 hp	480V × 3.40A × 1.732	2,827 VA
(c) Largest Motor 25%	11,639 VA × 25%	+2,910 VA
Motor Loads		17,376 VA

Step 2: *Determine the continuous loads.*

(1) General Lighting (given)	20,000 VA × 125%	25,000 VA
(2) Industrial Dryers	10 kVA × 3 × 125%	+37,500 VA
Continuous Load		62,500 VA

Step 3: *Determine the feeder overcurrent protection [215.3]. The overcurrent protective device must be sized at 125 percent of the continuous loads, plus the noncontinuous loads.*

(1) Noncontinuous Loads	89,212 VA
(2) Motor Loads	17,376 VA
(3) Continuous Loads	+62,500 VA
	169,088 VA

Step 4: *Convert to amperes to size the overcurrent device.*

$I = VA/(E × 1.732)$

I = 169,088 VA/(480V × 1.732)

I = 169,088 VA/831V

I = 203A

Note: Conductor and overcurrent protection is as follows:

Service Size = 225A [240.6]

Use a 4/0 AWG conductor rated 230A at 75°C [110.14(C)(1)(b)(1) and Table 310.16].

Answer: *(c) 203A*

Unit 8—Conclusion

This unit showed that the calculations used to size services for commercial and industrial buildings do not include the same demand factors as those allowed for dwelling units.

Article 220 is not the only *Code* article in which service calculation requirements are contained. We referred to Article 440 for hermetic air-conditioning equipment, Article 430 for motors, Article 550 for mobile home parks, and Article 630 for electric welders. When performing commercial service calculations, be sure to look over the details and the scope of the project to ensure you apply all the appropriate *NEC* articles to your installation.

Keep in mind which (and when) certain demand factors can be applied to size commercial services. When dealing with continuous loads, remember to use a 125 percent multiplier for the phase conductors. That multiplier also applies to the continuous duty portions of loads when determining the actual service conductor sizing for commercial occupancies. The neutral conductor only needs to be sized at 100 percent of the continuous and noncontinuous loads when it is not connected to an overcurrent protective device [210.19(A)(1) Ex 2 and 215.2(A)(1) Ex 2]. Optional calculations are allowed for some commercial installations, so be sure to read problems carefully so you will employ the correct method.

UNIT 8

REVIEW QUESTIONS

Please use the 2023 *Code* book and this textbook to answer the following questions.

PART A—GENERAL COMMERCIAL DEMAND LOADS

8.2 General Lighting Load, Examples [Table 220.42(A)]

1. What is the general lighting load for a 10,000 sq ft exercise center?
    (a) 11 kVA
    (b) 14 kVA
    (c) 17 kVA
    (d) 19 kVA

2. What is the general lighting load for a 200,000 sq ft hospital?
    (a) 320 kVA
    (b) 330 kVA
    (c) 340 kVA
    (d) 350 kVA

3. What is the general lighting load for a 500,000 sq ft office?
    (a) 420 kVA
    (b) 530 kVA
    (c) 650 kVA
    (d) 770 kVA

4. What is the general lighting load for a 50,000 sq ft retail store?
    (a) 75 kVA
    (b) 80 kVA
    (c) 95 kVA
    (d) 100 kVA

5. What is the general lighting load for a 100,000 sq ft school?
    (a) 150 kVA
    (b) 160 kVA
    (c) 170 kVA
    (d) 180 kVA

8.3 General Lighting Load Demand Factors [Table 220.45]

6. What is the general lighting demand load for a 100,000 sq ft hotel?
    (a) 66 kVA
    (b) 71 kVA
    (c) 77 kVA
    (d) 81 kVA

7. What is the general lighting demand load for a 200,000 sq ft hotel?
    (a) 126 kVA
    (b) 136 kVA
    (c) 146 kVA
    (d) 156 kVA

8. What is the general lighting demand load for a 20 unit motel, each unit is 750 sq ft?
    (a) 11 kVA
    (b) 13 kVA
    (c) 15 kVA
    (d) 17 kVA

9. What is the general lighting demand load for a 100,000 sq ft storage warehouse?
    (a) 66 kVA
    (b) 76 kVA
    (c) 86 kVA
    (d) 96 kVA

10. What is the general lighting demand load for a 250,000 sq ft storage warehouse?

   (a) 125 kVA
   (b) 135 kVA
   (c) 145 kVA
   (d) 156 kVA

8.4 Number of General Lighting Circuits

11. How many 20A, 120V branch circuits is required for a parking lot containing fifty 500 VA/120V luminaires?

   (a) 10 circuits
   (b) 11 circuits
   (c) 13 circuits
   (d) 14 circuits

12. How many 20A, 120V branch circuits are required to supply the general lighting load for a 100 ft × 200 ft department store?

   (a) 10 circuits
   (b) 12 circuits
   (c) 13 circuits
   (d) 16 circuits

13. How many 20A, 120V branch circuits are required to supply the general lighting load for a 20,000 sq ft convention center?

   (a) 10 circuits
   (b) 12 circuits
   (c) 13 circuits
   (d) 16 circuits

8.5 Sign Circuit [220.14(F)]

14. The feeder/service demand load for conductor sizing of a commercial sign circuit is _____.

   (a) 1,200 VA
   (b) 1,500 VA
   (c) 1,600 VA
   (d) 1,700 VA

8.6 Multioutlet Receptacle Assemblies [220.14(H)]

15. What is the branch circuit load for 20 ft of fixed multi-outlet assembly where appliances are likely to be used at the same time?

   (a) 1,800 VA
   (b) 2,400 VA
   (c) 3,000 VA
   (d) 3,600 VA

16. What is the branch circuit load for 20 ft of fixed multi-outlet assembly where appliances are unlikely to be used at the same time?

   (a) 650 VA
   (b) 670 VA
   (c) 690 VA
   (d) 720 VA

8.7 Receptacle Demand Load [220.14(I) and 220.47]

17. What is the demand load for 50 receptacle outlets in a commercial occupancy?

   (a) 9 kVA
   (b) 10 kVA
   (c) 11 kVA
   (d) 12 kVA

18. What is the demand load for 100 receptacle outlets in a commercial occupancy?

   (a) 10 kVA
   (b) 12 kVA
   (c) 14 kVA
   (d) 16 kVA

19. What is the demand load for 150 receptacle outlets in a commercial occupancy?

   (a) 14.5 kVA
   (b) 16.5 kVA
   (c) 18.5 kVA
   (d) 19.5 kVA

PART B—OFFICE, MOBILE HOME, KITCHEN, RESTAURANT, AND SCHOOL EXAMPLES

8.10 Mobile Home Parks [550.31]

20. What is the demand load for a mobile home park containing 25 homes?

    (a) 96 kVA
    (b) 106 kVA
    (c) 116 kVA
    (d) 119 kVA

21. What is the demand load for a mobile home park containing 25 homes, each having a calculated demand load of 14 kVA?

    (a) 96 kVA
    (b) 106 kVA
    (c) 116 kVA
    (d) 116 kVA

22. What is the demand load for a manufactured home park with facilities for forty-two sites? The system is 120/240V, single-phase.

    (a) 621A
    (b) 632A
    (c) 644A
    (d) 652A

8.11 Kitchen Equipment and Restaurants

Kitchen Equipment Load, Commercial [220.56]

23. What is the service demand load for one 15 kW water heater, one 15 kW booster water heater, one 10 kW oven, and two 5 kW deep fryers in a commercial kitchen?

    (a) 25 kW
    (b) 30 kW
    (c) 35 kW
    (d) 40 kW

24. What is the service demand load for one 15 kW water heater, one 15 kW booster water heater, two 10 kW oven, and two 10 kW deep fryers and two 5 kW deep fryers in a commercial kitchen? See

    (a) 46 kW
    (b) 48 kW
    (c) 50 kW
    (d) 52 kW

Restaurant—Optional Method [220.88]

25. What is the demand load for an all-electric restaurant that has a total connected load of 350 kVA using the optional method?

    (a) 165 kVA
    (b) 175 kVA
    (c) 180 kVA
    (d) 185 kVA

26. What is the demand load for an all-electric restaurant that has a total connected load of 400 kVA using the optional method?

    (a) 210 kVA
    (b) 215 kVA
    (c) 220 kVA
    (d) 225 kVA

27. What is the demand load for an all-electric restaurant having a connected load of 500 kVA using the optional method?

    (a) 250 kVA
    (b) 260 kVA
    (c) 270 kVA
    (d) 280 kVA

8.12 School Optional Method Load Calculations [220.86]

28. Using the optional method, What is the demand for a 6,000 sq ft school having a total connected load of 150 kVA at 480Y/277V, three-phase?

    (a) 125A
    (b) 150A
    (c) 175A
    (d) 200A

29. Using the optional method, What is the demand load for a 10,000 sq ft school having a total connected load of 200 kVA at 277/480V, three-phase?

    (a) 150A
    (b) 175A
    (c) 200A
    (d) 225A

30. Using the optional method, What size service conductor is required for a 15,000 sq ft school having a total connected load of 400 kVA at 480/277V, three-phase?

    (a) 250 kcmil
    (b) 300 kcmil
    (c) 400 kcmil
    (d) 500 kcmil

PART C—WELDER CALCULATIONS

8.13 Arc Welders

Branch-Circuit Conductors—Arc Welders [630.11(A)]

31. What TW conductor is required for a nonmotor-generator arc welder that has a primary current rating of 30A with a duty cycle of 40 percent?

    (a) 12 AWG
    (b) 10 AWG
    (c) 8 AWG
    (d) 6 AWG

32. What TW conductor is required for a nonmotor-generator arc welder that has a primary current rating of 40A with a duty cycle of 30 percent?

    (a) 12 AWG
    (b) 10 AWG
    (c) 8 AWG
    (d) 6 AWG

33. What TW conductor is required for a motor-generator arc welder that has a primary current rating of 30A with a duty cycle of 40 percent?

    (a) 12 AWG
    (b) 10 AWG
    (c) 8 AWG
    (d) 6 AWG

34. What TW conductor is required for a motor-generator arc welder that has a primary current rating of 40A with a duty cycle of 30 percent?

    (a) 12 AWG
    (b) 10 AWG
    (c) 8 AWG
    (d) 6 AWG

Feeder Conductors—Arc Welders [630.11(B)]

35. What is THW feeder required for five 30A nonmotor-generator arc welders with duty cycles of 30 percent, terminals are rated 75°C?

    (a) 4 AWG
    (b) 1 AWG
    (c) 1/0 AWG
    (d) 2/0 AWG

36. What is THW feeder required for five 50A nonmotor-generator arc welders with duty cycles of 50 percent, terminals are rated 75°C?

    (a) 4 AWG
    (b) 3 AWG
    (c) 1/0 AWG
    (d) 2/0 AWG

37. What is THW feeder required for five 30A motor-generator arc welders with duty cycles of 30 percent, terminals are rated 75°C?

    (a) 4 AWG
    (b) 3 AWG
    (c) 2 AWG
    (d) 1 AWG

38. What is THW feeder required for five 50A motor-generator arc welders with duty cycles of 50 percent, terminals are rated 75°C?

    (a) 2 AWG
    (b) 1 AWG
    (c) 1/0 AWG
    (d) 2/0 AWG

8.14 Resistance Welders

Branch-Circuit Conductors—Resistance Welders [630.31(A)(2)]

39. What TW conductor is required for a 40A resistance welder with a duty cycle of 30 percent?

    (a) 12 AWG
    (b) 10 AWG
    (c) 8 AWG
    (d) 6 AWG

40. What TW conductor is required for a 30A resistance welder with a duty cycle of 50 percent?

    (a) 12 AWG
    (b) 10 AWG
    (c) 8 AWG
    (d) 6 AWG

Feeder Conductors—Resistance Welders [630.31(B)]

41. What is THW feeder is required for five 40A resistance welders with duty cycles of 30 percent, terminals are rated 75°C?

    (a) 4 AWG
    (b) 3 AWG
    (c) 2 AWG
    (d) 1 AWG

42. What is THW feeder is required for five 30A resistance welders with duty cycles of 50 percent, terminals are rated 75°C?

    (a) 4 AWG
    (b) 3 AWG
    (c) 2 AWG
    (d) 1 AWG

PART D—LIGHT INDUSTRIAL CALCULATIONS

8.15 Light Industrial Calculations

A store 80 ft by 60 ft, or 4,800 ft², has 30 ft of show window. There are a total of 80 duplex receptacles. The service is 120/240V. Actual connected lighting load is 7,000 VA, all of which for this example is considered continuous.

43. What size service is required?

    (a) 126A
    (b) 135A
    (c) 145A
    (d) 152A

An industrial building provides power to a remote building with the following loads:

- Electric-discharge Lighting, 11,600 VA at 277V used continuously
- Twenty-two receptacles, 20A at 125V, supplied by a separately derived system
- Air compressor, 5 hp at 460V, three phase
- Grinder 1.5 hp at 460V, three phase
- Three arc welders, (nameplate: 23 amperes, 480V, 60 percent duty cycle)
- Three industrial process dryers, 480V, three phase, 15 kW each (continuous use)

44. What size service is required?

    (a) 126A
    (b) 132A
    (c) 145A
    (d) 152A

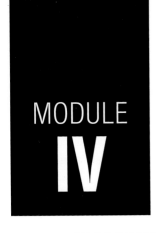
The following 25-question random order Practice Exam will test your knowledge of Module IV—Advanced *NEC* Calculations.

Please use the 2023 *Code* book and this textbook to answer the following questions.

Want to practice online? Scan the QR code to access these questions online to get familiar with the online environment in which you'll most likely be taking your exam.

UNIT 7—PRACTICE EXAM

PART A—OPTIONAL METHOD LOAD CALCULATIONS [ARTICLE 220, PART IV]

7.2 Multifamily Dwelling Optional Method [220.84] Examples

Use the following information for the next four questions. A multifamily dwelling equipped with electric cooking and space heating or air conditioning has 40 dwelling units. The area of each dwelling unit is 840 ft². Each dwelling unit is equipped with:

- Electric range, 8 kW at 120/240V
- Four electric space heaters, 1.5 kW at 240V
- Electric water heater, 2.5 kW at 240V

1. What size service is required for the 40 dwelling units?

   (a) 735A
   (b) 857A
   (c) 964A
   (d) 1,028A

2. What size service neutral is required for the 40 dwelling units?

   (a) 374A
   (b) 457A
   (c) 564A
   (d) 673A

PART B—STANDARD METHOD LOAD CALCULATIONS [ARTICLE 220, PART III]

7.3 General Lighting and General-Use Receptacle Demand Load [220.41 and 220.45]

3. What is the general lighting, general-use receptacle, small-appliance, and laundry circuit demand load for a 15-unit apartment building, each 1,000 sq ft?

   (a) 37 kVA
   (b) 39 kVA
   (c) 41 kVA
   (d) 44 kVA

7.4 Appliance Demand Load [220.53]

4. Using the standard method, what is the appliance demand load for a 16-unit multifamily building, each unit contains a disposal (940 VA), a dishwasher (1,250 VA), and a water heater (4,500 VA)?

   (a) 78 kVA
   (b) 80 kVA
   (c) 84 kVA
   (d) 88 kVA

7.5 Dryer Demand Load [220.54]

5. Using the standard load calculation method, what is the service demand factor for ten 4 kW dryers?

    (a) 25 kW
    (b) 29 kW
    (c) 31 kW
    (d) 33 kW

7.6 Single-Phase Dryers on Three-Phase Service [220.54]

6. What is the demand load for fifteen 5.5 kW dryers on a 208Y/120V three-phase service?

    (a) 38.52 kW
    (b) 39.55 kW
    (c) 41.25 kW
    (d) 43.52 kW

7.7 Single-Phase Ranges on Single-Phase Service [220.55]

Table 220.55, Column C—Over 8¾ kW to 12 kW

7. What is the demand load for thirty 16 kW ranges?

    (a) 46 kW
    (b) 48 kW
    (c) 50 kW
    (d) 54 kW

7.8 Single-Phase Ranges on Three-Phase Service [220.55]

8. What is the demand load for 24 ranges rated 14 kW on a 208Y/120V three-phase service?

    (a) 51 kW
    (b) 57 kW
    (c) 64 kW
    (d) 73 kW

7.9 Air-Conditioning and Heating Demand Load

9. What is the demand load for a 25-unit multifamily building using the standard method? Each unit has heat-pump air-conditioning of 12A/240V containing 6 kW supplemental electric heating.

    (a) 200 kVA
    (b) 210 kVA
    (c) 215 kVA
    (d) 223 kVA

7.10 Service Conductor Sizing [Table 310.16]

10. What size aluminum service conductor is required for a multi-family building that has a total demand load of 260 kW for a 208Y/120V, three-phase system? The conductors are paralleled in three raceways.

    (a) Three–300 kcmil AL
    (b) Three–350 kcmil AL
    (c) Three–500 kcmil AL
    (d) Three–700 kcmil AL

7.12 Two-Family (Duplex) Dwelling Units Load Calculations [220.85]

11. Using the optional method, What is the demand load for a duplex where each-unit is 1,100 sq ft and contains:

    - Dishwasher, 11A at 120V
    - Disposal, 8A at 120V
    - Water heater, 3.5 kW at 240V
    - Range, 9 kW at 120/240V
    - Air-conditioning, 1 hp at 120V
    - Heating, 5 kW at 240V

    (a) 147A
    (b) 155A
    (c) 167A
    (d) 177A

PART C—NEUTRAL LOAD CALCULATIONS

7.13 Neutral Demand Load—Dryers and Ranges [220.61]

Dryer Neutral Demand Load

12. What is the neutral load for fifty 4 kW dryers?

    (a) 38 kW
    (b) 41 kW
    (c) 44 kW
    (d) 47 kW

Range Neutral Demand Load

13. What is the neutral demand load for twenty 15 kW ranges?

    (a) 28 kW
    (b) 30 kW
    (c) 32 kW
    (d) 34 kW

UNIT 8—COMMERCIAL CALCULATIONS

PART A—GENERAL COMMERCIAL DEMAND LOADS

8.2 General Lighting Load, Examples [Table 220.42(A)]

14. What is the general lighting load for a 100,000 sq ft school?

    (a) 150 kVA
    (b) 160 kVA
    (c) 170 kVA
    (d) 180 kVA

8.3 General Lighting Load Demand Factors [Table 220.45]

15. What is the general lighting demand load for a 20 unit motel, each unit is 750 sq ft?

    (a) 11 kVA
    (b) 13 kVA
    (c) 15 kVA
    (d) 17 kVA

8.4 Number of General Lighting Circuits

16. How many 20A, 120V branch circuits are required to supply the general lighting load for a 100 ft × 200 ft department store?

    (a) 10 circuits
    (b) 12 circuits
    (c) 13 circuits
    (d) 16 circuits

8.6 Multioutlet Receptacle Assemblies [220.14(H)]

17. What is the branch circuit load for 20 ft of fixed multi-outlet assembly where appliances are likely to be used at the same time?

    (a) 1,800 VA
    (b) 2,400 VA
    (c) 3,000 VA
    (d) 3,600 VA

8.7 Receptacle Demand Load [220.14(I) and 220.47]

18. What is the demand load for 150 receptacle outlets in a commercial occupancy?

    (a) 14.5 kVA
    (b) 16.5 kVA
    (c) 18.5 kVA
    (d) 19.5 kVA

PART B—OFFICE, MOBILE HOME, KITCHEN, RESTAURANT, AND SCHOOL EXAMPLES

8.10 Mobile Home Parks [550.31]

19. What is the demand load for a mobile home park containing 25 homes, each having a calculated demand load of 14 kVA?

    (a) 96 kVA
    (b) 106 kVA
    (c) 116 kVA
    (d) 116 kVA

8.11 Kitchen Equipment and Restaurants

Kitchen Equipment Load, Commercial [220.56]

20. What is the service demand load for one 15 kW water heater, one 15 kW booster water heater, one 10 kW oven, and two 5 kW deep fryers in a commercial kitchen?

    (a) 25 kW
    (b) 30 kW
    (c) 35 kW
    (d) 40 kW

Restaurant—Optional Method [220.88]

21. What is the demand load for an all-electric restaurant that has a total connected load of 350 kVA using the optional method?

    (a) 165 kVA
    (b) 175 kVA
    (c) 180 kVA
    (d) 185 kVA

8.12 School Optional Method Load Calculations [220.86]

22. Using the optional method, What is the demand for a 6,000 sq ft school having a total connected load of 150 kVA at 480Y/277V, three-phase?

    (a) 125A
    (b) 150A
    (c) 175A
    (d) 200A

PART C—WELDER CALCULATIONS

8.13 Arc Welders

Branch-Circuit Conductors—Arc Welders [630.11(A)]

23. What TW conductor is required for a motor-generator arc welder that has a primary current rating of 30A with a duty cycle of 40 percent?

    (a) 12 AWG
    (b) 10 AWG
    (c) 8 AWG
    (d) 6 AWG

8.14 Resistance Welders

Feeder Conductors—Resistance Welders [630.31(B)]

24. What is THW feeder is required for five 30A resistance welders with duty cycles of 50 percent, terminals are rated 75°C?

    (a) 4 AWG
    (b) 3 AWG
    (c) 2 AWG
    (d) 1 AWG

PART D—LIGHT INDUSTRIAL CALCULATIONS

8.15 Light Industrial Calculations

A store 80 ft by 60 ft, or 4,800 ft², has 30 ft of show window. There are a total of 80 duplex receptacles. The service is 120/240V. Actual connected lighting load is 7,000 VA, all of which for this example is considered continuous.

25. What size service is required?

    (a) 126A
    (b) 135A
    (c) 145A
    (d) 152A

MODULES III-IV

NEC CALCULATIONS *CODE* AND SECTION INDEX

The following is a reference index for the calculations covered in Modules III and IV. It displays the *Code* rule found in the 2023 edition of the *National Electrical Code* as well as the section in this book that is referenced, so you can go to that section to review questions for those topics.

WHAT'S THE NEXT STEP?

Follow the wheel and see how to take your career to the next level

Never stop learning...

To be a success, you have to remain current, relevant, and marketable. Your individual success is a function of your education and the key is continuous self-improvement, even if just a little each day. Here is a great map to make sure you have taken all the steps to complete your electrical education.

Mike Holt

MikeHolt.com/NextStep

STEP #1 THEORY

STEP #2 UNDERSTANDING THE NEC

STEP #3 BONDING AND GROUNDING

STEP #4 ELECTRICAL EXAM PREP

STEP #5 SOLAR PHOTOVOLTAIC SYSTEMS

STEP #6 MOTOR CONTROLS

STEP #7 ELECTRICAL ESTIMATING

STEP #8 LEADERSHIP

STEP #9 BUSINESS MANAGEMENT

ABOUT THE AUTHOR

Mike Holt—Author

Mike Holt
Founder and President
Mike Holt Enterprises
Groveland, Florida

Mike Holt is an author, businessman, educator, speaker, publisher and *National Electrical Code* expert. He has written hundreds of electrical training books and articles, founded three successful businesses, and has taught thousands of electrical *Code* seminars across the U.S. and internationally. His dynamic presentation style, deep understanding of the trade, and ability to connect with students are some of the reasons that he is one of the most sought-after speakers in the industry.

His company, Mike Holt Enterprises, has been serving the electrical industry for almost 50 years, with a commitment to creating and publishing books, videos, online training, and curriculum support for electrical trainers, students, organizations, and electrical professionals. His devotion to the trade, coupled with the lessons he learned at the University of Miami's MBA program, have helped him build one of the largest electrical training and publishing companies in the United States.

Mike is committed to changing lives and helping people take their careers to the next level. He has always felt a responsibility to provide education beyond the scope of just passing an exam. He draws on his previous experience as an electrician, inspector, contractor and instructor, to guide him in developing powerful training solutions that electricians understand and enjoy. He is always mindful of how hard learning can be for students who are intimidated by school, by their feelings towards learning, or by the complexity of the *NEC*. He's mastered the art of simplifying and clarifying complicated technical concepts and his extensive use of illustrations helps students apply the content and relate the material to their work in the field. His ability to take the intimidation out of learning is reflected in the successful careers of his students.

Mike's commitment to pushing boundaries and setting high standards extends into his personal life as well. He's an eight-time Overall National Barefoot Waterski Champion. Mike has more than 20 gold medals, many national records, and has competed in three World Barefoot Tournaments. In 2015, at the tender age of 64, he started a new adventure—competitive mountain bike racing and at 65 began downhill mountain biking. Every day he continues to find ways to motivate himself, both mentally and physically.

Mike and his wife, Linda, reside in New Mexico and Florida, and are the parents of seven children and seven grandchildren. As his life has changed over the years, a few things have remained constant: his commitment to God, his love for his family, and doing what he can to change the lives of others through his products and seminars.

Special Acknowledgments

My Family. First, I want to thank God for my godly wife who's always by my side and for my children.

My Staff. A personal thank you goes to my team at Mike Holt Enterprises for all the work they do to help me with my mission of changing peoples' lives through education. They work tirelessly to ensure that, in addition to our products meeting and exceeding the educational needs of our customers, we stay committed to building life-long relationships throughout their electrical careers.

The National Fire Protection Association. A special thank you must be given to the staff at the National Fire Protection Association (NFPA), publishers of the *NEC*—in particular, Jeff Sargent for his assistance in answering my many *Code* questions over the years. Jeff, you're a "first class" guy, and I admire your dedication and commitment to helping others understand the *NEC*.

ABOUT THE ILLUSTRATOR

Mike Culbreath—Illustrator

Mike Culbreath
Graphic Illustrator
Alden, Michigan

Mike Culbreath has devoted his career to the electrical industry and worked his way up from apprentice electrician to master electrician. He started working in the electrical field doing residential and light commercial construction, and later did service work and custom electrical installations. While working as a journeyman electrician, he suffered a serious on-the-job knee injury. As part of his rehabilitation, Mike completed courses at Mike Holt Enterprises, and then passed the exam to receive his Master Electrician's license. In 1986, with a keen interest in continuing education for electricians, he joined the staff to update material and began illustrating Mike Holt's textbooks and magazine articles.

Mike started with simple hand-drawn diagrams and cut-and-paste graphics. Frustrated by the limitations of that style of illustrating, he took a company computer home to learn how to operate some basic computer graphics software. Realizing that computer graphics offered a lot of flexibility for creating illustrations, Mike took every computer graphics class and seminar he could to help develop his skills. He's worked as an illustrator and editor with the company for over 30 years and, as Mike Holt has proudly acknowledged, has helped to transform his words and visions into lifelike graphics.

Originally from South Florida, Mike now lives in northern lower Michigan where he enjoys hiking, kayaking, photography, gardening, and cooking; but his real passion is his horses. He also loves spending time with his children Dawn and Mac and his grandchildren Jonah, Kieley, and Scarlet.

ABOUT THE MIKE HOLT TEAM

There are many people who played a role in the production of this textbook. Their efforts are reflected in the quality and organization of the information contained in this textbook, and in its technical accuracy, completeness, and usability.

Technical Writing

Mario Valdes is the Technical Content Editor and works directly with Mike to ensure that content is technically accurate, relatable, and valuable to all electrical professionals. He plays an important role in gathering research, analyzing data, and assisting Mike in the writing of the textbooks. He reworks content into different formats to improve the flow of information and to ensure expectations are being met in terms of message, tone, and quality. He edits illustrations and proofreads content to "fact-check" each sentence, title, and image structure. Mario enjoys working in collaboration with Mike and Brian to enhance the company's brand image, training products, and technical publications.

Editorial and Production

Brian House is part of the content team that reviews our material to make sure it's ready for our customers. He also coordinates the team that constructs and reviews this textbook and its supporting resources to ensure its accuracy, clarity, and quality.

Toni Culbreath worked tirelessly to proofread and edit this publication. Her attention to detail and her dedication is irreplaceable. A very special thank you goes out to Toni (Mary Poppins) Culbreath for her many years of dedicated service.

Cathleen Kwas handled the design, layout, and typesetting of this book. Her desire to create the best possible product for our customers is greatly appreciated, and she constantly pushes the design envelope to make the product experience just a little bit better.

Vinny Perez and **Eddie Anacleto** have been a dynamic team. They have taken the best instructional graphics in the industry to the next level. Both Eddie and Vinny bring years of graphic art experience to the pages of this book and have been a huge help updating and improving the content, look, and style our graphics.

Dan Haruch is an integral part of the video recording process and spends much of his time making sure that the instructor resources created from this product are the best in the business. His dedication to the instructor and student experience is much appreciated.

Video Team

Special thank you to **Ron Pelkey**, Master Electrician and Instructor from Pinellas Park, Florida, for attending this video recording as a guest, and contributing his time and energy to help us, and thanks to **Power Design Inc.** for their support.

The following special people provided technical advice in the development of this textbook as they served on the video team along with author **Mike Holt**.

Boyd Bindrup
Electrical Contractor/Instructor
Ogden, UT

Boyd Bindrup launched his electrical career at age 12 by working for his father's company during the summers and earning $0.75 per hr. He began his electrical apprenticeship in Ogden Weber Technical College but left to attend Salt Lake Community College for his last two years of training. After finishing school, he obtained his Journeyman license and, 2 years later, his Master Electrician license.

Boyd is an Electrical Contractor license holder for Creative Times Inc. (CTI Electric) which does commercial and military electrical work. He has been an Instructor at Ogden Weber Tech College since 1994, having taught over 1,400 classes and trained thousands of electricians. He's a Utah, Idaho and Colorado Master Electrician, and his credentials include LEED AP BD+C, Lightning Protection Master Installer/Designer #1447, Vindicator Certified Security Installer, Cathodic Protection Installer CP1 NACE 56675, Fiber Optics Installer #FOIUT216, and SKM Arc Flash Power Tools trained.

Boyd is devoted to learning and passing on the knowledge to current and future electrical professionals. He is passionate about the direction of the profession and is active politically in the industry.

Boyd and his wife Rebecca reside in Ogden Canyon and are parents to six children. His hobbies include CrossFit and Xterra triathlon.

Daniel Brian House
Vice President of Digital and Technical Training
Mike Holt Enterprises, Instructor, Master Electrician
Brian@MikeHolt.com
Ocala, Florida

Brian House is Vice President of Digital and Technical Training at Mike Holt Enterprises, and a Certified Mike Holt Instructor. He is a permanent member of the video teams, on which he has served since the 2011 *Code* cycle. Brian has worked in the trade since the 1990s in residential, commercial and industrial settings. He opened a contracting firm in 2003 that designed energy-efficient lighting retrofits, explored "green" biomass generators, and partnered with residential PV companies in addition to traditional electrical installation and service.

In 2007, Brian was personally selected by Mike for development and began teaching seminars for Mike Holt Enterprises after being named a "Top Gun Presenter" in Mike's Train the Trainer boot camp. Brian travels around the country teaching electricians, instructors, military personnel, and engineers. His experience in the trenches as an electrical contractor, along with Mike Holt's instructor training, gives him a teaching style that is practical, straightforward, and refreshing.

Today, as Vice President of Digital and Technical Training at Mike Holt Enterprises, Brian leads the apprenticeship and digital product teams. They create cutting-edge training tools, and partner with in-house and apprenticeship training programs nationwide to help them reach the next level. He is also part of the content team that helps Mike bring his products to market, assisting in the editing of the textbooks, coordinating the content and illustrations, and assuring the technical accuracy and flow of the information.

Brian is high energy, with a passion for doing business the right way. He expresses his commitment to the industry and his love for its people in his teaching, working on books, and developing instructional programs and software tools.

Brian and his wife Carissa have shared the joy of their four children and many foster children during 25 years of marriage. When not mentoring youth at work or church, he can be found racing mountain bikes or SCUBA diving with his kids. He's passionate about helping others and regularly engages with the youth of his community to motivate them into exploring their future.

John Mills
Master Electrician/Instructor
Miami Springs, Florida

John Mills is an instructor for Mike Holt Enterprises, and is a Certified Electrical Contractor, Certified Inspector, Plan Reviewer, and CBO. John started in the electrical trade in 1980 as a helper, attended an ABC Apprenticeship Program, and then worked his way up to Master Electrician. He's been an instructor for 30 years, teaching master and journeyman exam preparation courses and Florida State certification courses.

John resides in Miami, Florida with his wife Corina and their four sons. His hobby is working with wood and metal, and he enjoys turning wooden bowls, making things for his children, and building furniture. John enjoys fishing, family picnics, and taking vacations with his family.

Eric Stromberg, P.E.
Electrical Engineer, Instructor
Eric@MikeHolt.com
Los Alamos, New Mexico

Eric Stromberg has a bachelor's degree in Electrical Engineering and is a professional engineer. He started in the electrical industry when he was a teenager helping the neighborhood electrician. After high school, and a year of college, Eric worked for a couple of different audio companies, installing sound systems in a variety of locations from small buildings to baseball stadiums. After returning to college, he worked as a journeyman wireman for an electrical contractor.

After graduating from the University of Houston, Eric took a job as an electronic technician and installed and serviced life safety systems in high-rise buildings. After seven years he went to work for Dow Chemical as a power distribution engineer. His work with audio systems had made him very sensitive to grounding issues and he took this experience with him into power distribution. Because of this expertise, Eric became one of Dow's grounding subject matter experts. This is also how Eric met Mike Holt, as Mike was looking for grounding experts for his 2002 Grounding vs. Bonding video.

Eric taught the *National Electrical Code* for professional engineering exam preparation for over 20 years, and has held continuing education teacher certificates for the states of Texas and New Mexico. He was on the electrical licensing and advisory board for the State of Texas, as well as on their electrician licensing exam board.

Eric now consults for a Department of Energy research laboratory in New Mexico, where he's responsible for the electrical standards as well as assisting the laboratory's AHJ.

Eric's oldest daughter lives with her husband in Zurich, Switzerland, where she teaches for an international school. His son served in the Air Force, has a degree in Aviation logistics, and is a pilot and owner of an aerial photography business. His youngest daughter is a singer/songwriter in Los Angeles.

Mario Valdes, Jr.
Technical Content Editor Mike Holt Enterprises,
Electrical Inspector, Electrical Plans Examiner,
Master Electrician
Mario@MikeHolt.com
Ocala, Florida

Mario Valdes, Jr. is a member of the technical team at Mike Holt Enterprises, working directly with Mike Holt in researching, re-writing, and coordinating content, to assure the technical accuracy of the information in the products. He is a permanent member of the video teams, on which he has served since the 2017 *Code* cycle.

Mario is licensed as an Electrical Contractor, most recently having worked as an electrical inspector and plans examiner for an engineering firm in South Florida. Additionally, he was an Electrical Instructor for a technical college, teaching students pursuing an associate degree in electricity. He taught subjects such as ac/dc fundamentals, residential and commercial wiring, blueprint reading, and electrical estimating. He brings to the Mike Holt team a wealth of knowledge and devotion for the *NEC*.

He started his career at 16 years old in his father's electrical contracting company. Once he got his Florida State contractor's license, he ran the company as project manager and estimator. Mario's passion for the *NEC* prompted him to get his inspector and plans review certifications and embark on a new journey in electrical *Code* compliance. He's worked on complex projects such as hospitals, casinos, hotels and multi-family high rise buildings. Mario is very passionate about educating electrical professionals about electrical safety and the *National Electrical Code*.

Mario's a member of the IAEI, NFPA, and ICC, and enjoys participating in the meetings; he believes that by staying active in these organizations he'll be ahead of the game, with cutting-edge knowledge pertaining to safety codes.

When not immersed in the electrical world Mario enjoys fitness training. He resides in Pembroke Pines, Florida with his beautiful family, which includes his wife and his two sons. They enjoy family trip getaways to Disney World and other amusement parks.